T0406285

# The Palgrave Handbook of Crisis Leadership in Higher Education

"This is a must-read handbook, especially important at a time of exceptional challenges for all when the world is engulfed in multiple crises. It is a book that is not only relevant for academics and leaders in education, going well beyond that; it gives all readers some insightful ideas about what we can do to stop things from falling apart, building a well-founded sense of hope. Most importantly, it invites readers to think."

—Stefan Popenici, *Academic Lead, Quality Initiatives, Charles Darwin University, Australia*

"A phoenix rising from the ashes that captures hope and better things to come as leaders manoeuvre their way out of the multiple crises worldwide is the image that best captures this unique read. Previously muted voices across continents come alive through the text and are simultaneously embedded in a sophisticated theoretical framing of crises leadership that is enlightening and instructive for all. The diverse narratives articulate challenging circumstances across familiar and unfamiliar contexts but also provide possibilities for regeneration and renewal, which is a refreshing quality of this unique publication."

—Tania Aspland, *Vice President (Academic), Kaplan Business School and Kaplan Higher Education, Australia*

"Organisational crises are inevitable, challenging and oftentimes unexpected. Their urgent and effective resolution, therefore, demands leaders with a nuanced skillset, hence the profound importance of this handbook. It is an impressively comprehensive and contemporary compendium contextualised for leadership professionals in higher education who will no doubt value these trusted insights as they navigate the complex landscape in the years ahead."

—James Adonopoulos, *Academic Dean, Kaplan Business School and Kaplan Higher Education, Australia*

"A very timely and thoughtful discussion that portrays a system in crisis worldwide. The book raises real questions to think about as academics, leaders, and citizens. The type of leadership put in place in times of crisis is discussed thoroughly by local experts, which is key to this endeavour. It allows us to think about the type of leadership we are exercising and whether it is sustainable. Are we just reacting or building for the future? There are many good examples of effective leadership in extremely challenging circumstances and beyond COVID-19. We should all learn from the innovative models of leadership presented whilst accepting that we need to redefine the concept going forward, allowing more capacity for growth."

—Fotini Diamantidaki, *Associate Professor, Language Learning and Intercultural Communication, University College London, UK*

"This handbook has a laudable global coverage and offers invaluable guidance for leaders in higher education. Its post-COVID outlook and multifaceted approach to crisis—from environmental to AI challenges—provide practical, forward-thinking strategies. Emphasising learning leadership, this indispensable resource is key for navigating and shaping the evolving landscape of the higher education sector."

—Susie Khoo, *President, Kaplan Singapore*

"This perennial gem of a book explores the multifaceted crises plaguing higher education in the 21st century, notably the COVID-19 pandemic, environmental challenges, socioeconomic and political issues. The authors from 33 international sources trace historical shifts in the rapidly evolving purpose and structure of universities, from Humboldt's holistic vision to the neoliberal, business-oriented models of today. They emphasize the detrimental impact of managerialism, advocating for crisis leadership to balance the efficiency and well-being of academic professionals."

—Bina Rai, *Senior Lecturer, Department of Biomedical Engineering, National University of Singapore*

"An indispensable guide for educational leaders navigating the storm. This groundbreaking book on crisis leadership in education transcends borders, featuring insights from authors across more than 20 countries, from every continent. It meticulously explores the profound challenges of our time, dissecting various leadership styles and their impact on higher education's resilience in an era of polycrises. A timely and essential read for those steering educational institutions through turbulent times."

—Martin Grünert, *Dean, Academic Services, Kaplan Singapore*

"This work is encyclopaedic. It is undoubtedly the most complete work in the field I have read to date. I have no doubt it will become a standard reference work. It ranges widely in its selections, drawing upon the results of research conducted with small groups as well as on large institutions and organisations. Moreover, the organisation and syntheses of what is presented are excellent. Overall, the work is an extremely important contribution to the area of leadership."

—Tom O'Donoghue, *Professor Emeritus, The University of Western Australia*

"The Palgrave Handbook of Crisis Leadership in Higher Education is an ambitious, timely and essential resource for all who want to understand and navigate the complex challenges facing higher education today. Its comprehensive global approach to addressing multifaceted crises—from pandemic impacts to those caused by the neoliberalisation of higher education—makes it an invaluable guide for academics, policymakers, and leaders. This handbook is not just a collection of insights; it offers inspiration for strategic thinking and resilient leadership in times of unprecedented change."

—Can Seng Ooi, *Professor in Cultural and Heritage Tourism, University of Tasmania, Australia*

"Distinctive, fresh and completely of the moment and beyond, this Handbook serves an important purpose—that of providing rare insights into exemplars of crisis leadership, and not just management, at a time when higher education is in a state of 'permacrisis'. The sweep and scale of the global exemplars outlining what is considered and done, as encapsulated across 33 chapters, are impressive and significant and make this Handbook an important achievement for the authors and a critical source of reference for any leader."

—Renée Tan, *Associate Professor, Singapore University of Social Sciences, Singapore*

Jürgen Rudolph · Joseph Crawford ·
Choon-Yin Sam · Shannon Tan
Editors

# The Palgrave Handbook of Crisis Leadership in Higher Education

palgrave
macmillan

*Editors*
Jürgen Rudolph
Kaplan City Campus
Kaplan Singapore
Wilkie Edge, Singapore

Choon-Yin Sam
Kaplan City Campus
Kaplan Singapore
Wilkie Edge, Singapore

Joseph Crawford
University of Tasmania
Newnham, TAS, Australia

Shannon Tan
Kaplan City Campus
Kaplan Singapore
Wilkie Edge, Singapore

ISBN 978-3-031-54508-5 ISBN 978-3-031-54509-2 (eBook)
https://doi.org/10.1007/978-3-031-54509-2



This Palgrave Macmillan imprint is published by the registered company Springer Nature Switzerland AG
The registered company address is: Gewerbestrasse 11, 6330 Cham, Switzerland

Paper in this product is recyclable.

*For Clara, my love*

*—Jürgen Rudolph*

*For the lockdown friends that kept us sane enough to survive it*

*—Joseph Crawford*

*For Sam Choon-Keong, my beloved brother*

*—Choon-Yin Sam*

*For my parents, who planted the seed of curiosity in my mind and nurtured it into a flourishing tree of knowledge*

*—Shannon Tan*

# Contents

# List of Figures

**Prospecting Educational Leadership in the Wake of COVID-19: An Aotearoa/New Zealand Narrative Study**



**From Crisis to Learning Leadership? Singapore's Unique Journey Through COVID-19 and Beyond**



**Leaders in Crisis: Philippine Educational Leaders Sustaining Learning in Higher Education Institutions During and Beyond the Pandemic**



**Management of Higher Education Learning and Teaching Through Crisis: A Benchmark for Improved Future Learning in Uganda**

# List of Tables

## Higher Education and COVID-19: An Adaptive Approach in Thailand



## Leaders in Crisis: Philippine Educational Leaders Sustaining Learning in Higher Education Institutions During and Beyond the Pandemic



## Caution, Conception, and Repercussion: Re-examining Higher Education Leadership in Perilous Times in Uzbekistan

# Introduction: Higher Education in Crisis

Jürgen Rudolph, Joseph Crawford, Choon-Yin Sam, and Shannon Tan

> To say the current era is one of crisis borders on cliché. Habitual and familiar, this crisis differs from the dystopian of George Orwell or Aldous Huxley, or hell in the paintings of Bosch or the last days of Earth as told in the Book of Revelations. It is unlike Europe during the Black Death or Central Asia as it faced the galloping Golden Horde. Here, instead, we inhabit a world in free-fall and yet we are along for the ride. (Bastani, 2020, p. 19)

J. Rudolph
Kaplan City Campus, Wilkie Edge, Kaplan Singapore, #02-01 Wilkie Edge, Singapore
e-mail: jurgen.rudolph@kaplan.com

J. Crawford
University of Tasmania, Newnham, TAS, Australia
e-mail: joseph.crawford@utas.edu.au

C.-Y. Sam
Kaplan City Campus, Wilkie Edge, Kaplan Singapore, #02-01 Wilkie Edge, Singapore
e-mail: choonyin.sam@kaplan.com

S. Tan (✉)
Kaplan City Campus, Wilkie Edge, Kaplan Singapore, #02-01 Wilkie Edge, Singapore
e-mail: Shannon.Tan@kaplan.com


J. Rudolph et al. (eds.), *The Palgrave Handbook of Crisis Leadership in Higher Education*, https://doi.org/10.1007/978-3-031-54509-2_1

## Introduction

The dominant theme characterising the early twenty-first century is undeniably *crisis* (Popenici, 2023). In 2020, the global COVID-19 pandemic had morphed into what may be best described as a *polycrisis* (a convergence of multiple intersecting, simultaneously occurring crises: Tooze, 2021) inside of a *mess* (Ackoff, 1997): not just a crisis of continuity of learning, but also health, economic, social, and political crises; a "crisis like no other" (IMF, 2020). COVID-19 may also be described as the first major crisis of the Anthropocene (an era defined by the fallout from our unbalanced relationship with nature) (Rudolph et al., 2021). An escalating climate crisis poses a grave threat to humanity's existence on Earth (Tan & Rudolph, 2023), and one which tertiary institutions are attempting to respond to. Moreover, as Popenici (2023) eloquently posits:

> We have a humanitarian crisis, where millions deal with extreme poverty, famine, racism, and injustice, all disputing our commitments to stated ideals and questioning the very idea of humanity. We have a migration crisis with impacts across the world. We have a political crisis, with new fascist regimes and wars arising in the last few years. We have an energy crisis and massive imbalances with impact across the world. We also have a worldwide crisis of liberal democracy, a social crisis, a crisis of inequality, and a public health crisis. Most importantly, we have a crisis of ideas. (p. 1)

Our time of polycrisis has also been described as one of *permacrisis*, "the feeling of living through a period of war, inflation, and political instability" and Collins Dictionary's word of the year in 2022 (Bushby, 2022). While we do not subscribe to a full-fledged pedagogism—the naïve optimism that places excessive confidence in education as the main remedy for all social problems—we also do not advocate a reproductionist perspective—where schools are seen primarily as tools of the capitalist state to reinforce social inequalities (see Schugurensky, 2014). Moving beyond the binaries of pedagogism versus reproductionism, it would appear that redefining the essence of a well-rounded higher education that surpasses the confines of mere job readiness or intellectual prowess to address the multiple crises of our time has never been as important as it is now. A challenge many governments (e.g., the Australian Universities Accord Process) aspire to address. Alas, even pedagogists must face the reality that higher education itself has long been engulfed in crisis.

In fact, whenever and wherever we look, academics have historically diagnosed higher education to be in crisis. Purpel (1989, p. 1) observed that since time immemorial, notions of crisis have been associated with serious critiques of educational practices, providing "an astonishing resonance with contemporary displeasure, anxiety, and even horror over the present and future prospects of our educational system". To select a few examples, in 1992, Salmi (1992, p. 19) diagnosed that higher education was in crisis due to "an alarming situation of uncontrolled growth of enrollments and expenditures against a background of diminishing financial resources, a decline in the quality of teaching and research, and a rising problem of mismatch and graduate unemployment". In the United States, at various times, a crisis of ballooning tuition fees and student debt has been diagnosed (Blumenstyk, 2015), in addition to curricular fragmentation, a decline in academic standards and liberal learning, and a widespread neglect of undergraduate education in favour of scholarly research and unprecedented financial woes (Lucas, 1998). As significant aspects of contemporary higher education depend on globalisation not only in terms of student mobility and internationalisation initiatives, but also for collaborative research and knowledge networks, the current trends of nationalism and populism are bound to adversely affect the higher education landscapes, particularly in low per-capita income countries (Altbach & de Wit, 2020). Popenici (2023, p. 3) diagnoses "multiple crises of higher education in the English-speaking Western world: an ideological, an intellectual, a managerial, and an ethical crisis". He warns against the "most common answer to all these major challenges": "a religious expectation that technology will provide the panacea, the perfect silver bullet that can end these problems" (Popenici, 2023, p. 3).

When we conceptualised this Handbook, we were well aware that the crisis experienced by higher education predated the novel coronavirus pandemic that took hold of the world from late 2019. In key higher education exporting countries such as the United States, the United Kingdom, and Australia, shrinking government budgets contributed to exacerbated crisis and mess in higher education (Fleming, 2021). The neoliberal university's dark side includes despair, depression, chronic stress and anxiety, self-harm, and, in extreme cases, suicides among students and academics. The neoliberalisation of society has led to the 'businessification' of universities, where higher education has been revamped as an 'industrial complex' and a leading export sector, resulting in the phenomenon of the 'edu-factory', where a premium is charged for employability outcomes, in line with the cult of work (Fleming, 2021). The pandemic amplified these pre-existing higher education crisis symptoms. The cliché of never letting a good crisis go to waste has been viewed as part of higher education leaders' ideology (Fleming et al., 2021).

How did it ever come to this sorry state of higher education? The modern university has undergone several shifts. The first shift was Wilhelm von Humboldt's nineteenth-century ideal of higher education as a holistic combination of research and teaching in an environment of academic freedom in order to transform students into autonomous individuals and global citizens. Although Humboldt's vision constituted an important breakthrough (that was by and large adopted by the early twentieth-century US liberal university and elsewhere), the university envisaged and enacted by him was still elitist and dominated by white male privilege, among other flaws (Fleming, 2021; Fleming et al., 2021).

In a second shift, after the end of the Second World War, the commercialisation of higher education accelerated when international organisations like the OECD and the World Bank started to influence higher education with a 'solutionist' emphasis on educational technology as a cure-all (Popenici et al., 2023). A third historical shift that occurred starting around the 1960s was the so-called academic revolution that led to the massification of university admission (Fleming, 2021). In a fourth shift, the academic revolution eventually led to a counter-revolution and the birth of the neoliberal university from the mid-1980s onwards, exhibiting increasing top-down managerialism and the metrification of academic work. The fifth shift to an edu-factory (and even further removed from Humboldt's ideal) is an acceleration of the neo-corporatised university due to the COVID-19 pandemic (Fleming et al., 2021).

Branson and Marra (see Chapter 5 in this volume; Hill, 2023) have raised concerns about the growing influence of managerialism within universities. This trend is not limited to New Zealand or Australia, but is observable in universities worldwide. Managerialism, in this context, refers to an administrative approach characterised by excessive bureaucracy with a strong focus on cost-cutting and efficiency. They argue that this approach has led to rising administrative costs and demotivated academics.

These managerial practices can compromise the primary mission of universities, which is to foster a conducive learning environment for both staff and students. In contrast to managerialism, the concept of 'strategic leadership' involves positioning the organisation for success while also empowering, caring for, and inspiring its staff. This approach seeks to balance the need for efficiency with the well-being and motivation of academic professionals.

One significant consequence of managerialism is the centralisation of control over policies and resources, often directed from the top down. Decision-making authority is largely concentrated within central leadership, limiting the autonomy of academics. Communication predominantly flows from the top down, although some consultation may occur. However, those providing input often face restrictions in terms of the data available to them and tight timeframes for feedback. This limited consultation and constrained communication contribute to a growing erosion of trust between academics and universities.

Indeed, a significant transformation has taken place broadly within the higher education landscape, leading universities to increasingly resemble commercial enterprises. This shift is well-documented in scholarly works by Washburn (2005), Arum and Roksa (2010), Brandon (2010), Carey (2015), Blum (2016), Davidson (2017), and Caplan (2018). Since the mid-1980s, federal research funding in the United States has plateaued, while the need for financial capital to enhance facilities and attract top-tier faculty, driven by heightened competition, has surged. Consequently, higher education institutions have been compelled to pursue market efficiency and seek alternative funding sources, such as academic-industry partnerships and increasing student enrollments.

As universities vie to attract and retain fee-paying students, they have sometimes resorted to questionable practices. These practices include simplifying curricula, compromising on meritocratic admission principles, and inflating grades. These actions have led to an oversupply of graduates who, unfortunately, lack the skills and knowledge necessary for the workplace. This trend is undeniably risky; however, educational leaders, facing confusion and desperation, often prioritise short-term interests over their educational mission as they eagerly seek more students, thus preventing them from doing what is truly necessary.

So, what exactly should a university's ultimate goal be? Within academic institutions, various academic leaders hold differing views. Some consider a university to have a unique mission: preserving subjects that may not be in high demand but are deemed culturally or academically important. They value the study of subjects like classics of French and Chinese literature, even if computer sciences and business administration appear more lucrative. On the other hand, some primarily view students as a source of revenue and assert that a university should appear as attractive as possible to a large number of students. Profitability is their bottom line, and student attraction is their primary objective.

However, the majority find themselves somewhere in between these extremes. They recognise the influence of market dynamics while also understanding the importance of transmitting culture from one generation to another and safeguarding the study of classics, even when they may be out of favour. These institutions face the challenging task of maintaining a delicate balance between their educational objectives and commercial goals.

One problem with leaning too far towards the commercial aspect of the business is that it can result in prioritising students' interests above all else. This can lead to students being rewarded with diplomas or degrees without demonstrating the capability to solve complex problems. In extreme cases, students may obtain qualifications without submitting assignments or attending classes simply by paying for the degree. In such a transactional model, students see their university education as a financial exchange where cash is traded for a diploma.

## Crisis Leadership

This Handbook takes a broad lens of crisis leadership. One which acknowledges the polycrisis that is occurring inside of higher education. Universities and tertiary institutions are not purely unique in their regular and frequent engagement with multiple simultaneous crises, but their resilience in response, their capacity to engage, and the nature of the crisis are different. Ackoff coined the term 'mess' as a whole system of problems so interconnected that removing one single problem to manage on its own would do irreparable damage to the system itself (see Mitroff & Kilman, 2021b). Quite a dire proposition that has been proposed in large and wicked problems like homelessness, and more recently the COVID-19 pandemic. In the design of this text, we asked scholars to engage with how types of leadership might play a role in influencing higher education navigation through polycrisis among the mess. And, as can be seen in the following chapters, there were varied approaches taken to unpacking crises like COVID-19, belonging, and managerial creep.

For most scholars, engaging with sectoral conversations required engaging with the foundational question of whether the matter at hand was *indeed* a crisis, and what approach to leadership best explained the current approach or acted as the best future solution. For this, we drew on Riggio and Newstead's (2023) model of crisis, although some authors in this text drew on alternate sources. In their model, they speak to the need for crises to be low in probability, public, have high consequence, force rapid action, be temporally situated, ethically laden, novel, and ambiguous, and emotionally laden. In higher education in the twenty-first century, COVID-19 is a quick example that comes to mind (e.g., Andrew et al., 2021), but also may extend to epidemics of black plague, Spanish Flu, SARS, Influenza A, and the Middle

Eastern Respiratory Syndrome (Crawford, 2023a). These forced institutional actions—often in localised areas—and disrupted in different levels. They required leadership to respond.

In this text, we invited scholars to think beyond the conventional language of leadership in higher education, where 'leadership' is a term synonymous with senior management (e.g., College *leadership* teams, and Senior *leadership* teams) and focus more on what it means to be a lead—with or without formal positional power. We are not the first to comment on the need for distinction. That is, to get to the heart of how organisations respond effectively (or not) to crises, scholars ought to start with leaders. This could be the transformative practices of a teacher influencing and inspiring their students to senior managers enacting empathy and sincerity—practices of an authentic leader. It could also be about the student who takes action to build informal teams of peers to feel connected during lockdowns. These stories of leadership transcend traditional and formal institutional structures, but remain prominently underrepresented in the higher education leadership literature. There is a need for good leaders in higher education (Crawford, 2023b), but likely not more people in management roles.

With this in mind, we acknowledge that scholars will approach crisis leadership from diverse perspectives, natural in an increasingly evolving landscape of crisis. Riggio and Newstead (2023) speak to five key recursive competencies of crisis leadership including communicating, sensemaking, decision-making, coordinating teamwork, and facilitating learning. Although, not all of these are able to be treated the same, with communication through social media, artificial intelligence, and other technologies requiring effective management during crisis (Mitroff & Kilman, 2021a). Comments like these are perhaps even more pertinent with the advent of tools like ChatGPT (see Tan et al.'s Chapter 8 in this volume), where artificial intelligence-mediated communication has gone well beyond Mitroff and Kilman's earlier comments.

Crisis leadership in higher education is more than Vice Chancellors and Rectors deploying human and financial resources towards a crisis—this is management. Instead, creating psychological safety and supporting staff and students to be heard and supported is crisis leadership. During the COVID-19 pandemic, and particularly during the emergency remote teaching window, rapid decision-making and 'captains calls' were normal inside of institutions. While it can be difficult to ascertain the degree of consultation or engagement with the views and values of staff, these are important areas for further analysis. In some of the chapters in this text, we see scholars having taken up the invitation to be critical about these experiences adopting diverse approaches to leadership from authentic, transformational, crisis, complexity, and learning leadership, among others. Approaching crises from contextually relevant styles of leadership is essential to effectively evaluating and responding.

## Purpose and Relevance

The purpose of our Handbook is to provide a reference work of crisis leadership in higher education that goes beyond the COVID-19 pandemic and also includes other global challenges. The pandemic has been an unprecedented crisis and turbo-charged the digitalisation of higher education. With the perspective of our Handbook having a long shelf life, our focus is *post*-pandemic, that is, on recommendations and directions for the future. In this volume, we explore a comprehensive range of topics in the context of higher education during the post-COVID-19 era. This includes a theoretical overview of crisis leadership (Riggio & Newstead), discussions on neoliberalism (Andrew and Ismail & Aljunied), managerialism (Branson & Marra), and environmental challenges (E. Tan), as well as in-depth analyses of intersectionality (Klein), the impact of artificial intelligence (Tan et al.), the effects of the Ukraine conflict (Sedochenko & Shyyan), and the various crises in higher education employment (Waring).

In conceptualising this Handbook, we were mindful that generalising the global landscape of higher education, which includes over 20,000 universities and 200 million students, is unwise due to the significant variations in resources and purposes across public and private higher education institutions (Altbach & de Wit, 2020). Vast differences are not only evident across borders but also within countries, making broad generalisations less than useful. Consequently, we collate a systematic, global view of the higher education situation during the pandemic, explore post-pandemic possibilities, and provide recommendations for the 'new normal'. A specific focus in these endeavours is to understand the role educational leadership has on institutional and educational responses. Our project provides detailed country-level analyses from 23 countries on all continents, providing educational leadership perspectives not only during the pandemic but also looking beyond it.

The countries selected by us use in-country experts. The nations are not just the 'usual suspects', but in many cases, they are under-researched, and that holds important lessons for technologically less-advanced countries. The scope includes countries that are more familiar to a general readership, such as the United Kingdom, the United States, Australia, and New

Zealand. In addition, the two most populous countries in the world are included: China and India. Moreover, under-researched countries such as Brazil, Cambodia, Egypt, Ghana, Greece, Ireland, Malaysia, Mozambique, Nigeria, Papua New Guinea, Philippines, Singapore, Sri Lanka, Thailand, Türkiye, Uganda, and Uzbekistan serve as interesting contrasts. For instance, government and higher education institutions' resources and student access to the Internet and online learning differ drastically. The benefits of the country chapters are the support of scholars who are progressing through and beyond the pandemic to view how their country's responses compare to other nations and to support informed knowledge-sharing across jurisdictional boundaries.

We fill a gap in the literature. Thus far, no books have been published that look at higher education globally during and beyond the pandemic from an educational leadership perspective—a key tenet of publishable academic work on COVID-19 in higher education (Crawford, 2021). As university leaders around the world are trying to envisage the future of higher education, they are in need of a book that provides succinct overviews of the varied experiences in select countries around the globe, as well as critical reflections and recommendations. The readership is higher education lecturers, university leaders (presidents, deans, heads of departments), students, parents, government and accreditation bodies, and anybody interested in reflecting over the past two-plus years in higher education and the road ahead.

Our book is the first Handbook on the topic of crisis leadership in higher education from a global perspective. There are two US-centric books on crisis leadership in higher education worth mentioning. First, there is Gigliotti's (2019) single-authored, relatively thin book (the main text has 146 pages) on *Crisis leadership in higher education* that was written pre-pandemic. Second, there is an edited book by Weaver et al. (2022), entitled *Acute Crisis Leadership in Higher Education*, that focuses on the perspectives of US higher education leaders during the first half of 2020.

## Pathways Out of the Malaise: A Brief Overview of the Book

The chapters in this volume offer national case studies and contribute hugely to the literature emerging on crisis leadership in the 2020s. Emerging research in this space to date suggests no one-size-fits-all model of crisis leadership can be applied to such crises since it is multifaceted and requires an all-encompassing effort (Balasubramanian & Fernandes, 2022). Indeed, crisis leaders must "demonstrate multiple-leadership styles simultaneously to meet the changing needs of an organization and its employees", demonstrating compassion, supporting courageous action, and communicating with openness (Balasubramanian & Fernandes, 2022, p. 24). What is clear is that the future must deflect neoliberalism and build on what is known from current crisis management to generate and adopt fresh ways of crisis leadership, arguably starting with compassion. Academic leadership is inextricably enmeshed in neoliberalism as affective capitalism (Nehring & Brunila, 2023). Leaders must not be acquiescent zombies (Ryan, 2012). We are at an urgent juncture. In Fleming's words: "beleaguered by managerial bloat, business bullshit and a Covid-compromised economic environment, the idea of the modern university might soon be coming to an end" (2021, p. 19). What replaces it will benefit from the insights in this volume.

In the following, we provide an overview of the remainder of the book. There are nine thematic chapters and 23 country-specific chapters from all continents. Rather than summarising the chapters one by one, we provide more of a bird's eye view in showing their connections and overarching themes. Our Handbook has two major sections: thematic and country chapters. The thematic chapters provide insightful perspectives on the multifaceted challenges and responses in higher education leadership during times of crisis. They provide a crisis leadership framework (Chapter 2), critique neoliberalism and managerialism (Chapters 3–5), discuss the environmental and exclusion crises (Chapters 6 and 7), and the ones brought upon by generative artificial intelligence, war, and changing features of the labour market (Chapters 8–10). Three of the thematic chapters can be regarded as hybrid in the sense that they focus on both themes and countries: neoliberalism in Malaysia (Chapter 4), higher education and war in Ukraine (Chapter 9), and multiple crises in higher education employment in Australia (Chapter 10).

Newstead and Riggio's Chapter (2) underscores the importance of effective crisis leadership in the face of unexpected and high-stakes situations, setting the tone for the Handbook by providing a conceptual framework of crisis leadership that many chapters have referred to. Andrew's and Ismail & Aljunied's contributions (Chapters 3 and 4) delve into the pervasive influence of neoliberalism, highlighting how it perpetuates a state of crisis in higher education. The transition from traditional academic leadership to managerialism, critiqued by Branson and Marra (Chapter 5), reflects a significant shift in the higher education landscape. Eunice Tan's Chapter (6) brings environmental education to the forefront, emphasising the urgent need for higher education leaders to address the Triple-C crises of COVID-19, conflict, and climate change. Klein's exploration of intersectionality (Chapter 7) provides a nuanced understanding of exclusion crises in higher education, which are based on classism, racism, sexism, and ableism. Samson Tan et al. address the profound impact of generative AI on education, examining its implications for teaching, learning, and academic integrity. Chapters (9 and 10) by Sedochenko and Shyyan, and Waring offer complementary perspectives by exploring the unique challenges faced by higher education in Ukraine amidst war and Australia's struggles with economic and pandemic-related crises.

The 23 country chapters are organised alphabetically, but we discuss them here by continents. A glance at various indices, such as the World Bank's Ease of Doing Business Index, UNDP's Human Development Index, the World Economic Forum's Global Competitiveness Report, the IMF's GDP rankings, Freedom House's Freedom in the World Report, or the World Happiness Report, would show the vast diversity of the countries represented in this volume (e.g., Freedom House, 2023; Helliwell et al., 2023; United Nations Development Programme, 2022; World Bank, 2021; World Economic Forum, 2020). According to the latest data, for instance, Singapore is the world's richest and most competitive country (Stolarchuk, 2023; World Economic Forum, 2020), and New Zealand is the easiest place to do business (World Bank, 2021). With three members of our editorial team located in Singapore and one in prosperous Australia, it is easy to forget that the rest of the world is hugely diverse. Without delving deeply into statistics, it may have to suffice here to state that three of the countries discussed in this Handbook (Mozambique, Nigeria, and Uganda) rank lowly in the Human Development Index, which comprises data on life expectancy, years of schooling and per-capita gross national income (United Nations Development Programme, 2022).

African countries are notoriously under-researched, so we are particularly pleased that we were able to include chapters on five African countries: Egypt (which, thanks to its unique geography, could have alternatively been counted as Asian), Ghana, Mozambique, Nigeria, and Uganda (see Chapters 14, 15, 21, 23, and 30). Together, the selected African countries provide a rich tapestry of experiences and insights into the complex dynamics of crisis leadership in higher education. For the selected African countries, common themes emerge. These themes are similar to other nations, and the variations largely depend on economic, political, and socio-cultural factors. The forced transition to online and distance teaching during the COVID-19 pandemic highlights the challenges and opportunities in all countries. Additional themes are crisis management and leadership—including strategic decision-making, policy formulation, and managing institutional changes and educational equity and accessibility in the context of online learning, limited resources, and technological disparities. Another theme is the impact on stakeholders through financial challenges, the disruption of traditional teaching methods, and the well-being of students and staff. Finally, there is a discussion of introducing new teaching methodologies and the potential for long-term changes in the education sector post-pandemic. Together, these chapters underscore the importance of crisis leadership in higher education, not only in managing immediate disruptions but also in shaping the future of education in a rapidly changing world.

With Asia being the largest and most populous continent, it is appropriately represented by the highest number of countries in our volume: Cambodia, Hong Kong and China, India, Malaysia, Papua New Guinea, Singapore, Sri Lanka, Thailand, The Philippiness, Türkiye, Uzbekistan (Chapters 13, 17, 18, 20, 24, 25, 26, 27, 28, 29, and 33). Similar to the African chapters, these chapters also feature the recurring themes of adaptation to online learning and teaching, crisis management and educational leadership, challenges of equity and access in higher education, the impact of COVID-19 on educational systems and stakeholders, and the future of higher education post-pandemic. Asia is an incredibly diverse continent. Our volume contains Asian insights from the two most populous nations, China (Chapter 17) and India (Chapter 18), a post-Soviet nation (Uzbekistan: Chapter 33), a highly developed nation-state (Singapore: Chapter 25) and countries that, at the time of writing, are emerging from multiple crises, such as, for instance, Sri Lanka (Chapter 26). The authors explore the diverse and complex challenges faced by educational institutions and leaders across Asian countries during times of crisis, particularly during and after the COVID-19 pandemic.

Many international readers may be less familiar with the above-mentioned African and Asian case studies. Our volume also contains perhaps more recognisable country studies from Australasia (Australia and New Zealand), the Americas (Brazil and the United States), and Europe (Greece, Ireland, and the United Kingdom). From the rapid or not-so-rapid transition to remote and hybrid learning models to addressing issues of access and equity, each chapter highlights the critical role of higher education leadership in navigating through turbulent times. The authors discuss the impact of the pandemic and other crises on students and faculty, including mental health concerns and the challenges of maintaining academic quality and engagement. Furthermore, the chapters provide insights into the long-term effects of the pandemic on the higher education landscape, underscoring the need for sustainable recovery strategies and visionary leadership.

Together, the 33 international contributions in this Handbook paint a vivid picture of the global higher education sector's journey through crisis, resilience, adaptability, innovation, and transformation, offering valuable lessons for future crisis leadership in higher education institutions around the world. They weave a narrative that not only illustrates the complexities of crisis leadership in higher education but also illuminates pathways for effective response and adaptation. Combined, the chapters highlight the critical role of leadership in not only navigating immediate challenges but also shaping the future trajectory of higher education in a rapidly evolving global context.

Finally, we would like to express our heartfelt thanks to all contributors to this Handbook for trusting us and going through numerous revisions of their texts. It has been our honour and pleasure to lead this truly global effort. We hope that this Handbook will serve as a critical resource for educators, policymakers, and higher education leaders striving to navigate and transform higher education in turbulent times.

## References


Ackoff, R. (1997). Systems, messes and interactive planning. *The Societal Engagement of Social Science, 3*, 417–438.

Altbach, P., & de Wit, H. (2020). Postpandemic outlook for higher education is bleakest for the poorest. *International Higher Education, 102*, 3–5.

Andrew, L., Wallace, R., & Sambell, R. (2021). A peer-observation initiative to enhance student engagement in the synchronous virtual classroom: A case study of a COVID-19 mandated move to online learning. *Journal of University Teaching & Learning Practice, 18*(4), 14.

Arum, R., & Roksa, J. (2010). *Academically adrift: Limited learning on college campuses*. University of Chicago Press.

Balasubramanian, S., & Fernandes, C. (2022). Confirmation of a crisis leadership model and its effectiveness: Lessons from the COVID-19 pandemic. *Cogent Business & Management, 9*, 1–31. https://doi.org/10.1080/23311975.2021.2022824

Bastani, A. (2020). *Fully automated luxury communism*. Verso Books.

Blum, S. (2016). *'I love learning. I hate school': An anthropology of college*. Cornell University Press.

Blumenstyk, G. (2015). *American higher education in crisis?: What everyone needs to know*. Oxford University Press.

Brandon, C. (2010). *The five-year party: How colleges have given up on educating your child and what you can do about it*. Benbella Books.

Bushby, H. (2022, November 1). Permacrisis declared Collins Dictionary word of the year. *BBC News*. https://www.bbc.com/news/entertainment-arts-63458467

Caplan, B. (2018). *The case against education: Why the education system is a waste of time and money.* Princeton University Press.
Carey, K. (2015). *The end of college: Creating the future of learning and the university of everywhere.* Riverhead Books.
Crawford, J. (2021). During and beyond a pandemic: Publishing learning and teaching research through COVID-19. *Journal of University Teaching & Learning Practice, 18*(3). https://doi.org/10.53761/1.18.3.2
Crawford, J. (2023a). COVID-19 and higher education: A pandemic response model from rapid adaption to consolidation and restoration. *International Education Journal: Comparative Perspectives, 22*(1), 7–29.
Crawford, J. (2023b). The need for good leaders in higher education. *Journal of University Teaching & Learning Practice, 20*(1), 1–7.
Davidson, C. (2017). *The new education: How to revolutionize the university to prepare students for a world in flux*. Basic Books.
Fleming, P. (2021). *Dark academia. How universities die*. Pluto Press.
Fleming, P., Rudolph, J., & Tan, S. (2021). 'Never let a good crisis go to waste': An interview with Professor Peter Fleming on dark academia, the pandemic and neoliberalism. *Journal of Applied Learning and Teaching, 4*(2), 110–120.
Freedom House. (2023). *Freedom in the world: Country and territory ratings and statuses*. https://freedomhouse.org/countries/freedom-world/scores
Gigliotti, R. A. (2019). *Crisis leadership in higher education.* Rutgers University Press.
Helliwell, J. F., Layard, R., Sachs, J. D., De Neve, J.-E., Aknin, L. B., & Wang, S. (2023). *World happiness report 2023.* Sustainable Development Solutions Network. https://happiness-report.s3.amazonaws.com/2023/WHR+23.pdf
Hill, P. (2023, October 26). Perils our universities: Rise of managerialism. *The Post*. https://www.thepost.co.nz/nz-news/350097483/perils-our-universities-rise-managerialism
IMF. (2020, June). *World economic outlook update*. https://www.imf.org/en/Publications/WEO/Issues/2020/06/24/WEOUpdateJune2020
Lucas, C. J. (1998). *Crisis in the academy: Rethinking higher education in America.* Palgrave Macmillan.
Mitroff, I., & Kilman, R. (2021a). Crisis: A major systems problem. In I. Mitroff & R. Kilman (Eds.), *The psychodynamics of enlightened leadership: Coping with chaos* (pp. 13–19). Springer Link.
Mitroff, I., & Kilman, R. (2021b). Wicked messes: The ultimate challenge to reality. In I. Mitroff & R. Kilman (Eds.), *The psychodynamics of enlightened leadership: Coping with chaos* (pp. 21–24). Springer Link.
Nehring, D., & Brunila, K. (2023). *Affective capitalism in academia: Revealing public secrets.* Bristol University Press.
Popenici, S. (2023). *Artificial Intelligence and learning futures: Critical narratives of technology and imagination in higher education.* Routledge.
Popenici, S., Rudolph, J., Tan, S., & Tan, S. (2023). A critical perspective on generative AI and learning futures: An interview with Stefan Popenici. *Journal of Applied Learning and Teaching, 6*(2), 311–331.

Purpel, D. (1989). *The moral & spiritual crisis in education: A curriculum for justice and compassion in education.* Bergin & Garvey.

Riggio, R., & Newstead, T. (2023). Crisis leadership. *Annual Review of Organizational Psychology and Organizational Behavior, 10*, 201–224.

Rudolph, J., Tan, S., & Aspland, T. (2021). Editorial 4(2): Black swan or grey rhino? Reflections on the macro-environment of higher education during the pandemic. *Journal of Applied Learning and Teaching, 4*(2), 6–12.

Ryan, S. (2012). Academic zombies: A failure of resistance or a means of survival? *Australian Universities Review, 54*, 3–11.

Salmi, J. (1992). The higher education crisis in developing countries: Issues, problems, constraints and reforms. *International Review of Education, 38*, 19–33.

Schugurensky, D. (2014). A social worker, a community development worker and an adult educator walk into a bar: On strange bedfellows and social pedagogy. *Postcolonial Directions in Education, 3*(2), 360–395.

Stolarchuk, J. (2023, November 4). Singapore tops list of world's richest countries. *The Independent Singapore.* https://theindependent.sg/singapore-tops-list-of-worlds-richest-countries/

Tan, E., & Rudolph, J. (2023). Strategic sustainability in the Anthropocene. In A. de Moraes (Ed.), *Strategic management and international business policies for maintaining competitive advantage* (pp. 256–270). IGI Global.

Tooze, A. (2021). *Shutdown. How Covid shook the world's economy.* Viking.

United Nations Development Programme. (2022). *Human development report 2021–22: Uncertain times, unsettled lives: Shaping our future in a transforming world.* Retrieved from https://hdr.undp.org/system/files/documents/global-report-document/hdr2021-22pdf_1.pdf

Washburn, J. (2005). *University, Inc.: The corporate corruption of American higher education.* Basic Books.

Weaver, G. C., Rabbitt, K. M., Summers, S. W., Phillips, R., Hottenstein, K. N., & Cole, J. M. (Eds.). (2022). *Acute crisis leadership in higher education: Lessons from the pandemic.* Routledge.

World Bank. (2021). *Doing business: Ease of doing business score.* https://data.worldbank.org/indicator/IC.BUS.EASE.XQ

World Economic Forum. (2020). *The global competitiveness report 2020.* https://www.weforum.org/publications/the-global-competitiveness-report-2020/competitiveness-rankings/

# Headwinds of Crisis

# Crisis Leadership in Higher Education

Toby P. Newstead and Ronald E. Riggio

## Introduction

For the most part, universities are sedate environments, with centuries-old traditions. Yet, crises can arise at any time and cause serious disruptions to the campus and its constituents, with evidence to suggest the higher education sector is experiencing crises in increasing frequency and severity. In past decades, universities in the USA have witnessed increasingly frequent crises relating to gun violence and mass shootings (Wang & Hutchins, 2010). In early 2020, the rapid spread of the COVID-19 pandemic threw universities around the world into turmoil (Zhang et al., 2022, and covered extensively in this volume). And, in the wake of the COVID-19, universities face increasingly complex financial crises due to the persisting disruptions caused by the pandemic, while raging labour disputes add additional pressures to many crisis-fatigued universities (Duffy, 2023). Given the multitude of potential crises in higher education, from shootings to scandals, severe weather events, accidents, and data breaches, it is imperative that leaders in higher education be adequately prepared to meet the multifaceted challenges brought on by crises.

T. P. Newstead (✉)
University of Tasmania, Hobart, TAS, Australia
e-mail: toby.newstead@utas.edu.au

R. E. Riggio
Kravis Leadership Institute, Claremont McKenna College, Claremont, CA, USA
e-mail: ronald.riggio@claremontmckenna.edu





J. Rudolph et al. (eds.), *The Palgrave Handbook of Crisis Leadership in Higher Education*, https://doi.org/10.1007/978-3-031-54509-2_2

## What Are Crises?

Crises are unexpected and disruptive events that threaten an organisation's viability and significantly impact an organisation's operations, reputation, and/or stakeholder well-being. In the context of higher education, crises can take many forms, ranging from natural disasters and pandemics to financial mismanagement, cybersecurity breaches, live-shooter events, labour disputes and strikes, class-action lawsuits, and "acts of God," such as increasingly frequent extreme weather events. Regardless of the specific type of disruption, it is the unexpectedness and severity of an occurrence's consequences that define it as a crisis.

Riggio and Newstead (2023) articulate eight defining dynamics of crises. Here we elucidate five that are particularly salient to the higher education sector. *First*, to be a crisis, the event must be unexpected (Riggio & Newstead, 2023; Wu et al. 2021). A fire service expects to respond to fires regularly; therefore, a fire does not represent a crisis to them. However, a fire within a packed lecture hall or university gymnasium would be unexpected and easily become a crisis. A key function of crisis management is to foresee and plan for possible crises, this might include establishing and practising fire drills and no doubt fires have broken out in university facilities before. Thus, fires are not completely novel, however, a fire is still unexpected in that it is not part of the operational objectives or "business as usual" of a university campus or classroom. Therefore, when a fire breaks out on campus, it could well end up as a crisis for the university, whereas it is unlikely to be experienced as a crisis for the fire crews that respond, as responding to fires is part of their usual operational objectives.

The *second* dynamic is that a crisis is public (James & Wooten, 2005). Crises threaten the viability of an organisation. If no one finds out about the event or issue, there is unlikely to be any substantial immediate threat to the organisation. For example, if a student is sexually harassed by their professor but the assault is dealt with immediately and kept private in accordance with the victim's wishes, the event is unlikely to eventuate as an organisational crisis. However, if there are efforts to cover up the assault by other members of the university, and it eventually attracts external attention and ends up in a media storm, it could well threaten the organisation's reputation and viability and therefore become a crisis.

The *third* defining dynamic of a crisis is that it is of high consequence (Riggio & Newstead, 2023; Weick, 1988). If a tech failure results in one student losing their assignment, it is unlikely to become an organisational crisis. However, a tech failure resulting in all student data being made public represents a much higher consequence and could well result in an organisational crisis. The fourth dynamic of crises that is particularly salient to the higher education sector is that crises are novel and ambiguous. If the event has happened before, if it is known and expected, it probably does not qualify as a crisis. For example, it is reasonable to expect that, while unfortunate, instances of underage drinking will occur within higher education institutions. Therefore, it is reasonable for higher education organisations to plan and prepare for such events making them unambiguous and unlikely to qualify as an organisational crisis. In contrast, the emergence of generative artificial intelligence is poised to completely transform the higher education landscape with students suddenly able to have artificial intelligence tools complete almost any written or graphic output to high standards that are nearly indistinguishable from human-generated outputs. This poses novel and ambiguous challenges that could easily thrust universities into crises regarding assurance of learning and academic integrity.

The *final* dynamic that is vital for the higher education sector to consider is the ethically and emotionally laden nature of crises (Alpaslan & Mitroff, 2021; Riggio & Newstead, 2023). Crises demand trade-offs and decisions that will invariably leave some stakeholders worse off than others. Crises also entail loss—the loss of security, knowingness, assets, routines, resources, safety, time, money, health, and sometimes even the loss of life. These losses, coupled with the ethical and moral implications of said losses often being borne unequally among different stakeholders, can result in high levels of emotion and often distress among organisational members. This is evident in the varied and widespread ethical and emotional consequences of the COVID-19 crisis on university campuses around the globe (Fernandez & Shaw, 2020), and is discussed at length in this volume. The diverse and arguably vulnerable stakeholder base of the higher education sector demands that crisis managers and leaders carefully consider the ethical and emotional implications of the crises they encounter and the responses they implement.

Crises are not new, but they are occurring more frequently and becoming more complex. As such, they require careful attention, planning, and preparation, which are typical functions of good crisis management. Crises are also multifaceted and complex, meaning they require leadership as well as management. While closely related, crisis management and crisis leadership are distinct, and the distinction is important within the higher education sector.

## What Is Crisis Leadership?

In the higher education sector, as in other sectors, crisis leadership and crisis management are often conflated, when in fact, they are distinct. Crisis management is usually focused on the predictable and knowable aspects of crises (e.g., Mitroff, 2005). Crisis management includes planning, preparation, and often accounts for much of the immediate response in relation to implementing known responses to planned for crises (Riggio & Newstead, 2023). An example of this is when a live-shooter event occurs on a university campus in the USA. While tragic, and arguably avoidable, these crises occur with some regularity. Therefore, many American universities now have planned responses for live-shooter events. These may include lock-down processes, evacuation drills, expedited reporting and emergency response communication, and advanced training for designated crisis response team members. Following the event, the university may have processes in place for debriefing victims and resuming operations. All these plans and processes are aspects of crisis management. Crisis management is, for the most part, enshrined in legitimate authority. Crisis management is about the formal processes, the execution of plans, and hierarchical structures.

Crisis leadership, on the other hand, is different. While crisis management is about planning and process implementation in an effort to control and mitigate known threats, crisis leadership comes into play when the crisis is completely novel, when there are challenges to implementing planned approaches, and/or in the aftermath of a crisis when the complexities of recovery unfold. Crisis leadership is about the myriad interpersonal and communication competencies, strategic foresight and execution, prudent decision-making, mission focus, emotion regulation, and values alignment of those tasked, either formally or informally, with navigating their teams and organisations through crises.

The distinction between crisis management and crisis leadership is particularly important within the higher education sector because of the unique nature of HE workforces and the complexities of the higher education institutional stakeholder base, which includes students, faculty, staff, alumni, industry partners, local and state governments, federal government, and the broader community—each of which is itself composed of diverse sub-groups. In the following section, we explore the distinctiveness of crisis leadership within the higher education sector.

## Leading Through Crisis in Higher Education

Crises in higher education can have far-reaching impacts on a range of dimensions, including academic programmes, financial stability, institutional or sector reputation, and stakeholder relationships and well-being. For instance, a natural disaster such as a hurricane or earthquake may disrupt academic operations and research activities, leading to delays and potential financial losses. In contrast, a cyberattack that results in the theft of sensitive data can damage an institution's reputation and undermine the trust of stakeholders. Here we outline three key challenges related to leading well through crises in higher education.

First, higher education organisations tend to have hierarchical, bureaucratic structures (Murphy, 2009), which can hinder the need for agile, cross-silo responses to crises. This poses a distinctive challenge to crisis leadership in higher education institutions because leaders must actively cultivate communication channels and networks that bridge across these siloed entities. Coordinating and encouraging the free flow of communication throughout the organisation is crucial to effective crisis leadership. Leaders within higher education must have the savvy to navigate—and where necessary, circumvent—often cumbersome structures of bureaucracy in order to achieve rapid, agile decisions, and take prudent action.

Second, the higher education sector tends to be staffed largely by independent knowledge workers, who can be especially hard to engage (Byrne & McDonagh, 2017), retain (Selesho & Naile, 2014), and involve in the training, development, and planning required to cultivate crisis leadership capability. Managing academics during a crisis can be especially challenging due to their highly specialised knowledge, deep commitment to academic freedom and independence, and often individualistic and competitive nature. Academics are trained to question authority and push back against approaches that do not align with their own perspectives or research. This can make them resistant to directives from leadership during a crisis, as they may perceive them as compromising their academic integrity or independence, posing distinct challenges to crisis leaders' efforts to engage in the collective sensemaking needed to navigate crises. Furthermore, the collaborative nature of research and teaching in higher education can be disrupted by crisis-induced changes, further challenging crisis leaders' capability in relation to coordinating teamwork. Thus, the unique nature of the higher education workforce poses distinct challenges for crisis leadership.

The third key challenge to crisis leadership in the higher education context has to do with students. Students represent the primary clients of the higher education sector and represent an immensely complex, ever-evolving cohort to whom higher education institutions owe a duty of care to provide conditions that support not only educational attainment, but also physical and mental safety and well-being. This means that crisis leaders within the higher education sector are responsible for a large, diverse, arguably vulnerable stakeholder base. Here, the emotional competencies of crisis leaders are called upon as well as their ability to be transparent in the means and ends of their decision-making and actions.

## A Case in Point: Tulane University's Response to the Hurricane Katrina Crisis

The crisis caused by Hurricane Katrina at Tulane University in August 2005, is a good example of both the difference between crisis management and crisis leadership, as well as addressing the three core crisis leadership challenges encountered in the higher education sector. Tulane University, in New Orleans, Louisiana, USA, is no stranger to hurricanes. The university had encountered them before and had fully prepared to close down the campus and evacuate students in the event of a hurricane. Katrina, however, was an unexpected crisis event. The levees designed to hold back flood waters broke, and it created an unanticipated disaster, causing massive damage, and closing the campus for months.

The magnitude of Katrina exceeded all crisis management plans and required the university administration and staff to face unexpected dilemmas and engage in adaptive, crisis leadership. The leadership team, including the university's president and top-level administrators met daily. Vice President for Student Affairs, Cynthia Cherrey, said, "the way we used to work changed. Every day the leadership team met to consider all possibilities. Cell phone towers went down, so we had to overcome communication difficulties."

The university's crisis management plans had arrangements with other universities, such as Mississippi's Jackson State University, to move and house students, but the devastation was so great that many new partnerships were needed. For example, the School of Medicine was relocated to Houston for a year. While 600 students were sent to Jackson State, many more students required housing, and many faculty and staff had their houses destroyed. Out-of-the-box, adaptive thinking led to the decision to bring a rented cruise ship to the nearby Mississippi River to house students, faculty, and staff, and it became a makeshift "living and learning" community.

Once the magnitude of the damage was realised, crisis decision-making was needed. Prior to the hurricane, decision-making was decentralised. It was decided that there needed to be a centralised structure to manage recovery operations and communication to the many stakeholders (i.e., students, parents, alumni, faculty, etc.). The leadership team set a goal of bringing everyone back to campus by January 1, 2006. Rather than making decisions based on financial or legal concerns, the leadership team made decisions based on what were the right things to do for the stakeholders.

Throughout the crisis, the leadership team engaged in sensemaking based on the changing conditions. Clear and constant communication was emphasised and decisions were made based on the best possible evidence. The university leaders reached out to others—universities, tech companies, businesses—to help out. As the campus reconstruction took place, and people moved back to the university, the leadership team continued to adapt and innovate. They realised that there was a need for human contact, after so many of the university's population had been relocated and/or worked remotely. Town hall meetings were held. As VP Cherrey stated, "when we eventually came back, the hardest part was transitioning to the new reality. Everyone thought things would be the same as before, but it wasn't."

The university's president decided that a process of renewal was needed and a plan was put into place to come back better than before. Relying on lessons learned from the crisis, Tulane University became more "student-centric" and more oriented to helping the surrounding community, which was greatly affected by the massive hurricane, rebuild. As with the University, the goal was to improve conditions for both the campus community and the larger, local community.

## Conclusion

As illustrated above, crises in the higher education sector can present both immense challenges and promising opportunities for leaders. Effective crisis leadership requires transparent, responsive, adaptive, and empathetic communication with myriad stakeholders, as well as a willingness to make difficult decisions that prioritise stakeholder well-being and the long-term viability of the institution. By successfully navigating crises, leaders can sometimes turn negative events into valuable learnings that can increase the resilience of their organisations into the future.

At the heart of effective crisis leadership in the higher education sector is a commitment to the well-being of students and communities. Higher education institutions have a crucial role to play in developing the next generation and contributing to society as a whole. Leaders must recognise the importance of the "whole person" and prioritise the mental, emotional, and physical health of their students, faculty, and staff. By taking a person-centred approach, crisis leaders in the HE sector can foster a sense of resilience and unity that can help institutions navigate and endure the crises that are sure to occur.

Leaders in the higher education sector will continue to face many complex and potentially devastating crises. However, by learning from past crises and maintaining a person-centred approach, leaders can prepare themselves to respond effectively. Future leaders must develop a deep understanding of the unique needs, priorities, strengths, and vulnerabilities of their institutions. They must also continually scan and remain responsive to the broader environmental, economic, cultural, and political contexts in which they operate. To effectively lead their higher education institutions through inevitable future crises, leaders need to continually cultivate their individual and collective competencies in sensemaking, prudent decision-making, coordinating teamwork, facilitating learning, and clear, multi-directional communication (Riggio & Newstead, 2023). And, they must actively dismantle systems and processes that hinder rather than support the agility that is needed in times of crisis. By focusing on these competencies, maintaining a person-centred approach, and continually scanning for potential crises, higher education leaders will be best placed to effectively lead their organisations through crises.

## References

Alpaslan, C., & Mitroff, I. (2021). Exploring the moral foundations of crisis management. *Technological Forecasting and Social Change, 167*, 120713.

Byrne, O., & MacDonagh, J. (2017). What's love got to do with it? Employee engagement amongst higher education workers. *The Irish Journal of Management, 36*(3), 189–205.

Duffy, C. (2023). University staff strike over insecure work as 'anger and discontent' builds on campus. *ABC News*, Australian Broadcast Corporation. https://www.abc.net.au/news/2023-05-04/university-unions-strike-across-australia-over-pay-work/102298204. Accessed 25 May 2023.

Fernandez, A., & Shaw, G. (2020). Academic leadership in a time of crisis: The Coronavirus and COVID-19. *Journal of Leadership Studies, 14*(1), 39–45.

James, E., & Wooten, L. (2005). Leadership as (Un) usual: How to display competence in times of crisis. *Organizational Dynamics, 34*(2), 141–152.

Mitroff, I. (2005). Why some companies emerge stronger and better from a crisis: Seven essential lessons for avoiding disaster. *AMACOM*.

Murphy, M. (2009). Bureaucracy and its limits: Accountability and rationality in higher education. *British Journal of Sociology of Education, 30*(6), 683–695.

Riggio, R., & Newstead, T. (2023). Crisis leadership. *Annual Review of Organizational Psychology and Organizational Behavior, 10*(1), 201–224. https://doi.org/10.1146/annurev-orgpsych-120920-044838

Selesho, J., & Naile, I. (2014). Academic staff retention as a human resource factor: University perspective. *International Business & Economics Research Journal (IBER), 13*(2), 295–304.

Wang, J., & Hutchins, H. (2010). Crisis management in higher education: What have we learned from Virginia tech? *Advances in Developing Human Resources, 12*(5), 552–572.

Weick, K. (1988). Enacted sensemaking in crisis situations. *Journal of Management Studies, 25*(4), 305–317.

Wu, Y., Shao, B., Newman, A., & Schwarz, G. (2021). Crisis leadership: A review and future research agenda. *The Leadership Quarterly, 32*(6), 101518.

Zhang, L., Carter, R., Jr., Qian, X., Yang, S., Rujimora, J., & Wen, S. (2022). Academia's responses to crisis: A bibliometric analysis of literature on online learning in higher education during COVID-19. *British Journal of Educational Technology, 53*(3), 620–646.

# Neoliberalism and the Crisis in Higher Education

Martin Andrew

## Introduction: Crisis of the Neoliberal

In *Dark Academia*, Fleming (2021) pointed out that even prior to COVID-19, "modern universities were… gravely ill" (p. 2). This chapter posits that higher and vocational education have long faced and continue to face a more insidious crisis than COVID: coping with the fallout from neoliberal capitalist logic. This 'logic' is not of crisis leadership or any leadership but new public management (NPM), a "handmaiden" of neoliberalism (Treagar et al., 2022). Under NPM, Ward (2012) demonstrated that market-oriented, outcomes-focused strategies are applied to higher educational (HE) institutions. NPM privileges the needs of 'the organisation' over those of its employees, academics, and education workers and subjugates its workers to 'the market' (Chomsky, 1999). This logic, demanding that the market decides everything, including social concerns such as HE, requires continuous cost-cutting and drives the workforce to maximise corporate capital. It pivots on 'efficiency' and 'accountability'. It leads to an "overloading of responsibilities" for the 'schizophrenic' university and equally multiple subjects/workers (Shore, 2010, p. 20). Ball (2003, p. 224) declared: "Performance has no room for caring". As Andrew et al. suggested (2023), aligning with COVID-era crisis leadership researchers Balasubramanian and Fernandes (2022), what is

M. Andrew (✉)
College of Work-Based Learning, Otago Polytechnic|Te Kura Matatini ki Otago (Te Pūkenga), Dunedin 9022, New Zealand
e-mail: martin.andrew@op.ac.nz





J. Rudolph et al. (eds.), *The Palgrave Handbook of Crisis Leadership in Higher Education*,
https://doi.org/10.1007/978-3-031-54509-2_3

needed is compassion, not the apparatus of NPM. Provided compassion does not become a commodity, its application in leadership can repersonalise the individual, repurpose shared enterprise, and revalidate community.

Neoliberalism was itself seen as a solution to a global economic crisis; nonetheless, it was an engineered solution to problems attributed to a very different age. It was an ideological response against Marxism, socialism, state planning, and Keynesian interventionism (Hofmeyr, 2021). In the 2020s, it is considered '24/7 capitalism' or 'late capitalism' (Crary, 2014). McBride (2022) pathologises neoliberalism as capitalism's global 'variant'. In this era, the pandemic foregrounded that HE stakeholders were forced to implement crisis management and leadership strategies and techniques across their enterprises. This was most notable concerning viable and resilient hybrid and e-programme delivery. This, in turn, sped up the disruptive but inevitable digitisation agenda of Education 3.0, contributing to the somnambulism of late capitalism (Crary, 2014).

## Learning for the Future

As we emerge from this time of plague, we collectively wonder what, if anything, HE leaders have learned. At this juncture, it appears likely that higher education providers will default to their pre-pandemic authoritarian neoliberalist settings and, for instance, pull learners and workers back to the physical campus in an unimaginative show of consumerist bums on paid-for seats in a restored free market (Andrew, 2023). To paraphrase Balasubramanian and Fernandes (2022), the general response lies in the unchanging needs of the organisation as an organ of profit-driven capital. However, many learners' and employees' needs and views on flexible work and the nature of productivity and its impacts have changed. This is arguable because those stakeholders in management and leadership know little else and default to what they thought worked before, such as perfunctory performance and research quality measurements. Shore (2010) saw measurement/funding exercises as the most heinous trespasses of neoliberalism, fuelling "institutional rivalry and internal divisions" (p. 25), rifts still evident today. Many academics believe such measures should be discredited as an inviable and corruptible measure from an obsolete era.

There are precedents to the pessimistic suspicion about the super-resilience of neoliberal ideology. History holds precedents. Lafer (2004) thought 9/11 would focus attention on the ability of workers to challenge corporate prerogatives, but it did not happen. The war on terror, in actuality, furthered the neoliberalist agenda. After the Great Financial Crisis (GFC) of 2008, neoliberalism overcame, experiencing what Hofmeyr (2021) calls an "un-death" (p. 593); like the cockroach, it "defies demise". The GFC may have revealed neoliberalism as "unsustainable given the imperative of protecting the known forms of life on Earth" (Saad-Filho, 2021, p. 181). Still, it led to 'the Great Stagnation' and the widespread anti-democratic anomie that led to Trumpism and post-truth. Still, the ideology was visibly torn: if its principles of rational autonomy were true, there would be no state bail-outs, no corporate welfare—strategies used to keep business alive during COVID-19. Governments would make it up with post-COVID austerity (Saad-Filho, 2021).

The 2011 nuclear accident at the Fukushima Daiichi Nuclear Power Plant in Ōkuma, Japan, might have scuttled neoliberalism. However, Garrick (2014) wrote: "alarmingly, we so often appear to return to 'business as usual', as if nothing had happened" (p. 151). He writes: "rapacious corporate greed, avarice and corruption lurk ever close to the surface" (p. 152). Such critique could apply to the fickleness of neoliberal crisis leadership in the Capitalocene, the climate crisis/emergency (Moore, 2016; Saad-Filho, 2021). Gildersleeve (2017, p. 286) shows neoliberalism, "the ubiquitous *modus operandi* of the Anthropocene", is *itself* the crisis, evident in the production and performance of neoliberal knowledge imperatives. He argues that the crisis of hegemonic, neoliberal doxa is that they exert a "stranglehold" (Gildersleeve, 2017, p. 286); that is, they are still as "entrenched and normalized" as Shore (2010, p. 19) had described. Neoliberal doxa certainly was still aflame when Giroux published *Neoliberalism's war against higher education* (2019). COVID, Saado-Filho (2021) discerns, changes "the transformation of the *crises in neoliberalism* into a *crisis of neoliberalism*" (p. 186). Via a Foucauldian critique, Hofmeyr (2021) writes of neoliberalism: "the very reason it becomes so pervasive, and indeed hegemonic, is because it is 'reasonably justified' – as are so many measures to which we have grown accustomed post 9/11 and in our present reality of COVID-19" (p. 593).

*This* crisis in higher education looks likely to continue to be and has long been, the neoliberalist default setting for crisis management, as Garrick (2014) and others identified. However, without hope, there would be no story. Without hope, Apple (2013) wrote, in an imagined conversation with Stephen Ball, "our research can simply lead to cynicism or despair" (p. 207). He argues that we need an organic public sociology where the scholar/activist takes action. In like vein, Denzin (2010) encouraged those still hopeful to "seek a critical sociological imagination that inspires and empowers persons to act on their utopian impulses" (p. 18). Giroux (2003, p. 91) called it a "critical pedagogy of educated hope". In that space, this chapter explores the features of the neoliberalised university that the post-COVID world need not re-embrace. Apple (2013) concludes with a still-utopian vision of the potential of positive education, sustainability, inclusion, decolonisation, and wellbeing as key discourses increasingly apparent in pandemic-era scholarship. They indicate spaces of future hope for a virtues-led and wellbeing knowledge economy. Ten years and one pandemic on, these things are still what we need.

## The Ruined University

Experienced by insider researchers, the university under neoliberalist capitalism has been characterised with such epithets as the 'ruined university' (Readings, 1996), 'the schizophrenic university' (Shore, 2010), 'whackademia' and 'the troubled university' (Hil, 2012), the 'toxic university' (Smythe, 2017), and 'dark academia' (Fleming, 2021). 'Academic incivility' with its 'bully culture' (Twale & DeLuna, 2008) dominates. Neoliberalism valorises workers' social time for delivery or production (Mau, 2023), performance-managing individuals' efficiencies. Mau's late Marxist critique opens out the de- and impersonalisation that are defining features of neoliberalist capitalism. In a real-world artefact of dark academia's eviscerating change management at Unitec Institute of Technology in Auckland, Cooke (2018) identified "a neoliberal takeover" (p. 16) with zero consultation: "there is only the opportunity to influence anything where the executive leadership team is the least interested—namely in the areas of direct hands-on teaching and learning" (p. 16). This artefact survives as a counternarrative of institutional death at the hands of bureaucrats. It serves as a placeholder for what seemed to happen everywhere in the sector during the perma-crises of the 1990s. Our generation remembers 'the annual crisis', usually another restructure, a further rationalisation; 2023 has been arguably worse.

The ruined university's neoliberal discourse is one thing to critically 'resist' if educators and their allies are to proceed with integrity—though with caution (Bottrell & Manathunga, 2019). Ideally, this occurs within organic public sociology to identify 'fracture points' and their impacts and, with fresh understandings of crisis leadership models, to suggest ways of leading sustainably. In a digitised, Web 3.0 world of transformed production and labour, we meet the intersection of 'cognitive capitalism' (Peters & Bulut, 2011) with its fallacy that a digital economy, a commodity misconfigured by neoliberalist capitalism as messianic, saves labour time and maintenance costs

(Washburn, 2005). Tynan et al. (2015) concluded that instructors providing 'quality teaching' are driven to work "out of hours" (p. 11). Digital and cognitive capitalisms are founded on "the accumulation of immaterial capital, the dissemination of knowledge and the driving force of the knowledge economy" (Moulier-Boutang, 2011, p. 52). Interestingly, the importance of trust and community emerges consistently in the e-pedagogy literature as humane affordances building learner resilience.

For authentic educators, however, the cost is loss of wellbeing in response to an ethos of gallant overwork, particularly in administrivia (Gill, 2009; Sparkes, 2007; Acton & Glasgow, 2015; Viitala et al., 2015; Barker, 2017). In addition to teaching, service, and research, they are also administration workers, upholding compliance regulations in the name of 'quality assurance' or 'excellence'. Giroux (2009, p. 673) wrote: "the appeal to excellence… functions like a corporate logo, hyping efficiency while denuding critical thought and scholarship of any intellectual, civic, and political substance". Bertram (2020a) contends that we are too deep to unmesh ourselves from the crisis of neoliberalism and threaten to lapse into a "new feudalism" (p. 85). The impact of dynastic corporatisation on academic identities and the symptoms of the resultant crisis inform the infrastructure of this chapter. I present storied themes, with each story both valorising key activists/scholars and functioning as a cautionary tale.

## Methodological Approach

Drawing on the methodological technique of subjective academic narrative, I use embodied autoethnography (Sparkes, 2007, 2018) to bring into the academy and the world of professional practice storied retellings of dynamic knowledge practices, linking theorising and lived experience (Arnold, 2012). I access the story behind the master narrative figured by those in power (Andrew, 2020). Such autoethnographies mine personal experience to indicate broader cultural experience, making "characteristics of a culture familiar for insiders and outsiders" (Ellis et al., 2010, para. 3). A conscious use of languaging, often borrowed from scholarship, brings emotion and compassion back to the narrative to compensate for reductive neoliberalist weaselling of such words as 'rationalisation', 'quality', and 'excellence'.

Methodologically, I bring my storied reality to discussing key themes in the discourse of higher education in crisis. This approach acknowledges the multiple experiences, observations, and water cooler conversations, both my own and those of others, in the space of data (Sparkes, 2007). Like Shore

(2010), I may do this with rigour since I have participated in numerous higher educational contexts over a thirty-plus-year period, my service to higher education coinciding with the slippage of higher education into neoliberal capitalism. Apple (2013, p. 206) calls this participation an act of "bearing witness" that supports critical understanding through acts of relating. This relational narrative approach views knowledge as a human and cultural construction, an agreed-upon map or model (Polkinghorne, 1997). The key themes from the scholarship on the crisis of neoliberal capitalism serve as compass points on my map or components of my model.

The themes covered in the storied sequence of narratives, each representing a pillar of neoliberal ideology covered dramatically in literature, are *the schizophrenia of higher education* (Shore, 2010), *corporatisation* (Giroux, 2001, 2002, 2009, 2014, 2017, 2019; Fleming, 2021), *the terrors of performativity* (Ball, 2003), *perverse audit culture* (Craig et al., 2014), *academic zombies* (Ryan, 2012), *resisting neoliberalism* (Bottrell & Manathunga, 2019), and *hope and other choices* (Barcan, 2013). The final section takes us to a space where we might contemplate strategies for challenging the ideology behind a crisis more insidious than that of the COVID-19 pandemic.

## The Schizophrenia of Higher Education

Critiquing the neoliberal agenda of a global knowledge economy, Shore (2010) imaged the modernised university as 'schizophrenic', where education is an individual's private economic investment rather than a contributor to any sense of 'common good'. Under the logic of this agenda, universities become transnational business corporations rather than liberal sites of critical enquiry fostering autonomous and agential citizenries. The university is "a palimpsest: a scholarly community, a bureaucracy and a transnational corporation" (Barcan, 2013, p. 42). It is also increasingly a real estate empire masquerading as an institution of learning (Andrew, 2023). Beyond being educational and critical, the university's (or rather *multi*versity's) roles became social, symbolic, economic, *and* political—metaphorical hydra heads and hence the 'schizophrenic'. To satisfy multiple masters, Thornton (2020, p. 12) argues in a dystopian critique, serves only "to reify enterprise, capital accumulation and promotion of the self within the neoliberal economy". Opposing technologies coenact to construct governable subjects: "a technology of *agency* and a technology of *performance*" (Davies & Petersen, 2005, p. 93). Lorenz (2012) titles the article 'If you're so smart, why are you under surveillance'? Trust is the critical victim of the schizophrenic university.

This schizophrenia is evident in the discourse. Bertram (2020b) identifies a discursive feature of neoliberal logic as its "outrageous misuse of language to cover up a corporate free-for-all". Its agendas are declared by nominalisations such as 'intensification', 'privatisation', 'marketisation', and 'metricisation' (Barker, 2017). Lorenz (2012, p. 600) argued that new public management "parasitises the everyday meanings of (its) concepts…and simultaneously perverts all their original meanings". The discourse of the multiverse marketplace replaced the university's language of researching, teaching, learning, and service.

Shore (2010) shows that the language of neoliberal logic imported such terms as 'quality assurance', 'performance management', 'mission statement', 'audit culture', and 'international benchmarking', leading to a commercialisation of academic research and labour, a massification of the student body, and a fragmented identity for the university and educators. The disciplines of free market fundamentalism replaced those of the liberal university, now 'schizophrenic'. In government statements, "the language of 'investment', 'opportunity', 'enterprise', 'assets' and 'returns' is paramount" (Shore, 2010, p. 19). In Australia, Cooper (2007) described "knowledge capitalism" and "academic Darwinism" and nails the schizophrenia:

> While once the university stood apart from the society it framed and interpreted, it now stands in direct competition with a society made over in its image: a technologically-enhanced knowledge-driven form of the social whose commitment to ceaseless innovation and commodity creation leaves the university little ground on which to stand apart, or to defend more traditional values.

## Corporatisation

Drawing on the work of Milojević (1998), Shore (2010) identified the corporate university as one of six current models of university governance competing for the organisation's soul. Along with the post-disciplinary polyversity, the global electronic university model is most triggered by crisis leadership post-COVID-19. Three others are to some degree nostalgic: the university as a place of academic leadership and scholarly sanctuary, the university as a cultural coordinator for citizenship, and the university as a community-based institution. Even in the post-COVID world, the university as a corporation remains dominant.

The fact that the word 'corporation' has at its root 'body' is a gift to those who, like myself, dissect its corpse (Andrew, 2019), its symptoms (Fleming, 2021), and the remaining zombie culture (Whelan et al., 2013). Bakan's book and documentary *The Corporation* (2003) anatomised the corporation's personality type as pathologically psychotic, which Tregear et al. (2022) see as current in Australian universities. The monetised, efficiency-driven university is corporocratic; employees are intrinsically untrustworthy. The corporatist-managerial approach to institutional governance leads to the commodification of knowledge, and those involved in 'delivery' and "management models of decision-making replace faculty governance" (Giroux, 2002, p. 106).

Giroux (2001, 2002, 2009, 2014, 2017, 2019) is the most persistent critical voice on the budgetary, ideologic, and political corporatisation of HE. Such corporatisation threatens democratic participation, liberatory public good, and critically informed citizenship. His metaphors are Foucauldian (discipline, power, panopticon, symbolic violence) and military: hostile takeover, invasion, war, chains, and more symbolic violence. His writing is always evocative: "As the university is annexed by defence, corporate, and national security interests, critical scholarship is replaced by research for either weapons technology (e.g., Ray Guns) or commercial profits" (Giroux, 2009, p. 673).

In Giroux's world of Bush and Obama-era USA circa 2009, there is evidence of corporations having their tendrils in everything in HE. Student debt is corporatised. Corporations sponsor and capture students for a duration by paying their fees. Teaching labour is outsourced, corporate-tyle, leading to casualisation and precariousness (Standing, 2011). Corporate downsizing expels excess workers. Top-down corporate power structures control education workers and measure their productivity: annual performance reviews, research assessment exercises, or competitive rankings, for instance (Shore, 2008). Corporate metrics mete out punishments and rewards. Everything is evaluated. VC salaries are cast on corporate CEO scales. The likes of Barnes and Noble corporatise university bookshops. Researcher honesty is a commodity for sale. Corporations exert pressure on universities not to publish research not in their interests. University publishing is annexed and aggregated by monied corporations like Elsevier, Kluwer, Springer, Taylor, & Francis (Allen, 2017), and corporate identities lurk behind measurement engines like Scopus. Corporate culture is inscribed within course management systems and everyday software sold to universities and made by such vested interests as the Microsoft Corporation. Microsoft 360 embeds corporate affordances of espial, enabling data collection to inform the disciplinary processes of those rendered unruly. Corporations like Fox News and the Cato Institute, fired by populism, declaim universities as temples of radicalism and critical race theory and demand their closure (Fleming, 2021). Sped-up corporate time replaces reflective slow time:

> Faculty interaction is structured less around collective solidarities built upon practices that offer a productive relationship to public life than around corporate-imposed rituals of competition and production that conform to the "narrowly focused idea of the university as a support to the economy". (Giroux, 2009, p. 683, citing Sharp, 2002, p. 280)

The corporate university extends beyond Giroux's America, though his invective remains the most powerful. Sharp (2002), like Cooper (2007), wrote in the Australian context, where Sims (2019) believes Australian academics endure the harshest managerialism in the world, though Shore (2010) claims the same for New Zealand. The fact that neoliberalist ideology hardwires bullying into its organisational structure underscores a rise in claims of being bullied (Sims, 2019) and underpins motives for taking voluntary redundancy during regular cost-cutting crises (Joseph, 2015; Andrew, 2020). As democracy's nemesis, its vicious tools include competitiveness rather than collaboration and a consequent culture of fear.

## The Terrors of Performativity

The loss of the educator's soul in a Faustian bargain to Mephistopheles/ neoliberalist logic informs Ball's 2003 critique of the terrors of performativity. With its audit regimes and surveillance technologies, this logic quantifies and controls academic labour (Burrows, 2012; Lorenz, 2012). Ball (2003, p. 216) evoked 'performativity' as an active concept designating "a technology, a culture and a mode of regulation" where individuals' or organisations' performances are enactments of 'quality'. "As such", he wrote, "they stand for, encapsulate or represent the worth, quality or value of an individual or organization". In short, beyond *publish or perish* is *perform, produce, and profit*—both your own and ours. This is the capitalistic 'cult' of performance (Micali, 2010). It has "a corrosive effect on people's sense of professionalism and autonomy" (Shore, 2008, p. 292). Tregear et al. (2022, p. 45) write:

> Values that an academic might seek routinely to profess to uphold in one's work such as a commitment to reason, objectivity, public responsibility, and the pursuit of knowledge are routinely compromised, thwarted, trivialised, or dismissed by those above them.

Remembering that, like 'quality', 'excellence' is a non-neutral term (Giroux, 2009), the neoliberalised "performative worker", is "a promiscuous self, an enterprising self, with a passion for excellence" (Ball, 2003, p. 16). This promiscuity takes the form of wantonly reaping grants and outputs to release the university from obligations to fund research internally and to reward those who contribute most to such regimes as Australia's ERA (Australian government, Excellence in Research for Australia, 2023). In Australian contexts, I witnessed research heads putting forward their applications and those of cronies, vying to be the alpha in the "academic star complex" (Fleming, 2021, p. 116) while denying early/mid-career non-crony academics, Fleming's "nobodies" (p. 116), any access. Regimes of performativity were brought in to ensure only the shiniest trinkets made it to the magpie's nest.

This promiscuity harnesses those inclined to 'the entrepreneurship of the self', a term Foucault (1982) employed to identify those who use a capacity for personal leverage, using power to ensure that the playing field is *not* level. Such individuals are prone to narcissism, insecurity, envy (Fleming, 2021), qualities not conducive to collegiality or compassion. More positively, Foucault's 1982 '*homo oeconomicus*' can be construed as individuals possessed of/by the ability to actively shape and manage their subjectivities by leveraging their capacity for 'technologies of the self'. These technologies consist largely of a market-savvy talent for making cost/benefit calculations to measure decisions, choices, and actions. These entrepreneurs are self-reliant (Bröckling, 2016). While the Foucault of *Discipline and punish* (1995) still watches us today, we cannot suborn late '70s Foucault to give a critique of neoliberalism: his context maps a very different terrain (for example, German Ordoliberalism) and for very different explorative purposes (Bröckling, 2016; Hofmeyr, 2021). Nevertheless, with Hofmeyr (2021), I believe some of his terminologies serve to elucidate a critical understanding of such issues as governmentality, particularly the notions of technologies, both of domination and the self, the latter allowing us to conceive of the individual as simultaneously a seeming free agent of self-transformation and a product of power both imposed and internalised. Thus, *homo oeconomicus*.

While some argue that the entrepreneurial spirit supports creative risk-takers (Christiaens, 2019), increased emphasis on the individual over community and competition over collaboration are major contributors to workplace toxicity (Smythe, 2017; Fleming, 2021). Dirty tricks, like constant rescheduling and being wilfully absent for scheduled meetings, became part of the neoliberal toolkit (Vaillancourt, 2020). In Australian universities in the 2010s, we were told not to conduct collaborative research as it diluted the organisation's ERA points, but to publish individually for bonus points. Within this regime, those actors who 'perform' thrive, even if they may seem like servants to a "puppet master" in a neoliberal circus, to borrow a metaphor from Thornton's (2020) critique of entrepreneurship of the self in the schizophrenic law faculty. Those who inhabited this subjectivity, Giroux (2002) wrote, are "competitive self-interested individuals vying for their material and ideological gain" (p. 429). Even today, few see such viciousness as negative.

Research becomes more an exercise of compliant *homo oeconomicus* identity than any authentic conception of 'excellence' or making a critical or transformative difference. As Roberts (2007) wrote: "research is a competitive, self-interested, instrumental, outputs-oriented process" (p. 362). No one has surpassed Roberts' (2007) description of the aforementioned puppet:

> The ideal citizen… is a sophisticated, competitive, innovative and enthusiastic participant in the global economy, ever ready to apply what he or she knows (from research or other activities) to the goal of creating… a "prosperous and confident nation". (p. 363)

Those with a gift for self-fashioning, for talking themselves up, for fabrication, thrive. They are agile bodies, theoretically "robust, resilient, responsive, flexible, innovative, and adaptable" (Gillies, 2011, p. 210), not that the neoliberalised university allows authentic scope for those ideals (Ryan, 2012). Further, the neoliberalised subject has bought into the rhetoric tying the work of the individual/*homo oeconomicus* to the patriotic national good. But surely such individuals are docile? Elsewhere Foucault (1995) defines the docile body as one that may be subjected, used, transformed, and improved. While I am one who calls out the puppet, there are many who would praise the hero.

## Perverse Audit Culture

As Foucault (1995 but from 1975) would concur, constant scrutiny and surveillance undermines academics' sense of self (Shore, 2010). Managerialist regimes of performativity, Ball (2003, p. 15) argued, required "practitioners to organize [our]selves as a response to targets, indicators and evaluations". Ball decries how "lists, forms, grids, and rankings work to change the meaning of educational practice – what it means to teach and learn – and our sense of who we are in terms of these practices – what it means to be an educator, and to be educated" (Ball, 2003, p. 6). Those not naturally fashioned as *homo oeconomicus* may view audit culture as 'perverse' (Craig et al., 2014) because, as Burrows (2012) pinpointed, it enacts competitive market processes, turning academia into a site of gladiatorial combat.

Audit culture persists in performance management, teacher evaluation, and research metricisation systems. Research 'impact' represents an extension of the trend to apply performance and audit cultures to HE. Gunn and Mintrom (2016) maintain that the merit of research is judged according to its economic and social benefits. 'Impact' is a proxy for return on investment (Gunn & Mintrom, 2016). In Cheek's critique (2017, p. 222), "a journal article in a high-impact-factor journal may have no impact at all" since the accepted article rides on the calculated reputation of the journal. Such anomalies are meaningless but measured by-products of the relentless competition driving research marketplaces. It is a game, "the rankings rodeo" (Cheek, 2017, p. 224). Get ahead or be in debt. Lazzarato (2013) argues neoliberalism subjectifies the body politic as "indebted" known only through debt of economic or temporal capital. Not enough research points last year? You lose your research hours.

Academics are leaders, specialists, or experts in pedagogy, mentoring, curriculum, and research in HE contexts. They are active contributors to service their communities, working as reviewers, editors, conference organisers, assessors, examiners, and in affiliated functions. Under neoliberal agendas, the definition of 'service' is stretched into administrative issues beyond reasonable academic remit but tied to the neoliberal buzzwords. Shore (2010, p. 16) argues that regimes of 'quality assurance' mean assessment criteria must be measurable. Bröckling (2016) reminds us that 'quality' means customer orientation and interminable self-optimisation. He admits: "the fear of failure becomes irresistible" (xviii). Quoting Power (1996), Shore's (2010, p. 27) vision entails "scrutinising mountains of documentation, producing lengthy paper trails for review, and various other technologies of 'auditability'". Riemer (2016, p. 39) writes: "every aspect of academics' professional activity is destabilised – or, rather, constituted – by an incessant round of assessment, evaluation and control".

Educators are passionate about working for transformations for learners and stand ever accountable; the worm in the fruit is administrivia. For many, the straw breaks the camel's back because the governmentalised audit culture embedded in administrivia trails marks the academic as untrustworthy and slack (Roberts, 2007). Performance reviews enact a biopolitical situation where professors who resist administrivia are deemed lazy (Gildersleeve, 2017). This pattern indicates a broad trend—the de-professionalisation and proletarianisation of academic work (Radice, 2008). Moreover, after COVID-19, as we find our feet again, it only increased (Tregear et al., 2022). Fill in the spreadsheet of zombification.

## Academic Zombies

The danger of accepting the story as inevitable is that "the rhetoric of managerialism can change the way academics see themselves" (Joseph, 2015, p. 158), leading them away from self-belief and self-care. Educators unable to become *homo oeconomicus* either become sick, engage in acts of underground resistance/solidarity, or leave 'voluntarily' (Andrew, 2020). They may become 'nervous wrecks' (Barker, 2017), suffering survivor guilt (Sutton, 2019). Survivor guilt comes from the self-knowledge that they may have betrayed themselves and embraced repression. The nervous wrecks linger in toxic workplaces, repressed but usually economically pressured. Although nervous wrecks are ethically torn, their choice to remain perpetuates the systems of repression. They trot off to Employee Assistance Programmes (EAP) for counselling and look at the health and wellbeing website to build resilience (Morrison & Guth, 2021). Many of us carry hidden injuries (Gill, 2009), but few complain about how much it hurts (Viitala et al., 2015). In my experience, 'Human Relations' or 'People and Culture' may conduct reviews of faculty culture and outsource the job to some consultant with one degree of separation from the CEO/VC. Thus, staff distress is weaponised by change management (Tregear et al., 2022). Miscreants will be witch-hunted, scapegoated, spied on, and expelled, and survivors trot off for their quota of EAP.

The above narrative demonstrates another option: becoming a zombie (Ryan, 2012; Whelan et al., 2013). The zombies wait for the dawn of a new era in suspended animation (Ryan, 2012) and compliantly await takeover by technocratic Artificial Intelligence (Whelan et al., 2013). In contrast, the *homo oeconomicus* 'ninjas' (Barker, 2017) become 'starlets' (Fleming, 2017) and aspirational alphas. Foucault might see the ninjas as compliant but self-regulated individuals leveraging power by embracing the entrepreneurial possibilities of the corporate culture. Davies and Petersen (2005) show how representing the neoliberal as individual capital ultimately forestalls all resistance via compliance. In Smythe's 'zombie leadership' (2017), the zombies are co-opted subjects, surviving repression by sacrificing integrity but unable to do otherwise as they are captured by academic capitalism. This zombification heralds our welcome to the post-truth university, threatening to slip towards undemocratic economic liberalism (McBride, 2022).

## Resisting Neoliberalism

> Resistance is no longer an option, it is a necessity. (Giroux, 2014, p. 57)

Withers and Wardrop (2014, p. 6) describe the 'devastated' university: "scoundrels have infiltrated the academy—bureaucrats, managers and marketing 'experts'—some of whom know very little, or even care about education". This would seem to be a status quo where the authentic educator might resist, insisting on their passion for learning and refusing to be deemed capital. Yet the reason why those inside the university resist resisting is fear: fear of loss of job, income, position, and privileged voice as social conscience (Sims, 2019, 2020). "Fear becomes a form of paralysis", writes Ryan (2012, p. 4). But fear is real. Tregear et al. (2022, p. 45) write: "staff who reasonably question managerial decisions can find themselves stripped of their capacity to function in, let alone enjoy, their workplace". This is not just the history of NPM; it is happening now. COVID-19 is the perfect subterfuge for change management.

Ryan (2012) shows that in Australia, forms of individual withdrawal and acts of resisting managerialism, like laughing at student evaluations and performance management software, were the commonest modes of resistance (Anderson, 2008). And the mantra, "I'll just focus on my learners"—the ostrich as a resister. Even Bröckling (2016) admits three options are available: exhaustion, irony, and passive resistance, as in Ball and Olmedo's (2012) study of self-care ethics. There are likely more 'nervous wrecks' in academe worldwide than we imagine.

Yet numerous scholars (Apple, Giroux, Denzin), books (Withers & Wardrop, 2014; Bottrell & Manathunga, 2019; Tett & Hamilton, 2021), presses (Polity Press), and journal special editions call for resistance. Peleas and Peleas (2011, p. 420) make a call to arms in *Cultural Studies ↔ Critical Methodologies:*

> We are called forth to work guided by but beyond the abstract ideals we cherish into the nuts and bolts of grass roots politics, into the toil of activist labour,

into daily talk with friends and neighbours to promote with as much persuasion as we can muster alternative visions based on a pedagogy of hope and progress.

Many studies describe concrete strategies in the spaces of pedagogies of hope and hew public sociology, and many, epitomised by the *Social Alternatives* 2022 special edition entitled *It's time: the reform of Australian public universities*, deliberately reclaim multiple authorship as a strategy of solidarity (Hill et al., 2022a).

Strategies might be global or specific. Global calls include Di Maggio et al.'s (2021) urge for "new strategies, embracing solidarity, mutual aid, a sense of societal responsibility, empathy towards the others, and, overall, inclusion and sustainability within and beyond national borders" (p. 257), or any call for vision via the lenses of feminism, environmentalism, democratic equality, and market accountability to civil society (Jones & O'Donnell, 2019). Like most cited authors in this chapter, we create activist counternarratives (Goodall, 2010), at the very least as an elegiac legacy; but leaving behind our stories has not changed the future. Our quest for ethical reformation and reengagement leaves us vulnerable to charges of self-indulgence (Clarke & Knights, 2015). Trust me, there are places in the Twittersphere where minions laugh at academics in hell.

Specific calls include Gildersleeve's (2017) impetus to become a 'responsible methodologist' or a 'lazy academic'. In another special edition of *Cultural Studies ↔ Critical Methodologies*, Cheek (2017) advises researchers to publish where their work has reached, not according to top-down impact factors, and to mentor new generations of researchers, using conferences as a site of positive, not egotistical networking. We can embrace 'slow scholarship' (Hartman & Darab, 2012), practice the 'quieter' intellectual virtues (Skea, 2021), and dare to self-care (Ball & Olmedo, 2012). We can self-fashion by appearing 'lazy' (Gildersleeve, 2017) or 'irresponsible' (Ball & Olmedo, 2012, p. 88) as actions denying performance culture. We may cast ourselves as agents of resistance and agency in our minds as a survival strategy. We can resist careerism and the panoptic-like gaze it affords (Clarke & Knights, 2015). We can claim the identity of our colleague, *homo academicus* (Skea, 2021), and foster vulnerability to force the organisation's professed duty of care (Morrison & Guth, 2021). We can practice passive resistance collectively: re-imagine power, deny the validity of metrics, and regain power over how to define our productivity, our value, and our humanity (Ball & Olmedo, 2012). Nevertheless, we cannot storm the Bastille, bring out the guillotine, and put the aggressors on trial.

## Hope and Other Choices

> Universities do not have to undergo a living death. They can and must contribute to the health and wellbeing of society, ensuring that students are prepared for jobs but also with a critical awareness of the changing world around them. (Hil et al., 2022a, p. 3)

The crisis of leadership discussed here—the ongoing impact of 'reasonably justified' neoliberal capitalism (Hofmeyr, 2021)—consists not in what and how leaders learned from COVID-era crises; but rather in what they chose not to learn. Saad-Filho (2021) cogently outlines the policy lessons. Current scholarship offers opportunities to reflect and to understand that every learner in higher or vocational education sits at a critical moment "characterized by globalization, the hegemony of neoliberal politics, rapid technological advancements, precariousness, and unemployment" (Di Maggio et al., 2021, p. 259). In any sustainable way forward, enabling learners' transformative agency must be at the centre (Abson et al., 2017). In the face of crisis, our changing world, including that of HE, requires transformative intervention in such leverage points as reconnecting people to nature, positively restructuring institutions, and rethinking knowledge creation in light of sustainability (Abson et al., 2017). It needs to move away from leadership models aligned with neoliberalist logic. It needs to understand resilience as a function of sustainability, not a challenge to kick back into an exponential growth curve. Within HE crisis management narratives, we witness resilience in action, forgetting that 'resilience', the ability to be constantly ready for unpredicted opportunities, is a 'responsibilised' commodity (Bottrell, 2013) that sidesteps corporate responsibility, blames individual staff, and demobilises their support networks (Morrison & Guth, 2021).

Barcan (2013) examined the possibilities and politics of 'hope' in the neoliberal university, emphasising collegiality, intellectual honesty, critique, and courage. Through the discipline of hope, we can redefine the limits of productivity, enveloping productive inefficiency. We can reclaim pauses, becoming models of reflective, ethical academic beings. We can embrace multiplicity: many ways to be academic, including accepting that originality is as mythical as mastery: finding our voices and places is the thing. Kenway et al. (2014, p. 2) emphasise our need to "critically, imaginatively, positively and optimistically" move beyond the doom and gloom of critiques of the neoliberal university and look to "a new economy of hope, where [our] precious resources and their strategic utilisation combine to achieve a multiplier effect, spreading hope back through the university sector globally". Many discourses of the neoliberal university land on 'hope' with distant echoes of critical pedagogy, Paulo Freire, Bell Hooks, and Raymond Williams's 1989 notion of 'resources of hope' (Tett & Hamilton, 2021). Via Williams (1989) and Tett and Hamilton (2021), they are familiar, reflective of Barcan (2013), but worth listing here:

- Finding ways to create dialogic, emancipatory spaces;
- Prioritising learner perspectives;
- Harnessing communication technologies;
- Explicit sharing of core values among practitioners;
- Fostering Creativity;
- Collaborating with new groups who share similar values;
- Using both horizontal (peer alliances) and vertical (institutional) strategies to pressure for change;
- Developing and encouraging a "knowledge commons";
- Sharing responsibility for promoting education as a common good;
- Using educational research itself as a resource for hope and for making change.

Visions of hope are not enough. Activist narratives are not enough. Writing to be on the good side of history records but does not impact. What Wardrop and Withers call "making-learning-creating-acting" (p. 6) comes closer. Instead of calls to action, we need action itself.

Speeding up 'late Capitalism' and succession planning for neoliberalism is underway (Hil et al., 2022b). The pandemic revealed the limitations of neoliberalism like never before (Saad-Filho, 2021). Alternatives to neoliberalism are 'new social settlement' (Jones & O'Donnell, 2019) and 'Building Back Better' (McBride, 2022). There are challenges: "solutions are either not obvious or, if they are, will be hard to achieve within the framework of existing political and economic systems" (McBride, 2022, p. 11). Connell (2022, p. 76) lists ways of current change: "circulation of leadership, decentralization of power, deliberative bodies, election of representatives, participatory decision-making, inclusive discussions of policy".

Voices of economics researchers anticipate an end: "capitalism may undermine itself by being too successful" (Jaffee, 2020). The sustainable, inclusive, green, compassionate economy future will be a hard sell. Petersen (2012) sees the "monsters astray in the flesh", neoliberal managers, the zombies most needing decapitation. Progressive institutional changes are necessary (McBride, 2022), perhaps starting with New Zealand's 'iron cage' and Australia's 'straitjacket'. COVID has opened up the reality (Andrew et al.,

2020). Neoliberalism's stranglehold is weakening. McBride (2022, p. 208) writes:

> Neoliberalism's record is dismal. Its intellectual foundations are discredited. Powerful interests continue to support it, but the concepts it was built on, such as the efficiency and superiority of the private sector when compared to the public sector, that markets know best, and that austerity is sound public policy, are unconvincing.

Saad-Filho (2021, p. 186), in a detailed internationalist political economy critique of the limitations of neoliberalism post-COVID, concludes the need for "a politics of humanity and hope, organised around the defining concerns of the left with equality, collectivity and economic and political democracy, against (a, by now, clearly zombie form of) neoliberalism". Zombiedom moves from the academic to the university to neoliberalisation itself.

How do we move from zombiedom to enacted hope in HE? Fresh crisis leadership models for the post-dystopia McBride (2022) sees are needed. According to Balasubramanian and Fernandes (2022), compassion and care are the most significant constructs in building a crisis leadership model; authentic resilience comprises the second. Third is openness and communication. It is clear that the traction researchers on virtuous leadership currently have will enable crisis leadership modelling to impact three core effects: behaving ethically, experiencing happiness, and enhancing productivity (Wang & Hackett, 2015). The virtues these researchers foreground are courage, temperance, justice, prudence, humanity, and truthfulness. Such an authentic but virtue-led approach might delimit the effects of neoliberal leaders, but research on how that can happen continues (Newstead et al., 2019).

Ethical university leadership can also be impacted if it turns back to two of Milojević's (1998) possible models: the university as a cultural coordinator, prioritising indigenous learners and ways of doing and being, and the university as a community-based institution with both models being integrated towards community belonging (Crawford et al., 2023; Tice et al., 2021). Imagining for Australia a forward-thinking governance system like those found in South America, for instance, Hil et al. (2022b, p. 68) write:

> Academics, students and the wider public should have a direct influence on policy directions, ideally anchoring them in social justice and human rights principles that are cognizant of human need in the face of escalating global crises.

Indigenous ways of being are increasingly finding traction in Aotearoa/New Zealand, Australia, and Canada, and Sàmi education in Finland has brought the values of respect, self-determined autonomy, and compassion to education in the world's happiest country (Keskitalo et al., 2012). However, neoliberalism is still oppressive (Nehring & Brunila, 2023). The journey begins in childhood, where, in Aotearoa/New Zealand, *kapa haka* (performing arts) situates song and dance in embodied learning; *kapa haka* seeds cultural values and embeds virtues. Fraser (2014) writes of the inclusion of "emotional involvement—love, compassion, caring, trust, and passion. They also involve *mana* (respect, prestige), *ihi* (essential force), *wehi* (awe), ownership, resistance, a sense of security and empathy" (p. 125). Within Mātauranga Māori, the lived theories and practices of Aōtearoa Māori, we also find *aroha* (love, compassion, empathy), and *wairua* (capacity for spirituality) as principles for reconstructing teams as *whānau,* family groupings. *Whanaungatanga* (nurturing and community-building practices) is foundational to how we treat each other, along with the leaderly qualities of *āwhinatanga* (empathy-based interpersonal care), *manaakitanga* (respect and care among relationships), and *kotahitanga* (unity, looking for what unites us). Kotahitanga; union. "Join the union" (Connell, 2022, p. 79).

For us, this is not a return to the past; it is a recognition that authenticity has long been incompatible with neoliberalism. It's up to us. Let these not be missed opportunities.

## References

Abson, D., Fischer, J., Leventon, J., Newig, J., Schomerus, J., Vilsmaier, I., von Wehrden, H., Abernethy, P., Ives, C., Jager, N., & Lang, D. (2017). Leverage points for sustainability transformation. *Ambio, 46*, 30–39.

Acton, R., & Glasgow, P. (2015). Teacher wellbeing in neoliberal contexts: A review of the literature. *Australian Journal of Teacher Education, 40*(8), 98–114.

Allen, M. (2017). Qualitative publishing in a neoliberal universe and university. *Cultural Studies ↔ Critical Methodologies, 17*(3), 214–220.

Anderson, G. (2008). Mapping academic resistance in the managerial university. *Organization, 15*(2), 251–270.

Andrew, J., Baker, M., Guthrie, J., & Martin-Sardesai, A. (2020). Australia's COVID-19 public budgeting response: The straitjacket of neoliberalism. *Journal of Public Budgeting, Accounting and Financial Management, 32*(5), 759–770.

Andrew, M. (2019). Double negative: When the neoliberal meets the toxic. In D. Bottrell & C. Manathunga (Eds.), *Resisting neoliberalism in higher education: Volume 1. Seeing through the cracks* (pp. 59–81). Palgrave Macmillan.

Andrew, M. (2020). Behind voluntary redundancy in universities: The stories behind the story. *Australian Universities' Review, 62*(2), 14–24.

Andrew, M. (2023). Neo-neoliberalist capitalism, intensification by stealth and campus real estate in the modern university in Aotearoa/New Zealand. *Journal of Applied Learning & Teaching, 6*(2), 1–9. Advanced online publication. https://doi.org/10.37074/jalt.2023.6.2.16

Andrew, M., Dobbins, K., Pollard, E., Mueller, B., & Middleton, R. (2023). The role of compassion in higher education practices. *Journal of University Teaching & Learning Practice, 20*(3), 1. https://doi.org/10.53761/1.20.3.01

Apple, M. (2013). Between traditions: Stephan Ball and the critical sociology of education. *London Review of Education, 11*(3), 206–217.

Arnold, J. (2012). Teaching and learning about writing in the digital media culture: A subjective academic narrative. *International Journal of Asian Social Science, 2*(6), 950–960.

Australian Government. Excellence for Research in Australia (2023). *Excellence in research for Australia.* https://www.arc.gov.au/evaluating-research/excellence-research-australia

Bacan, J. (2003). *The corporation: The pathological pursuit of profit and power*. Free Press.

Balasubramanian, S., & Fernandes, C. (2022). Confirmation of a crisis leadership model and its effectiveness: Lessons from the COVID-19 pandemic. *Cogent Business & Management, 9*, 1–31. https://doi.org/10.1080/23311975.2021.2022824

Ball, S. (2003). The teacher's soul and the terrors of performativity. *Journal of Education Policy, 18*(2), 215–228.

Ball, S. (2012). Performativity, commodification and commitment: An I-spy guide to the neoliberal university. *British Journal of Educational Studies, 60*(1), 17–28.

Ball, S., & Olmedo, A. (2012). Care of the self, resistance and subjectivity under neoliberal governmentalities. *Critical Studies in Education, 54*(1), 85–96.

Barcan, R. (2013). *Academic life and labour in the new university: Hope and other choices.* Ashgate.

Barker, J. (2017). Ninjas, zombies and nervous wrecks? Academics in the neoliberal world of physical education and sport pedagogy. *Sport, Education and Society, 22*(1), 87–104. https://doi.org/10.1080/13573322.2016.1195360

Bertram, G. (2020a). Why the commerce act 1986 is unfit for purpose. *Policy Quarterly, 16*(6), 80–87.

Bertram, G. (2020b). Breaking out of neoliberalism's "iron cage". *Newsroom.* https://www.newsroom.co.nz/ideasroom/breaking-out-of-neoliberalisms-iron-cage

Bottrell, D. (2013). Responsibilised resilience? Reworking neoliberal social policy texts. *M/C Journal, 16*(5). https://doi.org/10.5204/mcj.708

Bottrell, D., & Manathunga, C. (Eds.). (2019). *Resisting neoliberalism in higher education: Volumes 1 & 2.* Palgrave Macmillan.

Bröckling, U. (2016). *The entrepreneurial self*. Sage.

Burrows, R. (2012). Living with the H-Index? Metric assemblages in the contemporary academy. *The Sociological Review, 60*(2), 355–372.

Cheek, J. (2017). Qualitative inquiry and the research marketplace: Putting some +s (pluses) in our thinking, and why this matters. *Cultural Studies ↔ Critical Methodologies, 17*(3), 221–226.

Chomsky, N. (1999). *Profit over people: Neoliberalism and global order*. Seven Stories Press.

Christiaens, T. (2019). The entrepreneur of the self beyond Foucault's neoliberal *homo oeconomicus*. *European Journal of Social Theory, 23*(4), 493–511. https://doi.org/10.1177/136843101985

Clarke, C., & Knights, D. (2015). Careering through academia: Securing identities or engaging ethical subjectivities? *Human Relations, 68*(12), 1865–1888.

Connell, R. (2022). Raewyn Connell on why and how universities need to change, and soon: Interview with Richard Hil. *Social Alternatives, 41*(1), 76–80.

Cooke, D. (2018). *Blind faith: Deconstructing Unitec 2015–2017*. Quality Public Education Coalition.

Cooper, S. (2007). Academic Darwinism: The (logical) end of the Dawkins era. *Arena Journal, 28*, 107–111.

Craig, R., Amernic, J., & Tourish, D. (2014). Perverse audit culture and the modern public University. *Financial Accountability and Management, 30*, 1–24.

Crary, J. (2014). *24/7. Late capitalism and the ends of sleep*. Verso.

Crawford, J., Allen, K.-A., Sanders, T., Baumeister, R., Parker, P. D., Saunders, C., & Tice, D. M. (2023). Sense of belonging in higher education students: An Australian longitudinal study from 2013 to 2019. *Studies in Higher Education, 49*, 395–409. https://doi.org/10.1080/03075079.2023.2238006

Davies, B., & Petersen, E. (2005). Neoliberal discourse in the academy: The forestalling of collective resistance. *Learning and Teaching in the Social Sciences*. http://ezproxy.uws.edu.au/login?url=10.1386/ltss.2.2.77/1

Denzin, N. (2010). *The qualitative manifesto: A call to arms*. Left Coast Press.

Di Maggio, I., Ginevra, C., Santilli, S., Nota, L., & Soresi, S. (2021). Life design for an inclusive and sustainable future. In M. L. Kern & M. L. Wehmeyer (Eds.), *The palgrave handbook of positive education* (pp. 251–270). Palgrave Macmillian. https://doi.org/10.1007/978-3-030-64537-3_10

Ellis, C., Adams, T., & Bochner, A. (2010). Autoethnography: An overview. *Forum Qualitative Sozialforschung/Forum: Qualitative Social Research, 12*(1), 10. http://nbn-resolving.de/urn:nbn:de:0114-fqs1101108

Fleming, P. (2017). *The death of homo economicus*. University of Chicago Press Economics Books.

Fleming, P. (2021). *Dark academia: How universities die*. Pluto Books.

Foucault, M. (1982). Technologies of the self. In L. H. Martin, H. Gutman, & P. Hutton (Eds.), *Technologies of the self: A seminar with Michel Foucault* (pp. 16–49). Tavistock Publications.

Foucault, M. (1986). *The care of the self*. Pantheon.

Foucault, M. (1995). *Discipline and punish: The birth of the prison* (A. Sheridan, Trans.). Vintage.

Foucault, M. (2008). *The birth of biopolitics. Lectures at the Collège de France 1978–1979* (M. Senellart, Ed., G. Burchell, Trans.). Palgrave Macmillan.

Fraser, T. (2014). Māori-Tūhoe epistemology: Sustaining tribal identity through Tūhoe performing arts. In New Zealand Qualifications Authority (Ed.), *Enhancing Mātauranga Māori and global indigenous knowledge* (pp. 118–135). NZQA.

Garrick, J. (2014). The limits of knowledge management in contemporary corporate conditions. *International Journal of Learning and Change, 7*(3/4), 141–155.

Gildersleeve, R. (2017). The neoliberal academy of the Anthropocene and the retaliation of the lazy academic. *Cultural Studies ↔ Critical Methodologies, 17*(3), 286–293.

Gill, R. (2009). Breaking the silence: The hidden injuries of neo-liberal academia. In R. Flood & R. Gill (Eds.), *Secrecy and silence in the research process: Feminist reflections* (pp. 228–244). Routledge.

Gillies, D. (2011). Agile bodies: A new imperative in neoliberal governance. *Journal of Education Policy, 26*(2), 207–223.

Giroux, H. (2001). *Beyond the corporate university: Culture and pedagogy in the new millennium.* Rowman & Littlefield.

Giroux, H. (2002). Neoliberalism, corporate culture and the promise of higher education: The university as a public sphere. *Harvard Educational Review, 72*, 423–463.

Giroux, H. (2003). Utopian thinking under the sign of Neoliberalism: Towards a critical pedagogy of educated hope. *Democracy and Nature, 9*(1), 91–105. https://doi.org/10.1080/1085566032000074968

Giroux, H. (2007). *The university in chains: Confronting the military-industrial-academic complex.* Paradigm Books.

Giroux, H. (2009). Democracy's nemesis: The rise of the corporate university. *Cultural Studies ↔ Critical Methodologies, 9*(5), 669–695. https://doi.org/10.1177/1532708609341169

Giroux, H. (2014). Public intellectuals against the neoliberal university. In N. Denzin & M. Giardina (Eds.), *Qualitative inquiry outside the academy* (pp. 35–60). Left Coast.

Giroux, H. (2017). Neoliberalism's war against higher education and the role of public intellectuals. In M. Izak, M. Kostera, & M. Zawadzki (Eds.), *The future of university education* (pp. 185–206). Palgrave.

Giroux, H. (2019). *Neoliberalism's war on higher education.* Haymarket.

Goodall, H., Jr. (2010). *Counternarrative: How progressive academics can challenge extremist and promote social justice.* Left Coast Press.

Gunn, A., & Mintrom, M. (2016). Evaluating the non-academic impact of academic research: Design considerations. *Journal of Higher Education Policy and Management, 39*(1), 20–30. https://doi.org/10.1080/1360080X.2016.1254429

Hamilton, M. (2020). *Resisting neoliberalism in education: Resources of hope*. https://wp.lancs.ac.uk/literacy-research-centre/2020/01/24/resisting-neoliberalism-in-education-resources-of-hope/

Hartman, Y., & Darab, S. (2012). A call for slow scholarship: A case study on the intensification of academic life and its implications for pedagogy. *Review of Education, Pedagogy and Cultural Studies, 34*(1–2), 49–60.

Hil, R. (2012). *Whackademia: An insider's account of the troubled university*. University of Sydney Press.

Hil, R., Pelizzon, A., & Baum, F. (2022a). It's time: The reform of Australian private universities. *Social Alternatives, 41*(1), 3–4. https://socialalternatives.com/issue/its-time-the-re-form-of-australian-public-universities/

Hil, R., Thompsett, F., Lyons, K., Joannes-Boyau, R., Lake, S., Lucas, A., McCallum, A., O'Connor, J., Pelizzon, A., Tregear, P., & Vodeb, O. (2022b). Over the horizon: Is there an alternative to neoliberal university governance? *Social Alternatives, 41*(1). https://socialalternatives.com/issue/its-time-the-re-form-of-australian-public-universities/

Hofmeyr, A. (2021). Foucault's analyses of neoliberal governmentality: Past investigations and present applications. *Etica & Politica, 23*(1), 589–616.

Jones, B., & O'Donnell, M. (2019). *Alternatives to neoliberalism: Towards equality and democracy*. Polity Press.

Joseph, R. (2015). The cost of managerialism in the university: An autoethnographical account of an academic redundancy process. *Prometheus, 33*(2), 1–25. http://dx.coi.org/10.1080/08109028.2015.109223.

Jaffee, D. (2020). Disarticulation and the crisis of neoliberalism in the United States. *Critical Sociology, 46*(1), 65–81. https://doi.org/10.1177/0896920518798122

Kelly, A. (2020). Rethinking the neoliberal university and its impact on students. *Journal of Academic Language and Learning, 14*(2), C1–C6.

Kenway, J., Boden, R., & Fahey, J. (2014). Seeking the necessary 'resources of hope' in the neoliberal university. In M. Thornton (Ed.), *Through a glass darkly: The social sciences look at the neo-liberal university* (pp. 259–281). ANU.

Keskitalo, P., Uusiautti, S., & Määttä, K. (2012). How to make small indigenous cultures bloom? Special traits of Samì education in Finland. *Current Issues in Comparative Education, 15*(1), 52–63.

Lafer, G. (2004). Neoliberalism by other means: The "war on terror" at home and abroad. *New Political Science, 26*(3), 323–346. https://doi.org/10.1080/0739314042000251306

Lazzarato, M. (2013). *The making of the indebted man* (Trans. J. Jordan). Semiotext(e).

Lorenz, C. (2012). 'If you're so smart, why are you under surveillance'? Universities, neoliberalism, and new public management. *Critical Enquiry, 38*, 599–629.

Mau, S. (2023). *Mute comparison: A Marxist theory of the economic theory of power*. Verso.

McBride, S. (2022). *Escaping dystopia: Rebuilding a public domain*. The Polity Press.

Micali, S. (2010). The capitalistic cult of performance. *Philosophy Today, 54*(4), 379–391.

Milojević, I. (1998). Women's higher education in the 21st century. *Futures, 30*(7), 693–704.

Moore, J. W. (2016). *Anthropocene or capitalocene? Nature, history and the crisis of capitalism.* PM Press.

Morrison, D., & Guth, J. (2021). Rethinking the neoliberal university: Embracing vulnerability in English law schools? *The Law Teacher, 55*(1), 42–56. https://doi.org/10.1080/03069400.2021.1872867

Moulier-Boutang, Y. (2011). *Cognitive capitalism.* Polity Press.

Nehring, D., & Brunila, K. (2023). *Affective capitalism in academia: Revealing public secrets.* Bristol University Press.

Newstead, T., Dawkins, S., Macklin, R., & Martin, A. (2019). The virtues project: An approach to developing good leaders. *Journal of Business Ethics, 15*, 1–18. https://doi.org/10.1007/s10551-019-04163-2

Peleas, R., & Peleas, M. (2011). A screed, a surrender, and a summons: Facing the political surround. *Cultural Studies ↔ Critical Methodologies, 11*(4), 418–420.

Petersen, E. (2012, July). Monsters astray in the flesh: A layered exploration of the im/possibilities of resistance-work in the neoliberalised university. *Paper presented at the Academic Identities Conference*, Auckland.

Peters, M., & Bulut, E. (2011). *Cognitive capitalism, education and digital labour.* Peter Lang.

Polkinghorne, D. (1997). Reporting qualitative research as practice. In W. Tierney & Y. Lincoln (Eds.), *Representation and the text: Reframing the narrative voice* (pp. 3–21). State University of New York Press.

Power, M. (1996). Making things auditable. *Accounting, Organizations and Society, 21*, 289–315.

Radice, H. (2008). Life after death? The Soviet system in British higher education. *International Journal of Management Concepts and Philosophy, 3*(2), 99–120.

Readings, B. (1996). *The university in ruins.* Harvard University Press.

Redden, G. (2017). John Howard's investor state: Neoliberalism and the rise of inequality in Australia. *Critical Sociology, 45*(4–5), 713–728. https://doi.org/10.1177/0896920517745117

Riemer, N. (2016). Academics, the humanities and the enclosure of knowledge: The worm in the fruit. *Australian Universities' Review, 58*, 33–41.

Roberts, P. (2007). Neoliberalism, performativity and research. *International Review of Education, 53*(4), 349–365.

Ryan, S. (2012). Academic zombies: A failure of resistance or a means of survival? *Australian Universities Review, 54*, 3–11.

Saad-Filho, A. (2021). Neoliberalism and the pandemic. *Notebooks: The Journal for Studies on Power, 1*, 179–186. https://brill.com/view/journals/powr/1/1/article-p179_179.xml?language=en

Sharp, G. (2002). The idea of the intellectual and after. In S. Cooper, J. Hinkson, & G. Sharp (Eds.), *Scholars and entrepreneurs: The university in crisis.* Arena.

Shore, C. (2008). Audit culture and illiberal governance: Universities and the politics of accountability. *Anthropological Theory, 8*(3), 278–299.

Shore, C. (2010). Beyond the multiversity: Neoliberalism and the rise of the schizophrenic university. *Social Anthropology, 18*(1), 15–29.

Sims, M. (2019). Neoliberalism and the new public management in an Australian university: The invisibility of our takeover. *Australian Universities Review, 61*(1), 21–30.

Sims, M. (2020). *Bullshit towers: Neoliberalism and managerialism in universities.* Peter Lang.

Skea, C. (2021). Emerging neoliberal academic identities: Looking beyond. *Homo economicus, Studies in Philosophy and Education, 40*, 399–414. https://doi.org/10.1007/s11217-021-09768-7

Smythe, J. (2017). *The toxic university.* Palgrave.

Sparkes, A. C. (2007). Embodiment, academics, and the audit culture: A story seeking consideration. *Qualitative Research, 7*(4), 521–550.

Sparkes, A. (2018). Autoethnography comes of age: Consequences, comforts, and concerns. In D. Beach, C. Bagley, & S. Marques da Silva (Eds.), *Handbook of ethnography of education* (pp. 479–499). Wiley.

Standing, G. (2011). *The precariat: The new dangerous class.* Bloomsbury Academic.

Sutton, M. (2019, 2 April). *Flinders university restructure has left surviving staff overworked, academics say.* ABC News. https://www.abc.net.au/news/2019-04-02/flinders-university-restructure-staff-overworked-academics-say/10958418

Tett, L., & Hamilton, M. (2021). *Resisting neoliberalism in education: Local, national and transnational perspectives.* Policy Press.

Thornton, M. (2020). The challenge for law schools of satisfying multiple masters. *Australian Universities Review, 62*(2), 5–13.

Tice, D., Baumeister, R., Crawford, J., Allen, K. A., & Percy, A. (2021). Student belongingness in higher education: Lessons for Professors from the COVID-19 pandemic. *Journal of University Teaching & Learning Practice, 18*(4), 2. https://doi.org/10.53761/1.18.4.2

Tregear, P., Guthrie, J., Lake, S., Lucas, A., O'Connor, J., Pellzzon, A., & Vodeb, B. (2022). 'Enough to make you sick!' Pathological characteristics of the Australian academic workplace. *Social Alternatives, 41*(1), 44–51.

Twale, D., & DeLuna, B. (2008). *Faculty incivility.* Jossey-Bass.

Tynan, M., Ryan, Y., & Lamont-Mills, A. (2015). Examining workload models in online and blended teaching. *British Journal of Educational Technology, 46*(1), 5–15.

Vaillancourt, A. (2020, January 14). 5 'dirty tricks' common in campus administration. *The Chronicle of Higher Education.* https://www.jobhakr.com/news/2020/1/17/5-dirty-tricks-common-in-campus-administration

Viitala, R., Tanskanen, J., & Säntti, R. (2015). The connection between organizational climate and wellbeing at work. *International Journal of Organizational Analysis, 23*(4), 606–620. https://doi.org/10.1108/IJOA-10-2013-0716

Wang, G., & Hackett, R. (2015). Conceptualization and measurement of virtuous leadership: Doing well by doing good. *Journal of Business Ethics, 137*(2), 1–25.

Ward, S. (2012). *Neoliberalism and the global restructuring of knowledge and education.* Routledge.

Washburn, J. (2005). *University Inc.: The corporate corruption of American higher education.* Basic Books.

Wardrop, A., & Withers, D. (2014). *The para-academic handbook: A toolkit for making-learning-creating-acting.* HammerOn Press.

Whelan, A., Walker, R., & Moore, C. (2013). *Zombies in the academy* (pp. 67–78). Intellect Ltd.

Williams, R. (1989). *Resources of hope*. Verso.

Withers, D., & Wardrop, A. (2014). Reclaiming what has been devastated. In A. Wardrop & D. Withers (Eds.), *The para-academic handbook: A toolkit for making-learning-creating-acting* (pp. 6–13). HammerOn Press.

# Beyond Academic Dehumanisation: Neoliberalism and the *'Good University'* in Malaysia

Fadhil Ismail and Khairudin Aljunied

## Introduction

Universities have been traditionally considered hallowed institutions responsible for the creation of knowledge for the betterment of states (Connell, 2019). They are respected for the guidance they provide on significant societal issues. They perform a critical role in developing agents of change vital for systemic reforms. As the world entered into an advanced industrial age after the Second World War, many countries reconstructed their higher education systems (de Wit & Altbach, 2021). Universities today are geared towards producing cutting-edge research while contributing to the socio-economic, political, and sustainability enhancement of the nation (Kohl et al., 2022). The highly mobile global labour market in the twenty-first century has compelled many universities to diversify their programmes to develop individuals with a broader knowledge base, more diversified skills, advanced analytical capacities, and complex communication skills (Engel & Yemini, 2020). In other words, universities have become indispensable cornerstones of modern civilisations and a purveyor of national progress (Kenway & Howard, 2022).

F. Ismail (✉)
Kaplan, Singapore
e-mail: fadhil.ismail@kaplan.com

K. Aljunied
National University of Singapore (NUS), Singapore, Singapore


J. Rudolph et al. (eds.), *The Palgrave Handbook of Crisis Leadership in Higher Education*,
https://doi.org/10.1007/978-3-031-54509-2_4

Be that as it may, this relentless pursuit of progress has been largely underpinned by a philosophy of economic rationality. Universities worldwide have significantly departed from their primary role as the conscience of society (Zajda & Rust, 2020). Instead, these revered institutions are steadily functioning like global corporations, with their overriding objective being to maximise profits and inform policies to influence economic prosperity. The recent COVID-19 crisis has laid bare the problems of higher education. Universities struggle to sustain themselves and remain relevant in a globalising world (Connell, 2020). They have generally failed to produce adaptive and resilient scholars and students who can withstand the shocks of failing economies and institutions (Trigueros et al., 2020). This distressing phenomenon can be observed partly in the stresses scholars and students face in the post-COVID-19 scenarios as higher educational institutions shift from online classes and meetings to hybrid arrangements (Knight et al., 2021; Rudolph et al., 2023; Tice et al., 2021). The global pandemic has accentuated the human cost of such neglect of universities, as evidenced by the prevalence of mental health problems and suicides among undergraduates globally (Uvais, 2021).

In this chapter, we develop the argument that universities in the Global South suffer from the problem of *academic dehumanisation* made worse by the pressures caused by the COVID-19 pandemic. Using Malaysia as our case study, academic dehumanisation broadly refers to a process where materialist and prestige-driven aspirations come in the way of ethical and balanced approaches to academic life. Academic dehumanisation involves prioritising status and branding rather than the welfare of scholars who are expected, ironically enough, to work harder year after year to meet the rising demands of the academe (Mason & Megoran, 2021). Academic dehumanisation promotes utilitarian management of higher educational institutions and focuses primarily on economic success and brand development (Darder, 2012). The overriding concern goes beyond enlightening knowledge seekers' minds, hearts, and souls. The goal is to publish extensively and market universities by any means necessary to be at the forefront of global institutional rankings. As such, we further argue that academic dehumanisation is a hegemonic condition plaguing universities in the Global South. It is, in fact, an aspiration that obstructs the creation of '*good universities*'.

The concept of a good university was first proposed by Raewyn Connell (2019). A frank critic of contemporary universities' deplorable state of affairs, Connell argues that universities have created and sustained widespread social inequalities. Her acerbic accusation of universities legitimising regressive policies favouring the powerful and the elite struck a chord with many in higher education who have suffered from such policies. Connell frames universities as "privilege machines" and laments that "individual departments can be pocket-sized tyrannies; income inequalities within universities are growing; hierarchies of rank and authority are usual" (Connell, 2019, pp. 104, 121). Connell's barb is directed not only against universities at the top of the global pecking order. Most universities have now come to terms with the neoliberal logic of individualised competition and market rationality at the expense of scholarly integrity (Brooks et al., 2016). Other scholars have also demonstrated how neoliberalism has resulted in the exploitation of academic labour, turning universities into sites of acute tensions between university management and faculty staff, causing high levels of occupation stress, personal insecurity, wage stagnation, and low job satisfaction (Latecka, 2023).

This chapter underlines Cornell's critique and further shows that academic dehumanisation has its roots deeply buried in the colonial past. Connell argues that historically, universities have served the elite class and exerted control by influencing policy research agendas that are predominantly Eurocentric and solely crafted to promote Western intellectual traditions (Connell, 2019). This continued hegemony tightens its vice-like grip on marginalised populations and, tragically, exacerbates social and economic inequalities. Using Malaysia as our case study, we highlight how colonial powers founded universities in the Global South and how these powers wrapped their oppressive tentacles in a vice-like grip around the country. Malaysia has inherited such colonial schemes (Nah, 2003). Following that, we examine the predominance of STEM subjects in the overall focus of Malaysian universities. Developmental and nation-building goals initially drove this focus but were soon taken over by the pressures of neoliberalism, largely defined and described in Western terms. As this chapter shall demonstrate, leadership within the university system has also been influenced and conditioned through the surreptitious consolidation of colonial values and ideologies and, currently, by neoliberalism. The injudicious adoption of such styles of thought and management of the academe have kept universities in the Global South still dependent on the West, which set the standards defining what "successful universities" should be (Marginson & Sawir, 2006). Attempts at decolonising universities severely fell short of their objectives. Good universities in Malaysia eventually succumbed to academic dehumanisation.

## Academic Dehumanisation in the Global South: A Brief History

The "Global South" refers to Latin America, Asia, Africa, and Oceania regions. It has also been called the "Third World" to denote underdeveloped and developing countries (Atkinson, 2021; Haug et al., 2021). These countries have been stifled with a myriad of societal challenges, exacerbated by poorly functioning economies, and, more often than not, involve politically or culturally marginalised populations. It is treated as a periphery to countries that govern the world system (Whetstone & Yilmaz, 2020). These countries include, among others, western Europe and the United States. Most former colonies in the Global South are heavily dependent on or have invested in the schemes of their Euro-American colonisers (Smiet, 2022). The Global South, therefore, also refers to a coalition of nations attempting to overcome the effects of neo-colonialism and chart new destinies of their own. It is indeed a profound endeavour to remedy and recover previously colonised peoples' human rights, liberty, and equality (Dados & Connell, 2012).

The problems of education and other realms of life in the Global South, including education, have been extensively examined by postcolonial theorists (Tenzin & Lee, 2022). These theorists highlight the abuse of education by the European colonial powers as a means to civilise and modernise colonised peoples. The aim was to instil in the minds of the coloniser, the superiority of Western ways of thinking and living compared to local cultures, values, and traditions (Hennessey, 2022). Concepts such as humanism, enlightenment, and civilisation were used as ideological tools to impose Western values and ways of knowing on other cultures (Sullivan & Hickel, 2023). Formal education was the most effective way these concepts were imbibed (Dei, 2019). In so doing, European colonial powers consigned native educational systems to secondary importance, couching such age-old institutions of learning and pedagogical methods as regressive, outmoded, traditional, and unsuitable for modern life (Moyo, 2020; Willinsky, 1998).

The creation of nation-states in the Global South since the 1940s did not dismantle the legacies, power structures, and relationships rooted in the history of imperialism and colonial rule (Patel & McMichael, 2004). Postcolonial theorists assert that formerly colonised countries continued to be exploited and subjugated by European nations by producing graduates from Western elite schools and universities (Hickling-Hudson et al., 2004). These graduates return to their home countries, importing Eurocentric ideas they studied while overseas. Little wonder then that, as graduates of elite universities such as the University of Sorbonne, University of Barcelona,

University of Cambridge, University of Oxford, and Harvard University, many founders of nation-states in the Global South replicated the educational policies of their former European colonial powers (Rangan, 2022). They modelled their public universities upon their alma mater and produced civil servants who looked at universities in Europe and North America as pinnacles of knowledge. These elites, who later became leaders, were also responsible for perpetuating the core–periphery development model in their home countries and pushing it to its logical conclusions (Gabriel, 2015; Ricart-Huguet, 2021). One example is that religious educational institutions were deemed inferior to secular schools and universities (Ul-Haq, 2022). Colonialism may have left, but these elites sustained colonial knowledge philosophies through higher education and the maintenance of a Western-style civil service (Ricart-Huguet, 2021).

To be sure, manifestations of colonial authority continue to characterise these countries, lingering in higher education institutions and governing structures (Bhambra, 2021). Founded as they were under colonial rule, universities in the Global South purveyed the ideas of the powers that had previously subjugated them (Thorpe, 2022). They remained beholden to the standards defined by the United Kingdom, the United States, France, Spain, and Germany and to a lesser extent, Italy, Portugal, and Belgium. The United Kingdom and the United States emerged as dominant powers in shaping universities' careers in the Global South after the formal end of colonialism (Kohli, 2019). Decolonising the universities remains an unfinished and contested project, as it pitched elites bent on entrenching colonial forms of knowledge and power against socially conscious scholarly communities desiring autonomy in structuring curricula and determining their criteria for success (Bhambra et al., 2018).

The case of universities in Malaysia is illustrative of the salient observations made by postcolonial theorists. The British colonial period in Malaysia began in 1786, establishing a trading post in Penang (Loh, 2023). The British colonists established a mainstream education system that, in a way, acted like a production mill producing streams of workers, including miners, peasants, manual labourers, and fishermen who worked, some for their entire lives, for the sole purpose of supporting colonial capitalism and sustaining the British Empire (Knowles, 2022). One of the chief architects behind the creation of this second stream of education was Richard O. Winstedt (Wong, 2021), who established the Sultan Idris Training College in 1922 "to train all Malay teachers in gardening and elementary agriculture, so that they may introduce scientific methods of the West in the most remote villages" (Seng, 1975, p. 29). The British education system also sought to produce a class of civil servants who thought, spoke, and behaved like the colonisers (Coté, 2020) and became the elites of the British education system in Malaysia. They were *white* but not quite. They were educated but, in fact, subservient to the people who colonised them and worked alongside the colonisers to keep the majority population in states of subjugation with pockets of this educated class conditioned by the system in thinking that they were actually on equal footing with their British masters given their social status. The Afro-American civil rights leader, Malcolm X, described this class of people as *house negroes* who were more able servants than the *field negroes* who were menial labourers (Taylor, 2019). The disturbing similarities between the description of the educated natives in Malaysia by the British and the *field negroes* as described by Malcolm X here are apparent.

Other than sending many locals to British universities to train them in the manners and ways of English, the colonial government also established several institutions of higher learning in Malaysia; the earliest was the University of Malaya (UM). Founded in 1949, the UM merged the King Edward VII College of Medicine and the Raffles College in Singapore (Lee & Tan, 1996). The university was established to train a new generation of professionals and leaders who would support and sustain the British colonial administration (Gabriel, 2015).

It is safe to argue that the colonial powers hoped that the leaders they selected and developed through these institutions would fulfil certain vital functions. They would play instrumental roles in fashioning a vision providing direction and guidance to a nation's political organs, economic establishments, or educational institutions (Regmi, 2022). In this article, we further state that educational leadership in the postcolonial period involved establishing and implementing policies in national schools and universities that maintained the British colonising vision. Most educational leaders trained in the colonial ways of frames of thought were placed at the forefront of policy implementation in postcolonial Malaysia. They consolidated and strengthened colonial instruments and structures already inherent within the country's education systems (Gabriel, 2015; Joseph, 2014).

As discussed, Malaysian public universities were closely modelled after the British university system, which emphasised the teaching of science, technology, and engineering (Mukherjee & Wong, 2011). The British system considered science and technology as key mechanisms for economic development and national progress, and this consideration was reflected in the development of the curricula of the university. Science and technology were, to the British, the most potent instruments to manage their empire and maintain their grip over their lost colonies (Marsden & Smith, 2004). These systems were established not for the benefit of local societies but were hubs that justified the legitimacy of the British Empire and the forms of knowledge that flowed from its tentacles. Since the Europeans were at the forefront of most modern scientific discoveries, countries in the Global South, including Malaysia, relied on the West to keep up with the latest technological, medical, and other science-related advances (Bennett & Hodge, 2011).

Hence, like all other universities in the Global South, Malaysian public universities face the challenge of breaking out of the British system. Since the 1960s, many of these universities have focused on Malay language instruction in mathematics, science, and technology and sought to heighten their research capacities. Malaysian public universities have expanded widely into social sciences and humanities research to instil a strong sense of nationhood. However, by the beginning of the twenty-first century, Malaysian public universities have been placed under great pressure by political-economic instabilities at the domestic level on the one hand and the push towards globalisation on the other (Norazlan et al., 2020). The legacy of colonialism continues to cast a dark shadow over the institutional branding of universities in Malaysia today. This shadow still looms over many universities in the country where a higher emphasis on education for capitalistic ends has grown stronger. Tight constraints on budget, a haphazard approach towards corporatisation, and brain drain have added to the strains suffered by university administration (Anees et al., 2021; Lee, 2004).

Additionally, due to the forces of globalisation since the turn of the twentieth century, the existing twenty Malaysian public universities have been plugged into a neoliberal system that structures their modus operandi in ways almost similar to colonial times but more intense than ever before as the world becomes increasingly connected through digital technologies (Lee, 2016). Some voices have requested a more balanced approach to incorporating neoliberal policies into public universities. Still, the English language and publications in that medium of instruction are generally regarded as a symbol of academic prestige and progress. In the next section, we dive deeper into the effects of neoliberalism in Malaysian universities.

## Neoliberalism and the Fates of Malaysian Public Universities

Neoliberalism in the university system is characterised by privatising education and the marketisation of knowledge (Noui, 2020). This ideology emphasises competition between students, scholars, and institutions. Neoliberalism in higher education entails high performance in the realm of publications. The notion of "publish or perish" has taken on a new meaning with the advent of neoliberalism (Madikizela-Madiya, 2023). Every academic is expected to show evidence of publications in internationally indexed journals, mostly in English. This is aside from having to teach and carry out many administrative duties. For some academics lacking proficiency in the English language, such criteria in judging academic success promote the rise of precarity (Albayrak-Aydemir & Gleibs, 2023; Lee & Lee, 2013). Academics working in neoliberal universities are often left without long-term prospects or constant insecurity. The university management perceives them, or they perceive themselves, as objects and tools to be placed under high pressure to perform at their optimum levels or else be replaced by new staff. In other words, at the core of the neoliberal conception of higher education is the dehumanisation of the academe. It treats them as *animated tools*. Managers of the neoliberal university might claim that their staff matters or that they are, in fact, 'investors' in people and talent, but these 'people' are in reality treated like caricatures of real humans, mere manifestations of warped imaginations of 'Human Resource' departments of what *people* ought to be and their subjugated roles in these institutions (Mason & Megoran, 2021).

This commodification and commercialisation have shifted the traditional noble pursuit of universities towards an instrumentalist understanding of what constitutes knowledge. Knowledge is viewed in monetary terms. For the same reason, the focus of universities has become largely centred on STEM subjects (science, technology, engineering, and mathematics) (Hin, 2020) or research that is commercially viable and consonant with market and policy-based demands (Ha et al., 2020). A two-tier system is therefore developed in that faculties teaching STEM subjects are given the lion's share of university funding and attention because these are subjects that generate the largest number of publications and citations, which are key indicators put in place by global university-ranking companies such as Times and Quacquarelli Symonds (QS). Research on universities in the Global South and the West has uncovered problems of gender, class, and ethnic biases in most STEM faculties (Eaton et al., 2020). These faculties are dominated by mostly middle- and higher-class men belonging to ethnic groups that are privileged or seen as model minorities, as in the case of Asian students in the United States.

It is, however, important to consider that the very essence of the neoliberal investment in education is a deep desire to subjugate 'the university's commitment to the truth, critical thinking, and its obligation to stand for justice and assume responsibility for safeguarding the interests of young people as they enter a world of marked massive inequalities, uncertainty, exclusion, and violence at home and abroad' (Giroux, 2020, p. 12). This is a concern as institutions in higher education may be the only ones left offering a conducive environment for promoting intellectual thought, conducting critical discourse, and creating a safe, creative space for creative thought and innovation. It is distressing to observe how neoliberalism considers such a space as a threat and the concerted efforts taken to mitigate this threat by limiting this space for students to be realised as critical citizens (Kumar, 2012). In addition, it also restricted opportunities for faculty members to contribute towards policy formulation and reformation of governing structures (Giroux, 2020, p. 12).

This push towards neoliberalism in higher education has been particularly pronounced in Malaysia. Since 2013, women have been underrepresented in subjects such as mathematics, science, and engineering in the twenty Malaysian public universities, even though the number of women enrolled as students in these universities has been higher than men. Low recruitment, the imposition of glass ceilings, and the rising demands of publications and grant applications stifle women's advancement, especially among those with families (Goy et al., 2018). Neoliberalism in Malaysian public universities has also caused rising inequalities. Students from privileged backgrounds are more likely to have access to high-quality education, causing marginalised communities to be left behind and, often, reduced to jobs in secondary labour markets. This is because the emphasis on marketability and profitability means that education becomes more expensive, and those who cannot afford it are excluded from the system. Even though Malaysian public universities provide generous subsidies to needy students, much is needed to ensure a more equitable system of admitting students from the minority population (Muftahu et al., 2023).

Furthermore, state policies prioritising the marketability of education have also resulted in the neglect of non-STEM subjects, the underfunding of public universities, and the commodification of students. The result is a Malaysian public university system exacerbating the decline of the philosophical and theoretical disciplines. The social sciences and humanities are downplayed, regarded as not commercially viable and less likely to produce profitable research outcomes. Since the outbreak of the COVID-19 pandemic, the burden of maintaining financial sustainability and revenue diversification, coupled with falling student numbers, has resulted in more support given to STEM subjects than the humanities and the social sciences (Jaafar et al., 2023). As a result, the humanities and social sciences, subjects that were once viewed as fundamental for nation-building and providing the soft skills for graduates to flourish in societies, receive little acknowledgement.

This lack of recognition of the importance of humanities and social sciences is barely unique to Malaysia, but it has been a new trend within the global education system. In Japan, for example, many social sciences and humanities departments have been closed down or suffered from huge cuts (Grove, 2015).

The effects of this are universities losing their relevance as sites of intellectual and cultural production. Instead, they are becoming mere training grounds for the workforce operating like a mechanistic production line. The liberal arts departments are, ironically, the chief victims of neoliberalism. We want to emphasise here, however, that STEM education is vital in Malaysia for a few reasons. The first is that STEM education is critical for the nation's developmental goals as these subjects fuel innovations and creative industries (Chua & Choong, 2019). Secondly, STEM subjects are critical for developing the skills necessary for the workforce to support a knowledge-based economy, which Malaysia sees as vital for its future. Next, STEM education is central to addressing the lack of skilled workers, given that Malaysia has recently suffered from a shortage of skilled workers in STEM fields (Kaur et al., 2020). Such a shortage of skilled workers will prove to be a significant obstacle to the development of Malaysia's economy. Finally, STEM education is necessary to produce a workforce capable of addressing global challenges such as climate change, food security, and energy security Mudaly & Chirikure, 2023). With the increasing importance of STEM education to the economy, the Malaysian government has taken steps towards making significant investments in STEM education in recent years. The National STEM Movement was launched in 2017 to promote STEM education and attract potential undergraduates to pursue STEM-related qualifications (Foi & Kean, 2022).

Several Malaysian universities have also established STEM-related programmes and initiatives (Halim et al., 2021). STEM subjects were seen as essential for developing the skills necessary to support the colony's infrastructure (Chin, 2019). For example, The University of Technology Malaysia is another institution that has made significant investments in STEM education and is working closely with American universities towards that end (UTM-MIT Blossoms, 2015). The university offers undergraduate and graduate engineering, computer science, mathematics, and physics programmes. However, despite their obvious benefits, the focus on STEM subjects can also be perceived as preserving the colonial legacy of producing a skilled class of civil servants to run the country and continue to be beholden to the empire. In addition, this focus on STEM education is also critical for international recognition and to be accepted as part of a recognised body of knowledge-producing global institutions (Jia & Park, 2022). Being part of this body would mean being part of well-known ranking systems such as QS Universities rankings, Times Higher Education rankings, and US Universities rankings and, consequently, developing global institutional branding and recognition for Malaysian universities (Crew, 2019).

The rankings of Malaysian public universities have been increasing through the years, partly because they pushed towards the predominance of STEM subjects. However, the upkeep of many facilities of most public universities has been in decline as the concern is with producing marketable research and less with ensuring a conducive environment for all (Abdullah, 2017). The latest QS World University rankings list the University of Malaya among the world's top 70 universities. In Asia, it is among the top 10 (QS World University Rankings, 2023). Other public universities in Malaysia, such as the Universiti Sains Malaysia, Universiti Putra Malaysia, and Universiti Teknologi Malaysia, are also rising through the world rankings. Even so, this chase for rankings has been at the expense of establishing a 'good university'. A more humane and equitable approach to university life and education has achieved a high ranking. A recent study of 191 academics in Malaysian Research Universities (MRUs) found that their workload has increased over the years and was supercharged by the COVID-19 pandemic. Job satisfaction has plummeted dramatically. The researchers observe that "the faculty members of these MRUs may face more occupational issues than previously known since university management teams are dealing with the pressure of participating in fierce competition with their institutional peers" (Janib et al., 2021, p. 89). The effects of neoliberalism on Malaysian academics have become more dire and place the management teams under more pressure to perform, which likely leads to the dehumanisation of the university and its people.

## Conclusion

Seen as a highly complex societal institution, the university is core to a nation's economic development and a symbol of economic rationality. The idea of the university as an institution for conserving, understanding, extending, and disseminating intellectual, scientific, cultural, and artistic heritage in society synonymous with the growth of civilisation has changed in recent years (Benner, 2020). With the advent of neoliberalism, the university concept has become a commodified and commercialised institution tasked primarily to contribute to the country's economic development. One of the primary effects of the neoliberal approach is the dehumanisation of university education. Universities are increasingly being seen as institutions that serve the market's needs rather than as spaces for critical inquiry, social transformation, and human flourishing. Such an intent is not only detrimental towards developing an equitable and ethical education system, but it erodes humanistic values, leaving societies decimated and destroyed, incapacitating human will, the core value of what civilisations in the past were all about.

The Malaysian higher education system has made steady progress in taking up the neoliberal approach to education. Malaysian education system aims and is determined to become one of the best in the world (Sia & Adamu, 2020). However, educational outcomes and quality have continued to deteriorate despite the significant improvements in support, access, and attainment (Haider et al., 2020; Nasri, 2022). Malaysia's dependency on the standards placed by former colonising nations is responsible for this decline. As highlighted earlier in the article, it is a concern that the leaders within the education system merely set out to sustain the colonial education system due to their ways of thinking instead of striving towards reforming it.

A sustained humanistic education system can remove the colonial fetters of Malaysian universities and mitigate the dehumanisation causing their decline towards the realisation of good universities (Engel & Yemini, 2020). If properly understood and applied, establishing good universities can aid in the decolonising efforts of education systems and universities in Malaysia. It can facilitate a more inclusive and equitable approach to education that recognises and respects the diversity of cultural and intellectual traditions worldwide. Good universities can undo the oppressive structures of colonialism, remove the shackles of colonial legacies, and promote a more just society.

We want to conclude by reiterating Edward Said's critical argument that only humanism can answer and remedy the injustices brought about by colonialism and its avatars: "Humanism is the only – I would go so far as saying the final – resistance we have against the inhuman practices and injustices that disfigure human history" (Said, 1978, p. xxix). The deep-rooted problems brought about by colonialism and neoliberalism heightened as a result of academic dehumanisation can only be undone when we begin to recognise that universities are the nerve-centres of humanity. Only then can the idea of the good university be realised, and the fetters of colonial legacies be completely removed from these hallowed institutions.

## References


Abdullah, D. (2017). Public universities and budget cuts in Malaysia. *International Higher Education, 91*, 15–17.

Albayrak-Aydemir, N., & Gleibs, I. H. (2023). A social-psychological examination of academic precarity as an organisational practice and subjective experience. *British Journal of Social Psychology, 62*(Suppl. 1), 95–110. https://doi.org/10.1111/bjso.12607

Anees, R. T., Heidler, P., Cavaliere, L. P. L., & Nordin, N. A. (2021). Brain drain in higher education. The impact of job stress and workload on turnover intention and the mediating role of job satisfaction at universities. *European Journal of Business and Management Research, 6*(3), 1–8. https://www.ejbmr.org/index.php/ejbmr/article/view/849

Atkinson, C. (2021). Theme-based book review: The global south and complexity. *International Journal of Public Administration, 44*(8), 699–704. https://doi.org/10.1080/01900692.2020.1744646

Benner, M. (2020). Becoming world class: What it means and what it does. In S. Rider, M. A. Peters, M. Hyvönen, & T. Besley (Eds.), *World class universities: A contested concept* (pp. 25–40). Springer Nature Singapore. https://doi.org/10.1007/978-981-15-7598-3_3

Bennett, B., & Hodge, J. (2011). *Science and empire: Knowledge and networks of science across the British Empire* (pp. 1800–1970). Palgrave Macmillan UK. https://books.google.com.sg/books?id=O2KADAAAQBAJ

Bhambra, G. K. (2021). Colonial global economy: Towards a theoretical reorientation of political economy. *Review of International Political Economy, 28*(2), 307–322. https://doi.org/10.1080/09692290.2020.1830831

Bhambra, G. K., Gebrial, D., & Nişancıoğlu, K. (2018). *Decolonising the university*. Pluto Press.

Blossoms, U.-M. (2015). *UTM-MIT blossoms*. UTM Centre for Advancement in Digital and Flexible Learning. https://utmcdex.utm.my/utm-mit-blossoms/

Brooks, R., Byford, K., & Sela, K. (2016). Students' unions, consumerism and the neoliberal university. *British Journal of Sociology of Education, 37*(8), 1211–1228. https://doi.org/10.1080/01425692.2015.1042150

Chin, Y. F. (2019). Malaysia: From hub to exporter of higher education and implications. *International Journal of Business and Social Science, 10*(2), 48–54.

Chua, Y. L., & Choong, P. Y. (2019). Interactive STEM talk and workshop outreach programme-by students, for students: A Malaysian context. *2019 IEEE 11th International Conference on Engineering Education (ICEED).*

Connell, R. (2019). *The good university: What universities actually do and why it's time for radical change*. Bloomsbury Publishing.

Connell, R. (2020). COVID-19/sociology. *Journal of Sociology, 56*(4), 745–751. https://doi.org/10.1177/1440783320943262

Coté, J. J. (2020). Colonial education: Colonials and the colonised in "colonies of settlement" and "colonies of exploitation". In *Handbook of historical studies in education: Debates, tensions, and directions* (pp. 259–276).

Crew, B. (2019). World university rankings: Explained. *Nature Index*. https://www.nature.com/nature-index/news-blog/world-university-rankings-explainer-times-higher-education-arwu-shanghai-qs-quacquarelli-symonds

Da Wan, C., Sirat, M., & Razak, D. A. (2015). The idea of a university: Rethinking the Malaysian context. *Humanities, 4*(3), 266–282. https://www.mdpi.com/2076-0787/4/3/266

Dados, N., & Connell, R. (2012). The global south. *Contexts, 11*(1), 12–13. https://doi.org/10.1177/1536504212436479

Darder, A. (2012). Neoliberalism in the academic borderlands: An on-going struggle for equality and human rights. *Educational Studies, 48*(5), 412–426. https://doi.org/10.1080/00131946.2012.714334

de Wit, H., & Altbach, P. G. (2021). Internationalisation in higher education: Global trends and recommendations for its future. *Policy Reviews in Higher Education, 5*(1), 28–46. https://doi.org/10.1080/23322969.2020.1820898

Dei, G. J. S. (2019). Neoliberalism as a new form of colonialism in education. In *Confronting educational policy in neoliberal times* (pp. 40–58). Routledge. https://www.taylorfrancis.com/chapters/edit/10.4324/9781315149875-4/neoliberalism-new-form-colonialism-education-george-sefa-dei

Eaton, A. A., Saunders, J. F., Jacobson, R. K., & West, K. (2020). How gender and race stereotypes impact the advancement of scholars in STEM: Professors' biased evaluations of physics and biology post-doctoral candidates. *Sex Roles, 82*(3), 127–141. https://doi.org/10.1007/s11199-019-01052-w

Engel, L. C., & Yemini, M. (2020). Internationalisation in public education offers hope for future citizenship. *Humanistic Futures of Learning*, 105.

Foi, L. Y., & Kean, T. H. (2022). STEM education in Malaysia: An organisational development approach? *International Journal of Advanced Research in Future Ready Learning and Education, 29*(1), 1–19.

Gabriel, S. P. (2015). The meaning of race in Malaysia: Colonial, postcolonial and possible new conjunctures. *Ethnicities, 15*(6), 782–809. https://doi.org/10.1177/1468796815570347

Giroux, H. (2020). *Neoliberalism's war on higher education* (2nd ed.). Haymarket Books.

Goy, S. C., Wong, Y. L., Low, W. Y., Noor, S. N. M., Fazli-Khalaf, Z., Onyeneho, N., Daniel, E., Azizan, S., Hasbullah, M., & GinikaUzoigwe, A. (2018). Swimming against the tide in STEM education and gender equality: A problem of recruitment or retention in Malaysia. *Studies in Higher Education, 43*(11), 1793–1809. https://doi.org/10.1080/03075079.2016.1277383

Grove, J. (2015). Social sciences and humanities faculties 'to close' in Japan after ministerial intervention. *Times Higher Education*. https://www.timeshighereducation.com/news/social-sciences-and-humanities-faculties-close-japan-after-ministerial-decree

Ha, C. T., Thao, T. T. P., Trung, N. T., Van Dinh, N., & Trung, T. (2020). A bibliometric review of research on STEM education in ASEAN: Science mapping the literature in Scopus database, 2000 to 2019. *Eurasia Journal of Mathematics, Science and Technology Education, 16*(10), em1889.

Haider, K., Kerio, G. A., & Kazimi, A. B. (2020). Higher education in Pakistan and Malaysia: A comparative analysis of their education policies in the modern era of technology. *Global Educational Studies Review, 3*, 103–113.

Halim, L., Nam, L. A., & Shahali, E. H. M. (2021). STEM education in Malaysia: Policies to implementation. In *STEM education from Asia* (pp. 33–48). Routledge.

Haug, S., Braveboy-Wagner, J., & Maihold, G. (2021). The 'global south' in the study of world politics: Examining a meta category. *Third World Quarterly, 42*(9), 1923–1944. https://doi.org/10.1080/01436597.2021.1948831

Hennessey, J. L. (2022). Teaching European colonial history in a "humanitarian superpower": Presentations of colonialism in Swedish middle-school textbooks. *Journal of Curriculum and Pedagogy*, 1–25. https://doi.org/10.1080/15505170.2022.2124331

Hickling-Hudson, A., Matthews, J., & Woods, A. (2004). Education, postcolonialism and disruptions. *Disrupting Preconceptions: Postcolonialism and Education, 3*(2), 1–16.

Hin, K. K. (2020). PISA 2018 and Malaysia. *International Journal of Advanced Research in Education and Society, 2*(3), 12–18.

Jaafar, J. A., Latiff, A. R. A., Daud, Z. M., & Osman, M. N. H. (2023). Does revenue diversification strategy affect the financial sustainability of Malaysian public universities? A Panel data analysis. *Higher Education Policy, 36*(1), 116–143. https://doi.org/10.1057/s41307-021-00247-9

Janib, J., Mohd Rasdi, R., Omar, Z., Alias, S. N., Zaremohzzabieh, Z., & Ahrari, S. (2021). The relationship between workload and performance of research university academics in Malaysia: The mediating effects of career commitment and job satisfaction. *Asian Journal of University Education, 17*(2), 85–99. https://doi.org/10.24191/ajue.v17i2.13394

Jia, N., & Park, J. (2022). Institutional brand construct and university sustainability. In T. Savelyeva & G. Fang (Eds.), *Sustainable tertiary education in Asia: Policies, practices, and developments* (pp. 163–175). Springer Nature Singapore. https://doi.org/10.1007/978-981-19-5104-6_10

Joseph, C. (2014). Education politics in postcolonial Malaysia. In *Equity, opportunity and education in Postcolonial Southeast Asia* (p. 101). Routledge.

Kaur, A. H., Gopinathan, S., & Raman, M. (2020). Work-in-progress—Role of innovative teaching strategies in enhancing STEM education in Malaysia. In *2020 6th International Conference of the Immersive Learning Research Network (iLRN)*.

Kenway, J., & Howard, A. (2022). Elite universities: Their monstrous promises and promising monsters. *Curriculum Inquiry, 52*(1), 75–96. https://doi.org/10.1080/03626784.2021.1994837

Knight, H., Carlisle, S., O'Connor, M., Briggs, L., Fothergill, L., Al-Oraibi, A., Yildirim, M., Morling, J. R., Corner, J., Ball, J., Denning, C., Vedhara, K., & Blake, H. (2021). Impacts of the COVID-19 pandemic and self-isolation on students and staff in higher education: A qualitative study. *International Journal of Environmental Research and Public Health, 18*(20), 10675.

Knowles, L. C. A. (2022). *Economic development of the British overseas empire.* Routledge.

Kohl, K., Hopkins, C., Barth, M., Michelsen, G., Dlouhá, J., Razak, D. A., Abidin Bin Sanusi, Z., & Toman, I. (2022). A whole-institution approach towards sustainability: A crucial aspect of higher education's individual and collective engagement with the SDGs and beyond. *International Journal of Sustainability in Higher Education, 23*(2), 218–236. https://doi.org/10.1108/IJSHE-10-2020-0398

Kohli, A. (2019). *Imperialism and the developing world: How Britain and the United States shaped the global periphery.* Oxford University Press.

Kumar, R. (2012). Neoliberal education and imagining strategies of resistance: An introduction. In R. Kumar (Eds.), *Education and the reproduction of capital. Marxism and education.* Palgrave Macmillan. https://doi.org/10.1057/9781137007582_1

Latecka, E. (2023). Humanising pedagogy: A politico-economic perspective. *Educational Philosophy and Theory, 55*(5), 634–651. https://doi.org/10.1080/00131857.2022.2032653

Lee, E., & Yong, T. T. (1996). *Beyond degrees: The making of the National University of Singapore.* Singapore University Press.

Lee, H., & Lee, K. (2013). Publish (in international indexed journals) or perish: Neoliberal ideology in a Korean university. *Language Policy, 12*(3), 215–230. https://doi.org/10.1007/s10993-012-9267-2

Lee, M. (2016). Reforms of university governance and management in Asia: Effects on campus culture. In *The Palgrave handbook of Asia pacific higher education* (pp. 261–277). https://doi.org/10.1057/978-1-137-48739-1_18

Lee, M. N. N. (2004). Global trends, national policies and institutional responses: Restructuring higher education in Malaysia. *Educational Research for Policy and Practice, 3*(1), 31–46. https://doi.org/10.1007/s10671-004-6034-y

Loh, W. L. (2023). What is wrong with the historiography on colonialism in Malaya? Penang at the Periphery. *Journal of Contemporary Asia, 53*(1), 79–94. https://doi.org/10.1080/00472336.2022.2032276

Madikizela-Madiya, N. (2023). Transforming higher education spaces through ethical research publication: A critique of the publish or perish aphorism. *Higher Education Research & Development, 42*(1), 186–199. https://doi.org/10.1080/07294360.2022.2048634

Marginson, S., & Sawir, E. (2006). University leaders' strategies in the global environment: A comparative study of Universitas Indonesia and the Australian National University. *Higher Education, 52*(2), 343–373. https://doi.org/10.1007/s10734-004-5591-6

Marsden, B., & Smith, C. (2004). *Engineering empires: A cultural history of technology in nineteenth-century Britain*. Springer.

Mason, O., & Megoran, N. (2021). Precarity and dehumanisation in higher education. *Learning and Teaching, 14*(1), 35–59.

Moyo, L. (2020). *The decolonial turn in media studies in Africa and the Global South*. Springer Nature.

Mudaly, R., & Chirikure, T. (2023). STEM education in the global North and global South: Competition, conformity, and convenient collaborations [Review]. *Frontiers in Education, 8*. https://doi.org/10.3389/feduc.2023.1144399.

Muftahu, M., Annmali, D., & Xiaoling, H. (2023). Massification of higher education in Malaysia: Managing institutional equity and diversity. *Asian Journal of University Education, 19*(2), 352–364.

Mukherjee, H., & Wong, P. K. (2011). The National University of Singapore and the University of Malaya: Common roots and different paths. In *The road to academic excellence: The making of world-class research universities* (pp. 129–166).

Nah, A. M. (2003). Negotiating indigenous identity in postcolonial Malaysia: Beyond being 'not quite/not Malay.' *Social Identities, 9*(4), 511–534.

Nasri, N. M. (2022). Context setting: Malaysia, Indonesia and Japan. In *Culturally responsive science pedagogy in Asia* (pp. 18–30). Routledge.

Norazlan, N., Yusuf, S., & Al-Majdhoub, F. M. H. (2020). The financial problems and academic performance among public university students in Malaysia. *The Asian Journal of Professional & Business Studies, 1*(2), 1–6.

Noui, R. (2020). Higher education between massification and quality. *Higher Education Evaluation and Development, 14*(2), 93–103. https://doi.org/10.1108/HEED-04-2020-0008

Patel, R., & McMichael, P. (2004). Third worldism and the lineages of global fascism: The regrouping of the global South in the neoliberal era. *Third World Quarterly, 25*(1), 231–254. https://doi.org/10.1080/0143659042000185426

QS World University & Rankings. (2023). *About Universiti Malaya (UM)*. https://www.topuniversities.com/universities/universiti-malaya-um

Rangan, H. (2022). Decolonisation, knowledge production, and interests in liberal higher education. *Geographical Research, 60*(1), 59–70. https://doi.org/10.1111/1745-5871.12510

Regmi, K. D. (2022). The enduring effects of colonialism on education: Three praxes for decolonising educational leadership. *International Journal of Leadership in Education*, 1–19. https://doi.org/10.1080/13603124.2022.2098379

Ricart-Huguet, J. (2021). Colonial education, political elites, and regional political inequality in Africa. *Comparative Political Studies, 54*(14), 2546–2580. https://doi.org/10.1177/0010414021997176

Said, E. W. (1978). *Orientalism* (1st ed.). Pantheon Books.

Sia, J. K. M., & Adamu, A. A. (2020). Facing the unknown: Pandemic and higher education in Malaysia. *Asian Education and Development Studies, 10*(2), 263–275.

Seng, P. L. F. (1975). *Seeds for separatism: Educational policy in Malaya 1874–1940*. Oxford University Press.

Smiet, K. (2022). Rethinking or delinking? Said and Mignolo on humanism and the question of the human. *Postcolonial Studies, 25*(1), 73–88. https://doi.org/10.1080/13688790.2022.2030595

Sullivan, D., & Hickel, J. (2023). Capitalism and extreme poverty: A global analysis of real wages, human height, and mortality since the long 16th century. *World Development, 161*, 106026. https://doi.org/10.1016/j.worlddev.2022.106026

Rudolph, J., Tan, S., Crawford, J., & Butler-Henderson, K. (2023). Perceived quality of online learning during COVID-19 in higher education in Singapore: Perspectives from students, lecturers, and academic leaders. *Educational Research for Policy and Practice, 22*(1), 171–191. https://doi.org/10.1007/s10671-022-09325-0

Taylor, J. (2019). Laugh! The revolution is here: Humor and anger in the speeches of Malcolm X. *Journal for the Study of Radicalism, 13*(2), 159–186.

Tenzin, J., & Lee, C. (2022). Are we still dependent? Academic dependency theory after 20 years. *Journal of Historical Sociology, 35*(1), 2–13. https://doi.org/10.1111/johs.12355

Thorpe, R.-A. (2022). The idea of a postcolonial university. *PRISM: Casting New Light on Learning, Theory and Practice, 4*(1), 4–14. https://doi.org/10.24377/prism.ljmu.0401211

Tice, D., Baumeister, R., Crawford, J., Allen, K. A., & Percy, A. (2021). Student belongingness in higher education: Lessons for Professors from the COVID-19 pandemic. *Journal of University Teaching & Learning Practice, 18*(4), 2. https://doi.org/10.53761/1.18.4.2

Trigueros, R., Padilla, A. M., Aguilar-Parra, J. M., Rocamora, P., Morales-Gázquez, M. J., & López-Liria, R. (2020). The influence of emotional intelligence on resilience, test anxiety, academic stress and the Mediterranean diet. A study with university students. *International Journal of Environmental Research and Public Health, 17*(6), 2071. https://www.mdpi.com/1660-4601/17/6/2071

Ul-Haq, S. (2022). Reversing the colonial warp in education: A decolonial encounter with Muhammad Iqbal. *Higher Education, 84*(2), 399–414. https://doi.org/10.1007/s10734-021-00773-w

Uvais, N. A. (2021). 'Coronaphobia' among undergraduate students: A pilot survey study. *Asia Pacific Journal of Public Health, 33*(8), 990–991. https://doi.org/10.1177/10105395211007645

Whetstone, C., & Yilmaz, M. (2020). Recreating the third world project: Possibilities through the fourth world. *Third World Quarterly, 41*(4), 565–582. https://doi.org/10.1080/01436597.2019.1702457

Willinsky, J. (1998). *Learning to divide the world: Education at empire's end*. University of Minnesota Press.

Wong, W. W. W. (2021). *Sir Richard Winstedt and the historical creation of Malaya and Tanah Melayu in the twentieth century* (Doctoral dissertation). The Australian National University (Australia).

Zajda, J., & Rust, V. (2020). Current research trends in globalisation and neoliberalism in higher education. In J. Zajda (Ed.), *Globalisation, ideology and neoliberal higher education reforms* (pp. 1–9). Springer Netherlands. https://doi.org/10.1007/978-94-024-1751-7_1

# Addressing the Real Crisis in Today's Higher Education Leadership

Christopher M. Branson and Maureen Mara

## Introduction

Many would share Wu and colleagues (2021) view of what constitutes a crisis as being "events that leaders and organisational stakeholders perceive as unexpected, highly salient, and potentially disruptive" (p. 2). From this view, the impact of COVID-19 could be classified as a crisis in today's higher education sector. Arguably, however, the distinction proffered by Williams et al. (2017) between crisis-as-event and crisis-as-process calls this somewhat superficial assessment of the impact of COVID-19 into question. A crisis-as-event is an unpredictable and unexpected discrete event such as an accident, a natural disaster, or an act of terrorism or sabotage. In such circumstances, these authors propose that leadership aims to recover, adjust, and restore the status quo.

In contrast, the crisis-as-process draws attention to the evolution of a crisis over time. This view recognises that many crises emerge from ongoing ignorance, avoidance, inattention, or incapacity by those in positions of leadership

C. M. Branson (✉)
Educational Leadership, La Salle Academy, Australian Catholic University, Sanctuary Cove, QLD, Australia
e-mail: Christopher.Branson@acu.edu.au

M. Mara
Leadership and Organisational Culture Consultant, Leadership Consultancy, Hamilton East, New Zealand
e-mail: mmarra@inleadership.co.nz



J. Rudolph et al. (eds.), *The Palgrave Handbook of Crisis Leadership in Higher Education*,
https://doi.org/10.1007/978-3-031-54509-2_5

responsibility. This crisis-as-process approach describes how leaders often facilitate the incubation of a crisis due to "erroneous assumptions, complex information and stimuli, norms of inattentiveness to signals, and a reluctance to imagine worst-case scenarios" (Riggio & Newstead, 2023, p. 16).

We argue that this latter view, crisis-as-process, needs to be adopted if the real problems faced by higher education institutions are to be properly and effectively addressed. Simply returning higher education institutions to the status quo that existed just before the impact of COVID-19, which is the action of leadership following a crisis-as-event, would be tantamount to invoking systematic sabotage. Such thoughtlessness would further undermine higher education institutions' reputation, credibility, and sustainability.

In support of these claims, this chapter will describe how COVID-19 exposed several crucially important pre-existing higher education crises and then link these to managerialism's prevalence. The chapter then proceeds to describe how these crises can be overcome by returning higher education to its core purpose—the creation and the dissemination of knowledge—while also explaining how this change necessitates moving from a product-based to a service-based business model in which the needs of the students and thus, by necessity, the well-being of the staff take priority. The chapter concludes by describing how this change to the business model requires an entirely different understanding of the nature and practice of higher education leadership, founded upon relationships rather than command, control, and management.

## How COVID-19 Exposed the Pre-existing Higher Education Crisis

Despite the relatively recent COVID-19 pandemic, there is a plethora of research literature describing and analysing its impact on higher education institutions. In these publications, it is posited that, with the advent of COVID-19, those in higher education leadership positions suddenly had to attend to unprecedented, serious issues concerning deficient online learning experiences, extensively diminished enrolments, large-scale staff reductions, and inadequate income channels. In and of themselves, such salient and disruptive issues seem to coalesce to present an unheralded crisis. However, we will describe how the genesis of these institutionally debilitating issues pre-existed the emergence of the COVID-19 pandemic. COVID-19 was simply a catalyst, the tipping point, and not the primary creator of these critical issues.

According to the research by Mete et al. (2022), the worldwide ban on face-to-face teaching wrought by COVID-19 "led more than two million students to complete their studies online" and added that most higher education institutions around the world "were not prepared for this crisis or successful with online teaching" (p. 144). Herein lies the real cause of this aspect of the COVID-19 crisis—the mismanagement of online learning during the decade before the COVID-19 outbreak. Throughout this time, higher education institutions worldwide continually expanded their use of various forms of online learning, including distance, remote, e-learning, and multimode learning (Zhang et al., 2022). However, despite this relatively lengthy online learning experimentation and implementation, most higher education institutions faced unprecedented logistical and cultural turmoil when transitioning to large-scale online learning (Garcia-Morales et al., 2021). The need to accelerate this transition caused by COVID-19 laid bare the prior professional learning deficiencies of higher education staff even though the use of technology in society, generally, and in education had already expanded exponentially (Blankenberger & Williams, 2020). Arguably, before the COVID-19 pandemic, most higher education leaders viewed online learning as a beneficial economic resource—maximising enrolments while decreasing staffing and facility costs. Hence, this severe lack of leadership foresight and planning resulted in extensive stress for staff due to a lack of preparation and support, widespread student dissatisfaction due to a perception of deficient technical and learning support, and seriously inadequate technical and digital resources to deliver the required array of online learning activities, experiences, and assessments. In short, a decade or more of scant strategic regard and financial investment had left online learning underdeveloped and exposed higher education institutions as backward in providing a twenty-first-century learning service.

Moreover, this uncritical commitment to economic benefit has dominated higher education enrolment policies more broadly throughout this century. A blind commitment to financial growth through increased student enrolments, particularly of higher fee-paying international students, had become the mainstay of many higher education institutions' annual budgets before the COVID-19 pandemic (Devlin & Samarawickrema, 2022). Focusing on an obviously narrow, vulnerable, and highly competitive income source was a high-risk and short-sighted approach to financial management and organisational leadership. This understanding was unequivocally illustrated by COVID-19's dramatic impact on higher education student enrolment populations. In response to having to re-configure budgets due to significantly decreased student enrolments, Blankenberger and Williams (2020) describe how these institutions have had to pause facilities projects, implement hiring restrictions, limit discretionary spending, eliminate targeted programme investments, defer maintenance, decrease classroom technology and infrastructure expenditure, request employees take leave or early retirements, and layoff large numbers of employees. Essentially, the fiscal inattentiveness of those in higher education leadership positions before COVID-19 led to drastic crisis management strategies being enacted during COVID-19, which ultimately may have a long-lasting detrimental impact on these institutions' nature and social status post-COVID-19.

An overdependence on government funding throughout the past 30 years is an additional example of how the impact of COVID-19 exposed higher education leaders' longer-term serious fiscal short-sightedness and mismanagement. In many countries, government sources provided both per-capita funding through partial payment of enrolment fees for non-international students and large research grant funding. This latter funding source was highly significant for higher education institutions because these are mostly relatively large research grants that can readily absorb the institution's mandatory administration cost, which could account for some 30% or more of the total research grant budget. For many other potential research grant providers, such an additional cost to a proposed research project's budget rendered it unsupportable. Importantly, although this income was generated from research projects, it was general income and extensively contributed to staffing, facilities, resources, and maintenance expenditures.

Given this overdependency, it is easy to see the dual fiscal blow that COVID-19 caused to higher education budgets. First, as enrolments dramatically decreased due to the absence of international students and other students forgoing tertiary studies during extended lockdown periods, per-capita government funding reduced accordingly. Secondly, in response to having to find ways to fund other dire COVID-19-related social and health-related needs, in addition to the incapacity of higher education institutions to conduct research due to lockdowns and social distancing, government grant-related funding was greatly reduced (Blankenberger & Williams, 2020; Mete et al., 2022). The serious implications of this re-direction or reduction in government funding resulted in higher education institutions having to cut expenditure costs severely. Furthermore, since large infrastructure projects are founded on contractual obligations, which renders them non-changeable, the only other expenditure cost that could accommodate sufficient reductions was that of staffing. Thus, higher education staff reductions in many countries were widespread and substantial, often resulting in the faculties that attract the lowest number of students—arguably, Arts and Social Sciences—being affected the most. Although this provided higher education leaders with a means for reducing their institution's budget deficits, it makes it extremely difficult to rebound back to its maximum capacity once enrolment numbers return to pre-COVID-19 levels. Simply, it might become impossible for these higher education institutions to ever return to their pre-COVID-19 level of functioning and social status.

Essentially, this discussion of three imperative consequences of the COVID-19 pandemic on higher education institutions illustrates that COVID-19 did not create these critical consequences but, instead, it only provided the environment in which the resultant outcomes of pre-existing inappropriate leadership practices became blatantly apparent. Thus, the substantial learning from the COVID-19 crisis for higher education leadership can only come from a deeper exploration of the deficiencies in such leadership that existed before the advent of COVID-19 (Lalani et al., 2021). It is only in this way that it is possible to get to the crux of the real crisis in contemporary higher education leadership.

## The Crux of the Real Crisis—Managerialism

To identify the pre-COVID-19 deficiencies in higher education leadership, it is first necessary to appreciate the pre-existing tertiary educational context. For much of the past 30 years, government policies around the world have required universities to account for the expenditure of public funds and provide evidence of value for money. Such government policies were generically termed 'New Public Management' (Chandler et al., 2002) or 'New Managerialism' (Deem, 1998) or 'Corporatisation' (Giroux et al., 2015). Essentially, these policies pressured higher education leaders to become far more managerial in their leadership practices. Anderson (2006) describes these managerial practices as the "incorporation of approaches, systems, and techniques commonly found in the private sector to the management and conduct of the public sector" (p. 578). Moreover, managerialism within a higher education context is aligned with causing a strong focus on international growth and rankings, increased reliance on private funding, massive investments in advertising campaigns, and the use of normative markers such as 'excellence' and 'best practice' (Branson & Marra, 2022).

Moreover, Branson and Marra (2022) explain in detail how a managerialist-led higher education culture is noted for its creation of rigidity at the expense of flexibility and innovation since the foundations of managerialism are command, control, and management. Thus, those in leadership positions who revert to managerialism seek to be in total command and the key decision-maker. They do not like surprises as this has the potential to lay bare for all to see the limitations of their decision-making capacity and their command imperfections. To avoid surprises, managerialists strive to create consistency and predictability in the belief that this gives them control over all that can happen in their organisation. The presumption is that achieving control means that nothing can happen that will be beyond their decision-making capacity to resolve to their satisfaction. The result is that, as described by many researchers (see, for example, Churchman, 2006; Dobbins et al., 2011; Hamlin & Patel, 2015; van Ameijde et al., 2009), the traditional higher education leadership practices that embraced academic freedom and research-informed learning were rapidly replaced by managerial principles adopted from the business world.

In response to this managerialist movement in universities worldwide, Vincent (2011) raised deep concern about its unchallenged ideological suitability and acceptability, whereby it invoked the assumption among its proponents that it provided a better form of all-encompassing leadership practice. It moved from the pragmatic to the hegemonic—from having a specific practical benefit when overseeing fiscal responsibilities to being the singular way to lead. Managerialism now masquerades as the only acceptable leadership reality and pervades deeply and unquestionably into the culture of higher education institutions (Branson & Marra, 2022). Hence, managerialism became the widely accepted approach to higher education leadership, and any alternative approach was treated with derision. Hence, higher education leaders have become far more concerned with income and budgets than wisdom, knowledge, and people.

This naïve adoption of managerialism has led to the development of a higher education culture in which market competitiveness and income-generating mechanisms have taken precedence and re-framed academic work (Branson et al., 2018). Hence, the institution's strategy, policy, and performance processes have become singularly directed towards striving to meet essentially economic outcomes. As a result, teaching loads were increased to generate more income, research priorities were predetermined around external grant sources, publication outputs were controlled according to relative contribution to international rankings, discipline reputations were hierarchically categorised according to public opinion and political preferences, and faculties were run like factories. Thus, many of our higher education institutions "have lost their soul … because their focus has shifted away from fully achieving their core purpose – the creation and the dissemination of knowledge – to production-line teaching and learning and income-based research"

(Branson et al., 2018, p. 130). These authors argue that the core purpose of a higher education institution must always remain "its capacity to discover new knowledge for the benefit of humanity and society through the dissemination and teaching of new insights, actions, judgements, and wisdom. To be the critic, the conscious, and the benefactor of society are outcomes that take time and so potentially defy the [limitations of managerialism]" (p. 130).

## Overcoming the Higher Education Crisis by Reclaiming Its Purpose

Informed by this understanding, we argue that this fallible higher education environment encompassed two inherently ruinous elements—leadership theory and the choice of a business model—and these two elements, not COVID-19, have caused the real crisis in today's higher education institutions.

Concerning the element of leadership theory, what these higher education leaders who continue to adopt managerialist practices are stubbornly ignoring is the growing business research literature refuting the credibility of such practices (see, for example, Branson et al., 2018; Hamel & Zanini, 2021). Should higher education leaders take the time to consult today's business research literature, they would find that it raises a concern about the concept of leadership lore: flawed managerial axioms, sayings, anecdotes, or beliefs that are so pervasive in leadership thoughts and practices that they erroneously achieve the status of immutable facts underpinning mandatory practice (Branson & Marra, 2022). Managerialism is no longer the recommended leadership theory in the corporate world. If higher education leaders are truly committed to adopting leadership practices aligned to that now strongly recommended in the business world, then they would not be so devoted to managerialism.

Contemporary leadership theory urges adopting a new, more relational approach to leadership to create a more inclusive, connected, and collaborative organisational culture (Branson et al., 2018). Nevertheless, in a managerialist-infused higher education culture, there is little evidence of leaders applying this new knowledge and practising appropriate critical thinking. It is grossly hypocritical that, on the one hand, higher education institutions expect their students to develop and apply new knowledge based on critical thinking. However, the same is not expected of its leaders. Hence, under the lingering application of debunked managerial strategies, higher education leaders are failing to adequately transform their institutions to meet today's social and economic demands. Indeed, these misguided and discredited leadership practices undermine the higher education institution's core purpose, essential role, and potential survival.

As previously described, for the past 30 years, governments worldwide have imposed heightened accountability measures upon higher education institutions. Regrettably, the response by these institutions was almost a unilateral introduction of a particularly harmful business model in place of their traditional administrative practices. Essentially, this particular business model is what the Harvard Business School calls a 'product-based' business model whereby the institution strives to produce its product (knowledge education) for as low a cost as possible while maintaining a reasonable level of quality. Also, this product-based business model implies that the institution then strives to sell as many units (i.e., increase enrolments) as possible for as high a price as possible to maximise its profit. This endeavour underscores why many higher education institutions have striven to maximise their international enrolment numbers since these students pay considerably higher study fees than domestic students. In contrast, the costs for the institution remain much the same.

The inherent dire fallacy in this business model choice is the apparent misjudgement that higher education provides a product when it offers a service. As argued above, the core purpose of a higher education institution is to create and disseminate new knowledge to its students, community, nation, and the world. Thus, these institutions are providing a service primarily to its students but also, secondly, to the community, nation, and world. In other words, the proper choice for higher education leaders, when forced by governments to adopt more fiscally accountable procedures, was to implement a service-based business model and not a product-based business model.

As described by Saarijärvi et al. (2014), the service-based business model "shifts the [institution's] attention from the sale of goods to the support of customer value creation" (p. 529). This model would be distinctive because it focuses the higher education institution's primary attention on the student's needs rather than its overall profit. This involves concentrating on offering and seamlessly integrating all the institutions' resources towards enhancing and enriching the students' educational experiences and everyday activities (Gaiardelli & Songini, 2021). Instead of aiming to sell knowledge in the form of tuition fees to most students, a higher education institution guided by a service-based business model becomes a proactive provider of a high-quality, student-focused learning environment. This entails the institution shifting from predominantly concentrating on its own needs to those of the students.

## Pinpointing the Prime Crisis in Higher Education: Student Unwellness and Attrition

Regrettably, many current higher education leaders employing a product-based business model make the false claim that their institution strives to place the students' needs as its highest priority. Most would point to the existence of some form of a survey gathering the student evaluation data of their learning and teaching experience. However, the reality is that only about 20% of students complete these surveys 40% of the time. Very few complete these surveys because most students see them as lacking specificity, relevance, or impact. These surveys do not include or address actual student needs. Hence, a plethora of research is now focusing on student wellness in higher education (Baik et al., 2019; Jones et al., 2021; Upsher et al., 2022).

Moreover, according to Huang and colleagues (2020, p. 2), "Among all of the populations that suffer from mental disorders, students at the tertiary education level have a higher incidence of mental health problems – including anxiety, depression, and other mental health conditions – than other age groups". The reasons provided in this study for this unacceptable level of unwellness are academic stress and related performance expectations, a lack of social support networks, unfulfilled desires for friendship, sexual harassment or assault, financial worries over tuition fees, clashes between work and study commitments, and unhealthy lifestyles. These are not issues being captured in student evaluation survey data.

More specifically, Jones et al. (2021) claim that "Sixty-one percent of UK university counselling services reported an increase in demand of at least 25% between 2012 and 2017" (p. 438). For many unwell students, leaving their studies is easier than persisting in an adverse culture. In their research into the issue of high attrition rates of first-year higher education students, Bye et al. (2020) point out that "new students are often largely expected to fend for themselves and … the institution should be augmenting the support available to transitioning students rather than relying on their external social and cultural capital" (p. 899). Hence, these authors posit that, for many first-year higher education students, the institution's culture and curriculum design appear foreign and unhelpful, significantly disregarding the student's need for a sense of belonging and connection (Crawford et al., 2023; Tice et al., 2021).

Also, while higher education institutions ardently embrace digital technology, inclusive of intelligent tutoring systems, virtual learning environments, mobile computing devices, and artificial intelligence-powered applications to increase enrolments nationally and internationally while decreasing costs associated with the provision of physical facilities, they ignore the negative consequences for both students and staff. Concern for the increasing prevalence of 'technostress' among students is the focus of Wang et al. (2021) research. Here, these authors describe how staff and students who are not used to the many and varied requirements associated with the application of technology-enhanced learning may experience technostress, which they define as "a maladaptation problem caused by individuals' incapability to cope with the demands of technology and changing requirements associated with the use of technology in their work in a healthy manner" (p. 1). Importantly, these authors add that "technostress can lead to a variety of negative consequences to individuals' psychological and physiological health, for instance, frustration, anxiety, and fatigue. It can further adversely affect their work, such as causing concentration problems, biasing their judgements of digital technology, and decreasing work performance" (p. 2).

The student's economic well-being is explicitly related to the higher education's commitment to a product-based business model. Essentially, the priority of the institution's fee structure is to do with profit-making and largely ignores its impact on students. An issue explored by Nissen et al. (2019) who found that "to meet rising costs of living and to minimise [student] debt, some students are taking on high levels of employment during the academic year [and this] is associated with declines in academic performance and higher rates of drop-out, which can affect students' career prospects" (p. 4). A specific example is cited by Thornton (2016) when describing growing unwellness concerns among Australian law students. Here, she describes how these law students, "are aggrieved that the high fees they pay are not connected to a superior education but to their anticipated earning capacity as graduates [and they] are commonly working several days per week or even full-time while enrolled in a full-time law course, a factor that further accentuates their distress" (p. 48). Importantly, Thornton concludes her discussion by arguing that managerialist-led higher education institutions "sloughs off responsibility for stress, leaving such problems to be borne by the individual student or resolved through the market" (p. 48).

However, Upsher et al. (2022) also acknowledge that any exploration of issues associated with student unwellness must consider the teacher–student relationship. They add that a lack of student wellness could result from poor staff well-being. Hence, the next section examines the relative cogency of this assumption by drawing on research literature which focuses on the influence of the profit-based business model on the role of higher education staff.

## Recognising the Complementary Crisis in Higher Education: Staff Disengagement and Burnout

Within the product-based business model in higher education, the students are cast as the consumers since they are the purchasers of the product. Hence, the staff become the service providers. Instead of being the initiators, producers, and distributors of new knowledge, as would be their role in a service-based business model, their role is largely relegated to that of a knowledge pedlar. The professional implications of this role change are profound because it impacts the nature and meaning of higher education teaching and higher education learning. Morris (2022) argued that "the marketisation of higher education results in pressures away from *inquisitive* learning and towards *acquisitive* study. The vision of education as transformation [inquisitive learning] accords student satisfaction a more major role than does a model of higher education as a marketised commodity [acquisitive learning]" (p. 10, italics in original). Moreover, this role change has also had a detrimental physical and psychological effect on higher education staff. For example, the research by Upsher et al. (2022) illustrates how higher education "staff burnout has escalated across the UK, resulting in increasingly poor mental health due to excessive workload, external audits, short-term contracts, and progression based on short-term outcomes" (p. 16).

However, as we argued at the outset of this chapter, concern about the crisis resulting from the detrimental impact of managerialism in higher education has been the focus of research worldwide. As previously described (see Branson et al., 2018), Shore's New Zealand study (2010) highlighted how managerialism not only greatly adds to the range and complexity of required staffing tasks but also often creates contradictory missions and, thus, priorities. Santiago and Carvalho (2012) explored the influence of managerialism on Portuguese academics and raised deep concern for the loss of autonomy and collegiality within the higher education workplace environment. Similarly, Sporn's (2010) Austrian higher education research recommended that managerialism reduces trust and respect throughout the institutions' culture. Weinberg and Graham-Smith (2012) criticised the application of managerialism in South African higher education and claimed it resulted in the loss of the institution's 'soul and its autonomy'. To add detail to this concern, Tsheola and Nembambula (2014) posit that managerialism has triumphed over transformational leadership in South African higher education, and this has decreased innovation, imagination, risk-taking, common sense, and experimentation, all of which are considered essential to the future development of the country.

More specifically, to summarise the crisis-creating impact of managerialism upon higher education, where the product-based business model predominates, the institution's market competitiveness and income-generating mechanisms take precedence and re-frame the academic work of the staff. The acknowledged pillars of managerialism are command, control, and manage achieved through mechanistic, ruled-based management practices inclusive of formalised policies, prescribed processes, regimented annual goal-setting and performance review systems, mandated role descriptions, imposed workplace networking structures, bureaucratised decision-making and communication channels, intensification of a dependency on contracted employment, and the like (Branson & Marra, 2021). This creates a coercive culture and strongly discourages higher education staff from working differently, being creative, taking risks, committing to any discretionary workload, and working cooperatively with others. Instead, they feel like a cog in a machine that is expected to continually churn out repetitive, predictable, largely mundane professional outputs for a seemingly predetermined, distant world. This is a far cry from research and scholarship being regarded as a unique, individualistic source of new knowledge, which produces a personal sense of meaning and purpose through a tangible sense of helping to create a better world.

The shift in both the expected outcomes and the systems they relate to also highlights the emotional response of higher education academics sensing the loss of a highly valued cultural characteristic—academic freedom. As Ayers (2014, p. 99) explains, "Today's [higher education institution] is a unique conjuncture in which discourses of strategy, efficiency, and managerial control meet a deeply sedimented culture of professional autonomy, academic freedom, and deliberative decision-making". While managerialism strives to create a more unified, distinctive, coalesced, whole institution that can be then considered a single organisation under centralised control, these very same practices have been the instrument of fragmentation, disunity, and derision because these have brought conflicting values and contrasting philosophical beliefs about what constitutes best practice to the fore (Branson et al., 2018). When the balance between the higher education leader's desired managerialist beliefs and principles is out of kilter with their academic staff's way of behaving and working, the result is the total undermining of the staff's ability to do their work in an engaged and purposeful way. In such a situation, staff become disengaged, and the student's learning experience is significantly lessened. The institution is in crisis. However, if a service-based business model is the solution for redressing this crisis, then what does this imply for higher education leadership practice?

## Leading Higher Education Institutions with Courage, Authenticity, and Wisdom

As an explicit acknowledgement of this higher education crisis, some institutions have introduced mentoring programmes (see Baik et al., 2019; Upsher et al., 2022). However, this deals with the symptom and not the cause. Mentoring implies that the mentee, either a student or staff member, has the problem, and a colleague or peer can fix it. It is essential to accept that the crisis is an institutional, cultural concern and not a personal issue if this seriously unacceptable crisis is to be fixed. Moreover, as an institutional culture concern, the leader can only rectify it. Cultural change begins with the leader, is promoted by the leader, is overseen by the leader, and is modelled by the leader. This necessitates that the higher education leader has the courage to lead such a dramatic cultural change, the authenticity to personally promote and model the change with sincerity and conviction, and the wisdom to create, support, and sustain the change.

To this end, higher education leaders wishing to adopt a service-based business model must radically transform how they understand their institution's culture and leadership practice. This requires the leader to see their institution as an ecosystem whereby each component of its functioning interacts in a co-dependent or interdependent relationship with every other component (Branson & Marra, 2022). Moreover, from this ecosystem perspective, "relationships are the pivotal determinant in achieving [the institution's] success. It is the diversity of quality relationships which shapes the essential productive interconnectivity both within the [institution] and with its external environment and, ultimately, determines not only the [institution's] level of productivity and, therefore, its longevity but also creates a work environment where people thrive" (p. 13). Informed by this ecosystem perspective, we argue that the development of a service-based business model in a higher education institution necessitates, first, that the leader adopts a transrelational approach to their leadership practice and, secondly, that the leader also embraces an anthropological understanding of their institutions' culture.

As defined (Branson et al., 2016, p. 155), a transrelational approach to leadership practice "is to move others, the organisation and the leader to higher levels of functioning by means of relationships". Although described in far more detail elsewhere (see Branson & Marra, 2021; Branson et al., 2018), within the confines of this chapter, we argue that the higher education leader's most effective source of influence upon those they are leading their 'power' to unite all in the achievement of a common vision, is the relationships that the leader creates with every person they are leading.

Furthermore, this influence derives from their ability to allow rather than to direct and is grounded in their staff remaining engaged and connected. Through recognising the importance of interactions as the ideal source of staff engagement, high performance, and innovation, these higher education leaders build 'correlation': the emergence of a common or shared institutional vision and a recognisable widespread pattern of positive organisational behaviour. Through this focus, everyone in the higher educational institution can find meaning and purpose in whatever is happening.

More specifically, we have described how this transrelational approach to higher educational leadership is founded upon five essential practical qualities. The first quality is that the leader must have the relevant knowledge, skills, and experiences to fulfil the role with wisdom and confidence. But then, when first appointed to the position, the leader must show that they have willingly become an integral member of the staff and community. This is about the leader building sustainable trust among those they are leading. Sustainable trust is built upon predictability, consistency, and authenticity. For a leader, this means interacting with the staff, building trusting relationships, talking with them, and understanding what is happening for them in their varied roles. This allows the leader to understand workloads and pressures, achievements and effort, the learning needs of the academic and professional staff, where there are gaps in knowledge and capability, how these can be overcome, and how to affirm and promote the institution. In essence, these interactions with staff acknowledge that there is always greater wisdom in the room than that of the leader—particularly if the room is full of academic experts. It also provides the platform for the leader to create professional networks and connections so that new ideas can flow and be shared to generate continual professional growth and development.

Then, upon this deepening familiarity, the leader must take every opportunity to praise, affirm, champion, and promote individuals and teams. Words of praise and affirmation from the leader for behaviour that mirrors desired beliefs, values, and aspirations are a powerful influence not only on the thoughts and actions of staff members but also for reinforcing their trustworthiness.

After this quality, the higher education leader can propose and nurture individual, team, department, and institutional growth and transformation. This commitment to a growing and transforming responsibility is about fostering dialogue with individuals, committees, departments, and staff that leads to insights about current beliefs, values, and practices in order to help the person, group, or institution to devise ways to enhance and improve learning, teaching, researching, and publication outcomes. In essence, this involves the capacity of the leader to create an institutional culture in which all are committed to actively and continuously improving or growing in some way towards a visionary ideal.

The final foundational leadership quality within a transrelational approach to higher education leadership is the need for the leader to develop a secure yet transcendent institutional environment. Once the staff are working better together towards achieving its vision through incremental improvement, the leader can draw the staff's attention to the changing nature and demands of the external higher educational and socio-communal environment. This involves all in the institution being supported in looking to the future to determine what must be initiated in the present. Without such a leadership eye on the future, higher education institutions will constantly be reactive to environmental demands such as those played out during the COVID-19 pandemic.

However, the leader of a higher education institution cannot have an explicit relationship with each staff member and every student, but their capacity to achieve this universal influence is by ensuring that the institution's culture is commensurate with a relational foundation to all interpersonal interactions. As mentioned above, we argue that this requires an anthropological understanding (see Branson & Marra, 2022) of their institutions' culture. Traditionally, organisational culture has been perceived from a sociological perspective. It is argued that "culture is a socially constructed attribute of organisations that serves as the social glue binding the organisation together" (p. 41). From this foundation, proponents of this perspective nominate certain key cultural elements (inclusive of certain roles, behaviours, values, beliefs, signs, symbols, etc.), which are then collated into a proposed universal construct for classifying the organisation's culture.

Moreover, according to this perspective, understanding the culture provides a framework for not only considering the factors that influence the culture but also identifying areas of strength and weakness. Furthermore, it is argued that understanding the culture in this way gives the leader the knowledge of how to control or change the culture. But this is not so. Due to the various cultural elements appearing as independent, distinct, and fixed, such a description maintains the confusion and ambiguity surrounding the nature of organisational culture, and, therefore, leaders remain reluctant to pursue trying to understand and work with their organisation's culture.

In contrast, our anthropological view of organisational culture explains how the culture emerges out of the everyday individual and personal aspirations, interpretations, and cognitions of those within the organisation. Understanding organisational culture "is about understanding the people begetting the culture. Thus, working with the culture is about working with the people. Changing the culture involves the leader helping the people to know why the culture needs to change and then supporting them in how they bring about the change" (Branson & Marra, 2022, p. 48). For the leader to truly know their organisation's culture, they must be personally relating, communicating, and dialoguing with others throughout the organisation to become aware of how the current culture is being felt, interpreted, and experienced.

This is not about the higher education leader trying to connect and interpret inexplicit institutional, cultural elements but rather coming to deeply know the culture simply by regularly talking with their leading employees. There is no need for the leader to be an expert cultural analyser; all it takes is for the leader to know how culture is formed and, thereby, be able to ask the right questions and seek the right information from staff members regularly. This means that it is not a mechanistic, formalised, periodic process of control, but rather, it is a humanistic, relational, daily way of leading. Moreover, this view mandates that the higher education leader needs to understand the institution's culture from its grassroots, from the phenomena upon which it is created, and not from its observable or espoused symptoms. Such a leader continually seeks honest, accurate, truthful, and insightful information from a wide variety of staff members about how they are experiencing and contributing to the culture as an individual or a team member.

Simply, understanding the institution's culture to have the knowledge and capacity to change it demands a relational approach. Moving from a product-based to a service-based business model requires the higher education leader to become a transrelational leader and, thereby, learn how to change their institution's culture through the myriad of diverse formal and informal relationships they can establish.

## Concluding Comments

While acknowledging that the COVID-19 pandemic has created a diverse array of serious disruptions in the higher education domain, we believe these hide rather than illuminate the factual crisis in higher education leadership. The factual crisis is in how higher education leadership is understood and practised. It is not how the leader will overcome the problems caused by COVID-19. As argued and described in this chapter, overcoming this crisis is founded on ensuring the higher education institution can be fully focused on achieving its core purpose—the creation and the dissemination of knowledge—which demands that its leader strives to establish a service-based culture formed upon collegial professional relationships throughout the institution. In effect, this demands that the higher education leader jettison managerialism and becomes fully committed to adopting a transrelational approach in all of their leadership practices.

## References


Anderson, G. (2006). Carving out time and space in the managerial university. *Journal of Organisational Change, 19*(5), 578–592.

Ayers, D. F. (2014). When managerialism meets professional autonomy: The university "budget update" as genre of governance. *Culture and Organization, 20*(2), 98–120.

Baik, C., Larcombe, W., & Brooker, A. (2019). How universities can enhance student mental well-being: The student perspective. *Higher Education Research & Development, 38*(4), 674–687. https://doi.org/10.1080/07294360.2019.1576596

Blankenberger, B., & Williams, A. M. (2020). COVID-19 and the impact on higher education: The essential role of integrity and accountability. *Administrative Theory & Praxis, 42*(3), 404–423.

Branson, C. M., Franken, M., & Penney, D. (2016). Reconceptualising middle leadership in higher education: A transrelational approach. In J. McNiff (Ed.), *Values and virtues in higher education research: Critical perspectives* (pp. 155–170). Routledge.

Branson, C. M., Marra, M., Franken, M., & Penney, D. (2018). *Leadership in higher education from a transrelational perspective*. Bloomsbury Publishing.

Branson, C. M., & Marra, M. (2021). Reclaiming the soul of the university in an agile corporate world. In T. M. Connolly & S. Farrier (Eds.), *Leadership and management strategies for creating agile universities* (pp. 129–143). IGI Global.

Branson, C. M., & Marra, M. (2022). *A new theory of organisational ecology, and its implications for educational leadership*. Bloomsbury Publishing.

Bye, L., Muller, F., & Oprescu, F. (2020). The impact of social capital on student well-being and university life satisfaction: A semester-long repeated measures study. *Higher Education Research & Development, 39*(5), 898–912. https://doi.org/10.1080/07294360.2019.1705253

Chandler, J., Barry, J., & Clark, H. (2002). Stressing academe: The wear and tear of the new public management. *Human Relations, 55*(9), 1051–1069.

Churchman, D. (2006). Institutional commitments, individual compromises: Identity-related responses to compromise in an Australian university. *Journal of Higher Education Policy and Management, 28*(1), 3–15.

Crawford, J., Allen, K.-A., Sanders, T., Baumeister, R., Parker, P. D., Saunders, C., & Tice, D. M. (2023). Sense of belonging in higher education students: An

Australian longitudinal study from 2013 to 2019. *Studies in Higher Education,* 1–15. https://doi.org/10.1080/03075079.2023.2238006

Deem, R. (1998). New managerialism in higher education: The management of performance and cultures in universities. *International Studies in the Sociology of Education, 8*(1), 47–70.

Devlin, M., & Samarawickrema, G. (2022). A commentary on the criteria of effective teaching in post-COVID-19 higher education. *Higher Education Research & Development, 41*(1), 21–32. https://doi.org/10.1080/07294360.2021.2002828

Dobbins, M., Knill, C., & Vögtle, E. M. (2011). An analytical framework for the cross-country comparison of higher education governance. *Higher Education, 62*(5), 665–683.

Gaiardelli, P., & Songini, L. (2021). Successful business models for service centres: An empirical analysis. *International Journal of Productivity and Performance Management, 70*(5), 1187–1212.

Garcia-Morales, V. J., Garrido-Moreno, A., & Martin-Rojas, R. (2021). The transformation of higher education after the COVID-19 disruption: Emerging challenges in an online learning scenario. *Frontiers in Psychology, 12*, 1–6.

Giroux, D., Karmis, D., & Rouillard, C. (2015). Between the managerial and the democratic university: Governance structure and academic freedom as sites of political struggle. *Studies in Social Justice, 9*(2), 142–158.

Hamel, G., & Zanini, M. (2021). Humanocracy. *McKinsey & Company, 18*, 1–5.

Hamlin, R. G., & Patel, T. (2015). Perceived managerial and leadership effectiveness within higher education in France. *Studies in Higher Education, 42*(2), 1–23.

Huang, L., Kern, M.L., & Oades, L.G. (2020). Strengthening university student wellbeing: Language and perceptions of Chinese international students. *International Journal of Environmental Research and Public Health, 17*, 5538, 1–18.

Jones, E., Priestley, M., Brewster, L., Wilbrahan, S. J., Hughes, G., & Spanner, L. (2021). Student well-being and assessment in higher education: The balancing act. *Assessment & Evaluation in Higher Education, 46*(3), 438–450. https://doi.org/10.1080/02602938.2020.1782344

Lalani, K., Crawford, J., & Butler-Henderson, K. (2021). Academic leadership during COVID-19 in higher education: Technology adoption and adaptation for online learning during a pandemic. *International Journal of Leadership in Education*, 1–17.https://doi.org/10.1080/13603124.2021.1988716

Mete, J. K., Das, R., & Chowdhury, A. (2022). Post-COVID-19 challenges and opportunities for Higher Education. *Journal of Higher Education Theory and Practice, 22*(9), 144–155.

Morris, K. V. A. (2022). Consumerist views of higher education and links to student well-being and achievement: An analysis based on the concept of autonomy as depicted in self-determination theory. *Journal of Further and Higher Education, 46*(6), 836–849. https://doi.org/10.1080/0309877X.2021.2011842

Nissen, S., Hayward, B., & McManus, R. (2019). Student debt and well-being: A research agenda. *Kōtuitui: New Zealand Journal of Social Sciences Online, 14*(2), 245–256. https://doi.org/10.1080/1177083X.2019.1614635

Riggio, R. E., & Newstead, T. (2023). Crisis leadership. *Annual Review of Organizational Psychology and Organizational Behavior, 10*(15), 1–24.

Saarijärvi, H., Grönroos, C., & Kuusela, H. (2014). Reverse use of customer data: Implications for service-based business models. *Journal of Services Marketing, 28*(7), 529–537.

Santiago, R., & Carvalho, T. (2012). Managerialism rhetorics in Portuguese higher education. *Minerva, 50*(4), 511–532.

Shore, C. (2010). The reform of New Zealand's university system: 'After neoliberalism.' *The International Journal of Higher Education in the Social Sciences, 3*(1), 1–31.

Sporn, B. (2010). Management of and in higher education institutions. *International Encyclopedia of education* (3rd ed., pp. 245–250). Elsevier.

Tsheola, J., & Nembambula, P. (2014). Governance of the South African university under democracy and the triumphalism of managerialism over transformational leadership. *Mediterranean Journal of Social Sciences, 5*(27), 1655–1666.

Thornton, M. (2016). Law student well-being: A neoliberal conundrum. *Australian Universities Review, 58*(2), 42–50.

Tice, D., Baumeister, R., Crawford, J., Allen, K. A., & Percy, A. (2021). Student belongingness in higher education: Lessons for Professors from the COVID-19 pandemic. *Journal of University Teaching & Learning Practice, 18*(4), 2. https://doi.org/10.53761/1.18.4.2

Upsher, R., Percy, Z., Cappiello, L., Byrom, N., Hughes, G., Oates, J., Nobili, A., Rakow, K., Anaukwu, C., & Foster, J. (2022). Understanding how the university curriculum impacts student well-being: A qualitative study. *Higher Education*, 1–20. https://doi.org/10.1007/s10734-022-00969-8

van Ameijde, J. D. J., Nelson, P. C., Billsberry, J., & van Meurs, N. (2009). Improving leadership in higher education institutions: A distributed perspective. *Higher Education, 58*, 763–779.

Vincent, A. (2011). Ideology and the university. *The Political Quarterly, 82*(3), 332–340.

Wang, X., Li, Z., Ouyang, Z., & Xu, Y. (2021). The Achilles heel of technology: How does technostress affect university students' well-being and technology-enhanced learning. *International Journal of Environmental Research and Public Health, 18*, 1–17. https://doi.org/10.3390/ijerph182312322

Weinberg, A.M., & Graham-Smith, G. (2012). Collegiality: Can it survive the corporate university? *Social Dynamics, 38*(1), 68–86.

Williams, T. A., Gruber, D. A., Sutcliffe, K. M., Shepherd, D. A., & Zhao, E. Y. (2017). Organisational response to adversity: Fusing crisis management and resilience research streams. *The Academy of Management Annals, 11*(2), 733–769. https://doi.org/10.5465/annals.2015.0134

Wu, Y. L., Shao, B., Newman, A., & Schwarz, G. (2021). Crisis leadership: A review and future research agenda. *The Leadership Quarterly, 32*(6), 1–22.

Zhang, L., Carter, R. A., Qian, X., Yang, S., Rujimora, J., & Wen, S. (2022). Academia's responses to crisis: A bibliometric analysis of literature on online learning in higher education during COVID-19-19. *British Journal of Educational Technology, 53*, 620–646.

# The Environmental Crisis and the Crisis in Environmental Education: Implications for Higher Education Leadership

Eunice Tan

## Introduction

> During disasters, you hear a lot of praise for human resilience. And we are a remarkably resilient species. But that's not always good. It seems a great many of us can get used to almost anything, even the steady annihilation of our own habitat. (Klein, 2020, p. 229)

The above statement by Naomi Klein expresses the contentious nature of our global climate emergency and its surrounding debates. Scientists have warned about the dire consequences of anthropogenic-induced climate change. Increasing numbers of environmental movements and young activists have intensified their pleas for action and positive change. Debates and polls regarding the politics of climate change and policymakers' (in)ability to address the climate emergency have been divergent. Public opinions and reactions have ranged from hopeful determination to profound despair, impassioned rage and blissful ignorance. Recently, scientists and the Intergovernmental Panel on Climate Change (IPCC, 2023) delivered an urgent warning in its Climate Change 2023 Synthesis Report—the time to act decisively for climate change is now. There is a dire need for more ambitious

E. Tan (✉)
Academic Division, SIM Global Education, Singapore Institute of Management, Singapore, Singapore
e-mail: eunicetan@sim.edu.sg



J. Rudolph et al. (eds.), *The Palgrave Handbook of Crisis Leadership in Higher Education*,
https://doi.org/10.1007/978-3-031-54509-2_6

action to mainstream equitable and effective climate action to secure a liveable, sustainable future for all. They warn that the current pace and scale of policies and strategies are woefully inadequate to tackle climate change. Transformational change is needed and needed now.

Likewise, Waeber et al. (2021) caution that accelerating anthropogenic pressures have put humanity on a collision course with the planet's ecosystem, biodiversity and more-than-human world, with detrimental consequences for all. Our planet is "clearly and unequivocally" facing a climate emergency (Gardner et al., 2021, p. 2). One would think that the warnings and perils of annihilation would be enough to scare us into taking action. Why do humans (and our leaders), a remarkably risk-averse species, not act on that risk? (Kluger, 2018). Can humanity (and our leaders and policymakers) awaken in time from its unsustainable, unsound sleepwalk into a global catastrophe and its destruction before it is too late? (Tan & Rudolph, 2023). To these questions, Klein (2020) suggests that "the idea that we humans cannot do what is required to confront the climate crisis because it is too much" is a fallacy advocated by "those whose interests it was for things to remain the same. Clearly when societies decide to treat an emergency as an emergency… all manner of possibilities instantly bloom" (p. xvi).

Notwithstanding, the recent intersecting Triple-C Crises of COVID-19, conflict (e.g., the war in Ukraine—see Sedochenko & Shyyan, 2024, in this volume) and climate change have had detrimental repercussions on people, society and the economy worldwide (United Nations, 2022). As the global community struggles with crisis fatigue in crisis-upon-crisis conditions, sound crisis leadership becomes paramount (Connor, 2010; Rozelle-Stone, 2022; Vandaele & Stålhammar, 2022). Thus, this chapter focuses on the thematic dimensions of the environmental crisis, environmental and sustainability education, and the significance of higher education leadership in the face of this climate emergency and sustained crisis.

The environmental crisis is a defining crisis of our generation, and its devasting effects are felt across the globe (United Nations, 2019). As Tregidga and Laine (2022) concede, "the environment is in crisis" (p. 1). However, despite broad acknowledgement and understanding of this emergency, humanity is still sluggish in realising (or accepting) the magnitude of the threats and pursuing realistic, actionable interventions. The time of living unsustainably must end if we are to reverse the damaging consequences we have caused to our planet's ecosystem, which we have pushed to the point of collapse. We have to move away from generation after generation of a distorted perception of life that constantly shifts the baselines of what is considered 'normal' for our planetary resources and ecological boundaries.

It is *not* normal and *cannot* be accepted as normal. Forcible transformations are needed to curtail current modes of human consumption and production (Tan & Rudolph, 2023).

Consequently, there is a need to push for greater climate action and the framing of stronger measures and transformations in humanity's relationship with the natural and more-than-human world. The higher education sector is no exception. Confronted with a world of crisis-induced change, Stickney and Skilbeck (2020) advocate the vital role of policymakers, researchers and educators in mobilising and pulling together stakeholders to address the climate crisis. Concurrently, mounting global concerns relating to sustainable development, climate and sustainability agendas have spurred heightened discourse about the role of education curricula, programmes and institutional leadership (Gluch & Månsson, 2021; Ryan et al., 2010; Shephard & Furnari, 2013; Singh & Segatto, 2020; Wamsler, 2020). In this respect, Waeber et al. (2021, p. 12) advocate for more constructive discourse and collaborative action since concerns such as "climate, poverty, and health are global affairs, which do not stop at political boundaries nor follow ideological trenches". Therefore, there is value in forwarding educational research agendas, instructional adjustments and the development of core competencies to address the environmental crisis.

Education is key in activating this transformation of people and society towards sustainability. Education for sustainability as a transformative approach spotlights the "educational vision to balance human and economic well-being with cultural traditions and reverence for the Earth's natural resources" (Chen et al., 2022, p. 1). However, whilst there has been heightened recognition and debates concerning the environmental-sustainability education nexus in recent decades, there has been limited discourse from the perspective of crisis leadership within higher education. Moreover, with the multifaceted nature, multi-disciplinary dimensions and multifarious interpretations of environmental crisis agendas, there is value in its investigation (Crawford & Cifuentes-Faura, 2022; Waeber et al., 2021). In this 'environmental century', it is vital for institutions of higher education to organise themselves to align to transdisciplinary sustainability agendas (Mulkey, 2017). However, most have not been successful in meeting this mandate. Likewise, Gardner et al. (2021) remark that the higher education sector "is not rising to the collective challenge with the urgency commensurate with the warnings" concerning the climate emergency, and is generally "continuing with business as usual" (p. 2). Given the potentially salient, disruptive and volatile nature of crises on an institution, its stakeholders and the broader community, the role of crisis leadership and the actions of leaders and policymakers during a crisis becomes critical (Riggio & Newstead, 2023; Wu et al., 2021). After a century of imprudent environmental policies and (in)action, environmental scientists, researchers and activists have been intensifying their warnings about the alarming consequences forecasted and the need to strengthen the capacities (and priorities!) of leaders and policymakers in addressing the growing climate crisis (Stickney & Skilbeck, 2020).

Therefore, the above thematic considerations and research gaps emphasise the value of obtaining the opinions of environmental educators and policymakers to better understand the issues and concerns impacting environmental education. This chapter presents preliminary data from a research-in-progress and broader study on sustainability education and policy-making in higher education. Data collection and analyses for this work are based on critical incident techniques (CIT) (Butterfield et al., 2005; Gluch & Månsson, 2021; Paraskevas et al., 2013; Viergever, 2019) utilised to gather critical analysis, feedback and reflections from higher education policymakers and educators involved in environmental and sustainability education and curricula. Specifically, it examines crisis leadership in higher education through the lens of environmental education. It is based on critical reflections as an analytical approach to investigate higher education leadership in the face of this climate emergency. The chapter begins with a critical review of the climate and environmental crisis, the evolution of global sustainability agendas, and its corresponding effects on environmental and sustainability education approaches. This is followed by discussing the implications and role of crisis leadership and policy-making in forwarding sustainability agendas in environmental education within the higher education space. Finally, an analysis and discussion of key findings are considered, which include (1) the challenges and barriers impacting the alignment and integration of sustainability into IHLs, (2) the perceived enabling and disabling factors impacting education for sustainability and (3) recommended areas of adjustments, based on the critical analysis. The resultant analysis can support future efforts in environmental education and the teaching and learning of sustainability in higher education to support climate emergency actions.

## Literature Review

### Environmental Education

The debates concerning environmental education within the higher education space are not new. However, the rhetoric relating to sustainable development and its implications in higher education has evolved significantly over the years (Fisher & McAdams, 2015; Ryan et al., 2010; Shephard & Furnari, 2013). Its fundamental role in sustainability and climate agenda has similarly developed within educational practices (Crawford & Cifuentes-Faura, 2022). As such, there is a need to investigate this evolution since humanity's and societies' perceptions and priorities change as their circumstances change. The key to meaningful environmental education within our ecologically damaged world is transforming values and mindsets and inspiring the next generation of learners to take a cognitive leap towards an environmental awakening and transform their paradigms of sustainability (Wamsler, 2020). Hence, in order to adequately appreciate and facilitate this perceptive leap, it is important for us first to review the evolution of sustainability education. Transformations in environmental education provide opportunities for prompting changes in attitudes, values and behaviours needed for our collective survival (Stickney & Skilbeck, 2020). Thus, sound integration of sustainability agendas within the higher education learning space is vital to address the socio-ecological challenges and climate emergency adequately.

Pedagogical approaches to sustainability education have evolved from education ***about*** sustainability (E*a*S: focused on knowledge and content) to education ***for*** sustainability (E*f*S: focused on developing values, capabilities and dispositions), wherein the advocacy for reforms and motivation to take action *for* sustainability is emphasised. Accordingly, E*f*S is a transformative approach to teaching and learning that underscores the need for critical reflection on beliefs and values and the affective transformations of learners (Chen et al., 2022). Correspondingly, education *for* the environmental crisis similarly requires addressing the crisis in environmental education outcomes and comprehending its implications on attitudinal transformations, sustainability values and the magnitude of generative forces (Vandaele & Stålhammar, 2022). The extant discourse regarding E*f*S generally posits that for us to transition towards a sustainable future, individuals' attitudes, values and perceptions towards sustainability must change so that long-term behavioural transformation in line with sustainable development goals may occur (Niebert, 2019). E*f*S also considers the embedded educational practices enabling sustainability and environmental knowledge development within disciplinary contexts (Crawford & Cifuentes-Faura, 2022). Per Shephard and Furnari (2013) and Cotton et al. (2009), an individual's sustainability-driven perceptions and priorities are viewed through personal lenses, backgrounds, values and belief systems. Under these circumstances, leaders' sustainability-driven interpretation and priorities will similarly influence the degree and focus of their sustainability initiatives. It will also define their role(s) as leaders, educators and policymakers within Institutes of Higher Learning (IHLs). With this in mind, Sandri (2022) posits that the policy- and decision-making priorities of IHL leadership will impact their support, development and/or approaches to sustainability-based curricula within teaching and learning practice.

Sustainability agendas have been emphasised at national and international levels within education policies and environmental education. However, Stickney and Skilbeck (2020) observe that whilst the value of embedding sustainability into educational programmes has been debated and emphasised in extant educational debates, policies and discourse, there is a paucity of extant discourse dedicated to the examination of specific environmental education practice, applications and learning outcomes. Likewise, other authors (Chen et al., 2022; Crawford & Cifuentes-Faura, 2022; Sandri, 2022; Shephard & Furnari, 2013) have noted that this predicament may be exacerbated since sustainability agendas may conflict with other politically, economically or developmentally driven contemporary educational objectives. Extant research observes that the multiplicity and contradictions in viewpoints concerning sustainability agendas in IHLs impose barriers impacting its alignment within the higher education space. These barriers may include but are not limited to (1) incongruence and/or limitations in relevant applications, (2) poor academic or institutional policy leadership, (3) competing and/or conflicting IHL agendas or policy-making priorities, (4) the adoption of unsuitable sustainability pedagogies, (5) diversity of curricular and disciplinary structures, (6) variances in teaching and/or methodological approaches, (7) availability of resources and competent change leaders and (8) non-conformity or divergence in measurements of sustainability learning outcomes (Adomßent et al., 2019; Cotton et al., 2009; Shawe et al., 2019; Singh & Segatto, 2020). Thus, whilst sustainability in higher education is not new, the discourse surrounding its intentions, implementation and strategies within teaching and curriculum development are discernibly diverse. Consequently, there is a need for sound leadership and cooperative and collaborative actions rather than policies and activities undertaken in isolation without consideration of national and international environmental agendas (Crawford & Cifuentes-Faura, 2022). As Niebert (2019) suggests, addressing the current global environmental challenges cannot be accomplished individually or in isolation but by enforcing collectively agreed social, political and economic decisions for transformation.

From an institutional perspective, this implies that sustainability educators, researchers and policymakers should not try to create a better world in independent isolation but instead engage with their present collectives (i.e., students and fellow researchers) to critically respond to and navigate our present and future more-than-human world (Decuypere et al., 2019). Per Gluch and Månsson (2021), there is value in critical reflexivity, wherein the lived experiences of players and the socio-environmental concerns and/or challenges impacting them are critically, reflectively and holistically examined. Niebert (2019, p. 1) stated that in order to ensure a sustainable future, "we need to transform societies...and changes in our mindsets, lifestyles, attitudes and the way we imagine industry and economy...and education must play a major role in bringing about these changes". The author's statement brings to light the critical role that we (people, policymakers, communities and future generations) as a (human) species, have in impacting multiple species (the more than human world) and the earth; that education is the key to transforming values (i.e., not just knowledge) and changing mindsets and behaviours.

However, as noted in the preceding literature, there are concerns about the severity of the environmental crisis, the predicaments of environmental education, and its (in)ability to achieve the lofty goals it has set out to accomplish. The Anthropogenic emergency we face is entrenched in the planetary scale of our human–environment actions and consequences (Tan & Rudolph, 2023). Consequently, Gardner et al. (2021) declare the need for educators, researchers and academics in IHLs to take decisive action and expand beyond their traditional academic roles to actively engage in, advocate for and influence policies addressing the environmental crisis. Whilst extant discourses concerning sustainability and environmental education within the higher education space have been intensifying, there is a need to explore its implications beyond teaching and learning agendas. We must concede that knowledge and awareness alone cannot activate long-term change and affirmative action. With the environment in crisis, strong policy leadership for the environment is needed in higher education. Thus, the next section of the chapter explores the thematic dimensions of crisis leadership and policy-making for the environment in higher education.

## Crisis Leadership and Policy-Making for the Environment in Higher Education

The works above regarding contemporary environmental education debated the importance of considering the implications of the role of educational leaders and policymakers in forwarding sound sustainability agendas in environmental education. There is a need to bridge the gaps and increased polarisation of academic and societal calls for action, urging policymakers to recognise the full repercussions of the current environmental crisis (Waeber et al., 2021). In order to centre the environmental emergency at the heart of the Triple-C crises, we need leaders with a strong sustainability mindset who will ensure that sustainability agendas are not marginalised or de-prioritised (Chen et al., 2022; Tregidga & Laine, 2022). Effective crisis leadership from industry, political and societal leaders is pivotal in managing crises and is often considered a true test of leadership (Wu et al., 2021). Concurrently, IHLs, as central hubs and leaders in education and research, are responsible for driving the transformations towards sustainability. Gardner et al. (2021, p. 2) coined the adage, "with knowledge comes responsibility", to assert that IHLs, as pivotal change agents, must speak out and take action during this planetary emergency. Concerning global climate emergency leadership, the urgency of enacting genuine calls for concrete action was emphasised in UN Secretary-General António Guterres's remarks at the 2019 Climate Action Summit, where he said,

> This is not a climate talk summit. We have had enough talk. This is not a climate negotiation summit because we don't negotiate with nature. This is a climate action summit… (our) generation has failed in its responsibility to protect our planet. That must change. The climate emergency is a race we are losing, but it is a race we can win. The climate crisis is caused by us – and the solutions must come from us. (United Nations, 2019)

The declaration and framing of the climate crisis as an emergency advocate the urgent need for stronger measures and firmer (and faster/more efficient) policy decision-making to immediately address humanity's relationship with the natural environment and more-than-human world (Tregidga & Laine, 2022). As Klein (2020) surmises, there is a dire need to awaken from the prevalent cognitive dissonance that obstinately denies the reality of the environmental crisis and climate emergency. "Treating an emergency like an emergency means all our energies can go into action, rather than into screaming about the need for action, which is what is happening now" (p. 285). Relatedly, Leal Filho et al. (2018) highlight the significance of macro- or national-level policy-making and the role of policymakers in influencing priorities in environmental education. Sustainability educators and policymakers play an important role as change agents within IHLs, higher education, and society (Gardner et al., 2021; Shawe et al., 2019). However, while rapid response and adaptation have increasingly become the dominant rhetoric of climate change policy discourse, significant constraints and barriers remain to its effective implementation (Connor, 2010). Thus, whilst there has been broad consensus about the role of education as the key to enacting change, successful implementation of sustainability agendas into educational programmes and policy requires the reorientation of environmental education towards transformational, attitudinal and values-based outcomes (Niebert, 2019). Chen et al. (2022) note that there are significant ideological differences in how educators and policymakers perceive, position and teach sustainability—ranging from a weaker sustainability (economic-centric) focus to a stronger sustainability (ecological and/or sociocultural-centric) focus. This, in turn, impacts their degree and depth of participation and/or support for environmental reform principles, political agency, critical reflection and activism for interventions. In this respect, Ryan et al. (2010) posit the significance of IHL leadership and policy-making and the role of government stakeholders in addressing the gaps between sustainability policy and practice integration. Likewise, Leal Filho et al. (2018) suggest that a lack of and/or absence of formal commitments, plans and/or strategies for including sustainability agendas into higher education may hamper its subsequent synergistic integration.

In addition to the barriers impacting the alignment of sustainability education within the higher education space discussed in the previous section (Adomßent et al., 2019; Cotton et al., 2009; Singh & Segatto, 2020), there are also further constraints generated by IHL leadership and policy-making dimensions. These predominantly result from observed deficits in (1) building strong sustainability collaborative networks, (2) the synergistic integration and dissemination of sustainability curricula, (3) funding, resources and expertise supporting sustainability initiatives, (4) support from government initiatives to promote sustainability and (5) poor engagement and interaction between academia and industry (Adomßent et al., 2019; Connor, 2010; Fisher & McAdams, 2015; Leal Filho et al., 2018). In this regard, Shawe et al. (2019) observe that sustainability concerns with educational agendas may not often be a policy priority for IHL leadership. This imposes significant challenges against efforts to enact E*f*S approaches in higher education.

Moreover, the perils of 'sustainability fatigue' and 'crisis fatigue' (Connor, 2010) may prompt a regression towards banality or avoidance. As Rozelle-Stone (2022) suggests, our moral attention (i.e., the ability to open up fully and empathise emotionally, cognitively and physically) gets unwittingly undermined when we become overwhelmed, helpless or strained from the realities of crisis-upon-crisis encounters. Consequently, what started as a compassionate understanding gradually or quickly became avoidance or banal. Therefore, the value of sound crisis leadership to mitigate crisis fatigue becomes all the more important (Riggo & Newstead, 2023). We are now at the crossroads of our planet's climate and sustainable future, and the need for strong leadership and critical action is now.

## Critical Incident Techniques for Policy-Making Activities and Processes

This literature review section discusses the potentiality of applying critical incident techniques (CIT) to facilitate the critical reflection and analysis of policy-making activities and processes. Since its inception by Flanagan (1954) almost seven decades ago, CIT has become a frequently used approach for critical reflection and analysis and an investigative tool in qualitative research across various disciplines (Butterfield et al., 2005; Viergever, 2019). Flanagan and colleagues (1954) drew on psychological principles, proceedings and analysis as the procedural roots for CIT. They suggest that CIT is well suited as the procedural guidelines for investigating human behaviour and activities to solve practical problems because it (1) outlines specific procedures for systematically collecting observed incidents (i.e., human activity) based on a set of defined criteria and after that (2) permits interpretations, predictions and analyses of consequences and/or outcomes from those observed effects. Within this context, CIT has been deemed suitable as an analytical approach and investigative tool within this study since it enables the critical analysis of policy-related activities and processes within environmental education. This is discussed in further detail in the methodology section.

As a tool developed to generate a functional description of an activity, CIT serves to (1) determine the aim(s) or objective(s) of the activity being studied and (2) specify the expected outcomes from those engaged in the activity (Butterfield et al., 2005). It also serves to investigate and analyse what helps or hinders the activity or experience under study, particularly those that result in participants' perceived satisfaction or dissatisfaction (Viergever, 2019). Whilst CIT was developed as a tool to structure and formulate the critical requirements of an activity under investigation, it has since evolved from its roots as a task-oriented analytical tool to encompass a flexible set of guiding principles capable of being adapted and modified to suit a range of specific investigative situations (Butterfield et al., 2005). Subsequently, other authors have adapted and extended the procedural protocols for CIT beyond just behavioural observations to include analysing and classifying human perceptions and observations, such as satisfying and dissatisfying factors, critical reflections, knowledge and informational transfer, and experiential outcomes (Butterfield et al., 2005; Gluch & Månsson, 2021; Paraskevas et al., 2013; Viergever, 2019). Whilst its applications and orientations may vary, based on the synthesis of suggested procedures from extant discourse, there are fundamentally five key steps when conducting analyses using the CIT: (1) State the aim(s), (2) Define the critical incident, (3) Data collection, (4) Data analysis and (5) Interpretation and reporting. These five progressive stages of investigation were similarly adapted in this study.

## Methodology

This chapter critically discusses some preliminary data from a research-in-progress and broader study on sustainability education and policy-making in higher education. It draws on critical incident analysis and reflections captured from participants who are educators and policymakers involved in environmental and sustainability education and curricula within IHLs. As discussed in the literature, the adaptation of CIT within this study enables the critical analysis of policy-related activities and processes within environmental education in higher education. CIT has been selected within this study as it is an analytical approach and investigative tool frequently used for critical analysis within qualitative research (Butterfield et al., 2005). As Viergever (2019) observes, applying critical incident techniques examines specific factors and/or dimensions that help or hinder a particular activity, process, or experience under study and/or the degree of satisfaction or dissatisfaction from participants.

Participants were recruited through snowball sampling, as this approach is suitable when there is a need to recruit study participants who fulfil a specific set of characteristics and/or experiences (Hennink et al., 2020). Likewise, Gluch and Månsson's (2021) study adapted CIT to investigate critical events affecting institutional sustainability practices and utilised a concise, nested process to investigate the enabling and disabling factors impacting institutional sustainability processes and narratives. As introduced in the prior section, this chapter examines the critical factors impacting education for sustainability and higher education crisis leadership in the face of the current climate emergency. To do this, the CIT approach was utilised, wherein feedback and critical reflections from higher education policymakers and educators actively involved in environmental and/or sustainability education and curricula were sought. To be eligible, participants needed to be teaching/have taught/be involved in developing a course at their IHLs that supports education for sustainability. In their critical reflections, participants were asked to share opinions regarding:

1. The factors impacting the alignment of sustainability agendas into higher education.
2. How education for sustainability initiatives were implemented at their institution.
3. The rationale for the course development and how it supports education for sustainability.
4. The different teaching and learning methods utilised to support education for sustainability.
5. Which aspects of the course were *most* valuable to education for sustainability
6. Which aspects of the course were *least* valuable to education for sustainability
7. Which/any aspects of the course would they change in order to support education for sustainability learning outcomes better
8. Any other comments and/or feedback they would like to share regarding education for sustainability agendas?

For this chapter and the focus of this handbook, only Questions 1, 2, 5, 6, and 7 are analysed and discussed. A total of 13 participants accepted the invitation to participate and submitted their reflections on an online qualitative, semi-structured pro forma administered through Qualtrics. Per Vasileiou et al. (2018), the qualitative sample of participants within this study is purposive and thus were selected under their positionality as sustainability educators and/or policymakers and based on their capabilities to offer richly textured information relevant to the study's thematic dimensions being investigated. In order to ensure the anonymity of participants, no names or personally identifying information were collected from participants. All information collected, coded and analysed are only reported in aggregated form. The resultant analysis is discussed in the following section.

## Discussion and Conclusions

The literature discussed in the preceding sections highlights the fundamental challenges and interdisciplinary complexities of integrating sustainability agendas in higher education. In order to realise sustainable development goals and address the climate crisis impacting people, society and the planet, there is a need for continuous improvements in sustainability education instruction, competencies and skills to nurture a change-promoting educational culture in higher education (Chen et al., 2022). However, prevailing institutional structures and participation or knowledge gaps may signal why sustainability continues to endure a niche or peripheral existence in many IHLs (Adomßent et al., 2019). As noted in the preceding literature, the multiplicity of viewpoints and priorities of IHLs and their institutional leaders and/or policymakers do influence the alignment and integration of sustainability agendas into higher education and IHLs (Adomßent et al., 2019; Cotton et al., 2009; Shawe et al., 2019; Singh & Segatto, 2020).

Participants in this study were asked to rank in order of significance (*1 for totally insignificant, 5 for totally significant*) 16 factors that may impose barriers impacting the alignment and integration of sustainability into higher education (Fig. 1). The results indicate that the top eight impacting factors perceived by participants were: (1) lack of qualified staff to lead and supervise sustainability initiatives, (2) lack of synergy in the adoption and diffusion of sustainability curricula, (3) lack of research funding to support sustainability initiatives, (4) lack of incentives to implement sustainability trajectories, (5) the ignorance of environmental impacts, (6) sustainability education being at the periphery, rather than as core curricula, (7) lack of strong institutional leadership towards sustainability agendas and (8) financial priorities of higher education business models. Per Waeber et al. (2021), the perceived action gap(s) impacting the alignment of sustainability into higher education represents a problem of differing attitudinal perceptions and values towards sustainability and a problem of ineffective strategies. The incongruence between the urgency and existential threat of the climate emergency and the lack of an efficient, coordinated decision- and policy-making process, sustainability reporting system and/or systematic approaches to reorienting sustainability initiatives (Gardner et al., 2021; Shawe et al., 2019; Waeber et al., 2021) challenge the expedient integration of sustainability into higher education.

In terms of the implementation of education for sustainability initiatives at their IHLs, the most common level of implementation indicated by the participants was at the institution-wide level (42%), followed by

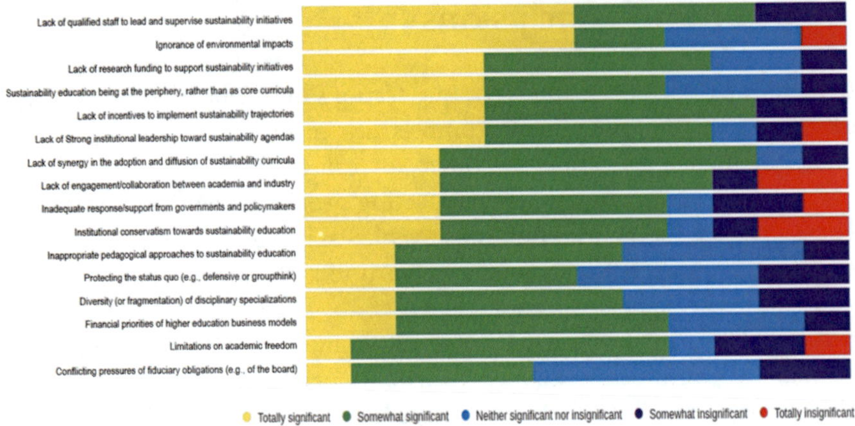


**Fig. 1** Ranking of factors impacting the alignment of sustainability into higher education (sorted by factors considered 'totally significant')

the college or department level (25%) and the programme or course level (25%). No participants' IHLs implemented the sustainability initiatives at the discipline or sectoral level. These findings are congruent with extant literature concerning the significance of the role of IHLs in supporting education for sustainability initiatives. Per Crawford and Cifuentes-Faura (2022), IHLs are increasingly recognised for their role in establishing and developing clear sustainability precedents and actions as key institutional players within their communities. Likewise, Ryan et al. (2010) and Stickney and Skilbeck (2020) emphasise the significance of IHL leadership, policymakers, researchers and educators in bridging the gaps between sustainability policy and practice integration to support efforts in addressing the climate crisis. In this respect, the ability of IHLs to re-align and re-organise themselves towards transdisciplinary education for sustainability is vital.

However, not all IHLs can achieve this mandate (Mulkey, 2017). Similarly, it was interesting to note that in this study, whilst there were strong institutional-led initiatives for implementing sustainability at participants' IHLs, none of their IHLs implemented sustainability initiatives at the discipline or sectoral level. From the participants' narratives, the findings support the notion that the majority of sustainability programmes and/or curricula developed at their respective IHLs, whilst supported by their institutional and/or college/departmental leadership, were predominantly driven by the sustainability orientations, advocacy or dedication of the faculty member(s) driving it.

In order to determine the effectiveness of an activity or process under investigation, it is important to engage in critical reflection. Within the context of this study, CIT is utilised as an investigative tool to analyse the participants' perceptions and observations about specific enabling (helpful) or disabling (hindering) factors and/or dimensions that impact the institutional sustainability processes and activities (Gluch & Månsson, 2021; Viergever, 2019). About the enabling factors, participants were asked to share which aspects of the course were *most* valuable to education for sustainability. Subsequently, participants were asked to share which aspects of the course were *least* valuable. A review and analysis of the participants' narratives indicate that the factors considered to be most valuable for education for sustainability predominantly related to the E*f*S dimensions (i.e., developing capabilities, changing mindsets, nurturing values and beliefs, affecting transformations of learners, inspiring calls for action).

In contrast, those considered least valuable are mainly related to aspects of E*a*S (i.e., content and knowledge about sustainability) (Fig. 2). Of course, it is important to acknowledge that to warrant a comprehensive and holistic understanding of sustainability concerns, both E*a*S and E*f*S learning concepts and activities are required. After all, foundational theoretical knowledge and conceptual content are fundamental concepts that scaffold higher-level learning and critical thinking.

The students' learning journeys through E*f*S-focused activities can foster deeper connections between sustainability conceptual knowledge learned and their inner individual transformations, consciousness and associated cognitive/emotional capacities (e.g., other- and self-awareness, mindfulness,

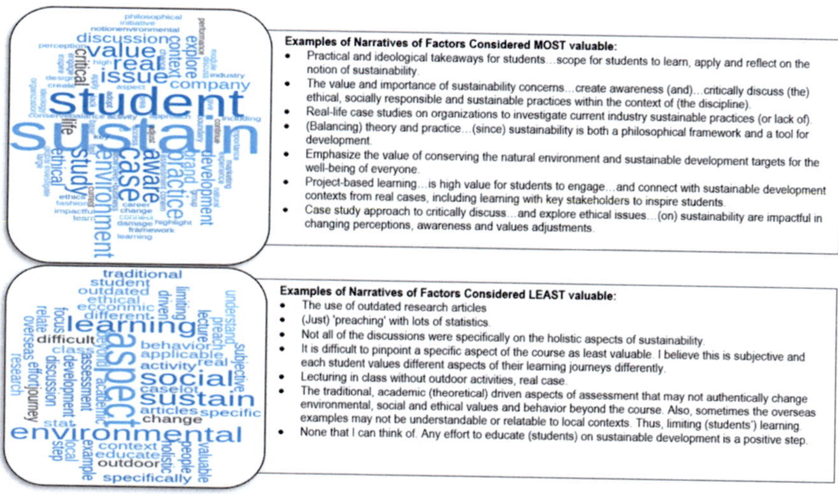


**Fig. 2** Aspects of the course *most* and *least* valuable to education for sustainability

compassion and empathy) towards sustainability (Wamsler, 2020). As highlighted by Fisher and McAdams (2015), the amount and type of coursework, curricula and programmes students undertake can impact their conceptualisations of sustainability. When the teaching and learning of sustainability are perceived to be limited in relevance or ambiguous to the learners' disciplines, it may be challenging to achieve optimal learning outcomes. Moreover, there is a need for some flexibility in curriculum content to engage learners on an individual level to approach sustainability in different ways (Cotton et al., 2009). Therefore, IHL educators and leaders must assess the impacts of the teaching and learning approaches most relevant to their disciplines. Similarly, Wamsler (2020) recommends that there is a need for a more holistic pedagogical perspective embedding sustainability agendas in higher education to address today's challenges adequately. Just as education is posited to be a powerful and proven vehicle to forward sustainability agendas, so is a need to consider the leadership roles of educators and policymakers at IHLs in enabling or hindering this.

One of the key aspects of CIT adapted for a study such as this is the capacity to investigate if the aims/objectives of the activity being studied have met its expected outcomes from those engaged in the activity and if any adjustments can be made to improve it (Butterfield et al., 2005). Thus, participants were asked to reflect on the aspects of their sustainability-related course/curriculum that they would like to change/hope to change. Based on the critical reflections and narratives shared by participants, the four most commonly articulated areas of improvement and/or adaptation suggested related to (1) adjustments in assessments to create more authentic, active learning and participative engagement of learners; (2) increasing the value and prominence of real-world learning, industry-relevant on-site visits and field studies; (3) the need to promote reflective and values-based activities and learning outcomes to aid attitudinal transformations; and (4) ensuring consistent and comprehensive scaffolding of sustainability education and actions across different disciplines and student engagement and/or learning activities.

It is not enough to simply make climate emergency declarations (Gardner et al., 2021). After all, actions speak louder than words. Thus, such declarations alone, with generic or weak sustainability initiatives and traditional approaches to teaching, learning and research, are "insufficient to trigger the transformative changes required at the necessary speeds" (Gardner et al., 2021, p. 2). Instead, engaged academics (and IHLs) should pursue academic activism, wherein those with the greatest skills and knowledge to address these crises will be explicitly recognised (and rewarded!) to provide leadership and engage in policy-making and political processes. Likewise, Shawe et al. (2019) advocate that sustainability initiatives and actions following a standardised institution-based (i.e., internally driven) approach will be less effective if external outreach is overlooked.

In times of crisis, the greatest obstacle impeding us is hopelessness, the fear that we are too late, that we have ignored it for too long, or that we have insufficient time to rectify such a herculean task (Klein, 2020). However, we must awaken from this despondence or apathy that has had a stranglehold on humanity's responses to the climate challenge for far too long. Instead, we should reach into it and galvanise it into constructive calls for action. In exploring the debates concerning the role of education in times of crisis, Vandaele and Stålhammar (2022) suggest a need to foster the cognitive, emotional and behavioural dimensions of hope as an existential necessity. Within this context, the multifaceted dimension of constructive hope can facilitate learners' ability to confront the socio-environmental threats of our time and positively undertake transformative action for sustainability. Likewise, it is not too late for us to utilise transformative educational strategies and approaches to transform mindsets, actions, lifestyles and societies through the appropriate approaches and adaption of education for sustainability (Niebert, 2019; Tregidga & Laine, 2022). As Klein (2020, p. 291) advises, we are at the cusp of a "new vision of what humanity can be… it's a vision that says that all of us, combined, make up the fabric of society. And when the future of life is at stake, there is nothing we cannot achieve". As increasingly advocated in contemporary global calls to action, the transformative moment for climate action is now, and purposeful crisis leadership is the key. So, let us (people, policymakers, communities and future generations), as a collective humanity, forge ahead together to reclaim a sustainable future for all.

## References


Adomßent, M., Grahl, A., & Spira, F. (2019). Putting sustainable campuses into force: Empowering students, staff and academics by the self-efficacy Green Office Model. *International Journal of Sustainability in Higher Education, 20*(3), 470–481.

Butterfield, L. D., Borgen, W. A., Amundson, N. E., & Maglio, A. S. T. (2005). Fifty years of the critical incident technique: 1954–2004 and beyond. *Qualitative Research, 5*(4), 475–497.

Chen, M., Pei, T., Jeronen, E., Wang, Z., & Xu, L. (2022). Teaching and learning methods for promoting sustainability in tourism education. *Sustainability, 14*(21), 14592. https://doi.org/10.3390/su142114592

Connor, L. H. (2010). Anthropogenic climate change and cultural crisis: An anthropological perspective. *Journal of Australian Political Economy, 66*, 247–267.

Cotton, D., Bailey, I., Warren, M., & Bissell, S. (2009). Revolutions and second-best solutions: Education for sustainable development in higher education. *Studies in Higher Education, 34*(7), 719–733.

Crawford, J., & Cifuentes-Faura, J. (2022). Sustainability in higher education during the COVID-19 pandemic: A systematic review. *Sustainability, 14*(3), 1879.

Decuypere, M., Hoet, H., & Vandenabeele, J. (2019). Learning to navigate (in) the anthropocene. *Sustainability, 11*(2), 547.

Fisher, P. B., & McAdams, E. (2015). Gaps in sustainability education: The impact of higher education coursework on perceptions of sustainability. *International Journal of Sustainability in Higher Education, 16*(4), 407–423.

Flanagan, J. C. (1954). The critical incident technique. *Psychological Bulletin, 51*(4), 327.

Gardner, C. J., Thierry, A., Rowlandson, W., & Steinberger, J. K. (2021). From publications to public actions: The role of universities in facilitating academic advocacy and activism in the climate and ecological emergency. *Frontiers in Sustainability, 2*, 679019.

Gluch, P., & Månsson, S. (2021). Taking lead for sustainability: Environmental managers as institutional entrepreneurs. *Sustainability, 13*(7), 4022. https://doi.org/10.3390/su13074022

Hennink, M., Hutter, I., & Bailey, A. (2020). *Qualitative research methods* (3rd ed.). Sage Publications.

Intergovernmental Panel on Climate Change (IPCC). (2023). *AR6 synthesis report: Climate change 2023*. https://www.ipcc.ch/report/ar6/syr/

Klein, N. (2020). *On fire: The (burning) case for a green new deal*. Simon & Schuster.

Kluger, J. (2018). Why we keep ignoring even the most dire climate change warnings? *Time Magazine*. https://time.com/5418690/why-ignore-climate-change-warnings-un-report/

Leal Filho, W., Pallant, E., Enete, A., Richter, B., & Brandli, L. L. (2018). Planning and implementing sustainability in higher education institutions: An overview of the difficulties and potentials. *International Journal of Sustainable Development and World Ecology, 25*(8), 713–721.

Mulkey, S. (2017). Higher education in the environmental century. *American Journal of Economics and Sociology, 76*(3), 697–730.

Niebert, K. (2019). Effective sustainability education is political education. *Journal for Research and Debate, 2*(4), 1–5.

Paraskevas, A., Altinay, L., McLane, J., & Cooper, C. (2013). Crisis knowledge in tourism: Types, flows and governance. *Annals of Tourism Research, 41*(2), 130–152.

Riggio, R. E., & Newstead, T. (2023). Crisis leadership. *Annual Review of Organizational Psychology and Organizational Behavior, 10*, 201–224.

Rozelle-Stone, R. (2022). When tragedy becomes banal: Why news consumers experience crisis fatigue. *The Conversation*. https://theconversation.com/when-tragedy-becomes-banal-why-news-consumers-experience-crisis-fatigue-187756

Ryan, A., Tilbury, D., Corcoran, P. B., Abe, O., & Nomura, K. (2010). Sustainability in higher education in the Asia-Pacific: Developments, challenges, and prospects. *International Journal of Sustainability in Higher Education, 11*(2), 106–119.

Sandri, O. (2022). What do we mean by 'pedagogy' in sustainability education? *Teaching in Higher Education, 27*(1), 114–129.

Sedochenko, A., & Shyyan, O. (2024). Crisis in higher education—Ukrainian realities. In J. Rudolph., J. Crawford., C. Y. Sam., & S. Tan (Eds.), *The Palgrave handbook of crisis leadership in higher education*. Palgrave.

Shawe, R., Horan, W., Moles, R., & O'Regan, B. (2019). Mapping of sustainability policies and initiatives in higher education institutes. *Environmental Science & Policy, 99*, 80–88.

Shephard, K., & Furnari, M. (2013). Exploring what university teachers think about education for sustainability. *Studies in Higher Education, 38*(10), 1577–1590.

Singh, A. S., & Segatto, A. P. (2020). Challenges for education for sustainability in business courses: A multi-case study in Brazilian higher education institutions. *International Journal of Sustainability in Higher Education, 21*(2), 264–280.

Stickney, J., & Skilbeck, A. (2020). Problematising 'transformative' environmental education in a climate crisis. *Journal of Philosophy of Education, 54*(4), 791–806.

Tan, E., & Rudolph, J. (2023). Strategic sustainability in the Anthropocene. In A. DeMoraes (Ed.), *Strategic management and international business policies for maintaining competitive advantage* (pp. 256–270). IGI Global.

Tregidga, H., & Laine, M. (2022). On crisis and emergency: Is it time to rethink long-term environmental accounting? *Critical Perspectives on Accounting, 82*, 102311. https://doi.org/10.1016/j.cpa.2021.102311

United Nations. (2019). The climate crisis—A race we can win. *United Nations Climate Action Summit*. https://www.un.org/sites/un2.un.org/files/2020/01/un75_climate_crisis.pdf

United Nations. (2022). Convergence of conflicts, COVID and climate crisis, jeopardise global goals. *United Nations News*. https://news.un.org/en/story/2022/07/1122112

Vandaele, M., & Stålhammar, S. (2022). "Hope dies, action begins?" The role of hope for proactive sustainability engagement among university students. *International Journal of Sustainability in Higher Education, 23*(8), 272–289.

Vasileiou, K., Barnett, J., Thorpe, S., & Young, T. (2018). Characterising and justifying sample size sufficiency in interview-based studies: Systematic analysis of qualitative health research over a 15-year period. *BMC Medical Research Methodology, 18*, 1–18.

Viergever, R. F. (2019). The critical incident technique: Method or methodology? *Qualitative Health Research, 29*(7), 1065–1079.

Waeber, P. O., Stoudmann, N., Langston, J. D., Ghazoul, J., Wilmé, L., Sayer, J., ... & Garcia, C. A. (2021). Choices we make in times of crisis. *Sustainability, 13*(6), 3578.

Wamsler, C. (2020). Education for sustainability: Fostering a more conscious society and transformation towards sustainability. *International Journal of Sustainability in Higher Education, 21*(1), 112–130.

Wu, Y. L., Shao, B., Newman, A., & Schwarz, G. (2021). Crisis leadership: A review and future research agenda. *The Leadership Quarterly, 32*(6), 101518.

# Intersectionality for Inclusion and Transformation in Higher Education Leadership

Mike Klein

## Introduction

To address intersectionality, this chapter will begin with personal and institutional challenges that will help to describe—if not precisely define—intersectionality. From there, aspects of the theory will be summarised through the work of major contributors and contextualised through scholarly critiques and challenges. The praxis of intersectionality—how theory and practice iteratively inform each other—will be explored through application and examples. The chapter identifies the challenges and promises of intersectionality for the exclusion crisis in higher education leadership.

A note on leadership in higher education: leadership is often assumed to be a noun, referencing a person with position and authority. Leadership can also be reframed as a verb, focusing on power dynamics as they operate between people, structures, and cultures in an organisation or a community. In addition, leadership can be enacted from the top down, bottom up, or inside out. Intersectionality for leadership in higher education is a conscientious and critical examination of power operations as they appear in identity categories that intersect with and complicate each other and concern the institution's structures, policies, and practices. Therefore, intersectionality will be more powerful in addressing leadership crises when democratising leadership employs it (Klein, 2016) as both a noun and a verb at all university levels.

M. Klein (✉)
Justice and Society Studies, University of St. Thomas, Saint Paul, MN, USA
e-mail: mcklein@stthomas.edu



J. Rudolph et al. (eds.), *The Palgrave Handbook of Crisis Leadership in Higher Education*, https://doi.org/10.1007/978-3-031-54509-2_7

I—the author of this chapter—am blond-haired, blue-eyed, white, straight, cis-gendered, male, middle-class, middle-aged, mid-western, US citizen, able-bodied, Christian, right-handed… all the dominant characteristics of a dominating society. Most of my identities carry socially constructed advantages, whereas the different identities of others in the same categories might carry socially constructed disadvantages. Taken together, these advantages and disadvantages complicate each other as they intersect in each of us and as we show up in different social contexts. As a leader in higher education, I need to figure out these power dynamics and more if I am to cross boundaries of identity and community and work towards inclusion and transformation in education. Stephen Brookfield calls this personal approach a "pedagogy of narrative disclosure to uncover white supremacy" (2020, p. 9), utilising appropriate self-disclosure to identify and illuminate power dynamics in racial discourse. Niki Latino (2016) describes an inclusive leadership framework with four key processes: discourse, self-reflexivity, meaning-making, and praxis. Such self-disclosure and comprehensive processes are part of the challenge and opportunity of intersectionality for inclusive leadership.

On an institutional level, intersectionality can be applied as a theoretical lens of analysis and as an action plan for addressing contemporary crises in higher education. The crisis of exclusion revolves around questions such as: Whom does higher education serve? Is the university for all, or only for some? These questions are ontological as higher education leadership clarifies self-understanding and identity. They are also existential as higher education leadership decides who will be included—or not—in an era of declining enrolment and broadening diversity of students whose identities might have been excluded from previous iterations of the university. Intersectionality as a theory can help to explain diversity beyond superficiality, equity grounded in historical and social contexts, and inclusion of the whole person while also addressing belonging and justice (Crawford et al., 2023; Tice et al., 2021). Intersectionality as action can guide leadership in challenging and changing structures, policies, and practices to take specific and tangible steps towards a more inclusive and less exclusive institution.

The promise of intersectional analysis is in understanding the socially constructed nature of identity advantages and disadvantages and understanding these power dynamics as more than just an additive (or subtractive) sum. The power differentials associated with each aspect of a person's identity complicate each other and can shift based on social context. Thus, intersectional analysis is more rigorous and nuanced than simplistic notions of identity politics. It is also more than a moral or ethical concern to recognise the whole person who shows up in the classroom or the university senate. It is a matter of praxis, applying intersectional theory to the university's work in its tangible structures and arrangements. For example, policy development is typically a one-size-fits-all approach and tends to focus on the issues of the dominant majority group. However, such policies will not address the lived experience of many constituents across their complex intersectional identities, especially in the case of identities that are made up of compounded disadvantages, meaning leadership may unintentionally sustain unjust policies, procedures, and practices without knowledge of their consequence or impact.

Leadership enacted in higher education requires regular intersectional analysis in and beyond the work of diversity, equity, and inclusion (DEI). One aspect of this intersectional analysis has led to redefinition of the work, noted in some institutions as DEAI to include *accessibility* (American Alliance of Museums, 2017) and in others as DEIB to include *belonging* (Grim et al., 2021) and DEIJ to include *justice* (Fife et al., 2021). DEI will be used in this chapter to reference the appropriately contested and unsettled definition of this work. The negotiation of these terms speaks to the dynamic need for intersectional analysis in DEI work to move beyond a technical and transactional approach so that issues of power are addressed. Without intersectional analysis, DEI work can be reduced to diversity alone—a focus on individual categorical differences—without accounting for the way these differences intersect and complicate each other, how recognition, power, and resources are equitably distributed, and how people in all of their complexity can be included as whole people without leaving disadvantaged aspects of their identity at the door.

Beyond DEI work, the university will be judged either as an institution for the elitist reproduction of social hierarchies or as a liberating educational force based on its willingness to address these factors in this critical moment of our collective history. Leadership in higher education regularly faces a choice between reproducing the world as it is (Bourdieu & Passeron, 1990) or transforming it. Neglecting this choice is a de facto decision for the status quo, and as Bishop Desmond Tutu declared, "neutrality favors the oppressor" (Brown, 1984, p. 19). Beyond the critique of neutrality, Sarah Ahmed, in her critical book *What's the Use?* states, "the system is working by stopping those who are trying to transform the system" (2019, p. 212). Given these institutional tensions, intersectionality for higher education leadership will necessarily and rightly be rooted in conflict over the proper role of education in society and the identities of people included or excluded in our institutions.

In this chapter, I will point to the role of intersectionality and intersectional analysis for higher education leadership based on my experiences as staff, faculty, diversity requirement committee co-chair, and programme director. Given my intersectional identities, I acknowledge the certainty of my misapprehension of some aspects of this theory and praxis because I necessarily fail to encounter them all in my person. I am sure to embody some of these failings in my own leadership. So, I write with humility to know myself better and how I contribute to the failures of higher education. I also write hoping to advance such work with allies and alongside those who read this chapter. I write to learn and to understand intersectionality in the political reality of the university—in the power dynamics of racism, classism, misogyny, heteronormativity, ableism, and more—so that I may better work with others across our differences to change these dynamics and to transform higher education.

Some readers might respond to this confessional introduction by skipping to the next chapter. Before you do, I would assert that until we all wrestle with the theoretical and practical implications of intersectionality, we will limit our potential for institutional and cultural change. Engaging in intersectional analysis and application is a step towards being a good ally in transformative education. I once heard a community organiser in New York City assert, "Your ally card is earned each day, conferred only by those at the centre of the struggle, and expires every night at midnight." So, I will conclude the introduction by stating that this work is urgent, lifelong, and relational. Intersectionality in higher education leadership requires humility, deep listening, and a willingness to learn from mistakes to transform ourselves and our universities into genuinely inclusive institutions so we can all thrive.

## Theory of Intersectionality

Given important critiques of the "whitening" of intersectionality (Bilge, 2013; Eguchi et al., 2021) and my own identity articulated above, this chapter acknowledges the origins of intersectionality and its continuing development in Black feminism. It is rooted in the works of Patricia Hill Collins, Kimberlé Crenshaw, and other Black feminist scholars and in reflections by activists/scholars such as Angela Davis, who understood intersectionality first through social movements and later in critical academic analyses. Patricia Hill Collins defines it this way: "The term intersectionality references the critical insight that race, class, gender, sexuality, ethnicity, nation, ability, and age operate not as unitary, mutually exclusive entities, but as reciprocally constructing phenomena that in turn shape complex social inequalities" (2015, p. 2). Kimberlé Crenshaw describes the dangers of ignoring intersectionality by identifying "political strategies that challenge only certain subordinating practices while maintaining existing hierarchies not only marginalise those who are subject to multiple systems of subordination but also often result in oppositionalising race and gender discourses" (quoted in Bilge, 2013, p. 406). This approach accounts for the intersections of such discourses. Angela Davis grounds intersectionality in the lived experience of social movements:

> behind this concept of intersectionality is a rich history of struggle. A history of conversations among activists within movement formations, and with and among academics as well. I mention this genealogy that takes seriously the epistemological productions of those whose primary work is organising radical movements because I think it's important to prevent the term "intersectionality" from erasing essential histories of activism. There were those of us who by virtue of our experience, not so much by virtue of academic analyses, recognised that we had to figure out a way to bring these issues together. They weren't separate in our bodies, but also they are not separate in terms of struggles. (Davis, 2016, pp. 29–30)

Davis identifies interrelated dimensions of intersectionality that are essential to its definition: the interplay of theory and practice and the relation between individual identities and social struggles reflecting intersectionality.

An early work on intersectionality addresses the concept in tangible terms, emerging from Black feminist analysis in Kimberlé Crenshaw's article "Demarginalising the intersection of race and sex: A Black feminist critique of antidiscrimination doctrine, feminist theory and antiracist politics" (1989). She examines antidiscrimination law and its "tendency to treat race and gender as mutually exclusive categories of experience and analysis" (p. 139). Legal precedent in antidiscrimination law was formed on case law that addressed either race or gender and not the intersection of the two identity categories. Cases addressing race were often premised on discrimination against Black men. Cases addressing gender were typically focused on White women. US Courts often restrict arguments to one category: "this single-axis framework erases Black women in the conceptualisation, identification, and remediation of race and sex discrimination by limiting inquiry to the experiences of otherwise privileged members of the group" (p. 140). Cases about Black men, gender discrimination in cases about White women represented race discrimination. The intersection of race and gender in Black Women was excluded from case law even though this intersection led to unique consequences not represented by the other categories.

Intersectionality emerged from Black feminist analysis, but tensions arose as the powerful concept was applied to the intersections of other identities. Some argued that the term was being appropriated and that its expansion beyond Black feminism would detract from the original critique. As intersectionality was applied in theory and practice to the intersections of multiple identity categories, this critique began to fade, yet the concept is still vigorously defended against minimisation and appropriation. Harris and Patton (2019) provide an overview and historical survey of these tensions.

Sirma Bilge has also been a staunch defender of the concept, and her critique should be heeded by higher education leaders who engage in the theory and practice of intersectionality:

> Intersectionality has been transformed by the confluence between neoliberal corporate diversity culture and identity politics in the last fifteen years and also acquired undeniable intellectual, political, and moral capital… which proved to be a fertile ground for opportunistic uses of intersectionality that I have dubbed "ornamental intersectionality". (Bilge, 2013, p. 408)

More recently, her critique might be applied to DEI work that is considered "virtue-signalling" or simply checking a box to satisfy management of institutional concerns rather than rigorous analysis or structural change to address socially constructed advantages and disadvantages institutionalised in higher education. Bilge has also defended intersectionality against another form of minimisation that higher education leaders must address: an intersectional analysis that avoids race:

> The appropriation of a whitened intersectionality needs to be countered by insistently emphasising intersectionality's constitutive ties with critical race thinking and (re)claiming a non-negotiable status for race and the racialising processes in intersectional analysis and praxis. (Bilge, 2013, p. 413)

She points to appropriations of intersectionality that decentre or remove race by recasting it as a primarily feminist concept and broadening its genealogy to a universal concept present in many social analyses before Black Feminist critique (Bilge, 2013). This de-politicisation renders intersectionality safe for institutional use by removing its racial critique and separating the concept from action central to its praxis. She also qualifies intersectional analysis to explain that whiteness is a socially constructed identity of advantage in most contexts, such that:

> 'whitening intersectionality' does not refer to the embodiment, skin color, or heritage of its practitioners, nor does it attempt to police the boundaries of who can legitimately do intersectionality and who cannot. (Bilge, 2013, p. 412)

Instead, whitening intersectionality is decentring or removing racial analysis from the concept, neutralising its change orientation, and citing white authors in priority or exclusion to "marginalised social actors—women of colour and queers of colour" (p. 412). Scholars representing non-white racial identities can participate in whitening intersectionality by these means. For higher education leadership, these are cautionary critiques about how to engage authentically and fully with a fraught concept, recognising its potential for cultivating a truly inclusive higher education community while avoiding pitfalls that are likely recognised and well-known to faculty, staff, and students who embody identities representing overlapping social disadvantages. Intersectionality is a challenging concept that leadership might be tempted to avoid. However, your constituents are not shying away from this analysis, and leaders will be better able to respond to community context and promote inclusivity by learning this urgent yet lifelong analysis.

Another aspect of Intersectionality is recognition of the importance of context. Sarah Ahmed aptly names this contextual component when she says it is:

> to think about and through the points at which power relations meet. A body can be a meeting point. A concern with meeting points requires that we attend to the experiential: how we experience one category [of identity] depends on how we inhabit others. (Ahmed, 2012, p. 14)

In a later work, Ahmed says, "I find intersectionality a profoundly useful way of understanding the complexity of social experience because of how intersectionality enables us to show how people's relation to one social category is affected by their relation to other social categories" (Ahmed, 2021, p. 317). Not only do the socially constructed advantages and disadvantages complicate each other in power relations and their consequences, but these intersecting identities also impact how we see the interaction of identity categories. A Latina student attending a predominantly white institution (PWI) may experience race as a primary identity, where in her community, gender was centred, and in her workplace, class. Such contextual shifts may be routine to people for whom many intersecting identities are disadvantaged, requiring daily negotiation of such power dynamics. Intersectional analysis can provide a theoretical lens to understand these dynamics and give a name to the negotiation of individual experiences. For higher education leaders, intersectionality can offer that same individual analysis, and perhaps more importantly, it can be applied beyond the individual to larger institutional dynamics.

Sarah Ahmed's book *Complaint!* (2021) peers into the role of grievance in illuminating institutional dynamics. Related to intersectionality, she states, "We have many struggles at universities because universities are occupied by many histories. If to complain within the institution is to struggle against it, then complaint shows, to use Angela Y. Davis' terms, 'the intersectionality of struggles' (Ahmed, 2021, pp. 23–24). Institutions are occupied by many histories and collective identities based on race, class, gender, ability, age, and other intersectional identity categories. Inclusive universities move beyond a superficial sense of unity, grounded in conformity or assimilation, to an inclusivity that recognises and allows - even promotes - differences to form a community that lives together across its differences. Often, those differences grind against the advantaged identity categories that may be normative but unacknowledged in our institutions: white, male, upper-class, legacy admissions (generations at the same institution) who seek education to prepare them to continue the current social arrangements of power and privilege. Of course, some institutions of higher education function with much different and even intentionally alternative normative identities (e.g., Historically Black Colleges and Universities in the US), yet such institutions may also prepare students to fit into or transform the status quo.

Intersectionality beyond individual analysis can also be deployed in such institutional and social contexts to analyse what Davis calls 'the intersectionality of struggles':

> Initially intersectionality was about bodies and experiences. But now, how do we talk about bringing various social justice struggles together, across national borders? So we were talking about Ferguson and Palestine. How can we really create a framework that allows us to think these issues together and to organise around these issues together?" (Davis, 2016, pp. 29–30)

The struggles are for recognition and redistribution of power and resources. When we address inclusivity in higher education in an authentic and substantial way, this is what it means: recognition of the identities that have been disadvantaged and redistribution of advantages based on that recognition.

Intersectionality, in summation, is a theoretical concept tied to action, an analysis of praxis that leads to the reordering of higher education structure and culture. Perhaps this is why it can be approached with concern and fear by leadership and why it is often dismissed or tokenised in deference to the status quo. This entire volume is evidence that we cannot assume an unchanging and static approach to leadership in higher education. Intersectional analysis is an important tool for cultivating a dynamic and inclusive university.

## Praxis of Intersectionality

So, what does intersectionality look like in practice for higher education? First, it looks like praxis—iterations of theory and action in regular dialogue. It looks like ongoing individual development and ongoing institutional reordering. It looks like the world beyond the walls of the campus. It looks like an inclusive and dynamic re-energising of the social purpose of higher education.

Institutional leaders are regularly confronted with decisions to minimise crises related to racism, misogyny, ableism, et cetera, or to address them publicly. Behind that leadership decision is an underlying normative commitment to universities as sites of social reproduction or social transformation. Without a conscientious decision between these two fundamental commitments, a de facto choice is made for the status quo: uncritical reproduction of the social order and these embedded identity-based inequities.

Conflicts, discrimination, and abuses related to the power dynamics socially constructed in intersectional identities are commonly experienced in higher education; they are reproduced and reinforced in universities. Pierre Bourdieu stated that formal educational institutions:

> produce and reproduce the institutional conditions whose existence and persistence (self-reproduction of the system) are necessary both to the exercise of its essential function of inculcation and to the fulfilment of its function of reproducing a cultural arbitrary which it does not produce (cultural reproduction), the reproduction of which contributes to the reproduction of the relations between the groups or classes (social reproduction). (Bourdieu & Passeron, 1990, p. 54)

Higher education is not only a stage for actors to play out advantages and disadvantages; it is also a script and a director for reproduction or transformation.

Complicating this tension is the conflict avoidance common in leadership. Each new crisis comes with the temptation to sweep problems under the rug, to avoid bad publicity, and to minimise disruption to the function and flow of the institution. Because intersectionality is an analysis of socially constructed identity-based power, it might be used in leadership for either reactionary and tactical management of crises—"ornamental intersectionality" (Bilge, 2013, p. 408)—or it can be used for proactive and strategic institutional change. Regular and critical self-reflection on the purpose of using intersectional analysis should accompany understanding and practice.

For example, if you wonder about your university's reproductive or transformative nature, especially for constituents who embody multiple disadvantaged identities, consider this exercise: rewrite each word of your university mission statement to express its opposite intent. Where the mission says "critical thinking," replace it with "conformity." If it promotes change, replace that verbiage with "taking your place in the world as it is." Suppose it addresses diversity, substitute uniformity. Then, ask representatives of many constituencies, especially those disadvantaged or marginalised, to reflect on which one is more aligned with their experience: the actual mission statement or its opposite. Mission statements are typically aspirational and inclusive by nature. Our institutions both strive towards their vision and fail to live up to it regularly, which is the work of leadership. Differential responses to the mission and its opposite may begin to shed light on the advantaged and disadvantaged identities that intersect in their social experience of power at your institution.

A reflexive leader understands that education is shaped by the social realities that underlie educational institutions. To examine how power operates in our school settings and larger social and political contexts, leadership can critically reflect on the normative assumptions at the core of our learning communities, including assumptions about power, how it is used or misused, and what identities are included and excluded. This approach can uncover hegemonic values that underlie the structures, policies, and practices that advantage some and disadvantage others. Our institutions have histories of serving some and excluding or ignoring others. Until those values are examined and attendant structures, policies, and practices are reviewed in the light of intersectional analysis, we are likely to reproduce them, not through malicious ill will but through institutional inertia that maintains notions of "who we are" and "how we do things here." Leadership can examine what we take for granted or assume as natural, uncovering advantages for some identities and disadvantages for other identities:

> Critical reflection is, quite simply, the sustained and intentional process of identifying and checking the accuracy and validity of our [leadership] assumptions. We all work from a set of orienting, stock assumptions that we trust to guide us through new situations. Some of these are explicit and at the forefront of our consciousness. Other assumptions are much more implicit. Implicit assumptions soak into consciousness from the professional and cultural air

around you. Consequently, they're often harder to identify. (Brookfield, 2017, p. 7)

As we critically reflect on the inequities in hegemonic values, structures, policies, and practices, we can "push back against this exploitation by changing structures and alerting others to its presence" (Brookfield, 2017, p. 9). This is central to the work of diversity officers and others specifically charged with institutional DEI work. However, it is required of all leadership in the university if it is to be more than ornamental. In her book *On being included*, Sarah Ahmed aptly describes "Diversity practitioners as institutional plumbers; they develop an expertise in how things get stuck, as well as where they get stuck" (Ahmed, 2012, p. 32). Higher education leaders can see this work as uncomfortable critique and extra work, or they can see themselves as partners in this institutional plumbing. Critical assessment of power distribution can either be normatively challenged as "deviant, immoral, or unpatriotic" (Brookfield, 2017, p. 249) or normatively encouraged and valued as a skill in sophisticated social relations and active citizenship. As partners in the work of inclusivity, institutional leaders can promote equitably flows of power to constituents rather than allowing power blockages by unexamined constructions of disadvantage.

Like most organisations, educational institutions tend to see inclusion as an additive process: "we need more of them to be with us." An additive approach avoids critical reflection on the change required to include rather than assimilate new or underrepresented identities in the university. Intersectionality can promote an integrative approach to inclusion by examining the advantaged construction of identities included in "we" and the disadvantaged identities that compose concepts of "them." The current conception of "we" can be expanded and changed to include those previously excluded, marginalised, or assimilated as much as the overlapping disadvantages of identities considered "them" are considered and addressed. Inclusion is often limited to asking others to become us by presuming they will leave at the door aspects of themselves that diverge from predominant organisational norms. Authentic inclusion moves towards integrating people into evolving institutions with integrity as whole people and inclusive of all of their identity categories. Respecting and recognising all identities is central to democratic commitments to living across our differences and distributing power equitably so that everyone may contribute to a truly inclusive learning community.

## Examples

One example of this work for inclusivity through intersectional analysis is the urgent, late, and only emerging work addressing settler colonialism in higher education for historical and contemporary Indigenous people. Intersectionality in this socially constructed context might acknowledge identity categories that are most relevant in the original and ongoing oppression of Indigenous peoples, including suppression of cultural identity, language, and religion by secular and religious institutions; historical displacement from land that continues to be manifested as poverty and exploitation; inequities in law enforcement and legal proceedings; fetishisation of Indigenous women and non-binary people; and cultural appropriation of sacred traditions and objects for education, entertainment, and profit. All these dynamics can be reproduced by higher education uncritically, perhaps with more ignorance than overt malice, yet in ways that sustain ongoing injustices and lead to real and continuing harm.

### Tobacco Policy

As a practical example, my university wanted to support the physical health of its entire community by instituting a zero-tolerance policy towards tobacco use on campus. This policy had unintended consequences for a small group of students and employees. Many Indigenous peoples in North America use forms of tobacco as a central prayer practice, some carrying it in a sacred pouch for daily prayer and thanksgiving. In a casual conversation, an Anishinaabeg student mentioned that she would never carry her prayer bundle on campus for fear that security would take it as they enforced the tobacco policy. This concern was a reflection of her intersectional identities: as a woman facing a mostly male security force, as an Indigenous person on a predominantly white campus, as a student potentially challenging leadership at a predominantly white settler colonial institution on Indigenous (Dakota) land, and as a religious minority at a Catholic university with its fraught historical and contemporary relationship to Indigenous people. The intersections of gender, race, Indigeneity, and religion all played a role in her concern. Some identity categories were more or less primary to her concern depending on context, such as gender and race with security personnel or student status and religious identity with administrators.

When I brought the issue to a university leader with the authority to change the policy, they responded with surprise, concern, and a willingness to address it. They briefly looked to a peer institution and quickly added an addendum to the policy to grant an exception for Indigenous students. It was a well-intentioned response; however, it reinforced a disadvantage for religious minorities who would need an exception and special permission to practice their spirituality where the religious majority did not. It required the student to ask permission from the administrators she found intimidating or uninformed, and it presumed that security personnel would know and respect this policy change. After identifying these still complicating and disadvantaging factors, a task group was convened to reconsider the policy. The final revision first expressed support for the religious freedom of all students. Then instead of putting the onus on a student to ask permission to practice their religion, the responsibility was accepted by university leadership to educate themselves about this practice and to disseminate this information to campus security so that they would understand this important exception to the health policy. This situation also highlighted the need to educate a campus largely ignorant of the historical and contemporary Indigenous peoples whose homeland is occupied by the university. When I asked this student for feedback on the chapter she commented, "Ultimately Indigenous students are constantly reminded that they are not wanted (by all) at educational institutions, and these spaces were never made for them to access" (personal communication, July 19, 2023). This is what the institutional work of inclusion and transformation looks like in the practice of higher education leadership.

Such work is a step in the right direction, based on an intersectional policy analysis, with implications for additional review of policies in light of diverse and intersecting identities. It also raises questions about the policy formation process and its critical role in cultivating an inclusive campus. Some task force participants saw this as an unreasonable commitment of time and resources for a very small number of students and employees. Others argued that this was the least the university could do as it began examining its role in settler colonialism and the continuing suppression of Indigenous peoples and practices in our region. Intersectionality is about complicating simple formulations of identity for more equitable approaches to inclusion. Intersectionality is also complicated by the seemingly endless complexity of overlapping identity categories and the socially constructed advantages and disadvantages of identity categories in shifting social contexts. Such work might seem monumental at first and unwieldy in its all-encompassing challenge to entrenched values, structure, policy, and practice. Intersectionality is, however, a more rigorous pursuit of truth and a more just accounting of the structures of oppression that advantage some and disadvantage others. If university leadership wants to shift from reproducing structures of injustice to challenging injustices embedded in its structure, this is one aspect of that work.

## Interest Convergence: Enrolment

Another example of intersectional analysis and praxis lies in the interest convergence principle of Critical Race Theory (Harris et al., 2019) as it relates to the US and many countries of the Global North, which are facing a "demographic cliff" (MacGregor, 2022a) of declining enrolments in higher education. Universities in many countries face an enrolment crisis based on the declining number of traditional college-age students (e.g., white middle-class or upper-middle-class students). This is leading some universities to commit to diversity, equity, and inclusion (DEI) work to attract students who have not traditionally attended their institutions and sustain enrolment. Hopefully, the work of DEI is not only instrumental or ornamental and in service to enrolment, but there is an interest convergence between these two areas of university life.

Critical Race Theory (CRT) has been much politicised in the US, but this should not detract from its central tenets that emerge from critical legal scholarship (much like intersectionality) and has developed into theory and praxis, "studying and transforming the relationship among race, racism, and power" (Harris et al., 2019, p. 3). According to Harris et al. (2019), the basic tenets of CRT include:

- racism is common and ordinary rather than aberrational
- interest convergence is behind most advances or setbacks regarding racism
- race and racism are socially constructed
- differential racialisation accounts for the changing construct of race over time
- intersectionality identifies the complexity of overlapping and complicating identity categories
- the voice-of-color thesis suggesting knowledge and narratives unique to racial identity.

This chapter focuses on one of the tenets—intersectionality—and the next example in particular focuses on "interest convergence," another tenet. Interest convergence claims the alignment of material benefit across advantaged and disadvantaged groups as the condition for the advancement of racial justice or lack of alignment as the condition for inaction or retrenchment. Scholars like Derrick Bell "argued that civil rights advances for blacks always seemed to coincide with changing economic conditions and the self-interest of white elites" (Harris et al., 2019, p. 22). The demographic cliff of declining enrolments in higher education is a particular interest convergence between DEI initiatives and enrolment management. It holds potential for a deeper commitment to transformational diversity, equity, and inclusion work or the development of transactional initiatives that may be ornamental, tokenising, virtue-signalling, and instrumentalising.

The headline catching the attention of higher education leadership is "Falling student enrolment is a key trend in Global North" (MacGregor, 2022a). One strategy to curtail the effects of this trend has entailed recruiting international students to make up for declines in domestic student demographics. While this may seem like a simple answer to a numerical problem, it is a more complex normative question that intersectionality may address in part. The primary identity of international students for university leadership may be their country of origin; however, international students are complex individuals with intersectional identities. They are also confronted by host country social contexts that layer advantages and disadvantages onto their many identities, such as race, gender (identity or expression), class, language, religion, et cetera. University leadership may view international students as a promising approach to enrolment issues, but is the university, its students, and its faculty prepared to receive them? Will international students be orientated not only to potentially positive cultural differences but also to racism, sexism, homophobia, classism, and other identity-based oppressive dynamics in their new host country? An intersectional analysis may help higher education leadership understand how to develop an inclusive process, cultivate an inclusive campus, and understand why retention of international students may be an issue.

A more intersectional praxis will identify this interest convergence, develop a more holistic approach to recruitment and retention of international students, and consider them as whole persons who will likely require changes in university structures, policies, and practices to meet their interests. If higher education leaders do not address this interest convergence, a follow-up headline may be the signpost for future trends: "Higher education report charts rise of the Global South" (MacGregor, 2022b). The article states:

> World student numbers have now passed 200 million. But the number of students in the Global North peaked in 2011 and has been going down since, to around 58.3 million in 2018. Meanwhile, the number of students in the Global South has almost doubled, from some 78 million in 2006 to 150 million in 2018.

Intersectionality that is ornamental or instrumental may initially seem like a good public relations or recruitment strategy. However, students and employees who have spent their lifetimes negotiating advantages and disadvantages will see through transactional approaches and tokenising efforts, however well-intended. Higher education will be better served as leaders learn about intersectionality as a theory and learn how to integrate it into their leadership practice.

Because intersectional analysis attends to power dynamics associated with identity categories that overlap and complicate each other, in the interest convergence of DEI work and enrolment management, intersectional analysis can promote a nuanced approach to recruiting, integrating, and retaining international students on multiple levels. For example, focusing on just one identity category for recruiting new student populations might create tensions among the target group and the existing university population. A Predominantly White Institution (PWI) that develops a recruitment plan for high school students who are African international students (a single identity category) without considering distinctions related to intersecting identity categories of class, religion, nationality, or normative family structures will create more problems than they solve for students and for the institution. Wealthy, middle-class, or poor students will have different educational expectations. Christian and Muslim students will have very different needs in practising their faith traditions, including food, sacred spaces, and accommodations for holidays. Black students whose families have been citizens of the country for generations and Black students who are new immigrants will look for different kinds of support as they navigate a PWI. An intersectional approach will promote recognising differences and advantages and disadvantages in overlapping intersectional identities. It will identify ways these advantages and disadvantages have been reproduced in the privileging of traditional and, therefore, normative identities of existing students and faculty while misunderstanding or ignoring the complexities of identities that are new to campus or that remain the numerical minority. If not, they will remain othered from normative assumptions of who "our" students are, what they strive for, and what they need from our institution.

As mentioned above, this crucial need for intersectional analysis is grounded in whether the existing institution expects itself to change as new populations are included or if people representing new categories are expected to conform to the institution's existing normative values and practices. If diversity is reduced to "us" as the existing population and "them" as newcomers, then inclusion will be reduced to assimilation. This is a denial of intersectional complexity and an expectation of conformity, the "individual fit" (Ahmed, 2012) that problematises the person instead of the institution. Instead, higher education institutions can decide on the core identity and mission they commit to sustaining (reproducing) while anticipating that students and faculty representing new identity categories will bring novel ideas, different expectations, and divergent needs that will transform aspects of the institution. The interest convergence between DEI work and enrolment management may lead to the reproduction of the university or the transformation of the university as it engages more fully and adeptly with its social reality.

As the lens of intersectional analysis becomes familiar, higher education leadership can become more adept at understanding intersectional distinctions and acting on the potential for transformation. This is urgent yet lifelong work beginning too late for current students, staff, faculty, and administrators who do not feel free to bring their whole selves to our campus. Neglect of this work will reproduce the injustices and oppression embedded in the structures of our institutions and, therefore, in our societies, stifling individual development and flourishing while inhibiting collective agency to meet the pressing needs of our day. Efforts to cultivate a more inclusive institution can advance the academy's work and create the conditions for students to become agents of change for a more just and inclusive society.

## Conclusion

For higher education leadership, the choice between the reproduction of the status quo and exclusion transformation through inclusion is urgent and even existential. Understanding intersectionality is an important reflection of identity and mission, addressing the social construction of advantages and disadvantages embedded in our institutions. It is a daunting challenge, yet resources exist and can be developed in university human resources and faculty development offices. New programmes are emerging in formal educational settings, and informal education is happening in community and social movement spaces. Leadership in higher education can and should avail themselves of these opportunities to develop intersectional understanding, analysis, and practice through ongoing professional development. Such crucial work cannot be left to individual DEI professionals and offices on campus. Authentic inclusivity in higher education requires leadership from those in positional authority alongside institution-wide engagement by leadership enacted in the faculty, staff, alumni, boards, and students.

Our incoming students may be more adept at this analysis than most university leadership will ever be. Current students have come of age willing to struggle with such identity-based inequities, perhaps more than ever before. They will expect to find a place in our universities as whole people and not just as the partial categories of identity that conform to the norm. They will challenge us to live up to the transformational power of education, and they will presume that lessons in the classroom will be reflected in their institution's leadership. We will strive and sometimes fail to do this work well. However, through this work, we deepen our understanding and develop our practice of intersectionality for authentic inclusion in our universities and for the transformation of higher education.

## References

Ahmed, S. (2012). *On being included: Racism and diversity in institutional life*. Duke University Press.

Ahmed, S. (2021). *Complaint!* Duke University Press. https://doi.org/10.1515/9781478022336

American Alliance of Museums. (2017). *Facing change: Insights from the American Alliance of Museums' diversity, equity, accessibility, and inclusion working group.* American Alliance of Museums.

Bilge, S. (2013). Intersectionality undone. *Du Bois Review: Social Science Research on Race, 10*, 405–424.

Bourdieu, P., & Passeron, J. C. (1990). *Reproduction in education, society, and culture.* Sage.

Brookfield, S. D. (2017). *Becoming a critically reflective teacher* (2nd ed.). Jossey-Bass.

Brookfield, S. D. (2020). Using a pedagogy of narrative disclosure to uncover white supremacy. *New Directions for Adult and Continuing Education, 165*, 9–19. Spring Wiley Periodicals, Inc.

Brown, R. M. (1984). *Unexpected news: Reading the Bible with third world eyes* (1st ed.). Westminster Press.

Collins, P. H. (2015). Intersectionality's definitional dilemmas. *Annual Review of Sociology, 41*(1), 1–20. https://doi.org/10.1146/annurev-soc-073014-112142

Crawford, J., Allen, K.-A., Sanders, T., Baumeister, R., Parker, P. D., Saunders, C., & Tice, D. M. (2023). Sense of belonging in higher education students: An Australian longitudinal study from 2013 to 2019. *Studies in Higher Education*, 1–15. https://doi.org/10.1080/03075079.2023.2238006

Davis, A. Y. (2016). *Freedom is a constant struggle: Ferguson, Palestine, and the foundations of a movement.* Haymarket Books.

Eguchi, S., Abdi, S., & Calafell, B. M. (2021). *De-whitening intersectionality: Race, intercultural communication, and politics*. Lexington Books.

Fife, D., Stephens, M. N., Lyons, A., & Huang, M. (2021). Leader responsibility for diversity, equity, inclusion & justice in academic libraries: An exploratory study. *The Journal of Academic Librarianship, 47*(4), 102361. https://doi.org/10.1016/j.acalib.2021.102361

Grim, V., Davenport, M. Y., Brown, O. G., Hinton, K. G., & Howard-Hamilton, M. F. (2021). *Unleashing suppressed voices on college campuses: Diversity issues in higher education*. Peter Lang.

Harris, J. C., & Patton, L. D. (2019). Un/doing intersectionality through higher education research. *The Journal of Higher Education, 90*(3), 347–372. https://doi.org/10.1080/00221546.2018.1536936

Klein, M. (2016). *Democratising leadership counter-hegemonic democracy in organisations, institutions, and communities*. Information Age Publishing Inc.

Latino, N. (2016). Leadership at the intersection. In P. Felten, & B. Barnett. (Eds.), *Intersectionality in action: A guide for faculty and campus leaders for creating inclusive classrooms and institutions* (pp. 25–35). Stylus Publishing, LLC.

MacGregor, K. (2022a). Falling student enrolment is a key trend in Global North. *University World News*. https://www.universityworldnews.com/post.php?story=20220318140456226

MacGregor, K. (2022b). Higher education report charts rise of the Global South. *University World News*. https://www.universityworldnews.com/post.php?story=20220311151815827

Tice, D., Baumeister, R., Crawford, J., Allen, K. A., & Percy, A. (2021). Student belongingness in higher education: Lessons for Professors from the COVID-19 pandemic. *Journal of University Teaching & Learning Practice, 18*(4), 2. https://doi.org/10.53761/1.18.4.2

# Riding the Generative AI Tsunami: Addressing the Teaching and Learning Crisis in Higher Education

Samson Tan, Jürgen Rudolph, and Shannon Tan

## Introduction

Artificial intelligence (AI) is a rapidly evolving field that is in the process of transforming various aspects of higher education, such as teaching, learning, assessment, and administration. AI can be defined as the ability of machines or systems to perform tasks that normally require human intelligence, such as reasoning, problem-solving, decision-making, and learning (Russell & Norvig, 1995). Generative AI refers to advanced algorithms capable of creating content or data patterns similar to, or indistinguishable from, those generated by humans, encompassing activities such as text generation, image creation, and predictive modelling. However, critics caution that it is deceptive to equate generative AI with human intelligence: "There is no creativity,

The original version of the chapter has been revised. A correction to this chapter can be found at https://doi.org/10.1007/978-3-031-54509-2_34

S. Tan
Development Division, Institute for Adult Learning Singapore, Singapore, Singapore
e-mail: samsontanyt@ial.edu.sg

J. Rudolph · S. Tan (✉)
Kaplan, Singapore
e-mail: shannon.tan@kaplan.com

J. Rudolph
e-mail: Jurgen.Rudolph@kaplan.com


J. Rudolph et al. (eds.), *The Palgrave Handbook of Crisis Leadership in Higher Education*, https://doi.org/10.1007/978-3-031-54509-2_8

no critical thinking, no depth or wisdom in what generative AI gives users after a prompt: it is just plausible text with good syntax and grammar, and this is all that it is" (Popenici, 2023b, p. 6).

Adopting AI in higher education is not a straightforward process, and it requires a comprehensive consideration of the opportunities and challenges that AI brings to the educational context. Our chapter aims to support educators and policymakers in responding to AI's impact on higher education, especially in assessment and graduate employment, so that they can judiciously incorporate AI into their strategies. Our chapter adds an important layer to the handbook's focus on crisis leadership in higher education. Pervasive polycrises (the climate crisis, the COVID-19 pandemic, and the war in Europe, to mention but a few)—mark the contemporary era and appear to embody a unique state of continual decline and uncertainty (Popenici, 2023a). Amidst these concurrent crises, the higher education sector is currently experiencing ideological, intellectual, managerial, and ethical challenges, with a misguided reliance on technology, particularly AI, being perceived as a panacea, thus highlighting an urgent need for critical scrutiny and innovative solutions (Popenici, 2023a).

Our chapter begins by providing a brief history of AI and its application in education, tracing its origins from the early attempts to use computer programs to simulate human intelligence and to provide intelligent tutoring systems (ITS), which are computer-based systems that can provide personalised instruction and feedback to learners based on their individual needs and goals, to the current developments of using data-driven and adaptive approaches to enhance learning outcomes and experiences (Luckin et al., 2016). Since late 2022, the popularisation of generative AI has exacerbated the existing crises in higher education. The proliferation of AI chatbots, capable of acing graduate-level exams, is shaking up higher education and the job sector, necessitating a revamp in assessment methods to foster responsible chatbot use and enhance critical thinking (Firat, 2023). Concurrently, the integration of AI tools in the workforce is reshaping tertiary education, potentially reducing the demand for certain roles and steering curricula towards a collaboration with AI advancements, away from traditional teaching and learning approaches.

The incorporation of AI in higher education (HE) offers tools capable of swiftly handling complex tasks, from summarising texts to editing source codes (Rudolph et al., 2023a). However, this development has catalysed a crisis marked by heightened academic dishonesty and ethical dilemmas surrounding academic integrity and plagiarism, notably exacerbated by AI systems like ChatGPT, which have been implicated in student misconduct (Mohammadkarimi et al., 2023; Rasul et al., 2023; Sullivan et al., 2023).

As we stand at the crossroads, we urge a re-evaluation of teaching modalities and assessment methodologies in HE, emphasising adaptive, personalised learning to maintain the authenticity and originality of student work, even as the landscape of AI in higher education becomes increasingly volatile and competitive.

Our literature review delves into the transformative impact of advanced chatbots, with a special focus on ChatGPT, within the higher education landscape. We scrutinise pertinent issues, including the burgeoning concerns of plagiarism, discipline-focused dialogues, unfolding debates on co-authorship, media narratives, and potential strategies for AI integration in teaching and learning. Our study draws upon the theoretical underpinnings of Riggio and Newstead's (2023) framework on crisis leadership, coupled with Preskill"s and Brookfield (2009) notion of learning leadership, to provide a comprehensive lens to evaluate the phenomena at hand. Moreover, we offer an overview of the mushrooming generative chatbot industry, analysing the foray of platforms like ChatGPT, Bing Chat, Bard, and Baidu's Ernie in higher education. Among these, GPT-4 stands out with its unparalleled capabilities; Bing Chat facilitates access to real-time data; Bard is a nascent entity with potential; and Ernie is poised to capture the Chinese market despite censorship hurdles.

Lastly, we suggest recommendations that can help higher education leaders and teachers adopt AI in higher education. Our recommendations address higher education's multiple stakeholders and three additional dimensions: pedagogy, policy, and culture. These dimensions contain sub-sets of considerations that higher education leaders can use to guide the decision-making and implementation process related to using AI.

## A Brief History of AI in Higher Education

The genesis of artificial intelligence (AI), initially a subject of science fiction, advanced significantly in the 1950s, driven by Turing's (1950) seminal insights into machine computation. Early progress was confined to a few entities due to technological barriers and steep costs. A milestone occurred in 1956 with the Dartmouth Summer Research Project on Artificial Intelligence (DSRPAI), orchestrated by Newell & Simon (1956) and McCarthy et al. (1955), who defined AI as machines displaying human-like intelligence. Yet, the field faced ongoing definitional ambiguity, with the focus varying between AI's capabilities and the underlying algorithms, marking the onset of an intense period of AI development (Tan, 2020, 2023b).

In the two decades after DSRPAI, AI flourished, driven by improved computer accessibility and the progression of machine learning algorithms, especially in data processing and language translation, attracting government attention (Haenlein & Kaplan, 2019). Yet, advancements in natural language processing and abstract thinking lagged. By the early 1970s, education technologists started investigating AI's capacity to enhance educational methodologies (du Boulay, 2016). Higher education began incorporating AI to uplift teaching, learning, and governance, underscored by the advent of Intelligent Tutoring Systems (ITS), rooted in the 1960s, proficient in customising learning experiences (Robot, 2020). Nonetheless, the enthusiasm waned, challenged by AI's struggle to emulate human cognition and language comprehension. Constrained by inadequate computational prowess and intricate language semantics, the sector witnessed reduced funding and a prolonged research hiatus (Metz, 2022).

In the second AI age of the 1980s, augmented algorithmic resources and boosted funding revitalised AI. Feigenbaum (1981) pioneered expert systems, simulating human expert decision-making, extensively utilised in various industries. Despite initial hopes, many objectives remained unfulfilled, resulting in reduced funding and a diminished public presence of AI (Metz, 2022). AI prospered in the 1990s and 2000s, notably with IBM's Deep Blue defeating chess champion Gary Kasparov in 1997 and Dragon Systems launching speech recognition on Windows (Coniam, 1999). The continual rise in computing power facilitated further milestones like Google's Alpha Go triumphing over Go champion Ke Jie (Bory, 2019), embodying a cycle of AI advancements meeting computational capabilities before awaiting hardware progression. Recent developments have seen the fusion of enhanced computing power and big data analytics, fostering sophisticated AI algorithms capable of self-improvement (Tan, 2023b). This convergence has ignited discussions on the evolving AI landscape and introduced varied techniques, from data-centric machine learning to psychological model-based decision-making processes.

At present, AI software pervades various sectors, including personalised tutoring and immersive virtual reality learning experiences, enhancing online collaboration and educational outcomes (Yang & Evans, 2019). AI tools offer multifaceted benefits in higher education (Ismail et al., 2023), from facilitating student learning to aiding teacher administrative tasks and informing system-level insights for more targeted student support (Rudolph et al., 2023a). This technological progression prompts a re-evaluation of the dynamics within higher education, necessitating a reshaping of learning and teaching methodologies and policies.

## AI Futures and Higher Education

The Fourth Industrial Revolution, fuelled by emerging technologies, led to unprecedented growth in AI. It can potentially transform how we live, work, and interact with each other. AI is rapidly becoming ubiquitous, with applications in various industries, including healthcare, finance, and education. It has the potential to revolutionise how humans and machines interact, creating more intelligent and efficient systems. Educators working in the field of Artificial Intelligence in Education (AIEd) have been investigating the uses of AI for creating learning technologies for improving education since the early 1970s (du Boulay, 2016; Tan, 2023b). In the past 30 years, the academic community associated with AIEd has examined and deliberated the potential benefits of AI, especially when used in conjunction with other emerging technologies, such as immersive technologies (Tan, 2023c).

ChatGPT was launched in November 2022, taking the world by storm. The application is based on OpenAI's Generative Pretrained Transformer (GPT) language model, which produces text that can be indistinguishable from text produced by humans (Rudolph et al., 2023a). At the same time, ChatGPT generated considerable anxiety and concerns even among the tech community. Due to significant investments in OpenAI, Microsoft was the first to capitalise on ChatGPT's power by integrating it with its Bing search engine and has further plans for ChatGPT to be integrated with other Microsoft applications (Rudolph et al., 2023b). With ChatGPT's successful debut, other companies are scrambling to cash in on the gold rush of generative AI. The unchecked proliferation of generative AI, such as ChatGPT, has led the G7 leaders to stress the importance of establishing and adopting international technical standards for trustworthy AI as lawmakers of rich countries concentrate on the emerging technology (Komiya & Mukherjee, 2023). It also has created a crisis in higher education.

### Higher Education's AI Crisis

The introduction of generative AI in higher education has brought benefits, such as summarising and explaining complex concepts, fixing bugs in the source code of computer programs, writing texts and providing translation in record speed. Despite generative AI's educational benefits, its rapid, continued evolution constitutes a crisis. In January 2023, the New York Department of Education announced a ban on the use of ChatGPT due to a violation of academic integrity (Rosenblatt, 2023). Students committing academic offences with ChatGPT were widely reported in different geographies (Levin, 2023). Such incidents brought public attention and an unprecedented discussion on the impact of AI on learning and teaching. Academics are concerned with ethical issues involving academic integrity, plagiarism, detection of authenticity, and originality of students' work. The playing field is becoming more open and volatile as tech giants such as Alphabet, Baidu, and Alibaba join the generative AI bandwagon. This will increase competition and lead to faster innovation in the generative AI space. Companies will need to move quickly and invest heavily in order to stay ahead of the competition. As a result, the market will become more dynamic and unpredictable (Rudolph et al., 2023b).

Yang et al. (2019) criticised the uniform approach to teaching, advocating for a shift to adaptive, personalised learning, underscored by enhanced AI technology. They highlighted the current educational strategies' shortcomings in offering real-time, student-centric feedback. Consequently, higher education institutions are considering revamping assessment and evaluative methods, fostering policies that uphold integrity and guide educators effectively. There are widespread concerns that AI technology in education could lead to more cheating and academic dishonesty (Chaka, 2023; Hassoulas et al., 2023; Sullivan et al., 2023). With the ability to easily access information and answers online, there is a worry that students will be more tempted to cheat on assignments and exams.

## Theoretical Framework

There has been a fast-exploding academic literature on large language model-based chatbots and their impact on higher education. Our recent article provided a review of the English-language academic literature and considered Chinese journal articles (Rudolph et al., 2023b). This chapter focuses on generative AI-related assessment, learning, and teaching issues that exacerbate the ongoing higher education crisis. Our literature review uncovered the following major themes: (1) assessment and plagiarism concerns, (2) discipline-specific considerations, (3) research, co-authorship, and crediting issues, (4) higher education discourses in popular and social media, and (5) teaching and learning.

First, ChatGPT has raised grave concerns about assessment and plagiarism. ChatGPT seriously threatens the credibility of short-form essays as an assessment method (Yeadon et al., 2023). Various tests were conducted regarding ChatGPT's efficacy in assessment performance. There is a widespread consensus that student assessments need to be changed. Crawford et al.

(2023) exhorts faculty to ask students to demonstrate their comprehension by applying their knowledge to complex cases. The literature is generally sceptical on the current reliability of detection tools of generative chatbots' creations (Perkins, 2023). ChatGPT-generated text cannot reliably be detected by traditional anti-plagiarism software such as iThenticate and Turnitin and by generative AI detection software (Chaka, 2023; Gimpel et al., 2023). Second, there have been disciplinary discussions in a wide variety of fields. In medicine, already ChatGPT-3.5 performed well in the United States Medical Licensing Examination (USMLE) (Gilson et al., 2022). ChatGPT-3.5 was able to pass a U.S. Bar Exam, and GPT-4 performed even better (Katz et al., 2023). It has been fascinating to observe how fast the chatbots have been improving in 2023. After initially showing glaring weaknesses in mathematics, GPT-4 has since been recommended as a learning tool in calculus and statistics (Santandreu et al., 2023).

Third, much literature explores ChatGPT in relation to research and authorship. While some examples of ChatGPT-co-authored academic articles and editorials exist, this practice is highly controversial and prohibited by many journals (Stokel-Walker, 2022; Thorp, 2023). Nonetheless, the critically informed use of ChatGPT and LLMs, in general, could be useful in reducing researchers' workload (Xaves & Shefa, 2023). Fourth, the discourse on chatbots and higher education is prominently reflected in news and social media. Sullivan et al. (2023) analysed news articles discussing university reactions, academic integrity, AI limitations, and prospects for student learning. They noted a gap in public discourse concerning ChatGPT's potential to enhance engagement and success, particularly among underprivileged students, coupled with a scant representation of student perspectives (Sullivan et al., 2023). Conversely, TikTok content mostly portrays a favourable discourse on employing ChatGPT in higher education, emphasising practical applications like assisting with essay writing and coding. However, these discussions often overlook significant ChatGPT shortcomings, including its predisposition to produce hallucinations and biases (Haensch et al., 2023; Tlili et al., 2023). Finally, teaching and learning were also thematised. ChatGPT can boost student learning, and AI, when implemented cautiously and thoughtfully, can help instructors create new teaching materials and reduce their workload to support strategies that improve student learning (Mollick & Mollick, 2023). Mills et al. (2023) propose adopting open educational practices, which foster collaboration and adaptability through digital platforms, facilitating cross-institutional cooperation and enabling a swift, equitable approach to navigating the evolving landscape of AI in higher education.

This chapter primarily hones in on crisis leadership, a relatively nascent yet significant field given the complex global crises of the present times (Riggio & Newstead, 2023). Several theories, including crisis management theory and complexity leadership theory, help unravel the intricacies of this domain, emphasising adaptive responses, quick decision-making, and the pivotal role of a leader's personal attributes in navigating crises (Riggio & Newstead, 2023). Generative AI, similar to the preceding COVID-19 pandemic, epitomises a polycrisis, necessitating a coordinated and innovative approach from multiple stakeholders. In this context, Riggio and Newstead (2023) pinpoint five central competencies for crisis leadership, emphasising learning facilitation, a concept aligned with Preskill and Brookfield's (2009) "learning leadership".

## War of the Chatbots and the Crisis of Assessment in Higher Education

The big chatbot battle appears to be largely between Microsoft and Alphabet (*The Economist*, 2023). Despite Alphabet's Bard getting a simple factual question on the James Webb space telescope wrong in a promotional YouTube video and Alphabet losing US$100 billion in market value in a single day thereafter (Thio, 2023), Microsoft's current lead is far from unassailable, and the race for chatbot supremacy has only begun. We proceed to provide some background about ChatGPT (based on GPT-3.5 and 4), Bing Chat, Alphabet's Bard, and Baidu's Ernie as examples of dominant names that are relevant to our higher education focus.

### ChatGPT

OpenAI, the organisation behind ChatGPT, underwent a fundamental change from a not-for-profit organisation to a commercial business model in less than four years between 2015 and 2019, consequently raising doubts about its continued "openness" (Metz, 2022; Rudolph et al., 2023a). ChatGPT's seemingly boundless applications (writing essays in a hundred different languages, composing speeches in the style of a famous person, summarising documents, writing code, learning from prior exchanges, answering trivia questions, passing legal and medical exams, etc.) have captured the world's imagination. They are the source of the tech hype cycle on steroids. However, among the many weaknesses of ChatGPT are the lack of currency (no knowledge of events after September 2021), the lack of reliable sources, errors of both reasoning and fact, its being prone to hallucinations (making things up), and the danger of automating such systems to generate misinformation on an unprecedented scale (Marcus & David, 2023; Rudolph et al., 2023a).

Unlike the launch version of ChatGPT, which currently continues to be freely available, the latest version of ChatGPT (based on GPT-4 that was released on March 14) is a subscription service (at a monthly recurring fee of US$20). OpenAI (2023) has shown care in GPT-4's avoiding answers to questions or requests that ask it to create harmful content—including advice or encouragement for self-harm behaviours, graphic material such as erotic or violent content, harassing, demeaning, and hateful content, content useful for planning attacks or violence, and instructions for finding illegal content. GPT-4's performance in test-taking constitutes a major improvement over its third iteration. It can score among the top ten per cent of students on the Uniform Bar Examination in the US, between 1300 and 1410 (out of 1600) on the SAT and a "five (out of five) on Advanced Placement high school exams in biology, calculus, macroeconomics, psychology, statistics and history" (Metz & Collins, 2023).

## Other Chatbots

In February 2023, Microsoft unveiled a revamped Bing search engine featuring ChatGPT (Ortiz, 2023). Bing Chat, powered by the GPT-4 language model grounded in Bing data, signifies a pivotal advancement, addressing some limitations of ChatGPT. Bing Chat surpasses the knowledge cutoff of September 2021 and has internet access, thus offering more accurate and current responses as it constantly receives new data. Consequently, it promises users more current conversations. Also in February 2023, Alphabet unveiled Bard, a chatbot driven by Google's LaMDA, a language model akin to Microsoft's GPT. Initially available in the US and UK, Bard has a dedicated website and will gradually extend its reach to other countries and languages. Although perceived as Alphabet's response to Microsoft's advancements (Rudolph et al., 2023b), Bard presents certain limitations. Notably, it cannot generate computer code or handle follow-up questions, restricting the complexity of conversations it can engage in and marking it as less versatile compared to ChatGPT (De Vynck & Tiku, 2023).

In March 2023, Baidu introduced Ernie, also known as *wenxin yiyan*, a chatbot adept at understanding Chinese culture, trained on a massive amount of web, voice, and image data, along with a knowledge graph encompassing 550 billion facts (Yang, 2023). While capable of generating pictures and composing poems in the Tang dynasty style, it avoids answering queries about President Xi Jinping and occasionally exhibits errors in elementary math tasks (Baptista, 2023). Due to tense Sino-US relations and stringent censorship norms, Ernie might lag behind ChatGPT in development despite its proficiency in various Chinese dialects (Che & Liu, 2023). Nonetheless, Baidu aims to dominate the local market by capitalising on ChatGPT's unavailability in China, potentially outmanoeuvring domestic competitors like Tencent and Alibaba and harnessing valuable consumer insights (Huang, 2023).

## The Crisis of Assessment and Graduate Employment

The impact of chatbots on higher education is widely debated, as GPT-4 has passed graduate-level exams in various disciplines (Metz & Collins, 2023). Roivainen (2023) estimated ChatGPT's Verbal IQ at 155, ranking it in the top 0.1% of test-takers. Institutions have banned ChatGPT or returned to traditional assessments (e.g. Wood, 2023). However, banning chatbots is challenging since Microsoft is integrating the technology into its products (Vanian, 2023). With AI detection software being unreliable, some instructors actively use chatbots for specific purposes (Mollick & Mollick, 2023).

Our multi-disciplinary test reveals that chatbots do not perform as well as expected in a wide variety of assignments (see Rudolph et al., 2023b). Recommendations for assessments include teaching responsible chatbot usage (Crawford et al., 2023), requiring students to declare chatbot involvement (Gimpel et al., 2023), emphasising integrity and accountability, allowing students to write about personal interests (McMurtrie, 2022), using authentic assessments (Ifelebuegu, 2023), and incorporating AI tools into assignments (Mills, 2023a).

Additionally, educators should resist returning to closed book exams, innovate assessment formats, avoid attempting to out-design chatbots, acknowledge the limitations of AI detection software, incorporate a mentoring and coaching process, rethink rubrics, and place a greater emphasis on critical thinking and creativity (Gimpel et al., 2023; Pani et al., 2023; Rudolph, 2023a). Lastly, they should focus on motivation and the writing process, emphasising the intrinsic rewards of writing and its contribution to intellectual growth (Mills, 2023b).

In the context of evolving societal and technological landscapes, the concept of work is undergoing significant transformations, raising questions about future disparities and the sustainability of current employment structures. Throughout history, the perception of work has varied significantly, with it being viewed as both a necessity for the less privileged and undesirable for the affluent (Susskind, 2021). The rise of generative AI threatens to exacerbate existing inequalities, as demonstrated by the startling wealth accumulation among a small elite and the grim realities the impoverished populace faces globally face (Adarkwah et al., 2023; Rudolph et al., 2023c). With the integration of AI in various sectors, there is a looming reshuffling in the job market. This necessitates a critical reassessment of the values attributed to different forms of work and a redefinition of what constitutes meaningful employment (Rudolph et al., 2023c).

The advent of generative AI technologies has fast-tracked the reshaping of the job landscape, a shift previously anticipated to be gradual, starting with physical labour jobs. The recent advancements in AI have surpassed expectations, impacting sectors involving cognitive and even creative tasks, altering tasks ranging from coding to content creation (Thio, 2023). This technological surge potentially threatens a vast spectrum of jobs, prompting a need to rethink strategies to prevent growing income inequalities and job displacement. The education sector is seen as a potential growth area, demanding a shift in skill sets towards more cognitive abilities such as analytical and creative thinking (World Economic Forum, 2023). Amidst this, the conversation veers towards implementing universal basic income or similar concepts, aiming to cushion the impact of the changing job landscape and to reconsider the societal role and perception of work (Susskind, 2021). Moreover, the narrative encourages reflection on the direction in which society is heading, whether towards a "fully automated luxury communism" (Bastani, 2020) or a "Turing trap" (Brynjolfsson, 2022), where the misuse of technology could have tragic consequences (Rudolph et al., 2023c).

## Conclusion

With the convergence of the surge in computing power and big data analytics since the 2010s, AI has become a heady mix of real technological advances, unfounded hype, wild predictions, and legitimate concerns for the future (Metz, 2022; Tan, 2023b). Considering the current generative AI hype, it is difficult to assess whether we are at a historic, revolutionary time in AI development (Rudolph et al., 2023b). As it stands, generative AIs constitute a new step in AI's capabilities. While there is a broad consensus that there is not yet any artificial general intelligence (AGI), generative AI could represent a significant step towards that goal, prompting tech celebrity Elon Musk and AI experts such as Max Tegman and Geoffrey Hinton to call on governments to impose a temporary moratorium on the development of generative AIs (Rudolph et al., 2023b). Overall, we may be witnessing a significant inflexion point in AI development that may have important implications for our future. It remains unclear what kind of future humanity can expect from the extensive application of generative AIs. It is clear, however, that all stakeholders will need to work together to ensure that AI benefits outweigh the costs. Generative AI has the potential to be used for good and bad, depending on who is in control of it. It is imperative that we explore its potential responsibly and with caution.

It is likely that the current versions of the generative AI chatbots are only the beginning of a lengthy journey towards increasingly powerful generative AIs that would impact higher education and beyond (Rudolph et al., 2023b). In the future, these tools may potentially transform a student's journey through academia, including aspects such as admission, enrollment, career services, and other aspects associated with higher education. Our earlier articles (Rudolph et al., 2023a, 2023b) contain many recommendations for higher education leaders, faculty, and students in terms of leveraging generative AI chatbots to enhance and innovate teaching and learning. There is a need for experimentation and caution, and most of our recommendations revolve around risk management, safeguards, innovation, and experimentation. Before we provide additional recommendations on how to use generative AI in higher education, we revisit the previous ones organised by recommendations regarding (1) higher education assessments, (2) teaching and learning, (3) students, and (4) higher education leaders (Rudolph et al., 2023a, 2023b). While crisis leadership largely comes from the top (Riggio & Newstead, 2023), learning leadership will also have to come from below, behind, and among (Brookfield & Preskill, 2009), thus including multiple stakeholders such as teachers and students (see Rudolph et al., 2024, in this Handbook).

To foster academic integrity and engage students deeply in the learning process, educators should encourage responsible chatbot usage and transparent AI tool application in research and writing tasks (Crawford et al., 2023; Gimpel et al., 2023). It is crucial to blend traditional assessments with innovative formats such as oral presentations and collaborative projects while also integrating AI discussions to illuminate the limitations of AI-generated content and emphasise the value of human insight (Mills, 2023a). Simultaneously, it is imperative to nurture critical thinking, creativity, and personal accountability, steering clear of attempting to 'out-design' chatbots, an exercise in futility in the long run (Mills, 2023b; Rudolph et al., 2023b).

In the contemporary educational sector, it is essential to guide and train students on responsible and critical use of chatbots in their learning processes, including aiding in the creation of diverse learning materials and enhancing critical reflection skills (Gimpel et al., 2023; Mollick & Mollick, 2023). Educators are urged to foster deeper relationships with students, encouraging respectful and engaged discourse while educating them to discern and critique authoritative-sounding misinformation potentially generated by AI tools like ChatGPT (Mills, 2023b). A vigilant approach towards AI interactions, including debunking anthropomorphic tendencies and the capacity to discern "gibberish" presented as factual information, is essential in nurturing well-rounded, critical thinkers (Mills, 2023b; Rudolph et al., 2023b).

Students must foster digital literacy and ethical engagement with AI tools, understand academic integrity policies, utilise AI for enhancing employability, and incorporate them as writing partners, not as a source of plagiarisable content (Rudolph et al., 2023a). Emphasising critical and creative thinking, they should utilise AI tools responsibly in various learning aspects, including coding and addressing real-world issues, while continuously reflecting on personal learning goals and being cautious of the misinformation potential in AI-generated content (Gimpel et al., 2023; Rudolph et al., 2023b).

Higher education institutions are advised to foster multi-stakeholder dialogues, including representatives from various sectors, to integrate the insights gleaned into concrete guidelines, regulations, and educational materials, emphasising the pivotal role of digital literacy education which encompasses a range of AI tools (Gimpel et al., 2023; Rudolph et al., 2023a). Moreover, it is vital to prevent faculty overwork, to initiate faculty and student training workshops focusing on AI tool utility and academic integrity, and to update existing academic policies to clearly delineate the acceptable use of AI tools in higher education settings (Crawford et al., 2023; Rudolph et al., 2023b).

We organise our additional recommendations for governmental and higher education leaders into three categories: (1) Enhancing pedagogical innovation in higher education, (2) regulating AIEd through policies, and (3) developing a culture of innovation in higher education. First, organisations ought to utilise AI to enhance higher education by addressing key challenges, including accessibility, equity, and quality. AI tools can automate numerous tasks for teachers, including assessments and plagiarism detection, consequently diminishing their workload (Tan, 2023a). Furthermore, teachers can employ AIEd systems to track students' progress and facilitate personalised instruction based on the analytical insights derived from student data patterns, thereby optimising individual student engagement and attainment (du Boulay, 2016). AIEd systems, through bespoke feedback and guidance, promise a personalised learning journey, catering to individual learning styles and paces, facilitating students in realising their utmost potential (Quixal & Meurers, 2016). Moreover, the predictive abilities of algorithms within AIEd systems enable timely interventions by accurately anticipating students' risk of failing or abandoning a course, ensuring continuous evaluation of student progress (Cope & Kalantzis, 2017). Second, system-facing AI applications, such as ChatGPT, which witnessed accelerated development post-COVID-19, aid academic administrators in overseeing large-scale trends like institutional attrition. This growth calls for revamped policies to leverage benefits, including the automation of mundane tasks, while mitigating the potential risks associated with job displacement (Thio, 2023). Consequently, policymakers are urged to take several crucial steps to navigate this new landscape.

A collaborative endeavour between governments and regulatory entities is imperative to guide responsible AI development, harmonising its foreseeable benefits and potential pitfalls (Rudolph et al., 2023b; Tan, 2023b). This initiative should be accompanied by the establishment of ethical standards and adaptive guidelines, facilitating the responsible and fair implementation of AI and data in the educational sector (Buckingham Shum et al., 2019). Furthermore, fostering a culture of human-centric and inclusive AI application in education is pivotal, aiming to enhance teacher resources and ensure accessibility for all students. This approach necessitates encouraging partnerships between educational stakeholders and AI specialists to integrate and appraise AI within educational strategies ethically. To further nurture a community adept in AI, crafting curricula and training modules for students and teachers is essential to foster responsible usage and a profound understanding of potential biases and ethical dimensions. Lastly, advancing the quality and reach of AI-enabled higher education is vital, warranting concerted efforts in research and infrastructure investments with an emphasis on data analytics and crafting AI-supportive learning environments (Cowling et al., 2023). Finally, to foster positive perspectives towards AI in education, it is paramount that higher education institutions build a culture grounded in trust, respect, and collaboration, mirroring the core values of both the organisation and the wider society. This endeavour necessitates enlightening stakeholders about the capabilities and implications of AI, incorporating a nuanced understanding of its potential benefits and risks tailored to the unique educational environment.

It is essential to ensure the responsible deployment of AI systems, with a strong focus on data security, privacy, and compliance with relevant legal frameworks (Berendt et al., 2020). This should be coupled with fostering cooperation and the exchange of knowledge among stakeholders, utilising AI to amplify these initiatives. In addition, promoting diversity should be a priority, tasking AI system development with the reduction of bias and the amplification of diversity within educational spheres. Equally important is stimulating innovation by aiding stakeholders in investigating the potential of AI-based systems to spearhead progressive learning methodologies (Tan, 2023a). To optimise AI's potential in reshaping industries, organisations should foster an open and supportive AI culture, constantly updating themselves with recent research while ensuring ethical and responsible technology application with necessary safeguards (Tan, 2023b). This proactive approach will facilitate capitalising on AI's evolving potential while mitigating associated risks.

## References

Adarkwah, M., Amponsah, S., van Wyk, M., Huang, R., Tlili, A., Shehata, B., Metwally, A. H. S., & Wang, H. (2023). Awareness and acceptance of ChatGPT as a generative conversational AI for transforming education by Ghanaian academics: A two-phase study. *Journal of Applied Learning and Teaching, 6*(2), 1–16. Advanced online publication. https://doi.org/10.37074/jalt.2023.6.2.26

Baptista, E. (2023, March 20). Baidu's Ernie writes poems but says it has insufficient information on Xi, tests show. *Reuters*. https://www.reuters.com/technology/baidus-ernie-writes-poems-says-it-has-insufficient-information-xi-tests-show-2023-03-20/

Bastani, A. (2020). *Fully automated luxury communism*. Verso Books.

Berendt, B., Littlejohn, A., & Blakemore, M. (2020). AI in education: Learner choice and fundamental rights. *Learning, Media and Technology, 45*(3), 312–324.

Bory, P. (2019). Deep new: The shifting narratives of artificial intelligence from Deep Blue to AlphaGo. *Convergence, 25*(4), 627–642.

Buckingham, S., Ferguson, R., & Martinez-Maldonado, R. (2019). Human-centred learning analytics. *Journal of Learning Analytics, 6*(2), 1–9.

Brynjolfsson, E. (2022). The Turing trap: The promise & peril of human-like artificial intelligence. *Daedalus, 151*(2), 272–287.

Chaka, C. (2023). Detecting AI content in responses generated by ChatGPT, YouChat, and Chatsonic: The case of five AI content detection tools. *Journal of*

*Applied Learning and Teaching, 6*(2) 1–11. Advanced online publication. https://doi.org/10.37074/jalt.2023.6.2.12

Che, C., & Liu, J. (2023, March 16). China's answer to ChatGPT gets an artificial debut and disappoints. *The New York Times.*

Coniam, D. (1999). Voice recognition software accuracy with second language speakers of English. *System, 27*(1), 49–64.

Cope, B., & Kalantzis, M. (2017). Conceptualising e-learning. In B. Cope & M. Kalantzis (Eds.), *E-learning ecologies* (pp. 1–45). Routledge.

Cowling, M., Crawford, J., Allen, K.-A., Wehmeyer, M. (2023). Using leadership to leverage ChatGPT and artificial intelligence for undergraduate and postgraduate research supervision, *Australasian Journal of Educational Technology.* Ahead of Print.

Crawford, J., Cowling, M., & Allen, K.-A. (2023). Leadership is needed for ethical ChatGPT: Character, assessment, and learning using Artificial Intelligence (AI). *Journal of University Teaching & Learning Practice, 20*(3), 02.

De Vynck, G., & Tiku, N. (2023, March 21). Google's catch-up game on AI continues with Bard launch. *The Washington Post*. https://www.washingtonpost.com/technology/2023/03/21/bard-google-ai/

du Boulay, B. (2016). Artificial intelligence as an effective classroom assistant. *IEEE Intelligent Systems, 31*(6), 76–81.

Feigenbaum, E. (1981). *Expert systems in the 1980s. State of the art report on machine intelligence.* Pergamon-Infotech.

Firat, M. (2023). What ChatGPT means for universities: Perceptions of scholars and students. *Journal of Applied Learning and Teaching, 6*(1), 57–63. https://doi.org/10.37074/jalt.2023.6.1.22

Gilson, A., Safranek, C., Huang, T., Socrates, V., Chi, L., Taylor, R., & Chartash, D. (2022). *How well does ChatGPT do when taking the medical licensing exams? The Implications of large language models for medical education and knowledge assessment.* Preprint. medRxiv.

Gimpel, H., Hall, K., Decker, S., Eymann, T., Lämmermann, L., Mädche, A., Röglinger, R., Ruiner, C., Schoch, M., Schoop, M., Urbach, N., & Vandirk, S. (2023, March 20). *Unlocking the power of generative AI models and systems such as GPT-4 and ChatGPT for higher education: A guide for students and lecturers.* University of Hohenheim.

Haenlein, M., & Kaplan, A. (2019). A brief history of artificial intelligence: On the past, present, and future of artificial intelligence. *California Management Review, 61*(4), 5–14.

Haensch, A., Ball, S., Herklotz, M., & Kreuter, F. (2023). *Seeing ChatGPT through students' eyes: An analysis of TikTok data.* arXiv preprint arXiv:2303.05349

Hassoulas, A., Powell, N., Roberts, L., Umla-Runge, K., Gray, L., & Coffey, M. (2023). Investigating marker accuracy in differentiating between university scripts written by students and those produced using ChatGPT. *Journal of Applied Learning & Teaching, 6*(2), 1–7. Advanced online publication. https://doi.org/10.37074/jalt.2023.6.2.13

Huang, Z. (2023, March 21). China's first major chatbot doesn't need to be as good as ChatGPT. *Bloomberg*. https://www.bloomberg.com/news/newsletters/2023-03-21/baidu-s-ernie-bot-aims-to-be-first-in-chatgpt-free-market-in-china

Ifelebuegu, A. (2023). Rethinking online assessment strategies: Authenticity versus AI chatbot intervention. *Journal of Applied Learning and Teaching, 6*(2), 1–8. Advanced online publication. https://doi.org/10.37074/jalt.2023.6.2.2

Ismail, F., Tan, E., Rudolph, J., Crawford, J., & Tan, S. (2023). Artificial intelligence in higher education. A protocol paper for a systematic literature review. *Journal of Applied Learning and Teaching, 6*(2), 56–63.

Katz, D., Bommarito, M., Gao, S., & Arredondo, P. (2023). *Gpt-4 passes the bar exam.* Available at SSRN 4389233.

Komiya, K., & Mukherjee, S. (2023, May 20). G7 calls for adoption of international technical standards for AI. *Reuters*. https://www.reuters.com/world/g7-calls-adoption-international-technical-standards-ai-2023-05-20/

Levin, J. (2023). Student caught cheating using AI on final: Academic integrity policy updated. *The Commentator*. https://yucommentator.org/2023/01/students-caught-cheating-usingai-on-final-academic-integrity-policy-updated/

Luckin, R., Holmes, W., Griffiths, M., & Forcier, L. (2016). *Intelligence unleashed: An argument for AI in education.* Pearson Education.

Marcus, G., & David, E. (2023, January 10). Large language models like ChatGPT say the darnedest things. *Communications of the ACM*. https://cacm.acm.org/blogs/blog-cacm/268575-large-language-models-like-chatgpt-say-the-darnedest-things/fulltext

McCarthy, J., Minsky, M., Rochester, N., & Shannon, C. (1955). A proposal for the Dartmouth Summer Research Project on Artificial Intelligence. *AI Magazine, 27*(4), 1–12.

McMurtrie, B. (2022, December 13). AI and the future of undergraduate writing. *The Chronicle of Higher Education*. https://www.chronicle.com/article/ai-and-the-future-of-undergraduate-writing

Metz, C. (2022). *Genius makers*. Penguin.

Metz, C., & Collins, K. (2023, March 14). 10 ways GPT-4 is impressive but still flawed. *The New York Times*. https://www.nytimes.com/2023/03/14/technology/openai-new-gpt4.html

Mills, A. (2023a). *AI text generators. Sources to stimulate discussion among teachers*. https://docs.google.com/document/d/1V1drRG1XlWTBrEwgGqd-cCySUB12JrcoamB5i16-Ezw/edit#heading=h.qljyuxlccr6

Mills, A. (2023b). ChatGPT just got better. What does that mean for our writing assignments? *Chronicle of Higher Education*. https://www.chronicle.com/article/chatgpt-just-got-better-what-does-that-mean-for-our-writing-assignments?emailConfirmed=true&supportSignUp=true&supportForgotPassword=true&email=drjuergenrudolph%40gmail.com&success=true&code=success&bc_nonce=ppl84ovfdhi8axuyk590ko&cid=gen_sign_in

Mills, A., Bali, M., & Eaton, L. (2023). How do we respond to generative AI in education? Open educational practices give us a framework for an ongoing process. *Journal of Applied Learning and Teaching, 6*(1), 16–30. https://doi.org/10.37074/jalt.2023.6.1.34

Mohammadkarimi, E. (2023). Teachers' reflections on academic dishonesty in EFL students' writings in the era of artificial intelligence. *Journal of Applied Learning and Teaching, 6*(2), 1–9. Advance online publication. https://doi.org/10.37074/jalt.2023.6.2.10

Mollick, E., & Mollick, L. (2023, March 17). *Using AI to implement effective teaching strategies in classrooms: Five strategies, including prompts.* https://doi.org/10.2139/ssrn.4391243

Newell, A., & Simon, H. (1956). The logic theory machine—A complex information processing system. *IRE Transactions on Information Theory, 2*(3), 61–79.

Ortiz, S. (2023, March 16). What is the new Bing? Here's everything you need to know. *ZDNET*. https://www.zdnet.com/article/what-is-bing-with-chatgpt-heres-everything-we-know/

Pani, B., Crawford, J., & Allen, K.-A. (2023). Can generative artificial intelligence foster belongingness, social support, and reduce loneliness? A conceptual analysis. In Z. Lyu (Ed.), *Applications of Generative AI*. Springer Nature.

Perkins, M. (2023). Academic Integrity considerations of AI Large Language Models in the post-pandemic era: ChatGPT and beyond. *Journal of University Teaching & Learning Practice, 20*(2), 07.

Preskill, S., & Brookfield, S. D. (2009). Learning as a Way of Leading: Lessons from the Struggle for Social Justice. Jossey-Bass.

Popenici, S. (2023a). *Artificial Intelligence and learning futures: Critical narratives of technology and imagination in higher education.* Routledge.

Popenici, S. (2023b). The critique of AI as a foundation for judicious use in higher education. *Journal of Applied Learning and Teaching, 6*(2), 1–7. Advanced online publication. https://doi.org/10.37074/jalt.2023.6.2.4

Quixal, M., & Meurers, D. (2016). How can writing tasks be characterized in a way serving pedagogical goals and automatic analysis needs? *Calico Journal, 33*(1), 19–48.

Rasul, T., Nair, S., Kalendra, D., Robin, M., de Oliveira Santini, F., Ladeira, W., ... & Heathcote, L. (2023). The role of ChatGPT in higher education: Benefits, challenges, and future research directions. *Journal of Applied Learning and Teaching, 6*(1), 41–56. https://doi.org/10.37074/jalt.2023.6.1.29

Riggio, R. E., & Newstead, T. (2023). Crisis leadership. *Annual Review of Organizational Psychology and Organizational Behavior, 10*, 201–224.

Robot, R. (2020, July 31). How intelligent tutoring systems are changing education. *Medium.* https://medium.com/@roybirobot/how-intelligent-tutoring-systems-are-changing-education-d60327e54dfb

Roivainen, R. (2023, March 28). I gave ChatGPT an IQ Test. Here's what I discovered. *Scientific American.* https://www.scientificamerican.com/article/i-gave-chatgpt-an-iq-test-heres-what-i-discovered/

Rosenblatt, K. (2023, January 5). ChatGPT banned from New York City public schools' devices and networks. *NBC News*. https://www.nbcnews.com/tech/tech-news/new-york-citypublic-schools-ban-chatgpt-devices-networks-rcna64446

Rudolph, J., Tan, S., & Tan, S. (2023a). ChatGPT: Bullshit spewer or the end of traditional assessments in higher education? *Journal of Applied Learning and Teaching, 6*(1), 342–363. https://doi.org/10.37074/jalt.2023.6.1.9

Rudolph, J., Tan, S., & Tan, S. (2023b). War of the chatbots: Bard, Bing Chat, ChatGPT, Ernie and beyond. The new AI gold rush and its impact on higher education. *Journal of Applied Learning & Teaching, 6*(1), 364–389. https://doi.org/10.37074/jalt.2023.6.1.23

Rudolph, J., Tan, S., & Aspland, T. (2023c). JALT Editorial 6(1): Fully automated luxury communism or Turing trap? Graduate employability in the generative AI age. *Journal of Applied Learning and Teaching*, *6*(1), 7–15. https://doi.org/10.37074/jalt.2023.6.1.35

Russell, S., & Norvig, P. (1995). A modern, agent-oriented approach to introductory artificial intelligence. *Acm Sigart Bulletin, 6*(2), 24–26.

Santandreu, D., Smail, L., & Kamalov, F. (2023). Enough of the chit-chat: A comparative analysis of four AI chatbots for calculus and statistics. *Journal of Applied Learning and Teaching*, *6*(2), 1–15. Advanced online publication. https://doi.org/10.37074/jalt.2023.6.2.22

Stokel-Walker, C. (2022). AI bot ChatGPT writes smart essays-should academics worry? *Nature*. https://doi.org/10.1038/d41586-022-04397-7

Sullivan, M., Kelly, A., & McLaughlan, P. (2023). ChatGPT in higher education: Considerations for academic integrity and student learning. *Journal of Applied Learning and Teaching*, *6*(1), 31–40. https://doi.org/10.37074/jalt.2023.6.1.17

Susskind, D. (2021). *World without work: Technology, automation and how we should respond*. Penguin.

Tan, S. (2020). Artificial intelligence in education: Rise of the machines. *Journal of Applied Learning and Teaching, 3*(1), 129–133. https://doi.org/10.37074/jalt.2020.3.1.17

Tan, S. (2023a). Exploiting disruptive innovation in learning and teaching. In *Learning intelligence: Innovative and digital transformative learning strategies: Cultural and social engineering perspectives* (pp. 149–176). Springer Nature Singapore. https://doi.org/10.1007/978-981-19-9201-8_4

Tan, S. (2023b). Harnessing Artificial Intelligence for innovation in education. In *Learning intelligence: Innovative and digital transformative learning strategies: Cultural and Social Engineering Perspectives* (pp. 335–363). Springer Nature Singapore. https://doi.org/10.1007/978-981-19-9201-8_8

Tan, S. (2023c). Harnessing immersive technologies for innovation in teaching and learnings. In *Learning intelligence: Innovative and digital transformative learning strategies: Cultural and social engineering perspectives* (pp. 305–334). Springer Nature Singapore. https://doi.org/10.1007/978-981-19-9201-8_7

*The Economist.* (2023, January 30). The race of the AI labs heats up. https://www.economist.com/business/2023/01/30/the-race-of-the-ai-labs-heats-up

Thio, S. (2023, February 24). ChatGPT: Has artificial intelligence come for our jobs? *The Business Times*.

Thorp, H. (2023). ChatGPT is fun, but not an author. *Science, 379*(6630), 313.

Tlili, A., Shehata, B., Adarkwah, M. A., Bozkurt, A., Hickey, D. T., Huang, R., & Agyemang, B. (2023). What if the devil is my guardian angel: ChatGPT as a case study of using chatbots in education. *Smart Learning Environments, 10*(1), 15.

Turing, A. (1950). The use of metaphor and counterfactual thinking Computer Machinery and Intelligence. *Mind, 54*(236), 433–460.

Vanian, J. (2023, March 16). Microsoft adds OpenAI technology to Word and Excel. *CNBC*. https://www.cnbc.com/2023/03/16/microsoft-to-improve-office-365-with-chatgpt-like-generative-ai-tech-.html

Wood, P. (2023, March 2). Oxford and Cambridge ban ChatGPT over plagiarism fears but other universities choose to embrace AI bot. *Inews*. https://inews.co.uk/news/oxford-cambridge-ban-chatgpt-plagiarism-universities-2178391?ITO=newsnow

World Economic Forum. (2023). *Future of jobs report 2023*. https://www3.weforum.org/docs/WEF_Future_of_Jobs_2023.pdf

Xames, M., & Shefa, J. (2023). ChatGPT for research and publication: Opportunities and challenges. *Journal of Applied Learning and Teaching, 6*(1), 390–395. https://doi.org/10.37074/jalt.2023.6.1.20

Yang, S., & Evans, C. (2019, November). Opportunities and challenges in using AI chatbots in higher education. In *Proceedings of the 2019 3rd International Conference on Education and E-Learning* (pp. 79–83).

Yang, S., Tian, H., Sun, L., & Yu, X. (2019, June). From one-size-fits-all teaching to adaptive learning: The crisis and solution of education in the era of AI. *Journal of Physics, 1237*(4), 042039.

Yang, Z. (2023, March 22). The bearable mediocrity of Baidu's ChatGPT competitor. *MIT Technology Review*. https://www.technologyreview.com/2023/03/22/1070154/baidu-ernie-bot-chatgpt-reputation/

Yeadon, W., Inyang, O., Mizouri, A., Peach, A., & Testrow, C. (2023). The death of the short-form physics essay in the coming AI revolution. *Physics Education, 58*(3), 035027.

# Crisis in Higher Education—Ukrainian Realities

Alevtyna Sedochenko and Olena Shyyan

## Introduction

Educational leadership has been the subject of scholarly awareness in Ukraine for many years. The current context, characterised by a combination of reforms, pandemic-related outcomes, and war, has disrupted the entire educational system and has far-reaching societal implications. This chapter aims to provide an overview of key milestones in Ukraine's higher education (HE) development, particularly regarding recent developments under the pandemic and military actions. The authors share some insights on emerging trends in Ukrainian and European higher education, which could serve as a starting point for a broader international discussion of the issues.

For the preparation of the chapter, we reviewed policy papers, legal acts, and publications on the official websites of the Ministry of Education and Science of Ukraine, which develops and implements public policy in the field of education. An examination of scientific research carried out by scholars from both domestic and international sources (Antoniuk, 2023; Berezhna & Prokopenko, 2020; Fimyar, 2008; Galynska & Bilous, 2022; Goodman, 2013; Gryshkova, 2019; Kokarieva, 2019; Koshmanova & Ravchyna, 2008; Kutsyuruba & Kovalchuk, 2015; Nikolaev et al., 2023; Popovych et al.,

A. Sedochenko (✉)
Kyiv, Ukraine

O. Shyyan
Lviv State University of Physical Culture, Lviv, Ukraine


J. Rudolph et al. (eds.), *The Palgrave Handbook of Crisis Leadership in Higher Education*, https://doi.org/10.1007/978-3-031-54509-2_9

2022; Shevchuk & Shevchuk, 2022; Shyyan & Shyyan, 2022; Stukalo & Simakhova, 2020; and others) has been utilised to analyse the overall aspects of issues and advancements in Ukrainian higher education and education reforms, including during the pandemic and the war. The foundation of the research on educational leadership is based on a review of the works of Bush (2011), Bergman et al. (2012), Kezar and Holcombe (2017), Kalashnikova and Orzhel (2019), Riggio and Newstead (2023), Janovac and Virijević Jovanović (2022), Crayne and Medeiros (2021), Balasubramanian and Fernandes (2022), and others.

The authors also analysed publications and materials from public discussions and conferences on the topics related to HE development, HE in crisis, and educational and crisis leadership. This helped to formulate relevant questions and identify new areas of inquiry or potential collaborations. The statistics and data presented in the chapter are based on open data analysis from the State Statistics Service of Ukraine (SSSU), the Unified State Electronic Database on Education (USEDE), analytical reports from the Institute of Educational Analytics (SSI 'IEA') and some independent research.

The chapter is divided into five sections. The first section provides an overview of higher education in Ukraine. The second elaborates on educational leadership models. The third section reviews the context of the HE development in Ukraine since 1991, while the fourth addresses the impact of crises, such as the COVID-19 pandemic and warfare. Finally, the fifth section discusses potential trends and recommendations for higher education and education leadership in crisis.

## Background

Higher education is widely regarded as an essential component of economic growth and the primary source of intellectual potential in society. In Ukraine, citizens have the right to obtain higher education free of charge in state and municipal institutions under established higher education standards. The state also supports training specialists with higher education in priority areas such as the economy, fundamental and applied scientific research, and education.

Ukraine has established state standards that set requirements for higher education programmes applicable to all programmes at a given level of higher education and speciality. These standards are developed per the National Qualifications Framework and evaluate the quality of higher education and the outcomes of educational activities conducted by higher education and research institutions.

Higher education programmes are available at several levels, including the primary level, with a short cycle of study, leading to the award of the educational and professional degree of 'junior bachelor'; the first bachelor's level leading to the degree of 'bachelor'; the second level leading to the degree of 'master'; the third level, educational-scientific/educational-creative, leading to the degrees of 'doctor of philosophy' or 'doctor of arts', and the highest scientific level leading to the degree of 'doctor of science'. As of the beginning of 2022, approximately 984,000 individuals were pursuing higher education at the junior bachelor's, bachelor's, and master's levels in Ukraine. In 2021, up to 44% of bachelor's degree graduates enrolled in master's programmes. Ukrainian higher education institutions employed about 135,200 people and enrolled 67,300 international students (Nikolaev et al., 2023).

All higher education institutions in Ukraine are classified into three types: colleges, universities, and academies/institutes. Colleges only train junior bachelor's and first-level (bachelor's degree) students. Universities offer training at all higher education levels and can be either multi-sectoral or sectoral. Institutes and academies train students at the first and second levels and the third and higher scientific levels for specific specialities. They can also be exclusively sectoral (specialised or technological). As of 2018, there were up to 320 universities, institutes, and academies, as well as 45 colleges in Ukraine. Of these, 78% were state-owned or municipal, which accounted for approximately 87% of higher education students (Nikolaev et al., 2023). In the 1990/1991 academic year, there were 170 university students per 10,000 people in the population. This number has almost doubled to 314 university students per 10,000 people in 2018/2019 academic year.

The Ministry of Education and Science of Ukraine is responsible for the formation of public policy in the field of higher education. Higher education institutions (HEIs) are granted autonomy in implementing educational, scientific, financial, and economic activities per the legislation and the institution's charter. The legislation governing HE in Ukraine is based on the Constitution of Ukraine, as well as laws such as the "On Education" law (2017), the "On Higher Education" law (2014), the "On Scientific and Scientific-Technical Activities" law (2015), and other regulatory legal acts. Furthermore, Ukraine enters into international treaties following the procedure established by law.

## Education Leadership in Times of Crisis

Leadership is crucial in driving changes within the education landscape, achieving desired outcomes, and ensuring growth. In Ukraine, enacting the law "On Higher Education" and the ongoing reforms in the education system, transitioning from a Soviet-style approach to a democratic one, have sparked significant interest in educational leadership. Discussion on educational leadership in higher education has transformed due to changes in the sector and its surroundings. The focus has expanded beyond traditional management practices, such as the managerial style, effective administration, organisational planning, and resource management. It has also gone beyond the instructional style, which prioritises pedagogical expertise, instructional strategies, and teaching–learning methods. The discussion now encompasses various leadership styles tailored to meet different educational settings' unique needs and challenges in various situations. The shift in focus reflects a recognition that effective educational leadership requires a nuanced understanding of the complex dynamics and diverse contexts in which educational systems and institutions operate.

Kalashnikova and Orzhel (2019) suggest that the transformational process requires significant leadership capacity, which can be provided as 'shared leadership'. Bush (2007, 2011) proposes a 'collegial' leadership model that combines three of his leadership models. This model incorporates 'transformational leadership' elements, emphasising the importance of nurturing organisational members' commitments, competencies, and capabilities. It also includes 'participative leadership', which involves democratic processes and shared decision-making. The model also incorporates 'distributed leadership', which leverages the expertise of individuals and acknowledges their leadership in specific domains, fostering collaborative environments. This involves the emergence of co-leaders in addition to formal or positional leaders, giving them more room for initiative, ownership, and freedom of thinking and allowing for self-realisation and self-fulfilment (Kezar & Holcombe, 2017). To exercise the leadership models based on collegial principles, specific skills and attitudes are required, including adaptability, creativity, collaboration, flexibility, interdependence (Kezar & Holcombe, 2017), consensus building, positive group interaction, team member satisfaction (Bergman et al., 2012).

Most leadership models have traditionally focused on stable and 'normal' circumstances. However, there is arguably no situation where leadership becomes more crucial than during times of crisis. A distinct leadership response is required in situations characterised by uncertainty, instability, and emergencies demanding immediate action. This response often entails being flexible and adaptable, making rapid and sound decisions, and mobilising resources quickly (Riggio & Newstead, 2023). Furthermore, influential leaders should consider the human elements involved—the emotions, behaviours, and reactions that are both influenced by and influential in a crisis. It is important to recognise that individuals emotionally impacted by the crisis may find even simple tasks challenging, and high-stress situations can cause typically rational individuals to act irrationally. Leaders must delve deeply into the crisis and tap into the potential for individual achievement (Klann, 2003).

Klann (2003) suggests that every crisis leader should concentrate on key elements: communication, clarity of vision and values, and caring. Elaborating on crisis leadership, Riggio and Newstead (2023) identify key competencies needed for leadership in times of crisis, including sensemaking, decision-making, communication, coordination of resources, teamwork, and facilitating learning. These key crisis leadership competencies are required no matter the type or scale of the crisis and should be factored into leader selection and development.

Janovac and Virijević Jovanović (2022) consider charismatic leadership the most effective and applicable model in uncertain crises that necessitate swift and drastic changes. This leadership style entails possessing a clear vision, providing inspiration, exhibiting determination, and embodying a specific set of behaviours, attitudes, and values that followers adopt. Charismatic leaders are more inclined than others to take risks, make bold decisions, and prioritise motivating their followers to achieve exceptional outcomes. Their distinctively optimistic and change-oriented approach inspires their followers, enabling charismatic leaders to effectively implement their vision (Crayne & Medeiros, 2021). In his work, Bush (2007) outlines moral leadership as a significant model that emphasises leaders' values, beliefs, and ethics, which their followers translate and perceive. The charismatic leadership model underscores the essential role of leaders' moral foundations in shaping their leadership approach and influencing the ethical climate within their organisations.

In their study, Balasubramanian and Fernandes (2022) discuss the concept of situational leadership within a crisis. They emphasise that each leadership style faces challenges when dealing with significant uncertainty during a crisis. For instance, when time is limited, transformational leadership may not be suitable since it requires time to build consensus. Similarly, charismatic leadership can have negative consequences during a crisis, as these leaders often prioritise their own needs, seek attention, and disregard the perspectives of other organisational members. Leaders must be capable of transitioning between or demonstrating multiple styles simultaneously. The situational leadership approach encourages leaders to assess their team members, consider various factors in their work environment, and select the leadership styles that align best with their goals and circumstances. The key dimensions of crisis leadership can be identified: adaptiveness, openness, and communication; compassion and care; resilience and courage; decisiveness; consultation and collaboration; and employee (team members) empowerment.

Riggio and Newstead (2023) also highlight the importance of leaders and their organisations practising adaptive approaches to navigate challenges effectively. In times of crisis, regardless of its nature or origin, it becomes crucial for organisational members to collaborate in developing innovative and adaptable solutions. This entails fast information sharing, generating and evaluating various courses of action, fostering functional and constructive conflict among diverse members, and having the ability to pivot rapidly. Leadership is not solely a top-down process initiated by the leader; it emerges from the intricate interplay between individuals—leaders, followers, and other stakeholders—and the dynamic contexts in which this interplay occurs.

The Ukrainian educational landscape has been marked by significant upheavals, including the effects of COVID-19 and the war, which started in a hybrid form in 2014 and then as warfare since 2022. To navigate these crises through extremely challenging times, education leaders must adapt their strategies accordingly and lay the foundation for a resilient and sustainable education system in the future.

## The Context of Higher Education in Ukraine

Ukraine gained independence in 1991 following the collapse of the Soviet regime. However, the country has since been struggling to move closer to the rest of Europe amidst mixed post-communist legacies and external influences from both the East (Russia) and the West (Europe, USA) (Fimyar, 2008). With a population of nearly 42 million, Ukraine has been constantly experiencing structural, institutional, and economic crises, leading to frequent (and sometimes chaotic) transformations in various social spheres, including education (Kutsyuruba & Kovalchuk, 2015). Ukraine's national higher education system has undergone several stages of development, transitioning from a post-Soviet model to a more European-oriented one. Ukraine has taken steps towards becoming a more open society that is compatible with European education systems (Khustochka, 2009). Nonetheless, the inherited

'Soviet' multilevel education system could not effectively respond to rapid global changes and requirements of new nation-building, with issues such as overgrown bureaucracy, residual financing, and lack of support to teachers compromising education's contribution to society (Stepko, 2004).

Profound educational reforms were necessary to address these issues, including the structural organisation of secondary schools and universities, curricula, and teacher and educational administrator training programmes at all levels (Koshmanova & Ravchyna, 2008). Ukraine's education system has undergone significant changes due to the country's transition from an administrative command economy to a socially oriented market economy and the shift from totalitarian ideology to democracy and pluralism.

The old Soviet model of managerial leadership, with its authoritarian, administrative, and functionary approach, was focused on existing activities rather than visioning a better future. This approach was suitable for school leaders working in centralised systems as it prioritises the efficient implementation of external imperatives, notably those prescribed by higher levels within the bureaucratic hierarchy (Bush, 2007). In the context of a tremendous political shift followed by a continuous multidimensional reform process, the managerial type of leadership was unlikely to yield successful results. New education leadership able to envision and enact transformative solutions had to become indispensable for navigating higher education through these times of change.

The entire educational system, which includes higher education, has progressed through multiple stages of its formation under the era of independence. The period from 1991 to 2000 was characterised by the development and implementation of the state national programme "Education: Ukraine in the 21st Century" (1992). The programme outlined strategic tasks, priority areas, and main directions for reforming the educational sphere, including higher education. It aimed to de-ideologise and update the content of higher education, form a regulatory framework to ensure the evolution of the higher education system under new conditions and initiate the diversification of ownership of higher education institutions (state, municipal, private). Recommendations for the licensing and accreditation of higher education institutions were also developed. This period marked a turning point from the Soviet educational model to the European one. Although, for many years, Soviet and post-Soviet traditions have perpetuated the managerial leadership model in education, characterised by centralisation, limited academic freedom, discouragement of independent thinking, and the political involvement of university leaders. These traditions have hindered the development of democratic leadership models in education, causing a delay in their establishment and implementation.

The subsequent stages, from 2000 to 2005 and 2005 to 2014, brought Ukraine's HE system closer to the international standards. During 2000–2005, the four levels of training—junior specialist, bachelor, specialist, and master—were established. From 2005 to 2014, Ukraine began integrating into the global educational community, intensifying contacts with foreign educational and scientific institutions. During this period, we have also witnessed increased student mobility due to mutual recognition of higher education diplomas by countries that have signed the Bologna Declaration. The need to align with EU standards and implement the principles of the Bologna Process has determined the direction of higher education reform in Ukraine (Goodman, 2013; Kutsyuruba & Kovalchuk, 2015). Since 2005, Ukraine has been a member of the European Higher Education Area (EHEA), which has set out the principles of academic freedom, integrity, student and staff participation in higher education governance, civic responsibility in and for higher education, and institutional autonomy for complex implementation (NAGA, 2019).

Integrating into the European educational community under the Bologna Declaration necessitated efficient administration, organisational planning, and resource allocation, which aligned well with the strengths of managerial leaders. Several external factors initially drove the development of democratic university leadership models in Ukraine due to the Bologna Process. For example, it included increasing competition from European universities for international students, as highlighted by Kalashnikova and Orzhel (2019). Ukrainian students choose foreign universities to pursue international diplomas and global job opportunities. To remain competitive in the educational services market, Ukrainian HEIs must demonstrate excellence and leadership, enhance quality, and adopt rigorous marketing and internationalisation strategies.

Additionally, HEIs have a growing role in driving societal change and problem-solving, which requires additional competencies from their leaders and staff. The transformations in the higher education sector and its surroundings involve HEIs' internal and external stakeholders. Managing the transformational processes requires significant leadership capacity, which can be provided through shared leadership (Kalashnikova & Orzhel, 2019). However, despite certain successful endeavours to initiate the development of democratic educational leadership at both institutional and sectoral levels, there has been a lack of significant progress in transitioning from managerial to collegial leadership. The transformation towards the leadership styles that encourage initiative, active engagement, interdependence, creativity, collaboration, compassion, and care among team members and students has not gained strong momentum at that time.

The next stage of higher education reform in Ukraine is believed to have occurred between February 2014 and February 2022, coinciding with the Euromaidan civil protests of 2013–2014 and the Russian hybrid aggression against Ukraine, which started in 2014. During this stage, the higher education system has been further reformed and developed based on the principles of the Bologna Process. In 2014, the adoption of the new Law of Ukraine's "On Higher Education" introduced new requirements aimed at enhancing the professionalism of teachers and student training, modernising the content of education, enriching the education process with active forms of learning, promoting mobility and flexibility in higher education, deepening its integration into the international scientific space, and stimulating self-development and self-improvement for both teachers and students. Even though the 2014 "Law on Higher Education" represented a significant stride towards disassembling the centralised structures of the past, it granted greater autonomy without the corresponding accountability mechanisms or financial flows. Without a strategy for higher education development, HE institutions use their autonomy to achieve individual goals rather than working to achieve a broader goal for the system and the nation (Shyyan & Shyyan, 2022).

Furthermore, the higher education sector has encountered a notable dearth of visionary leaders capable of providing a clear direction, engaging in sense-making, facilitating information exchange, fostering shared understanding, promoting open communication, and facilitating effective collaboration among multiple stakeholders. There was a pressing need for university leaders who could foster alignment and coordination among diverse individuals and groups, all working towards a common purpose.

Higher education reform has been hindered by half-hearted efforts, leading to a substantial disparity between policy proposals and their actual implementation. As mentioned in the Higher Education Development Strategy for 2021–2031, the problems in the sector are interconnected and exacerbate one another. There are mismatches of the content and quality of HE with the actual needs of the society, unsatisfactory financial support, insufficient autonomy, shortage of qualified personnel of HE institutions, and weak integration of Ukrainian HE into the global and European educational and scientific space. To a great extent, the unsatisfactory performance of higher education institutions stemmed from the inability of educational leaders to manage change. Along with the flawed laws and lack of resources, there was also a failure to provide a clear and holistic vision for the educational reforms by the educational leaders. The inability to manage resistance to change and political compromises led to the deceleration of the reform process by 2020.

Despite some notable accomplishments, Ukraine's higher education field currently faces numerous challenges that require prompt resolution. These challenges include enhancing the quality of education to foster the development of contemporary competencies, adapting training programmes and qualifications to meet the evolving needs of the labour market, modernising the educational process by integrating digital technologies and embracing global educational trends, elevating the level of scientific research conducted at universities, and actively engaging in internationalisation efforts. Additionally, there is a need for increased participation in educating the adult population. As highlighted by Antoniuk (2023), these pressing issues emphasise the urgency for proactive measures to address the existing shortcomings and pave the way for a more progressive and globally competitive higher education system in Ukraine.

Ukrainian higher education remains outdated for the main part. It has lost some positive features of the Soviet-era educational system and has not gained distinctive modern characteristics. Ukrainian universities are still too reliant on state decisions. Many proclaimed transformations are not fully implemented and only entail superficial changes akin to a facade. The activities of HEIs are regulated by numerous and constantly changing decrees and instructions, which are often unnecessary and too formal. During this time, most Ukrainian higher education institutions were reorganised from regular institutes into universities without changing their internal structure, requirements for teaching quality, or focus on students' knowledge (Gryshkova, 2019).

The 'stalling reforms' and the years following COVID-19 and the war presented unprecedented challenges to the Ukrainian higher education system, urgently requiring education leaders capable of effectively coping with these challenges and solving complex problems in crises.

## Higher Education in Crisis

### Higher Education in the Pandemic

The COVID-19 pandemic forced students, academic staff, and management to adapt to new circumstances quickly that they had never experienced before (Rudolph et al., 2023; Tice et al., 2021; Wilson et al., 2020). In 2020–2021, most classes were either temporarily cancelled and replaced with forced vacations or transferred to a distance learning format. The different levels of quarantine restrictions required different modes of operation, ranging from partially open (in certain regions, for certain grades, with hybrid learning, etc.) to entirely online mode. During long quarantine periods, online, distance, and blended learning became the only chance for higher education institutions in Ukraine to continue their operations. As a result, distant forms converted from supplementary to traditional in-person ones into the main forms of education overnight.

The "new normality" has become a challenge and a transformative experience for teachers and students. Before the pandemic, 61.1% of teachers used online learning tools sometimes or some of its elements, while 23.3% had no previous online experience, and 13.7% had experience and constantly taught online (Stukalo & Simakhova, 2020). The pandemic forced teachers to update their digital skills quickly to continue the educational process. Despite the lack of experience among some teachers, up to 80% of the lecturers could organise online education relatively quickly during the lockdowns and further digitise educational processes and content (Stukalo & Simakhova, 2020). The increased use of technology aims to deliver teaching, support students, and provide new forms of student assessment (Stukalo & Simakhova, 2020).

Although online educational tools and methodologies are still essential, for example, many distance learning classes have not been adapted to the new format and continue to be held in a traditional face-to-face style. This can mean online lectures lasting for 1.5 hours or several lecture classes in a row, which exhausts participants (Nikolaev et al., 2023). This reflects a lack of access to technology-enhanced learning facilities, technical equipment, multimedia, and other necessary devices for educational institutions, teachers, and students. Additionally, the lack of developed digital skills and knowledge in creating methodologically rigorous online educational products has perplexed teachers when creating online courses without or with minimal external help.

Emerging pedagogical trends are primarily marked by changing positions of teachers and communication between teachers and students. Online and distance education has shifted the role of university teachers from being a person who 'owns' knowledge and 'delivers' it to students in classes to becoming a facilitator of independent students' learning in various forms. The renewed involvement of a teacher is a mentor-consultant who coordinates the learning process and constantly improves their skills and capacity (Berezhna & Prokopenko, 2020). Another trend is the increased power-sharing between an instructor and a student, which involves changing the roles of both the teacher and the student. The primary goal is cultivating and nurturing student autonomy while facilitating enhanced peer interactions through social networks, asynchronous discussions, feedback, and other effective means (Stukalo & Simakhova, 2020).

At the same time, distance education has brought about several favourable factors that help students create their study schedules. When asked about the positive aspects of distance education, 75.8% of students indicated the ability to study anywhere, 64% mentioned the ability to study at any time, and 62.1% pointed out mobility. However, 42% of students wanted to study in university classrooms in person (Popovych et al., 2022). In addition, the ability to do homework at an individual pace is another positive factor worth mentioning (Stukalo & Simakhova, 2020).

However, negative factors of education digitalisation also should not be neglected. As 71.4% of the respondents mentioned, online and distance education may not help develop communication skills and teamwork, and there is no personal contact between students (Popovych et al., 2022). The virtual educational space can hardly provide students with a real social environment to practice their skills. In contrast, a traditional university provides an open space for gaining life experience. Additionally, 44% of the respondents mentioned low motivation for students to study online (Popovych et al., 2022).

Surveys conducted by the State Education Quality Service at the end of the 2019/2020 and 2020/2021 academic years indicate that the attitude of teachers and students towards the distance format has begun to change since the spring of 2020. In the fall of 2020, 61.2% of respondents recognised the quality of educational services provided by higher education institutions as improved compared to the previous period of distance learning. A survey conducted in the spring of 2021 showed an increase in all indicators, and almost 90% of higher education institution managers indicated that the quality of educational services had improved (Nikolaev et al., 2023).

Nonetheless, the entire higher education system in Ukraine failed to make a full and systematic transition to distance learning as a 'new normal' during the pandemic academic years. It was generally believed that after lifting the quarantine restrictions, education would return to 'business as usual'. This resulted in problems with funding, lack of technical resources, insufficient access to licensed software and poor adaptation of training programmes and courses to distance formats. Many teachers were not aware of effective teaching methods in the distance format, so they remained extremely limited in their use of these methods (Nikolaev et al., 2023).

However, it may be highlighted that these transformations raise interest in the concept of instructional leadership, which strongly emphasises the effective management of teaching and learning as the central activities of educational institutions. Instructional leadership focuses on studying, experimenting, and promoting effective tools and methods for the professional development of teachers, as well as facilitating the students' growth. It involves equipping teachers with the necessary resources, skills, and support to promote student success. In light of recent educational developments, characterised by the active development of distance learning and the need for effective online and hybrid communication between teachers and students, instructional leadership has taken on an additional dimension. These advancements might further enhance the role of instructional leadership in meeting the evolving needs of educators and learners.

## Higher Education in War

The warfare that followed the years of COVID-19 has further disrupted the education system in general and higher education in particular. The large-scale open military aggression that began in February 2022 was a continuation of the hybrid military actions that started in February 2014 with the annexation of Crimea by the Russian Federation and the beginning of the covert annexation of the eastern territories of Ukraine (Donetsk and Luhansk regions). About 7% of Ukraine's territory was occupied in 2014. Therefore, turmoil had started much earlier than the pandemic crisis for HEIs in the southern and eastern parts of the country. Up to 20 universities from Donetsk, Luhansk, and Crimea were relocated to the territories controlled by the government of Ukraine. As of the end of 2022, about 24,000 students and 3000 academics were affected in higher education institutions relocated to the government-controlled territory in 2014 (Nikolaev et al., 2023). Antoniuk (2023) mentions that at that time, the Ukrainian state initially did not initiate the evacuation of these institutions. Thus, relocation and revival of the universities in new locations was carried out on the initiative and due to the teams' efforts of the educational institutions themselves. There are also some universities which were relocated twice from occupied areas in 2014 and 2022.

The war has significantly impacted the entire higher education system in Ukraine, with most universities facing territorial dispersion of their students and staff and being forced to switch to distance or blended learning. The situation was particularly critical for universities located in areas of active military action, where students and staff were forced to evacuate. As a result of intense shelling, higher education infrastructure suffered varying degrees of damage, with up to 11% of all HEIs in Ukraine affected, either damaged or destroyed (Shevchuk & Shevchuk, 2022). Between March and May 2022, 25 independent higher education institutions and 19 separate structural units of various universities were relocated, and over 54,000 students and almost 7000 teachers are now studying and working there, respectively (Nikolaev et al., 2023). The experience of HEI relocation in 2014 helped to manage the relocations in 2022.

Although warfare has directly affected all Ukrainian higher education institutions, regardless of their location, the educational process began to resume in mid-March 2022, only three weeks after the start of the military actions. Mostly, the learning process took place remotely or in a mixed format, in synchronous and asynchronous modes. The practical skills acquired during the pandemic in organising educational processes under quarantine restrictions helped to switch to online learning quickly. They facilitated the resumption of education in HEIs under the war circumstances. In 2022–2023, all universities in Ukraine continue their operations, with most students resuming their studies. Many higher education institutions (57%) have shifted to providing educational services exclusively online, while 41% have adopted a hybrid format combining face-to-face and online instruction (Antoniuk, 2023). Institutions operating in rear regions manage to join internal mobility programmes and invite students to study at safer locations. It is worth noting that the experience of the online teaching and learning process acquired during the pandemic, even with the destruction of institutions' infrastructure, helped them to continue their activities during the war.

However, many new challenges emerged during the war. There is a need for creating safe access to education facilities, as not all institutions have shelters and protective constructions. Constant artillery shellings and missile attacks, frequent interruptions in power supply and unstable internet access, and shortage of technical resources for online teaching and learning were reported by nearly 40% of respondents (Antoniuk, 2023). Additionally, only half of the educational institutions have the necessary resources to facilitate inclusive online education for individuals with special educational needs and disabilities. These obstacles underscore the need for concerted efforts and support to ensure the continuity and accessibility of education in the face of adversity (Antoniuk, 2023).

The invasion of Ukraine by Russia on February 24, 2022 resulted in one of the largest population displacements in history and one of the biggest challenges for Ukraine and Europe. Nearly 14 million people were compelled to leave their homes due to the hostilities. Within various universities, the percentage of internally displaced students or those who went abroad ranged to 30%. Unfortunately, almost 24,000 students did not resume their studies for various reasons. Additionally, up to 30% of teachers in some universities also became internally displaced or sought refuge in other countries (Antoniuk, 2023).

Consequently, thousands of students and educators from higher education institutions found themselves internally displaced persons or seeking asylum in other countries, facing different living conditions and emotional challenges. The student population is expected to decline, as many high school students and teachers may not return to Ukraine and choose to remain abroad. Moreover, considering the ongoing warfare, frequent air raids, and the targeting of Ukraine's energy infrastructure and civil objects, it is unlikely that a swift return will be facilitated. Instead, a new wave of migration may appear more likely.

Expanding upon the challenges faced by students and teachers during times of war, Galynska and Bilous (2022) specifically highlight psychological factors. Exposure to war, death, displacement from home, uncertainty, and pessimistic expectations about the future result in many individuals losing concentration, increased stress, and apathy. These factors negatively impact the ability and capacity to teach and learn effectively. However, it has been mentioned that higher education has the potential to mitigate the adverse effects experienced by students due to the conflict of war, offering them a sense of hope and a positive outlook for the future. Education plays a crucial role in bolstering the confidence and motivation of university students. In this regard, the role of educational leaders becomes indispensable. They play a vital part in providing guidance and motivation, creating an environment fostering resilience and growth, and restoring a sense of normalcy amidst challenging circumstances. By addressing the psychological well-being of students and teachers, educational leaders can contribute to the overall recovery and rebuilding efforts in post-war scenarios.

Hostilities' impact and consequences on the higher education system are devastating. Damaged and destroyed infrastructure and premises of higher education institutions, as well as the loss of educational and research equipment, make it difficult (if not impossible in some cases) to continue offline, blended, and online education, laboratory work, and research. Significant losses of staff and students at HEIs have been observed. The base for educational practice has narrowed due to the curtailment of training and production facilities (centres, complexes, etc.) and leading Ukrainian enterprises. Projected learning losses are enormous due to long-term hardships and compounding negative effects.

Challenging circumstances have compelled numerous education managers to assume participative, charismatic, and moral leadership roles. In these extraordinary situations, they are forced to make swift and effective decisions, take genuine ownership, and manage risks. Resilience becomes crucial as leaders must demonstrate courage and motivate others to join them at the forefront of unprecedented risks and challenges. In this way, education leaders, albeit somewhat forcedly, demonstrate their ability to act as effective crisis managers. They possess diverse competencies and display a cohesive blend of leadership styles, enabling them to guide their institutions and teams through times of crisis effectively.

Despite the threatening trends, Ukrainian higher education institutions continue to operate and provide educational services. Like the pandemic, Ukraine's HE system may have an opportunity to emerge from this crisis stronger, more adapted to the new conditions, and eventually reformed and modernised (Nikolaev et al., 2023). The war has compelled higher education leaders to take on crucial roles in mobilising and adapting their institutions and teams to the new challenges and conditions. This experience should catalyse reevaluating approaches to restoring and modernising Ukraine's higher education system and education leadership. However, it should not be just an improvement of the existing system, which in many respects is a legacy of the Soviet Union, but the creation of an innovative model of higher education that can respond to the challenges of modern society (Antoniuk, 2023).

## Conclusions

Since 2020, the Ukrainian higher education system has been in a constant crisis, accompanied by the long-run inconsistent reformation processes, which started in the 1990s. The transformation processes, which were already difficult, have been significantly complicated by two years of the pandemic and education during warfare, dating back to 2014 and particularly intensified in 2022. However, these crises have accelerated the pace of reforms that would have otherwise taken years to implement in non-crisis times.

The years of education in crisis have created a basis for an unprecedented natural experiment in which education innovations are being tested and evaluated, and it has highlighted what is unnecessary while also revealing what has been effective. Many of the innovations introduced during the crisis years will continue. At the same time, emerging trends already determine universal future development vectors for higher education.

Distance education has emerged as an exceptional opportunity to maintain an uninterrupted educational process despite destabilising factors. Additionally, this trend reflects a broader movement towards increasing the overall digitalisation of education and society. Therefore, the level of digitalisation for teachers and students should also be increased to support the implementation of information technologies in the educational process. Specifically, teachers must be trained in effective online teaching methods and in creating online courses. Moreover, research programmes should focus on developing practical, self-contained distance and blended learning methods rather than merely supplementary ones. Distance learning can serve as a full-fledged form of higher education for certain fields of study, providing students with the opportunity to study and work simultaneously to gain practical experience. To meet these evolving needs, universities must adopt flexible and robust educational models that can adapt to the different stages of the "new normal" state.

When analysing the benefits of online learning, it becomes clear that they all revolve around the freedom and autonomy this mode of education provides. As such, these advantages are unlikely to diminish in the future. Educational programmes, methods, and technologies should thus be designed with flexible learning in mind, providing students with greater freedom and independence. Achieving this requires teaching students to learn independently and practice self-discipline and self-motivation effectively. Furthermore, teachers must possess expertise in their subject and be able to serve as facilitators of the educational process and mentors to their students.

Beyond the classroom, learning losses can have serious long-term consequences. Therefore, developing new monitoring and measurement methodologies is important to identify and quickly address any learning gaps or losses. Additionally, a mechanism should be developed to identify potential threats and mitigate their negative impact. Introducing and enhancing various models of lifelong learning and creating conditions for their implementation at different levels can help students close their learning gaps independently or with the help of teachers, tutors, or mentors. The network of higher education institutions needs to be improved and developed to provide ample opportunities for academic mobility of teachers and students, both domestically and internationally, and to foster active collaboration between higher education institutions and businesses.

In times of transformation and crises, leadership plays a crucial role. The unique challenges and complexities that arose during the reformation period and the times of crisis demonstrated the limitations of traditional leadership approaches. This embraces the idea of modern leadership models that allow for effective management of modernisation and diverse challenges in the higher education sector. Education leaders at all levels must reflect and learn from experience and critically examine their practices, roles, duties, and responsibilities during the crisis. It will help to activate a much-needed reevaluation of education leadership concepts and to advocate for necessary systemic changes to enhance the resilience and responsiveness of education leadership under volatile and unsustainable conditions. This may involve policy reforms, resource allocation, and structural adjustments to better support and develop education leaders who can navigate crises effectively and facilitate their teams' and students' resilience, growth, and development. It is equally important for strengthening the sustainability of higher education institutions in the face of diverse challenges and current and future transformations.

As Ukraine emerges from the crisis, its education system will never change. Rather than rebuilding it, a new foundation must be established with a new educational culture, models, technologies, forms, and methods. This will involve modernising the higher education system, creating a new network of higher education institutions, and the emergence of new educational leaders who can lead the way.

## References

Antoniuk, V. (2023). Perspective chapter: The war as a factor of upheavals and transformations in higher education: Experience of Ukraine. In *Higher education-reflections from the field*. IntechOpen. https://doi.org/10.5772/intechopen.109688

Balasubramanian, S., & Fernandes, C. (2022). Confirmation of a crisis leadership model and its effectiveness: Lessons from the COVID-19 pandemic. *Cogent Business & Management, 9*(1), 2022824.

Berezhna, S., & Prokopenko, I. (2020). Higher education institutions in Ukraine during the Coronavirus, or COVID-19, outbreak: New challenges vs new opportunities. *Revista Romaneasca Pentru Educatie Multidimensionala, 12*(1Sup2), 130–135.

Bergman, J. Z., Rentsch, J. R., Small, E. E., Davenport, S. W., & Bergman, S. M. (2012). The shared leadership process in decision-making teams. *The Journal of Social Psychology, 152*(1), 17–42.

Bologna National Report Ukraine. (2009). *Home*. http://www.ond.vlaanderen.be/hogeronderwijs/bologna/links/National-reports-2009/National_Report_Ukraine_2009.pdf

Bush, T. (2007). Educational leadership and management: Theory, policy, and practice. *South African Journal of Education, 27*(3), 391–406.

Bush, T. (2011). *Theories of educational leadership and management.* Sage Publications.

Crayne, M. P., & Medeiros, K. E. (2021). Making sense of crisis: Charismatic, ideological, and pragmatic leadership in response to COVID-19. *American Psychologist, 76*(3), 462–474.

Fimyar, O. (2008). Educational policy-making in post-communist Ukraine as an example of emerging governmentality: Discourse analysis of curriculum choice and assessment policy documents (1999–2003). *Journal of Education Policy, 23*(6), 571–594.

Galynska, O., & Bilous, S. (2022). Remote learning during the war: Challenges for higher education in Ukraine. *International Science Journal of Education & Linguistics, 1*(5), 1–6.

Goodman, B. A. (2013). Ukraine and the Bologna Process: Convergence, pluralism, or both? *Paper presented at the 12th Berlin Roundtables on Transnationality, Berlin.*

Gryshkova, R. (2019). Leadership in Ukrainian educational dimension. *Advances in Social Science, Education and Humanities Research, 318*, 251–256.

Janovac, T. D., & Virijević Jovanović, S. R. (2022). The effects of charismatic leadership of the Eastern European cultural cluster in crisis situations. *Kultura Polisa, 19*(3), 156–175.

Kalashnikova, S., & Orzhel, O. (2019). University leadership development: Lessons from Ukraine. *International Scientific Journal of Universities and Leadership, 2*(8), 133–143.

Kezar, A. J., & Holcombe, E. M. (2017). *Shared leadership in higher education: Important lessons from research and practice.* American Council on Education.

Khustochka, O. (2009). *Teacher training in Finland and Ukraine: Comparative analysis of teacher training systems* [Master's Thesis, University of Oslo].

Klann, G. (2003). *Crisis leadership: Using military lessons, organisational experiences, and the power of influence to lessen the impact of chaos on the people you lead*. CCL Press.

Kokarieva, A., Khomenko-Semenova, L., Glushanytsia, N., Ievtushenko, I., & Odarchenko, R. (2019). *Information and communication technologies in the professional training of engineers.* International Workshop on Conflict Management in Global Information Networks, Lviv, Ukraine.

Koshmanova, T., & Ravchyna, T. (2008). Teacher preparation in a post-totalitarian society: An interpretation of Ukrainian teacher educators' stereotypes'. *International Journal of Qualitative Studies in Education, 21*(2), 137–158.

Kutsyuruba, B., & Kovalchuk, S. (2015). Stated or actual change in policy terrain? Review of the literature on the Bologna process implementation within the context of teacher education in Ukraine. *Journal of Ukrainian Politics and Society, 1*, 33–57.

Law of Ukraine "On Higher Education". (2014). (English). http://erasmusplus.org.ua/vyshcha-osvita-v-ukraini.html

Law of Ukraine "On Education". (2017). (English). https://mon.gov.ua/ua/npa/law-education

Ministry of Education of Ukraine. (1992). *Ukraina XXI Stolittya: Derzhavna Nastional'na Prohrama' OSVITA'* [Ukraine of 21 century: The state national program of education]. Ministry of Education.

NAGA. (2019). *Statement of the national agency for higher education quality assurance regarding the current government's attempts to eliminate the gains of higher education reform and to suspend the integration of Ukraine into the EHEA.* https://en.naqa.gov.ua

Nikolaev, E., Riy, H., & Shemelynets, I. (2023). *Higher education in Ukraine: Changes due to the war: An analytical report.* Borys Grinchenko Kyiv University.

Popovych, V., Stadnyk, A., & Vanyushina, O. (2022). Higher education in the convention of the COVID-19 pandemic: Challenges and threats. *GRANI, Sociology, 25*(2), 65–71.

Riggio, E. R., & Newstead, T. (2023). Crisis leadership. *Annual Review of Organizational Psychology and Organizational Behavior, 10*, 201–224.

Rudolph, J., Tan, S., Crawford, J., & Butler-Henderson, K. (2023). Perceived quality of online learning during COVID-19 in higher education in Singapore: Perspectives from students, lecturers, and academic leaders. *Educational Research for Policy and Practice, 22*(1), 171–191. https://doi.org/10.1007/s10671-022-09325-0

Shevchuk, A., & Shevchuk, I. (2022). Educational analytics through the prism of war: Challenges and opportunities for higher education in Ukraine. *Economy and Society, 39.* https://economyandsociety.in.ua/index.php/journal/issue/view/39

Shyyan, O., & Shyyan, R. (2022). Teacher education in Ukraine: surfing the third wave of change. In *The Palgrave handbook of teacher education in Central and Eastern Europe* (pp. 527–551). Springer International Publishing.

Stukalo, N., & Simakhova, A. (2020). COVID-19 impact on Ukrainian higher education. *Universal Journal of Educational Research, 8*(8), 3673–3678.

Stepko, M. (2004). *Reports from new members of the Bologna Process: Ukraine.* Paper presented at the Conference of European Ministers Responsible for Higher Education.

Tice, D., Baumeister, R., Crawford, J., Allen, K. A., & Percy, A. (2021). Student belongingness in higher education: Lessons for Professors from the COVID-19 pandemic. *Journal of University Teaching & Learning Practice, 18*(4), 2. https://doi.org/10.53761/1.18.4.2

Wilson, S., Tan, S., Knox, M., Ong, A., Crawford, J., & Rudolph, J. (2020). Enabling cross-cultural student voice during COVID-19: A collective autoethnography. *Journal of University Teaching & Learning Practice, 17*(5), 3. https://doi.org/10.53761/1.17.5.3

# Managing Multiple Crises in Higher Education Employment: The Case of Australia

Peter Waring

## Introduction

On most established metrics, the Australian Higher Education sector is largely successful on the global stage, with multiple public universities entrenched in highly ranked positions within global league tables, a strong national higher education participation rate (44%) (Clare, 2022), enviable research performance and an international education industry that ranks as Australia's fourth most valuable export (see Crawford et al., 2024 in this volume). Just beneath this pristine image, though, lies a more complex and less attractive reality of talent shortages, precarious employment, industrial grievances, acute managerialism and corporatisation. Calls for Australia's universities to become 'more business-like' (Parker et al., 2021) appear to have been met—at least in terms of the less enviable characteristics of businesses. The causes of the Janus-like nature of the Australian higher education sector are complex and multi-faceted. The decline in Federal funding for the sector incentivised Universities to grow their international student revenues through onshore and off-shore expansion. These efforts coincided with growing student mobility, especially from China, to create an export education sector worth $40 Billion by 2019.

P. Waring (✉)
Murdoch Singapore Pte Ltd, Singapore 169662, Singapore
e-mail: P.Waring@murdoch.edu.au


J. Rudolph et al. (eds.), *The Palgrave Handbook of Crisis Leadership in Higher Education*, https://doi.org/10.1007/978-3-031-54509-2_10

The booming Australian international sector proved a double-edged sword for many Australian universities. Though it provided greatly needed resources at a time of falling government support, it also created a dependency on international student revenue to support core activity and a concentration risk centred on Chinese students within a narrow range of courses. The onset of the global pandemic tested this dependency. It forced the sector to go 'cold turkey' as borders were slammed shut, and the Morrison government advised international students to 'go home' (Ross, 2020). This, in turn, created an unprecedented crisis for Australian universities as they simultaneously managed the challenges of delivering under COVID-19 restrictions with greatly reduced international student revenue. Given that labour costs are the most significant portion of the sector's cost base, it was obvious that universities' employment arrangements would be tested as leaders responded to the crisis.

This chapter analyses these sectoral responses and pressures in the context of crisis leadership. The first section details the pre-COVID-19 trends in employment relations in Australian Higher Education and the consequences of pressures to adopt practices and managerial behaviours common with neo-liberalism and New Public Management (Andrew, 2024 in this volume; Lyons & Dalton, 2011). The responses and strategies of University leaders are examined in light of the shifting sands of reduced Federal funding, the pursuit of global ranking success and growing international student mobility.

The second section examines the COVID-19 crisis period of 2020–2022 and the leadership responses concerning employment relations. This section describes how common pressures nonetheless produced divergent responses among Australian university leaders. The merits of these divergent responses are evaluated from strategic and operational perspectives. The final section analyses the post-COVID-19 period and explores how Australian university leaders are positioning their approaches to employment relations in this period. In 2023, most Australian universities are engaged with or about to commence bargaining over employment relations. Therefore, it is instructive to examine bargaining strategies and approaches to employment relations issues to conclude the varied approaches of University leaders. These strategic approaches can tell us much about leadership responses to short and longer-term unfolding crises.

## The Pre-COVID-19 Era

Through Government reform, population growth and the passing of statutes, the Australian Higher Education Sector has become a key sector of the economy, generating substantial wealth and employment for metropolitan and regional centres. There are some forty Australian Universities, which, on average, are much larger than comparative institutions in the UK or Canada, for instance, in terms of average enrolment, revenues and on- and off-shore business operations. In 1988, the sector enrolled approximately 440,000 students; in 2022, 1.6 million students were enrolled, including domestic and international students (Goodman, 2022). Annual revenues of some of Australia's larger institutions regularly exceed a billion dollars. In contrast, the annual salaries of Vice Chancellors at most institutions are comparable to the seven-figure salaries received by the CEOs of some of the larger Australian corporations. University strategies, in the two to three decades prior to the pandemic, were arguably subject to coercive and convergent pressures to achieve legitimacy through the pursuit of improved global rankings and, in the case of their Business Schools, the attainment of coveted badges of validation from organisations such as AACSB and EQUIS.

Declining public expenditure on the sector in real terms also led to institutional mimicry in international education, with all Australian universities developing similar structures and strategies to grow international student enrolment aggressively. These approaches proved successful, with Australia emerging as one of the three top global study destinations for international students. Importantly, international student fee income grew substantially. By 2019, international education was Australia's fourth largest export, valued at $40.3 billion (Department of Education, 2023a, 2023b, 2023c, p. 1), which helped offset declining public funding. The growth of international student revenues has been startling over the previous three decades. Peetz et al. (2023, p. 10), citing Horn (2020), state that the proportion of Australian university revenue from international students grew from 6% in 1995 to 24% by 2018.

This expansion in international fee revenues did not prevent isomorphic pressures, arguably creating homogeneity in the employment relations characteristics of institutions (DiMaggo & Powell, 1983). Indeed, Ryan (2009) and Croucher & Lacy (2022) provide a compelling argument that the growth of international education as a leading Australian export industry led to the commodification and corporatisation of Australian higher education, with deleterious consequences for academic values and academic employment. Commercial imperatives combined with the neo-liberalist discourse around productivity, accountability, performance and metrics resulted in University governance mirroring private sector corporate governance values and behaviours (as Ismail and Aljunied's [2023] discussion of higher education in Malaysia in this volume demonstrates, these trends are not unique to Australia). This was buttressed by an increasing executives from the private sector taking positions on Australian University Councils and Senates. These developments were also encouraged by the Howard Coalition Government, which led Australia between 1996 and 2007 and pushed for similar neoliberal reform to public sector industrial Relations (Macdonald, 1998; see Andrew, 2024; Ismail & Aljunied, 2023 in this volume). Popenici (2022, p. 83) has savagely criticised these developments, stating that "universities became unrecognisable in a relatively short time… (turning) into a space of managerial gibberish, ruled by pseudo-managers eager to adopt solutions that lead to the demise of universities".

One important human resource initiative widely adopted at this time was the performance management of Vice Chancellors and other senior university leaders with cascading key performance indicators (KPIs) that were typically focused on limited commercial and reputational (via rankings) targets. Other elements of the corporate world, such as 'bonuses' for senior university leaders, became more prevalent to incentivise and reward the achievement of KPIs.

For academics and professional staff, these developments have helped alter university employment characteristics in common ways. Perhaps ironically, despite all Australian universities engaging in enterprise-based bargaining over wages and conditions, homogeneity of key employment trends has largely been the outcome. Two critical trends are worth explaining here: the introduction of academic workload models and the growth in casualisation and precarious employment across the sector.

The shift from the previous practice of decentralised and collegial management of academic work to more centralised and systematised management of academic work has proved to be a fundamental and far-reaching change in the Australian Higher Education sector. In this near-universal transformation, academic work is broken down into constituent elements and then incorporated into normative models in which academics' actual work is applied against the normative model to determine if there are deficits or surpluses. The identification of deficits results in an increased workload. The compelling nature of this approach is that it offers the opportunity to distribute work fairly across objective categories. The critique of this approach, however, is that it is essentially Taylorist in design as it strengthens the prerogative of management to continuously increase work intensity, leading to burnout and stress (Lyons & Ingersoll, 2010). Additionally, the normative model often fails to capture the nuances of academic work that are linked to differences between disciplines.

Another discernible trend in employment relations in thc Australian Higher Education sector has been the growth of insecure or precarious academic employment. Casualisation has grown significantly as a means for universities to manage teaching in particular, where casuals receive no leave entitlements and fewer workplace rights. Although casual and other precarious employment has grown substantially in Australia, the Higher Education sector has been one of the heaviest users of such temporary employment. In 2013, Ryan (2009) estimated that casual academics were responsible for more than 50% of all teaching activity and up to 80% of all first-year teaching. More recently, Carey (2023), drawing on Victorian university annual reports from 2022, has indicated that just over 50% of all academics employed in universities in Victoria are employed on casual contracts. One of the drivers for this growth has been the growth of onshore and off-shore full-fee-paying international students. They suggest that the increased use of casual academics has been used by university management "as a buffer against the vagaries and oscillations in the global education market" (p. 3).

For some casual academics, the flexible nature of casual employment undoubtedly meets interests in supplementing income while allowing time for other employment or caring responsibilities. Yet for others, casual employment means fluctuating income, reduced entitlements, financial insecurity, and lack of recognition and professional development opportunities.

The continuing degradation of academic employment in Australia over these decades has, unsurprisingly, been observed in academic research (Barnes et al., 2013; Popenici, 2022) and in campaigns led by the National Tertiary Education Union, which represents both academic and professional staff across the sector. Moreover, the 2008 Bradley Review of Australian Higher Education acknowledged that the resourcing of public universities had come under pressure, with staff-student ratios 'growing markedly from 12.9 in 1990 to 20.3 by 2005' (Bradley Review, 2008). Further, the Bradley Review pointed to the ageing of the academic workforce and the challenge Australian universities face in recruiting and retaining staff with diminishing and uncertain revenue streams.

This pre-pandemic context could be described as a slow-moving crisis within Australian Higher Education where university leaders were required to deliver more with fewer government-sourced resources while being incentivised to grow alternative revenue streams and boost productivity. The answer to these challenges was often found in the aggressive pursuit of full-fee-paying international students, especially from a few source countries.

The Australian Department of Education (2021) noted that 2020 China and India accounted for 57% of international higher education enrolments 2020, up from 46% in 2010. This created a significant dependency on fee-paying international students from just two countries, with the Department of Education noting that "One risk to sustainable growth in international education enrolments is not adequately managing potential overexposure to particular markets" (Department of Education, 2022, p. 1).

Concentration risk was also evident in the field of study, with international students making up 65% of enrolments in Information Technology courses and 54% of all enrolments in management and commerce courses (Department of Education, 2023a, 2023b, 2023c, p. 4). Meanwhile, the two top source markets, China and India, accounted for most postgraduate enrolments in Information Technology.

While these risks were known and referred to within the higher education sector, they remained *largely* existential until the onset of the global pandemic in early 2020. It is accurate to use the adverb 'largely' because leading up to the outbreak of the COVID-19 virus, there have been concerns expressed on the significant dependency of some Australian universities on full-fee-paying Chinese international students. Some of these concerns were connected to national security issues, with Australia passing the *Foreign Interference Act* in 2018 to stymie the capacity of the Chinese government to exert influence in various sectors in Australia, including, most notably, the higher education sector (*Reuters*, 2023).

The next section examines the emergency COVID-19 period from March 2020 until the end of 2022. It particularly explores the employment relations responses to the crisis from Australian university leaders, which arguably diverged during this period.

## The COVID-19 Global Pandemic and Australian Higher Education

The once-in-a-century COVID-19 global pandemic is perhaps the 'black-swan' event of the twenty-first century (Rudolph et al., 2023). Much is and will be analysed and debated about the virus's origins, impact and ongoing consequences for years. As of May 2023, The World Health Organisation had estimated total global fatalities at just under 7 million, while more than three-quarters of a billion people had been infected by the virus (WHO, 2023).

A comprehensive interrogation of the pandemic's political, social and economic consequences is beyond this chapter's scope. Instead, this section will focus on the immediate implications for Australian universities, the responses by leaders and especially the strategic choices made concerning employment relations.

As Crawford et al. (2020) have noted, the initial institutional responses to the emergence of COVID-19 were largely focused on maintaining continuity of learning in response to government restrictions on group size and the need to manage the health and welfare of staff and students. In some higher education sectors, this meant partial online delivery through what could be described as emergency 'satisficing' strategies in which existing online platforms were repurposed for online delivery but with few, if any, changes to curricula and very little in the way of investment in staff training (see Crawford et al., 2024 in this volume). This frequently required intense efforts from academics and professional staff to accomplish in days what would have ordinarily required many months. As the pandemic ensued, improvements were made to online delivery and greater consideration was given to staff training, the online experience for students and student welfare more generally (Tice et al., 2021).

As the public health crisis ensued, strict border entry restrictions were imposed, denying new international students entry to Australia. Indeed, international student arrivals fell from 143,810 in the year to July 2019 to just 40 in 2020 (Peetz et al., 2023). International students already in Australia faced especially perilous times as many of the sectors in which they hold part-time jobs (such as Hospitality and Retail) came under enormous economic pressure and began to downsize. Their vulnerability was magnified by the fact that international students typically lack the family support structures of domestic students and cannot access welfare payments. Therefore, many Australian Universities were forced to provide financial support to these students when revenue from new international students collapsed. The advice offered by Prime Minister Morrison in April 2020 was not especially comforting as he urged international students in Australia to 'go home'. Moreover, the financial crisis created by COVID-19 was accentuated by the additional spending required on health and hygiene measures and greater investment in Information Technology to maintain continuity of learning.

As public health measures (such as lockdowns and restrictions on gatherings) were implemented, it was clear that the Australian labour market would very quickly deteriorate without government support. The then Morrison Coalition Federal Government moved to introduce the 'Job Keeper' policy—an enormously expensive wage subsidy that cost more than $88 Billion in its first year of operation (Borland & Hunt, 2023). As Clibborn (2021) states, this was largely a result of the urgings of businesses, unions and academics for a wage subsidy to be introduced, and indeed, the then Treasurer expressed his reluctance to implement such a large-scale government intervention. Job Keeper payments (initially $750 per week per employee) were made to eligible employers for full-time employees who were covered by the programme and also eligible self-employed people (Borland & Hunt, 2023, p. 110). Some 3.66 million workers received Job Keeper payments; however, universities were deemed, by design, ineligible to receive the payments (Karp, 2020). By contrast, some organisations of more dubious public benefit, such as casinos, received many millions of dollars in Job Keeper payments (Hatch, 2021). This ineligibility led Peetz et al. (2023) to claim that the conservative Morrison government had deliberately excluded the sector from Job Keeper as part of its culture war on progressive universities. Peetz et al. (2023, p. 11) state "Despite their neoliberal turn, Australian universities were not neoliberal enough".

Universities, facing the collapse of international student revenue and increased costs without support from the Australian government, unquestionably faced a significant crisis which was almost entirely novel and presented challenges and variables for which there were no known precedents (Riggio & Newstead, 2023). Horn has estimated that Australian universities lost $3–$4.6 Billion in 2020 due to closed borders, and these losses continued to mount in 2021 as borders largely remained firmly shut to international students. Faced with difficult choices, almost all institutions began to shed casual academic labour and not renew short-term contracts. According to Little and Stanford (2021), approximately 39,000 jobs were lost across the sector between 2020 and 2021, including 36,000 full-time jobs. This problematic context highlighted the moral and ethical dilemmas, which are often typical of low-probability, high-risk events. For university leaders, institutional survival during this time demanded difficult decisions involving trade-offs and costs for some stakeholders.

Given this once-in-a-generation challenge, the National Tertiary Education Trade Union (NTEU) chose to be proactive by urging an industry-wide arrangement known as the "National Job Protection Framework" aimed at maximising employment security while also allowing for temporary pay cuts, deferred salary costs and other cost savings (Peetz et al., 2023, p. 11). This partnership or concession bargaining approach represented a unique strategic choice and departure for the Union that has historically focused on improving wages and conditions for its members. The motivation of the NTEU's leadership in promoting such a concession-bargaining strategy was fundamentally related to the daunting wave of job losses visible on the horizon. By making unprecedented concessions on wages and flexibility, the NTEU's leadership hoped to mitigate as many job losses as possible. The National Job Protection Framework was also designed to give the NTEU greater oversight of university restructuring processes. As the then President of the NTEU stated at the time, the framework was constructed to ensure that the Union 'simply did not passively accept job losses' (Vassiley & Russell, 2021).

The National Job Protection Framework proved highly controversial within the Union and among many of its members, and its proposals were vigorously debated. Indeed, Vassiley and Russell (2021) note that resolutions opposing the concession bargaining strategy were passed at most NTEU branches in Australia. Union members opposed to the plan argued that reducing wages and conditions would not guarantee that jobs would be saved. It was also controversial among universities, with many choosing not to sign up for the framework agreement out of concern about providing the NTEU with oversight arrangements—especially concerning financial matters (Peetz et al., 2023).

As a consequence of this opposition, the NTEU leadership abandoned the pursuit of a national agreement for the Job Protection Framework but continued to negotiate similar local arrangements with individual universities (for example, the Universities of Tasmania and Wollongong; Western Sydney University; University of Western Australia; La Trobe University and Queensland University of Technology). Vassiley and Russell (2021) have indicated that these arrangements typically entailed wage cuts of between 2 and 10% and other concessions, such as the compulsory purchasing of leave and the removal of holiday loadings. It is difficult to assess whether these arrangements mitigated job losses than at Universities without Union framework agreements. Vassiley and Russell (2021) claim that there is no evidence that they had this effect (neither is there good evidence that they did not have this impact); however, what is significant is that university leaders in these institutions were prepared to partner with the Union to help manage the crisis whereas others were not prepared to do so. Furthermore, Vassiley and Russell (2021) acknowledge that a few universities did not sign up to framework agreements with the NTEU, where there were few job losses.

The divergent approaches concerning managing labour and operating costs during the emergency period of COVID-19 may reflect the extraordinary nature of the crisis that befell the Australian Higher Education Sector. University leaders may have had to achieve similar cost efficiencies when faced with unprecedented challenges. However, the divergent paths taken reflect not only the characteristics of each institution but also the character of leadership at each institution. Arguably, this divergence has continued into the post-emergency COVID-19 era, detailed in the next section.

## The Post-Emergency COVID-19 Era and Australian Higher Education

On the 5th of May 2023, the World Health Organisation declared an end to the emergency phase of COVID-19 (Lenhano, 2023), citing the steep reduction in the global hospitalisation and death rate from COVID-19. The announcement came many months after Australia had removed most pandemic health restrictions and lifted border controls. From at least the second half of 2022, Australian Universities had largely resumed pre-COVID-19 campus activities, and international students were returning to Australia in significant numbers.

Indeed, by the first semester of 2023, there was overwhelming evidence of a sharp rebound in international student arrivals in Australia, with 546,678 international students studying there as of February 2023—26% more than in February 2022. Much of this surge was again concentrated in a few countries, including China, India and Nepal (Department of Education, 2023a, 2023b, 2023c), where demand for Australian higher education had been pent up through the emergency COVID-19 period. The Australian Government (addressing both business and university interests) added fuel to this demand by extending post-study work rights for a further two years for international graduates with certain qualifications and increasing the allowable hours that international students may work from 40 to 48 hours per fortnight (Department of Education, 2023c).

The concentration of international students from a few source countries has prompted the Australian government to develop a diversification index to illustrate the mix of student enrolments at each Australian university. Additionally, the Government has suggested that it will require universities to develop diversification action plans designed to encourage universities to develop strategies to diversify their international student cohorts. These are fairly 'light touch' initiatives, though, which are unlikely to do much to mitigate against the same sectoral risks that proved so damaging in 2020–2022.

Given that university public funding arrangements are yet to be substantially altered, university leaders will welcome the growth in international fee revenue as they seek to rebuild after the COVID-19 period and as they address demands for improved employment relations. In 2022–2023, most of Australia's public universities were bargaining with the NTEU to renew enterprise agreements. The NTEU's key campaign demands focused on improving employment security (especially converting insccure university jobs into ongoing full-time jobs), fairer workloads and increased pay—15% over three years to address the cost of living concerns (Hare, 2022).

Several concluded enterprise agreements suggest that the Union has been reasonably successful in achieving pay settlements close to its initial objective. For example, the University of Technology Sydney settled on a pay rise of 14.75% and created 110 new full-time positions for casual academic staff (NTEU, 2023). Western Sydney University also settled on pay rises approximating 11.5% and creating 150 new full-time positions open to casual employees (WSU, 2022).

There is some evidence that the divergent approaches to employment relations encountered during the COVID-19 era have continued. Some university leaders, for instance, have attempted to bypass the Union by proposing new enterprise agreements directly to staff. At Griffith University, for instance, management proposed to staff without the support of the NTEU, which was subsequently rejected (*Times Higher Education*, 2022). Similar attempts were made at the University of Newcastle, Curtin University and Charles Darwin University, which were all subsequently rejected (Newcastle Weekly, 2023).

Other university leaders, perhaps for strategic reasons or due to observed failures elsewhere, have avoided this path and instead worked closely with unions to strike new agreements. At Flinders University in South Australia, for instance, a new enterprise agreement was quietly negotiated without industrial action (*Campus Morning Mail*, 2023).

It is clear that without structural change to sectoral funding arrangements, university leaders will continue to face difficult choices and occasional crises in higher education employment. This has been acknowledged by the NTEU, which has proposed a Higher Education Secure Future Fund (which would be seeded with $500 million by the Federal Government). The purpose of the fund would be to help mitigate the financial impact of future crises like the pandemic. A portion of the interest of the fund the NTEU suggests could also be used for future workforce development and helping to convert casual jobs into ongoing positions (NTEU, 2023).

The NTEU's proposal formed part of their submission to an Australian review of higher education known as the 'Australian University Accord'. According to the Labour-led Federal Government, the Accord aims to develop a long-term plan for Australia's higher education sector. Its terms of reference include meeting the country's knowledge and skills needs; enhancing access and opportunity to quality higher education; reviewing funding arrangements and the contribution of higher education to the community; exploring opportunities to connect vocational and higher education; enhancing quality and sustainability and delivering new knowledge and innovation (Clare, 2022).

During the global pandemic, the higher education sector's experience has added piquancy to the Australian University Accord process. There is an opportunity to conceive of more balanced funding arrangements and perhaps a set of strategic choices that help cultivate sustainable international education and prevent the adverse consequences so keenly felt in the emergency COVID-19 period.

## Concluding Thoughts

The global pandemic was the 'blackest' of black-swan events. Although there had been warnings over many years that a global pandemic to rival that of the twentieth century's Spanish Flu could emerge at any time, these cautions, for the most part, went unheeded. The world was generally unprepared for the breath-taking assault on global political, economic and health systems caused by a few strands of malevolent Ribonucleic Acid (RNA). The unfolding crisis shared many of the dynamics of crises documented by Riggio and Newstead (2023). It was a low-probability event with high consequences that was also novel and characterised by high ambiguity requiring rapid responses.

For the Australian Higher Education Sector, the crisis was acutely felt, in large part due to the significant dependency that had been built up over several previous decades on full-fee-paying international students from a small number of South and East Asian source countries worth around $12 billion a year to the sector (Vassiley & Russell, 2021)—up to a third of universities' revenue base (Littleton & Stanford, 2021). To deploy a metaphor, the rapid border closures represented the removal of the last supporting beam in the 'Jenga Tower' that international education had become. As international education revenues came crashing down and operating costs shot up, university leaders found themselves in a fully blown crisis without any established 'playbook' to fall back on. As Riggio and Newstead (2023) have argued, decision-making in such crises often tests leaders by posing complex ethical dilemmas where the consequences for stakeholders may be adverse.

In this case, the crisis led to tens of thousands of job losses in a sector already characterised by high levels of insecure employment and claims of work intensification and wage theft. What was particularly interesting about the COVID-19 crisis was that it produced more divergent processes and outcomes in higher education employment relations than had been seen through successive enterprise bargaining rounds. Some University leaders took steps to work with unions to mitigate job losses, while many others saw no other option but to cut labour costs.

In the post-emergency COVID-19 era, the same pressures appear to be again building in Australian international education. There appears to be a level of 'path dependency' and institutional mimicry, where Australian university leaders, once more, appear to have little choice but to aggressively compete for international full-fee-paying students from the same narrow set of source countries. A fresh approach to international education may be required to address these risks by facilitating and incentivising entry into new markets and market segments through transnational education and innovative delivery models. There is also merit in the NTEU's idea of establishing a national Higher Education Fund as a 'rainy day' sovereign wealth fund to address future crises. Perhaps this model could be stretched further by considering how such a fund (or a portion of it) could be used to reinvest in a more stable international education sector. For instance, a small levy on onshore international students could be invested in shared offshore campuses, enabling Australian universities to reach a broader market of 'immobile international students'.

The Albanese Federal Government has set in motion (through the proposed Universities Accord) a process which, optimistically, will generate frank assessments of the challenges and a plethora of novel ideas for the future. All hopes now rest on this Australian University Accord to address structural funding arrangements and workplace arrangements that will best support a flourishing higher education system in Australia in the decades to come.

## References

Andrew, M. B. (2024). Neoliberalism and the crisis in higher education. In J. Rudolph, J. Crawford, C. Y. Sam, & S. Tan (Eds.), *The Palgrave handbook on crisis leadership in higher education*. Palgrave Macmillan.

Barnes, A., Macmillan, C., & Markey, R. (2013). Maintaining union voice in the Australian university sector: Union strategy and non-union forms of employee participation. *Journal of Industrial Relations, 55*(4), 565–582.

Borland, J., & Hunt, J. (2023). JobKeeper: An initial assessment. *The Australian Economic Review, 56*(1), 109–123.

*Campus Morning Mail*. (2023). No muss, no fuss at Flinders U. www.campusmorningmail.com.au

Carey, A. (2023, May 30). Poor swots who have to beg: The great divide for casual university staff. *Sydney Morning Herald*.

Clare, J. H. (2022). *'The Bradley Oration', Speech by Minister for Education*. www.ministers.education.gov.au

Clibborn, S. (2021). Australian industrial relations in 2020: COVID-19, crisis and opportunity. *Journal of Industrial Relations, 63*(3), 291–302.

Crawford, J., Allen, K., & Cowling, M. (2024). Australian higher education in perpetual crisis? A narrative of crisis leadership in universities. In J. Rudolph, J. Crawford, C. Y. Sam, & S. Tan (Eds.), *Palgrave handbook on crisis leadership in higher education*. Palgrave Macmillan.

Crawford, J., Butler-Henderson, K., Rudolph, J., Malkawi, B., Glowatz, M., Burton, R., Magni, P., & Lam, S. (2020). COVID-19: 20 countries higher education intra-period digital pedagogy responses. *Journal of Applied Learning & Teaching*, *3*(1), 9–28. https://doi.org/10.37074/jalt.2020.3.1.7

Croucher, G., & Lacy, W. (2022). The emergence of academic capitalism and university neoliberalism: Perspectives of Australian higher education leadership. *Higher Education, 83*, 279–295.

Department of Education. (2021). *Australian strategy for international education 2021–2030*. Australian Government. www.education.gov.au

Department of Education. (2022). *International student diversity at Australian universities* (Discussions Paper). Australian Government. www.education.gov.au

Department of Education. (2023a). *International student monthly summary*. www.education.gov

Department of Education. (2023b). *Review of Australia's higher education system—Terms of reference*. Australian Government. www.education.gov.au

Department of Education. (2023c). *Extended post-study work rights for international graduates*. www.education.gov.au

DiMaggo, P., & Powell, W. (1983). The iron cage revisited: Institutional isomorphism and collective rationality in organisational fields. *American Sociological Review, 48*(2), 147–160.

Hare, J. (2022). Academics union pushes for 15pc wage increase. *Australian Financial Review*.

Hatch, P. (2021). Casino group Star awards executive bonuses while pocketing JobKeeper. *Sydney Morning Herald*. www.smh.com

Ismail, F., & Aljunied, K. (2023). Beyond academic dehumanisation: Neo-Liberalism and the good university in Malaysia. In J. Rudolph, J. Crawford, C. Y. Sam, & S. Tan (Eds.), *Palgrave handbook on crisis leadership in higher education*. Palgrave Macmillan.

Goodman, J. (2022). Why universities urgently need a new business model. *Australian Financial Review*. www.afr.com

Karp, P. (2020). Australian universities angry at final twist of the knife excluding them from jobkeeper. *The Guardian*. www.theguardian.com

Lenhano, M. (2023). WHO declares end to COVID-19's emergency phase. *Nature*. www.nature.com

Littleton, E., & Stanford, J. (2021). An avoidable catastrophe: Pandemic job losses in higher education and their consequences. *The Australia Institute Centre for Work*. www.australiainstitute.org.au

Lyons, M., & Dalton, B. (2011). Australia: A continuing love affair with the new public management. In S. Phillips & S. Smith (Eds.), *Governance and regulation in the third sector*. Routledge.

Lyons, M., & Ingersoll, L. (2010). Regulated autonomy or autonomous regulation? Collective bargaining and academic workloads in Australian universities. *Journal of Higher Education Policy & Management, 32*(2), 137–148.

Macdonald, D. (1998). Public sector industrial relations under the Howard government. *Labour & Industry, 9*(2), 43–59.

Newcastle Weekly. (2023). *NTEU rejects Newcastle Uni management's offer*. www.newcastleweekly.com.au

NTEU. (2023). *Union unveils future fund plan for better universities*. NTEU Media Release.

Parker, L., Martin-Sardesai, A., & Guthrie, J. (2021). The commercialised Australian public university: An accountingized transition. *Financial Accountability & Management, 39*(1), 125–150.

Peetz, D., O'Brady, S., Westar, J., Coles, A., Baird, M., Cooper, R., Charlesworth, S., Pyman, A., Ressia, S., Strachan, G., & Troup, C. (2023). Control and insecurity in Australian and Canadian universities during the COVID-19 pandemic. *Relations Industrielles, 77*(2), 1–21.

Popenici, S. (2022). *Artificial intelligence and learning futures: Critical narratives of technology and imagination in higher education*. Routledge.

*Reuters*. (2023). Australia's foreign interference laws designed for China—Former PM Turnbull. www.reuters.com

Riggio, R. E., & Newstead, T. (2023). Crisis leadership. *Annual Review of Organizational Psychology and Organizational Behavior, 10*, 201–224.

Ross, J. (2020). Time to go home, Australian PM tells foreign students. *Times Higher Education*. www.timeshighereducation.com

Rudolph, J., Tan, S., Crawford, J., & Butler-Henderson, K. (2023). Perceived quality of online learning during COVID-19 in higher education in Singapore: Perspectives from students, lecturers, and academic leaders. *Educational Research for Policy and Practice, 22*(1), 171–191. https://doi.org/10.1007/s10671-022-09325-0

Ryan, S. (2009). *Academic business: Tensions between academic values and corporatisation of Australian higher education in graduate schools of business* [Ph.D. Thesis, Macquarie University].

Tice, D., Baumeister, R., Crawford, J., Allen, K. A., & Percy, A. (2021). Student belongingness in higher education: Lessons for Professors from the COVID-19 pandemic. *Journal of University Teaching & Learning Practice, 18*(4), 2. https://doi.org/10.53761/1.18.4.2

*Times Higher Education.* (2022, December 13). University, union share points in enterprise agreement showdown. www.timeshighereducation.com

Vassiley, A., & Russell, F. (2021). Concession-bargaining in Australian higher education: The case of the national jobs protection framework. *Labour & Industry, 31*(4), 439–456.

Western Sydney University. (2022). *Western Sydney University staff vote to support new Enterprise Agreements.* www.wsu.edu.au

World Health Organisation (WHO). (2023). *COVID-19 statistics.* www.who.int

# National Cases of Crisis

# Australian Higher Education in Perpetual Crisis? A Narrative of Crisis Leadership in Universities

Joseph Crawford, Kelly-Ann Allen, and Michael Cowling

## Introduction

Australian higher education has typically performed above its weight class globally. For a country of approximately 26 million people and 42 universities, the nation exceeds global averages. In 2023, Australia was the 55th largest country by population (Worldometer, 2023), and in 2021 it was the thirteen largest economy (World Bank, 2023). For clarity, it represents 0.33 per cent of the world's population, and 1.7 per cent of the world's global economy. In research terms however, it represents the 9th largest country by citations since 1996, and has ranged from 5 to 7th largest since 2014 (Scimago, 2023). Australia represents 17 per cent of the top 100 universities in the Times Higher Education Impact Rankings (2022) and represents seven of the top 100 universities by teaching quality (Times Higher Education, 2022). In contextual terms, earliest evidence indicates University of Oxford

J. Crawford (✉)
University of Tasmania, Launceston, TAS, Australia
e-mail: joseph.crawford@utas.edu.au

K.-A. Allen
Monash University Melbourne, Melbourne, VIC, Australia
e-mail: allen@monash.edu

M. Cowling
Central Queensland University, Rockhampton, QLD, Australia
e-mail: m.cowling@cqu.edu.au


J. Rudolph et al. (eds.), *The Palgrave Handbook of Crisis Leadership in Higher Education*, https://doi.org/10.1007/978-3-031-54509-2_11

was teaching in 1096, Harvard College was founded in 1636, and the University of Sydney was founded in 1850. So, despite the smaller economy and population, and a much younger higher education sector, Australia is quite successful as a global provider of higher education.

The success of Australian higher education has required resilience in the face of continued crisis, from government decrees to for university massification and lofty targets of 50 per cent of the Australian population receiving a tertiary education to the COVID-19 pandemic, and more recently the authentication crisis presented by ChatGPT's emergence. Many of these challenges lack a unique Australian origin, but have required a uniquely Australian response. This chapter provides a critical review of twenty-first-century Australian higher education through the lens of crisis leadership, and offers a look at the ways in which crisis leadership and management have been applied to contemporary crises in universities. The release of the Australian Universities Accord (2024) also offers an important signpost for more work in and around sector leadership.

The critical review presented in this chapter is important in its identification of leadership practices that have, and have not, been successful in Australian universities. This chapter affords a conceptual assessment of practical efforts made by those in senior management positions to enact leadership in response to crisis. It concludes with possible policy and leadership development responses that may support greater resilience when an unexpected and unpredictable crisis presents itself.

## Crisis Leadership

Crisis leadership is not a new concept in organisational, political, or educational leadership literature or practice. Passow (1953) discussed the need for more than crisis leadership being needed in educational settings. Tyler (1956) wrote of the crisis leadership of the Industrial Workers of the World, established in 1905 as a revolutionary industrial union. In this historical analysis, Tyler (1956) articulates that the union was highly effective in its crisis leadership practices but failed to offer practical benefits to its followers and members in between crisis events. Perhaps, this imbalance described why the organisation's member year-on-year turnover was discussed as so high.

Higher education has been no exception to this rule. In the University of Missouri case (Fortunato et al., 2018), historical context brought forth racial tension that resulted in the President and Chancellor departing. From 1347, University of Oxford students fled to their country residents to wait out the end of the Black Death (Crawford, 2023). With their books in bags—the laptops and lockdown equivalent—they pursued their learning from remote settings, and returned when it was safe to do so. In the U.S., Woolridge (2023) postulates of the impending crisis of losing educational superpower status. While, as we go on to discuss, definitions of crisis vary, it is evident that the higher education sector globally has experienced its fair share of crisis. And indeed, made attempts to respond through the enactment of crisis leadership.

There are two key crisis leadership studies that inform our approach to this chapter. First, Riggio and Newstead (2023) provide a critical review and propose a five-phase iterative loop of crisis leadership: sensemaking, decision-making, coordinating teamwork, facilitating learning, and communicating. This process supports crisis leaders to quickly determine the status of the crisis (sensemaking), make decisions with a bounded rationality frame, communicate openly and sincerely, coordinate team efforts while leading navigation, and facilitate practices of learning to identify vulnerabilities and establish immediate and future resilience. In this book (see Chapter 2), the authors apply this framework to higher education.

The second study is a systematic and bibliometric review. In this study, Wu et al. (2021) summarise the existing literature on crisis leadership, identifying 168 manuscripts between 1970 and 2020 that discuss crisis leadership. They identify that crisis leadership research has grown exponentially over recent years, and identify four key areas of need for future research. First, leader emotional management in crisis contexts, with a focus on cognitive and behavioural processes overrepresented in the literature. Second, the need to take a stronger process view of crisis leadership over static leadership responses. Third, Wu et al. (2021) identify a diverse range of crises that have been studied—from global financial crisis to leadership deaths and product harms—and the value that could arise in examining differences across crisis contexts. Fourth, the need for greater consideration to how leaders are selected during times of crisis, and differences that effect how followers appraise and experience leadership during crisis.

## Contemporary Crises

Since the new millennium, Australian higher education continues to experience crisis. While not exhaustive, this chapter examines the current crises taking grasp of the higher education and forcing leaders to respond in turn. These include the global massification agenda, the unexpected epidemics and pandemics, the emergence of artificial intelligence (Crawford et al., 2023; Kelly et al., 2023; Perkins, 2023) and authentication crisis, the belonging crisis, and the economic toll of continued expectations of agility. While we write of these as independent crises for readability, it would be inappropriate to claim these are mutually exclusive and independent in nature. Many of the crises discussed below coexist and Australian higher education crisis leaders are likely to need to respond to multiple crises concurrently.

## The Massification of Education Crisis

When considering the design of higher education institutions, three forms commonly appear in the literature: elite, mass, and universal (Trow, 2007). These paradigmatic lenses shape how the contemporary institution develops courses, assesses applications of prospective students, and the nature of research it conducts. In countries with elite education approaches, they might aspire to support up to 15 per cent of the population; historically an approach Australian higher education has adopted. Mass, or massified, education targets educating between 16 and 50 per cent of the population, and universal education seeks full participation in tertiary institutions.

> Over the last 30 years, Australia has moved from an elite system of higher education to a mass system. [...] Australia may achieve a government target of 40 per cent higher education attainment for 25 to 34 year olds by 2025. As a result, universities take students who would not previously have gone on to higher education. (Norton, 2013, p. 5)

In 1989, only 7.9 per cent of the population were educated with bachelor's degrees in Australia, and this progressively increased to 30.1 per cent in 2020 (Statista, 2023). In 2021, this rose significantly to 50.2 per cent, and 50.8 per cent in 2022. This while seeming to be a form of slow progression towards increasing participation has also influenced the way programmes of study are offered. In recent years, larger participation has meant students who are less prepared and from non-traditional backgrounds are entering university. Students of this nature tend to require different forms of support that universities have not historically been accustomed to. For example, online, indigenous, part-time, mature-age, and remote students tend to have the lowest completion rates in Australia (Cherastidtham & Norton, 2018). And there is a decline in four-year completion rates experienced between 2015 (45.3 per cent) and 2017 (42.5 per cent: Joseph, 2023).

While university leaders would have considerable awareness of their student engagement, student success, attrition, and completion rates, the requirement for crisis leadership appears in the context of connecting the crisis challenge and solution. The current solution for some universities has been to change the educational bar which students must jump to graduate. Foster (2015) writes of the slide of academic standards in Australia, and the need for reform. Hare (2022a) cites the Australian Productivity Commission's review of the Gonski Reforms that the domestic primary and high school students have declined in international standards. And Hare (2022b) goes on to describe the problem as a 'national crisis'. For universities, this means domestic students that will be less prepared for university education in the future; and perhaps that the education graduates the sector produces are not educated in a way that is likely to resolve the problem.

This crisis exists at both the supply and the demand end of higher education, where the quality of incoming students (e.g., reduced international education standards, particularly in regional and underserved populations), and the types of teachers graduating are creating a cycle that will require educational crisis leadership to respond to. Crises can sharply expose the weaknesses and vulnerabilities of a system (Riggio & Newstead, 2023), and in this case, there is perhaps a need for greater facilitation of learning and the coordination of national university resources to respond. While it is perhaps an appropriate pursuit to seek to educate and sustain half of the Australian population as well-educated civic leaders, the approximately 5.80 per cent compound growth rate of the sector since 1989, and the burgeoning of education from 2019 to 2020 has identified a significant mismatch between the types of curricula developed and the student cohort needs.

## Epidemics and Pandemics

The COVID-19 pandemic wrote a challenging narrative of higher education leaders. The first virus in Wuhan, China in late 2019 forced universities deeply connected in transnational education to their knees rapidly and without discrimination (Eri et al., 2021). Martin (2020) wrote of the need for revising engagement and interaction pursuits for the symptom of higher education moving online, and of the mismatch between Australian academics' skills and expectations for online teaching delivery. For those embedded in higher education during the pandemic, these were found to be not new comments. Instead, most institutions as attested across this book (see Chapter 25) experienced similar turbulence.

Yet, the epidemics and pandemics facing higher education are not new, but COVID-19 was perhaps the largest by effect. Instead, in lamenting the effect of COVID-19, Crawford (2023) documents references to the Black Death (1347–1351), Spanish Flu (1918–1919), SARS (2002–2003), Influenza A (2009), and the Middle Eastern Respiratory Syndrome (2012) as examples of localised and international outbreaks that affected higher education. In recent memory, Feast and Bretag (2005) discuss the impact that SARS had on their Australian university case study. This model, however, resembled a response similar to a smaller-scaled response to COVID-19, and this was relatable to narratives of Oxford students taking texts to their houses during the Black Death. These moments created a need for rapid and immediate response from educational leaders, and applied judgement with limited knowledge in unknown contexts. That takes crisis leadership. Interestingly, there were important examples of crisis leadership portrayed by female leaders in the COVID-19 pandemic (Wilson & Newstead, 2022), perhaps related to glass-cliff theory challenges that appear in precarious leadership roles (Ryan et al., 2016).

While the COVID-19 pandemic has been covered in considerable depth from broad learning and teaching and financial lens, it has received much less crisis leadership than studies on the Global Financial Crisis and similar (e.g., Knight & McCabe, 2015; Liu et al., 2017), with studies discussing Australian leadership during this time common (e.g., Liu, 2015, Liu et al., 2015; Xu et al., 2013). The impact of SARs had limited explicit discussion of crisis leadership, but in the primary study reporting on it, leadership was mentioned explicitly once, in relation to lack of awareness of who was responsible for implementing the contingency plan:

> This resulted in both frustration for administrative staff, and a sense of helplessness at the perceived lack of leadership from senior management at the local level. (Feast & Bretag, 2005, pp. 72–73)

In one narrative review, 14 manuscripts were identified on resilience in higher education during pandemics, and nine of these were published in 2020 contrasted to two on SARs, and one on H1N1 (de los Reyes et al., 2022). In the Australian context, the ratio is perhaps similar, with primary research on educational responses to pandemics and epidemics largely limited to COVID-19. It is perhaps clear that elements of the Riggio and Newstead (2023) model are applied in various forms in this context. The first capability discussed in the iterative model is sensemaking, and in this case, universities were quite separate in their approaches to sensemaking and decision-making initially. As chronicled in Crawford et al. (2023), Australian university responses included rapid cleaning practices after first cases, and for many of the older and higher ranked universities conservative and slower responses. Smaller and more regional universities seemed to opt towards rapid online delivery, commonly termed 'emergency remote teaching', and others actioned decisions of physical distancing in classrooms. In later extensions, Crawford (2023) argued there were three common initial decisions made including (a) digitalisation, (b) delayed commencements, and (c) responding to government mandate minimums only. These practices followed varied applications of the pace of sensemaking institutions were able to engage with, and for many it seems the pandemic was perceived as the same level of risk as the earlier SARS outbreak. Those institutions whose efforts were radical and whose decisions were quick tended to receive better 2020 student experience survey scores than those who acted with legal minimums first (QILT, 2020). The communication efforts were widespread, and used scaled media from senior university managers to students and staff. In the university sector, it seemed regular email distributions and online webpages were the most common. Despite evidence students have poor email access habits, during the pandemic periods it seemed much more effective.

The coordination of resources for universities is likely to be the subject of examination in contemporary literature. Universities spoke of likely financial collapse (Marshman & Larkins, 2020), but in recent years, profits of universities and significant redundancy practices tell a different story (Andrew, 2020; Cassidy, 2023; Hare, 2022c), with some universities posting operational surpluses and revenue at record levels. Perhaps an area for greater critique however was sector-wide teamwork and learning practices. Researchers and educators across Australia were consistently testing and revising assumptions of effective learning and continuity of learning. Yet, these were disparate and largely shared at the institutional level rather than from national perspectives. This led to organisations whose structures were poorly set up for online and digital education with staff forced by circumstance to engage in new forms of work without time for training or deep support (e.g., online pedagogy). As Cowling et al. (2022) and others began to distinguish, there was an important and missing step between digitisation (replication of face-to-face content online) and digital pedagogy (designing learning for an online delivery and student cohort). Despite the sheer volume of literature on COVID-19 education in the Australian context, it was not clear whether these were used to drive decision-making or facilitate learning in universities. To make this point clear, a simple search of Web of Science (on 24 May 2023) at the abstract level with keywords 'COVID-19' AND 'higher education' AND 'Australia' yielded 62 results, Google Scholar yields 59,400 results (at the full-text level).

By Riggio and Newstead's (2023) definition, a crisis must be low probability, public, high consequence, force rapid action, temporal, morally and ethically laden, have novelty and ambiguity, and be emotionally laden. Yet, in the case of pandemics there is likely a natural expectation that these will perhaps occur again, and while the consequences of future pandemics are likely to be more known and organisations now produce pandemic response plans, there is still much to be learned about how Australian universities handled the pandemic, and indeed should respond and plan for future pandemics. Decisions of leadership development for crisis and pre-emptive resilience-building are perhaps critical outcomes from the COVID-19 pandemic, and should have been outcomes of previous pandemics.

## Authentication and Integrity Crisis

Into a world already rocked by the massification crisis, and the crisis caused by the COVID-19 pandemic and the shift to online teaching, in late 2022 another crisis loomed, the rise of tools that leveraged Large Language Modelling (LLM) to produce generated text from a large corpus of collected Internet data. Led by the OpenAI tool ChatGPT becoming available to use in November 2022, these tools—collectively christened Generative artificial intelligence (AI), and including not only text generation but also video and image generation variants—exploded in early 2023, with a slate of opinion pieces (Colbran et al., 2023), panel discussions, and dedicated conferences (e.g., Informa Connect, 2023) cropping up quickly to discuss how these products might change education.

In line with the model proposed by Riggio and Newstead (2023), this process very much represents the first stage of sensemaking they identify, with educators around the world trying to determine how this tool might be used in education. And while there was much discussion on how the tool might be used to enhance both the student and teacher experience, there was also clearly concern about the impact that these new Generative AI tools might have on the (so-called) traditional education experience. In particular, one thread of narrative focused very much on authentication, and how to ensure that students didn't use this tool to write their assignments for them.

Authentication as a concern in higher education is not a new concept, and in fact as far back as 2015 in Australia, projects such as the Transforming Exams (2019) project funded by the Australian National Office of Learning & Teaching looked at how we could provide a more authentic assessment model to students while still ensuring that these students were completing their own work. More recently, the rise of plagiarism checking software such as TurnItIn as well as the prevalence of concern about contract cheating (Dawson et al., 2020) and the response to it (Awdry et al., 2022) have shown that the academy is still concerned about this.

But Generative AI caused this concern to amplify significantly. Providing very low barriers of entry to students to use the tool, educators became quickly concerned that students would generate their assignments rather than writing them themselves, with some circles calling for a return to high-stakes invigilated assessment, either written (as a closed book exam) or oral (as a viva) as a way to ensure authentication of students. Others discussed mechanisms to 'ChatGPT-proof' assessment, asking students to include real-world examples, engage in higher order thinking, or simply include things that ChatGPT is not (yet) good at such as diagrams, with little regard for the appropriateness of this learning design.

The solution to this concern appears to be to reconsider the process of learning design in line with this new change. And this is where the industry appears to be heading, in line with Riggio and Newstead (2023)'s second and third stages related to 'decision-making, and coordinating teamwork'. A prime example of this is the work of Brooker et al. (2018) in the MOOC context, but there is also early work in other venues considering how teachers and AI can work together for student advantage (Koh et al., 2021). While mapping to the crisis framework is promising for this crisis, it remains to be seen whether teamwork, learning, and communication will follow, and what form these will take, in line with the work in the chapter on artificial intelligence as crisis in this book (see Chapter 8).

## Belonging Crisis

Loneliness, a subjective sensation that arises from the disparity between desired and actual social relationships, is a global concern, particularly among students (Cacioppo et al., 2015). Despite the digital era opening new avenues for communication and connection, loneliness remains a substantial issue (Bu et al., 2020; Surkalim et al., 2022; Weissbourd et al., 2021). This issue is particularly pronounced among students in higher education institutions, especially since the advent of COVID-19, which necessitated physical distancing measures and precipitated a shift towards online learning (Dingle et al., 2022; Hopp et al., 2022; Weber et al., 2022). Prior to the pandemic, numerous studies had already identified loneliness as a prevalent issue among university students (Diehl et al., 2018; Hysing et al., 2020; Özdemir & Tuncay, 2008). Factors contributing to these feelings can include transitioning to a new environment, being away from family and friends, academic pressures, and financial stress (Zahedi et al., 2022). The pandemic amplified feelings of loneliness for many students as traditional social activities and face-to-face interactions were curtailed (Besser et al., 2022; Werner et al., 2021 ). Students often found themselves studying from home or confined to their rooms with limited opportunities for social interaction (Geary et al., 2023; Son et al., 2020).

Loneliness can coincide with a lack of belonging—an individual's innate desire for interpersonal connections, association with social entities such as the university community, and the sense of inclusion, acceptance, and value within a particular setting or group (Allen, 2020; Arslan, 2021; Baumeister & Leary, 1995; Hagerty & Williams, 1999). Extensive research suggests that the COVID-19 pandemic has adversely impacted the sense of belonging among university students (Lederer et al., 2021; Tice et al., 2021; Xie et al., 2020). The pandemic led to sudden changes in the learning environment, with many institutions transitioning to remote or hybrid learning models (Xie et al., 2020). This shift reduced face-to-face interaction, restricted access to campus resources, and disrupted community events and social activities, all of which are crucial contributors to a sense of belonging (Lederer et al., 2021; Reuter et al., 2021).

The high prevalence of loneliness and the diminished sense of belonging among students in higher education indicate that expectations around human connection and the need for relationships with others lie at the core of the issue. Despite being surrounded by peers and having multiple channels of communication, students are seeking a deeper sense of belonging (Potts, 2021; Tice et al., 2021). University leaders must therefore strive to create environments that facilitate these meaningful relationships and cultivate a sense of belonging. Allen and Furlong (2021) emphasised the importance of leveraging this sense of belonging as a response to loneliness, particularly in the context of global loneliness, a pressing social issue. Additionally, as Lim et al. (2021) have noted, belonging and loneliness are likely two complex and intertwined constructs. Low belonging and increased loneliness in student populations are a critical issue for university leaders.

In parallel, mental health concerns among students have seen a surge, with several sources reporting that 1 in 4 students experience mental health problems (Browne et al., 2017; Ochnik et al., 2021; Sheldon et al., 2021). This complex issue is shaped by a multitude of factors, including societal pressures, academic expectations, and personal circumstances. Alarmingly, suicide has become the second leading cause of death in young adults, highlighting the gravity of mental health issues in this demographic (Centers for Disease Control and Prevention [CDC], 2023).

In addition, students and academics alike are reporting unprecedented levels of stress. The pressures of academic life, coupled with the uncertainty following the COVID-19 pandemic, have created what has been referred to as a mental health crisis (Salimi et al., 2023; Wathelet et al., 2020). Issues such as food and financial insecurity further compound these challenges, making it difficult for students to focus solely on their academic pursuits (Owens et al., 2020; Weaver et al., 2020). The demand for psychological help among students has increased at such a dramatic rate that the available mental health services and resources are struggling to meet the demand (Salimi et al., 2023).

Higher education leaders have a pivotal role to play in this context. By promoting positive mental health practices, providing supportive resources, and addressing pressing issues such as food and financial insecurity, they can create an environment that not only fosters academic success but also supports the overall wellbeing of students. It is a task that requires a concerted effort and a recognition of the complex interplay of factors affecting student mental health. The widely established compelling links between a sense of belonging and mental health (Arslan et al., 2020; Dingle et al., 2022; Gopalan et al., 2022) underscores its importance as a critical focus area for university leaders.

Despite various initiatives, many universities continue to grapple with the challenge of fostering a sense of belonging among their students (Meehan & Howells, 2019). This is not for lack of trying, but rather due to a notable lack of interventions and resources specifically designed to nurture a sense of belonging in the higher education context (Thomas, 2012). Unfortunately, the interventions currently available for fostering belonging in universities seem to be disproportionately fewer than those offered for younger age groups. Yet the compelling evidence emerging from mental health statistics indicates that the need for such interventions in higher education is just as crucial, if not more so (Lipson et al., 2022).

While means of building belonging do exist in higher education (e.g., Walton et al., 2023; Van Herpen et al., 2020) the scale of the issue calls for a more comprehensive and proactive approach. Higher education leaders must recognise and address this significant gap, using evidence-based strategies to foster a stronger sense of community and connection among students. The works of Wu et al. (2021) and Riggio and Newstead (2023) provide a useful framework for understanding the ongoing concerns surrounding threats to belonging and loneliness in higher education, underlining the critical need for responsive measures. Drawing from crisis leadership theories and methodologies could be instrumental in this context. By viewing the belonging crisis as a significant and pressing issue, leaders can use the strategies and insights from crisis leadership research to inform their approaches, ultimately creating more supportive university environments where students can thrive and feel a sense of belonging.

## Economic Crisis

While not a critical contribution from this chapter, it would be remiss of the authors to not highlight a critical crisis contributor in the Australian context. Andrew (2020) writes of the ruined and the toxic university narrative in contemporary literature, and its explicit nature in Australian and New Zealand higher education. These perhaps representative in part of crisis responses (e.g., see section on pandemics and epidemics), are also a response to an unstable economic environment for Australian universities. An examination of 89 government budget decisions was used by Universities Australia (2017) to argue that Australian universities have covered 3.9 billion AUD of budget recovery between 2011 and 2017, despite a 29 per cent increase in student places between 2009 and 2015. The economic landscape in Australia, like many other nations has seen growth in government debt, although this is currently at around 40 per cent of GDP, a figure lower than the United States, France, and Canada among others (IMF, 2022). In parallel, there is growing evidence of community sentiment that university quality of education is declining related to funding (The Age, 2003; Tomazin, 2008), including the flow-on effect for teacher education (Sakkal, 2023; Tudge, 2021). Andrew and Oonagh (Chapter 22), in this book, speak more to this in the New Zealand context, and Waring (Chapter 10) on this in the Australian context. This is an important component likely affecting the way the crisis is appearing in the Australian higher education system worthy of further research.

# The Australian Crisis Leader?

It appears that despite the prevalence and complexity of crisis in Australian higher education, leaders are poorly prepared to respond. Among our review, we identified limited evidence pertaining to proactive responses for crisis. This included most crisis activity being addressed on a case-by-case basis, with a response driven by an external force pressuring decision-making. Indeed, there have been many other influencers driving crisis response and requiring crisis leadership that were not discussed in this chapter.

One example of an initially proactive response was into sexual assault and harassment on campus, following the Hunting Ground documentary in the

U.S., with an Australian Human Rights Commission survey (2017) finding 51 per cent of students experienced sexual harassment, and 6.9 per cent experienced sexual assault at least once in 2015–2016. In a following review (SRC, 2021), these numbers were much lower for sexual assault or harassment 'since commencing at university', although these surveys may not be comparable. What is evident is that despite initiating of a crisis in 2016, students report not respecting the academic processes for resolution. In 2021, after reporting sexual assault only 29.7 per cent were satisfied with the process, and 41.3 per cent for sexual harassment reporting. This satisfaction perhaps signals more effort is needed, given reporting rates declined from 13 per cent to 5.6 per cent for sexual assault. The proactivity does not seem to have yet resolved this problem, with crisis activity continuing.

Indeed, there is perhaps a need for more effective crisis leadership and general forms of adaptive leadership needed among university executives to better prepare them for an environment where crisis is likely to be the 'new normal'. The Riggio and Newstead (2023) model may provide a useful foundation alongside styles of leadership well suited to rapid decision-making. It is also perhaps evident that the underlying administration and bureaucracy of universities have failed to build agility to support rapid adaption where required. In this case, the eternal Australian challenge of appointments based on front-line competency rather than management or leadership capability has perhaps produced administrators poorly equipped to deal with crises in ways equivalent to well-trained managers and leaders. To illustrate, of the eight Vice Chancellors in the Group of Eight (most prestigious universities), seven of eight were promoted into university leadership following academic careers, with at least three still research active. While not necessarily an issue that they are academics, it was difficult to identify formal management or leadership qualifications for these individuals responsible for organisations with multi-billion-dollar asset bases and thousands of staff. This perhaps serves as an important starting point for contemporary higher education resilience-building.

Equally as notable is the opportunity to examine organisational leader capability in key areas such as empathy, emotional intelligence, and ethical decision-making. While these may not always form components of management curriculum, they seem closely aligned to the crisis leadership model discussed. This may be particularly important in current times, with rapid changes to staff and student profiling, volume, and expectations on the post-pandemic curve. This may be developed progressively, but also may include opportunities for drills and simulations in similar ways that medical students or military soldiers are taught to prepare for medical emergencies or wartime, respectively. Existing emergency management preparation training and development may also have some answers to developmental questions in this area (e.g., Waugh Jr & Streib, 2006).

## Conclusion

In this chapter, we discussed a series of key crises that have taken shape in contemporary higher education. Whether the common crisis of the day—the COVID-19 pandemic—or others less obvious from loneliness, artificial intelligence insurgence, or sexual assault on campus these require sustained leadership in response. From the brief review of a few of these key crises against a model of crisis leadership, we saw a need for more cohesive development, planning, and organisational design supportive of adaptability and sustainability of institutions and people within. While perhaps a negative assessment of higher education, we approached this research from a perspective of facilitating learning, a key end-state to approach in crisis leadership. Each of these crises had useful opportunities for the sector to grow and build a more sustainable, healthy, and flourishing climate for students, staff, and community stakeholders. And Australia can perhaps continue to lead a global response to the rollercoaster of higher education crises.

## References

Australian Universities Accord. (2024). Final Report. Canberra, Australia: Australian Government. Viewed 23 February 2024. https://www.education.gov.au/australian-universitiesaccord

Andrew, M. (2020). Behind voluntary redundancy in universities: The stories behind the story. *Australian Universities Review, 62*(2), 14–24.

Allen, K. A., & Furlong, M. (2021). Leveraging belonging in response to global loneliness special issue: Belonging and loneliness. *Australian Journal of Psychology, 73*(1), 1–3. https://doi.org/10.1080/00049530.2021.1875532

Allen, K. A. (2020). Commentary: A pilot digital intervention targeting loneliness in youth mental health. *Frontiers in Psychiatry, 10*, Article 959. https://doi.org/10.3389/fpsyt.2019.00959

Arslan, G. (2021). Loneliness, college belongingness, subjective vitality, and psychological adjustment during coronavirus pandemic: Development of the College Belongingness Questionnaire. *Journal of Positive School Psychology, 5*(1), 17–31. https://doi.org/10.31234/osf.io/j7tf2

Arslan, G., Allen, K. A., & Ryan, T. (2020). Exploring the impacts of school belonging on youth wellbeing and mental health among Turkish adolescents.

*Child Indicators Research, 13*(5), 1619–1635. https://doi.org/10.1007/s12187-020-09721-z

Awdry, R., Dawson, P., & Sutherland-Smith, W. (2022). Contract cheating: To legislate or not to legislate-is that the question? *Assessment & Evaluation in Higher Education, 47*(5), 712–726.

Baumeister, R. F., & Leary, M. R. (1995). The need to belong: Desire for interpersonal attachments as a fundamental human motivation. *Psychological Bulletin, 117*(3), 497–529. https://doi.org/10.1037/0033-2909.117.3.497

Besser, A., Flett, G. L., & Zeigler-Hill, V. (2022). Adaptability to a sudden transition to online learning during the COVID-19 pandemic: Understanding the challenges for students. *Scholarship of Teaching and Learning in Psychology, 8*(2), 85–105. https://doi.org/10.1037/stl0000198

Brooker, A., Corrin, L., De Barba, P., Lodge, J., & Kennedy, G. (2018). A tale of two MOOCs: How student motivation and participation predict learning outcomes in different MOOCs. *Australasian Journal of Educational Technology, 34*(1).

Browne, V., Munro, J., & Cass, J. (2017). The mental health of Australian university students. *Journal of the Australian & New Zealand Student Services Association, 25*(2), 51–62.

Bu, F., Steptoe, A., & Fancourt, D. (2020). Who is lonely in lockdown? Cross-cohort analyses of predictors of loneliness before and during the COVID-19 pandemic. *Public Health, 186*, 31–34. https://doi.org/10.1016/j.puhe.2020.06.036

Cacioppo, S., Grippo, A. J., London, S., Goossens, L., & Cacioppo, J. T. (2015). Loneliness: Clinical import and interventions. *Perspectives on Psychological Science, 10*(2), 238–249.

Cassidy, C. (2023, March 3). Australian university sector makes record $5.3bn surplus while cutting costs for Covid. *The Guardian.*

Centers for Disease Control and Prevention. (2023). *Facts about suicide.* https://www.cdc.gov/suicide/facts/index.html

Cherastidtham, I., & Norton, A. (2018*). University attrition: What helps and hinders university completion* (Grattan Institute Background Paper No. 2018-08).

Colbran, S., Beer, C., & Cowling, M. (2023, January 29). The ChatGPT challenge: Regulate or liberate. ChatGPT can enhance learning when combined with critical thinking and more authentic holistic assessment. *Campus Morning Mail*. https://campusmorningmail.com.au/news/the-chatgpt-challenge-regulate-or-liberate/

Cowling, M. A., Crawford, J., Vallis, C., Middleton, R., & Sim, K. N. (2022). The EdTech difference: Digitalisation, digital pedagogy, and technology enhanced learning. *Journal of University Teaching & Learning Practice, 19*(2), 1–13.

Crawford, J. (2023). COVID-19 and higher education: A pandemic response model from rapid adaptation to consolidation and restoration. *International Education Journal: Comparative Perspectives.* Ahead of Print.

Crawford, J., Butler-Henderson, K., Rudolph, J., Malkawi, B., Glowatz, M., Burton, R., ... & Lam, S. (2020). COVID-19: 20 countries' higher education intra-period digital pedagogy responses. *Journal of applied learning & teaching, 3*(1), 1–20.

Crawford, J., Cowling, M., & Allen, K. A. (2023). Leadership is needed for ethical ChatGPT: Character, assessment, and learning using artificial intelligence (AI). *Journal of University Teaching & Learning Practice, 20*(3), 02. https://doi.org/10.53761/1.20.3.02

Dawson, P., Sutherland-Smith, W., & Ricksen, M. (2020). Can software improve marker accuracy at detecting contract cheating? A pilot study of the Turnitin authorship investigate alpha. *Assessment & Evaluation in Higher Education, 45*(4), 473–482.

de los Reyes, E. J., Blannin, J., Cohrssen, C., & Mahat, M. (2022). Resilience of higher education academics in the time of 21st century pandemics: A narrative review. *Journal of Higher Education Policy and Management, 44*(1), 39–56.

Diehl, K., Jansen, C., Ishchanova, K., & Hilger-Kolb, J. (2018). Loneliness at universities: Determinants of emotional and social loneliness among students. *International Journal of Environmental Research and Public Health, 15*(9), Article 1865. https://doi.org/10.3390/ijerph15091865

Dingle, G. A., Han, R., & Carlyle, M. (2022). Loneliness, belonging, and mental health in Australian university students pre-and post-COVID-19. *Behaviour Change, 39*(3), 146–156. https://doi.org/10.1017/bec.2022.6

Fortunato, J., Gigliotti, R., & Ruben, B. (2018). Analysing the dynamics of crisis leadership in higher education: A study of racial incidents at the University of Missouri. *Journal of Contingencies and Crisis Management, 26*(4), 510–518.

Eri, R., Gudimetla, P., Star, S., Rowlands, J., Girgla, A., To, L., Li, F., Sochea, N., & Bindal, U. (2021). Digital resilience in higher education in response to COVID-19 pandemic: Student perceptions from Asia and Australia. *Journal of University Teaching and Learning Practice, 18*(5), 7.

Feast, V., & Bretag, T. (2005). Responding to crises in transnational education: New challenges for higher education. *Higher Education Research & Development, 24*(1), 63–78.

Foster, G. (2015). The slide of academic standards in Australia: A cautionary tale. *The Conversation*. https://theconversation.com/the-slide-of-academic-standards-in-australia-a-cautionary-tale-40464

Geary, E., Allen, K. A., Gamble, N., & Pahlevansharif, S. (2023). Online learning during the COVID-19 pandemic: Does social connectedness and learning community predict self-determined needs and course satisfaction? *Journal of University Teaching & Learning Practice, 20*(1). https://ro.uow.edu.au/jutlp/vol20/iss1/13

Gopalan, M., Linden-Carmichael, A., & Lanza, S. (2022). College students' sense of belonging and mental health amidst the COVID-19 pandemic. *Journal of Adolescent Health, 70*(2), 228–233. https://doi.org/10.1016/j.jadohealth.2021.10.010

Hagerty, B. M., & Williams, A. (1999). The effects of sense of belonging, social support, conflict, and loneliness on depression. *Nursing Research, 48*(4), 215–219. https://doi.org/10.1097/00006199-199907000-00004

Hare, J. (2022a, September 14). Gonski's 319b reforms fail to improve school performance: PC. *Australian Financial Review.* https://www.afr.com/work-and-careers/education/gonski-school-reforms-given-poor-report-card-20220913-p5bhn8

Hare, J. (2022b, September 30). Why Australia's students keep falling behind. *Australian Financial Review.* https://www.afr.com/work-and-careers/education/why-australia-s-students-keep-falling-behind-20220928-p5blna

Hare, J. (2022c, February 13). Pandemic-hit units cut up to 27,000 jobs in a year. *Australian Financial Review.* https://www.afr.com/work-and-careers/education/university-jobs-slashed-as-pandemic-forces-students-away-20220211-p59vqn

Hopp, M. D., Händel, M., Bedenlier, S., Glaeser-Zikuda, M., Kammerl, R., Kopp, B., & Ziegler, A. (2022). The structure of social networks and its link to higher education students' socio-emotional loneliness during COVID-19. *Frontiers in Psychology, 12,* Article 733867. https://doi.org/10.3389/fpsyg.2021.733867

Hysing, M., Petrie, K. J., Bøe, T., Lønning, K. J., & Sivertsen, B. (2020). Only the lonely: A study of loneliness among university students in Norway. *Clinical Psychology in Europe, 2*(1), 1–16. https://doi.org/10.32872/cpe.v2i1.2781

Informa Connect. (2023, May 24). *Artificial intelligence in Education Conference.* https://www.informa.com.au/event/conference/education/artificial-intelligence-in-education-conference/

International Monetary Fund [IMF]. (2022). *Helping people bounce back.* International Monetary Fund. https://www.imf.org/en/Publications/FM/Issues/2022/10/09/fiscal-monitor-october-22

Joseph, R. (2023). *ATAR's rising relevance: Admission standards and completion rates.* The Centre for Independent Studies.

Knights, D., & McCabe, D. (2015). 'Masters of the Universe': Demystifying leadership in the context of the 2008 global financial crisis. *British Journal of Management, 26*(2), 197–210.

Lederer, A. M., Hoban, M. T., Lipson, S. K., Zhou, S., & Eisenberg, D. (2021). More than inconvenienced: The unique needs of US college students during the COVID-19 pandemic. *Health Education & Behavior, 48*(1), 14–19. https://doi.org/10.1177/1090198120969372

Lim, M. H., Allen, K. A., Furlong, M. J., Craig, H., & Smith, D. C. (2021). Introducing a dual continuum model of belonging and loneliness. *Australian Journal of Psychology, 73*(1), 81–86. https://doi.org/10.1080/00049530.2021.1883411

Lipson, S. K., Zhou, S., Abelson, S., Heinze, J., Jirsa, M., Morigney, J., Patterson, A., Sing, M., & Eisenberg, D. (2022). Trends in college student mental health and help-seeking by race/ethnicity: Findings from the national healthy minds study, 2013–2021. *Journal of Affective Disorders, 306*, 138–147. https://doi.org/10.1016/j.jad.2022.03.038

Liu, H. (2015). Constructing the GFC: Australian banking leaders during the financial 'crisis.' *Leadership, 11*(4), 424–450.

Liu, H., Cutcher, L., & Grant, D. (2015). Doing authenticity: The gendered construction of authentic leadership. *Gender, Work & Organization, 22*(3), 237–255.

Liu, H., Cutcher, L., & Grant, D. (2017). Authentic leadership in context: An analysis of banking CEO narratives during the global financial crisis. *Human Relations, 70*(6), 694–724.

Kelly, A., Sullivan, M., & Strampel, K. (2023). Generative artificial intelligence: University student awareness, experience, and confidence in use across disciplines. *Journal of University Teaching & Learning Practice, 20*(6). https://doi.org/10.53761/1.20.6.12

Koh, J., Cowling, M., Jha, M., & Sim, K. N. (2021). *A proposal to measure the impact of automated response systems on meeting student learning outcomes* (pp. 149–154). ASCILITE Publications.

Marshman, I., & Larkins, F. (2020). *Modelling individual Australian universities resilience in managing overseas student revenue losses from the COVID-19 pandemic.* University of Melbourne.

Martin, L. (2020). *Foundations for good practice: The student experience of online learning in Australian Higher Education during the COVID-19 Pandemic.* Australian Government Tertiary Education Quality and Standards Agency.

Meehan, C., & Howells, K. (2019). In search of the feeling of 'belonging'in higher education: Undergraduate students transition into higher education. *Journal of Further and Higher Education, 43*(10), 1376–1390.

Norton, A. (2013). *Keep the caps off! Student access and choice in higher education.* Grattan Institute.

Owens, M. R., Brito-Silva, F., Kirkland, T., Moore, C. E., Davis, K. E., Patterson, M. A., Miketinas, D. C., & Tucker, W. J. (2020). Prevalence and social determinants of food insecurity among college students during the COVID-19 pandemic. *Nutrients, 12*(9), Article 2515. https://doi.org/10.3390/nu12092515

Özdemir, U., & Tuncay, T. (2008). Correlates of loneliness among university students. *Child and Adolescent Psychiatry and Mental Health, 2*, Article 29. https://doi.org/10.1186/1753-2000-2-29

Ochnik, D., Rogowska, A. M., Kuśnierz, C., Jakubiak, M., Schütz, A., Held, M. J., Arzenšek, A., Benatov, J., Berger, R., Korchagina, E. V., Pavlova, I., Blažková, I., Aslan, I., Çınar, O., & Cuero-Acosta, Y. A., & Cuero-Acosta, Y. A. (2021). Mental health prevalence and predictors among university students in nine countries during the COVID-19 pandemic: A cross-national study. *Scientific Reports, 11*(1), Article 18644. https://doi.org/10.1038/s41598-021-97697-3

Passow, A. (1953). A conception of educational leadership. *Teachers College Record, 54*(6), 1–7.

Perkins, M. (2023). Academic Integrity considerations of AI Large Language Models in the post-pandemic era: ChatGPT and beyond. *Journal of University Teaching & Learning Practice, 20*(2). https://doi.org/10.53761/1.20.02.07

Potts, C. (2021). Seen and unseen: First-year college students' sense of belonging during the COVID-19 pandemic. *College Student Affairs Journal, 39*(2), 214–224. https://doi.org/10.1353/csj.2021.0018

Reuter, P. R., Forster, B. L., & Kruger, B. J. (2021). A longitudinal study of the impact of COVID-19 restrictions on students' health behavior, mental health and emotional well-being. *Peer J, 9,* Article e12528. https://doi.org/10.7717/peerj.12528

Ryan, M. K., Haslam, S. A., Morgenroth, T., Rink, F., Stoker, J., & Peters, K. (2016). Getting on top of the glass cliff: Reviewing a decade of evidence, explanations, and impact. *The Leadership Quarterly, 27*(3), 446–455.

QILT. (2020). 2020 SES national report. *QILT.*

Sakkal, P. (2023, January 20). Call for focus on teaching as academic results slide despite $300b school funding deal. *The Sydney Morning Herald.* https://www.smh.com.au/education/call-for-focus-on-teaching-as-academic-results-slide-despite-300b-school-funding-deal-20230119-p5cdwu.html

Salimi, N., Gere, B., Talley, W., & Irioogbe, B. (2023). College students mental health challenges: Concerns and considerations in the COVID-19 pandemic. *Journal of College Student Psychotherapy, 37*(1), 39–51. https://doi.org/10.1080/87568225.2021.1890298

Scimago. (2023). Scimago journal and country rank. *Scimago.* https://www.scimagojr.com/countryrank.php?order=ci&ord=desc&year=2013. Accessed 1 May 2023.

Sheldon, E., Simmonds-Buckley, M., Bone, C., Mascarenhas, T., Chan, N., Wincott, M., ... & Barkham, M. (2021). Prevalence and risk factors for mental health problems in university undergraduate students: A systematic review with meta-analysis. *Journal of affective disorders, 287*, 282–292.

Social Research Centre [SRC]. (2021). *2021 national student safety report*. Social Research Centre.

Son, C., Hegde, S., Smith, A., Wang, X., & Sasangohar, F. (2020). Effects of COVID-19 on college students' mental health in the United States: Interview survey study. *Journal of Medical Internet Research, 22*(9), Article e21279. https://preprints.jmir.org/preprint/21279

Statista. (2023). Share of population who hold a bachelor level degree or above in Australia from 1989 to 2022. *Statista.* https://www.statista.com/statistics/612854/australia-population-with-university-degree/#:~:text=Over%20the%20past%2020%20years,both%20public%20and%20private%20institutions. Accessed 1 May 2023.

Surkalim, D. L., Luo, M., Eres, R., Gebel, K., van Buskirk, J., Bauman, A., & Ding, D. (2022). The prevalence of loneliness across 113 countries: Systematic review and meta-analysis. *BMJ, 376,* Article e067068. https://doi.org/10.1136/bmj-2021-067068

The Age. (2003, January 12). Uni standards falling: Report. *The Age*. https://www.theage.com.au/national/uni-standards-falling-report-20030112-gdv1xe.html

Thomas, L. (2012). Building student engagement and belonging in Higher Education at a time of change. *Paul Hamlyn Foundation, 100*(1–99).

Tice, D., Baumeister, R., Crawford, J., Allen, K. A., & Percy, A. (2021). Student belongingness in higher education: Lessons for Professors from the COVID-19 pandemic. *Journal of University Teaching & Learning Practice, 18*(4), Article 2. https://doi.org/10.53761/1.18.4.2

Times Higher Education (2022). *Impact rankings 2022.* Times Higher Education. https://www.timeshighereducation.com/impactrankings#!/length/25/locations/AUS/sort_by/rank/sort_order/asc/cols/undefined. Accessed 1 May 2023.

Tomazin, F. (2008, November 20). University standards on the decline, admit teachers. *The Sydney Morning Herald*. https://www.smh.com.au/national/university-standards-on-the-decline-admit-teachers-20081119-6bm1.html

Transforming Exams. (2019). *Transforming exams: A scalable examination platform for BYOD invigilated assessment.* http://www.transformingexams.com/guides.html

Trow, M. (2007). Reflections on the transition from elite to mass to universal access: Forms and phases of higher education in modern societies since WWII. In J. Forest & P. Altbach (Eds.), *International handbook of higher education* (pp. 243–280). Springer.

Tudge, A. (2021, June 22). To reverse decline in school standards, focus on teacher training. *Ministerial Opinion Editorial*. https://ministers.dese.gov.au/tudge/reverse-decline-school-standards-focus-teacher-training

Tyler, R. (1956). The rise and fall of an American radicalism: The I. W. W. *The Historian, 19*(1), 48–65.

Universities Australia. (2017, April). The facts on university funding. *Universities Australia.* https://www.universitiesaustralia.edu.au/wp-content/uploads/2019/05/University-Financing-Explainer-April-2017.pdf

Riggio, R. E., & Newstead, T. (2023). Crisis leadership. *Annual Review of Organizational Psychology and Organizational Behavior, 10*(1), 201–224.

Van Herpen, S. G., Meeuwisse, M., Hofman, W. A., & Severiens, S. E. (2020). A head start in higher education: The effect of a transition intervention on interaction, sense of belonging, and academic performance. *Studies in Higher Education, 45*(4), 862–877. https://doi.org/10.1080/03075079.2019.1572088

Walton, G. M., Murphy, M. C., Logel, C., Yeager, D. S., Goyer, J. P., Brady, S. T., Emerson, K. T. U., Paunesku, D., Fotuhi, O., Blodorn, A., Boucher, K., Carter, E., Gopalan, M., Henderson, A., Kroeper, K. M., Murdock-Perriera, L. A., Reeves, S., Ablorh, T. T., Ansari, S. … & Krol, N. (2023). Where and with whom does a brief social-belonging intervention promote progress in college? *Science, 380*(6644), 499–505.https://doi.org/10.1126/science.ade4420

Wathelet, M., Duhem, S., Vaiva, G., Baubet, T., Habran, E., Veerapa, E., Debien, C., Molenda, S., Horn, M., Grandgenèvre, P., Notredame, C.-E., & D'Hondt, F. (2020). Factors associated with mental health disorders among university students in France confined during the COVID-19 pandemic. *JAMA Network Open, 3*(10), e2025591. https://doi.org/10.1001/jamanetworkopen.2022.49342

Waugh, W., Jr., & Streib, G. (2006). Collaboration and leadership for effective emergency management. *Public Administration Review, 66*, 131–140.

Weaver, R. R., Vaughn, N. A., Hendricks, S. P., McPherson-Myers, P. E., Jia, Q., Willis, S. L., & Rescigno, K. P. (2020). University student food insecurity and academic performance. *Journal of American College Health, 68*(7), 727–733. https://doi.org/10.1080/07448481.2019.1600522

Weber, M., Schulze, L., Bolzenkötter, T., Niemeyer, H., & Renneberg, B. (2022). Mental health and loneliness in university students during the COVID-19 pandemic in Germany: A longitudinal study. *Frontiers in Psychiatry, 13*, Article 848645. https://doi.org/10.3389/fpsyt.2022.848645

Weissbourd, R., Batanova, M., Lovison, V., & Torres, E. (2021, February). *Loneliness in America: How the pandemic has deepened an epidemic of loneliness and what we can do about it.* Making Caring Common Project. https://mcc.gse.harvard.edu/reports/loneliness-in-america

Werner, A. M., Tibubos, A. N., Mülder, L. M., Reichel, J. L., Schäfer, M., Heller, S., Pfrrmann, D., Edelmann, D., Dietz, P., Rigotti, T., & Beutel, M. E. (2021). The impact of lockdown stress and loneliness during the COVID-19 pandemic on mental health among university students in Germany. *Scientific Reports, 11*(1), Article 22637. https://doi.org/10.1038/s41598-021-02024-5

Woolridge, A. (2023, April 18). America's educational superpower is fading. *Bloomberg.* https://www.bloomberg.com/opinion/articles/2023-04-18/higher-education-in-the-us-faces-a-systemic-crisis

Worldometer. (2023). Countries in the world by population (2023). *Worldometer.* https://www.worldometers.info/world-population/population-by-country/. Accessed 1 May 2023.

World Bank. (2023). *GDP (current US$).* World Bank Group. https://data.worldbank.org/indicator/Ny.Gdp.Mktp.Cd?most_recent_value_desc=true. Accessed 1 May 2023.

Wilson, S., & Newstead, T. (2022). The virtues of effective crisis leadership: What managers can learn from how women heads of state led in the first wave of COVID-19. *Organizational Dynamics, 51*(2), 100910.

Wu, Y. L., Shao, B., Newman, A., & Schwarz, G. (2021). Crisis leadership: A review and future research agenda. *The Leadership Quarterly, 32*(6), 101518.

Xie, X., Siau, K., & Nah, F. F. H. (2020). COVID-19 pandemic–online education in the new normal and the next normal. *Journal of Information Technology Case and Application Research, 22*(3), 175–187. https://doi.org/10.1080/15228053.2020.1824884

Xu, Y., Carson, E., Fargher, N., & Jiang, L. (2013). Responses by Australian auditors to the global financial crisis. *Accounting & Finance, 53*(1), 301–338.

Zahedi, H., Sahebihagh, M. H., & Sarbakhsh, P. (2022). The magnitude of loneliness and associated risk factors among university students: A cross-sectional study. *Iranian Journal of Psychiatry, 17*(4), 411–417. https://doi.org/10.18502/ijps.v17i4.10690

# Multifaceted Post-Pandemic Pedagogical Challenges and Leadership: The Case of Brazilian Universities

Ailson J. De Moraes and Carlos A. Teixeira

## Introduction

Brazil is considered a country of continental dimensions, with a territorial extension of 8,514,876 square kilometres. Its area corresponds to approximately 1.6% of the entire planet's surface, occupying 5.6% of the Earth's landmass, 20.8% of the total area of the Americas, and 48% of South America. Due to its vast territory, Brazil possesses a wide environmental and climatic diversity, as well as a rich cultural diversity (Fischmann, 2005), and, for the purpose of this chapter, considerable diversity in the field of education as well. Brazil displays climatic, economic, social, and cultural differences among its five regions: North, Northeast, Midwest, Southeast, and South.

The origin of Brazilian cultural formation is primarily linked to indigenous peoples, enslaved African Blacks (during the colonial period), and European immigrants. Italian, Japanese, German, Polish, and Arab immigrants, among others, add to Brazil's cultural diversity. In more recent times, due to global humanitarian crises, Brazil has also been receiving refugees from various countries (De Moraes & Teixeira, 2020). The majority are

A. J. De Moraes (✉)
Royal Holloway, University of London, London, UK
e-mail: A.J.DeMoraes@rhul.ac.uk

C. A. Teixeira
Independent Researcher, São Paulo, Brazil
e-mail: cteixeira@alumni.usp.br





J. Rudolph et al. (eds.), *The Palgrave Handbook of Crisis Leadership in Higher Education*, https://doi.org/10.1007/978-3-031-54509-2_12

Venezuelans (78.5%), Angolans (6.7%), and Haitians (2.7%), among other nationalities (UNHCR, 2019).

## Perspectives on Brazil

In 1969, Lambert published the book "The two Brazils", discussing the modernity of the central-southern and southern regions in contrast to the backwardness and poverty of the Northeast. The book portrays the perception of a Brazil of the central, south-eastern, and southern regions impacted by European immigration, compared to a Brazil, specifically the northeast region, marked predominantly by a population of former African slaves. The focus of the book is to analyse Brazil from the perspective of economic development and the nation's pursuit of becoming a society driven by economic dynamism, contrasting with its colonial past. The book does not address educational issues directly; however, it provides a hint that there are educational differences among Brazil's different regions.

To better understand Brazil, it would be relevant to read four books written by Freyre (1968, 2001, 2002, 2004). These books record significant changes that occurred in the Brazilian economy and politics in the twentieth century. Freyre's earlier books were marked by optimism for a brighter future for Brazilian democracy, resulting from events in the 1930s when the oligarchies were excluded from power and the country was undergoing a phase of modernisation. Freyre (1968) discusses the challenge of unifying the populations of the different Brazilian regions into a single, superior standard, considering the ethnic and cultural pluralism that characterises the nation. These books, like Lambert's (1959) work, also do not specifically address education in Brazil, but they provide insights into understanding the history of education in the country.

## The Context of Brazilian Education in Relation to COVID-19

In terms of the educational context in Brazil, Ribeiro (1968, 1995) presents us with what he considers facets of Brazil resulting from a process of adaptation and differentiation of its people. He portrays a country represented by creole, *caboclo* (Mestizo of mixed white and Brazilian Indian parentage), *sertanejo* (inhabitants of the north-eastern hinterland, the *agreste* or rural areas), *caipira* (referring to the free and poor people of the countryside of the Midwest and Southeast of Brazil), and southern cultures. A single book chapter would not suffice to present the myriad concepts within Ribeiro's thought on *Brasis* where he describes a creole Brazil, a *caboclo* Brazil, a *caipira* Brazil, a *sertanejo* Brazil, and a southern Brazil, each with their own cultural and consequently educational characteristics (Souza & Silva, 2021). To understand Brazilian culture, one must consider the diverse *Brasis* within the country itself, with its people formed from the deculturation of local indigenous inhabitants, enslaved Africans from Africa, and Europeans, each adapting their customs to survive in this new land.

Considering this viewpoint, it is not an easy task to present a consensus on how Brazilian universities dealt with the educational demands posed by the COVID-19 pandemic. Given Brazil's historical context as a vast nation divided into five expansive regions, achieving unanimity is challenging, even in light of the general guidelines laid out by the Ministry of Education through Resolutions and Opinions, which have been available since April 2020. These guidelines can be accessed under the COVID-19 section on the Ministry of Education's Portal (Ministério da Educação [MEC], 2023).

## An Overview of the Context of What Happened in Brazil in Terms of COVID-19

A complex interplay of public health policies, government actions, political controversies, and socioeconomic challenges marked Brazil's response to the COVID-19 pandemic. Initially, the federal government, under the populist leadership of President Jair Bolsonaro, downplayed the severity of the virus and emphasised economic concerns, leading to delayed and conflicting containment measures (Reuters, 2020). The lack of a unified national strategy resulted in varying approaches at the state level, contributing to the rapid spread of the virus, especially in densely populated urban areas (Scientific American, 2021). The health system faced overwhelming pressures, with shortages of hospital beds, medical supplies, and healthcare personnel (CNN, 2021).

Brazil's government also encountered challenges in vaccine procurement and distribution, exposing logistical and infrastructure weaknesses that called for effective leadership (CNN, 2021). The emergence of the highly transmissible P.1 variant added to concerns about vaccine effectiveness and global health (Nature, 2021). Vulnerable communities, including Indigenous populations and residents of informal settlements, were disproportionately affected due to limited access to healthcare and information, necessitating strong leadership (Amnesty International, 2020). The pandemic exacerbated socioeconomic inequalities, leading to increased unemployment, poverty, and food insecurity, highlighting the importance of leadership (BBC News, 2021; Financial Times, 2020). Political tensions emerged as conflicting approaches between the federal government and state governors, scientists, and public health experts led to public protests and controversies, underscoring the need for effective leadership (Council on Foreign Relations, 2021). This multifaceted landscape underscores the intricate challenges Brazil faced in navigating the COVID-19 pandemic.

## Contextualising the COVID-19 Pandemic Within the Brazilian Political Scenario

The COVID-19 pandemic has had a profound impact on Brazil, and understanding this impact requires a contextual analysis within the country's complex political scenario. This analysis sheds light on the governmental responses, challenges faced, and implications for public health. The Brazilian political landscape, under the leadership of then-President Bolsonaro, initially downplayed the severity of the pandemic and prioritised economic concerns over public health (Reuters, 2020). Bolsonaro's scepticism towards containment measures and vaccination strategies led to delayed and conflicting responses, as well as disagreements with state governors, scientists, and public health experts (Council on Foreign Relations, 2021). These divisions contributed to a fragmented approach to pandemic management.

The lack of a unified national strategy resulted in varying approaches at the state level, which further complicated the pandemic response (Scientific American, 2021). The health system faced immense pressures, including shortages of hospital beds, medical supplies, and healthcare personnel (CNN, 2021). The weaknesses in Brazil's healthcare infrastructure were exposed, necessitating significant investments and reforms to meet the demands of the pandemic (Smith, 2021).

The Brazilian government faced challenges in vaccine procurement and distribution, revealing logistical and infrastructure weaknesses (CNN, 2021). The emergence of the highly transmissible P.1 variant added to concerns about vaccine effectiveness and global health (Nature, 2021). Brazil's ability to secure and distribute vaccines was a critical component of pandemic control and required effective political and logistical leadership. Vulnerable communities, including Indigenous populations and residents of informal settlements, were disproportionately affected due to limited access to healthcare and information (Amnesty International, 2020). The pandemic exacerbated existing socioeconomic inequalities, leading to increased unemployment, poverty, and food insecurity, underscoring the critical role of leadership in addressing these disparities and providing support to mitigate the pandemic's impact (BBC News, 2021; Financial Times, 2020). The government's role in addressing these disparities and providing support was crucial in mitigating the pandemic's impact.

Between the declaration of the pandemic in the country and its revocation on May 23, 2021, the Ministry of Health in Brazil witnessed a series of changes in leadership, reflecting the profound challenges in managing the crisis. Notably, the Ministry saw four ministers during this period, with one of them, medical doctor Nelson Teich, serving for just under a month. The first two Ministers of Health, medical doctors Luis Henrique Mandetta and Nelson Teich, left their positions due to disagreements with how President Bolsonaro wanted to handle the pandemic, highlighting the complexities of aligning political and medical perspectives.

The third Minister of Health, military general Eduardo Pazuello, served from May 15, 2020, to March 15, 2021, amid widespread criticism for his subservience to President Bolsonaro and his approach to health policy, particularly in the context of vaccine procurement and delays in negotiations with vaccine manufacturers. During his tenure, a protocol for treating COVID-19 was launched, recommending the use of the drug hydroxychloroquine in alignment with the President's preferences, which ran counter to both Brazilian and global medical-scientific guidelines. This decision underscored the challenge of balancing political directives with scientific expertise and the consequences of such decisions in a public health crisis.

Under the leadership of Marcelo Queiroga, the last of the four ministers to serve during the COVID-19 pandemic, clashes emerged with public health experts, infectious disease specialists, biologists, and other professionals regarding measures adopted by the Ministry of Health, particularly concerning vaccination. Brazil has a broad and respectable tradition of mass immunisation (Benchimol, 2001; Gadelha & Azevedo, 2003; Gadelha et al., 2020). The establishment of the National Health Surveillance Agency (ANVISA) in 1999 was inspired by the Food and Drug Administration (FDA) in the USA (Brasil, 1999; Costa et al., 2008). However, for the first time in the last 50 years and coincidentally during the COVID-19 pandemic, the country faced a deconstruction of its public health policy and setbacks in other vital areas (Carneiro, 2022; Gomes & Costa, 2021; Gomide et al., 2023; Indursky, 2020; Silva & Ziviani, 2020).

These transitions and policy choices within the Ministry of Health during the pandemic period exemplify the intricate nature of leadership and decision-making in a crisis (Smith, 2021). They highlight the complexities of managing public health, where political, medical, and scientific dimensions intersect, and where the implications of leadership decisions can have far-reaching effects on the population's well-being (Johnson & Brown, 2020). This complex interplay of leadership, politics, and public health decision-making underscores the importance of effective governance (Smith, 2021) and the need for a unified and evidence-based approach to addressing health crises (Adams & Walls, 2019).

## Transparency Challenges and Data Initiatives Amidst the Brazilian COVID-19 Pandemic

Amidst the COVID-19 pandemic, due to a lack of transparency from the government regarding the supply of national data related to the disease, the Consortium of Media Vehicles (CVI) was created as an exceptional measure on June 8, 2020. It aimed to daily disseminate the number of COVID-19 deaths and cases based on information generated in the 26 states of Brazil and the Federal District (Poder360, 2020).

On November 18, 2011, the Access to Public Information Law (LAI—12.527) was promulgated. This law requires public agencies to disclose information such as revenues, contracts, bids, reports, and other relevant data in compliance with Article 37 of the Brazilian Constitution of 1988, which provisionally addresses transparency as one of the principles to be followed by the government, enabling citizens to monitor administrative actions. Gomes & Santos (2021) explain the formation of the CVI in response to amendments made to the LAI in January 2019, expanding the number of officials who would decide on data secrecy. In addition, they note the issuance of a provisional measure by the Federal Government that suspended response deadlines for government information requests. Ribeiro (2020) attributes the formation of the CVI to the denial by the Public Prosecutor's Office of the right to contest negative decisions. The Coronavirus Panel—Ministry of Health reports that in Brazil, there have been 37,789,040 confirmed cases of COVID-19, leading to the death of 705,494 Brazilians (Brazil, 2023).

Contextualising the COVID-19 pandemic within the Brazilian political scenario underscores the significance of leadership, the need for a unified national strategy, and the imperative for investment in public health infrastructure. These aspects have played a central role in Brazil's response to the pandemic and its ability to manage the associated challenges effectively. President Bolsonaro's initial prioritisation of economic interests over public health created divisions, delayed responses, and strained healthcare systems (Council on Foreign Relations, 2021; Reuters, 2020).

The challenges in vaccine procurement, the emergence of variants, and their disproportionate impact on vulnerable communities underscored the critical importance of leadership in addressing disparities (Amnesty International, 2020; Nature, 2021). Transitioning health ministers exemplified the intricate nature of decision-making during a crisis and the challenge of balancing political directives with scientific expertise (Smith, 2021).

Transparency initiatives empowered citizens to scrutinise government actions, emphasising the vital role of data in effective governance (Gomes & Santos, 2021; Poder360, 2020; Ribeiro, 2020). Brazil's experience serves as a stark reminder that effective leadership, unified strategies, and transparency are essential for tackling health crises (Adams & Walls, 2019; Smith et al., 2014). These lessons have global relevance and should guide future pandemic responses. However, it is essential to recognise that the negative aspects of populist leadership, as seen in President Bolsonaro's downplaying of the pandemic's severity and prioritisation of economic concerns over public health, significantly hindered an effective response to the crisis (Johnson & Brown, 2020; Reuters, 2020).

This case underscores the vital importance of governmental actions and leadership in managing health crises. Government responses shape the trajectory of a pandemic and influence public health outcomes. Effective governance, as evidenced in countries that have successfully controlled the spread of COVID-19, plays a central role in mitigating the impact of such crises. These governments adopted science-driven strategies, prioritised healthcare infrastructure, and demonstrated transparency in their communication with the public. The absence of these elements, as seen in Brazil's experience, results in confusion, inadequate healthcare, and a prolonged pandemic (Adams & Walls, 2019). This comparison highlights the significance of strong government leadership in crisis management and emphasises the importance of lessons learned from Brazil's challenges.

## The Response of Brazilian Public Universities to the COVID-19 Pandemic

In this section, we will address how Brazilian public universities have dealt with the challenges posed by the COVID-19 pandemic. Our literature review used the Scientific Electronic Library Online (SciELO) database, an open-access digital library of scientific journals (Parker et al., 1998). The SciELO portal offers free access to articles written in Portuguese, Spanish, and English.

In the initial analysis of the documents retrieved using the descriptors "COVID-19" and "University" in the SciELO Database, 140 documents were retrieved. 81 irrelevant articles were excluded for various reasons, leaving 59 that underwent further analysis. All five regions of Brazil were represented in the remaining documents. Figure 1 presents the number of selected articles for Brazil's five regions (Table 1).

Brazil's public universities are classified into federal and state institutions. The country comprises 69 federal public universities and 41 public state universities. In Brazil, a public university is defined as entirely tuition-free. According to the Higher Education Census published in 2020, there are a total of 2608 higher education institutions in the country, of which 2306 are private and 302 are public (including 192 standalone higher education institutions that are not universities). Out of the total number of enrolments in higher education, which stands at 8,604,526, the majority, 6,524,108, are

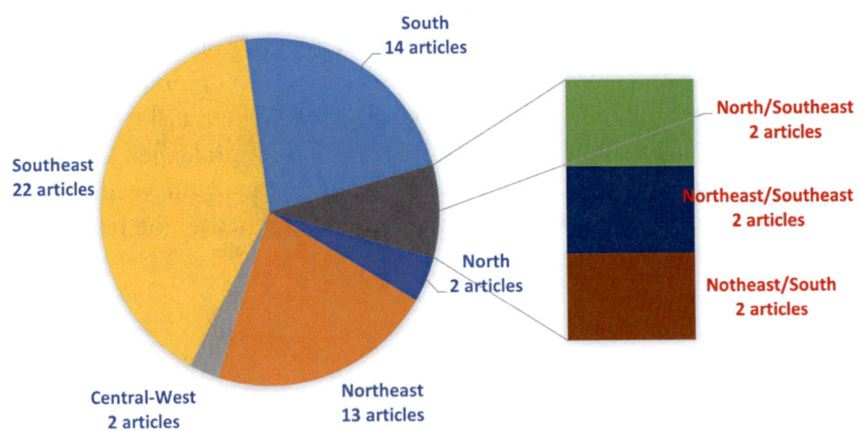


**Fig. 1** Number of published articles by region

Table 1 Classification of articles by focus

| Focus | Articles |
|---|---|
| Articles reporting studies with undergraduate and graduate students in the health field | 28 |
| Articles reporting studies with undergraduate students in the Humanities field | 9 |
| Articles reporting studies with undergraduate students in the Exact Sciences | 2 |
| Articles reporting research on the mental health of faculty and students | 10 |
| Articles reporting research with faculty and students in other areas unrelated to mental health | 6 |
| Articles reporting research with indigenous and quilombola undergraduates | 1 |
| Articles specifically addressing how Brazilian public universities dealt with the COVID-19 pandemic | 3 |

in private institutions. The census also revealed that 386,073 educators are working in higher education in Brazil (Brazil, 2020).

The highest-ranked Brazilian universities are primarily located in the South/Southeast regions. The fact that the highest-ranked university in the Northern region of Brazil is positioned at 29th place in the ranking is indicative in the context of Brazil's historical development and the disparity in development between the Southern/Southeastern regions compared to the lesser development in the Northern/Northeastern regions (RUF, 2019).

Sobe (2020) sheds light on the issue of remote learning and internet access. He discusses how COVID-19 has caused not only a crisis in health but also in the economy, politics, and education. COVID-19 crisis has revealed both promises and weaknesses in the use of distance learning technologies, and existing inequalities in access have been exacerbated (Sobe, 2020). He emphasises that digital connectivity must be understood as an expanded right to education and essential for continuous learning. Sobe's (2020) insights contribute to understanding the challenges and opportunities faced by Brazilian universities in adapting to the pandemic.

The analysis of articles retrieved from the SciELO Database reveals that Brazilian public universities across different regions have grappled with various aspects of the COVID-19 pandemic. This includes addressing issues related to remote learning, internet access, inequality, and the overall impact on education. The research highlights the diversity of responses and approaches taken by universities to navigate the challenges posed by the pandemic, shedding light on their efforts to ensure the continuation of education and research during this unprecedented global crisis. Examining these articles offers valuable insights into comprehending the Brazilian context, notably as a nation situated within the Global South. This context raises the issue of criticism regarding the hegemonic epistemology of science articulated by first-world countries, especially those in the Northern Hemisphere, that use English as the language of scientific communication. This perspective implies that science is only valid if expressed in the lingua franca of science, which is English (Santos & Meneses, 2010). Despite these criticisms, it is important to recognise that limitations in digital connectivity have affected the Brazilian university community.

Most of the analysed articles focused on remote teaching in health-related fields, particularly medicine. For instance, Motta-Passos et al. (2023) report that undergraduate students at the University of the State of Amazonas (Northern Region of Brazil) rated the experience of remote learning as unsatisfactory, with those living in remote areas of the state being the most affected due to inconsistent internet access. Students highlighted the lack of concentration as the most detrimental aspect of remote classes, as many attended classes primarily from their own bedrooms.

In comparative terms, Pesce & Vazquez (2022) conducted a study involving undergraduate students in the Humanities field at the Federal University of São Paulo to evaluate the Emergency Home Activities (ADE) regime implemented during the COVID-19 pandemic. The results indicated a decline in the overall quality of ADE courses compared to in-person instruction, failing to meet the expectations of most students. However, students viewed remote learning as a damage-control measure in light of the impossibility of in-person classes and the risk of delays in course completion. They also noted that synchronous classes resembled traditional classroom settings the most and suggested that mechanisms like discussion forums promoting interactions between students and faculty could have been better utilised. The ADE format, nevertheless, is considered by Arieira et al. (2009) to be superior to tutor-mediated Distance Learning (DL).

It is interesting to highlight that, despite the students residing in São Paulo, considered a global city due to its economic dynamism and available services, this research revealed that 81.4% of students had adequate internet connections, 65% had exclusive access to a computer, 62% claimed to have a suitable study space at home, and the average monthly per capita family income was approximately US$276 (Ministério da Educação [MEC], 2023).

These articles provide insights into the challenges faced by Brazilian universities during the COVID-19 pandemic, particularly in terms of remote learning, internet access disparities, and the complex interplay between technological, economic, and educational factors that influence the effectiveness of remote education strategies. About six million Brazilian students, from preschool to postgraduate levels, do not have internet access (Nascimento et al., 2020).

Regarding remote learning during the COVID-19 pandemic, a study conducted with students and professors from the School of Medicine at the Federal University of Pernambuco (Northeast region of Brazil) found that access to remote learning was not a problem for students, nor a hindrance for professors in delivering their lessons. 96% of students and 94% of professors have computer and internet access. However, when it comes to professors, only 53% had taught online classes before the start of the remote period. Although 88% considered themselves capable of teaching distance courses, 35% said they had obstacles that made it impossible to prepare or teach online classes. As for students, only 3% felt insecure about using digital devices and resources, and 66% of them had already participated in an online course (Campos Filho et al., 2022).

Serra et al. (2022) address emergency remote learning in the curriculum component of the postgraduate programme on "Didactic Training in Nursing and Health". This study brings up the reflection that educators need more than just scientific knowledge and technical mastery of tools for remote teaching. They also need training that encompasses ethical–political, conceptual, cultural, relational, and attitudinal knowledge to avoid reproducing the banking education model described and criticised by Freire (2016), which is limited to mere content transmission.

In a remarkable study, Souza (2021) addresses the response to COVID-19 by Brazilian federal universities. Souza, who currently holds the position of Secretary of Higher Education (SESU, 2023) at the *Ministry of Education of Brazil (MEC), was the creator and coordinator of the "CORONAVIRUS Portal: Monitoring the Federal Higher Education Network". This portal contains data on MEC's actions in response to the COVID-19 pandemic, as well as the "Biosafety Protocol for the Resumption of Activities in Federal Education Institutions" (*Ministério da Educação, 2020).

The first Ordinance by the Ministry of Education in response to the COVID-19 emergency was issued on March 11, 2020 (Souza, 2021). This Ordinance established the Operational Emergency Committee of the Ministry of Education (COE/MEC) with the aim of managing issues related to COVID-19 that had an impact on education in Brazil. The committee was also tasked with real-time monitoring of public education networks, discussing and defining measures to combat the spread of the new coronavirus, following the guidelines of the Ministry of Health, and coordinating measures for the return to normalcy. This Committee was also responsible for gathering information for the diagnosis of the emergency operation, enabling the establishment of goals and areas of focus; analysing the historical situation and the unfolding of similar events in order to support decision-making; planning actions, defining stakeholders, and determining the adoption of measures to mitigate threats and restore the normal situation; and monitoring the implementation of proposed measures and assessing the need for review and planning. The decisions made within the scope of the Committee aimed to guide the actions of educational institutions at the federal, state, and municipal levels, while respecting the autonomy of all involved.

An Ordinance issued on March 17, 2020, allowed for the replacement of in-person classes with digital (online) classes during the COVID-19 pandemic. This regulation reserved the right to determine which courses should be replaced, respecting the autonomy of the institutions and allowing for changes to the academic calendar, as well as addressing other provisions. In the Ordinance issued on April 1, 2020, educational institutions were exempted from the obligation to observe the minimum days of effective academic work for the academic year.

On July 27, 2020, Resolution No. 39 was adopted, suspending instalments and addressing the renegotiation of debts of contracts from the Student Financing Fund (Fies), established in 2001, with the aim of providing financing to students in non-free higher education programmes. Due to Ordinances No. 544, issued on June 16, 2020, and No. 617, issued on August 3, 2020, which addressed the replacement of in-person classes with digital classes in response to the pandemic situation, access to the internet by vulnerable students became a critical issue. In response to the COVID-19 pandemic, the Ministry of Education (MEC) took several measures to address the challenges faced by Federal Higher Education Institutions in Brazil. One of these measures was the establishment of the Operational Emergency Committee of the Ministry of Education (COE/MEC) on March 11, 2020. The committee's purpose was to manage issues related to COVID-19 affecting education in Brazil. It was responsible for real-time monitoring of public education networks, discussing and defining measures to combat the spread of the virus, and coordinating actions for the return to normalcy. The Committee also gathered information for emergency operation diagnosis, planned actions, analysed historical situations, and monitored the execution of proposed measures.

Further measures included ordinances and resolutions issued by the MEC. For instance, an ordinance on March 17, 2020, allowed the replacement of in-person classes with online classes during the pandemic. Another ordinance on April 1, 2020, exempted educational institutions from the obligation of minimum days of academic work for the affected academic year.

To address internet accessibility, the "Alunos Conectados" (Connected Students) project was initiated, providing internet access to vulnerable students. This project distributed approximately 165,000 internet access packages to students with a family per capita income of up to half the minimum wage (US$138). Additionally, the MEC implemented the digital issuance and registration of academic diplomas and documents, aiming to streamline the process and save time and costs.

Considering the shift to online education due to the pandemic, the MEC launched the National Digital Certificate Program in March 2021, providing digital certificates for students, teachers, and administrative staff. This programme integrated with the Academic Federated Community (CAFe), representing potential savings in the millions by automating academic processes.

In accordance with the law addressing the health emergency caused by the coronavirus, the MEC issued Ordinance No. 383 on April 9, 2020. This ordinance allowed for the exceptional early graduation of students in Medicine, Nursing, Pharmacy, and Physiotherapy programmes who had completed at least 75% of the internship or supervised training hours during the health emergency.

As the COVID-19 situation evolved and contagion rates increased, many Federal Education Institutions shifted to remote activities, planning and adapting their operations to ensure the safety of students and staff. A collaboration between the Secretariat of Higher Education of the Ministry of Education and various universities aimed to develop an online system for managing data and artefacts of Big Data Analytics to generate transparency and governance information for public administration.

As a result, the "Coronavirus Dashboard" was launched on April 20, 2020, encompassing 69 federal universities and 41 institutions of professional and technological education within the federal network. This online platform provided real-time information about the actions and operations of Federal Educational Institutions during the COVID-19 health emergency. The dashboard offered transparency and management capabilities by offering information in various categories, organised into eight main sections: epidemiological data; digital inclusion; operations of 107 federal universities; operations of federal institutes; general dashboard; biosafety protocol; measures for addressing the crisis; and early graduation. This service, which allowed for tracking and monitoring of information, was accessible through this dashboard during the period of emergency measures. It offered insights into various aspects of the institutions' responses to the COVID-19 situation, including health data, digital inclusion efforts, operational status, biosafety measures, and more. However, the service ceased to exist once the emergency measures were concluded.

The retrieved articles provide a comprehensive view of how Brazilian universities addressed the multifaceted challenges posed by the COVID-19 pandemic. These challenges encompassed issues of remote learning, digital connectivity disparities, and the intricate interplay of technological, economic, and educational factors affecting the efficacy of remote educational strategies. The research reveals diverse responses and approaches undertaken by universities across different regions of Brazil, shedding light on their efforts to ensure the continuity of education and research during an unprecedented global crisis. The articles also offer insights into the Brazilian context, particularly as a nation within the Global South. This context raises important discussions about the potential hegemony of scientific epistemology articulated by first-world countries, often in English, as a marker of validity (Santos & Meneses, 2010). Despite these considerations, it is crucial to acknowledge the impact of digital connectivity limitations on the Brazilian university community.

Sobe (2020) brings international perspectives into the discussion, highlighting the broader impacts of the pandemic beyond health, encompassing economics, politics, and education. Sobe (2020) emphasises the promises and challenges of distance learning technologies, underscoring the importance of equitable digital connectivity as a fundamental right for education. His insights contribute significantly to understanding the opportunities and obstacles that Brazilian universities faced in adapting to the pandemic.

Notably, the research underscores regional disparities in article representation. While the South/Southeast regions dominate in terms of publication output, the North/Northeast regions also contribute valuable insights, addressing issues such as remote learning quality, digital access, and regional challenges. Furthermore, the research has spotlighted specialised fields like medicine and humanities, highlighting varying student experiences and perspectives within different disciplines. Ultimately, the analysed articles collectively provide a rich panorama of the Brazilian university experience during the pandemic, unveiling both the resilience and limitations of higher education institutions. They underscore the importance of addressing digital inclusion, enhancing remote learning strategies, and fostering a holistic approach that recognises the diverse socioeconomic and regional contexts within Brazil. As the nation navigates the ongoing challenges of COVID-19 and beyond, these insights can inform future policies and strategies to build a more resilient and equitable educational landscape in the country, and even in different countries worldwide.

The response of Brazilian public universities to the COVID-19 pandemic has been a subject of great significance, as these institutions play a critical role in the nation's education, research, and public health infrastructure. This response, shaped by both internal university policies and external government directives, has been instrumental in navigating the challenges brought about by the pandemic. Brazil, being one of the hardest-hit countries by the pandemic, had to grapple with the complex interplay of public health, politics, and education. Brazilian universities, historically known for their commitment to research and innovation, had to adapt swiftly to the new reality. According to Neves and Martins (2016), 55.9% of Brazilian universities are public institutions, further highlighting their importance in managing the crisis.

At the onset of the pandemic, these universities faced several critical challenges. Their response included measures such as transitioning to online learning platforms, cancelling or postponing in-person academic activities, and implementing strict health and safety protocols on campus Ribeiro & Sousa (2021).

The role of Brazilian public universities in research and data collection also became pivotal. Universities, particularly those with strong medical and scientific departments, were instrumental in conducting COVID-19 research, clinical trials, and the production of diagnostic tests (Silva & Pereira, 2020). This demonstrates their potential for contributing to public health and for providing evidence-based solutions during crises. However, it is crucial to acknowledge that these responses were not without their challenges. The digital divide in Brazil meant that not all students had equal access to online education. This inequality was a cause for concern and led to debates about the role of public universities in bridging these gaps (UNESCO, 2020).

Moreover, the pandemic revealed the need for increased investment in public higher education in Brazil. Financial limitations posed obstacles to ensuring students had access to the necessary resources for remote learning and maintaining adequate healthcare infrastructure on campus (Afonso et al., 2020). The response of Brazilian public universities to the COVID-19 pandemic reflects their significance as critical actors in the country's education, research, and public health systems. The adaptability and resilience demonstrated during these challenging times underscore the importance of these institutions in shaping Brazil's future responses to crises.

## Navigating the Post-COVID Era: Leadership, Governance, and Strategy in Brazil

In the post-COVID era, Brazil's leadership faces the formidable task of reassessing government strategies to rebuild a healthier and more resilient nation. The pandemic has laid bare critical weaknesses in Brazil's public health infrastructure and governance, demanding a multifaceted response guided by evidence-based policies. Scholarly perspectives emphasise the following imperatives for leadership during this pivotal period:

1. **Strengthening public health infrastructure**: An academic consensus underscores the need for substantial investments in Brazil's public health sector. This includes expanding healthcare infrastructure, bolstering medical resources, and enhancing the nation's preparedness against future health crises (Costa & Louro, 2022; Santos et al., 2022).
2. **Data-driven decision-making**: In the academic discourse, there is a consistent call for leadership to prioritise transparency, science-based decision-making, and the establishment of an efficient data collection and analysis system. Reliable and real-time data are imperative for timely responses and informed policymaking (Alves & Pincay, 2021; Silva & Santos, 2020).
3. **Comprehensive vaccination strategies**: Scholars emphasise the importance of a well-structured vaccination strategy. Government leadership must ensure equitable access to vaccines, maintain a robust supply chain, and actively work to foster public trust in vaccination programmes (Machado et al., 2021; Araújo et al, 2023).
4. **Addressing social inequities**: Academic voices converge on the significance of mitigating socioeconomic disparities highlighted during the pandemic. This entails tackling educational inequalities, addressing income disparities, and working to provide equitable access to healthcare (Faria et al., 2023; Albuquerque & Ribeiro, 2020).
5. **Global collaboration**: The academic discourse underscores the importance of international cooperation and collaboration. Brazil's leadership should actively engage in global partnerships, sharing knowledge and resources to effectively combat global health threats (Carvalho & Araújo, 2020; Rolim, 2021).

Leadership in the post-COVID era in Brazil necessitates a comprehensive, strategic, and evidence-based approach to rebuilding the nation's health infrastructure and governance. These academic insights not only guide the response to the current pandemic but also prepare the nation for future health challenges in an increasingly interconnected world.

## Conclusion

The response of Brazilian public universities to the COVID-19 pandemic has been a subject of great significance, as these institutions play a critical role in the nation's education, research, and public health infrastructure. This response, shaped by both internal university policies and external government directives, has been instrumental in navigating the challenges brought about by the pandemic.

Brazil, being one of the hardest-hit countries by the pandemic, had to grapple with the complex interplay of public health, politics, and education. Brazilian universities, historically known for their commitment to research and innovation, had to adapt swiftly to the new reality.

At the onset of the pandemic, these universities faced several critical challenges. Their response included measures such as transitioning to online learning platforms, cancelling or postponing in-person academic activities, and implementing strict health and safety protocols on campus. These changes were made in alignment with directives from Brazil's Ministry of Education and Ministry of Health.

The role of Brazilian public universities in research and data collection also became pivotal. Universities, particularly those with strong medical and scientific departments, were instrumental in conducting COVID-19 research, clinical trials, and the production of diagnostic tests. This demonstrates their potential for contributing to public health and for providing evidence-based solutions during crises. However, it is crucial to acknowledge that these responses were not without their challenges. The digital divide in Brazil meant that not all students had equal access to online education. This inequality was a cause for concern and led to debates about the role of public universities in bridging these gaps. Moreover, the pandemic revealed the need for increased investment in public higher education in Brazil. Financial limitations posed obstacles to ensuring students had access to the necessary resources for remote learning and maintaining adequate healthcare infrastructure on campus.

In conclusion, the response of Brazilian public universities to the COVID-19 pandemic reflects their significance as critical actors in the country's education, research, and public health systems. The adaptability and resilience demonstrated during these challenging times underscore the importance of these institutions in shaping Brazil's future responses to crises. Nevertheless, it is essential to acknowledge that this response faced significant obstacles due to the negative aspects of populism in President Bolsonaro's leadership. His tendency to downplay the pandemic's seriousness and prioritise economic interests over public health directives complicated the situation, further accentuating the necessity for strong, science-based leadership in times of crisis. Leadership in post-COVID Brazil demands a comprehensive, strategic, and evidence-driven strategy to rebuild the country's health infrastructure and governance.

## References


ACNUR. (2021). *Refuge data in Brazil*. https://www.acnur.org/portugues/dados-sobre-refugio/dados-sobre-refugio-no-brasil/

Adams, J. G., & Walls, R. M. (2019). Supporting the health care workforce during the COVID-19 global epidemic. *JAMA, 323*(15), 1439–1440.

Afonso, J. R., Castro, K., Elacqua, G., Marotta, L., & Soares, S. (2020). *Impactos da pandemia sobre o orçamento educacional*. Banco Interamericano de Desenvolvimento (BID). Notas Técnicas IDB-TN-01983. Retrieved from https://issuu.com/fmcsv/docs/covid-19-financiamento-educacao-brasilimpactos-da

Albuquerque, M. V., & Ribeiro L. H. L. (2020) Desigualdade situação geográfica e sentidos da ação na pandemia da COVID-19 no Brasil. *ENSAIO Cadernos de Saúde Pública, 36*(12). https://doi.org/10.1590/0102-311X00208720. Retrieved from https://www.scielo.br/j/csp/a/YnJk6W34PYN9G5jp39kzCdy/?lang=pt#

Alexsandro, R. (2020). *Governos sacrificam transparência pública.* [Governments sacrifice public transparency]. Diário do Comércio. https://diariodocomercio.com.br/opiniao/governos-sacrificam-a-transparencia-publica/

Alves, T. A. L., & Pincay, C. M. G. (2021). Multilateralismo e cooperação internacional: o caminho que deve ser reforçado pelo Brasil no combate à pandemia/COVID-19. In *Revista Espirales, Edição Especial: Dossiê Covid-19 na América do Sul*. ISSN 2594-9721.

Araújo, S. R., Almeida, J. F. F., Rodrigues, L. F., & Machado, E. L. (2023). Preventable COVID-19 cases and deaths by alternative vaccination and non-pharmacological intervention policies in Brazil. *Revista Brasileira de Epidemiologia, 26*. https://doi.org/10.1590/1980-549720230054. Retrieved from https://www.scielo.br/j/rbepid/a/Csj3NQBSBj4rqDQ4qSdrNDM/?lang=en#

Arieira, J. D. O., Dias-Arieira, C. R., Fusco, J. P. A., Sacomano, J. B., & Bettega, M. O. D. P. (2009). Assessment of learning via distance education: The students' point of view. *Essay: Evaluation and Public Policies in Education, 17*, 313–340.

Benchimol, J. L. (coord). (2001). *Febre amarela: a doença e a vacina, uma história inacabada*. Editora Fiocruz. ISBN 85-85676-9-1.

Brasil. Lei n. 9.782, de 26 de janeiro de 1999. Define o Sistema Nacional de Vigilância Sanitária, cria a Agência Nacional de Vigilância Sanitária, e dá outras providências. Diário Oficial da União 1999; 26 jan.

Brasil. (2023). Coronavirus panel. https://covid.saude.gov.br

Brasil. (2020). Census of higher education. Retrieved from https://encurtador.com.br/ftGO6

Campos Filho, A. S. D., Ribeiro Sobrinho, J. M. D., Romão, R. F., Silva, C. H. N. D. D., Alves, J. C. P., & Rodrigues, R. L. (2022). Remote education at Brazilian university medical school during the pandemic. *Revista Brasileira de Educação Médica, 46*(1). https://doi.org/10.1590/1981-5271v46.1-20210243

Carneiro, R. (2022). O planejamento na esfera pública revisitado: lições, avanços e retrocessos desde a Constituição Federal de 1988 (CF/1988)—Planning in the public sphere revisited: Lessons, advances and setbacks since the Federal Constitution of 1988 (FC/1988). *Campo de Públicas: Conexões e Experiências, 1*(1), 30–50. Disponível em: http://fjp.mg.gov.br/v-1-n-1-2021-edicao-especial-sobre-planejamento

Carvalho, S. B. R., & Araújo, G. C. (2020, Jan–Apr). Internationalization management of higher education institutions. *Avaliação (Campinas), 25*(01). https://doi.org/10.1590/S1414-40772020000100007

Coêlho, C. R. J., & Silva, C. O. P. (2008). Constitutional mutation: The performance of the open society as a protagonist in the interpretation of the 1988 Brazilian constitution. *Journal of the Federal Public Defender's Office, 38*, 73–98.

Costa, E. A., Fernandes, T. M., & Pimenta, T. S. (2008). A vigilância sanitária nas políticas de saúde no Brasil e a construção da identidade de seus trabalhadores (1976–1999). *Ciência & Saúde Coletiva, 13*(3), 995–1004.

Costa, E. M., & Louro, A. (2022). *Desigualdades em saúde, desigualdades no território: desafios para os países de língua portuguesa em contexto de pós pandemia.* Centro de Estudos Geográficos. Instituto de Geografia e Ordenamento do Território. Universidade de Lisboa, Portugal.

Couto, C. G., & Arantes, R. B. (2006). Constitution, government and democracy in Brazil. *Brazilian Journal of Social Sciences, 21*, 41–62.

Council on Foreign Relations. (2021). Brazil's COVID-19 crisis.

De Moraes, A. J. & Teixeira, C. A. (2020). Migrants learning to become entrepreneurs: The case of migrants in the city of Sao Paulo, Brazil. In *Multidisciplinary approach to entrepreneurship education for migrants* (pp. 156–176). IGI Global.

Faria, L., Alvarez, R. E. C., & Santos, L. A. C. (2023). Desigualdades socioeconômicas na América Latina e Caribe: o futuro pós-pandemia para a formação profissional na saúde. *História, Ciências, Saúde-Manguinhos, 30*(suppl 1). https://doi.org/10.1590/S0104-59702023000100029. Retrieved from https://www.scielo.br/j/hcsm/a/qHRRn35ymQfpRPBWPVr8Rdm/?lang=pt#

Fischmann, R. (2005). Historical and legal remarks on cultural diversity and higher education in Brazil in the context of the school system. *Higher Education Policy, 18*, 375–395. https://doi.org/10.1057/palgrave.hep.8300094

Freire, P. (2016). *Pedagogy of autonomy: Necessary knowledge for educational practice* (53rd ed.). Peace and Land.

Freyre, G. (2001). *Casa-grande & senzala* (42nd ed.). Record.

Freyre, G. (2002). *Sobrados e Mucambos*. Record.

Freyre, G. (2004). *Ordem e Progresso*. Global Editora.

Freyre, G. (1968). *Brasis, Brasil e Brasília: Sugestões em torno de problemas brasileiros de unidade e diversidade e das relações de alguns deles com problemas gerais de pluralismo étnico e cultural*. Record.

Frigeri, M. (2014). SciELO: 15 anos de parceria com os periódicos científicos. *Ciência e Cultura, 66*(1).

Gadelha, C., & Azevedo, N. (2003). Vaccine innovations in Brazil: Recent experiences and structural constraints. https://doi.org/10.1590/S0104-59702003000500012

Gadelha, C. A. G., Braga, P. S. C., Montenegr, K. B. M., & Cesário, B. B. (2020). Acesso a vacinas no Brasil no contexto da dinâmica global do Complexo Econômico-Industrial da Saúde. *Cadernos de Saúde Pública, 36*(Suppl 2). https://doi.org/10.1590/0102-311X00154519. Retrieved from https://www.scielo.br/j/csp/a/DZrjZbq6GZFHzDQFFLGwhcb/#

Gomes, E. D., & Costa, D. L. X. (2021). The use os social management in the deconstruction of managerial conservativeism in public policies. *Revista Gênero E Interdisciplinaridade, 2*(03). https://doi.org/10.51249/gei02.03.2021.451. Retrieved from https://www.periodicojs.com.br/index.php/gei/article/view/451

Gomes, M. C. M. S., Crispino Santos, F. (2021). *A atuação do Consórcio de Veículos de Imprensa na pandemia de COVID-19 no Brasil*. Intercom—Sociedade Brasileira de Estudos Interdisciplinares da Comunicação, 44o Congresso Brasileiro de Ciências da Comunicação 4 a 9/10/2021. Retrieved from https://www.portalintercom.org.br/anais/nacional2021/resumos/ij01/mylla-claudia-marcolino-dos-santos-gomes.pdf

Gomide, A. A., Silva, M. M. S., Leopoldi, M. A. (2023). Políticas Públicas em Contexto de Retrocesso Democrático e Populismo Reacionário: Desmontes e Reconfigurações—Public Policies in the Context of Democratic Regression and Reactionary Populism: Dismantling and Reconfiguration. In Desmonte e Reconfiguração de Políticas Públidas (2016–2022)—Dismantling and Reconfiguring Public Policies (2016–2022). Instituto de Pesquisa Econômica Aplicada (Ipea)—Institute of Applied Economic Research (Ipea).

IBGE—Instituto Brasileiro de Geografia e Estatística. (2000). DF: IBGE, 225–226.

Indursky, F. (2020). O teatro do grotesco como cenário da desconstrução do Brasil—The theater of the grotesque as a scenario for the deconstruction of Brazil. *Revista da ABRALIN, [S. l.], 19*(3), 365–388. https://doi.org/10.25189/rabralin.v19i3.1730. Disponível em: https://revista.abralin.org/index.php/abralin/article/view/1730

Johnson, S. L., & Brown, J. S. (2020). Integrating clinical research into epidemic response: The Ebola experience. *Epidemics, 31*, 100387.

Johnson, N. F., Velásquez, N., Restrepo, N. J., Leahy, R., Gabriel, N., El Oud, S., Zheng, M., Manrique, P., Wuchty, S., & Lupu, Y. (2020). The online competition between pro-and anti-vaccination views. *Nature, 582*(7811), 230–233.

Lambert, J. (1959). *Os dois Brasis. Série VI—Sociedade e Educação.* INEP/CBPE.

Machado, R. C., Lopes, P. W., Silva, F. N., Santos, T. A. G. M., Prado, S. I., & Souza, A. R. (2021). Pandemias e COVID-19 transformam o mundo: uma análise de contextos. *Enfermagem Brasil, 20*(2). https://doi.org/10.33233/eb.v20i2.4442. Retrieved from https://convergenceseditorial.com.br/index.php/enfermagembrasil/article/view/4442

mec.gov.br. (2020, 2021, 2022). Conselho Nacional de Educação. Retrieved from http://portal.mec.gov.br/pec-g/33371-cne-conselho-nacional-de-educacao/90771-COVID-19

Melo, M. A. (2013). Mudança constitucional no Brasil: dos debates sobre regras de emendamento na constituinte à megapolítica. *Novos Estudos CEBRAP*, (97), 187–206.

Melo, Á., Carnut, L., & Melo, M. (2023). Continuum de desmontes da saúde pública na crise do covid-19: o neofascismo de Bolsonaro. *Saúde e Sociedade, 32*(1).

Ministério da Educação [MEC]. (2023). Portal do Ministério da Educação. http://portal.mec.gov.br/pec-g/33371-cne-conselho-nacional-de-educacao/90771-COVID-19

Ministério da Educação, Brasil. (2020). *Protocolo de biossegurança para retorno das atividades nas Instituições Federais de Ensino.* Secretaria de Educação Superior.

Motta-Passos, I., Martinez, M. L. L., Andrade, S. C. da S., Pinho A. C. dos S., & Martins, M. de A. (2023). Students' views on emergency distance learning at a medical and health sciences school. *Revista Brasileira de Educação Médica, 47*(1). https://doi.org/10.1590/1981-5271v47.1-20220261

Nascimento, P. A. M. M., Ramos, D. L., Melo, A. A. S., & Castioni, R. (2020). Instituto de Pesquisa Econômica Aplicada (Ipea). Acesso domiciliar à internet e ensino remoto durante a pandemia—Nota Técnica, Nº88. [Internet]. http://repositorio.ipea.gov.br/handle/11058/10228

Neves, C. E. B., Martins, C. B. (2016). Ensino superior no brasil: uma visão abrangente. In Jovens universitários em um mundo em transformação: uma pesquisa sino-brasileira/organizadores: Tom Dwyer ... [et al.]. Ipea/SSAP.

Parker, A. L. et al. (1998). SciELO: uma metodologia para publicação eletrônica. *Ciência Da Informação, 27*(2), 109–121, maio/ago 1998.

Pesce, L., & Vasquez, D. A. (2022, Jan–Apr). The remote learning experience during the Covid-19 pandemic: Determinants of student assessment in humanities courses at Unifesp. *Avaliação (Campinas), 27*(01). https://doi.org/10.1590/S1414-40772022000100010. Retrieved from https://www.scielo.br/j/aval/a/ScXyqLR49N8cNJ3WJnbQPJD/?lang=pt#

Poder 360. (2020). Jornais se unem para dar transparência a dados de COVID-19 no Brasil. Retrieved from https://www.poder360.com.br/midia/jornais-se-unem-para-dar-transparencia-a-dados-de-COVID-19-no-brasil/

Ranking Universitário Folha (RUF). (2019). https://ruf.folha.uol.com.br/2019/ranking-de-universidades/principal/

Reuters. (2020). Brazil president downplays coronavirus despite rising cases, sets bad example. *Reuters*. https://www.reuters.com/article/us-health-coronavirus-brazil-idUSKBN21B2GS

Ribeiro, A. (2020, 14 de maio de). Governos sacrificam a transparência pública. *Diário do Comércio*. https://diariodocomercio.com.br/opiniao/governos-sacrificam-a-transparencia-publica/

Ribeiro, D. (1968). The civilizing process: Stages of sociocultural evolution. In *The civilizing process: Stages of sociocultural evolution* (pp. 265–265). VHL Regional Portal Information and Knowledge for Health.

Ribeiro, D. (1995). *The Brazilian people: The formation and meaning of Brazil*. Company of Letters.

Ribeiro, R. O., & Sousa, F. N. T. (2021). The role of universities in building post-pandemic educational model. *Id on Line Revista Multdisciplinar e Psicologia, 15*(56), 776 –790. Julho/2021, ISSN 1981-1179. Retrieved from https://idonline.emnuvens.com.br/id/article/view/3172/4984

Rolim, M. C. L. (2021). Relações internacionais e governança da saúde global: Uma Análise de Políticas Sanitárias em Cenários de Enfrentamento das Pandemias. *Saúde Coletiva: Avanços e desafios para a integralidade do cuidado, 2,* 417–439. Retrieved from https://pdfs.semanticscholar.org/76ec/7f6f7d32f7c0bcdb58beb9114483d60f82d3.pdf

Santos, B. S., & Meneses, M. P. (2010). *Epistemologias do Sul*. Cortez.

Santos, P. P. G. V., Oliveira, R. A. D., & Albuquerque, M. V. (2022, Abr 11). Desigualdades da oferta hospitalar no contexto da pandemia da Covid-19 no Brasil: uma revisão integrativa. *Saúde debate, 46*(spe1). https://doi.org/10.1590/0103-11042022E122. Retrieved from https://www.scielosp.org/article/sdeb/2022.v46nspe1/322-337/pt/#

SciELO. (2022, setembro). Critérios, política e procedimentos para a admissão e a permanência de periódicos na Coleção SciELO Brasil. *SciELO*. Retrieved from https://www.scielo.br/media/files/20220900-criterios-scielo-brasil.pdf

Secretaria de Educação Superior (SESU). (2023). *Ministério da Educação*. Retrieved from http://portal.mec.gov.br/sesu-secretaria-de-educacao-superior

Serra, I. V. S., Lima, J. M. M., Silva, G. T. R., Santos, J. X. P., & Santana, L. S. (2022). Ensino Remoto na pandemia de Covid-19: um olhar sob a perspectiva de Paulo Freire. *Cogitare Enfermagem, 27*. https://doi.org/10.5380/ce.v27i0.84547. Retrieved from https://www.scielo.br/j/cenf/a/bgbhwPbzPqhXcGm8cWGyKNb/#

Silva, F. A. B., & Ziviani, P. (2020). O incrementalismo pós-constitucional e o enigma da desconstrução: uma análise das políticas culturais—Post-constitutional incrementalism and the enigma of deconstruction: an analysis of cultural policies. Repositório do Conhecimento do IPEA—IPEA Knowledge Repository. Disponível em: https://repositorio.ipea.gov.br/handle/11058/9802

Smith, K. F., Goldberg, M., Rosenthal, S., Carlson, L., Chen, J., & Chen, C. (2014). Global rise in human infectious disease outbreaks. *Journal of the Royal Society Interface, 16*(151), 20180620.

Smith, K. F., Goldberg, M., Rosenthal, S., Carlson, L., Chen, J., Chen, C., & Ramachandran, S. (2014, Dec 6). Global rise in human infectious disease outbreaks. *Journal of the Royal Society Interface, 11*(101), 20140950. https://doi.org/10.1098/rsif.2014.0950

Sobe, N. (2020). In Vidal, D. G., Bontempi Jr, B. A cosmopolitan intellectual: the trajectories of Noah Sobe in (the history of) education. *Seção: Entrevistas. Educação e Pesquisa, 46*. Retrieved from https://doi.org/10.1590/S1678-463420 2046002002

Souza, W. V. B. (2021). *Enfrentamento à COVID-19 nas universidades federais brasileiras: uma pesquisa-ação no Ministério da Educação.* Tese (Doutorado em Administração)—Universidade de Brasília, Brasília. Retrieved from http://reposi toriocovid19.unb.br/repositorio-produtos/enfrentamento-a-covid-19-nasuniver sidades-federais-brasileiras-uma-pesquisa-acao-no-ministerio-da-educacao/

Souza, F. C. S., & Silva, V. S. (2021). Conhecimentos tradicionais versus conhecimentos científicos? v. 5 n. Especial (2021): Saberes dos Povos e Comunidades Tradicionais na composição da EPT. https://doi.org/10.36524/profept.v5iEspecial.1104. Retrieved from https://ojs.ifes.edu.br/index.php/ept/article/view/1104

The United Nations High Commissioner for Refugees (UNHCR). (2019). Article 1, 1951 convention relating to the status of refugees. https://www.unhcr.org/3b6 6c2aa10.html

The United Nations High Commissioner for Refugees. UNHCR-ACNUR Brazil. (2019). https://www.acnur.org/portugues/dados-sobre-refugio/dados-sobre-ref ugio-no-brasil/

Vidal, D. G. & Bontempi Jr, B. (2020). A cosmopolitan intellectual: The trajectories of Noah Sobe in (the history of) education. Seção: Entrevistas. Educ. Pesqui. 46. https://doi.org/10.1590/S1678-4634202046002002

World Health Organization. (2020). *COVID-19 strategy update.* World Health Organization. https://www.who.int/publications/i/item/strategic-preparedness-and-response-plan-for-the-new-coronavirus

# Crisis Leadership in Cambodian Higher Education

Loeurt To

## Introduction

The COVID-19 pandemic has indeed unleashed unprecedented disruptions worldwide, affecting millions of people and plunging the world into a crisis. As of September 2023, the World Health Organization reported over 770 million confirmed COVID-19 cases and a tragic count of around 7 million lives lost to the pandemic (World Health Organization, 2023). The pandemic also disrupted over 220 million tertiary students worldwide (UNESCO, 2021). In Southeast Asia, the figure stands at over 61 million reported cases and over 800 thousand reported deaths (World Health Organization, 2023). In Cambodia, it impacted the livelihoods of more than 15 million people. As of September 2023, Cambodia reported a total of 138,941 confirmed cases of COVID-19, with 3056 deaths (World Health Organization, 2023). The crisis disrupted Cambodia's economic growth, particularly in key sectors critical to its economic stability, including tourism, the garment industry, manufacturing, and the construction sector. These sectors together constitute approximately 70% of Cambodia's GDP (Tansuchat et al., 2022). Tourism suffered the most, as the flow of tourists stopped completely due to border closures. This, in turn, resulted in the closure of restaurants, hotels, and businesses. At the same time, over 300 garment factories were forced to suspend

L. To (✉)
Faculty of Education, Dewey International University, Battambang, Cambodia
e-mail: loeurt@diu.edu.kh; loeurt_educ@yahoo.com





J. Rudolph et al. (eds.), *The Palgrave Handbook of Crisis Leadership in Higher Education*, https://doi.org/10.1007/978-3-031-54509-2_13

their operations, affecting approximately 200,000 factory workers (Tansuchat et al., 2022).

In combating the COVID-19 pandemic, Cambodia was successful in its vaccination campaign (Nozaki et al., 2023; Tao et al., 2022). It is one of the fastest ASEAN countries to provide vaccinations, behind Singapore as of September 2021 (Pramanick et al., 2021; Rudolph et al., 2023). According to the World Health Organization, as of September 2023, the country has administered a total of 47,601,597 vaccine doses, making it the second-highest contributor to vaccine distribution in Southeast Asia. The country has 15,287,370 individuals receiving at least one dose of COVID-19 vaccine and 14,659,514 individuals fully vaccinated, which is well over 90% of the total population (World Health Organization, 2023). This vaccination campaign underscores Cambodia's dedication to public health and its tireless efforts to combat the pandemic (Tao et al., 2022). The success is attributed to the political commitment of the government and the support from development partners in response to the crisis.

In response to the COVID-19 pandemic, the government of Cambodia also took leadership responses throughout various stages of the pandemic. According to a prior study, the progression of COVID-19 in Cambodia is classified into three pandemic development stages, each defined by the extent of transmission, the impact, and the corresponding response measures employed by the authorities (Chhim et al., 2023). First, the containment stage is the initial phase of the COVID-19 outbreak, characterised by effective control of the virus for over 12 months from January 27, 2020, to February 19, 2021, during which there were relatively fewer reported cases and recorded deaths. Second, the mitigation stage spanned over eight months, from February 20 to October 31, 2021. This stage is characterised by a large-scale community outbreak, leading to a significant increase in the number of reported cases and COVID-19-related deaths, with reported cases of 118,129 and 2781 reported deaths (Chhim et al., 2023). Third, the full reopening stage from November 1, 2021, is the situation in which the pandemic was largely under control. Throughout these three stages, higher education responded in alignment with the country's and the education sector's responses, which will be presented in this chapter.

## Context

Cambodia is a Southeast Asian country with a total population of 15.6 million, in which females are accounted for over 50% of the population (Ministry of Planning, 2020). The country shares a border with Thailand to the west and northwest, Laos to the northeast, Vietnam to the east and southeast, and the Gulf of Thailand to the southwest. The urban population accounts for 39.4% of the total population. As of 2019, the literacy rate of the population was 88.5%, with men at 91.1% and women at 86.2%. Cambodia's economy has experienced significant growth, with a pre-COVID-19 annual GDP growth rate of 7.7% (MoEYS, 2019). The country transited to a lower-middle income country in 2015 and envisions to transform to an upper-middle income country by 2030 and a high-income country by 2050 (MoEYS, 2019). In pursuit of the vision, Cambodia recognises the utmost importance of building a workforce equipped with relevant skills and up-to-date technology, ensuring they are well-prepared to keep pace with the rapid growth and integration within the ASEAN community (MoEYS, 2019). In this regard, higher education plays a role as a catalyst for the transformation and development envisioned by the country. By investing in human resource development and technological advancements, Cambodia will be prepared to unlock its industrial potential, positioning itself as a dynamic player in the region and paving the way for a prosperous and sustainable future.

Cambodia's higher education system has made significant quantitative progress in the last thirty years in response to the needs of a growing population in the post-conflict era. The number of HEIs has surged from less than ten HEIs in the early 1990s to over 130 by 2022, of which nearly two-thirds are private institutions (MoEYS, 2019, 2023). There were 209,059 recently enrolled students, of which 95,619 are women (MoEYS, 2023). This substantial growth was made possible through educational reforms in the late 1990s that allowed private sector involvement in education development, leading to an increase in enrolment (MoEYS, 2023). 16 ministries administer these HEIs, and the majority of them are under the supervision of two main ministries, the Ministry of Education, Youth and Sport (MoEYS), and the Ministry of Labor and Vocational Training (MoLVT), which account for two-thirds of the total number of HEIs (MoEYS, 2023). Despite the progress made, Cambodia's HE faces significant challenges that need to be addressed. These challenges encompass issues related to access, quality, equity, relevancy to the market needs, funding, and management and administration (MoEYS, 2019; UN, 2023). One of the reasons for these challenges lies in the lack of proper coordination among involved ministries (MoEYS, 2019) for an increasing number of ministries and government bodies providing higher education services, which causes a deficiency in quality control, administrative overlap, and information sharing. This fragmentation hinders the proper functioning and improvement of education quality.

During COVID-19, the higher education sector faced immense challenges and uncertainties, which added to the persistent challenges. Over 130 HEIs and over 200 thousand higher education students in Cambodia were interrupted. While some HEIs immediately adopted online learning to maintain their operation, others faced with inadequate internet infrastructure, limited readiness for online education, and hesitance to change (Cifuentes-Faura et al., 2021; Heng & Sol, 2021). Students also faced challenges when their institutions switched to online or hybrid teaching and learning due primarily to constraints on technology access and teaching methods (Eri et al., 2021). Despite the challenges faced by the institutions and students, the uncertainty of the COVID-19 pandemic forced HEIs throughout the country to transition to blended teaching and learning to maintain their operations since the situation was not under control, at least until mid-2022. This chapter aims to delve into the responses of Cambodian higher education to the COVID-19 crisis from early 2020 to mid-2022. This chapter intends to unpack several questions from a crisis leadership perspective: How has HE responded to the COVID-19 crisis? What are the lessons learned for HE leadership in responding to global crises? Through an analysis of data on governmental and institutional responses, this chapter seeks to provide valuable insights into how HE responded to the COVID-19 crisis, particularly from a leadership perspective.

## Crisis Leadership: Conceptual Framework

COVID-19 is indeed a global crisis as it emerged suddenly and as an unexpected event with a potential impact on human society all over the world. The pandemic's rapid spread and the profound effects it has had on public health, economies, and daily life in numerous countries highlight its global nature. Crises are perceived as challenging situations that can have detrimental effects on organisational operations and survival if not addressed promptly and effectively (Riggio & Newstead, 2023). According to Riggio and Newstead (2023), crises can be viewed from two perspectives: as a crisis-as-event and a crisis-as-process. The crisis-as-event represents discrete and infrequent occurrences, often unpredictable in nature, such as natural disasters and accidents.

Although these events may not happen frequently, their impact on organisations can be far-reaching and severe. On the other hand, the crisis-as-process perspective portrays crises as unfolding over time, with less sudden surprise or shock (Riggio & Newstead, 2023). These ongoing processes can negatively affect an organisation's operations and are often linked to issues such as corruption or dysfunctionality within the organisation itself. The COVID-19 pandemic can indeed be categorised as a crisis-as-event because it was a rare and sudden surprise. Inappropriate or delayed responses to such a crisis can have severe consequences, potentially leading to the collapse of societies and organisations where the crisis occurred. The COVID-19 crisis has directly impacted educational institutions, educational staff, and students in terms of teaching and learning, as well as their physical and mental health. This global crisis has disrupted traditional educational practices and necessitated significant adjustments to adapt to new modes of teaching and learning, causing various challenges and concerns for those involved in the education sector.

In a crisis situation, an inadequate and delayed response can have devastating consequences, potentially leading to organisational collapse (Riggio & Newstead, 2023). Thus, it requires crisis leadership to respond to the calamity. Crisis leadership refers to the ability of individuals or organisational leaders to navigate high-stress, unpredictable situations that threaten the organisation's viability, values, and performance (Riggio & Newstead, 2023). It entails making critical decisions rapidly amid ambiguity and uncertainty regarding the crisis's cause, impact, and resolution. Effective crisis leaders demonstrate emotional resilience, address the needs of stakeholders and victims, and handle undesirable outcomes. They respond to disruption and change, recognise high stakes, and take immediate corrective action. Crisis leaders in higher education could include national authorities such as the ministry, higher education institutions (HEIs), higher education staff, lecturers, student bodies, as well as stakeholders associated with HEIs. Crisis leadership essentially comprises five competencies for effectively managing the crisis, including sensemaking, decision-making, communication, coordinating teamwork, and facilitating learning. Each competency represents a critical aspect of crisis leadership, enabling leaders to effectively address crises, foster teamwork, and learn from experience to build a more resilient organisation. With these competencies, leadership entails providing clear direction, communication, and making decisions under time pressure while navigating pivotal challenges that can shape the organisation's future (Lalani et al., 2021).

## The Cambodian COVID-19 Response

### Emergency Response

The MoEYS implemented various measures to prepare for responding to the impending COVID-19 crisis before it reached the country in an effort to better understand the crisis within the education sector. The ministry assessed the COVID-19 situation and constantly disseminated information to education authorities and institutions across the nation to keep them informed about the evolving situation. For instance, in late January 2020, a directive was issued when the first COVID-19 case was detected, emphasising the importance of preventive measures and personal hygiene within educational institutions nationwide. The ministry also directed all Provincial Departments of Education (PDE) to reinforce preventive measures and enhance the well-being of students within educational institutions. Subsequently, when the first COVID-19 case was reported in Siem Reap, a densely populated city, the MoEYS quickly made the executive decision to close schools and educational institutions in that city and urged schools and students to remain extra-vigilant. The ministry urged all educational institutions to designate education staff responsible for COVID-19 prevention and hygiene promotion within their respective institutions. The ministry also called upon education authorities to intensify prevention measures, prepare for pandemic response, and collaborate closely with local health centres. These actions were implemented to safeguard public health and ensure the well-being of both students and educational staff during the COVID-19 pandemic. They also aimed to ensure that awareness of the potential impact of the pandemic was shared and understood. In preparation to minimise the risk of contracting the virus, the ministry permitted government departments and organisations to digitalise administrative documentation through platforms such as Telegram and WhatsApp. These initial actions aimed to provide relevant stakeholders with a clear understanding of the widespread nature of the disease and its potential impact on various sectors. Under the leadership of the ministry, these actions were intended to minimise the sudden shock of the disease's onset.

Additional measures were indeed taken in anticipation of responding to the escalating COVID-19 crisis. As the situation intensified, the MoEYS established a COVID-19 Combating Committee on March 14, 2020. This committee comprised key figures, including the Minister, Secretary of State, Deputy-Secretariate, General Directorate, Head of Department, and Deputy Head of Department. The MoEYS retained the flexibility to include more members as necessary to have a more diverse representation at all levels. The composition of this committee aimed to institutionalise a comprehensive response to the crisis, ensuring that everyone played a part in the collective effort. The committee's primary responsibility was to oversee and ensure accountability and efficiency in implementing COVID-19 prevention measures. As a leader in the ministry, the Minister of MoEYS also played a pivotal role in the National Committee for Combating COVID-19, which was formally established on March 18, 2020, underscoring the ministry's leadership in addressing the COVID-19 crisis. The National Committee for Combating COVID-19 (NCCC) comprises members from various ministries, which is crucial for a coordinated and effective response to the crisis. With the guidance of the ministry, HEIs were prompt in their response to the government's directives during the COVID-19 pandemic. While each institution adapted its response individually, a common thread was the dissemination of critical information to students, lecturers, and staff. They emphasised the importance of adhering to the Ministry of Health (MoH) guidelines, including practising social distancing and maintaining proper hygiene to ensure the well-being of everyone on campus. HEIs consistently shared COVID-19 information through various means, including official announcements, informative workshops, YouTube videos, and virtual sessions.

## National School Closures

When the MoEYS decided to close schools nationwide on March 16, 2020, HEIs across the country promptly complied, closing down their campuses and implementing strict access controls. This included mandatory QR code scanning for staff and students entering campus premises, which proved instrumental in efficient contact tracing for COVID-19. These collective efforts aimed to foster adherence to preventive guidelines, encouraging mask-wearing, social distancing, and maintaining cleanliness, especially during access to HEI premises. HE students who had recently travelled to countries with confirmed COVID-19 cases were required to trace their travel history. In cases where students were considered potential COVID-19 contacts or suspects, they were urged to contact the emergency number 115 for consultation and promptly inform the designated focal person at their respective institutions. Additionally, the directive mandated that provincial departments of education establish COVID-19 Combating Committee responsible for monitoring and reporting to the MoEYS daily through existing communication channels. The MoEYS made clear the communication channel within the sector, indicating upward and downward communication. The combating committee in the local area took responsibility for collaborating with other relevant stakeholders to communicate with HEIs—this directive aimed to mitigate the potential spread of COVID-19 within educational institutions and ensure public health. Following the closure of schools and educational institutions, the MoEYS implemented travel restrictions and limited the number of participants in any events or workshops to no more than 50 people. Missions outside of work zones were cancelled, and COVID-19 protocols were strictly enforced. The ministry urged students and teachers to follow the ministry's Facebook page and remain vigilant about the situation.

## Emergency Remote Teaching: The Shift to Blended Learning

As the COVID-19 situation worsened, the MoEYS announced an extension of the school closure without a specified end date. At the country-level decision, the MoEYS encouraged educational institutions to provide long-distance learning or e-learning. The minister of MoEYS mentioned that "We encourage schools at all levels, both public and private, to start thinking about teaching online" (Tom, 2020, para.4). This decision added financial pressure on HEIs (Chet & Sok, 2020). Each Higher Education Institution (HEI) had to establish a clear system to ensure the quality of e-learning and long-distance learning. The minister added that "online teaching curriculum educational institutions at all levels need to develop their own curricula because the condition of COVID-19 may last longer" (Tom, 2020, para.3). In Cambodia, higher education institutions (HEIs) responded to the COVID-19 pandemic with varying capacities, which depended on the resources and leadership capabilities of the institutions. The MoEYS directive to transition from traditional in-class learning left HEIs in a state of uncertainty, as blended learning or online learning had not been well-defined. However, according to Chet and Sok (2020), online learning is referred to as e-learning, online learning, and blended learning.

Before the extension of school closures, some higher HEIs promptly transitioned from traditional in-class teaching to an online or blended learning approach to ensure continuous teaching and learning. Meanwhile, other HEIs opted to wait for a more favourable on-campus reopening, expressing concerns about the quality of online learning because they faced challenges in making this transition due to limitations in technology capacity, tech infrastructure, and the readiness of teaching staff to adapt their pedagogical methods to online teaching (Chea et al., 2020; Sol, 2021). Data gathered from social media indicates that many private HEIs tended to adapt more quickly to online learning. This can be attributed to their favourable circumstances, including having adequate internet infrastructure, tech-savvy staff, institutional familiarity with technology, and strong institutional leadership. At the Royal University of Phnom Penh, a public HEI, the Faculty of Education stands out as an exemplar of swift institutional leadership response to transformation to online learning (Chet & Sok, 2020). The available data revealed their responsive actions, which included strategic planning, the establishment of online learning committees, the implementation of teaching and learning systems, capacity-building for staff, and training for both lecturers and students in the new learning environment, as well as monitoring and evaluation.

## Establishing Online Learning Committees

To manage the transition to online learning, HEIs established an Online Learning Committee to work on digital resolution during the COVID-19 pandemic (Chet et al., 2022). This committee diligently organised teams and defined clear roles for various online learning initiatives. For instance, shortly after the government extended school closures due to the ongoing COVID-19 situation, the leadership team of one HEI convened a series of meetings to devise solutions. This committee comprised vice presidents, deans, and department chairs. During these initial discussions, the committee addressed the challenges faced by the institution and its students. They considered the possibility of shifting to online classes, even though the institution had not previously experienced online learning. To explore alternative online learning platforms, the committee engaged in a comprehensive evaluation process. Ultimately, the decision was made to continue course delivery through e-learning, utilising Google Classroom as the chosen platform.

The committee also took on the main responsibility of ensuring the smooth operation of online teaching and learning. They developed academic policies, assessment policies, graduation policies, and student engagement policies. On the technical front, the committee focused on creating instructional manuals to facilitate online teaching and learning for both students and lecturers. In terms of pedagogy, they developed teaching guidelines specifically tailored for lecturers. These policies and guidelines established during the initial transition to online teaching and learning allowed for flexibility and creativity in course delivery, while a sub-committee system was also implemented. This sub-committee included representatives from the student body, academic committee, and technical committee, fostering close collaboration among various stakeholders throughout the COVID-19 pandemic.

## Building Learning Management Systems

Based on data from social media, several HEIs, predominantly private, emerged as leading in transitioning to blended learning during the initial school closures. Notable institutions like the American University of Phnom Penh (AUPP), Paññāsāstra University of Cambodia (PUC), CamEd Business School, University of Cambodia (UC), Phnom Penh International University (PPIU), Dewey International University (DIU), University of Puthisastra (UP), Build Bright University (BBU), and the National University of Battambang (NUBB), the Royal University of Phnom Penh (RUPP) (Chet & Sok, 2020; Chet et al., 2022) among others, proactively embraced this shift. These HEIs adopted a variety of learning platforms, with Google Classroom and Microsoft 365 being the most commonly used platforms, facilitating online teaching and learning experiences. Some institutions took an additional step by developing their own learning management systems to efficiently store and manage teaching materials. Others customised platforms like Moodle, providing students with valuable tools for learning and reviewing their lessons. In addition to these platforms, HEIs utilised various communication tools such as Google Meet, Zoom, VooV, Skype, Facebook Messenger, and Telegram to facilitate remote educational activities such as interactive online sessions or workshops. For example, the University of Human Resources offered its students a digital system on April 19 after testing it through Zoom and Google Classroom (Tom, 2020).

The university's online committee also carried out an experiment with the platform to establish a functional system. They conducted extensive tests of the system with university staff and students prior to rolling it out. Such preparation of the online learning system required time and effort as the system was relatively new and required thorough exploration of its functions. HEIs that used the free version of Google Classroom faced the challenge of self-exploration of the limited function. At the same time, those with subscription packages received support from the provider, allowing them to access more functions for teaching and learning. Testing the system before its official launch also took time to ensure its readiness. Once the platform was well-prepared, the online learning committee communicated the procedures for online learning to both lecturers and students.

## Capacity Building for Key Staff and Lecturers

HEIs faced considerable challenges when transitioning to online learning, primarily because staff members and lecturers lacked the necessary capacity for it. Despite some having prior experience with online learning, they were not adequately prepared for online teaching. The urgency imposed by the COVID-19 pandemic compelled staff members to actively engage with the online learning platform, striving to understand its functionality in order to provide support to both lecturers and students. In response to these challenges, HEIs provided capacity-building sessions for key staff, focusing on the functionality of the online learning management system. The goal was to equip them with the essential skills required for effective online collaboration and learning. Then, focal points of contact were designated for the implementation of the system to monitor and provide technical support to students and lecturers to access the learning platforms, ensuring that teaching and learning take place during the COVID-19 pandemic.

Lecturers and teaching staff were invited to orientation sessions focused on the functionality of the new online learning system. It is worth noting that a significant portion of HEIs, particularly private institutions, commonly employ contract-based full-time or part-time lecturers and staff. The latter hold primary responsibilities centred on course preparation and teaching. For many of these part-time lecturers, online teaching methods were unfamiliar, and the concept of online learning was entirely new. In response to these challenges, HEIs conducted ongoing orientation sessions aimed at enhancing the teaching effectiveness of faculty members and lecturers in the online environment. A series of consultation sessions followed, addressing various topics, including navigating the online platform, effective teaching methods, and assessment methods. Moreover, pedagogical orientation was provided to teaching staff and lecturers, covering online learning policies, guidelines, and assessment methods. Continuous feedback and improvement mechanisms were woven into each course to ensure an adaptable and evolving online learning experience, effectively addressing the unique challenges posed by online education.

## Student Engagement in Online Learning

In HE, students faced numerous challenges during the shift to online learning, including access to learning devices, internet connectivity issues, disruptions in their learning environment, and difficulties in maintaining engagement. A preceding study found that approximately 86% of HE students primarily relied on smartphones for their online learning, with nearly 90% depending on personal mobile data for connectivity (Heng et al., 2023). These challenges had the potential to impact the quality of online learning, a concern that higher education institutions (HEIs) needed to address when designing their learning systems and teaching methods. In response to these challenges, HEIs and lecturers strived to create a more flexible teaching and learning environment, acknowledging that it might influence educational quality. In addition, to ensure students could access online learning, HEIs facilitated engagement with online learning platforms, offering technical support and emotional guidance to students. Information about online learning was disseminated through a variety of channels, including social media and direct phone contact with students and their families. Orientation sessions about the online learning system were constantly provided, with in-person sessions offered for students less familiar with technology, all while adhering to COVID-19 protocols. HEIs leveraged various communication channels, including phone calls, Facebook Messenger, Facebook posts, WhatsApp, and, later, Telegram channels to ensure students were informed and could access online learning.

To students' engagement in online learning, the collective efforts of HEIs were necessitated. HE cultivated a culture of learning through collaboration with lecturers who regularly interacted with students in the learning process to gather feedback about their teaching and students' learning. For instance, HEIs considered adjusting online teaching methods to suit students' individual learning needs, thus ensuring a more suitable and effective learning experience. Once feedback was collected from both lecturers and students, HEIs made efforts to address the identified issues. Regarding pedagogical responses, lecturers played crucial roles in engaging students with adaptive methods tailored to students' learning situations. They adapted both synchronous and asynchronous teaching methods (Chea et al., 2020) by conducting real-time sessions through Zoom, Google Meet, and Microsoft Teams, as well as uploading videos and reading materials to the learning platform. Another strategy applied for enhancing online learning was the establishment of student learning communities (Chea et al., 2020) through Facebook groups, which allowed students to interact with each other not only for academic purposes but also to support their social well-being during the pandemic. Some HEIs facilitated the creation of Facebook groups for students to engage in collaborative learning, while some students took the initiative to form their own groups for learning.

## Online Teaching Recognition

In June 2020, in response to the severity of the COVID-19 situation, MoEYS announced the extension of school closures and the continuation of online learning for all HEIs. The ministry aimed to enhance quality online learning and HEIs were required to apply for an online education license from MoEYS. To obtain this license, HEIs had to meet a number of requirements, which included having clear online teaching mechanisms, a well-defined online teaching schedule, appropriate methods of assessment, an online teaching committee, online teaching guidelines and policies, and a prior report of online teaching. During this stage, MoEYS aimed to enhance the quality of online teaching, with Education Minister Hang Chuon Naron acknowledging that "digital education was still limited and unacceptable. The quality of education is not as good as in the classroom" (Tom, 2020, para. 6). The requirement for an online teaching license marked a positive step in Cambodia's transition to digital learning, representing a starting point for the new normal. While this requirement presented a challenge for HEIs, it is important to note that they did not start from scratch. They had already made significant strides by transitioning to online teaching in response to school closures. This requirement was one further step to formalise the existing online teaching practices that had initially emerged as a response to the closure of schools. In July 2020, the Ministry of Education, Youth, and Sport (MoEYS), in collaboration with development partners, developed the Cambodia Education Response Plan for the COVID-19 pandemic with the aim of responding to the crisis with responsibility, effectiveness, and efficiency. The plan serves as a coordinating tool that guides stakeholders and development partners to ensure the harmonisation of their responses across the sector (MoEYS, 2020). However, the decision to implement either online learning or blended learning was left to the discretion of individual institutions.

To officially run online learning, several HEIs promptly applied for this recognition and received approval from the ministry. Data retrieved from the Facebook pages of multiple HEIs demonstrated that these institutions presented structured e-learning plans to secure recognition. MoEYS acted in a rapid decision-making process and efficiently approved the recognition of online teaching for HEIs. Notably, institutions like UC, AUPP, and PUC were among the HEIs that obtained online teaching recognition certificates at an earlier stage.

## The Transition Back

### *School Reopening*

On September 26, 2020, MoEYS announced the reopening of HEIs after a prolonged period of closure. This decision was in response to the decreasing number of COVID-19 cases and concerns over the quality of online learning. In order to obtain approval for reopening, educational institutions were required to undergo assessments based on the Standard of Operation Procedure (SOP). Institutions that met the assessment criteria, closely adhered to MoEYS guidelines, and were prepared to invite MoEYS officials to inspect their campuses were granted permission to reopen. However, due to the rigorous standards, only a limited number of institutions with higher SOP ratings received immediate approval for reopening, while the majority had to await the second phase when they were ready and COVID-19 was more under control. For example, institutions that successfully obtained MoEYS approval for reopening included the University of Cambodia, which conducted campus inspections and formalised the process with the signing of a Memorandum of Understanding (MoU) before officially reopening on September 21, 2020. In a similar vein, the American University of Phnom Penh (AUPP) also underwent campus inspections by MoEYS officials to facilitate their reopening in the same month.

At this stage, with standard operating procedures (SOPs) restricting the number of students per classroom and mandating other necessary protocols, the leadership of each HEI and its online learning committee had to meticulously organise the teaching schedule and maintain clear communication with students. Some HEIs adopted hybrid methods, allowing limited numbers of students into the classroom. This approach necessitated the active involvement of university staff for effective management, and clear directions were essential. Additionally, feedback from students and lecturers was sought to inform the design of the learning system.

### *Second Nationwide School Closure*

On December 1, 2020, all schools and educational institutions faced a second closure due to the detection of a significant COVID-19 cluster. This closure lasted until November 1, 2021, and it had a continuing impact on the education system throughout the country. During this extended period of closure, HEIs and students remained impacted. However, as this phase progressed, they gradually experienced less shock as they had been in the crisis for a period of time. It was a time of reconsidering the improvements in teaching and learning systems, pedagogy, internet infrastructure, and policies, including those related to evaluation and assessment. In this phase, HE had collective actions to enhance online learning. For example, several online workshops, training sessions, and webinars were held both within and between institutions to facilitate the exchange of learning and teaching experiences during the COVID-19 pandemic. At the same time, educational videos by educational institutions and students promoted student engagement in online learning. This exemplified the collective leadership of HEIs as they adapted to the uncertainties of the crisis and worked towards establishing a new normal. During this period, some HEIs delayed the collection of fees from students because many students had lost their income and couldn't afford to pay. When HEIs eventually announced the resumption of fee collection, students reacted strongly. Some suggested that the schools should offer discounts for this period.

### *National Reopening of Educational Institutions*

In early November 2021, as COVID-19 came under control, the government lifted all travel restrictions, and all schools fully reopened. However, strict COVID-19 protocols remained in effect. To reopen their campuses, each Higher Education Institution (HEI) was required to be thoroughly prepared. Despite the government's permission for full school reopening, the MoEYS strongly urged all educational institutions to adhere to COVID-19 protocols and comply with three essential "do's" and three important "don'ts. Several workshops, such as those focusing on quality assurance practices during the COVID-19 pandemic, were organised. These workshops aimed to address the challenges, adaptations, and the way forward. They also provided insights into future improvements for online learning in the post-COVID-19 era.

## Discussion

The trajectory of COVID-19 in Cambodia between 2020 and mid-2022 was marked by significant fluctuations, demonstrating periods of both exacerbation and improvement. This complex evolution led to the categorisation of the pandemic into three distinct epidemiological phases: containment, mitigation, and full opening. Each phase was characterised by the extent of viral transmission, the impact on public health, and the corresponding response measures implemented by authorities. Throughout this dynamic landscape, Cambodia's higher education system responded in unique and adaptive ways tailored to the evolving stage of the pandemic.

These responses can be categorised into five main stages, which encapsulate the nuanced approach of Cambodia's HEIs to the crisis. In the *Initial Pre-Closure Phase,* national leadership took the helm in preparing for the impending outbreak and its potential impacts. HEIs played a critical role in comprehending the crisis and took it upon themselves to ensure that all relevant stakeholders within the sector were well-informed. Constant and rapid communication was diligently maintained. HEIs communicated extensively with staff, lecturers, and students about the pandemic, fostering a cautious and proactive approach to containing the disease. In the *First School Closure Period*, quick decision-making was paramount at both the national and institutional levels. The MoEYS made the decision to close schools and formed a national committee to respond to the crisis. At the provincial level, the education department created task forces to assist educational institutions in their response to the pandemic. HEIs responded rapidly by establishing an online learning committee, which aimed to support lecturers and students in the transition to remote learning. Clear channels of communication were established between MoEYS, the sub-national levels, and educational institutions to ensure the dissemination of accurate information while mitigating the spread of misinformation. At the institutional level, under the guidance of institutional leadership, active engagement of staff and students became the norm. For example, within the online learning committee, staff with diverse expertise collaborated to set up an online learning system, with students playing a pivotal role in promoting an understanding of the crisis and facilitating their engagement in online learning. MoEYS concurrently developed a comprehensive COVID-19 response plan, acting as a vital coordinating tool and guide for HEIs to harmonise their responses (e.g., Tice et al., 2021).

In the *Reopening Phase,* after a prolonged school closure, schools were cautiously reopened, necessitating strict adherence to Standard Operating Procedures (SOPs). In this stage, HEIs had to turn to a hybrid teaching model, with a limited number of students allowed in physical classrooms. Despite the substantial investment required, this approach empowered HEIs to innovate creatively in facilitating teaching and learning. In the *Second School Closure Period*, due to the resurgence of the crisis, educational institutions were once again compelled to close their physical campuses. This phase prompted a comprehensive re-evaluation of approaches, with a renewed focus on enhancing online learning as the primary alternative. HEIs were mandated to apply for an online teaching license, which demanded clear and functional teaching and learning infrastructure. This presented an opportunity for HEIs to further enhance their digital education systems. In the *Full Opening with COVID-19 Protocols* stage, the situation improved, and schools fully reopened, albeit under stringent adherence to COVID-19 protocols. Despite the resumption of on-campus teaching, the online learning system continued to operate, representing an ongoing commitment to providing flexibility and accessibility in education.

To conclude, amidst this intricate landscape, MoEYS demonstrated strong leadership by providing crucial guidance to educational institutions in their response to the crisis. This comprehensive response involved all education stakeholders, from the ministry to institutional and individual levels. MoEYS played a central role in assessing the crisis and its potential impacts, maintaining a consistent and clear communication channel regarding the crisis through various mediums. Moreover, the ministry made strategic decisions in consultation with the COVID-19 Combating Committee. The ministry facilitated a two-way communication channel between the national and local levels, ensuring the effective dissemination of relevant information and measures to enable a timely and effective response. A key strength of Cambodia's response to the COVID-19 pandemic was the allowance for flexibility and diversity within the combating committees. This approach enabled the utilisation of a wide range of expertise to address the crisis. This fostered a sense of ownership and collective action among relevant stakeholders. Institutional responses varied, largely contingent on organisational capacity, but they were all directed by MoEYS. Despite facing limitations in terms of financial and resource support, the sector displayed a deep political commitment to supporting HEIs. HEIs also acted swiftly by disseminating critical information to staff, lecturers, and students, fostering a shared understanding of the crisis and its potential consequences (Wilson et al., 2020). While responses differed among institutions, each institution harnessed available resources, both financial and human, to address the crisis. Online teaching emerged as a central approach, enabling HEIs to sustain their operations.

## References

Chea, S., Kieng, S., Leng, P., & Water, T. (2020). Pedagogy of online learning in Cambodia: Revisiting ideas of connection, engagement, attendance, and assessment. *AVI Policy Brief, 19*, 1–9.

Chet, C., & Sok, S. (2020). Dangers and opportunities related to the COVID-19 pandemic for higher education institutions in Cambodia. *Cambodia Journal of Basic and Applied Research (CJBAR), 2*(1), 20–26.

Chet, C., Sok, S., & Sou, V. (2022). The Antecedents and consequences of study commitment to online learning at higher education institutions (HEIs) in Cambodia. *Sustainability, 14*(6), 3184.

Chhim, S., Ku, G., Mao, S., Put, W. V., Van Damme, W., Ir, P., Chhorvann, C., & Or, V. (2023). Descriptive assessment of COVID-19 responses and lessons learnt in Cambodia, January 2020 to June 2022. *BMJ Glob Health, 8*(5). https://doi.org/10.1136/bmjgh-2023-011885

Cifuentes-Faura, J., Obor, D. O., To, L., & Al-Naabi, I. (2021). Cross-cultural impacts of COVID-19 on higher education learning and teaching practices in Spain, Oman, Nigeria and Cambodia: A cross-cultural study. *Journal of University Teaching and Learning Practice, 18*(5), 8.

Eri, R., Gudimetla, P., Star, S., Rowlands, J., Girgla, A., To, L., Li, F., Sochea, N., & Bindal, U. (2021). Digital resilience in higher education in response to COVID-19 pandemic: Student perceptions from Asia and Australia. *Journal of University Teaching and Learning Practice, 18*(5), 27.

Heng, K., & Sol, K. (2021). COVID-19 and Cambodian higher education: Challenges and opportunities. In *Online learning during COVID-19 and key issues in education* (pp. 31–48).

Heng, K., Sol, K., & Pang, S. (2023). Challenges and opportunities of online learning: Insights from Cambodian higher education during Covid-19. *Issues in Educational Research, 33*(2), 608–630.

Ministry of Planning. (2020). *General population census of the kingdom of Cambodia 2019: National report on final census results.*

Lalani, K., Crawford, J., & Butler-Henderson, K. (2021). Academic leadership during COVID-19 in higher education: Technology adoption and adaptation for online learning during a pandemic. *International Journal of Leadership in Education,* 1–17. https://doi.org/10.1080/13603124.2021.1988716

MoEYS. (2019). *Cambodia's education 2030 roadmap: Sustainable development—Goal 4.* Ministry of Education, Youth and Sport.

MoEYS. (2020). *Cambodia education response plan to COVID 19 pandemic.*

MoEYS. (2023). *Education congress.* Ministry of Education Youth and Sport. Retrieved from http://moeys.gov.kh/wp-content/uploads/2023/05/CRC_01_Final_Draft_EC_Report_2023_in_English_04042023-1.pdf

Nozaki, I., Hachiya, M., & Ikeda, C. (2023). COVID-19 vaccination program in Cambodia: Achievements and remaining challenges. *Global Health & Medicine, 5*(2), 92–98.

Pramanick, M., Choolani, M., & Seng, L. B. (2021). The epidemiology of COVID-19 in ten Southeast Asian countries. *Medical Journal of Malaysia, 76*(6), 783.

Riggio, R. E., & Newstead, T. (2023). Crisis leadership. *Annual Review of Organizational Psychology and Organizational Behavior, 10*(1), 201–224. https://doi.org/10.1146/annurev-orgpsych-120920-044838

Rudolph, J., Tan, S., Crawford, J., & Butler-Henderson, K. (2023). Perceived quality of online learning during COVID-19 in higher education in Singapore: Perspectives from students, lecturers, and academic leaders. *Educational Research for Policy and Practice, 22*(1), 171–191. https://doi.org/10.1007/s10671-022-09325-0

Sol, K. (2021). Rethinking higher education in Cambodia contemporary challenges and priorities in the post-COVID-19 era. *Journal of International Education, 27*, 46–60.

Tansuchat, R., Suriyankietkaew, S., Petison, P., Punjaisri, K., & Nimsai, S. (2022). Impacts of COVID-19 on sustainable agriculture value chain development in Thailand and ASEAN. *Sustainability, 14*(20), 12985.

Tao, N. P. H., Nguyen, D., Minh, L. H. N., Duong, V., Beaupha, C., Ahdal, T. A., & Huy, N. T. (2022). Cambodia achieved a high vaccination coverage for its population: A good example of a lower middle-income country. *Journal of Global Health, 12,* 03088. https://doi.org/10.7189/jogh.12.03088

Tom, M. (2020, April 20). Ministry of Education urges higher education institutions to launch online curriculum, but experts worry about quality. https://khmer.voanews.com/a/education-ministry-urges-online-classes-but-qualityquestions/5385279.html

Tice, D., Baumeister, R., Crawford, J., Allen, K. A., & Percy, A. (2021). Student belongingness in higher education: Lessons for Professors from the COVID-19 pandemic. *Journal of University Teaching & Learning Practice, 18*(4), 2. https://doi.org/10.53761/1.18.4.2

UN. (2023). *Transforming our world: The 2030 agenda for sustainable development*. United Nations. Retrieved March 14, 2023, from https://sdgs.un.org/2030agenda

UNESCO. (2021). *UNESCO COVID-19 education response* (COVID-19: Reopening and reimagining universities, survey on higher education through the UNESCO National Commissions, Issue).

VoA. (2020). *Ministry of Education urges higher education institutions to launch online curriculum, but experts worry about quality* (Malis & Tom, Trans.).

World Health Organization. (2023). *Cambodia*. Retrieved May 30, 2023, from https://covid19.who.int/region/wpro/country/kh

Wilson, S., Tan, S., Knox, M., Ong, A., Crawford, J., & Rudolph, J. (2020). Enabling cross-cultural student voice during COVID-19: A collective autoethnography. *Journal of University Teaching & Learning Practice, 17*(5), 3. https://doi.org/10.53761/1.17.5.3

# Communication Studies and Journalism Education in Egypt in Times of Multiple Crises

Carola Richter, Inas Abou Youssef, and Hanan Badr

## Introduction

This chapter focuses on crisis leadership in higher education in Egypt and zooms into (mass) communication studies and journalism education as one of its sectors. We take the forced transition to distance teaching during the pandemic and the post-COVID-19 situation as a case study and embed it in analysing the multiple crises higher education faces in Egypt. To substantiate our analysis, we rely on original focus group interview data collected from different mass communication faculty leaders during the pandemic in 2020 and afterwards in 2023. These leaders are responsible for managing the institutions by making decisions and implementing them. They are also key stakeholders in communicating between the ministerial and the university presidency levels and the student body. Thus, they can provide authentic insights into the current topics and conflicts that need to be dealt with in higher education.

C. Richter (✉)
Freie Universität Berlin, Berlin, Germany
e-mail: carola.richter@fu-berlin.de

I. A. Youssef
Ahram Canadian University, 6th of October City, Egypt

H. Badr
Paris-Lodron-University Salzburg, Salzburg, Austria
e-mail: hanan.badr@plus.ac.at



J. Rudolph et al. (eds.), *The Palgrave Handbook of Crisis Leadership in Higher Education*,
https://doi.org/10.1007/978-3-031-54509-2_14

In addition, the chapter features a critical review of the literature on higher education development in the mass communication and journalism education sector in Egypt. We divide the chapter into three main sections: The first section provides the context and historical trajectories that led to "multiple crises" in Egypt's mass communication and journalism education (building on Badr & Richter, 2022). The second section focuses on the time of the COVID-19 pandemic and how it accelerated the crisis. It also sheds light on the opportunities that have been discussed to overcome them (building on empirical studies in Abou Youssef & Richter, 2022). The third section provides a post-COVID evaluation from a leadership perspective and an outlook into the future crisis in Egyptian higher education.

## The Roads to a Crisis Situation in Mass Media and Journalism Education in Egypt

### The Development of Egyptian Higher Education

Egypt was a regional pioneer in mass communication studies in the Arab world and still has the largest community of researchers and students in the Middle East and North Africa (MENA) region. The professionalisation of the journalistic craft developed during the 1920s and 1930s, and Egyptian media and communication studies were founded during this time. The first journalism schools were established at the American University in Cairo in 1937 and Cairo University in 1939 (Richter & Badr, 2018).

The Faculty of Mass Communication at Cairo University, founded in 1974, is informally dubbed the "Mother Faculty" of all mass communication institutes in Egypt and most of the MENA region. It was the first faculty for journalism and mass communication in the Arab world and the alma mater for several generations of renowned journalists and professors (Abdelrahman, 1991).

For a long time, it has remained the only state-funded, fully developed faculty in Egypt. This has changed as new faculties were founded in the past few years. Three decades of neoliberal higher education reforms amid controlled privatisation and re-autocratisation (Barsoum, 2020; Kohstall, 2009) led to a dual structure of higher education—also in the communication and journalism sector—consisting of state-funded/public and private universities. In 2021, there were six faculties of mass communication, and half of Egypt's 31 public universities offered courses in communication studies (Badr & Richter, 2022). Public programmes are still mostly offered in departments within the Faculties of Arts, are more geographically dispersed than the private universities, and include regions like Upper Egypt (Assiut, South Valley or Minya University) and Lower Egypt (like Alexandria, Tanta or El-Menoufiya University). In the profit-driven private sector, more than 24 universities in Egypt offer degrees in communication or journalism studies (Badr & Richter, 2022). New institutes are still emerging. Private universities with established media and journalism studies include Modern Sciences and Arts University, 6th of October University, Al-Ahram Canadian University, Future University and British University in Egypt. Most of these universities offer BA programmes in communication studies, with some also offering MA programmes. In addition, there are newly established so-called National Universities and state universities with tuition fees, of which some also offer communication study programmes like Galala University.

## Leadership Hierarchies

The same kind of leadership hierarchy applies for all institutional strands—public, private or national. This reflects a traditional hierarchical leadership model (Uhl-Bien et al., 2007). At the top of the hierarchy is the Ministry of Higher Education and Scientific Research. Four bodies are related to the ministry: (1) the Supreme Council of Higher Education of Universities, (2) the Supreme Council of Higher Education in Private Institutions, (3) the Supreme Council of Higher Education in Private and National Universities and (4) the Supreme Council of Education in Technical Colleges. The Ministry of Higher Education and Scientific Research has a periodical meeting with each of the four bodies, discussing policies and proposing new regulations. The supreme councils also establish committees. These committees are responsible for setting up and revising the bylaws of the faculties. The committees also grant accreditation for the media and journalism schools' programmes every four years.

The second level in the structural hierarchy is the level of universities. On top here is the president of the university or institute and three vice presidents, one for education and students' affairs, one for graduate programmes and scientific research and one for environmental affairs and community services. A university secretary heads the administration. Private universities and institutes also have a board of trustees that is appointed to monitor the execution of plans and to suggest new policies.

On the third level, the level of media faculties and institutes, there is the dean and usually three vice deans appointed by the dean. They report their work to the faculty council and mirror the vice presidents' tasks on the faculty level. The number of vice deans might be extended, but each faculty must have at least three appointed to obtain their local quality assurance accreditation.

The academic affairs are primarily discussed in the respective departments that report to the faculty council, which consists of heads of departments, the vice deans, the dean and two or three public figures. When the faculty council approves a decision, the dean is responsible for its implementation. The dean also reports to the university council or the university president. Interestingly, when it comes to technical and administrative decisions, deans of public universities have more leverage in making decisions as long as it does not need a huge budget. In contrast, in private universities, the president or even the owner of the university has the upper hand which reflects a traditional leadership model and slows down decision-making. For example, at Ahram Canadian University, the implementation of the decisions takes rather long because the president of the university needs the approval of Al-Ahram News Organisation for all financial affairs, as they are the owners of the university. The president alone cannot access funds (I. Khoraby, personal communication, March 2023). Yet, while the decision-making processes on the leadership level are somewhat similar, the dual structure of the university system has brought up unresolved problems regarding inequality in education.

## Neoliberal Reforms and Precarious Working Conditions

Public journalism schools are chronically underfunded and overcrowded. Cairo University alone has 350,000 students enrolled in all faculties (DAAD, 2020). The Faculty of Mass Communication has about 4500 students in its Arabic- and English-language undergraduate and postgraduate programmes. In comparison, the faculty's facilities were originally designed to accommodate about 400 students only (Badr & Richter, 2022).

Public universities still attract top high school graduates because of their long-established reputation. Still, due to political reasons, the universities have to accept many students, double or even triple the size of available spots, overburdening the infrastructure (Badr & Richter, 2022). Thus, in public universities, the courses of study are very large in student number, and the teaching load is usually high. At the same time, salaries for the teaching staff are comparably low. Before the financial crisis in Egypt started in 2022, the basic monthly salary of a Ph.D. lecturer, who teaches about eight hours per week, was 400–900 US dollars in state universities, depending on rank and seniority, which can be considered a low, middle-class income. Private universities can reach double the rate of state universities in higher professor ranks, which often leads to a brain drain for these institutions.

Private tuition-based journalism programmes are better equipped than state universities and attract (economically) privileged students who have enjoyed private secondary education, enabling them to speak foreign languages (Badr & Elmaghraby, 2021). This leads to a class segregation of student strata. Yet, as postgraduate programmes at private universities are rarely accredited, a postgraduate bottleneck forces students back to public universities or leave Egypt to seek postgraduate degrees elsewhere.

Regarding the staff, overregulated and underfunded public universities leave little margin for creative and innovative teaching and research (Badr & Elmaghraby, 2021). Egyptian doctoral students hired as staff receive open-ended contracts with certain career opportunities, but they also must bear the main burden of teaching that overshadows research activity. Many professors must supplement their income with additional teaching at private universities or journalism, PR or consultancy professions. A brain drain to other countries, such as the Arab Gulf states, that offer better opportunities or higher salaries is common. These precarious work conditions often discourage (young) faculty from involving themselves in academic leadership affairs.

In addition to the problems resulting from a neoliberal transformation of the higher education sector, there are several political constraints. The social and political turbulences, starting with the Tahrir Revolution in 2011 and ending with a re-autocratisation and tightening of media freedoms after 2013, disrupted the media industry making it an uncertain and unattractive profession. Egypt is witnessing a strong media concentration in the hands of only a few (Badr, 2021). This concentration led to fewer job opportunities for graduates of mass communication and journalism studies and a preference for those with streamlined political attitudes. In addition, a systematic campaign led by prominent TV anchors advising high school graduates not to enrol in media schools because there would be no jobs for them. This reflects interest on the level of the political leadership to decrease newly graduated ambitious media practitioners entering the media institutions as they are satisfied with the loyal journalists dominating the scene at the moment. As a result, and to adapt to the current political realities, Egyptian journalism curricula often focus on pragmatic, hands-on technological skills and modern buzzwords with little critical perspective (Badr, 2021).

The COVID-19 crisis has accelerated this troublesome situation: teachers were overburdened with many students who had to be trained online, even in practical courses. The different infrastructural conditions in public and private universities increased student gaps. At the same time, these problematic situations forced the decision-makers on the ministry level to finally act, and it opened up opportunities to evade the hierarchical leadership model in Egyptian higher education.

## Accelerating the Crises and New Opportunities: The COVID-19 Implications

In previous decades, teaching communication studies and journalism in the Arab world focused mainly on face-to-face and rarely adopted online or distance learning methods (Alseady, 2019; Arafat, 2017; Helmy, 2020). Thus, mass communication departments and journalism schools in the Arab world faced a real challenge once the COVID-19 pandemic broke out in early 2020.

Even though for many years, Egypt considered itself a pioneer in journalism education and communication studies in the Arab world, it lagged regarding the adoption of technology-based methods of teaching due to a lack of (financial) resources, overload with students and lack of administrative support. It was not until 2005 that an e-learning unit opened in one of the regional universities in Egypt. As an exceptional programme, the mass communication faculty at Cairo University began a complete online master's programme in 2008. However, the faculty board refused to consider it a master's degree that qualifies graduates to apply for a Ph.D. Only when the whole world went into lockdowns in March 2020 did the Minister of Higher Education agree to embed distance learning as a recognised method of education and encouraged universities to adopt a hybrid teaching methodology.

Crises are "occurrences that threaten the fundamental operation or viability of an organisation" (Riggio & Newstead, 2023, p. 203) or a decision-making system, as we described it for the Egyptian higher education sector. The literature on leadership distinguishes between crisis as an event, such as the suddenly occurring COVID-19 pandemic, and crisis as a process, i.e., ongoing mismanagement (Riggio & Newstead, 2023). In the Egyptian case, both phenomena were intertwined: the immediate crisis caused by the pandemic accelerated the problems inherited from an unresolved leadership crisis over the past decades.

## Unregulated Transition

What could be observed at the beginning of the pandemic was an unregulated transition to distance teaching that resembled a laissez-faire or trial-and-error attitude at most institutions. The sudden shift was characterised by self-organisation and personal commitment, lacking a systematic pedagogical approach and a long-term leadership strategy. We conducted a focus group interview with nine participants at the public Cairo University and the private Ahram Canadian University in September 2020 to give us some insights on implementing and evaluating these measures (Abou Youssef & Richter, 2022). The focus group included, in particular, deans and vice deans of the communication studies faculties, representing the leadership on the third (faculty) level. According to the interviewees, both universities adopted open-source software on the internet as quickly and freely available tools. Neither department had any online learning management system (LMS), such as Blackboard. Although both departments shared the same vision, they took different paths of implementation, thus reflecting a take-over of somewhat autonomous leadership on the university or the faculty levels instead of waiting for ministerial decisions.

The mass communication faculty at Cairo University asked staff members to use whatever suitable tools. As the dean justified, "We did not want to panic the staff by imposing a specific online source on them" (H. Mustafa, personal communication, September 2020). The first steps included recording videos of lectures and uploading them on YouTube. "This was the most efficient and quickest way, since our studios are available and professors from any age range can come and record their lectures, then younger generations of assistant professors would upload the material on YouTube" (S. Awadely, personal communication, September 2020). Interactive methods differed among the staff, who mainly selected WhatsApp and Facebook groups to communicate with the students. The dean reported, "They preferred to choose tools they are familiar with." (H. Mustafa, personal communication, September 2020). Younger generations of professors used Zoom and Schoology because "they can easily master these applications", explained one assistant professor (K. Zaki, personal communication, September 2020); others refused to use any direct communication methods and relied on video and audio recordings of the lectures. "As the oldest school of media in the Arab world, we have especially older generation professors who were not convinced at all of distance learning as an educational method", added the vice dean (S. Awadely, personal communication, September 2020).

In contrast, Ahram Canadian University's department adopted one method to be applied by the entire faculty. They used Google Classroom for uploading lectures, assignments, and evaluations and utilised Zoom as an interactive tool to meet students in synchronous lectures, mirroring the old face-to-face schedule. As the dean explained, "We were able to transition to Google Classroom the next day. The decision was made because we had experience using Google Drive to upload materials and lectures for students, so somehow our students were familiar with the platform" (I. Abouyoussef, personal communication, September 2020). The vice dean added, "several training sessions were given to full-time professors, teaching assistants, and part-time professors. It took one-to-one training on how to use Zoom and Google Classroom" (I. Khoraby, personal communication, September 2020).

The focus group interview in September 2020 showed that the demand on the faculty leadership level was strong to integrate distance education and e-learning into future development plans for higher education (Wilson et al., 2020). It turned out that the COVID-19 crisis had accelerated a transformation process many had been waiting for. Participants highlighted that (increasingly) going online was a goal that faculty in many Egyptian universities had been trying to achieve but had been stopped by insufficient regulation and technical problems. In the middle of the lockdowns, the interviewed Egyptian faculty leadership already vowed a hybrid system by merging face-to-face education (50–60%) and e-learning (40–50%). This, they argued, would also help to solve long-lasting problems, such as dealing with overcrowded classrooms. They also hoped that such an approach could help the departments gain more international recognition by organising joint educational programmes in cooperation with other universities or international bodies that can be implemented remotely. Yet, this would require a comprehensive framework to redesign courses, adopt new learning strategies and evaluation tools and strengthen the administrative and technical units in the respective universities. One small step that Cairo University had taken at that time was the inclusion of Blackboard into regular teaching and its recognition as an examination tool.

During this unprecedented crisis and due to a lack of leadership decisions on the upper levels, the faculties seized the opportunity to push for change on their own terms. Riggio and Newstead argue that during a crisis, the leadership is required to "draw on normative power, seek collaboration, and actively engage in collective sensemaking" (2023, p. 207). However, these requirements were not or very slowly fulfilled on the ministerial level. While they decided on the modes of online teaching, the faculties addressed ministries and decision-makers on the political level regarding the legal problems of online teaching. Respondents in the focus group demanded that faculties' bylaws be updated to provide a legal framework for distance education and its procedures. During the pandemic, the existing regulations of many media schools conflicted with distance education. For example, in Egypt, up until the pandemic, students were required to attend 75% of classes and were obliged to complete final exams face-to-face. The ad hoc decisions and exceptions made during the pandemic were considered insufficient.

While the hierarchical leadership model clearly showed its limits during the pandemic, it allowed the experience of self-efficacy in leadership among faculty staff (Lalani et al., 2021). The participants in the focus group interview in 2020 concluded that the experience of applying online teaching had forced them to overcome obstacles and find immediate and practical solutions. In the end, this gave them more confidence. They also admitted that the experience proved that the younger staff is more ready to transition to online education. The pandemic had fostered cooperation among staff members, as some had previous experience utilising digital tools in teaching or uploading videos or e-books and took over these tasks to train their colleagues who were unfamiliar with those tools. Peer-to-peer training thus became a new asset that, at some points, also helped overcome generational hierarchies.

## Financial and Infrastructural Constraints

Another critical point that demanded leadership was Egypt's financial and infrastructural constraints. Given the financial hardships of many students but also of the faculties, the necessity of getting cheaper and more stable internet connections and a better infrastructure was strongly raised among the interviewees. Concrete suggestions were to prepare a central site through which universities could access the Internet free of charge and through which free or discounted Internet accounts for students could be provided. In addition, it was suggested that the necessary devices, such as laptops or computers for low-income students or those living in remote areas, should be provided. A dream of many participants in the focus groups was, therefore, to develop (or adapt) a nationwide online system for managing the educational process, which would include space for sharing scientific material, as well as channels for communication between students and faculty members, calendars, broadcasted lectures and other activities related to the educational process. This might also help to address the problem of faculty members' intellectual property rights being violated when scientific material is being shared for free on social media networks. This demand directly addressed the ministerial leadership.

The necessity of teaching online from a distance took Egyptian universities by surprise. Neither the infrastructure nor the legal framework was prepared, thus adding a new layer to Egyptian higher education's multiple crises. In our focus group interview, we observed, however, great flexibility and willingness to make distance teaching work, even without the proper frameworks. A lack of infrastructure and financial means proved the most relevant problem. Nevertheless, creative ideas were used by the staff to overcome this problem to some extent. Peer training and consultations helped to transfer skills, albeit this seemed to be an ad hoc measurement and has yet to be institutionalised by the universities. Interestingly, in our focus group discussion among the faculty leadership, the participants highlighted that they saw these changes as a move towards the modernisation of teaching.

## What Now? The Future of the Crises in Higher Education

In order to get a clearer impression of the post-COVID-19 pathways and the prospects in leadership, we organised another focus group in early 2023 with six deans, vice deans and one head of department of Egyptian mass media faculties. Among the participants were again interviewees from the faculty leadership that had taken part in the 2020 round (from Cairo University and Ahram Canadian University), but also leading faculty from the private October University for Modern Science and Arts, the Arab Academy for Science, Technology and Maritime Transport and the Higher Institute of Communication at El-Shourouk Academy took part. The participants thus represent the third level of leadership in higher education in Egypt, being the ones that implement the rules and regulations of the ministry and the university leadership on the programme level and receiving at the same time direct feedback from teaching staff and students.

### Acquisition of New Skills Fostered

From their management and leadership perspective, there have been indeed some positive outcomes resulting from the COVID-19 implications. After a long time of neglect of digital tools in Egyptian higher education, according to them, staff and students have acquired new skills in meaningfully using different online platforms and tools. In particular, faculty staff has benefitted from individual self-training and peer teaching to gain knowledge about various teaching strategies in relation to distance and online teaching. These skills and techniques are now being transferred to enhance teaching from a practical point of view: "Of course, the experience helped us to be more capable of controlling online classes, techniques of confirming attendance, uploading material, utilising online systems to detect plagiarism" (I. Khoraby, personal communication, March 2023). This leads to a hybridity of offline and online teaching strategies becoming the new normal. For example, professors create assignments or conduct quizzes, mid-term exams and questionnaires for quality assurance online—even in classes conducted in the physical presence (M. Saad, personal communication, March 2023). Thus, a remarkable gain in individual and institutional skills has been achieved that will impact teaching at least midterm. This was made possible only because on the upper level of decision-making, the Ministry of Higher Education has finally accepted hybridity in teaching, meaning that the uploading of material to LMS and the digital conduct of exams is not illegal anymore (S. Awadely, personal communication, March 2023; M. Saad, personal communication, March 2023). Nevertheless, even though this is what the faculty leadership had hoped for, it comes with strings attached and obviously with a deepening of inequalities among the different types of universities.

## Infrastructural Renewal Demanded

The ministerial decision to legalise online tools stimulated some private universities and institutes to invest in infrastructural renewal: "In our institute [the Higher Institute of Communication at El-Shorouk Academy], we gained a completely new internet network. Thus, we adopted a new system of online exams that is still applied in assignments and mid-terms until now because it proved successful to handle the huge numbers of students we have" (M. Saad, personal communication, March 2023). However, the already existing divide between better-off private, on the one hand, and underfunded public universities, on the other hand, has deepened regarding technological infrastructure and equipment. In the public Cairo University, for example, though they had adopted the Blackboard system in 2020 and 2021, this system was completely neglected after the decision to return to campus. "We also tried to adopt a hybrid system to minimise the number of students attending every week. But students staying in university dorms complained of not having good internet access, so now we are providing this hybrid system only to graduate students," says the vice dean (S. Awadely, personal communication, March 2023). As the problem of providing adequate infrastructure and equipment for all strata of students and in all universities has not been solved nor even tackled by the higher education leadership on the ministerial or university levels, the inequalities between different classes of students will deepen further.

## Programme Development Started

Regarding programme development, the interviewees mentioned that the forced transfer to online teaching helped media schools to strategically identify which topics and courses can easily be delivered online and which courses are better to conduct face-to-face. In particular, practical classes that teach TV or radio production or writing classes seem unsuitable for online delivery. These considerations were starting points for faculties and institutes for mass communication studies to consider redesigning their programmes. In Egypt, until the COVID-19 pandemic, all media schools—public or private—followed a tradition of dividing their programmes into three sections or departments, including respective study programmes: (1) (print and online) journalism, (2) radio and television, (3) advertising and public relations. This reflected a now outdated approach to classifying media production along specific techniques. The digital era has led to new realities, such as media convergence. This requires a multi-tasking media practitioner who can produce content for multiple platforms. At the same time, students should be able to analyse all kinds of communication processes in a platformised media environment. Finally, pushed by the COVID-19 implications, the respective committees about the supreme councils of the Ministry of Higher Education agreed to the necessity of changing all media studies programmes completely. Frames of reference for both undergraduate and graduate studies were set up. Media schools were asked to change their curricula to meet the standards of international media programmes. The committees declared that they would not accredit any media programmes that do not abide by the new frames of reference. While the private universities quickly used this new opportunity structure, the public university leadership faced more resistance from the older generation of professors who got used to traditional courses and textbooks and were not ready to begin something new. However, the new rules led to completely new programmes at public universities, which had only re-accredited their existing programmes for decades. Both representatives of the mass communication faculty's leadership at the public Cairo University in the focus group see this as a positive result: "The new programmes in Cairo University will link the graduates more with the demands of the market," says the head of the English (communication studies) department

(N. El Azrak, personal communication, March 2023), while the vice dean for education and student affairs seconds that "We have increasing numbers of students joining the digital media programme every year" (S. Awadely, personal communication, March 2023).

Yet, the new requirements also demand the students to take general courses such as sociology, psychology, geopolitics, human rights and principles of management, which have not yet been tailored for media and journalism students. Thus, students seem unable to relate them to their media studies curricula and complain about hardly benefitting from them (D. Othman, personal communication, March 2023). This problem is connected to a lack of trained teaching staff to allow for interdisciplinary teaching. At the same time, a specialised teaching staff that is mature in teaching, for example, data visualisation, digital journalism or topics on artificial intelligence, is also rare (S. Awadely, personal communication, March 2023). Given the precarious conditions for teaching faculty, including low salaries and overcrowded classes, finding adequate staff to implement the new programmes will be difficult. Even though the programmes are being redesigned and updated, the teaching crisis has not been solved yet.

## Communication and Feedback Loops to be Improved

One last major aspect has been addressed by the interviewees whose importance has been recognised during the pandemic: communication and feedback loops among the leadership levels and with the students. Communication is considered a key competence in (crisis) leadership (Riggio & Newstead, 2023) but was neglected in the COVID-19 crisis in Egypt. While internal faculty meetings are considered to be functional and successful, communication with other levels is seen as problematic. The meetings between the ministry's councils and the faculties had been reduced during COVID-19, albeit all faculties had submitted weekly reports. Only recently, these meetings are returning to a routine every month (S. Awadely, personal communication, March 2023; M. Saad, personal communication, 2023). But also, meetings between the university leadership and the faculty leadership are rather short in time and rarely solve any real problems. Deans and vice deans depend on random meetings with the president or the university owner to solve problems. In private universities, there is no clear communication routine with the president: "it always depends on personal relations, and it is up to the president to decide whom to meet and when" (I. Khoraby, personal communication, March 2023). At the same time, there is no institutionalised communication system with students except for their course evaluations or individual complaints. The Arab Academy has a vice dean for students' affairs dealing proactively with students' problems (D. Othman, personal communication, March 2023), while most other schools do not have a systemic communication process to deal with students. Again, private media schools are better off here because they are fewer in student numbers in comparison with public schools like Cairo University's mass communication faculty with its roughly 4500 students (S. Awadely, personal communication, March 2023).

## Conclusion

The multiple crises in the Egyptian higher education sector are persistent after COVID-19, mainly because of unresolved political and economic constraints that deepen structural inequalities in a two-tier system of public vs. private universities. Better technical equipment and digital infrastructures, as well as smaller courses with access to labs and studios, allow students in private institutions to get better training in media-related skills than their fellow students in public universities. Here, COVID-19 accelerated the crisis because new teaching skills and technologies have more sustainably been included only in private universities. The faculties' "dreams" of a comprehensive and inclusive national plan to provide e-learning platforms, a national learning management system and internet access points have not been fulfilled by the leadership on the ministerial level.

At the same time, COVID-19 also had positive implications, in particular, to finally convince the ministry to give up on outdated study programmes. The ministerial leadership has taken major steps to solve an education crisis by establishing innovative study programmes on digital and convergent media and the legalisation of the usage of digital tools in providing materials and conducting exams. Yet, their implementation is still accompanied by several problems, particularly the lack of trained and adequately paid teaching staff. The teaching crisis has not been addressed sufficiently on the leadership level by, for example, reducing the number of students in overcrowded faculties or paying suitable salaries.

Finally, the communication hierarchies among the leadership levels lack a meaningful inclusion of a bottom-up approach. Interestingly, during the COVID-19 pandemic, faculties had greater autonomy to search for suitable solutions and implement them ad hoc and were thus more flexible and innovative than in a strongly top-down regulated environment. This experience needs to be acknowledged and included in future strategies. In general, the multiple crises in Egypt's higher education sector can only be solved by a stronger commitment of the upper leadership levels to learn from the faculties' experiences. COVID-19 has provided a good starting point for reflecting on the failures of a neoliberal education policy and its problematic consequences concerning multiple inequalities, lack of infrastructure, overcrowded universities and saturated job markets, and outdated study programmes and teaching strategies.

## References


Abdelrahman, A. (1991). Arab world. In K. Nordenstreng & M. Traber (Eds.), *Promotion of educational materials for communication studies: Report of phase I of UNESCO/IPDC interregional project by IAMCR/AIERI*. The Department of Journalism and Mass Communication, University of Tampere.

Abou Youssef, I., & Richter, C. (2022). Distance Teaching in media departments in times of the COVID-19 pandemic. Experiences from six Arab countries. *Journal of Applied Learning & Teaching, 5*(2), 20–30. https://doi.org/10.37074/jalt.2022.5.2.5

Abouyoussef, I. (2020, September). *Dean of mass communication faculty*. Ahram Canadian University, Focus Group.

Alseady, T. M. (2019). The effectiveness of a blended e-learning program in developing the cognitive and practical skills of mass communication students in journalism photography [in Arabic]. *The Journal of Middle East Public Relations Research (Cairo University), 69*, 201–261.

Arafat, S. M. (2017). The attitudes of mass communication students towards e-learning and traditional learning: An applied research [in Arabic]. *The Egyptian Journal for Public Opinion Research (Cairo University), 16*(3), 61–112.

Awadely, S. (2020, September). *Vice dean for students' affairs, mass communication faculty*. Cairo University, Focus Group.

Awadely, S. (2023, March). *Vice dean for students' affairs, mass communication faculty*. Cairo University, Focus Group.

Badr, H. (2021). Egypt: A divided and restricted media landscape after the transformation. In C. Richter & C. Kozman (Eds.), *Arab media systems* (pp. 215–232). Open Book Publishers. https://doi.org/10.11647/obp.0238.13

Badr, H., & Elmaghraby, S. (2021). How higher education faculty in Egypt perceive the effects of Covid-19 on teaching journalism and mass communication: Perspectives from the global south. *Journalism & Mass Communication Educator, 76*(3), 394–411. https://doi.org/10.1177/10776958211025199

Badr, H., & Richter, C. (2022). Teaching journalism in Egypt: Captured between control and transformation. In D. Garrisi & X. Kuang (Eds.), *Journalism pedagogy in transitional countries* (pp. 91–109). Palgrave MacMillan.

Barsoum, G. (2020). When marketization encounters centralized governance: Private higher education in Egypt. *International Journal of Educational Development, 76*, 102264. https://doi.org/10.1016/j.ijedudev.2020.102215

DAAD. (2020). *Ägypten: Kurze Einführung in das Hochschulsystem und die DAAD-Aktivitäten.* [Report] DAAD. https://static.daad.de/media/daad_de/pdfs_nicht_bar-rierefrei/laenderinformationen/afrika/aegypten_daad_sachstand.pdf

El Azrak, N. (2023, March). *Head of English department, mass communication faculty*. Cairo University, Focus Group.

Helmy, I. (2020). The effectiveness of a proposed online curriculum in developing some writing skills for the radio of the educational media students in the faculty of specific education. [in Arabic] *The Egyptian Journal of Media Research (Cairo University), 72*, 249–315.

Khoraby, I. (2020, September). *Vice dean of graduate programs, mass communication faculty*. Ahram Canadian University, Focus Group.

Khoraby, I. (2023, March). *Vice dean of graduate programs, mass communication faculty*. Ahram Canadian University, Focus Group.

Kohstall, F. (2009). Free transfer, limited mobility: A decade of higher education reform in Egypt and Morocco. *Revue Des Mondes Musulmans Et De La Méditerrané, 131*, 91–110.

Lalani, K., Crawford, J., & Butler-Henderson, K. (2021). Academic leadership during COVID-19 in higher education: Technology adoption and adaptation for online learning during a pandemic. *International Journal of Leadership in Education,* 1–17. https://doi.org/10.1080/13603124.2021.1988716

Mustafa, H. (2020, September). *Dean of mass communication faculty*. Cairo University, Focus Group.

Othman, D. (2023, March). *Head of department at the language and communication department*. Arab Academy for Science, Technology and Maritime Transport, Focus Group.

Richter, C., & Badr, H. (2018). Communication studies in transformation—Self-reflections on an evolving discipline in times of change. In F. Kohstall, C. Richter, S. Dhouib, & F. Kastner (Eds.), *Academia in transformation. Arab and German Perspectives* (pp. 143–159). Nomos.

Riggio, R., & Newstead, T. (2023). Crisis leadership. *Annual Review of Organizational Psychology and Organizational Behavior, 10*, 201–224.

Saad, M. (2023, March). *Ex-dean of the higher institute of communication at El-Shorouk Academy*. Focus Group.

Uhl-Bien, M., Marion, R., & McKelvey, B. (2007). Complexity leadership theory: Shifting leadership from the industrial age to the knowledge era. *Leadership Quarterly, 18*, 298–318.

Wilson, S., Tan, S., Knox, M., Ong, A., Crawford, J., & Rudolph, J. (2020). Enabling cross-cultural student voice during COVID-19: A collective autoethnography. *Journal of University Teaching & Learning Practice, 17*(5), 3. https://doi.org/10.53761/1.17.5.3

Zaki, K. (2020, September). *Assistant professor, journalism department, mass communication faculty*. Cairo University, Focus Group.

# Leading Universities During COVID-19: Towards Understanding the Role of Educational Leadership in Ghana

Albert Amankwaa, Olivia Anku-Tsede, Desmond Tutu Ayentimi, Majoreen Osafroadu Amankwah, and Isaac Kosi

## Introduction

Ghana is situated on the coast of the Gulf of Guinea and shares borders with Togo, Burkina Faso, and Cote d'Ivoire. Before the COVID-19 pandemic, Ghana was one of the leading economies in sub-Saharan Africa (Amewu et al., 2020), partly due to its stable and thriving democracy and considerable natural resources, including gold, diamonds, cocoa, and oil. Ghana is also celebrated for its rich cultural heritage and colonial history—it was the first African country to gain independence from British colonisation on

A. Amankwaa (✉) · D. T. Ayentimi
University of Tasmania, Hobart, TAS, Australia
e-mail: albert.amankwaa@utas.edu.au

D. T. Ayentimi
e-mail: desmond.ayentimi@utas.edu.au

O. Anku-Tsede
Judicial Service of Ghana, Accra, Ghana
e-mail: oankutsede@googlemail.com

M. O. Amankwah
University of Ghana, Accra, Ghana
e-mail: moamankwah@ug.edu.gh

I. Kosi
University of Cape Coast, Cape Coast, Ghana
e-mail: ikosi@ucc.edu.gh



J. Rudolph et al. (eds.), *The Palgrave Handbook of Crisis Leadership in Higher Education*,
https://doi.org/10.1007/978-3-031-54509-2_15

6 March 1957. In higher education, Ghana was among the early colonies alongside Sierra Leone (Fourah Bay College) and Nigeria (Higher College at Yaba) to have higher educational systems established by the British. For example, in the early 1900s, students at Achimota School (established in 1927) who studied Intermediate Arts, Science, Engineering, and Economics took external examinations from London University (Tagoe, 2020). Interestingly, it was not until 1948 that the University College of the Gold Coast (now the University of Ghana) was eventually founded as a full degree-granting university in the colonies (Adekanmbi et al., 2021).

Historically, higher education in Ghana and formal education, more broadly, has been shaped by colonial and historical legacies, funding constraints, political polarisation, and the influence of cultural and economic idiosyncrasies, among others (Adekanmbi et al., 2021). Relatedly, studies on higher education in Ghana and Africa highlight how global and colonial institutional and development processes form the basis of education reforms without recognising the cultural, historical, and economic development trajectory (Zavale & Schneijderberg, 2022). For example, universities in Ghana and across Africa have regularly used Western institutional structures and curricula as a critical reference point. To this end, Mpofu and Ndlovu-Gatsheni (2020) contend that African higher education is still trapped in North American and European-centric thinking. Even though this style of higher education development may be illustrative and serve as a guide, an enduring systematic gap emerges, explicitly on how we can decolonise higher education to address the Global South unique social and economic needs.

Throughout the history of higher education in Ghana, funding has been a significant issue (Anamuah-Mensah et al., 2002). For example, the Education Sector Performance Report (2016) shows that government expenditure on higher education stood at 6.7% of gross domestic product (GDP) in 2012 and declined to about 5.3% in 2015. Another point of tension is that there is a wide discrepancy in education expenditure between technical education and other forms of education. The technical and vocational education subsector, in particular, has experienced relatively less policy commitment and financial attention (Ayentimi et al., 2018)—highlighting limited recognition of or lack of support for technical education in Ghana. In 2018, Ghana launched its Education Strategic Plan (ESP 2018–2030), which outlines specific delivery outcomes and actions in a sequence of four-year implementation plans. The ESP focuses on increasing learning outcomes and quality educational standards at all levels of education in Ghana. However, it is fair to say that government expenditure on education over the years has been erratic, with the highest being 6.7% of Gross Domestic Product (GDP) in

2012 and consequently declined to 3.9% of GDP in 2018 (Acquah, 2021; Ministry of Education, 2018). Given the erratic nature of higher education funding and the fact that the government typically provides between 50 and 55% of the total financial needs of the tertiary education subsector (Ministry of Education, 2018), there are substantial practical and policy concerns regarding the successful implementation of Ghana's long-term strategic education blueprint. The COVID-19 crisis may cast further doubts on the ESP's successful implementation and achieving its intended outcomes.

## COVID-19 in Ghana

Ghana recorded its first two cases of the COVID-19 virus on 12 March 2020, and by April 2021, the country had recorded an estimated 7000 cases and 34 deaths (Ministry of Health, 2023). The infection rate was shallow, and so was the rollout and rate of vaccination uptake across the country. The slow pace of vaccination rollout has been attributed to (1) delays in the arrival of vaccines from developed countries and (2) vaccine hesitancy among portions of the Ghanaian population. Some assumed that something may happen to them if they took the vaccine (World Health Organisation [WHO], 2023a, 2023b). This was quite surprising because vaccination against vaccine-preventable diseases is widespread in Ghana. Indeed, every child born in Ghana over the last two decades or so may have been vaccinated against vaccine-preventable diseases such as poliomyelitis and measles, among others. The hesitancy to take the COVID-19 vaccine may have been caused by cultural misconceptions about the vaccine and media misinformation, globally and locally (Botwe et al., 2022; WHO, 2023a, 2023b).

Nonetheless, Ghana is known to have managed the COVID-19 pandemic relatively well. As of November 2023, 27,959,283 vaccine doses had been administered, and about 70.8% of the target Ghanaian adult population (20.7 million) had been vaccinated (Ministry of Health, 2023). A total of 171,889 cases and 1,462 deaths had been recorded, with Greater Accra, the nation's capital, and Kumasi, the second-largest city, accounting for over 60% of confirmed cases and deaths (Ministry of Health, 2023).

Like many African countries, Ghana recorded low infection rates and deaths compared to many countries in Europe, the Americas, and Asia. For example, as of 17 July 2023, Africa, with a population of over 1.34 billion, only recorded an estimated 9,542,363 COVID-19 infections compared to 193,143,707 in the Americas, 275,747,929 in Europe and 61,193,230 in

South-East Asia. Likewise, Africa documented the lowest COVID-19 death rate being only 2.8% (175,399), whereas the Americas and Europe accounted for 47.8% (2,957,891) and 36.3% (2,244,732), respectively (WHO, 2023a, 2023b). This is despite most African countries relying heavily on Western partners for imports and vaccines. However, mandatory COVID-19 restrictions, social distancing rules, and international border closures led to disruptions in global supply chains, which led to dying economic consequences for countries in the region. The region's economic vulnerability has been demonstrated in several ways. The pandemic led to soaring inflation rates, public outcry for essential consumables and medical supplies, a total shutdown of schools, and disruption in education service delivery (Osabwa, 2022). The shutdown of schools and businesses was part of the World Health Organisation's (WHO) recommended measures to control the virus's spread and protect lives (WHO, 2023a, 2023b).

The pandemic impacted every sector of the Ghanaian economy (Boaheng, 2021), but perhaps the service industry, which includes the higher education sector, may have been the most affected. This is concerning given that the service sector alone contributes an estimated 46.6% (about US$35.7 billion in monetary terms) of Ghana's GDP (Ministry of Finance, 2023). Not surprisingly, Ghana's economy is currently experiencing a meltdown. A case in point is the current and ongoing financial aid/bailout negotiations with the International Monetary Fund (IMF). We note that many policy analysts and social commentators attribute the economic crisis to economic mismanagement and overborrowing by the government (Asante, 2023). However, given the import-driven nature of most African economies, the United Nations Development Programme's (UNDP) Regional Bureau for Africa rapid assessment report (2022) suggests that the Russian–Ukraine war may have further exacerbated the economic woes of many African economies, including Ghana.

## COVID-19 and Higher Education in Ghana

Globally, the COVID-19 pandemic has significantly impacted the higher education sector and, perhaps, a lasting shift in learning and teaching approaches (Parida et al., 2023). Correspondingly, much research has explored the Covid-19 pandemic and the higher education sector. For context, our search in the Scopus database for articles published in English between 2020 and 2023 revealed 566 studies with 'Covid-19' and 'higher education' in their title or abstract. Based on the results, we employed bibliographic coupling (documents and countries) in VOSviewer to generate maps of COVID-19 and higher education research from 2020 to 2023 (for an overview, see Fig. 1) and their geographical location (see Fig. 2). Scholars have, among others, sought to explore the implications of the COVID-19 pandemic on higher education from varying perspectives. The sheer volume of research interest in COVID-19 and the higher education sector in the last three years (as shown in Fig. 1) highlights the topical nature of the subject matter and the urgent need to advance the higher education sector in a new era. Not surprisingly, the bulk of the research so far, like many other research areas, is found in Western countries, with the United States and the United Kingdom leading the charge (see Fig. 2).

To fully understand COVID-19 and its implications on the higher education sector, it is essential that our knowledge reflects a global outlook of the issue, and that the data is mainly inclusive of non-western countries. In this chapter, we address this gap by providing insights into how educational leaders in Ghanaian universities are guiding their institutions to navigate the many challenges of the COVID-19 pandemic. The chapter highlights essential lessons for Ghanaian universities, educational leaders, and practitioners in the higher education sector. In Ghana, the pandemic has laid bare critical challenges and significant cracks in higher education, particularly in the university sector, but also uncovered new opportunities and potentially sustainable ways of advancing new forms of learning and teaching in the universities.

In this section of the chapter, we discuss some of the notable changes in the university sector in Ghana and some of the impacts of the pandemic on university education in Ghana. We focus solely on the university sector and categorise our discussions under the following broad themes: transitioning from face-to-face to online delivery, system changes and professional development issues, unequal access to learning and teaching, academic calendar disruptions, reduced enrolments, and financial implications.

## Transitioning from Face-to-Face to Online Delivery

Before the COVID-19 pandemic, learning and teaching in Ghanaian universities was predominantly limited to traditional face-to-face mode. We noted that some universities had learning management systems (LMS) or some online platforms that supported learning and teaching in a blended mode or hybrid approach. For context, face-to-face interactions and bridging social capital are integral parts of Ghana's social and cultural fabric. Relatedly, most

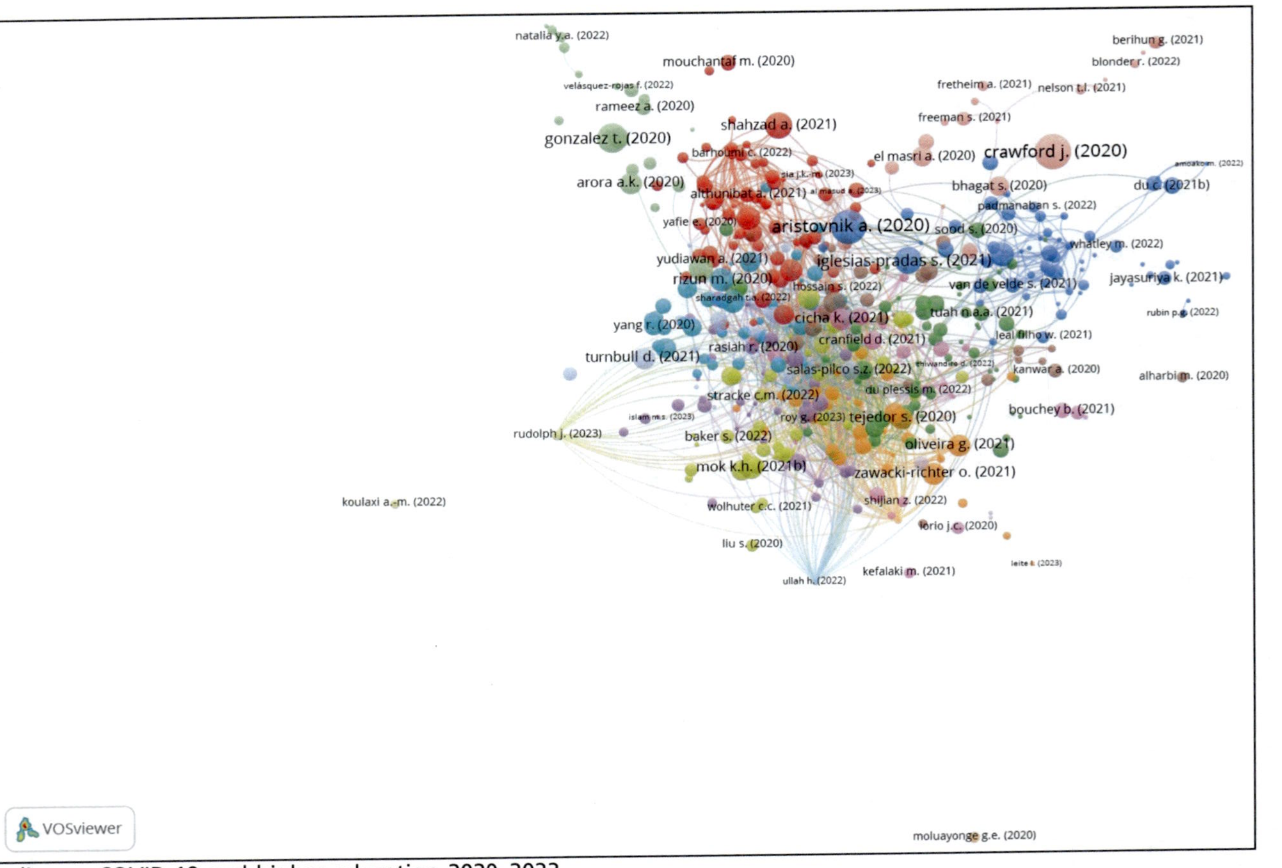


Fig. 1 Studies on COVID-19 and higher education 2020–2023

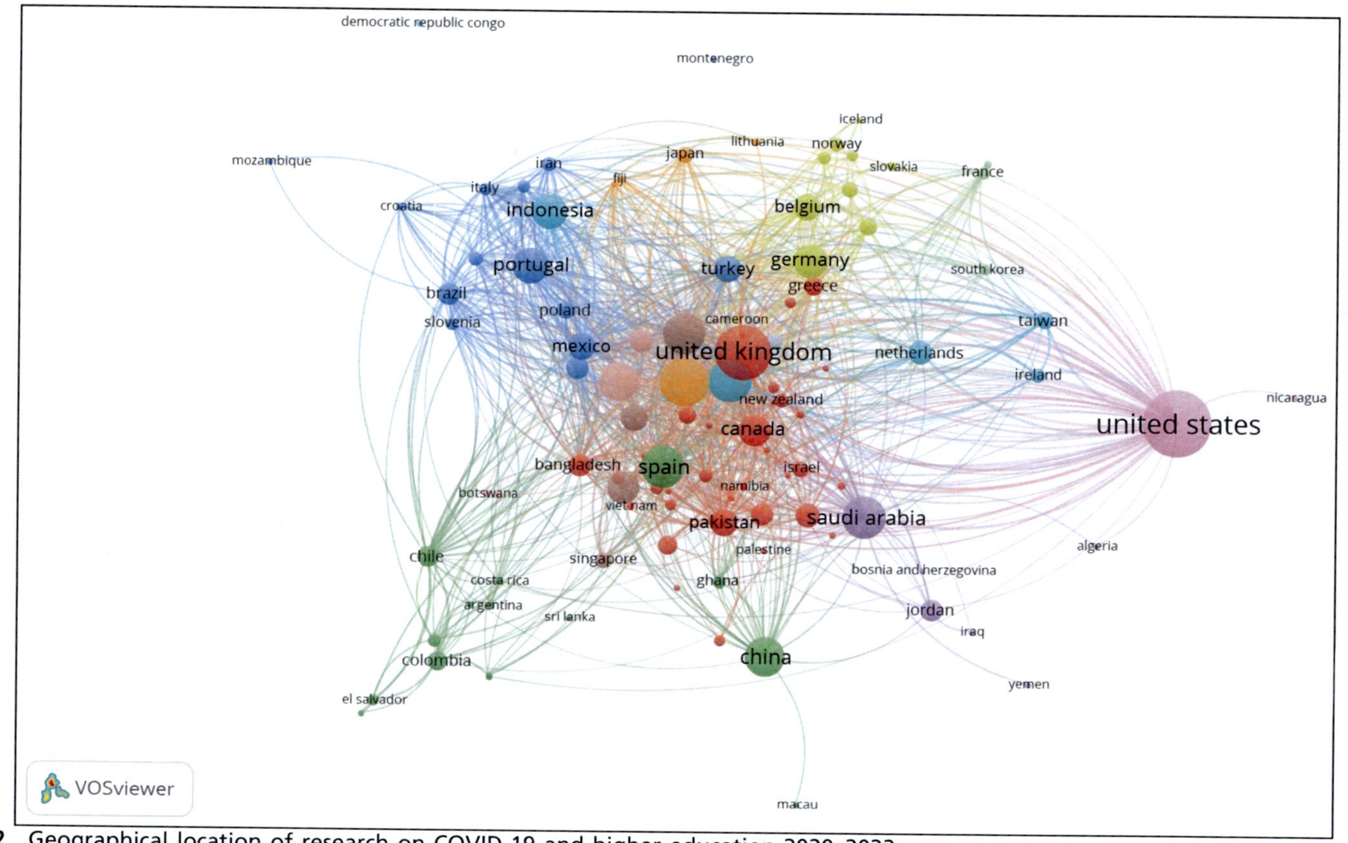


**Fig. 2** Geographical location of research on COVID-19 and higher education 2020–2023

university students prefer face-to-face, in-person lectures and tutorials to online classes. Sadly, the pandemic restricted all face-to-face social activities (Boaheng, 2021; Rudolph et al., 2023) following recommendations by the WHO to control the spread of the virus and protect lives (UNESCO, 2020).

Consequently, face-to-face learning and teaching became impracticable. They triggered a total closure or shutdown of universities that did not have existing LMS or online infrastructure to support remote learning and teaching activities. The closure of universities affected the entire education sector, though some piecemeal responses from universities helped minimise the severity of the crises in learning and teaching activities (Tsevi, 2021).

Most universities resorted to remote learning and teaching largely via meeting platforms such as Zoom, Skype, and Microsoft Teams. This was supported by emails, learning management systems (e.g., Moodle, Sakai, Vclass, et cetera.), and social media platforms (e.g., WhatsApp, Telegram, Facebook) to disseminate information on assignments and reading materials to students. While most universities were slowly able to assemble the basic Information, Communication and Technology (ICT) infrastructure needed to resume academic work immediately after the mandatory lockdown restrictions were eased, the transition from face-to-face to online learning and teaching was very challenging (Adekanmbi et al., 2021). Indeed, the transition has been described as 'emergency remote teaching' because it lacked the instructional design and content requirements of a well-planned online learning management system (Omari et al., 2022).

## System Changes and Professional Development Issues

Before the pandemic, most universities in developed countries (such as Australia) had LMS, including Blackboard, MYLO, or Moodle, to facilitate blended or hybrid learning and teaching for on-campus and distance students (Parida et al., 2023). As a result, lecturers, students, and administrators were familiar with using the different systems, tools, and technologies. In contrast, not all students, academic, and professional staff in Ghanaian universities had such familiarity with LMS. Consequently, there was the need to immediately develop staff capabilities to use the new online learning and teaching platforms (Zhao et al., 2021). It is important to recognise that professional development for academic and professional staff is essential for quality online engagement in developed and developing countries. That notwithstanding, Parida et al.'s (2023) study of Australian universities during the COVID-19 pandemic suggests that while universities continue to strive for quality learning and teaching and student engagement in the online environment, there seems to be limited focus or perhaps some haphazard approach to professional development of academic and professional staff. As noted elsewhere, most universities in Ghana had embraced the virtual mode of operation after the easing of mandatory lockdown and restrictions in 2020. Teaching had primarily moved online, along with seminars and research supervision, requiring lecturers and professional staff to swiftly adjust to the new normal of work and virtual interaction. In some universities, instructors and students had to attend multiple training sessions to be equipped with the basic digital capabilities and skills necessary for using online learning and teaching platforms (Zhao et al., 2021). Difficulties associated with using online platforms contributed to the slow transition to e-learning across the universities. Several factors undermined staff training coverage, including network connectivity issues, data acquisition problems, and the inability to acquire devices like laptops and smartphones (Biney, 2020).

## Unequal Access to Learning and Teaching

The COVID-19 pandemic uncovered the apparent inequalities in accessing learning and teaching in universities in Ghana. Restrictions on movement and social gatherings mean the pandemic aggravated inequalities in learning and teaching in the broader higher education sector (Adzovie & Jibril, 2022). Even though most universities in Ghana eventually rolled out some form of online learning and teaching arrangements, not all students could participate due to several challenges, including internet connectivity problems and the cost of internet data (Biney, 2020; Tsevi, 2021). In addition, the switch to online learning and teaching across universities in Ghana raised issues of quality education delivery standards and digital segregation concerns, as many students were underprivileged geographically, technologically, and economically (Osabwa, 2022). For example, the University of Ghana (i.e., Ghana's premier university) was the first to roll out its online LMS, SAKAI (Tsevi, 2021). Vodafone Ghana and MTN, two of Ghana's leading internet service providers, supported this initiative, extending free data to students to access the LMS (Adekanmbi et al., 2021). Moodle supported the transition to online learning and teaching for the University of Cape Coast. During these crucial times of changing learning and teaching conditions, the University of Cape Coast Library operated remotely for students to access library resources. Kwame Nkrumah University of Science and Technology (KNUST) adopted a two-way approach, which included the use of a virtual classroom (Vclass) platform and its Institute of Distance Learning (IDL) Centres in the various regional capitals as venues to distribute teaching and learning materials to students located in remote communities without access to internet connectivity. Similar arrangements were made with MTN and Vodafone Ghana to grant free data access to Lecturers to use Zoom to record student lectures. Despite all these initiatives from the various universities, students in remote communities (with poor networks or absence of internet connectivity) missed out on learning and teaching (Biney, 2020).

## Academic Calendar Disruptions

The COVID-19 pandemic led to the interruption of the academic calendar of universities in Ghana. Before the pandemic, most educational activities, including learning and teaching, occurred in and around lecture halls and laboratories. Following the pandemic, university work systems—both academic and administrative—were considerably modified/adjusted and, in some cases, halted (Wilson et al., 2021). A major change in the university system in Ghana was the introduction and implementation of a modular teaching system, a two-phase initiative limiting the number of students who attend lectures and tutorials on campus to maintain and enforce social distancing protocols. For the first phase, first and final-year students attended classes (lectures and tutorials) on campus for six weeks, followed by one week of revision and two weeks of examination. While the first and final-year students went on break, the second phase of the modular system commenced with second and third-year students attending classes on campus. Before the pandemic, the regular teaching period was thirteen weeks instead of the six weeks modular mode of instruction introduced during COVID-19 and the academic year, which conventionally starts between August and September and ends in May the following year across the various universities in Ghana, shifted to January due to the COVID-19 disruptions. This learning and teaching system disrupted the 2019/2020 academic year calendar and has had a knock-on effect on the university academic calendar to date.

The disruption of the academic calendar by the COVID-19 pandemic also led to the disruption of graduation ceremonies. Essentially, another area that saw a major shift was the mode and organisation of matriculation and graduation ceremonies across universities in Ghana. The COVID-19 pandemic led to the manifestation of a hybrid mode of organising matriculation and graduation ceremonies. This new approach allows only academic staff to be physically present at one location (face-to-face), whereas students participate via virtual mode at graduation and matriculation ceremonies. Only selected academic and management staff members can converge in person to ensure social distancing protocols are observed. These staff members include Heads of Departments, Deans, Directors of some units, and critical management officials. Other extra-curricular activities such as sporting events, hall week celebrations, and students' religious and student societies events were also halted as part of the protocols to manage the spread of the virus. Interestingly, the COVID-19 crisis compelled the student representative council to organise its elections using an online platform. Although this was not the first time in Ghanaian universities that students' elections were organised online, it was an opportunity to build confidence and trust in using technology in conducting elections.

Even though students and lecturers were able to transition to virtual teaching platforms during the 2020/2021 academic year, they encountered multiple challenges (Agormedah et al., 2020). For instance, because of poor internet connection, many students rarely paid attention to lessons during the online sessions. The online sessions also reduced the contact hours lecturers could have with students. Additionally, students with limited technology usage experience struggled to participate in online sessions and access learning materials effectively. It also led to some unpleasant situations, such as some students mistakenly turning on their cameras or unmuting themselves unknowingly, thereby publicising their private issues or lives. These incidents impacted the quality of learning and teaching as they regularly disrupted online class discussions and teaching activities. These disruptions further reiterate concerns about the quality and effectiveness of teaching via virtual platforms.

## Reduced Student Enrolments and Financial Implications

Globally, the pandemic has had a significant negative impact on international student enrolments. The number of international students admitted to universities in Ghana experienced a continuous decline during the pandemic. For context, before the pandemic, the University of Ghana, for example, admitted more than 745 international students annually to pursue various academic programmes. However, in the academic years following the pandemic, international students' enrolments dropped significantly to 409 students in the 2019/2020 academic year and 70 students in the 2020/2021 academic year. Only 158 international students are enrolled at the University of Ghana for the 2022/2023 academic year (International Programmes Office, 2023). Similar figures have been recorded in other public and private universities across Ghana.

The decline in international students' enrolment in Ghanaian universities is a major financial loss considering the huge number of international students' fees charged. Though private and publicly funded universities witnessed financial losses, private universities were the most affected; they suffered immense financial setbacks due to low enrolment, creating some financial challenges during the pandemic. While the government financially supported public universities, private universities struggled to raise revenue to pay their staff, which resulted in some staff resigning from the private universities (Institute of Statistical, Social and Economic Research [ISSER], 2020). Historically, private universities in Ghana cannot pay high salaries compared to publicly funded universities (ISSER, 2020). The pandemic exacerbated this situation as many private universities had to defer the payment of salaries for several months, and others had to institute half-salary arrangements. For example, some private universities implemented a 50% salary cut to only senior academic and non-academic members during the peak of the pandemic to navigate through the pandemic (ISSER, 2020; Teachout & Zipfel, 2020).

In Ghana, private university education is expensive, mainly as parents are required to pay full fees without any subsidy from the government. Thus, the target market for private universities is mostly students whose parents are engaged in private businesses. Interestingly, many of these parents lost their jobs and shut down their businesses during the pandemic. Therefore, they could not pay the school fees. Universities in Ghana initiated flexible payment plans for students during the pandemic despite the initiative negatively affecting their capacity to pay staff salaries, suppliers, and utility bills. The financial constraints witnessed by universities extended to job losses. Whereas no job losses were recorded in all publicly funded universities including casual employees, many private universities could not retain their staff, particularly part-time staff and permanent staff. As some permanent staff resigned voluntarily, many private universities could not renew permanent and part-time staff contracts.

## Response to COVID-19: The Role of Educational Leaders

A higher education institution constitutes a complex managerial organisation with decentralised services set up by relevant social laws that draw and exert influence from both regional and global communities (Dare & Saleem, 2022). Inferring from most societal organisations, higher education institutions like universities are led by institutional authorities, leaders, and/or government. University leaders and government agencies maintain legislation, provide official directives, and implement study activities. Actions of these leaders and government are thus essential to the general well-being of institutional members, students, teaching, and non-teaching staff (Constantia et al., 2021) and, more specifically, in times of global crisis. Riggio and Newstead (2023, p. 151) observe that "there is no situation where leadership is more important than during a crisis", such as the COVID-19 pandemic. During the COVID-19 pandemic, leadership became fundamentally critical not only for the performance of institutions but also for the very survival of these institutions. In one of the first assessments of complexity leadership and COVID-19, Uhl-Bien (2021) observed that "for all those who doubted the importance of leadership, the pandemic proves them wrong, adding that "leadership can be, literally, the difference between life and death" (p. 1400).

Indeed, the COVID-19 pandemic brought unprecedented challenges and complexities in the higher education sector in both the Global North and the Global South. Uhl-Bien (2021) notes that these complexities and challenges require that institutional leaders adapt quickly and creatively to provide solutions to protect the lives of their people and institutions. Relatedly, educational leaders in the higher education sector need to be more flexible and, perhaps, employ non-conventional leadership approaches to navigate these complexities. Drawing from complexity leadership theory and research, Uhl-Bien (2021) provides three guiding steps that can enable leaders and organisations to respond to challenges and pressures: (1) understanding complexity, (2) enabling adaptive responses, and (3) opening adaptive space. Using these steps as our frame, we discuss how educational leaders in Ghanaian universities responded to the COVID-19 crisis.

## Understanding Complexity During the COVID-19 Crisis

Complexity in institutions begins as pressures, usually taking the form of an adaptive challenge (Uhl-Bien, 2021; Uhl-Bien & Arena, 2017). An adaptive challenge is a problem without a known solution and requires new partnerships with people with conflicting views working independently towards a solution, in extreme cases, to survive (Uhl-Bien, 2021; Uhl-Bien & Arena, 2017). The onset of the COVID-19 pandemic disrupted the traditional role and practices of most institutional leaders and governments in delivering their mandates. The pandemic affected all kinds of social activities (Boaheng, 2021), including institutional leaders and government activities in higher education and Ghanaian society. The Ministry of Education and the Ghana Education Service (GES, 2020) acknowledge that disruptions in education delivery due to the COVID-19 pandemic endangered and reversed access to learning and teaching in Ghana. During the peak phase of the pandemic, the long-term higher educational demands exceeded the personal strengths and resources of institutional leaders and government within the country. As a result of the increased educational pressure on these leaders, they were vulnerable to their leadership roles, remote school navigation requirements, weariness, and significant tension on risks of both administrative and managerial roles. There was pressure on the government of Ghana to lock down the country and pressure educational leaders to close universities, mandate the wearing of masks on campus, and/or move all teaching and learning interactions online.

## Enabling Adaptive Responses

An adaptive response is an 'emergence dynamic' in complex situations (Uhl-Bien, 2021). The COVID-19 pandemic led to the emergence of adaptive responses when the pressures on government and education leaders meant that all stakeholders (i.e., government agencies and the people, educational leaders, lecturers, students, and administrators, et cetera.) needed to work collaboratively to follow all COVID-19 protocols (Lalani et al., 2021). For the government of Ghana, the first adaptive response was early partial and total lockdowns to restrict mobility and force the closure of businesses and schools. Another notable response was mandating the wearing of nose masks, enforcing social distancing rules, and the immediate rollout of traditional and social media campaigns for everyone to get vaccinated and adhere to COVID-19 protocols. In addition, the government initiated financial support programmes in the form of soft loans with manageable payment schedules to small and medium-sized enterprises (SMEs) to help moderate the losses due to mandatory lockdowns (Government of Ghana, 2020). Other adaptive responses include providing Ghanaians with free water and free electricity for three months (Antwi-Boasiako et al., 2021), establishing a COVID-19 Alleviation and Revitalisation of Enterprises Support (Ghana CARES), and the COVID-19 trust fund to purchase personal protective equipment (PPEs) for front-line workers in public sector organisations. Importantly, the initiative to supply PPEs to front-line workers was extended to private sector organisations, including private universities nationwide.

Several adaptive responses to the COVID-19 pandemic also emerged from educational leaders in the university sector. A major response was the transition of learning and teaching online using different technology platforms such as Microsoft Teams, Zoom, and Google Meet, among others (Tsevi,

2021). The universities nationwide first initiated the transition to online learning and teaching. At the same time, their counterparts at basic and secondary schools were t Another response was the adoption of and/or investment in online LMS platforms such as SAKAI (University of Ghana), Moodle (University of Cape Coast), and the use of a virtual classroom (Vclass) [KNUST]. Even though prior evidence suggests some students' inability to fully focus on their studies in a virtual learning atmosphere without the standard academic relationships (Biney, 2020), the learning management platforms ensured that learning and teaching continued while maintaining social distancing protocols. Finally, and perhaps the most enduring adaptive response in our estimation, has been the change of the university academic calendar to make up for lost time and accommodate academic disruptions.

## Opening Up Adaptive Space

The uncertainties and complexities in the world require that leaders not only understand but also be open to the idea of flexible systems and agile operating processes that offer opportunities for new thinking and ideas. Drawing from prior complexity leadership research, Uhl-Bien (2021) highlights the need for leaders to open adaptive space for unconventional ways of doing things to generate creative solutions to complex problems. According to Uhl-Bien (2021), adaptive space offers the context and environment for people and systems to interact and create novel solutions to problems during complex times like the COVID-19 crisis. We note that the unexpected nature of a crisis such as COVID-19 may mean the opening of adaptive space is forced on leaders or emerges naturally. Indeed, there were several instances in the Ghanaian university sector where there was a natural opening of adaptive space in response to the COVID-19 crisis. They include universities and educational leaders working with faculty, students, and parents to agree to move learning and teaching online and re-adjust the university academic calendar to accommodate the disruptions caused by the COVID-19 crisis. Other examples include universities and educational leaders working with faculty, professional staff, and students to implement new learning management systems and with faculty and professional staff to agree to new working-from-home arrangements regarding social distancing protocols. These indicate that for the higher education sector to thrive during a global crisis such as the COVID-19 pandemic, educational leaders must work with or, at least, allow for context that offers opportunities for new partnerships with people with conflicting views working independently towards a solution. Altogether, the COVID-19 crisis offers evidence of how educational leaders may lead their institutions and save their members' lives by loosening formal systems and rigid formalities in times of crisis.

## Conclusion

When the COVID-19 pandemic struck in early 2020, the education sector in Ghana faced significant disruptions. The closure of the various educational institutions disrupted the academic calendar, which tremendously affected learning and teaching while negatively impacting low-performing students and graduating students. This consequently led to unavoidable stress, depression, fear, and anxiety for some students due to cancellation and postponement of events such as examinations, project work defence, and graduation ceremonies. The increasing isolation level and the absence of in-person interaction during school and graduation ceremonies made students express mixed feelings. Though the COVID-19 pandemic primarily laid bare the lack of proactiveness of universities in Ghana to embrace technology in education delivery, the leadership shown by educational leaders of these universities to promptly transition to online learning and teaching highlights some capabilities of Ghanaian universities to adapt to complexities and challenges even under very extreme conditions.

The lessons for the management of universities in Ghana extend beyond the alternative mode of education delivery outside the traditional face-to-face but also include considerations around equal access to online learning opportunities and guaranteeing quality standards in education delivery. This pandemic offers many opportunities for universities in Ghana to embrace online learning technologies and to reinforce the need to incorporate e-learning and ICT mediation into the current distance learning programmes.

## Practical Implications

The COVID-19 pandemic has exposed Ghana's poor investment in ICT infrastructure in the higher education delivery system. This condition almost triggered a total shutdown of university education institutions following the outbreak. Looking back, Ghanaian universities' introduction of the distance education model in the 1990s was expected to accelerate technology adoption and investment in and/or development of e-learning infrastructure in the university sector. However, this failed to materialise as learning and teaching in distance education continued to be structured around face-to-face interactions in most universities across the country. If e-learning and ICT mediation had been embedded in Ghana's distance learning programmes, the disruption witnessed in university education delivery during the COVID-19 pandemic could have been largely curtailed.

Flexible learning and teaching options remain key in this post-pandemic era. Educational leaders must continuously embrace flexibility in the learning and teaching processes by investing in ICT infrastructure and developing staff digital capabilities. The use of a hybrid approach for learning and teaching must be embraced by Ghanaian universities, not as a reaction to the crisis but as an ongoing pursuit to harness the benefits of emerging digital transformation. Ghanaian universities must support the hybrid learning and teaching system to extend access to education nationwide. This is an essential step towards the Sustainable Development Goal (SDG) 4: Ensuring inclusive and equitable education and promoting lifelong learning opportunities for all.

## References


Acquah, A. (2021). Higher education finance between Ghana and the United States. *Current Issues in Comparative Education, 23*(1), 90–108.

Adekanmbi, G., Kasozi, J. A., Seabelo, C., & Batisani, C. (2021). Pre-and post-COVID-19: Exploring issues of access in higher education in Botswana and Ghana. *Alliance for African Partnership Perspectives, 1*(1), 125–135.

Adzovie, E. D., & Jibril, A. B. (2022). Assessment of the effects of Covid-19 pandemic on the prospects of e-learning in higher learning institutions: The mediating role of academic innovativeness and technological growth. *Cogent Education, 9*(1), 2041222.

Agormedah, E. K., Henaku, E. A., Ayite, D. M. K., & Ansah, E. A. (2020). Online learning in higher education during COVID-19 pandemic: A case of Ghana. *Journal of Educational Technology and Online Learning, 3*(3), 183–210.

Amewu, S., Asante, S., Pauw, K., & Thurlow, J. (2020). The economic costs of COVID-19 in sub-Saharan Africa: Insights from a simulation exercise for Ghana. *The European Journal of Development Research, 32*, 1353–1378.

Anamuah-Mensah, J., Effah, P., & Sarkodie, A. (2002). *Meeting the challenges of education in the twenty first century: Report of the President's committee on review of education reforms in Ghana*. Ministry of Education.

Antwi-Boasiako, J., Abbey, C. O. A., Ogbey, P., & Ofori, R. A. (2021). Policy Responses to fight COVID-19: The case of Ghana. *Brazilian Journal of Public Administration, 55*(1), 122–139.

Asante, K. T. (2023). The politics of policy failure in Ghana: The case of oil palm. *World Development Perspectives, 31*, 100509.

Ayentimi, D. T., Burgess, J., & Dayaram, K. (2018). Skilled labour shortage: A qualitative study of Ghana's training and apprenticeship system. *Human Resource Development International, 21*(5), 406–424.

Biney, I. K. (2020). Experiences of adult learners on using the Sakai learning management system for learning in Ghana. *Journal of Adult and Continuing Education, 26*(2), 262–282.

Boaheng, I. (2021). Christianity and the COVID-19 pandemic: A pastoral and theological reflection from the Ghanaian context. *Journal of Pastoral Theology, 31*(2–3), 224–237.

Botwe, B., Antwi, W., Adusei, J., Mayeden, R., Akudjedu, T., & Sule, S. (2022). COVID-19 vaccine hesitancy concerns: Findings from a Ghana clinical radiography workforce survey. *Radiography, 28*(2), 537–544.

Constantia, C., Christos, P., Glykeria, R., Anastasia, A.-R., & Aikaterini, V. (2021). The impact of COVID-19 on the educational process: The role of the school principal. *Journal of Education, 203*(3). 00220574211032588.

Dare, P. S., & Saleem, A. (2022). Principal leadership role in response to the pandemic impact on school process. *Frontiers in Psychology*, 3976.

Ghana Education Service (2020). *Covid-19 coordinated education response plan for Ghana*. https://www.ges.gov.gh/wp-content/uploads/2020/04/EDUCATION-RESPONSE-PLAN-TO-COVID-19-IN-GHANA-APRIL-2020-1.pdf

Ghana Health Service (2023). *COVID-19: Ghana's outbreak response management updates*. https://www.ghs.gov.gh/covid19/#

ISSER. (2020). *State of the Ghanaian economy report 2020*. https://www.isser.ug.edu.gh/publication/sger-2020

Lalani, K., Crawford, J., & Butler-Henderson, K. (2021). Academic leadership during COVID-19 in higher education: Technology adoption and adaptation for online learning during a pandemic. *International Journal of Leadership in Education, 1–17*. https://doi.org/10.1080/13603124.2021.1988716

Ministry of Education. (2018). *Education sector analysis 2018*. https://www.globalpartnership.org/node/document/download?file=document/file/2019-05-ghana-education-sector-analysis.pdf

Ministry of Finance (2023). *The budget statement and economic policy of the Government of Ghana for the 2023 financial year*. https://www.mofep.gov.gh/sites/default/files/budget-statements/2023-Budget-Statement-V5.pdf.

Mpofu, B., & Ndlovu-Gatsheni, S. (2020). *The dynamics of changing higher education in the global south*. Cambridge Scholars Publishing.

Omari, E. B., Salifu Yendork, J., & Ankrah, E. (2022). University students' perspectives on the benefits and challenges of emergency remote teaching during the Covid-19 pandemic in Ghana. *Education and Information Technologies, 28*, 6093–6113.

Osabwa, W. (2022, February). Coming to terms with COVID-19 reality in the context of africa's higher education: Challenges, insights, and prospects. In *Frontiers in education* (Vol. 7, p. 643162). Frontiers.

Parida, S., Dhakal, S. P., Dayaram, K., Mohammadi, H., Ayentimi, D. T., Amankwaa, A., & D'Cruz, D. (2023). Rhetoric and realities in Australian universities of student engagement in online learning: Implications for a post-pandemic era. *The International Journal of Management Education, 21*(2), 100795.

Riggio, R. E., & Newstead, T. (2023). Crisis leadership. *Annual Review of Organizational Psychology and Organizational Behavior, 10*, 201–224.

Rudolph, J., Tan, S., Crawford, J., & Butler-Henderson, K. (2023). Perceived quality of online learning during COVID-19 in higher education in Singapore: Perspectives from students, lecturers, and academic leaders. *Educational Research for Policy and Practice, 22*(1), 171–191. https://doi.org/10.1007/s10671-022-09325-0

Tagoe, C.N.B. (2020). Higher education systems and institutions, Ghana. In P. N. Teixeira & J. C. Shin (Eds.), *The international encyclopaedia of higher education systems and institutions*. Springer.

Teachout, M., & Zipfel, C. (2020). The economic impact of COVID-19 lockdowns in sub-Saharan Africa. *International Growth Centre, 1*(1), 1–16.

Tsevi, L. (2021). COVID-19 and higher education in Ghana: The case of a public higher education institution. *International Journal of Multidisciplinary Perspectives in Higher Education, 6*(1), 150–155.

Uhl-Bien, M., & Arena, M. (2017). Complexity leadership: Enabling people and organisations for adaptability. *Organisational Dynamics, 46*(1), 9–20.

Uhl-Bien, M. (2021). Complexity and COVID-19: Leadership and followership in a complex world. *Journal of Management Studies, 58*(5), 1400.

UNDP RBA. (2022). *Impact of the war in Ukraine on Africa*. Rapid Assessment by the Regional Bureau for Africa, UNDP—24 May 2022_0.pdf.

UNESCO. (2020). *Global education monitoring report 2020*. https://www.unesco.org/en/articles/global-education-monitoring-gem-report-2020.

University of Ghana (2023). *International Students Programme Office*. Legon, Accra-Ghana.

WHO. (2023a). *Tackling hesitancy to boost COVID-19 vaccine uptake in Ghana*. https://www.afro.who.int/countries/ghana/news/tackling-hesitancy-boost-covid-19-vaccine-uptake-ghana

WHO. (2023b). *WHO coronavirus (COVID-19) dashboard | WHO coronavirus (COVID-19) dashboard with vaccination data*. https://www.who.int/emergencies/diseases/novel-coronavirus-2019?adgroupsurvey={adgroupsurvey}&gclid=CjwKCAjwyY6pBhA9EiwAMzmfwe_ihPxOpsBAL9cfiNhH-iLfo_Ub5jI8Mn_5fWimRk_lVj3g4rkG5RoCycAQAvD_BwE

Wilson, S., Tan, S., Knox, M., Ong, A., Crawford, J., & Rudolph, J. (2020). Enabling cross-cultural student voice during COVID-19: A collective autoethnography. *Journal of University Teaching & Learning Practice, 17*(5), 3. https://doi.org/10.53761/1.17.5.3

Zavale, N. C., & Schneijderberg, C. (2022). Mapping the field of research on African higher education: A review of 6483 publications from 1980 to 2019. *Higher Education, 83*(1), 199–233.

Zhao, Y., Llorente, A. M. P., & Gómez, M. C. S. (2021). Digital competence in higher education research: A systematic literature review. *Computers & Education, 168*, 104212.

# Crisis Leadership in Greek Higher Education

Margarita Kefalaki

## Introduction

COVID-19 will remain a historical point of our era, both for its negative but mostly for its positive consequences in education. Education systems around the world were swift to react and adapt (Rudolph et al., 2021). COVID-19 affected the operation of school units in Greece, with a great impact on teaching and learning methods to leadership practices and actions (Eliophotou Menon, 2021). Nevertheless, apart from its negative effects, this crisis stimulated innovative practices and directions within the education sector, examining the approaches in support of education and training continuity and distance learning solutions (UN, 2020).

Higher education leadership during COVID-19 in Greece, as in most European and non-European (Bonk et al., 2020), faced unexpected challenges. So, the need for quick decisions to adapt to a new reality was crucial. In reality, HEIs were unprepared to face these inconveniences (Bonk et al., 2020). Educators in Greece were obliged to adapt their pedagogical style and curriculum to a new online teaching environment. They also needed to invent ways to build mutual trust and understanding with and among their students (Kefalaki et al., 2021). Post-crisis leadership is a priority for universities on a

M. Kefalaki (✉)
Communication Institute of Greece, Moschato, Greece
e-mail: president@coming.gr



J. Rudolph et al. (eds.), *The Palgrave Handbook of Crisis Leadership in Higher Education*,
https://doi.org/10.1007/978-3-031-54509-2_16

global level. Post-pandemic leadership sector will need to recognise and define carefully what is to remain (Crawford, 2021). Universities in Greece need to respond to the global competition among universities around the world.

This Chapter aims to add to the existing literature on recommendations and directions for successful post-crisis leadership in the Greek HEIS. To address this objective, the content of this study is based on critical reviews of the literature and my personal experience as an educator since 2007. In the first section, I present how Greek academia functions, focusing on the characteristics of post-COVID-19 leadership. Then, I propose specific actions for successful post-COVID-19 leadership in the Greek HEIs.

## Higher Education Institutions (HEIs) in Greece

Education in Greece (see Table 1) is free in all public schools and universities. Greek universities are owned and funded by the Greek Government. Thus, they are defined as public institutions and enjoy institutional autonomy. At the moment, there are no student fees, with few exceptions (master courses and Hellenic Open University), and national legislation determines university budgets, procurement, financial oversight, and employment (Bourantas et al., 2001; Katharaki & Katharakis, 2010). Students' entrance to HEIs depends solely on general examination results and on choice by the students at the preferred university. The students' number registering with HEIs is set by the Minister of Education.

To better know Greek public HEIs, it is important to note that they preserve an obsolete educational system, producing scientists according to the demands of nineteenth-century society and are not adapted to the changing

**Table 1** Summary of the Greek education system

| Age | | Years |
|---|---|---|
| 18 years old+ | **Higher Education**<br>Panepistimio (after 18 years old) | |
| 12–18 years old | **Secondary Education**<br>Called *Gimnasio* and *Lykio* | 6 years (3 years *Gimnasio* + 3 years *Lykio)*<br>Compulsory Education |
| 6–12 years old | **Primary Education**<br>Dimotiko/Primary Schools | 6 years<br>Compulsory Education |
| 4–6 years old | **Pre-school Education**<br>Nipiagogeia/Kindergarten | 2 years<br>Compulsory Education |

environment and the knowledge society (Trivella & Nasiopoulos, 2015). Then, speaking of academic leaders (rector, senate/council, and deans) in a practical sense, they still seem to act more like administrators than proper leaders (Kabouridis & Kakarelidis, 2011).

## Academic Leadership in Greece

Due to the complexity of HEIs and their multi-faceted mission of teaching, conducting research, and contributing to society, managing change in academia after COVID-19, is a profound challenge for academic leaders (Dumulescu & Mutiu, 2021). Especially as the COVID-19 crisis had a strong and deep impact on Greek higher education (Kefalaki et al., 2021). Universities have been confronted with various new issues and obligations toward students, staff, and academic audiences (Crawford et al., 2023; Tice et al., 2021).

Then, it is also that higher education institutions around the world experience profound changes in their missions and functions, due to accelerating globalisation, technological advances, and public demands for accountability (Pham et al., 2019). Even if public universities in Greece have strong conservative policies, they need to keep up with the European university's standard and quality guidelines (ESG, 2015) in order to survive. The question that remains among all the organisations and ministries involved is how to take forward quality assurance in the European Higher Education Area and provide a firm basis for successful implementation. Having at the moment negligible funds, Greek universities need to adapt to the global competition among universities to be able to function offering quality knowledge and opportunities to their students, their staff, and society as a total.

Universities in Greece are not used to working with leadership concepts and rules to ameliorate their product and quality of sharing knowledge, when their core mission (Greek law, 1268/1982) is the production and transmission of knowledge through research and teaching. Greek Universities are indeed not familiar with the concept of leadership (Whitchurch, 2007). Academic leaders are elected based on their academic and scientific prestige, and not on their expert knowledge, and managerial background, which can be a barrier in the leadership role (Pérez et al., 2011). Knowing that for expert knowledge implementation success, the result of the combined effects of high-quality decisions and effective implementation processes is needed (Rune, 2007), I can clearly say that this is not the case for higher education leadership in Greece.

According to Freidericou and Folerou-Tserouli (1991), an academic leader in Greece has transactional leadership characteristics, which means that he/she is focused on short-term goals and favours structured policies and procedures that generally tend to be rather inflexible and opposed to change. Xatzipanagiotou (2003) also claims that academic leaders in Greece work in a traditional and bureaucratic way without actually taking the initiative to introduce changes. Saitis (1997) was driven at this same conclusion, supporting that school heads are more traditionally bureaucratic and serve less as leaders. I personally agree with these views, judging from my own experience.

To understand the problems that appeared in the process of democratisation and modernisation of Greek universities, it is important to look at factors beyond the sphere of education. There is indeed a need for long-term planning and the examination of all processes taking place in tertiary education, considering the wider socioeconomic, political, and cultural context (Zmas, 2015). The constantly expanding state mechanism and the political party interests this has served (Zmas, 2015) has certainly a great role to play in the process of democratisation and modernisation of Greek universities.

Then, to identify the functionality of the Greek educational system, it is important to refer to laws concerning universities. A description proposed by Zmas (2015) can help: Article 16 of the Greek Constitution (1975), apart from securing the freedom to teach and research in Greek universities, clarifies how they intend to have a public character and be self-managed. Then, Law 1268/1982 (GMNERA 1982) reinforces the democratic character of Greek tertiary education. Its first Article clarifies that the mission of a university is to shape responsible 'human beings' with scientific, social, cultural, and political awareness who will receive a comprehensive education appropriate for their scientific and professional careers. The same article indicates the importance of academic freedom in teaching and research. Also, it includes a beneficial provision regarding the self-managed character of the universities, offering students and other members of the academic community the possibility to participate in matters of university governance. In this way, it abolishes the management of universities by specific individuals, which is a direct result of the wider responsibilities afforded to professors. In reality, the self-managed character of universities is weak in practice, as the decisions taken internally have to be approved at a central level, i.e. by the Ministry of Education. Therefore, state control remains powerful at a time when university funding is almost exclusively based on public funds. Additionally, initiatives that permit universities to connect with the job market to raise funding remain unrealised (Zmas, 2015).

Law 3374/2005 (GMNERA 2005) aims to create evaluation mechanisms in Greek universities. Since 2005, it appears that most of the universities' departments have started to establish procedures for internal and external evaluation. The external evaluation reports regarding the effort of the Greek universities to provide services of high quality were positive despite the adverse framework of their operation. Improvements have also been observed in the implementation of Laws 3374/2005, 3549/2007 and 4009/2011, which intended to familiarise the Greek universities with 'European and international practices'. An increasing number of universities were at the time (2005–2011) setting Development Academic Planning, with strategic objectives such as the production of innovative knowledge and research, effectiveness, international recognition, and financial and administrative autonomy, which were aligned with the aim of the EU to modernise the tertiary sector of its member-states (Zmas, 2015).

Nowadays, higher education institutions seem to have understood the urgent need to engage an external leader in order to adapt and respond to the global competition among universities. Law 4957/2022 (Article 18) for higher education in Greece refers to the existence of an executive director/manager (in Greek *«εκτελεστικός διευθυντής»*), who will ensure the efficient administrative and financial operation of the university and will also be responsible for the implementation of the strategic plan and the annual target setting. Specific points of Law 4957/2022 indicate the implication of innovative practices and proper leadership in Greek higher education institutions. More particularly, articles 18, 67, 131, and 224, explain this specific need: Article 18 gives details on the responsibilities of the university's executive director, explaining that this type of leader is the head of the university's organic units and ensures the smooth and efficient administrative and financial operation and the implementation of the strategic plan and annual targets of the institute. Additionally, the executive director coordinates and supervises the implementation of the university's digital transformation plan and the university's promotional actions and cooperates with all the organic and academic units in order to monitor actions and recommend measures to improve their effectiveness. He/she also proposes an annual report of activities. Then, Article 67 describes the actions and procedures of innovative distance education. Moreover, Article 131 refers to the University's Research and Innovation Centres (in Greek: *Πανεπιστημιακά Κέντρα Έρευνας και Καινοτομίας*) that has for mission, among other things, the development of research within the framework of the National Strategic Research, Technological Development and Innovation and the development of the National Smart Specialisation Strategy.

Then, article 224 refers to the Institution's Strategic Plan. More particularly, it explains that Higher Educational Institutions (HEIs) need to prepare a multi-year strategic plan for academic development in accordance with the national strategy programme for higher education (Law 4653/2020, A' 12, Article 14) and the national strategy for research and innovation. Paragraph three refers to the implementation of the university strategic plan, proposed with a duration of at least four years, which includes an annual target-setting programme, the planning of each target, and the measures for its implementation. Finally, in paragraph four of Article 224, we read that the strategic plan may be reformed during its validity in accordance with the universities' needs and conditions, the changes in the national strategy for higher education, the national strategy for research and innovation, as well as the developments at the European and international higher education area. Based on Law 4957/2022, we understand that the Greek government has finally understood the importance of an executive director/leader in higher education. The academic leader seems able to respond to any crisis and help higher education institutions innovate, organise and survive in a competitive global market. It remains to be seen if and how what is proposed in this new Law will be put into practice.

The current academic leaders in Greece struggle to balance corporate management styles with the more traditional, democratic approach of collegial leadership. Although it appears to be an almost impossible demand for a university leader to provide the qualities required of a CEO or senior business manager, in conjunction with those of an academic leader of significant reputation, it also seems difficult for universities in Greece to choose between academic or purely corporate style leaders (Kabouridis & Kakarelidis, 2011). The ideal profile for a higher education leader, and the qualities required to undertake such a role, appear to be very different from those of the past. As described by Kabouridis and Kakarelidis (2011), members of the academic staff still perceive the members of the governing bodies to be distinguished scholars even if they have no experience in business, commerce, production, or administration. At the moment, there is a need for a systematic curricula revision that will result in better employability of graduates at all levels—focus on competences and learning outcomes, increasing transparency and flexibility, and involving partners. This will also strengthen the knowledge triangle—teaching, research, and innovation—as part of the drive for excellence (Kabouridis & Kakarelidis, 2011).

## What Post-Crisis Leadership for Greek Academia?

> This (pandemic) is an opportunity to radically reconsider our view of the educational system. —Greek HEIs educator's view

Crisis leadership is the capability to lead under extreme pressure (Hayes James & Perry Wooten, 2011). A crisis of enormous scale that spreads quickly, leading to a feeling of loss of control, disorientation, and severe emotional disturbance (Forster et al., 2020) is in need of effective crisis leadership (Riggio & Newstead, 2023). As a result, the post-COVID-19 crisis leadership era is a needed tool for academic leaders (Lalani et al., 2021). Schechter et al. (2022) suggest that crisis leadership should be implemented as a core component of national standards for educational leadership and more particularly, that it should be incorporated into academic leaders' preparation and professional experiences. I couldn't agree more as this is crucial for the development of academia, and also there are many crisis situations academics will have to deal with in the future.

Recent developments such as the financial crisis and the COVID-19 pandemic strongly point to the need for re-examining the role of the academic leader in cases where he/she and the university in general face unprecedented challenges (Eliophotou Menon, 2021). The COVID-19 crisis has highlighted that education needs reform to better train teachers in new methods of education delivery (UN, 2020). It has been a reminder for all the education stakeholders, universities, and educators to understand the importance of academic leadership. The educational system has been affected and will continue to be affected by various categories of crisis. Crises present multiple, ongoing, and often critical demands, requiring leaders to perform a variety of roles and be able to respond appropriately (Harris & Jones, 2020). The move to distance learning for Greek Universities has been both a challenge and an opportunity to expand flexible learning modalities, setting the stage for a sustained shift towards more online learning in the future. From the onset of the pandemic, educators were immediately tasked with implementing distance learning modalities, often without sufficient guidance, training, or resources. In many contexts, educator's professional development moved online via Web-based class meetings and messaging applications. Papanaum's (1995) research shows that most of the academic leaders in Greece, are dissatisfied about their limited training opportunities. Organised training courses on how to become an effective academic leader will certainly help higher education post-crisis leadership become more effective.

Strengthened executive leaders, governing boards and administrative staff/processes with weakened and smaller consultative bodies will result in increased importance of institution-wide strategy, increased internal and external accountability and diversified funding sources, adaptation and upgrade of infrastructure (Kabouridis & Kakarelidis, 2011). As emphasised earlier, this paper is an approximation based on the changed environment and directions of the EU for tertiary education (Kabouridis & Kakarelidis, 2011). Needless to say, a detailed constitution on a HEI's organisation chart should be devised and any contradictions eliminated. But as a basic prerequisite, universities need more autonomy through changed legal frameworks (Kabouridis & Kakarelidis, 2011).

It is true that leadership and strategy are key elements in any quality framework (Sallis, 2014). Educational institutions need well-worked-out strategies proposed by well-trained academic leaders to deal with the competitive and results-oriented environment in which they operate. Of course, academic leadership practices may vary across universities according to their differing organizational culture, tradition, mission etc. (Dumulescu & Mutiu, 2021). There are many different leadership styles and variables that differentiate one university from another (missions, circumstances, cultures, external environmental factors), this is why there is not a simple formula to follow. Academic leaders are called to keep the university functioning effectively, responding to the needs of a complex environment where students, staff, and other stakeholders are involved (Doyle & Brady, 2018). An effective academic leader possesses the ability to view situations and challenges from multiple, and sometimes contradictory perspectives in order to encompass the full array of options for decision-making and policy development (Taylor & Machado, 2006).

In the process of designing future universities, academic leaders play an essential role (Dumulescu & Mutiu, 2021). COVID-19 made Greek academic leaders act under high psychological pressure (pressure of time, ambiguity, lack of information, stress), with great expectations from members of various organisations for constant reassurance and support that increased the difficulty of the decision-making process. Creative thinking, learning fast from experience, and decentralised decision-making are, at the time of the post-crisis era, important tools for academic leaders' decision-making process (Dumulescu & Mutiu, 2021).

Crises like COVID-19 also illuminated some deep fault lines in the way that education systems previously operated and have shifted academic leadership towards distributed, collaborative, and network practices (Harris, 2020). Kalavros (2007) and Mpotnias (2010) concluded that school management requires a participative leadership model. A survey questionnaire by Sfakianaki et al. (2018) demonstrated that academic leaders mainly adopt a specific participative style. Findings indicate that the teacher-leader who follows the participatory process shows concern for the student and the learner and thus can ensure educational quality, promoting Total Quality Management (TQM) principles such as continuous improvement and student satisfaction. TQM is recognised as a generic management tool applicable to any organisation (Kumar et al., 2011) that can contribute to quality education. However, the combination of different leadership styles is essential because an effective leader adapts his/her style to the characteristics of the group, the maturity of its members, the work to be carried out, and the environment. There are some leadership styles that can be followed by academic leaders, depending on the needs of each university. Schechter et al. (2022) reported areas by academic leaders as a response to various crises and proposed leadership guidelines. Nevertheless, the participative model is, indeed, judging from my personal experience in universities, a model that can be well integrated into Greek academic reality.

Then, the Crisis Communication lifecycle phases (Freimuth et al., 2022) (a) precrisis, (b) initial, (c) maintenance, (d) resolution, and (e) evaluation is an important tool for Greek higher education stakeholders to deal with crises. The evaluation phase can contribute to the post-crisis leadership in Greek higher education, as lessons learned can be applied and maintained. After the COVID-19 crisis, educators are able to evaluate the communication plan performance, examine the lessons learned, and finally determine specific actions to improve a possible crisis plan. Additionally, to move forward, academic leaders need to become technologically savvy and well-informed (Harris & Jones, 2020). This is also the case for the Greek academia. Academic leaders need to be discerning about the digital products they choose and to be careful about striking a balance between technology and pedagogy (Hargreaves & Fullan, 2020). Pedagogy is the key to effective learning, and while technology has a part to play, it is the human dimension of effective teaching and leadership that can make a difference (Harris & Jones, 2020). We also need to be reminded that education leaders are directly shaping the performances of their students, possessing different roles inside the university (Toker, 2022). This is why it is important to support educators' wellbeing, social-emotional competences, and resilience before, during, and after the crisis (UNESCO, 2020). Self-care must be a priority for all academic leaders, as it is by remaining healthy that they will be able to support others (Harris, 2020).

Support of the process of learning is also essential for post-pandemic crisis leadership in Greece. Remote learning strategies should pay attention to how students learn, as students do not learn by passively consuming content

(Andaleeb & Priyamvada, 2020). Practice should be coupled with feedback that explicitly communicates about aspect(s) of students' performance and should be compared to specific learning goals. Such feedback would help students progress based on their needs (Andaleeb & Priyamvada, 2020). Initiating communication and exchange with other universities around the world is also important for effective post-crisis leadership in the Greek higher education sector. This could, for example, take place with the correct organisation of international academic conferences, where students and academics would be involved, learn, and exchange (Kefalaki, 2013). Academic leaders could, in this way, benefit from receiving information on good practices from academics around the world and also share opportunities to meet and exchange. Additionally, monitoring learning behaviours and outcomes is key to informing education policy and correcting it over time (Andaleeb & Priyamvada, 2020). Using mobile phone surveys, tracking usage and performance statistics from learning platforms and apps, and implementing rapid learning assessments to identify learning gaps could, among other things, help monitor progress in education (Andaleeb & Priyamvada, 2020) and lead to an effective post-crisis leadership.

Additionally, it is important for a successful education leader to organise data collection on educators' needs, capacities and gaps. Innovative continuous assessment methods have received a lot of attention from universities around the world since student progress can be monitored with mobile phone surveys, tracking usage and performance statistics from learning platforms and apps, and implementing rapid learning assessments to identify learning gaps (Alam & Tiwari, 2021). Education leaders should use such methods to understand any capacity and gap and try to ameliorate the existing situation. Last but not least, listening to the voices of all concerned (UN, 2020), is essential for effective post-crisis leadership in Greek higher education. Education stakeholders, educators, parents, and students need to communicate and exchange views with a common interest to be able to provide education opportunities to improve and innovate universities.

## Conclusion

The pandemic has made it crystal clear that leaders around the globe have to navigate global crises and has ensured that crisis leadership is an important tool for HEIs around the world. Education leaders have a pivotal role to play in navigating a safe, principled, and collective passage (Harris, 2020), especially in the post-crisis era. Education leadership is critically important to better define principles and priorities and provide opportunities for the sector of education. In this Chapter, we add to the literature concerning strategies and practices for successful post-pandemic crisis leadership for the Greek HEIs. The main conclusion of this research is that academic leaders in Greece should use innovative managerial concepts, be open to innovative practices, and adapt to the new needs of universities as businesses, which means open business opportunities and better prospects for their students, academics, and the society as a total. This is how HEIs can maintain a competitive advantage in a global complex environment.

Public universities in Greece, previously operating in quasi-monopolistic positions in higher education systems, nowadays come across global competition (Kabouridis & Kakarelidis, 2011). Universities are becoming international enterprises that offer educational services beyond their territorial state boundaries. This is the reason that there is a significant pressure on universities to become efficient and responsive, to be able to operate in a more competitive environment. Universities need to make major organisational changes, with the help of an adequate academic leader (executive director) to become financially self-sustaining, and to maintain their educational character in a good level at the same time. Examining if and how an executive director (academic leader), proposed in the new universities Law (4957/2022) that is about to take place at this moment (September–October 2023) in Greek HEIs, will be able to build an appropriate post-crisis leadership environment, is certainly a theme of research to follow.

## References


Alam, A., & Tiwari, P. (2021). Implications of COVID-19 for low-cost private schools. UNICEF, Issue Brief, 8.

Andaleeb, A., & Priyamvada, T. (2020). Putting the 'learning' back in remote learning. Policies to uphold effective continuity of learning through COVID-19. UNICEF, Issue brief.

Bonk, R., Kefalaki, M., Rudolph, J., Diamantidaki, F., Rekar Muno, C., Karanicolas, S., Kontoleon, P., & Pogner, K.-H. (2020). Pedagogy in the time of pandemic: From localisation to glocalisation. *Journal of Education, Innovation and Communication, 2*(SI1), 17–64.

Bourantas, D., Lioukas, S., & Papadakis, P. (2001). University evaluation systems in Greece: Athens University of Economics and Business. *An internationalization* quality review. Quality Assessment, OECD.

Crawford, J. (2021). During and beyond a pandemic: Publishing learning and teaching research through COVID-19. *Journal of University Teaching & Learning Practice, 18*(3), 6–13.

Crawford, J., Allen, K.-A., Sanders, T., Baumeister, R., Parker, P., Saunders, C., & Tice, D. (2023). Sense of belonging in higher education students: An Australian longitudinal study from 2013 to 2019. *Studies in Higher Education, 49*(3), 395–409. https://doi.org/10.1080/03075079.2023.2238006

Doyle, T., & Brady, M. (2018). Reframing the university as an emergent organization: Implications for strategic management and leadership in Higher Education. *Journal of Higher Education Policy and Management, 40*(4), 305–320.

Dumulescu, D., & Mutiu, A. (2021). Academic leadership in the time of COVID-19—Experiences and perspectives. *Frontiers in Psychology, 12*, 648344. https://doi.org/10.3389/fpsyg.2021.648344

Eliophotou Menon, M. (2021). Transformational leadership at times of crisis: The case of school leaders in Greece. *European Journal of Educational Management., 4*(1), 1–11.

Forster, B., Patlas M., & Lexa F. (2020). Crisis leadership during and following COVID-19. *Canadian Association of Radiologists' Journal 2020, 71*(4), 421–422.

Freiderikou, A., & Folerou-Tserouli, F. (1991). *The teachers of Elementary school.* Epsilon Books.

Freimuth, V., Eberl-Lefko A., Weinberg, L., Williams, E., Wood, C., & Zawislanski A. (2022) (Eds.). *Crisis and emergency risk communication.* Center for Disease Control and Prevention.

Greek Law For the structure and operation of Higher Education Institutions. 1268/1982—FEK 87/A/16-7-1982.

Hargreaves, A., & Fullan, M. (2020). Professional capital after the pandemic: Revisiting and revising classic understandings of teachers' work. *Journal of Professional Capital and Community, 5*(3/4), 327–336.

Harris, A. (2020). COVID-19: School leadership in crisis? *Journal of Professional Capital and Community, 5*(3/4), 321–326.

Harris, A., & Jones, M. (2020). COVID 19—School leadership in disruptive times. *School Leadership & Management, 40*(4), 243–247.

Hayes James, E., & Perry Wooten, L. (2011). Crisis leadership and why it matters. *The European Financial Review*, pp. 60–64.

Kalavros, B. (2007). *Perceptions and attitudes of teachers in primary education on their participation in the teachers' association.* The Case of the Teachers of West Piraeus, HOU, Athens.

Kabouridis G., & Kakarelidis G. (2011). *Academic leadership in Greek higher educational institutions under economic and social crisis.* 2nd WIETE Annual Conference on Engineering and Technology Education, Pattaya, Thailand.

Katharaki, M., & Katharakis, G. (2010). A comparative assessment of Greek universities' efficiency using quantitative analysis. *International Journal of Educational Research. Science Direct, 49*(4), 115–128.

Kefalaki, M. (2013). Intercultural communication, a key factor for a successful International academic conference. In *3rd International Conference on Tourism and Hospitality Management [conference session]. International Conference on Communication and Management*.

Kefalaki, M., Nevradakis, M., & Li, Q. (2021). Cross-cultural effects of COVID-19 on higher education learning and teaching practice: A case study from Greece. *Journal of University Teaching & Learning Practice, 18*(5), 73–89. https://doi.org/10.53761/1.18.5.5

Kumar, R., Garg, D., & Garg, T. (2011). TQM success factors in North Indian manufacturing and service industries. *The TQM Journal, 23*(1), 36–46.

Lalani, K., Crawford, J., & Butler-Henderson, K. (2021). Academic leadership during COVID-19 in higher education: Technology adoption and adaptation for online learning during a pandemic. *International Journal of Leadership in Education,* 1–17. https://doi.org/10.1080/13603124.2021.1988716

Mpotnias, K. (2010). *The existence of a collective participatory management and its efficiency in primary schools of Aigion* [Doctoral Decertation, University of Patras].

New Horizons in Higher Education Institutions: Strengthening the quality, functionality and connection of A.E.I. with society and other provisions [translation by M. Kefalaki]. *Official Journal of the Greek Government*. Number 141. 21 July 2022. Law 4957/2022.

Papanaoum, Z. (1995). *The address of the school. Theoretical analysis and empirical investigation.* Kyriakides Brothers SA.

Pérez, S., Saritas, O., Pook, K., & Warden, C. (2011). Ready for the future? Universities' capabilities to strategically manage their intellectual capital. *Foresight, 13*(2), 31–48.

Riggio, R., & Newstead, T. (2023). Crisis leadership. *Annual Review of Organizational Psychology and Organizational Behavior, 10*, 201–224. https://doi.org/10.1146/annurev-orgpsych-120920-044838

Rudolph, J., Itangata, L., Tan, S., Kane, M., Thairo, I., & Tan, T. (2021). Bittersweet' and 'alienating': An extreme comparison of collaborative autoethnographic perspectives from higher education students, non-teaching staff and faculty during the pandemic in the UK and Singapore. *Journal of University Teaching and Learning Practice, 18*(8), 10.

Rune, L. (2007). Using power to install strategy: The relationships between expert power, position power, influence tactics and implementation success. *Journal of Change Management, 7*(2), 143–170.

Sallis, E. (2014). *Total quality management in education.* Taylor & Francis.

Schechter, C., Da'as, R., & Qadach, M. (2022). Crisis leadership: Leading schools in a global pandemic. *Management in Education.* British Educational Leadership, Management & Administration Society, 1–8.

Sfakianaki, E., Matsiori, A., & Giannias, D. (2018). Educational leadership and total quality management: Investigating teacher leadership styles. *International Journal of Management in Education, 12*(4), 375.

Taylor, J., & Machado, M. (2006). Higher education leadership and management: From conflict to interdependence through strategic planning. *Tertiary Education and Management, 12*, 137–160. https://doi.org/10.1007/s11233-006-0003-3

Tice, D., Baumeister, R., Crawford, J., Allen, K. A., & Percy, A. (2021). Student belongingness in higher education: Lessons for Professors from the COVID-19 pandemic. *Journal of University Teaching & Learning Practice, 18*(4), 2. https://doi.org/10.53761/1.18.4.2

Toker, A. (2022). Importance of leadership in the higher education. *International Journal of Social Sciences & Educational Studies, 9*(2), 230–236.

Trivellaa, L., & Nasiopoulos, K. (2015). Knowledge management strategy within higher education. The case of greece. Science Direct. *Procedia—Social and Behavioral Sciences, 175*, 488–495.

UNESCO. (2020). Supporting teachers and education personnel during times of crisis. *UNESCO Education Sector*. Issue note no. 2.2.

Whitchurch, C. (2007). The changing roles and identities of professional managers in UK higher education. *Perspectives: Policy and Practice in Higher Education, 11*(2), 53–60.

Xatzipanagiotou, P. (2003). *The administration of the school and the involvement of teachers in the decision-making process*. Kyriakides Bros SA.

Zmas, A. (2015). Financial crisis and higher education policies in Greece: Between intra- and supranational pressures. *Higher Education, 69*, 495–508.

# The Challenges of COVID-19 for Higher Education and the Implication to the Post-epidemic Era—Perspectives from China and Hong Kong

Chu Kwong Alex Chan and Sin Manw Sophia Lam

## Introduction

The emergence of the COVID-19 virus has profoundly impacted the global landscape. Wuhan, China, announced the first lockdown in January 2020, and many other countries subsequently adopted this approach. After three years of battling against the pandemic, the Director-General of the World Health Organisation, Tedros Adhanom, announced that COVID-19 may no longer be considered an international public health emergency in 2023. In retrospect, what has been the epidemic's impact on higher education in Hong Kong?

Hong Kong's anti-epidemic effectiveness is satisfactory in terms of numbers. As of March 18, 2023, Hong Kong has recorded 2,884,209 COVID-19 cases, with a death toll of 13,472, considerably lower than that of European and American countries (Worldometer, 2023). As a part of China, Hong Kong has adhered to China's lead in implementing anti-epidemic policies, ranging from early 'absolute elimination' to 'dynamic elimination', rendering it one of the world's most conservative and strongest resistance to epidemic regions. However, Hong Kong is also a highly outward-oriented,

C. K. A. Chan · S. M. S. Lam (✉)
Department of Chinese Language Studies, The Education University of Hong Kong, Hong Kong, China
e-mail: ssmlam@eduhk.hk

C. K. A. Chan
e-mail: cchukwong@eduhk.hk



J. Rudolph et al. (eds.), *The Palgrave Handbook of Crisis Leadership in Higher Education*,
https://doi.org/10.1007/978-3-031-54509-2_17

open economy that strives to maintain its status as an international financial centre. The government attempted to align with international standards while maintaining effective communication with China. Such an approach has resulted in occasional indecisiveness in policymaking, leading to slower response and recovery than other countries, including China. In March 2023, Hong Kong finally lifted all its anti-epidemic measures and is one of the last regions in the world to rescind mask mandates (Siddharth, 2023).

The Hong Kong government has primarily relied on legislative and enforcement measures to combat the pandemic. During severe outbreaks, the government implemented a work-from-home policy for civil servants exceeding four months while refraining from interfering with private enterprises' operations. However, to safeguard students' well-being, the Hong Kong Education Bureau mandated that primary and secondary schools and kindergartens transition to online learning for more than 50% of school days during the pandemic. Higher education institutions largely followed suit by offering online courses and remote access to campus resources. Educational institutions have faced significant challenges in adapting to ensure student safety while providing learning opportunities. This article examines the impact of the pandemic on higher education in Hong Kong and analyses potential long-term changes to the university ecosystem.

## Literature Review

Since the outbreak of COVID-19, there has been a rapid increase in research literature related to higher education. As the pandemic continues to evolve, the discourse and research have developed from focusing on single-country and single-institution cases to discussions with broad significance and a global perspective (Crawford et al., 2020). While the former approach has helped increase our understanding of the pandemic through various institutional cases (Bao, 2020; Karalis & Raikou, 2020), its drawback is that it focuses on specific local environments and may not apply to other environments, leading to a myopic view that overlooks the bigger picture (Rudolph et al., 2023). However, these exploratory studies have laid the foundation for a broad exploration of the pandemic's impact on higher education and established consensus and shared understanding. Thus, building on previous research, this study takes a macro perspective to reexamine the impact of the epidemic on higher education leadership in the past and its enduring effects.

The COVID-19 pandemic has presented higher education leadership with a crisis encompassing various dimensions. Its sudden and unexpected nature caught most institutions off guard, necessitating urgent decisions and actions to shift to online learning, cancel events, and implement safety measures (Hermann, 1963). The repercussions of the pandemic on higher education have been severe, affecting students, faculty, finances, and operations in ways that threaten institutions' fundamental functioning (Crawford, 2023; Wu et al., 2021). The situation created by the pandemic is novel and ambiguous, lacking clear precedents or answers for higher education leaders. Consequently, the pandemic and leaders' responses have attracted significant public attention through media coverage and scrutiny, eliciting strong emotions among students, faculty, and other stakeholders (James et al., 2011). Overall, the COVID-19 pandemic exhibits key characteristics defining organisational crises, including being unexpected, time-pressured, high-consequence, ambiguous, public, emotionally charged, and requiring decisive leadership action (Riggio & Newstead, 2023).

Given the unprecedented challenges posed by the COVID-19 pandemic, effective crisis leadership is crucial for higher education institutions to navigate the crisis successfully. Effective crisis leadership demands making sense of critical information, making rapid decisions, and strategically adapting (Weick, 1988). Leaders should provide confident, transparent communication that frames the crisis and outlines a path forward, creating clarity and order. Their decisions should be grounded in facts and expertise while actively soliciting input from diverse stakeholders through inclusive decision-making processes (Wilson & Newstead, 2022). In times of high uncertainty, crisis leadership requires a combination of calm rationality, clear direction-setting, empathetic connection with stakeholders, and agility to adjust to rapidly changing circumstances. Leaders must possess the capability to comprehend fluid situations, learn and decide swiftly, and adapt strategically through reoriented sensemaking and decision-making. This approach helps minimise conflict and maintain organisational cohesion and trust (Lau & Cobb, 2010; Pearson & Mitroff, 1993).

Effective crisis leadership necessitates competencies such as critical sensemaking, rapid decision-making, and strategic reorientation. These competencies enable leaders to comprehend complex and ambiguous situations, make well-informed decisions, and adapt promptly to changing circumstances. However, leaders may encounter challenges applying these competencies effectively without a clear framework to guide their decision-making processes.

Butler-Henderson et al. (2020) have introduced a four-stage model of pandemic response, which can guide higher education institutions in their decision-making processes. The first stage is Adaptation, which involves swiftly adapting core business processes to the new situation caused by the pandemic. In the context of higher education, this could include the rapid transition to online teaching and learning, the modification of course content, and the implementation of new assessment methods. The second stage is Improvement, which involves optimising existing teaching models to enhance their efficiency and effectiveness. This could include redesigning courses to suit online delivery better, improving communication channels between faculty and students, and using advanced technologies to enhance teaching and learning experiences. The third stage is Innovation, which involves exploring and implementing new teaching models better suited to the current situation. This could include the development of new online courses, the use of virtual reality technologies for hands-on learning, and the creation of more flexible learning pathways that cater to the diverse needs of students. The fourth and final stage is Restoration, which involves repositioning the role and status of higher education in society. This could include the development of new partnerships and collaborations with other institutions and stakeholders, reevaluating the value and purpose of higher education, and identifying new opportunities for growth and development.

This four-stage model provides a theoretical framework for higher education institutions to evaluate their responses to the pandemic and develop effective strategies. The model has been applied in various countries and institutions (e.g. Crawford et al., 2021; Hawley et al., 2021; Mishra et al., 2021; Wilson et al., 2020), providing a coherent and clear narrative of the impact of the pandemic on higher education from different perspectives. By identifying key issues, developing response strategies, and evaluating the effectiveness of these strategies, higher education institutions can effectively navigate the challenges posed by the pandemic and emerge stronger and more resilient.

Universities faced significant challenges in helping students who were forced into virtual learning, with many lacking effective methods to ensure that all students could access and benefit from online learning opportunities (Neuwirth et al., 2021). The shift to virtual learning has also exacerbated existing inequalities in higher education, with disadvantaged students facing greater challenges accessing and succeeding in online learning environments (Marinoni et al., 2020). Butler-Henderson et al. (2020) conducted a study of responses from universities in 20 regions to the COVID-19 pandemic, including the situation in Hong Kong. The findings revealed that the degree of epidemic prevention measures and the preparedness of universities for online teaching varied significantly across different regions. During online teaching, some teachers needed more systematic information technology training to be equipped to deal with the new teaching model, highlighting the importance of providing adequate training and support to educators during times of crisis (Rasind & Yadav, 2020).

Nevertheless, while the study was conducted at the early stages of the pandemic, other studies in Hong Kong focused on the mobility, desires, and challenges of international students studying in Hong Kong (Mok et al., 2021, 2022). However, these studies have yet to attempt to provide a comprehensive portrayal of the various developmental phases that higher education has undergone during the pandemic. This study aims to fill this gap in the literature and pave the way for a better understanding of the post-pandemic era.

This study utilises the Butler-Henderson et al. (2020) framework to analyse the impact of the pandemic on higher education in Hong Kong. This region has been significantly affected by the anti-epidemic measures implemented by mainland China. Additionally, this study will evaluate the applicability of the four stages of pandemic response to Hong Kong's unique environment and examine other issues and developments that are worthy of attention beyond the scope of this framework. The research questions that this study seeks to address are as follows:

Research question 1: What are the developmental stages of higher education during the pandemic?
Research question 2: How do anti-pandemic policies in mainland China impact the responses and operations of universities in Hong Kong?

## Methodology

This study employs a qualitative research approach to investigate the challenges that COVID-19 has posed to higher education and the implications for the post-epidemic era in mainland China and Hong Kong. The study reviews existing literature and analyses secondary data from media sources, including newspapers, university websites and government announcements. The content analysis of these sources allowed the identification of common themes and patterns related to the impact of the pandemic on higher education, such as the shift to online learning, changes in student enrolment, and financial difficulties faced by institutions (Cohen et al., 2017). The analysis of media sources also provided information on higher education institutions' responses to these challenges, such as developing new teaching methods and implementing new policies and procedures. Additionally, the analysis of media sources allowed for the identification of differences in the impact of the pandemic on higher education in mainland China and Hong Kong, providing a more comprehensive understanding of the challenges faced by the universities. Maintaining validity and reliability of analysing media sources is crucial for ensuring the accuracy and credibility of research findings (Scott & Morrison, 2005). To achieve this, the researchers employed robust and methodical approaches, cross-checked their findings with other sources, utilised multiple coders, and diligently documented the analysis process (Robson, 2011). These practices ensure the research findings' transparency, consistency, accuracy, and credibility when analysing media sources.

## Findings

Based on the Butler-Henderson et al. (2020) framework, the impact of COVID-19 on higher education in Hong Kong can be divided into the following four stages.

### Exploration: January to March, 2020

In 2003, Hong Kong was struck by the Severe Acute Respiratory Syndrome (SARS), resulting in 1755 confirmed cases and 299 deaths, making it the second-highest confirmed case globally (WHO, 2003). The outbreak persisted for about six months. Upon the emergence of COVID-19, most Hong Kong citizens believed it was similar to SARS and were on high alert. Regarding the situation during the SARS outbreak, universities promptly suspended classes and switched to online teaching with no teaching activities scheduled on campus from February to March (CUHK, 2020; The University of Hong Kong, 2020). It is believed that reducing contact between teachers and students was an effective measure to prevent the spread of the virus. Higher education leaders can solicit alternative ways of seeing, thinking, and making informed and sensible decisions (Riggio & Newstead, 2023). In addition, drawing on the experience with SARS, people were optimistic that the new virus would be eradicated by summer, and online teaching was initially considered a short-term measure that served as emergency remote teaching (Hodges et al., 2020).

At this stage, the primary objective for universities was to maintain teaching. Although universities could switch to online teaching and remote work, the systems and policies still needed to be fully developed or tested. Most institutions initially chose Zoom, a free and user-friendly platform, for online teaching. However, the software was exposed to security issues such as data leakage, which also impacted Hong Kong. This was evidenced by the intrusion during online exams at the Chinese University of Hong Kong, and adult videos were played during an online lecture (*Sing Tao Daily*, 2020). The prolonged suspension of in-person schooling and the shift to entirely online teaching were novel and ambiguous situations. Leaders had no precedents or established processes for resolving these challenges but responded promptly to the incidents (Riggio & Newstead, 2023).

The significant characteristic during this period was that online teaching was merely a stopgap for universities to maintain the most basic form of teaching. This needs a fundamental and autonomous application of online teaching by educators or a direction of emphasis for universities (Hong Kong Economic Times, 2020). Lingnan University, surveyed in May 2020, found that more than 60% of university students believed that online teaching was less effective than traditional teaching. Many teachers transferred their presentations from classrooms to students' screens, and teaching was mainly focused on the direct delivery of learning content, with little research on teaching methods that matched virtual modes and few other activities, such as group discussions. Some teachers could not grasp basic skills, such as opening software or sharing screens (HK01, 2022).

Mainland Chinese students studying in Hong Kong faced a challenging situation during the outbreak of the COVID-19 pandemic. At the onset of the pandemic, most Mainland students returned home. Many students opted to stay in Hong Kong as online teaching was implemented. In certain cases, universities went as far as advising Mainland students to avoid returning to Hong Kong (The Education University of Hong Kong, 2020) or implementing restrictions that prohibited Mainland students from residing in student dormitories (The Hong Kong Polytechnic University, 2020). The rapid onset of the pandemic compelled higher education leaders to make swift decisions and take action, which inevitably shaped the direction and impact of the crisis (Riggio & Newstead, 2023). As a result, students from mainland China stayed home and attended online lectures. Due to the cross-border nature of online courses, mainland students encountered numerous technical difficulties, such as slow network speed and software compatibility issues. For instance, the most commonly used online teaching platform in Hong Kong, Zoom, has certain restrictions on its use in Mainland China and stopped providing services to China in August 2020 (Unwire, 2020). Similarly, MEET, provided by Google, is not accessible in China. During the early stages of the pandemic, universities needed help to provide appropriate support for Mainland students, which may have contributed to less satisfactory learning outcomes and experiences for these students than their local counterparts.

In conclusion, the initial phase of online teaching in Hong Kong during the COVID-19 pandemic involved rapid adaptation to an unprecedented situation. Online teaching served as a temporary solution to maintain basic instruction, but the lack of preparedness, limited technological infrastructure, and inexperience led to a suboptimal learning experience for many students. The challenges faced by Mainland students underscored the importance of universities offering comprehensive support for cross-border online teaching throughout the ongoing pandemic.

## Stabilisation: April to August 2020

The COVID-19 pandemic rapidly spread across the globe, though there was a lack of transparency from China regarding the outbreak. By February 2020, the number of confirmed cases and deaths had surpassed the SARS outbreaks. The consequences of the epidemic were high and unexpected (James et al., 2011). This led to the continuation of school closures in Hong Kong. In late May 2020, the government announced that primary and secondary schools would resume classes.

However, with their autonomy to implement policies, universities decided to continue online teaching and quickly realised that online teaching would likely become the norm for the foreseeable future. Crises often expose weaknesses but also provide opportunities for management teams to identify strengths and discover better ways of working. Through such crises, it becomes evident that various forms of support are necessary to adapt to and improve online teaching practices. Therefore, empowering others to navigate the crisis becomes crucial (Riggio & Newstead, 2023). The measures taken during this period mainly involved upgrading hardware, software, and online teaching methods. The significant increase in network traffic resulting from the transition to online teaching required universities to improve their network speed and Wi-Fi stability.

To accomplish this, universities procured modern computer systems, microphones, and video cameras. In addition to hardware upgrades, universities took an active role in optimising commonly used teaching software and integrating these tools into existing Learning Management Systems (LMS) using plugins (e.g. Behavioral Analytics, Panopto) to facilitate their use by teachers and students. These measures aimed to enhance the overall quality of online teaching and ensure that students could have an effective and engaging learning experience (Tice et al., 2021). To facilitate effective use of teaching software, for example, Zoom and MS Teams, universities offer various modes of training to staff, such as seminars, training courses, and open lectures. These training programmes enable educators to employ more interactive and engaging teaching methods, such as group discussions, voting, and chat room features on the platforms. Online teaching removes functions such as mutual support and supervision among students. This makes creating a classroom atmosphere that promotes learning challenging. By utilising these tools, educators were able to create a more immersive and collaborative learning experience for students in the online environment. Additionally, more small-scale assessments were arranged during the teaching process to enable teachers to grasp student progress better and promote learning. Leaders in higher education have been actively searching for lessons that can help various stakeholders, particularly instructors, to improve and recover from online teaching (Riggio & Newstead, 2023).

The programmes most affected during this period, such as healthcare, education, social work, and hotel management, mandate students to undertake internships as a prerequisite for obtaining the requisite professional qualifications. However, the COVID-19 pandemic has ushered in numerous destabilising factors that have impacted the internship experience. As such, university management has been confronted with a conundrum: ensuring that students meet their internship requirements and graduate on time while minimising the attendant negative consequences. Medical programmes have been greatly impacted, particularly due to the high-risk environment of hospitals. Clinical rotations, including shadowing doctors and observing surgeries, have become impossible for medical and nursing students. Clinical internships have been rendered infeasible, leading to the need for conducting case studies through video conferencing. The lack of clinical experience has caused anxiety among many medical students regarding their prospects (*Cable News*, 2020). Despite the persistent shortage of medical personnel and urgent demand for human resources in the pandemic response, universities have been compelled to enforce timely graduation for students. Universities have tried to arrange internships and maintain communication with regulatory agencies, such as the Social Work Registration Board and the Education Bureau.

Although medical social work faced significant challenges, the majority of other programmes, such as school services and non-governmental organisations, were able to transition to online delivery (Jump, 2021). With primary and secondary schools and kindergartens resuming online classes in April, faculties of education in universities arranged for students to complete their teaching internships remotely. Education universities also flexibly schedule on-site internships, including allowing for online teaching formats (*Oriental Daily*, 2020). Student evaluations of the internship experience are mixed. According to a survey of 877 university students, only 52% completed their internships (Sky Post, 2020), with more than half conducted online (*Sing Tao Daily*, 2020). In the process of professional qualification certification, the university management coordinated teamwork and fulfilled a central role in soliciting diverse perspectives and expertise in coordinating the efforts of myriad others (Riggio & Newstead, 2023). They facilitated discussions and proactively addressed communication among the qualification awarding institutions, internship industry organisations, and students.

During this period, universities have focused primarily on enhancing the effectiveness of online teaching. University instructors have acquired proficiency in online teaching and explored relevant pedagogical strategies. Furthermore, university policies regarding hardware and software upgrades, internship contingency measures, and backup plans have been matured and stabilised to ensure uninterrupted student learning despite the pandemic challenges. Despite facing unprecedented situations, such as suspended hospital internships and halted classes in primary and secondary schools, universities have responded promptly. While not without flaws, particularly in internship arrangements requiring compromises, universities have made maximum efforts to safeguard students' professional qualifications. The experiences gained during this period have laid a solid foundation for future pandemic-related preparations, enabling universities to respond more effectively to similar situations and ensure continuous education for their students.

## Maturity: September 2020–November 2021

This phase spanned a significant period, and the overall pandemic situation in Hong Kong is under control. There were calls for a reopening, and several studies by scholars indicated that school closures were less effective in controlling the spread of the virus than social distancing measures (Yuen, 2020). After nearly a year of online teaching, teachers and students became proficient in the software and learning models used for online teaching, and classes proceeded smoothly. At that time, many students from China remained on the Mainland, and universities implemented a hybrid mode of teaching, allowing students to choose between online and face-to-face classes, with online classes being the primary mode of instruction. Teachers had become adept at the pedagogical methods of online classes, and online teaching gradually became the 'new normal'. Universities also began to recognise that even after the pandemic ends, the education revolution it initiated will persist. The popularity of online courses increases the proportion of virtual teaching (Wu, 2020) and accelerates the hybrid teaching model (Wu, 2020).

While the universities have stabilised and become proficient in online teaching, it is understood that there is still a need to enhance the quality of virtual instruction further. Accordingly, the Education Bureau and the Quality Assurance Council allocated an additional USD 21.2 million to assist universities in developing sustainable virtual teaching strategies. These strategies include enhancing hardware specifications, providing teacher training, promoting student interaction and communication in online classes, exploring new teaching methods, platforms, and facilities, and promoting the integration of virtual teaching into internships (*Sky Post*, 2020). During this phase, teacher training shifted from the technical operation of single classroom software to integrating different apps, such as Nearpod, Padlet, and Kahoot!, to improve the lack of interaction in online classes (Burton, 2019; Yeo, 2019). These apps enable both online and offline students to complete classroom activities or exercises simultaneously, reducing the division between the two. By adopting these new strategies and tools, universities could further improve the quality of online teaching and ensure that students receive an effective and engaging learning experience. Simultaneously, universities have also begun supporting students through their extracurricular experiences to facilitate a holistic university experience beyond academics alone. Universities have progressed beyond merely maintaining basic teaching operations during the early stages of the pandemic to restoring students' on-campus experiences and providing comprehensive support under feasible conditions. University leaders have frequently engaged in emotionally appropriate, present, and open communication with various stakeholders to ensure their voices are heard and their needs are acknowledged. The management has employed various means of communication to engage with staff, students, and the public, including policy decisions and emotional management. Open communication has been a vital tool for university leaders to address the concerns of stakeholders during the pandemic (Riggio & Newstead, 2023).

Nevertheless, this period revealed a noticeable disparity in the understanding of Mainland Chinese academic qualification recognition among management in local universities. Nonetheless, their response to the situation has been prompt. According to Chinese regulations, overseas students must undergo full-time education abroad for their degrees to be recognised by the Ministry of Education. As a regulated overseas region, Hong Kong falls under this mandate. However, due to the border closure between Mainland China and Hong Kong, Mainland Chinese students have faced significant challenges in attending classes in Hong Kong. Despite the Ministry of Education having subsequently eased the relevant restrictions, it is pertinent to note that the regulations were rescinded in January 2023, along with the reopening of China's border (China Study Abroad Network, 2023).

On the other hand, it is noteworthy that from January to July 2021, there was a significant increase of 126% of Mainland Chinese students pursuing higher education in Hong Kong compared to the same period in the previous year (EIC Education, 2022). Furthermore, the Immigration Department of Hong Kong has reported a 59% increase in the number of Mainland Chinese students who were granted student visas to study in Hong Kong between 2020 and 2021. This trend could be attributed to Hong Kong's strict pandemic control measures, making it a relatively safer destination than other regions such as the U.S., Europe, and Australia (Chen & Chao, 2021). Also, Hong Kong's reputation as an international city with several globally recognised universities, coupled with its relatively affordable tuition fees, has been a driving factor for Mainland Chinese students to pursue higher education there. However, the subsidised degree programmes in Hong Kong have a quota for Mainland Chinese students, while self-financed master's degree programmes do not. As a result, universities either expanded the admission quota for Mainland Chinese students or eagerly established new master's degree programmes targeting this group. Further research is expected to determine the impact on the overall academic landscape of Hong Kong in the post-COVID era.

In this phase, the universities provided more diversified support and extended university life experiences for students. This period has also seen an influx of high-end Mainland Chinese talent applying to study master's and above courses in Hong Kong, which helps to stabilise the development of local universities. Currently, Hong Kong is experiencing a wave of emigration, resulting in the loss of some of its talented individuals. The increment of graduates from the Mainland provides a supplement to the workforce.

## Restoration: December 2021–March 2023

When the semester started in September 2021, most universities in Hong Kong had resumed face-to-face teaching, and many had organised face-to-face orientation camps for students. However, this has also led to small-scale outbreaks and raised concerns among the public (*Sing Tao Daily*, 2022). The experience garnered from the pandemic over the past few years, and the universities have demonstrated their ability to respond to the challenges posed by the pandemic through the implementation of hardware, software, and institutional arrangements. The onset of the fifth wave of the pandemic in December 2021 resulted in a surge of daily more than ten thousand infections and the collapse of the healthcare system. Yet, the universities swiftly activated emergency response measures, including transitioning from face-to-face to hybrid or fully online teaching within a week and suspending all activities aimed at a return to normalcy. Notably, these measures were implemented without adversely impacting students' academic progress.

Over the past three years, online teaching has emerged as the primary mode of instruction, facilitating well-organised implementation of fundamental teaching activities. Following two brief periods of face-to-face teaching resumption and subsequent rapid switches back to online teaching, universities have realised that this pattern may persist, leading to a prolonged timeframe for a complete return to 100% face-to-face instruction. Universities have emphasised the importance of enhancing teachers' information technology literacy and developing pedagogical strategies based on Technological Pedagogical Content Knowledge (TPACK). Notably, the Virtual Teaching and Learning (VTL) project initiated by the Faculty of Humanities at the Education University of Hong Kong represents a significant effort to incorporate innovative teaching approaches and leverage technology to enhance education quality.

The VTL project consists of two phases, focusing on customising teaching materials to suit different disciplines while providing an extensive range of multimedia resources. Multimedia materials, including virtual reality (VR), augmented reality (AR), online games, and e-books, have become prominent features of the VTL project. These materials offer students an immersive and interactive learning experience that complements traditional classroom instruction. VR and AR, for example, provide students with simulated environments to explore complex concepts and theories more tangibly. On the other hand, E-books offer a convenient platform for students to access course materials, catering to those who prefer digital formats. The VTL project represents a forward-looking approach to teaching, aiming to leverage technology to enhance the quality and accessibility of education. By offering diverse multimedia resources and customising teaching materials for different disciplines, students can engage with course content more dynamically and interactively. These innovative learning modes and teaching materials play a guiding and directional role in shaping future teaching models in higher education.

The pandemic provided an unexpected learning opportunity facilitated by university leaders to promote innovative e-teaching practices and prepare for impending pandemic crises (Riggio & Newstead, 2023). It has significantly accelerated the adoption of electronic teaching, as the vast majority of courses have transitioned to online or hybrid modes of teaching. The widespread use of online teaching platforms was previously viewed as a 'niche' practice, primarily in more traditional academic disciplines. However, despite their distinct starting positions, the pandemic has compelled educators across disciplines to converge towards enhancing remote instruction. This convergence has resulted in a shift in paradigm from a reactive stance of adaptation to a proactive quest for mastery in enhancing teaching methodologies.

Furthermore, the pandemic has provided a roadmap for the future development of higher education in the post-pandemic era. The importance of incorporating technology in education has been highlighted, and the need for continued innovation in teaching methodologies has been emphasised. As such, the pandemic has catalysed change, accelerating technological innovation and challenging traditional educational models. Ultimately, the pandemic has underscored the need for higher education institutions to adapt to the rapidly changing educational landscape as they strive to provide a high-quality and accessible education to students in the future.

## Discussion and Conclusion

Upon examining the response of Hong Kong's tertiary institutions to the epidemic, it can be observed that their strategies generally align with the four stages proposed by Butler-Henderson et al.'s (2020) framework. The variances observed among university management teams, and their initial indecisiveness can be traced back to government policies. Nonetheless, the root cause of such dubiety could be attributed to the Hong Kong government's unwavering adherence to the policies of the Chinese government. It is particularly salient during the Exploration stage. Owing to the lack of transparency in the latter's governance, even though Hong Kong has established a reputation for its agility in responding to crises, the management of the pandemic became an impotent and passive affair in the absence of adequate information. The university management teams recognised that proactively formulating their contingency plans would be more expedient than waiting for government policies. In this respect, Hong Kong's universities retain sufficient autonomy and can assume leadership roles. Therefore, following the Improvement stage, the universities developed innovative practices of hybrid, blended, and online teaching in higher education.

The pandemic has altered the teaching models regarding impacts on higher education teaching. In the past decades, the digitisation of learning and teaching has been a central focus of the higher education agenda. However, before the pandemic, online learning was often considered an optional supplement to face-to-face instruction, and educational software and systems were primarily utilised as productivity tools and not fully integrated into pedagogy. The pandemic resulted in an unforeseen e-learning surge, accelerating universities' digital transformation worldwide. The pandemic fundamentally changed how universities supported students, as fully online learning became the only viable option for most courses during lockdowns.

Consequently, universities were driven to invest in new technologies and enhance their IT infrastructure to meet the increasing demand. Students and professors had to adapt swiftly to new technologies and teaching methods. The shift towards online learning is poised to gain even more significance.

One of the limitations of this study is the lack of investigation of the well-being and mental health of academic staff and students during the pandemic. Undoubtedly, the disruptive nature of digitalisation presented many unanticipated challenges in technology and pedagogy, and there is also concern for the well-being and mental health of academic staff and students. Nevertheless, we contend that the pandemic's online learning represents a unique opportunity to advance teaching and learning practices. Online learning allows universities to experiment with technology-enhanced teaching methods at scale, across different disciplines educational levels, and over extended periods, thereby presenting a timely opportunity to engage in innovative pedagogy. As such, it is the stage of Restoration and paved the way to the post-COVID era. As the pandemic subsides and the world finally returns to normalcy, it is hoped that higher education can emerge from this crisis with positive insights and begin anew.

## References

Bao, W. (2020). COVID-19 and online teaching in higher education: A case study of Peking University. *Human behavior and emerging technologies, 2*(2), 113–115.

Burton, R. (2019). A review of Nearpod—An interactive tool for student engagement. *Journal of Applied Learning and Teaching*, *2*(2), 95–97. https://doi.org/10.37074/jalt.2019.2.2.13

Butler-Henderson, K., Crawford, J., Rudolph, J., Lalani, K., & Sabu K. M. (2020). COVID-19 in higher education literature database (CHELD V1): An open access systematic literature review database with coding rules. *Journal of Applied Learning & Teaching*, *3*(2), 1–6. https://doi.org/10.37074/jalt.2020.3.2.11

Cable TV. (2020, September 8). Medical students are unable to practice for half a year and can only ask questions through online platform [Video]. *Youtube*. https://www.youtube.com/watch?v=t88j19ZDx1E

Chen, H., & Chao, L. (2021). Racial discrimination against Chinese in the U.S. and Chinese responses in the wake of the epidemic. *Journal of Oversea Chinese History Studies, 2*, 39–49.

Chinese Service Center for Scholarly Exchange [CSCSE]. (n.d.). *Announcement on adjustment of special certification rules for cross-border remote certificates during the epidemic*. https://www.cscse.edu.cn

Cohen, L., Manion, L., & Morrison, K. (2017). *Research methods in education* (8th ed.). Routledge.

Crawford, J. (2023). COVID-19 and higher education: A pandemic response model from rapid adaption to consolidation and restoration. *International Education Journal: Comparative Perspectives, 22*(1), 7–29.

Crawford, J., Andrew, M., Rudolph, J., Lalani, K., & Butler-Henderson, K. (2021). The cross-cultural effects of COVID-19 on higher education learning and teaching practice. *Journal of University Teaching & Learning Practice*, *18*(5), 73–89. https://doi.org/10.53761/1.18.5.5

Crawford, J., Butler-Henderson, K., Rudolph, J., Malkawi, B., Glowatz, M., Burton, R., Magni, P. A., & Lam, S. (2020). COVID-19: 20 countries' higher education intra-period digital pedagogy responses. *Journal of Applied Learning & Teaching*, *3*(1), 1–20. https://doi.org/10.37074/jalt.2020.3.1.7

EIC Education (2022). Report on studying in Hong Kong China. https://www.eic.org.cn/Report/hk_study_new_report_b/

Hawley, S. R., Thrivikraman, J. K., Noveck, N., Romain, T. S., Ludy, M. J., Barnhart, L., Chee, W. S. S. ., Cho, M. J., Chong, M. H. Z., Du, C., Fenton, J. I., Hsiao, P. Y., Hsiao, R., Keaver, L., Lee, H., Shen, W., Lai, C., Tseng, K., Tseung, W., & Tucker, R. M. (2021). Concerns of college students during the COVID-19 pandemic: Thematic perspectives from the United States, Asia, and Europe. *Journal of Applied Learning and Teaching, 4*(1), 11–20. https://doi.org/10.37074/jalt.2021.4.1.10

Hermann, C. F. (1963). Some consequences of crisis which limit the viability of organisations. *Administrative Science Quarterly, 8*(1), 61–82. https://doi.org/10.2307/2390887

Hodges, C. B., Moore, S., Lockee, B. B., Trust, T., & Bond, M. A. (2020*). The difference between emergency remote teaching and online learning.* https://vtechworks.lib.vt.edu/bitstream/handle/10919/104648/facdev-article.pdf?sequence=1

Hong Kong 01. (2022, April 7). Graduating from university under the epidemic, journalism and communication students sigh that they can't learn anything from internship, politics and administration graduates willing to move to greater bay area. *Hong Kong01*. https://www.hk01.com/18區新聞/756394/疫下大學畢業-傳理生嘆實習如白過-政政系畢業生願到大灣區發展

*Hong Kong Economic Times*. (2020, April 27). Educational institutions are switching to Teams to conduct online teaching. *Hong Kong Economic Times*. https://topick.hket.com/article/2627173/教育機構紛紛轉用Teams%20網上教學一Take過.

James, E. H., Wooten, L. P., & Dushek, K. (2011). Crisis management: Informing a new leadership research agenda. *The Academy of Management Annals, 5*(1), 455–493. https://doi.org/10.1080/19416520.2011.589594

Jump. (2021, January 22). Eight universities have been allocated resources to promote the development of online teaching. *Jump*. https://jump.mingpao.com/career-news/daily-news/網上教學新常態｜八大獲撥資源推網課發展-人手

Karalis, T., & Raikou, N. (2020). Teaching at the times of COVID-19: Inferences and implications for higher education pedagogy. *International Journal of Academic Research in Business and Social Sciences*, 10(5), 479–493.

Lau, R. S., & Cobb, A. T. (2010). Understanding the connections between relationship conflict and performance: The intervening roles of trust and exchange. *Journal of Organizational Behavior, 31*(6), 898–917. https://doi.org/10.1002/job.674

Marinoni, G., Van't Land, H., & Jensen, T. (2020). The impact of Covid-19 on higher education around the world. *IAU global survey report, 23*, 1–17. https://www.iau-aiu.net/IMG/pdf/iau_covid19_and_he_survey_report_final_may_2020.pdf

Mishra, S., Sahoo, S., & Pandey, S. (2021). Research trends in online distance learning during the COVID-19 pandemic. *Distance Education, 42*(4), 494–519. https://doi.org/10.1080/01587919.2021.1986373

Mok, K. H., Xiong, W., & Ke, G. (2022). Reimagining higher education in the post-COVID-19 era: Chinese students' desires for overseas learning and implications for university governance. *Higher Education Policy, 35*(3), 591–609. https://doi.org/10.1057/s41307-022-00273-1

Mok, K. H., Xiong, W., Ke, G., & Cheung, J. O. W. (2021). Impact of COVID-19 pandemic on international higher education and student mobility: Student perspectives from mainland China and Hong Kong. *International Journal of Educational Research, 105*, 101718. https://doi.org/10.1016/j.ijer.2020.101718

Neuwirth, L. S., Jović, S., & Mukherji, B. R. (2021). Reimagining higher education during and post-COVID-19: Challenges and opportunities. *Journal of Adult and Continuing Education, 27*(2), 141–156. https://doi.org/10.1177/1477971420947738

*Oriental Daily*. (2020, April 23). The prospective teachers may not able to graduate on time due to the suspension of the internship. *Oriental Daily*. https://orientaldaily.on.cc/cnt/news/20200423/00176_016.html

Pearson, C. M., & Mitroff, I. I. (1993). From crisis prone to crisis prepared: A framework for crisis management. *Academy of Management Perspectives, 7*(1), 48–59. https://doi.org/10.5465/ame.1993.9409142058

Rashid, S., & Yadav, S. S. (2020). Impact of Covid-19 pandemic on higher education and research. *Indian Journal of Human Development, 14*(2), 340–343. https://doi.org/10.1177/0973703020946700

Riggio, R. E., & Newstead, T. (2023). Crisis leadership. *Annual Review of Organizational Psychology and Organizational Behavior, 10*, 201–224. https://doi.org/10.1146/annurev-orgpsych-120920-044838

Robson, C. (2011). *Real world research: A resource for social scientists and practitioner-researchers* (4th ed.). Wiley-Blackwell.

Rudolph, J., Tan, S., Crawford, J., & Butler-Henderson, K. (2023). Perceived quality of online learning during COVID-19 in higher education in Singapore: Perspectives from students, lecturers, and academic leaders. *Educational Research for Policy and Practice, 22*(1), 171–191. https://doi.org/10.1007/s10671-022-09325-0

Scott, D., & Morrison, M. (2005). *Key ideas in educational research*. A&C Black.

Siddharth, S. (2023, February 23). When can Hongkongers stop wearing masks? *Hong Kong Free Press*. https://hongkongfp.com/2023/02/27/when-can-hongkongers-stop-wearing-masks/

*Sing Tao Daily*. (2020, April 28). CU's Zoom examination was hacked to broadcast pornographic videos with foul language. *Singtao News*. https://std.stheadline.com/realtime/article/1257520/即時-港聞-中大Zoom考試遭入侵-播色情影片講粗口

*Sing Tao Daily*. (2022, September 6). University students remove their masks to participate in OCAMP. One-third of students infected. *Singtao News*. https://std.stheadline.com/realtime/article/1870406/%E5%8D%B3%E6%99%82-%E6%B8%AF%E8%81%9E-%E5%A4%A7%E5%AD%B8Ocamp-%E9%99%A4%E7%BD%A9-%E4%B8%89%E5%88%86%E4%B8%80%E5%AD%B8%E7%94%9F%E6%84%9F%E6%9F%93

Sky Post. (2020, November 30). Nearly half of the university students were unable to do their internship due to the epidemic. *Sky Post*. https://skypost.ulifestyle.com.hk/article/2815970/

The Chinese University of Hong Kong. (2020). *Act together against Covid-19*. The Chinese University of Hong Kong. https://againstcovid19.cuhk.edu.hk/sc/

The Education University of Hong Kong. (2020). *Latest announcements*. The Education University of Hong Kong. https://newsemester.eduhk.hk/main/

The Polytechnic University of Hong Kong. (2020, February 15). *PolyU's arrangement for self-segregation in student hostels*. The Polytechnic University of Hong Kong. https://www.polyu.edu.hk/tc/media/media-releases/2020/0215_self-quarantine-arrangement-for-hall-students/

The University of Hong Kong. (2020, February 2). *Fight Covid-19*. The University of Hong Kong. https://fightcovid19.hku.hk/zh/category/hkunotice-zh/

Tice, D., Baumeister, R., Crawford, J., Allen, K. A., & Percy, A. (2021). Student belongingness in higher education: Lessons for Professors from the COVID-19 pandemic. *Journal of University Teaching & Learning Practice, 18*(4), 2. https://doi.org/10.53761/1.18.4.2

Unwire. (2020, August 3). Zoom exits China? Stopping direct service in China at the end of August. *Unwire*. https://unwire.hk/2020/08/03/zoom-stop-china-services-but-not-hong-kong/tech-secure/

Weick, K. E. (1988). Enacted sensemaking in crisis situations. *Journal of Management Studies, 25*(4), 305–317. https://doi.org/10.1111/j.1467-6486.1988.tb00039.x

Wilson, S., & Newstead, T. (2022). The virtues of effective crisis leadership: What managers can learn from how women heads of state led through the first wave of COVID-19. *Organisational Dynamics., 51*(2), 100910. https://doi.org/10.1016/j.orgdyn.2022.100910

Wilson, S., Tan, S., Knox, M., Ong, A., Crawford, J., & Rudolph, J. (2020). Enabling cross-cultural student voice during COVID-19: A collective autoethnography. *Journal of University Teaching & Learning Practice*, *17*(5), 3. https://doi.org/10.53761/1.17.5.3

World Health Organization. (2003). *The world health report 2003: Shaping the future*. World Health Organization. https://apps.who.int/iris/handle/10665/42789

Worldometers. (2023). Covid-19 coronavirus pandemic. Retrieved from https://www.worldometers.info/coronavirus/2023

Wu, Z. Z. (2020, July 6). How does the trend of virtual teaching disrupt university education? *HongKong01*. https://www.hk01.com/article/494437?utm_source=01articlecopy&utm_medium=referral

Wu, Y. L., Shao, B., Newman, A., & Schwarz, G. (2021). Crisis leadership: A review and future research agenda. *The Leadership Quarterly, 32*(6), 101518. https://doi.org/10.1016/j.leaqua.2021.101518

Yeo, E. Z. (2019). Bridging the gap in learning with the effective use of Kahoot!: A review. *Journal of Applied Learning and Teaching*, *2*(1), 69–71. https://journals.sfu.ca/jalt/index.php/jalt/article/download/85/73/311

Yuen, K. Y. (2020, March 10). The epidemic will only begin to abate when 70% of the population has antibodies. *Ming Pao*. https://health.mingpao.com/袁國勇:七成人有抗體-疫情始紓緩-現僅0-1%免疫-防/

# Transforming Educational Leadership in Indian Higher Education Ecosystem: Post-COVID-19 Perspectives

Sabu Karakka Mandapam, D. Senthil Kumaran, and Raghavan Vivek

## Introduction

India's University Education Commission, constituted in 1948, was the first initiative to establish higher education standards in India. Since 2001, India has rapidly expanded the higher education sector (Shamika et al., 2019). According to the University Grants Commission (UGC), 461 state universities, 125 deemed universities, 56 central institutions, and 432 private

The original version of the chapter has been revised. A correction to this chapter can be found at https://doi.org/10.1007/978-3-031-54509-2_34

S. K. Mandapam (✉)
Department of Health Information Management, Manipal College of Health Professions, Manipal Academy of Higher Education, Manipal - 576104, Karnataka, India
e-mail: sabu.km@manipal.edu

D. Senthil Kumaran
Department of Physiotherapy, Manipal College of Health Professions, Manipal Academy of Higher Education, Manipal - 576104, Karnataka, India
e-mail: senthil.kumaran@manipal.edu

R. Vivek
Department of Medical Laboratory Technology, Manipal College of Health Professions, Manipal Academy of Higher Education, Manipal - 576104, Karnataka, India
e-mail: vivek.rm@manipal.edu


J. Rudolph et al. (eds.), *The Palgrave Handbook of Crisis Leadership in Higher Education*, https://doi.org/10.1007/978-3-031-54509-2_18

universities operate in India (UGC, 2023). The Indian higher education (HE) system is the largest globally.

There are six categories of universities in India catering to the needs of post-secondary students: state public universities, state private universities, private deemed universities, institutes of national importance, central universities, and government-deemed universities. There is a large-scale variation of quality among HEIs, with the top hundred institutions in India concentrated within nine states of India.

The higher education ecosystem in the country, while robust, faced a setback due to the unexpected COVID-19 pandemic, mainly because of the digital divide. Both professional and non-professional education were significantly affected during this challenging period. The pandemic also brought to light various challenges. It provided valuable lessons, transforming the higher education sector and academic leadership in India propelling them to embrace new experiential levels.

This chapter provides an overview of the Indian Higher Education sector before the COVID-19 pandemic and delves into the significant impact and challenges brought about by the pandemic. It explores higher education institutions' responses to leadership transformation during this crisis and discusses various perspectives on futuristic leadership for the higher education ecosystem in India.

The methodology employed for this study involved conducting a literature search using the "single window search" tool at the Health Sciences Library of Manipal Academy of Higher Education, India. The search focused on English scholarly articles published between January 2019 and January 2023, using keywords such as "Leadership", "Higher Education", "India", and "Covid-19". Of the 3843 scholarly articles retrieved, 31 full-text eligible articles were shortlisted and included in the final review. Additionally, 19 relevant articles from various media and professional bodies obtained through Google search were also incorporated in the review. We will begin by outlining some characteristics of the higher education sector in India.

## Higher Education Enrolment Status in India

In India, the Gross Enrolment Ratio (GER) in higher education is below the global average of 36.7%. Various reports indicate that in the last two decades, there has been a steady increase in the GER, from a mere 8.1% GER in 2001 to 27.1% in 2019–2020. The increase in GER was largely due to the higher demand for higher education and the country's exponential growth of HEIs and Universities. The compounded annual growth rate of student enrolment was reported to be high (19.1%) for undergraduate programmes, followed by postgraduate programmes (12.2%), integrated programmes (9.8%), and Ph.D. programmes (8.5%) through the years 2015 to 2020. During this period, the highest enrolment rate was observed among state public universities, with a significant growth in female enrollment compared to male enrollment. The enrolment rate is higher among southern states and less among northern and eastern states. The national average for the number of colleges/institutions available for 100,000 people (18–23 years) stood at 30 in the year 2019–2020, with a range of seven (lowest) to 59 (highest) colleges available across 37 states (Department of Higher Education, 2021).

The Indian higher education system offers education and training across almost all disciplines (Gupta & Gupta, 2012). Agriculture and foreign language streams have registered the highest enrolment at the undergraduate level. Social science (0.78 million) and science and management streams (0.6 million) at the postgraduate level witnessed the highest enrolment. There have been over fifty thousand enrolments at the Ph.D. level in both Engineering Technology and Science streams. In the academic year 2019–2020, Indian HEIs witnessed a total enrolment of nearly fifty thousand international students from more than 165 countries, with the highest number of enrolments in Bachelor of Technology programmes. During the same period, there were over one hundred fifty thousand teaching faculty members across HEIs in India, with male faculty accounting for more than 57% of the total.

## Higher Education Regulations in India

The Indian higher education system is regulated and monitored by the central and state governments. The Ministry of Education (MoE) regulatory or professional councils at the central, and departments or councils of higher or technical education at the state level are the main policymakers in the higher education sector. University Grants Commission is the main governing body regulating and accrediting the HEIs in India, and it is the only grant-giving agency in the country with the tasks of providing financial support and ensuring standards in HEIs. Every professional domain has regulatory mechanisms established under specific professional councils to regulate and accredit the programmes. Nursing Council of India (1947), Dental Council of India (1949), Bar Council of India (1961), Rehabilitation Council of India (1986) and National Medical Commission (2020) are some of the key higher education regulators in India for various professional domains. The regulators' roles include promoting education, maintaining norms and standards for the conduct of programmes and running institutions and ensuring uniform curricular standards across all programmes and domains.

## Accreditation and Ranking

In India, the National Assessment and Accreditation Council (NAAC) conducts periodic assessments and accreditation of HEIs. NAAC was established in 1994 as an autonomous institution of the University Grants Commission. The NAAC evaluates HEIs to ensure they adhere to quality standards, including educational processes, syllabus coverage, teaching and learning methods, faculty, research, learning resources, infrastructure, organisational governance, financial stability, and student services. NAAC's core value framework includes contributions to national development, fostering global competencies, promoting the use of technology, and instilling a strong value system among students. Another important accreditation agency is the National Board of Accreditation, India (NBA), which was established in 1994 initially under the All-India Council of Technical Education. NBA is responsible for assessing the qualitative competencies of the engineering and technology, management, pharmacy, architecture, hotel management, and catering programmes from diploma to postgraduate levels. The National Board of Accreditation became an autonomous body in January 2010 and was accorded the permanent signatory status of the Washington Accord in June 2014.

The Institute of Eminence (IOE), a recognition scheme for HEIs in India, was established in 2017 as an initiative of the University Grants Commission to empower HEIs to excel in teaching and research. As of February 2023, eight institutions/universities in the public sector and four in the private sector were awarded the Institute of Eminence status. This is a game changer in the HE sectors in India as these institutions and universities have greater autonomy to establish various reforms which may raise the quality of education and research in the higher education sector. For example, HEIs with Institute of Eminence status enjoy enhanced autonomy in providing online programmes and setting up new off-campus centres and offshore campuses. This increased freedom empowers universities and institutions to offer education focusing on excellence and innovation. They can now deliver high-quality teaching, conduct pioneering research, and encourage academic exploration in well-established and emerging fields of knowledge, including interdisciplinary domains.

The National Institutional Ranking Framework (NIRF) is the established government mechanism for ranking HEIs in India. The Ministry of Human Resources, Government of India, established NIRF in September 2015 and provides a methodology to rank institutions nationwide. The ranking parameters include the broad categories of teaching and learning resources, research and professional practice, graduation outcomes, outreach and inclusivity, and perception, with differential weightage and multiple component metrics for each broad parameter (Ministry of Education, 2022).

## The Impact of the COVID Pandemic on Higher Education in India

The Indian higher education environment is distinctive and complicated due to the vast student population, restricted student–teacher ratio, diversified demographics, and obvious rural–urban split. The COVID-19 pandemic influenced admissions, exams, student internships, placements, and student mobility in Indian HEIs. In India, about 394 universities are situated in rural regions (Ministry of Education, 2019).

The sudden disruption in the HEIs affected nearly 280 million young learners students, especially in rural and remotely located areas where internet connectivity is a major constraint (Prakash et al., 2021; Siddesh & Gautami, 2021). The vast majority of HEIs were unprepared to transition from face-to-face teaching and learning to a completely online mode (Roy & Brown, 2022). Across the higher education system in India, institutions, faculty, and students have faced many hurdles in adopting a sudden transition to a virtual mode of teaching and learning (Yatreek, 2020). Suddenly, digital education has become the centre of discussion among every kind of HEIs. HEIs reacted to the situation and moved into the online mode of functioning with the use of all available ICT tools and ensured the steadiness of teaching–learning, research activities, and society services (Alamu et al., 2022; Jyoti & Ishani, 2020; Pravat, 2020). A surge in using readily available online education platforms, which were otherwise not popular among HEIs and students, was observed across the education sector. Teachers engaging students with online lectures, video conferencing, and assigning online activities quickly become the new norm across HEIs. Online applications such as Zoom, MS Teams, Google Meet, YouTube, Skype, etc., were widely used during the pandemic and a good number of HEIs invested in in-house online platforms for eLearning.

Within the higher education sector in India, certain areas have experienced notable challenges during this time. As highlighted in Jena (2020), these include:

i. Disruption of educational activities: The pandemic has significantly impeded various educational endeavours, causing disruptions in the normal functioning of academic institutions.
ii. Varied effects on academic study and professional development: The influence of the pandemic on academic study and professional development has been mixed, with some individuals facing obstacles while others have managed to navigate the situation with relative success.
iii. Severe impact on educational assessment: The educational assessment system has been severely affected, posing challenges in conducting fair and comprehensive evaluations of students' learning outcomes.
iv. Decreased employment opportunities: The pandemic has led to declining employment possibilities within the higher education sector, creating a challenging job market for graduates.

The periodic guidelines provided by the University Grants Commission on the conduct of exams, student progression, etc., have become a source of relief for thousands of students and HEIs (Seema, 2022; Shivarajappa, 2020; Souvik, 2022). The educational assessment system was the most severely affected academic activity as HEIs were forced to postpone or cancel the examinations and allowed students to progress to higher semesters based on the previous semester's performance (Parvat, 2020). Even the regulators could not provide a clear solution as HEIs have followed uneven assessment patterns. This has severely affected the student learning process.

The pandemic specifically made it difficult for teachers to generate assessment activities for remote learning and move to e-assessment mode. The ICT issues faced by faculties and students in India's higher education system were deeply ingrained in the system's technological and infrastructural shortcomings. Many educational institutions in India have not addressed infrastructural crises like poor pedagogical practices, poor student assessment patterns, irregularity in conducting classes, lack of functional transparency, etc., as reported by Dey & Alamman (2021). Kundu & Bej (2021) conducted a study among 200 Indian students pursuing higher education from different geographical locations. The study found that students' overall perception of e-assessment was moderate, with variations based on gender, academic level, stream of study, and economic background. Table 1 emphasises the most reported challenges HEIs faced nationwide during the COVID-19 pandemic.

The COVID-19 pandemic has also brought about notable positive changes in the higher education ecosystem in India, which could have enduring and beneficial effects on the HE system. One significant change is the shift in students' perceptions and adaptability to challenging educational situations.

**Table 1** Challenges reported across HEIs in India during the COVID-19 pandemic

**Academic factors**
- Academic dishonesty
- Curriculum design not conducive to online Practical training (STEM)
- Delay in the conduct of entrance examination and admissions
- Discourse of online teaching and learning
- ICT competency of students
- Incompetency of faculty in online teaching
- Lack of cooperation from faculty and students
- Lack of Scientific meetings
- Lack of peer learning
- Lack of digital resources
- Low capacity in digital and e-learning skills
- Online assessment & examinations
- Pedagogical challenges
- Research output
- Suspension of all practical activities

**Technological factors**
- Accessibility to electronic gadgets
- Affordability to gadgets
- Affordability to various technologies
- Cost of data
- Digital divide
- Internet connectivity
- Technological challenges

**Other factors**
- Different socio-economic conditions
- Employment opportunities
- Household circumstances (space constraints and distracting environment)
- Ineffective leadership
- Poor governance
- Psychological impact
- Timing of online sessions
- Weather conditions

E-learning and teaching have gained popularity and acceptance, opening doors for more engaging and active learning experiences (Kirti & Preeti, 2021; Niyaz et al., 2022; Shivangi, 2022; Sreshta, 2021). Academic leaders have been compelled to think beyond traditional educational models and develop resilience, becoming more strategic. Leadership will play a crucial role during this transformative phase for HEIs, as the widespread adoption of blended learning and learning management systems is expected with the resumption of face-to-face education (Mok, 2022; Roy & Brown, 2022). Other positive impacts on the Indian higher education system include acceptance of blended and personalised learning, widespread adoption of learning management systems, sharing and improved use of electronic learning materials, and initiatives for the new teaching–learning process witnessed across HEIs. Better time management, enhanced digital literacy, motivation for self-learning, and global exposure to online academic activities are some of the generally observed positive impacts among students and learners. HEIs have emerged to implement innovations in online assessments such as image-based assessment, online objective structure practical examination, verbal open-book method, and online viva-voce (Jindal, 2020; Nirupama et al., 2022). With the implementation of online education by central and state governments throughout different phases of the pandemic, there is now a pressing obligation for the government to ensure the availability of reliable communication tools, high-quality digital resources, and technology-assisted learning platforms. These measures are crucial for addressing the gaps during and after the pandemic.

During the reopening phase following the lockdown, HEIs encountered numerous challenges in teaching–learning. Many institutions transitioned to a hybrid mode, with physical sessions conducted under strict COVID-19 protocols, including social distancing and vaccination measures (Prakash et al., 2021; Sangita & Nandita, 2022). The University Grants Commission mandated that one-fourth of the curriculum be completed through online teaching, while the remaining curriculum required face-to-face interaction during the reopening phase. The government also allowed students to choose between remote or physical attendance for theory and practical classes based on prevailing COVID cases and regional restrictions. However, this arrangement presented challenges for academic leaders and faculty members due to infrastructure limitations, insufficient faculty resources, and a lack of suitable IT solutions to facilitate hybrid modes of classes, practical demonstrations, proctored exams, and evaluations. Moreover, HEIs faced significant hurdles in implementing strict protocols for isolating COVID-positive students within campus facilities, contact tracing, monitoring student health, and managing hostels. These challenges added complexity to the reopening phase and required diligent efforts from educational institutions to ensure the well-being of their students and staff.

## Response to COVID and Reforms in the Higher Education System in India

The Indian higher education system is challenged to reinvent itself to overcome obstacles in times of uncertainty posed by the pandemic (COVID-19) to deliver the education promised to the students. HEIs encountered uncharted territory as they switched to e-classrooms overnight while overcoming various other difficulties (Lalani et al., 2021). In addition to problems with curriculum, pedagogy, and evaluation, the availability of resources and access to education was the largest of these concerns. While there have been challenges, COVID-19 has also forced HEIs to rethink how to provide students with a complete and engaging classroom experience. This has sparked something of a revolution in the education industry.

Many HEIs in India operate as private entities, relying on self-funding and student tuition payments. The financial repercussions of the pandemic have been severe, impacting household finances and limiting student tuition payments. As a result, private HEIs faced considerable financial challenges. To ensure the continuity of educational programmes, private HEIs must devise cost-effective strategies and adopt academic continuity plans that do not exert undue pressure on their financial resources. Moreover, they are exploring innovative financing options to sustain operations during these difficult times. Considering the large number of students enrolled in private HEIs, any adverse financial impact on these institutions may affect the overall demand for education. HEIs must navigate the immediate effects of the pandemic on ongoing education while addressing resource constraints to expand and improve higher education in India in the long term. This includes increasing the gross enrolment ratio and promoting access to quality education for a broader population segment (Ministry of Education, 2019).

The closure of physical campuses during the pandemic had a profound impact on the majority of the students. The bulk of the students who were impacted by the COVID-19 crisis were undergraduate students. Thus, when planning for academic continuity in the context of Indian HEI, undergraduate studies were given a major priority. Moreover, over 50% of all enrolled students were from scheduled castes/tribes, other backward communities, and minority communities. A sizeable number of students who belonged to these communities were potentially more vulnerable to additional disadvantages in continuing their education during these challenging times (Tice et al., 2021).

The key role of government during the pandemic crisis was to provide the right technology, high-speed internet access, continuous power supply, et cetera, to allow effective teaching and learning. During the COVID pandemic, students and faculties had unlimited access to digital libraries, e-books, and journals (Naik et al., 2021; Pradip, 2021). The Prime Minster e-Vidya programme, by the Government of India provided education opportunities to 37 million students in higher education by allowing students access to educational content through television and radio during the nation-wide lockdown (Observer Research Foundation, 2020; Sudanshu, 2020). It also mooted the expansion of e-learning by relaxing open, distance, and online education regulatory frameworks and encouraged the top hundred universities to start online courses.

The Association of Indian Universities (AIU) implemented several initiatives to mitigate the adverse effects of COVID-19. These include online faculty development training for online teaching, national and international webinars, leadership talks, and online workshops on topics like assessment and evaluation and promoting social responsibility. To determine how well-prepared Indian HEIs are for online instruction, a survey of HEIs was conducted online. The "COVID-19 Response Tool Kit for Indian Higher Education Institutions" was a collaborative effort by the association of Indian universities to foster institutional resilience for academic planning and continuity. As a reference guide and checklist, this document assisted universities, colleges, and stand-alone institutions in achieving a more effective and organised reopening. The report guided higher education leaders and the academic community towards a more resilient future (Raj Kumar & Mittal, 2020).

The rapid transformation to online education with the timely support of UGC and the government by providing free online platforms and educational resources has assisted many HEIs and students (Pravat, 2020; Prakat, 2021; Roy & Brown, 2022). The important online education solutions extensively promoted by the Ministry of Education, Ministry of Human Resource and Development and University Grants Commission to support the HEIs during the COVID pandemic are highlighted in Table 2. Every HEIs has taken all possible measures to provide students with uninterrupted e-learning services and online resources (Chitkara, 2022; Lalitkumar & Hiresh, 2021). However, access to the internet and various digital gadgets among rural communities was a concern even with these initiatives.

**Table 2** Online solutions promoted during the COVID pandemic

| Online solution | Description |
|---|---|
| e-GyanKosh | A national-level digital depository to store and share the digital learning resources developed by the country's open and distance learning institutions |
| Gyandarshan | A web-based television channel devoted to educational and developmental needs for Open and Distance Learners |
| Gyandhara | An internet audio counselling service offered by IGNOU allows students to listen to live discussions by the teachers and experts on the topic of the day and interact with them through telephone, or email |
| Swayam | A programme designed to achieve access, equity, and quality in education. The Swayam platform facilitates the hosting of all classes of class nine until post-graduation taught in the classroom. This platform can be accessed by anyone, any place at any time free of cost |
| e-PG Pathshala | An MHRD initiative under its national mission on education through ICT. This platform provides high-quality, curriculum-based, interactive e-content in 70 subjects across all disciplines developed by professionals working in Indian universities and other research and development institutes across India |
| e-Adyayan | A platform that provides 700+ e-Books for the Postgraduate courses derived from e-PG Pathshala courses |
| e-Pathya | A software-driven course/content package for students pursuing postgraduate level education in distance learning as well as onsite learning mode with a provision for offline access |

(continued)

Table 2 (continued)

| Online solution | Description |
|---|---|
| National Digital Library of India (NDLI) | A national virtual source of multidisciplinary e-content for students, faculty, researchers, librarians, professionals, differently-abled users, and all other lifelong learners |
| e-Yantra | An embedded system with about 380 Labs |
| Virtual labs | Provides web-enabled curriculum-based experiments designed for remote operation. It has over a hundred virtual labs consisting of approximately 700+ web-enabled experiments designed for remote operation |
| e-ShodhSindhu | An assortment of e-journals, e-journal archives, and e-books on long-term access basis. It provides access to over ten thousand e-journals and over three hundred thousand e-books |
| National Educational Alliance for Technology (NEAT) | A Public–Private partnership model between the Government (through its implementing agency AICTE) and the Education Technology companies of India for the skilling of learners with the support of the latest technologies |
| SAKSHAT | An education portal for meeting all the education-related needs of students, scholars, teachers and lifelong learners |

## Higher Education and the Pandemic: Perspectives for Academic Leadership

The leaders of HEIs are responsible for nurturing students to become the future leaders of tomorrow (Sharma et al., 2022). The significant expansion of higher education in India after independence has brought numerous challenges for educational leadership. As HE leaders endeavour to transform institutions into top-ranked centres of excellence, they encounter both ethical challenges and those inherent to conventional leadership roles.

A qualitative study conducted among HEI leaders in India has identified four major academic leadership roles: boundary-spanning, fostering human talent, social influence, and operations. Within these roles, leadership responsibilities encompass developing vision and goals, fundraising, conservation, managing scholars, attracting students, social accountability, academics, and administration (Aggarwal & Avinash, 2020; Darshna & Kanika, 2020). The study emphasises the significance of addressing marginalisation and exclusion in higher education through "social inclusion" to elevate the global standing of Indian higher education. Moreover, it suggests that academic leaders should establish strong ethical quality measures from the outset rather than solely focusing on achieving world-class status for their institutions. By adopting such an approach, academic leaders can effectively shape academic and administrative affairs to ensure a thriving and inclusive higher education environment.

Globally, India is one of the countries faced with the longest period of closure of its higher education system during the COVID-19 pandemic. Due to a surge in COVID-19-positive cases, the Indian government declared a complete lockdown on March 24, 2020, which practically affected all aspects of public life (Jena, 2020; Seth, 2021). The government implemented successive phases of lockdown, extending the restrictions until 31 May 2020. Throughout this period, there were no opportunities for educational institutions nationwide to initiate their instructional activities. Consequently, the education industry faced significant disruptions due to the widespread impact of the COVID-19 pandemic. About 320 million students were impacted, and many were compelled to switch to online learning as a replacement (Seth, 2021). From June 2020 onwards, India started the unlock process in a phased manner. In phase II (1 July 2020 onwards), educational institutions were allowed to reopen with stringent COVID-appropriate protocols. However, the lockdown has been enforced by many states repeatedly during the unlocking phase to restrict the spread of COVID. By the end of February 2021, India was affected by a massive COVID wave, leading to a nationwide lockdown from 5 April to 15 June 2021. This entwining scenario of lockdown and unlock created a lot of disruption on all fronts, especially in the education sector.

The COVID-19 pandemic has posed serious obstacles to higher education in India. Managing the quickly changing environment and preserving the continuation of academic and administrative operations require excellent leadership. When remote work was introduced in higher education, it brought about a transformative shift and alleviated certain constraints within the sector. India's higher education system had largely lagged in adopting newer technology innovations within the teaching and learning process before the COVID-19 outbreak. Most HEIs were reluctant to get away with the chalk-and-board teaching mode, and a proper online learning management system was lacking in most HEIs. Adaptation to the best online platform, training the faculties on online teaching mode, training supporting staff and student training, scheduling and conducting online classes, lack of network, and conducting the online examination and evaluation were the major challenges the higher education leadership faced. As a result, educational authorities in India pooled their resources and developed an online education system to adapt to the circumstances of the COVID-19 pandemic.

The landscape of HEIs experienced significant complexity following the COVID-19 pandemic. HEI leaders found themselves navigating remote work arrangements and addressing unprecedented challenges. In India, educational leaders in higher education need to showcase exceptional leadership qualities and strategic approaches to tackle the multifaceted issues posed by the pandemic, as well as demonstrate a strong commitment to exploring innovative working arrangements that cater to the diverse educational needs of a large student body (Pravat, 2020).

In the wake of the COVID-19 pandemic, the landscape of higher education has undergone profound changes, necessitating a more complex and adaptive educational system. In this dynamic environment, the role of academic leaders in HEIs has become even more critical. These leaders have been tasked with managing their institutions remotely and steering them through the unprecedented challenges brought on by the global crisis. The following measures are worth considering to bring about a transformative impact:

i. Technology as a backup: Harnessing technology as a reliable backup method while prioritising the safety of all education stakeholders can contribute to the system's resilience.
ii. Empowering teachers: Inspiring teachers to go above and beyond for their students can make a significant difference. Encouraging professional growth and providing support can further enhance their dedication and effectiveness.
iii. Fostering student motivation: Encouraging students to embrace various means of learning and instilling a sense of enthusiasm can fuel their commitment to education. Creating engaging teaching methods, interactive learning materials, and supportive environments can nurture their passion for learning.
iv. Stakeholder feedback: Actively seeking feedback from all stakeholders, including students, teachers, parents, and administrators, is vital. Their perspectives and insights can guide decision-making and lead to improvements in educational practices.

v. Evaluating and redesigning strategies: Thoughtfully evaluating stakeholders' input and assessing current strategies' effectiveness can reveal areas for enhancement. The education system can adapt and improve by redesigning tactics based on these evaluations.
vi. Implementing innovative solutions: Embracing innovation and adopting new teaching, learning, and assessment approaches to overcome challenges can yield transformative outcomes. Emphasising creative solutions allows for the exploration of uncharted territories in education.

One of the primary responsibilities of academic leaders during this time is to continuously seek innovative ways to enhance the student's learning experience. With traditional in-person classes no longer feasible, leaders must embrace technological solutions to deliver course instructions effectively. Platforms like Google Classroom, Webex, and Zoom have emerged as valuable tools for remote instruction, enabling academic leaders to facilitate seamless interactions between students and educators (Lokanath et al., 2020).

Academic leaders are encouraged to explore alternative avenues for student–teacher interactions to foster a sense of connection and engagement in this virtual learning environment. This includes organising webinars, encouraging direct engagement through chat groups or texting, and creating opportunities for students to access additional resources for self-learning. Providing free access to comprehensive electronic manuals, especially in PDF format, with clear and explicit instructions can greatly enhance student comprehension and address their questions and concerns (Chaturvedi et al., 2021).

Beyond adapting to technological changes, academic leaders are also faced with implementing pedagogical modifications. The traditional lecture-based teaching model may no longer be suitable for distance learning, requiring academic leaders to support their teaching faculty in adopting innovative and interactive instructional approaches. Encouraging creativity and flexibility in teaching methodologies is essential to keep students engaged and motivated, regardless of the educational channel utilised.

Moreover, the pandemic has highlighted the importance of equipping students with essential life skills alongside academic proficiency. Academic leaders are now instrumental in fostering a holistic approach to education that goes beyond subject knowledge. Adaptability, critical thinking, problem-solving, and resilience are increasingly recognised as crucial components of a well-rounded education. Crises like the COVID-19 pandemic often arise unexpectedly, impacting every facet of life and presenting significant challenges. While the pandemic originated in China, its rapid spread necessitated a global collective response, calling for competent crisis leadership from HEI leaders. Throughout the COVID-19 pandemic, these leaders must demonstrate essential competencies, including sensemaking, decision-making, effective communication, team coordination, and the facilitation of continuous learning (Riggio & Newstead, 2023).

In the context of the education sector, particularly in HEIs, the complexity of the crisis is amplified due to interconnected stakeholders across the globe. Wu et al. (2021) aptly described this type of crisis as events that leaders and organisational stakeholders perceive as unexpected, highly salient, and potentially disruptive. India, with its diverse states encompassing social, cultural, and economic variations, can be likened to a microcosm of the world. Consequently, HEIs in India require even more effective and agile leadership to navigate the challenges posed by the crisis. Leadership at the national level in India has taken proactive measures to prepare and respond to the COVID-19 pandemic. A response toolkit has been developed, and leadership responsibilities have been decentralised to the state level to address the crisis effectively.

## The Way Forward for Indian Higher Education: Post-Pandemic Landscape

The Indian higher education sector is undergoing a significant transformational journey. This chapter has provided a comprehensive overview of the higher education landscape in India and delved into the profound influence of the COVID-19 pandemic on the sector. We have explored the wide-ranging impacts, reactions, and transformations of the pandemic on higher education in India.

Amidst the challenges posed by the pandemic, educational institutions have displayed remarkable resilience and innovation. They have taken proactive steps to accelerate the educational process by swiftly adapting and seizing opportunities. This chapter has shed light on the various actions undertaken to navigate the current difficulties and transform them into opportunities for growth and progress. Furthermore, the chapter has emphasised the pivotal role of leadership throughout this crisis. Leaders in higher education have played a crucial part in steering institutions through the challenges and uncertainties. Their perspectives and strategic decisions have been instrumental in guiding the sector during and after the pandemic.

India is actively striving to achieve the Sustainable Development Goals (SDGs) outlined in the 2030 agenda, which the Indian government embraced in 2015. As part of this global education development plan, India focuses on the SDG goal "Quality Education", aiming to provide equitable and inclusive access to high-quality education and promote lifelong learning opportunities for all by 2030. India mooted a National Education Policy (NEP) in 2020 as part of the effort. Experts in the education sector foresee that this new education policy will revolutionise all levels of education, including higher education in India. The higher education policy under the NEP envisions overcoming many existing challenges in the HE sector. The national education policy will provide a new vision for the Indian higher education system, transforming the quality of higher education and advancing holistic individuals. The reforms envisaged in national education policy are more relevant for the future and current milieu, considering the unexpected challenges the HE sectors faced during the COVID-19 pandemic. The policy will be expected to increase flexible pathways to higher education learning through credit transfers between multiple universities and the proposed academic credit bank (David, 2022; Prathamesh et al., 2022).

The institutional restructuring and consolidation proposed in the national education policy envisage phasing out single-stream HEIs and creating a system for multidisciplinary institutions of higher learning with superior teaching, research, and community engagement by 2040. The HEIs in India will transform into an integrated HE system combining specialised and occupational education. Autonomy and graded accreditation will enable the key stakeholders in the HE sector to establish more multidisciplinary HEIs nationwide. Implementing these measures will help rectify the imbalanced distribution of HEIs and tackle the challenges related to the gross enrolment ratio in the higher education sector. Adopting flexible and advanced curricula, credit and choice-based courses, community-based projects, and environmental and value-based training by HEIs will transform higher education into a holistic and multidisciplinary education system. The proposed Academic Bank of Credit (ABC) will allow a student to digitally stock the academic credits from multiple HEIs and utilise them to earn a degree from an HEI based on the credits earned. Open distance learning and online education equivalent to high-quality in-class programmes emphasised in the national education policy will allow thousands of underprivileged and socio-economically disadvantaged students to pursue their higher education from anywhere in the country.

Internationalisation is another focus area in national education policy, which entrusts top-ranked Indian universities to set up campuses outside India. Similarly, top-ranked global universities will be able to establish campuses in India. This will help HEIs to build more international collaborations, leading to student and faculty exchange, integration of cultural learning, and diversity. Leaders are working to fund solutions to the challenges resulting from the pandemic. The Government of India's post-pandemic budget for the financial year 2023 demonstrates a significant increase in fund allocation, particularly focused on enhancing the digital education ecosystem. Notably, the budget includes establishing a digital university, marking a promising beginning towards the digital transformation of education (Digital learning, 2022).

As the higher education sector continues this transformational path, it remains ever-evolving and responsive to the changing global landscape. The impact of the pandemic will continue to shape the future of higher education in India, and leaders, educators, and stakeholders need to remain forward-thinking and adaptive in this dynamic environment. The journey of higher education in India is marked by resilience, adaptation, and transformative leadership, laying the foundation for a brighter and more inclusive future in the face of unprecedented challenges.

## References


Aggarwal, K. K., & Sharma, A. C. (2020). *Re-envisioning higher education ecosystem in India.* Reimagining Indian Universities, 157. https://www.aiu.ac.in/documents/AIU_Publications/Reimagining%20Indian%20Universities/4.%20Re-Envisioning%20Higher%20Education%20Ecosystem%20In%20India%20Fostering%20Academic%20Leadership%20By%20K%20K%20Aggarwal%20Chairman,%20NBA%20&%20Avinash%20C%20Sharma%20Director,%20R&C,%20GGSIPU,%20New%20Delhi.pdf

Alamu, R., Roy, Y., & Das, S. (2023). The neglect of researchers during the first COVID-19 pandemic induced national lockdown in India: Inside the lives of JNU's research scholars. *Higher Education, 86*(2), 243–270. https://doi.org/10.1007/s10734-022-00927-4

Chaturvedi, S., Purohit, S., & Verma, M. (2021, June). Effective teaching practices for success during COVID 19 pandemic: Towards phygital learning. In *Frontiers in Education* (Vol. 6, p. 646557). Frontiers Media SA. https://doi.org/10.3389/feduc.2021.646557

Chitkara University. (2022, July 8). *Higher education in India: Challenges and opportunities.* By blog. https://www.chitkara.edu.in/blogs/higher-education-in-india-challenges-and-opportunities/

Darshna, V. B., & Kanika, T. B. (2020). Creating word class universities: Roles and responsibilities for academic leaders in India. *Educational Management Administration & Leadership, 48*(3), 570–590. https://doi.org/10.1177/1741143218822776

David, T. (2022, April 12). *India's higher education landscape.* NAFSA. https://www.nafsa.org/ie-magazine/2022/4/12/indias-higher-education-landscape

Department of Higher Education. (2021). *All India Survey on Higher Education (AISHE) reports.* Government of India. https://aishe.gov.in/aishe/viewDocument.action;jsessionid=D6A37869CAA9E5F8D86B1174C9F5CBA7?documentId=322

Dey, S., & Alamman, P. (2021). 'Covid batch': A case study on unethical assessment practices in selected higher educational institutions in Assam and West Bengal, India. *Journal of Applied Learning and Teaching, 4*(2), 130–134. https://doi.org/10.37074/jalt.2021.4.2.11

Digital Learning. (2022, March 30). *Education gets the "Big digital Push" with Union Budget FY-23.* https://digitallearning.eletsonline.com/2022/03/education-gets-the-big-digital-push-with-union-budget-fy-23/

Gupta, D., & Gupta, N. (2012). Higher education in India: Structure, statistics and challenges. *Journal of education and Practice, 3*(2). https://iiste.org/Journals/index.php/JEP/article/view/1146/1067

Jena, P. K. (2020). Impact of Covid-19 on higher education in India. *International Journal of Advanced Education and Research (IJAER), 5.* https://ssrn.com/abstract=3691541

Jyoti, B., & Ishani, B. (2020, October 5). *Impact of COVID-19 pandemic on higher education: A critical review.* Global University Network for Innovation. https://www.guninetwork.org/report/impact-COVID-19-pandemic-higher-education-critical-review

Mok, K. H. (2022). Impact of COVID-19 on higher education: Critical reflections. *Higher Education Policy, 35*, 563–567. https://doi.org/10.1057/s41307-022-00285-x

Kirti, D. L., & Preeti, S. (2021). The study of the impact of COVID pandemic on higher education with reference to management institutes in Pine, India. *Advances in Social Science, Education and Humanities Research, 661*, 108–121.

Kundu, A., & Bej, T. (2021). Experiencing e-assessment during COVID-19: An analysis of Indian students' perception. *Higher Education Evaluation and Development, 15*(2), 114–134. https://doi.org/10.1108/HEED-03-2021-0032

Lalani, K., Crawford, J., & Butler-Henderson, K. (2021). Academic leadership during COVID-19 in higher education: Technology adoption and adaptation for online learning during a pandemic. *International Journal of Leadership in Education,* 1–17. https://doi.org/10.1080/13603124.2021.1988716

Lalitkumar, P. P., & Hiresh, S. L. (2021). An overview of Indian higher education system: During & after COVID-19 pandemic period. *PalArch's Journal of Archaeology of Egypt, 18*(7), 2190–2195.

Lokanath, M., Tushar, G., & Abha, S. (2020). Online teaching-learning in higher education during lockdown period of COVID-19 pandemic. *International Journal of Educational Research Open, 1*, 100012. https://doi.org/10.29333/pr/9665

Ministry of Education (MoE). (2019). *All India Survey on Higher Education (AISHE) report 2018–19*. Government of India. https://www.education.gov.in/sites/upload_files/mhrd/files/statistics-new/AISHE%20Final%20Report%202018-19.pdf

Ministry of Education, (2022). *India rankings 2022—National institutional ranking framework*. Government of India. https://www.nirfindia.org/nirfpdfcdn/2022/pdf/Report/IR2022_Report.pdf

Naik, G. L., Deshpande, M., Shivananda, D. C., Ajey, C. P., & Manjunath, P. G. C. (2021). Online teaching and learning of higher education in India during COVID-19 emergency lockdown. *Pedagogical Research, 6*(1), em0090. https://doi.org/10.29333/pr/9665

Nirupama, A. Y., Chaudhari, S., Chittooru, C. S., Vani, K. Y., & Chittem, S. D. (2022). Undergraduate medical education in India during COVID-19 pandemic. *Current Medical Issues, 20*, 177–181. https://doi.org/10.4103/cmi.cmi_38_22

Niyaz, P., Habeeb, U. R., Mustafa, R. R., Abhinandan, K., Mahammad, T. P., & Shakira, I. (2022). COVID-19 and its impact on educational environment in India. *Environmental Science and Pollution Research, 29*, 27788–27804. https://doi.org/10.1007/s11356-021-15306-2

Observer Research Foundation. (2020, May 26). *Online higher education in India during the COVID-19 pandemic* [press release]. https://www.orfonline.org/research/online-higher-education-in-india-during-the-COVID-19-pandemic-66768/

O. P. Jindal Global University. (2020, June 29). *Impact of COVID-19 on higher education-challenges & opportunities*. The official blog. https://jgu.edu.in/blog/impact-of-COVID-19-on-higher-education-challenges-opportunities/

Parvat, K. J. (2020). Impact of COVID-19 on higher education in India. *International Journal of Advanced Education and Research, 5*(3), 77–81.

Pradip, K. D. (2021). Impact of pandemic COVID-19 on higher education—Indian context. *Universal Journal of Business and Management, 1*, 13–21. https://doi.org/10.31586/ujbm.2021.010102

Prakash, C. G., Deepayan, G., & Aditya, G. (2021). Higher education in India: Challenges and opportunities of the COVID-19 pandemic. *Asian Journal of Distance Education, 16*(1), 54–73. https://doi.org/10.5281/znodo.4643552

Prakat, K. (2021). The year lost to the pandemic: Reviewing the impact of COVID-19 on education in India. *Artha-Journal of Social Sciences, 20*(1), 51–60. https://doi.org/10.12724/ajss.56.4

Prathamesh, C., Kamal, M., Muhammad, M. A., Gaurav, D., Mukesh, S., & Utku, K. (2022). Online learning in COVID-19 pandemic: An empirical study of Indian and Turkish higher education institutions. *World Journal of Engineering, 19*(1), 58–71. https://doi.org/10.1108/WJE-12-2020-0631

Raj Kumar, C., & Mittal, P. (2020). *COVID-19 response tool kit for Indian higher education institutions*. https://www.aiu.ac.in/documents/index/COVID-19%20Response%20Toolkit%20for%20Indian%20Higher%20Education%20Institutions.pdf

Riggio, R. E., & Newstead, T. (2023). Crisis leadership. *Annual Review of Organizational Psychology and Organizational Behavior, 10*, 201–224. https://doi.org/10.1146/annurev-orgpsych-120920-044838

Roy, S., & Brown, S. (2022). Higher education in India in the time of pandemic, sans a learning management system. *AERA Open, 8*(1), 1–15. https://doi.org/10.1177/23328584211069527

Sangita, B., & Nandita, C. (2022). Impact of COVID-19 on higher education in India: A literature review. *Journal of Positive School Psychology, 6*(2), 4720–4724.

Seema, D. (2022). Challenges and opportunities in higher education. *International Journal of Advanced Research in Science, Communication and Technology, 2*(1), 551–553. https://doi.org/10.48175/568

Seth, Y. (2021). Challenges faced by higher education institutions amid Covid-19. *International Journal of Law Management and Humanities, 4*(3), 4951.

Shamika, R., Neelanjana, G., & Puneeth, N. (2019, November 27). *Reviving higher education in India*. Brookings. https://www.brookings.edu/research/reviving-higher-education-in-india/

Sharma, V., Poulose, J., & Maheshkar, C. (2022). Leadership styles in higher educational institutions in India—"A need for paradigm shift!". In *Role of leaders in managing higher education* (Vol. 48, pp. 59–81). Emerald Publishing Limited.

Shivangi, P. (2022, June 23). Online education and its consequences due to COVID-19. *Times of India*. https://timesofindia.indiatimes.com/readersblog/shivangipandey/online-education-and-its-consequences-due-to-COVID-19-43463/

Shivarajappa, M. (2020). Impact of pandemic COVID-19 on higher education in India—An empirical study. *International Journal of Research and Analytical Reviews, 7*(4), 557–565.

Siddesh, T., & Gautami, A. (2021). Impact of COVID on higher education in India. *Educational Resurgence Journal, 2*(5), 22–27.

Souvik, S. (2022). Possibilities and challenges of online education in India during the COVID-19 pandemic. *International Journal of Web-Based Learning and Teaching Technologies, 17*(4), 1–11. https://doi.org/10.4018/IJWLTT.285567

Sreshta, L. (2021, August 30). Multifaceted impact of COVID-19 on higher education of India. *The Siasat Daily*. https://www.siasat.com/multi-faceted-impact-of-COVID-19-on-higher-education-in-india-2115668/

Sudanshu, B. (2020, July 14). *A survey report COVID-19 and higher education*. National Institute of Educational Planning and Administration. http://www.niepa.ac.in/download/Final_14th%20July%20COVID%2019%20and%20Higher%20Education.pdf

Tice, D., Baumeister, R., Crawford, J., Allen, K. A., & Percy, A. (2021). Student belongingness in higher education: Lessons for Professors from the COVID-19 pandemic. *Journal of University Teaching & Learning Practice, 18*(4), 2. https://doi.org/10.53761/1.18.4.2

UGC (University Grants Commission). (2023). *Consolidated list of all universities.* Government of India. https://www.ugc.gov.in/oldpdf/Consolidated%20list%20of%20All%20Universities.pdf

Wu, Y. L., Shao, B., Newman, A., & Schwarz, G. (2021). Crisis leadership: A review and future research agenda. *The Leadership Quarterly, 32*(6), 101518. https://doi.org/10.1016/j.leaqua.2021.101518

Yatreek, G. B. (2020). The higher education scenario in India during COVID-19 pandemic. *Splint International Journal of Professionals, 7*(2), 81–82.

# The Emergency Response Framework (ERF) for the Republic of Ireland's Higher Education Sector: A Case Study of UCD's College of Business Global Campus

Matt Glowatz and Orna O'Brien

## Introduction

While the global pandemic created one of the largest periods of disrupted higher education study for all stakeholders in the HE sectors, University College Dublin (UCD) also experienced several small-scale events of disruption and crises in two of their transnational locations, which helped shape the approach in Ireland. Although this chapter focuses explicitly on UCD's College of Business (CoB) Global Campus's response to the global pandemic-related challenges and opportunities in its transnational education operations in Singapore, we additionally analyse the approach to crisis management and alternative programme delivery caused by unanticipated emergency events in both Hong Kong and Sri Lanka. This is a relatively new area of academic exploration, as outlined by Riggio and Newstead (2023, p. 201), who suggest that although crises are very complicated and of global consequence, crisis leadership "is a relatively underdeveloped field". Discussions by Riggio and Newstead (2023) and in this handbook (e.g. Crawford et al., 2020) are very useful in discussing the phases of a crisis. In this chapter, we hope to complement these resources with a practical heuristic to support education leaders in responding to future emergencies.

M. Glowatz (✉) · O. O'Brien
College of Business, University College Dublin, Dublin, Ireland
e-mail: matt.glowatz@ucd.ie

O. O'Brien
e-mail: orna.obrien@ucd.ie



J. Rudolph et al. (eds.), *The Palgrave Handbook of Crisis Leadership in Higher Education*,
https://doi.org/10.1007/978-3-031-54509-2_19

For its relatively small population of slightly more than 5 million (Central Statistics Office, 2023), the Republic of Ireland (RoI) has a relatively large number of 19 higher education institutions (HEI) spread across the country, catering to approximately 245,000 students from Ireland and across the world (Higher Education Authority, 2022). Although all HEIs fall under the overarching responsibility of the Irish Government's Department of Further and Higher Education, Research, Innovation and Science (Government of Ireland, 2023), most HEIs have independently implemented pandemic and other crisis-related response guidelines and policies. This approach—focusing on the recent global pandemic spanning two and half years—has created confusion and uncertainty among staff and student cohorts across both national and international campuses. It is not a recommendation for unified best practice implementation policies focusing on overall curriculum design and delivery approach, such as delivering curriculum content and administering assessment strategies utilising on-campus, online, or hybrid approaches.

This chapter is structured as follows. A detailed overview of UCD's College of Business Global Campus organisational structure and operations is provided. Secondly, the authors outline the recent emergencies UCD's CoB Global Campus had to address to draft the proposed emergency response framework before detailing UCD's initial response to the global COVID-19 pandemic. Initial emergency response observations, learnings, and generalised impact of crises on the HE sector are identified before elaborating on innovative digital initiatives to address identified impacts and challenges. Building upon Crawford et al.'s (2020) stages of response to the COVID-19 crisis, the chapter concludes by proposing a generic Emergency Response Framework (ERF) to be implemented by HEIs to respond to any unanticipated crisis emerging at some stage in the future. It is anticipated that the proposed ERF and other identified policy recommendations will provide other HEIs and government policy decision-makers with a unique opportunity to learn from the UCD CoB Global Campus approach to implement solid policies successfully counteracting crises in whatever shape or form they emerge for the higher education sector in both Ireland and abroad.

## Ireland—A Rich Higher Education Landscape

Ireland is often called the land of "Saints and Scholars". Walsh (2018) acknowledges there is no comprehensive academic review of higher education in the current Irish state from a historical stance. An Irish history of higher education has to be grounded in the larger debates about what a university is and the purpose of higher-level learning. UCD's founding father, John Henry Newman in 1852, first expressed these concepts in a series of lectures entitled "Discourses on the scope and nature of university education" (Walsh, 2018, p. 1). UCD, however, is not the oldest university in Ireland. The oldest university is the University of Dublin, which dates from 1592. As in many countries, the university landscape more widely reflects wider societal and political issues as Ireland fought for independence from the United Kingdom and looked for greater opportunities for Catholics. The 1908 Universities Act reflected a compromise between nationalist parties in Ireland and dominant forces in Britain. An important element of this Act, and subsequent Higher Education Acts in Ireland, is the autonomy of universities, which still is retained today and indeed influenced the response of institutions to the COVID-19 pandemic.

Irish higher education is often recognised as one of the reasons for the growth of the Irish economy (White, 2001), particularly its knowledge economy (Drudy, 2009). The announcement of free undergraduate fees in 1995 for citizens of Ireland, EU/EEA, and Switzerland was seen as a key change in policy and underpinned part of the success of the Celtic Tiger. A large infrastructure of institutions serves the Irish higher education sector. The Irish higher education sector moved in the 1960s from an exclusive, small number of institutions to mainly five institutions to forty years later, a "well diversified and well-developed provision of mass higher education" (White, 2001, p. vii). The universities, of which the University of Dublin (Trinity) and UCD are two, are state-supported and provide their awards. There are also publicly funded technological universities originating from the institutes of technology and the technical development of skills. They were awarded university status in 1971. The Higher Education Authority Act was instrumented to lead the overall strategic development of the area and to manage a coherent higher education with diverse, autonomous institutions. Other providers in higher education, including the more vocationally focused Further Education Colleges, are validated by Quality and Qualifications Ireland (QQI) and a few private institutions. All providers are intended to map their awards to a comprehensive National Qualifications Framework, which shows ten levels of education from certificate to doctoral level, which is intended to provide learners with a clear recognition structure and allow for the identification of routes of progression and transfer.

As outlined in a recent publication discussing 20 countries' higher education intra-period digital pedagogy responses (Crawford et al., 2020), neither the Irish Government nor the Irish HEI sector followed through an Ireland-wide unified, cohesive response to the pandemic. The origins of the diversity of response are in the autonomy recognised for institutions by the government and, more generally, by the higher education sector in Ireland. No mandate required the higher education sector to move from a 100% on-campus to a 100% online delivery method overnight, and not provide stakeholders with any best practice implementation guidelines. Despite some pressure for change, the universities in Ireland retain large-scale autonomy over their activities due to the Higher Education Act, 2022 and the Irish Universities Act 1997 (Higher Education Authority, 2023). In conclusion, it was left to the institutions to design, implement, and administrate innovative online-based pedagogical solutions as they saw fit, best meeting institution-specific needs and requirements.

## UCD College of Business, Global Campus

As stated above, University College Dublin is one of the oldest academic institutions in the Republic of Ireland. UCD is recognised as the strongest global institution, with 9500 students from over 152 countries represented (UCD, 2023a). The position as *Ireland's Global University* is reflected in the global curriculum, a global academic workforce, opportunities for in-programme travel, and the international student population. The UCD College of Business (CoB) is Ireland's largest and leading Business School, evidenced by alumni accomplishments, research achievements, international rankings, and accreditations. The CoB is a member of the elite Top 1% of global business schools granted the prestigious "Triple Crown Accreditation" by three of the largest and most influential business school accreditation organisations, namely the Association of Advance Collegiate School of Business (AACSB, USA), the Association of Master of Business Administration (AMBA, UK), and finally the European Quality Improvement Systems (EQUIS, EU). The College is consistently in Europe's top 30 business schools (UCD, 2023a).

The CoB comprises four schools: UCD Lochlann Quinn School of Business for undergraduate students, UCD Michael Smurfit Graduate Business School for graduate students, UCD College of Business Global Campus (previously known as the Centre for Distance Learning (CDL) for domestic part-time and transnational part-time and full-time programmes, and Smurfit Executive Development for its Executive Education programmes. The Global Campus business unit was established in 2002 with an active domestic and transnational student cohort exceeding 5000 registrations among its

Dublin campus and three global locations in Singapore, Hong Kong, and Sri Lanka. Since 2002, the Global Campus Alumni network has grown to over 10,000 active members across Southeast Asia (UCD College of Business Global Campus, 2023). In Dublin, located on the main and Blackrock UCD campus, Global Business is also responsible for an on-campus part-time undergraduate Diploma in Business Studies (DBS)/Bachelor of Business Studies (BBS) and online part-time postgraduate master's in science in Management (MSc Management) programmes. Outside of Ireland, UCD's Global Campus manages and delivers both full-time and part-time Bachelor of Business (BBS) programmes in Singapore covering nine distinct pathways/majors ranging from Digital Business to FinTech and Marketing. In comparison, the recently redesigned full-time and part-time Master of Science (MSc Management) caters for students interested in four pathways, such as Digital Marketing, FinTech, Management, or Project Management and Supply Chain Management. It also had an undergraduate programme offering in Sri Lanka and Hong Kong.

## Global Events Calling for Best Practice Emergency Response Policies

### The Global Pandemic (COVID-19)

As a global business school, global events have influenced the university and its approach to its delivery. The discussion here focuses on the response of UCD to its programme provision in Dublin and Singapore during the COVID-19 period. The approach here speaks largely to the experience of programmes managed by the College of Business, Global Campus. Different disciplines and colleges may have taken a different approach at different points in the crisis. Equally, it is not suggested that the COVID-19 pandemic was the only recent crisis that affected transnational education provided by UCD College of Business. This section demonstrates how the global nature of its operation influenced its response to the pandemic. Before looking at the programme provision from 2020 to 2023 in Dublin and Singapore, other recent crises in Hong Kong and Sri Lanka from 2019 to 2023 are briefly outlined. These crises impacted the ability and quality of the response to the pandemic in Singapore and Dublin.

## Sri Lanka Crisis

In Sri Lanka, emerging political upheaval in recent years, the devastating bomb attacks in 2019, wide-ranging corruption at all levels in politics and businesses, and a weakening of the local currency relative to the Euro have ultimately thrown Sri Lanka into an economic crisis (*BBC News*, 2023). Consequently, those unfortunate developments diminished the economic viability of operations in this location, requiring UCD to reconsider its partnership with the local higher education provider National School of Business Management (NSBM) Green University Town (NSBM, 2023). Further information on the Sri Lankan context is provided in this handbook by Edirisinghe et al. (2024).

## Hong Kong Crisis

Initially, the first period of demonstrations and disruptions across Hong Kong Island was recorded in June 2019, with a vast amount of people peacefully marching the streets of Hong Kong (Amnesty International, 2019; see Chan & Lam, 2024, in this handbook for a more in-depth insight into Hong Kong). Within a very short period, however, the protests escalated further, becoming the largest demonstrations in Hong Kong history to protest against the Hong Kong government's introduction of a bill to change the Fugitive Offenders Ordinance concerning extradition to mainland China (*BBC News*, 2019). Universities such as the Hong Kong Polytechnic University and the Chinese University of Hong Kong drew particular focus among demonstrators. For UCD, a major concern was warranted for the safety of students studying at its local facility managed by its higher education partner institution, Kaplan (Kaplan Higher Education Hong Kong, 2023).

## Timeline of Global Disruptions and Events

In conclusion, several global crisis events disrupted UCD's CoB Global Campus operations within and outside of the Republic of Ireland between 2019 and 2023, including the terrorist attacks in Sri Lanka at Easter 2019, followed by the Hong Kong Student Protests in November 2019. Even after the COVID-19 pandemic, another crisis arose for the College's transnational education offering with the economic crisis in Sri Lanka. In direct response to the incidents mentioned above, "Global Campus" developed crisis management guidelines and policies leading to the Emergency Response Framework outlined and discussed in the following sections.

## Methodology

This case study employs a qualitative research approach to document the concerns the COVID-19 pandemic has posed to higher education institutions and a framework for institutions and how they might respond to future crises. The approach to this study is a case study designed to allow for a comprehensive investigation into how the programmes in Dublin and Singapore at UCD College of Business Global Campus adapted to the COVID-19 pandemic. The discussion here makes for a suitable case study drawing on onsite observations and illustrative materials (Yin, 1981), including programme materials, newspaper articles, internal documents, institutional communications, and university website resources. These resources were reviewed using content analysis. Using these resources and investigating the trajectory of delivery throughout the pandemic allows for the opportunity for reflection. Boud et al. (2006) advocate the concept of "productive reflection" to address some of the complexities and uncertainties organisations encounter. As the case was explored, the concept of embedded collective reflection was also utilised. Cressey (2006) also outlines the advance of the concept of embedded collective reflection, which is associated with a progression from problem-solving within an organisation's setting, overseen by standardisation and control, to a greater emphasis on creativity and innovation through "reflective participation" in the workplace. The authors here are directly involved in the delivery of the programme and have taken this case as an opportunity for reflective participation in the programme's development.

## UCD and Global Campus' Immediate Response to the COVID-19 Pandemic

As COVID-19 spread quickly across the globe early in 2020, Singapore had confirmation of its first case on 23 January of that year, just before the Chinese New Year on 25 January. Many international students had travelled home for the Chinese New Year period, and it looked likely that students would either choose not to return to Singapore or be unable to return due to travel restrictions after the holiday period. Among other industry sectors severely impacted by the pandemic, it also brought about a sudden change in how tertiary education was delivered in Singapore (Rudolph et al., 2021, 2023; Tan et al., 2022) and across the globe. For UCD, the immediate priority was to enable students to continue with their studies despite the growing uncertainty in China and beyond. As an intended interim arrangement, UCD implemented a live broadcasted UCD Blackboard option from the classrooms for those students who had travelled overseas for Chinese New Year and could not attend classes in Singapore. It was anticipated to be a temporary solution as, at that time, there was an expectation that travel concerns and restrictions would be short-lived. Guidelines and instructional guides were rapidly disseminated to staff, and all classes proceeded as scheduled, using this new hybrid option. Higher education practitioners are proficient with this now, but at the time, implementing this within a week was very new. UCD colleagues observed the situation in Singapore closely, considering what impact it might have on delivery on campus in Dublin.

The first confirmed COVID-19 case in the Republic of Ireland was recorded on 29 February 2020 (RTE, 2020). Shortly afterwards, the Republic of Ireland's government announced the first lockdown, effectively closing the country overnight. UCD closed its physical infrastructure from 13 March until 29 March 2020 (Crawford et al., 2020; Leahy et al., 2020). On 16 March 2020, the Presidents of 21 Irish higher educational institutions, with the support of two student unions, disseminated a cohesive and consistent message through email to all registered students in Ireland in respective institutions offering advice on COVID-19 and nationwide procedures to be implemented in order to maintain a satisfactory and safe learning environment utilising innovative educational technologies (EdTech) enabling remote learning and assessment (Deeks, 2020). This message inevitably moved the entire Irish higher education sector from a traditional on-campus experience to 100% online education overnight and without any warning, providing no guidelines and policies to staff and students on effectively delivering online (Tice et al., 2021). Individuals were left to identify and implement best practices for their module and discipline. This called for the requirement to draft generic emergency response guidelines for future use. In time, a suite of online resources from UCD Teaching and Learning and the College of Business's Business eLearning Team (2023b).

In the context of one of Global Campus' domestic Dublin-based programmes, for example, both the Diploma of Business Studies (DBS) and bachelor's in business studies (BBS) on-campus teaching weekends were scheduled for Friday, 13 March 2020 and Saturday, 14 March 2020. While all classes were initially cancelled in response to UCD closing its infrastructure the same day, an agile approach was immediately adopted, and each lecturer was canvased to indicate their chosen date and mode of delivery for the content planned to be delivered that particular weekend. These programmes had previously offered supplementary online occasion sessions to students in the normal course of their studies, so there was expertise with online provision. The previous few months' experience in Singapore had assisted in migrating the domestic programmes over.

In Dublin, for these programmes, within two weeks, all content planned to be delivered in-person on the 13th and 14th of March had been delivered online utilising various platforms. Blackboard Collaborate Ultra was the most common platform used for live webinar delivery as it was integrated into UCD's Virtual Learning Environment (VLE) at the time. Asynchronous content—predominantly narrated PowerPoint slides—was also created and made available to students. Student support was migrated online almost immediately, and students could attend important staff support meetings with the Programme Managers and Student Advisor through Google Meet.

The Global Campus, as a result of the extensive programme management in China and Southeast Asia, had a range of staff resources already available, such as video tutorials on how best to use Blackboard Collaborate Ultra in the UCD teaching context, with accompanying guidebooks, and template study guides for online provision of modules to support teaching staff. These study guides provide a full overview of the module for students, including weekly readings, assessment guides, and topic overviews. When the pandemic forced the closure of campuses all over the world, these resources proved very helpful for both the Global Campus's overseas programmes in Singapore, Hong Kong, and Sri Lanka and, from March 2020, the domestic programmes, namely the Diploma in Business Studies (Dublin), Bachelor of Business Studies (Singapore, Dublin, and Hong Kong), Bachelor of Science (Sri Lanka) and Master of Science (Singapore, Dublin, and Hong Kong).

By the final teaching weekend of the academic year in April 2020, the intervening weeks they had given lecturers greater experience in the online space. They were more comfortable integrating question-and-answer sessions and more bespoke content intended to reflect the virtual setting instead of replicating face-to-face teaching in the online space, which was more of a trend with March 2020 online delivery. Over the summer of 2020, a greater proliferation of Zoom for video conferencing solutions became the platform of choice for the 2020/21 Academic Year. During 2020, the university investor in Zoom made accounts available to staff and students by default rather than by request. By the end of 2020, Zoom was fully integrated into the Brightspace platform and was the default online platform for UCD modules.

## Initial Emergency Response Observations and Learnings

On reflection, the early response of UCD would certainly echo what Crawford (2023) call "rapid adoption". Indeed, on the foot of the UCD case, it could be suggested that Crawford's multi-stage model could also be further developed to acknowledge the multiple activities required of each stage. These are proposed in the Emergency Response Framework below.

First, let us review the key observations of the UCD before building upon Crawford's (2023) helpful heuristic. While the adjustment to planning and delivery of online provision for students and staff was seismic, the standard of provision was largely maintained. Crawford (2023) observe that rigorous Quality Assurance is impossible due to rapid adaptation. However, at UCD, as there had been a foundation of previous technology expertise around the hybrid delivery of the programmes, it did limit internal concerns around potential quality issues. The move to introduce a hybrid and decompressed learning experience in the Summer of 2019, outlined above, was critical in allowing the rapid adoption of technology at UCD. As staff were familiar with some of the tools, there was less concern around quality as they might be for other institutions. Thus, delivery certainly was one of the immediate responses demanded, but developments around delivery were quickly followed by module assessment and evaluation.

The changes around assessment were monumental due to COVID-19. In Spring 2020, most modules were examined by a traditional examination hall in Singapore. All assessments then had to move to the online provision of social distancing restrictions onsite in Singapore and Dublin. There were some modules that made some small use of online exams prior to then. The end-of-February term examinations were scheduled in April 2020 (Singapore) and May 2020 (Dublin). The consideration to adapt examination papers and prepare advisories for students around taking online examinations, preparing a proforma examination document for students to prepare, guidance on academic integrity, and practical instructions on navigating online assessment were prepared. The earlier learnings from Singapore helped inform assessment plans in Dublin, which traditionally culminated in May and December each year.

As assessment procedures for programme-wide online assessment were established and UCD College of Business prepared for the second term in an online environment in 2020, the improvement phase was evident. Quickly, the areas of curriculum and evaluation (both module and programme) came to the fore. The curriculum required ongoing updates to ensure the changes in the dynamic business environment arriving from COVID-19 were reflected in what students were being taught, such as online retail developments and changes in work practices to include online and hybrid working. Curriculum update is an annual process in UCD each May, so this was relatively routine. Module and programme evaluation had to be migrated online. Previously, module evaluation, in particular, was completed in the classroom in hard copy format, which yielded high responses. This needed to be digitised in the online COVID environment. Equally, the evaluations themselves needed to be adapted to seek feedback from students regarding the online environment in which they participated in classes, were assessed and their overall programme experience. In both the curriculum and evaluation, consideration was made that one size did not fit all. Students had different needs, and different student groups had different needs at different points during the pandemic. UCD was conscious that full-time students could be struggling with the insular nature of being full-time students online, possibly away from families and in need of social support. This point of the students finding it harder to make social connections was also acknowledged by Wilson et al. (2020). This social connection between students during the pandemic remained critical (Finnegan, 2021). Equally, part-time students might struggle with working at home full-time, studying and possibly additional caring responsibilities, including home-schooling. To support students' overall well-being, initiatives utilising webinars with the student advisor and an occupational therapist for different cohorts were scheduled to ensure that students felt pastorally supported as much as possible during the pandemic period.

As the College navigated into the start of the academic year in 2020/2021, the consolidation phase commenced. This was the third term in Singapore and the second in Dublin in the online environment. The policy had begun to emerge after the experiences of the prior eight months of online provision. UCD as an institution was clearer in its expectations of programme provision, and there were several sets of data around student and programme evaluations about what was working and what required development. Communities of Practice emerged and communicated among members regarding the transfer of good practice.

As the experience of the present day in the academic year 2022/23 is considered, it is noted that the academic year in the Republic of Ireland commenced as it would have pre-pandemic and the full year with no interruption to delivery. In contrast, September 2022 saw the gradual and phased return to the classroom in Singapore. An initial hybrid approach was introduced in Singapore and will be gradually phased back to support a return to the classroom. This return contains elements of hybrid learning, with online provision, some recorded classes, and face-to-face delivery. This remains a watching brief as student expectations and regulatory requirements, in particular, emerge. The challenge at this phase, which UCD currently experiences across all campuses, is the assessment piece. How to rethink and redesign assessment in a manner that allows for a variety of modes of assessment, maintains the quality and rigour of the university, affords flexibility to students, and is particularly mindful of online assessment in the era of Artificial Intelligence (AI) (see Tan et al. (2024) in this volume). Of course, this restoration and the emergent issues listed have raised questions for the staff-support infrastructures for post-crises transnational education models. Again, this is very much a watching brief as trends emerge as student mobility and their resultant expectations of higher education.

UCD is still working through its restorative phase. While Crawford et al.'s (2020) model provides insight into the different stages of the pandemic response model, each phase itself demands a series of actions to take a comprehensive approach to a programme of study. In conclusion, many of the Global Campus's initial emergency response observations and learnings have been incorporated into the Emergency Response Framework discussed below. First, though, it is observed that central to each of the stages which UCD navigated through above was the role of technology, be it with Zoom as the online platform for delivery, online assessment, or digitalisation of evaluations. Before proposing the Emergency Response Framework, the role of technology before, during, and in the aftermath of the COVID-19 pandemic is explored.

## Role of Technology: Past—During Crises—Future

It is quite remarkable that with the COVID-19 pandemic in Ireland and elsewhere, the Hong Kong protests, the terror attacks and the more recent economic crisis in Sri Lanka, and the pervasive nature of COVID-19 at UCD's campuses around the globe, not a single student experienced a revision of their study schedule. The role of technology with the menu of options of hybrid, synchronous, asynchronous, digital scheduling, conferring tools, and diverse digital assessment mechanisms was the single factor attributable to this success. Acknowledging the evolution of digital teaching and learning technologies is now provided.

## Past

Technology focusing on educational technologies (EdTech) has traditionally played a less important role in higher education than today. The global higher education move to online provision has been well documented in the literature (Gopal et al., 2021; Pillai et al., 2021; Chakraborty et al., 2021). In the pre-pandemic era, EdTech was primarily regarded as a set of tools supporting academic and support staff with the delivery of both domestic and transnational modules, falling under the responsibility of the Global Campus business unit in UCD.

EdTech was utilised in the most basic form, not using it to its fullest potential. For instance, the overall module structure on VLE (Virtual Learning Environment: Blackboard and Brightspace) did not follow any best practices guidelines (e.g. structured folders, resource library, and discussion boards), resulting in some modules' VLE content simply displaying a generic module coordinator's/lecturer's welcome message and study guide, others listing some of the module's readings and lecture notes in digital format, while only a few incorporating more advanced tools to engage students digitally, such as VLE-administered discussion forums or online assessment in whatever shape or form (online examination or essay submission).

## During Crises

Although respective crises have immensely impacted the higher education sector, the strategic use of innovative technologies has helped institutions maintain the highest possible educational delivery standards. Both academic and support staff realised the true potential of EdTech with a particular focus on online module delivery, module assessment, and general module administration. For example, Global Campus utilised technologies quite effectively and efficiently during the crises above as follows:

- Combination of synchronous, asynchronous lectures and workshops
- Making lecture recordings available to students

- Support of a VPN (Virtual Private Network) for students studying while based in China during the pandemic
- Zoom and Google Meet supported walk-in clinics and other student support
- Developing interactive, multimedia, and Augmented Reality-enhanced study guides improving student motivation and engagement
- Using VLE to administrate discussion boards and wikis
- Moving from in-person to 100% online assessment
- Identifying alternative online assessment strategies linked with the module's overall learning outcomes, such as online or/and take-home written examinations, virtual group presentations, or creation of video productions.

However, using technology is not a silver bullet, as seen in Sri Lanka during the 2022 crisis. The Sri Lankan economic crisis immediately led to a country-wide electricity crisis lasting several years (*BBC News*, 2023). As a direct result, both electricity supply and internet connectivity were unstable, with many scheduled and unscheduled power cuts enforced by local Government authorities that triggered many challenges for Global Campus's stakeholders (lecturer, support staff, and students) around lecture delivery and online assessment (written examination) administration. Additionally, migrating traditional assessment components to online versions during the respective emergency events resulted in an increased number of suspected infringements of academic integrity and collusion cases among students, despite a student awareness campaign at the programme and module levels.

## Present and Future

Overall, observations and learnings from using technologies during crises offered invaluable insights into the pros and cons of digital-enabled emergency/crisis management in the higher education sector. Moving forward, using innovative EdTech will play an even greater role than in previous years. Consequently, the Global Campus team drafted an Emergency Response Framework (ERF) to help its stakeholders to respond to future emergencies more effectively and efficiently while maintaining the best possible teaching and learning standards. Having identified and outlined major recent crisis situations, the next section will focus on the HE sector in more detail, firstly outlining the main impact categories of crises on the HE sector, followed by our Emergency Response Framework (ERF).

## Impact of Crisis Situations on the HE Sector

This part outlines the crises' key impacts on the HE sector in general, identifying key components to be included in the ERF outlined in subsequent sections. While the situation has mostly normalised (June 2023), there are still some ripples of the impact of the COVID-19 period on student transfers. This impact on the different themes of staff, students, teaching and learning infrastructures, and policy and strategy is now explored.

### Impact on Staff

- There has been a shift in staff recruitment and talent development. Regardless of subject area or knowledge field of education, such as business, science, arts, engineering, or business, to name a few, most sought-after staff will need proof of extensive knowledge of digital applications and initiatives to help the higher institution to say competitive while offering the best possible learning experience for students. The expectations of students, particularly those who are considered Generation Z, have rapidly changed, and the catalyst of COVID-19 has raised the bar for staff working with students and their level of proficiency.
- The university requirement for existing staff to upskill, gaining digital competencies similar to the above point.
- Staff well-being is becoming increasingly important as they learn to operate in a more and more digital environment. This also impacts their ability to support students in the online environment and manage student issues.
- Staff are becoming more proficient with the various learning design approaches (online, face-to-face, hybrid) and the flexibility students demand.
- Innovative curriculum design focusing on digital will impact staff time and workload management. Additionally, emerging new AI-driven applications will require staff to meet the demands of assessment to maintain—in the best possible way—academic integrity.

### Impact on Students

- Similar to the above-mentioned crisis impact on HE staff, students are required:

    To upskill, gaining digital competencies.

To embrace a mixed learning environment (online, face-to-face, hybrid) moving forward.

- Similar to creating and maintaining initiatives to improve staff well-being, HE institutions need to consider and implement initiatives to maximise student well-being and support students during periods of change.

## Impact on Teaching and Learning Infrastructure

- Structural change of units within the HE sector will require fundamental investment levels to keep up to speed with the latest digital technologies, focussing on electronic/hybrid learning.
- Change of use of existing learning spaces utilising relevant learning-related infrastructure components.
- An emerging mixed learning environment (online, face-to-face, hybrid) requires substantial investments to be undertaken, offering the most effective and efficient learning environment for all HE stakeholders.
- A more flexible teaching and learning infrastructure will be required to meet future crises and emergencies, allowing HEIs to react to the aforementioned more strategically.
- A recalibrated space for academics and ed-tech practitioners to innovate.

## Impact on Policies and Strategy

Fundamental change in teaching and learning policies and strategies moves to a mixed, more dynamic, agile learning environment model (online, face-to-face, hybrid, etc.).

Design and implement best practice curriculum reviews meeting emerging teaching and learning demands and requirements.

A more fundamental emergency response framework is needed to prepare HEI stakeholders for possible unanticipated crises arising in the future.

Having identified the main areas of unexpected crisis and emergency effects have had on the HE sector in the Republic of Ireland and beyond, the authors designed, tested, and implemented a generic Emergency Response Framework (ERF) discussed in more detail in the next section.

## UCD College of Business Global Campus Emergency Response Framework (ERF)

Considering all of the above-outlined aspects in the context of addressing unexpected crises that have an immediate impact on the higher education sector, the UCD College of Business Global Campus team designed and implemented the following Emergency Response Framework, updating both the programme's overall curriculum design and preparing the unit's stakeholders for possible future crisis scenarios. This framework complements Crawford et al.'s (2020) earlier model of an institution's response to the pandemic and demonstrates the multiple levels of activity attached to the stages.

As the ERP follows a proactive rather than reactive design, response time to emerging crises will be drastically reduced while maintaining operations and offering the best possible learning environment and experience for "Global Campus" student cohorts. Building not only the COVID-19 pandemic but also events in Hong Kong and Sri Lanka, the framework looks at the role of stakeholders. Often, as a crisis emerges, it is unclear who should take responsibility for what, and the emergent response can be chaotic. Presuming module coordinators follow the ERF process as shown in the "ERF Showcase" section below, the response to the circumstances will be structured and considered, with the framework outlining the tools to address emerging crises being flexible to move between several delivery options.

The ERF has been implemented for all of the Global Campus modules offered in our Singapore campus in partnership with Kaplan Singapore (2023), as well as the part-time programmes in Dublin and those other programmes in the Asian portfolio in Hong Kong and Sri Lanka.

### ERF Process

Overall, the following ERF process has been implemented with the main objective to minimise the risk of disruption to students' study and ensure a high-quality learning experience in the event of an emergency while continuing operations. The key objective is to ensure that once all students and staff are safe, a student's programme of study can continue in a high-quality learning environment during the period of study intended for the student. Having identified possible emergencies and analysed possible negative outcomes and associated challenges for Global Campus operations, stakeholders are encouraged to respond by following the ERF framework process.

## ERF Components

For each of the four core ERF components outlined and illustrated below, policy and decision-makers are required to analyse, respond to, and mitigate identified emergencies.

1. **Stakeholders**
    a. Teaching staff
    b. Support staff
    c. Learner
    d. University Management
2. **Module Delivery Design (Timetable, Workload, Assessment Strategy)**
    a. Outline of overall module delivery (timeline)
    b. Consider the options for synchronous or/and asynchronous delivery depending on the content covered, the parameters of the situation, and staff/student interaction required to cover content, such as theoretical content, applied content, discussions, simulations, and group work.
    c. Pre-recorded learning units not requiring a great amount of teacher–student interaction will improve the learning experience as students can study material in their own time from any location, and it allows for potential issues, be it internet or electricity disruption, depending on the nature of the crisis.
    d. Review of the assessment of the module. Does the assessment require migration online, and if so, what revisions are required to the specification to allow for its assessment in the online environment? How is academic integrity safeguarded? What flexibility is required around access to the assessment if access to the online environment is disrupted?
    e. Enhanced student engagement activities, such as scheduled online Walk-in-Clinics aim to engage the whole class. At the same time, virtual office hours are designed to help and advise individuals addressing their specific questions.
3. **Module Delivery Environment/Infrastructure (On-Campus, Online, Hybrid)**
    a. Identification of the most suitable delivery method in line with delivery structure and learning material for each module's unit and the availability and expectations of students in their current environment.

4. **Module Learning Material**
    a. Migrating to 100% digital learning material will enable stakeholders to swiftly move from one digital learning environment to another whenever need be.
    b. Digital learning materials may include
        i. Digital versions (PDF) of traditional hardcopy readings
        ii. Multimedia content
        iii. Immersive learning experiences, such as Augmented Reality (AR) or/and Virtual Reality (VR) enhanced learning
        iv. Online simulations and gamification.

It is intended that this framework is considered not only at the module level but also at the programme level. This was a factor in the approach of the Global Campus response. Module coordinators were invited to consider the above at their module level. However, the Global Campus team would review each module's approach in light of the overall programme to ensure students had a consistent and suitable programme experience. This programmatic approach is vital for universities to ensure quality across the modules and that no aspect is overlooked. For example, at an operational level, taking a programme approach meant that students had a consistent learning environment. All online sessions were curated in Zoom for Education. The pathway to find each online class was the same. Equally, the students were trained in the netiquette expected at a programme level, which pervaded each module. This programme approach also came to the fore regarding assessment and ensuring a robust online assessment. A common set of guidelines was adopted, which governed all online exams and assessments with common procedures. It allowed the Global Campus team to ensure a variety of assessments was experienced by students and guaranteed programme learning outcomes were attained. This robust approach was also beneficial regarding the student support framework available to students (for more information, see Collins et al., 2022). So, despite the closure of the onsite campus facilities, students immediately had access to student support during high stress and uncertainty (Fig. 1).

## ERF Showcase

As mentioned in the previous section, ERF enables module coordinators to quickly address emerging crises with the help of innovative digital solutions while maintaining the highest teaching and learning standards for Global Campus students (Fig. 2).

**Fig. 1** Generic Emergency Response Framework (ERF) components

This Emergency Response Framework is intended to be dynamic. As institutions respond to a crisis, each stage should facilitate a review of the framework proposed above. Crawford et al. (2023) outline the four stages of the pandemic response model as rapid adaption, improvement, consolidation, and restoration. Each of these phases presents new challenges and considerations. Using the Emergency Response Framework to explore each module, in the totality of a programme, ensures that all necessary considerations are made by university management.

UCD and other institutions have a unique opportunity to harness what was learnt and develop emergency response strategies that could lead to the development of implementation templates (as outlined above) to be utilised by HEI stakeholders. The development of an HEI's set of widely accepted templates will not only enable stakeholders to respond quicker, however, also to implement response strategies more effectively. Every emergency will naturally be different, but a common starting point is a high tool to fast-track

**Pre-Module Planning**

- Approximately six weeks before the welcome lecture
  - Design interactive study guide and save as PDF
  - Design and implement a sound assessment strategy where each assessment component can be direclty linked to one or multiple module learning outcome(s)
  - Delivery and assessment structure communicated to students outlining any possible contingency plans in the event of an unexpected crisis situation.
  - Setup VLE section (Content folders, Reading folder with all module readings in digital format, assignment submission links and folders, Zoom meeting room for all online content deliveries)

**Module Delivery**

- 4 weeks before on-campus delivery
  - Live online welcome lecture (Zoom) which will also be recorded for students with potential VPN, internet connectivity, or electricity issues.
- On-Campus module delivery (typicaly four consecutive days).
- 2 - 3 weeks after final on-campus lecture
  - Live onlinemodule wrap-up and closing lecture (Zoom) which will also be recorded for students with potential VPN, internet connectivity, or electricity issues.
- Student Walk-In sessions (Face2Face while on campus and online after the main module delivery.

**Post-Module Administration**

- Approximately between four and six weeks after the online closing lecture
  - Download and check all assignment submissions with the VLEs plagiarism detection tool
  - Grade assignments and enter grades into Gradebook to be reviewed and approved by the UCD College of Business exam board
  - Export module's VLE content to be re-used for the module's next delivery

**Fig. 2** Pre-module, module delivery, and post-module administration flow

the best possible response. Digital upskilling strategies with associated initiatives are required for HE stakeholders to embrace unexpected changes to their teaching and learning environments caused by crises.

## Conclusion

This chapter identifies and outlines the Emergency Response Framework (ERF) implemented by the UCD College of Business Global Campus in response to recent local and global crises and emergencies that had an enormous impact on the higher education sector, demanding all stakeholders to draft, test, and implement institution-wide response policies and best practice guidelines to counteract future crises or emergencies. One of UCD's key selling points is that it is positioned as Ireland's global university, which promises a global learning experience and curricula. In this instance, the university's global positioning helped develop a good foundation for the emergency COVID-19 presented for the students' programme of study and an efficient, quality experience.

While a global pandemic is unlikely to impact higher education again in the immediate future, a range of social, political, and geographical crises remain a possible reality. An institution with a developed Emergency Response Framework, which is considered at all four stages of adoption, improvement, consolidation, and restoration, as suggested by Crawford et al. (2020), remains best placed to respond and achieve its primary objective, to support its students to continue their studies in the highest quality learning environment possible. The heuristic offered here with the ERF seeks to build upon our understanding of the phases of an institution's response to demonstrate a conceptual tool to prepare and respond to any future crises that might emerge from the dynamic economic, political, and social global environment and impact the higher education sector.

## References


Amnesty International. (2019, n.d.). *Hong Kong's protests explained*. https://www.amnesty.org/en/latest/news/2019/09/hong-kong-protests-explained/

*BBC News*. (2019, November 28). *The Hong Kong protests explained in 100 and 500 words*. https://www.bbc.com/news/world-asia-china-49317695

*BBC News*. (2023, March 29). *Sri Lanka: Why is the country in an economic crisis?* https://www.bbc.com/news/world-61028138

Boud, D., Cressey, P., & Docherty, P. (Eds.). (2006). *Productive reflection at work: Learning for changing organisations*. Routledge.

Central Statistics Office. (2023, March 30). *Press statement census of population 2022—Summary results*. Central Statistics Office Ireland. https://www.cso.ie/en/csolatestnews/pressreleases/2023pressreleases/pressstatementcensusofpopulation2022-summaryresults/

Chakraborty, P., Mittal, P., Manu, S. G., Yadav, S., & Arora, A. (2021). Opinion of students on online education during the COVID-19 Pandemic. *Human Behaviour and Emerging Technologies*, 1–9.

Collins, K., Dooley, D., & O'Brien, O. (2022). A reflection on evolving student support in a post-pandemic higher education environment. *Journal of Applied Learning & Teaching, 5*(2), 42–50. https://doi.org/10.37074/jalt.2022.5.2.6

Crawford, J. (2023). COVID-19 and higher education: A pandemic response model from rapid adaption to consolidation and restoration. *International Education Journal: Comparative Perspectives, 22*(1), 7–29.

Crawford, J., Butler-Henderson, K., Rudolph, J., Malkawi, B., Magni, P., Glowatz, M., Burton, R., & Lam, S. (2020). COVID-19: 20 countries' higher education intra-period digital pedagogy responses. *Journal of Applied Learning & Teaching, 3*(1), 1–19. https://doi.org/10.37074/jalt.2020.3.1.7

Cressey, P. (2006). Collective reflection and learning. In D. Boud, D. P. Cressey, & P. Docherty (Eds.), *Productive reflection at work: Learning for changing organisations*. Routledge.

Deeks, A. (2020, March 16). *Email message to students from presidents of Irish universities and institutes of technology*. Email to Students.

Drudy, S. (2009). Education and the knowledge economy: A challenge for Ireland in changing times. In S. Drudy (Ed.), *Education in Ireland*. Dublin.

Finnegan, M. (2021). The impact on student performance and experience of the move from F2Fto online delivery in response to COVID-19: A case study in an Irish higher education institute. *All Ireland Journal for Higher Education, 13*(1), 1–23.

Gopal, R., Singh, V., & Aggarwal, A. (2021). Impact of online classes on satisfaction and performance of students during the pandemic period of COVID-19. *Education and Information Technologies, 26*, 6923–6947.

Higher Education Authority. (2022, n.d.). *Annual report 2021*. Higher Education Authority Ireland. https://hea.ie/assets/uploads/2023/04/Annual-Reports.pdf

Government of Ireland. (2023, n.d.). *Department of higher education, innovation, and science* (Ireland). https://www.gov.ie/en/organisation/department-of-higher-education-innovation-and-science/

Higher Education Authority. (2023, June 17). *A high performing higher education system is an essential requirement in the development of creative, entrepreneurial people and the creation of new knowledge to support social, cultural and economic development*. Higher Education Authority. https://hea.ie/about-us/overview/

Leahy, P., Cullen, P., Lynch, S., & Kelly, F. (2020, March 12). Coronavirus: Schools, colleges and childcare facilities in Ireland to shut. *Irish Times*. https://www.irishtimes.com/news/health/coronavirus-schools-colleges-and-childcare-facilities-in-ireland-to-shut-1.4200977

Kaplan Higher Education Hong Kong. (2023, n.d.). *Master of science in digital marketing*. https://www.kaplan.com.hk/higher-education

Kaplan Singapore. (2023, n.d.). *About—University College Dublin*. Kaplan Singapore. https://www.kaplan.com.sg/university/university-college-dublin/

NSBM. (2023, n.d.). *National school of business management Green University Town*. NSBM. https://www.nsbm.ac.lk/

Pillai, K. R., Upadhyaya, P., Prakash, A. V., Ramaprasad, B. S., Mukesh, H. V., & Pai, Y. (2021). End user satisfaction of technology-enabled assessment in higher education: A coping theory perspective. *Education and Information Technologies*. https://doi.org/10.1007/s10639-020-10401-2

Riggio, R. E., & Newstead, T. (2023). Crisis leadership. *Annual Review of Organizational Psychology and Organisational Behavior, 10*(1), 201–224.

Rudolph, J., Itangata, L., Tan, S., Kane, M., Thairo, I., & Tan, T. (2021). 'Bittersweet' and 'Alienating': An extreme comparison of collaborative autoethnographic perspectives from higher education students, non-teaching staff and faculty during the pandemic in the UK and Singapore. *Journal of University Teaching and Learning Practice, 18*(8), 10.

Rudolph, J., Tan, S., Crawford, J., & Butler-Henderson, K. (2023). Perceived quality of online learning during COVID-19 in higher education in Singapore: Perspectives from students, lecturers, and academic leaders. *Educational Research for Policy and Practice, 22*(1), 171–191.

RTE. (2020, April 21). *Coronavirus in Ireland—A timeline*. RTE Ireland. https://www.rte.ie/news/2020/0421/1124382-covid-19-ireland-timeline/

Tan, S., Rudolph, J., Crawford, J., & Butler-Henderson, K. (2022). Emergency remote teaching or andragogical innovation? Higher education in Singapore during the COVID-19 pandemic. *Journal of Applied Learning and Teaching, 5*(Sp. Iss. 1), 64–80. https://journals.sfu.ca/jalt/index.php/jalt/article/view/475

Tice, D., Baumeister, R., Crawford, J., Allen, K. A., & Percy, A. (2021). Student belongingness in higher education: Lessons for Professors from the COVID-19 pandemic. *Journal of University Teaching & Learning Practice, 18*(4), 2. https://doi.org/10.53761/1.18.4.2

UCD. (2023a). *Study at UCD*. University College Dublin. www.ucd.ie/global/study-at-ucd/

UCD. (2023b). *T&L guides and resources during COVID-19*. University College Dublin, College of Business—Business eLearning. https://buselrn.ucd.ie/tl-guides-and-resources-during-covid-19/,

UCD College of Business Global Campus. (2023). *About UCD college of business global campus*. UCD. https://www.smurfitschool.ie/aboutus/globalcampus/

Walsh, J. (2018). *Higher education in Ireland, 1922–2016, politics, policy and power—A history of higher education in the Irish state*. Palgrave, Dublin.

White, T. (2001). *Investing in people: Higher education in Ireland from 1960 to 2000*. Institute of Public Administration.

Wilson, S., Tan, S., Knox, M., Ong, A., Crawford, J., & Rudolph, J. (2020). Enabling cross-cultural student voice during COVID-19: A collective autoethnography. *Journal of University Teaching & Learning Practice, 17*(5), 3. https://doi.org/10.53761/1.17.5.3

Yin, R. K. (1981). The case study as a serious research strategy. *Knowledge, 3*(1), 97–114.

# Issues and Challenges for Educational Leadership in the Implementation of ICT-Intensive Strategies for Higher Education in Post-Pandemic Malaysia

Rama Venkatasawmy and Peik Foong Yeap

## Introduction

Ongoing Information and Communication Technologies (ICT) advancement has continuously transformed curriculum delivery in Malaysian higher education, for instance, by multiplying teaching and learning channels and methods and supplementing face-to-face interactions with various online platforms. Since the first quarter of 2020, the COVID-19 pandemic triggered an acceleration of ICT-intensive strategies across the higher education institution (HEI) landscape in response to the repeated lockdown and closure of physical premises throughout Malaysia. The easing of restrictions in 2022 enabled face-to-face classes to resume, but the COVID-19 pandemic has irremediably altered long-lasting attitudes within local HEIs about teacher-centred learning practices. ICT-intensive approaches have become pretty much the new normal in post-pandemic Malaysia. To adjust past practices to better suit the current and future needs of educators and learners, educational leadership in Malaysian HEIs has had to manage the effective

R. Venkatasawmy
Callaghan, NSW, Australia
e-mail: rama.venkatasawmy@newcastle.edu.au

P. F. Yeap (✉)
Newcastle Business School, College of Human and Social Futures, University of Newcastle, Callaghan, NSW, Australia
e-mail: peikfoong.yeap@newcastle.edu.au



J. Rudolph et al. (eds.), *The Palgrave Handbook of Crisis Leadership in Higher Education*,
https://doi.org/10.1007/978-3-031-54509-2_20

implementation of ICT-intensive strategies in curriculum delivery, teaching and learning.

Using a combination of social, economic and technical perspectives, this chapter identifies some issues and challenges as well as discusses the practical implications for educational leadership in implementing ICT-intensive strategies within HEIs in post-pandemic Malaysia, such as pedagogic predicaments, professional development insufficiencies, leadership inadequacies and equity concerns.

## An Overview of the Evolution of the Malaysian Higher Education Landscape

The establishment of the first public university, namely the University of Malaya, in Kuala Lumpur right after independence in 1957 was the beginning of Malaysia's modern higher education system. The first phase of its evolution occurred from 1957 to 1970 (essential education frameworks and additional training), the second phase from 1970 to 1990 (democratisation of higher education) and the third phase from 1990 to the present (development of higher education ecosystems) (see Zain et al., 2017). HEIs have been defined by the Malaysian Ministry of Education as including public and private universities, university colleges, foreign university branches, polytechnics and community colleges.

By 2004, a Ministry of Higher Education (MOHE) was created separately from the Ministry of Education (MOE) with the "responsibility to oversee all aspects of the development of higher education in the country. This includes oversight of public and private universities, polytechnics, and community colleges, as well as furthering the national agenda for the export of Malaysian education" (Bajunid, 2011, p. 254). The relatively inexperienced MOHE then faced "tremendous challenges to regulate the private sector while maintaining direct control over public universities" (Ma et al., 2022, p. 843).

The launch of the National Higher Education Strategic Plan (2007–2020)—complemented with the guidelines of the National Higher Education Action Plan (2007–2010) for all stakeholders to follow—had the purpose of supporting Malaysia's achievement of developed nation status (see MOHE, 2007; Selvaratnam, 2016). The Malaysia Education Blueprint 2015–2025 (MOHE, 2015) was subsequently launched to nurture students' leadership qualities and higher order thinking abilities and prepare them to meet the economy's future needs. The higher education system has undergone multiple reforms accompanied by a remarkable amount of financial investment: “Malaysia has been generous in its support of higher education. Currently, the Malaysian government devotes over 20% of its expenditures to education at all levels and, in the latest Universitas21 Ranking of National Higher Education Systems, is ranked 12th in the world in terms of the resources committed to higher education” (Wan et al., 2017, p. 2135).

From the mid-1990s onwards, the government launched the National Information Technology Agenda (NITA), the National Information Technology Framework (NITF), the National Information Technology Strategic Agenda, the Strategic Trusts Agenda, the Strategic Trusts Implementation Committee (STIC) and the Multimedia Super Corridor Malaysia Project (MSC). Those played a central role in formulating strategies promoting ICT utilisation nationally and were integral to the goals of transforming Malaysian society into a ‘knowledge society,’ in line with the bigger plan of getting the country to eventually be on par with developed countries in terms of economic performance, technological advancement and quality of life (NITC, 2019a, 2019b; Yusuf & Nabeshima, 2009).

The combination of the abovementioned government initiatives contributed to integrating ICT-intensive strategies in higher education. By the 2010s, the adoption of rapidly changing trends in ICT intensified in Malaysian HEIs: “e-learning is used in smart schools, colleges, universities, and libraries. [...] Most universities have established their own e-learning systems by offering Internet-based degree programs and delivering online learning materials” (Sofiadin, 2014, p. 159). Integrating ICT-intensive strategies in higher education aims to equip graduates with new skills and necessary capabilities to transform Malaysia into a high-income economy, as advocated in the *Twelfth Malaysia Plan 2021–2025* (and earlier ones).

HEIs have been championed to perform a key role in achieving a ‘knowledge economy.’ “As a fast-growing and open economy, Malaysia faces the challenge of a more competitive employability landscape and the increased need for 21st-century skills, especially for higher education graduates, which remains a cornerstone in Malaysia’s development” (Rangel et al., 2018, p. 38). Strong strategic partnerships with international HEIs have been essential to nurture students’ international perspective and enhance the quality of the Malaysian higher education system (Flanders Investment & Trade, 2022). Rosnizah et al. (2022, p. 56) explain that the “number of international branch campuses reflects the well-structured higher education system under the education internationalisation agenda [...] first introduced in 2017 under the Malaysia Higher Education Strategic Plan 2007–2015. One of the strategies was to increase the quality of teaching and learning by focusing on leadership." By 2021, the *Twelfth Malaysia Plan 2021–2025* (2021, p. 360) highlighted that the "efforts undertaken to implement the 10 Transformational Shifts of the Malaysia Education Blueprint 2013–2025 (Higher Education) resulted in notable progress. [...]. Greater access to higher education was provided through 595 HEIs, comprising 20 public universities, 36 polytechnics and 104 community colleges as well as 435 private HEIs." Ma et al. (2022, p. 843) commented, however, while MOHE's ambition for Malaysia to become a regional education hub "has driven reforms towards technology-savvy education, the overall environment is less auspicious, with undertrained academic staff and legislative frameworks ill-suited to supporting the country's 'blended learning' model."

## The Impact of the COVID-19 Pandemic in Malaysia

Respiratory illness COVID-19 spread rapidly worldwide after being first identified in December 2019 in the Wuhan Province of the People's Republic of China. During the subsequent months following the first case of COVID-19 in Malaysia being reported on 25 January 2020, the number of infections skyrocketed nationwide, leading Muhyiddin Yassin, the Prime Minister at the time, to roll out a Movement Control Order (MCO) on 18 March 2020. All businesses, except for essential services, were required to close temporarily, and restrictions were placed on people's movement. The MCO was subsequently extended and implemented in different forms, such as the Conditional Movement Control Order (CMCO), the Recovery Movement Control Order (RMCO) and the Enhanced Movement Control Order (EMCO). Those measures were adjusted according to the varying rates of infection, mortality and vaccination in different states and territories. Throughout this period, the country's borders remained largely closed. The national vaccination campaign was deemed successful, considering that 84.1% of Malaysia's total population was vaccinated with at least two doses, and 50% subsequently took one booster shot. Vaccines made available freely to citizens and non-citizens alike included Cansino, AstraZeneca-Oxford, Sinovac and Pfizer-BioNTech. As COVID-19-related infections and deaths abated, the government implemented the National Recovery Plan (NRP) from 1 June 2021 onwards.

In June 2020, the government launched a Short-term National Economic Recovery Plan (PENJANA), with funds of RM35 billion, aimed to stimulate the country's economy through a 6-Phase Plan (6Rs): Resolve,

Resilience, Restart, Recovery, Revitalise and Reform (by 2022 Malaysia was in the Recovery phase). Forty initiatives in PENJANA focus on three key thrusts: Empower People, Propel Businesses and Stimulate the Economy. The Malaysian economy experienced a contraction of 4.5% during the third quarter of 2021, and to rebuild it, the Budget 2022 exercise allocated RM332.1 billion to anchor three key pillars: Strengthening Recovery, Building Resilience and Driving Reforms (Flanders Investment & Trade, 2022). While there was much concern about immediate economic fallout following the end of the pandemic phase, the Malaysian economy has nevertheless made good progress along the recovery path since 2022 (Flanders Investment & Trade, 2022).

## Curriculum Delivery, Teaching and Learning During the Pandemic Phase

The spread of the pandemic and the MCO considerably disrupted all activities throughout Malaysia, resulting in government services, businesses and HEIs being forced to shift towards technological leverage to maintain operations. As a result of the immediate response in higher education to transition from face-to-face practices, educators and students have been kept connected through online technologies "in processes such as enrolment, teaching and learning, communication and networking, student management, and course assessment" (Azizan et al., 2022, p. 246). Many HEIs embraced remote online teaching and learning and invested funds into online learning systems to maintain student engagement and minimise attrition rates during the pandemic's peak.

Because of repeated lockdowns, educators and students were compelled to utilise whatever ICT means available to them while operating entirely from domestic settings to continue teaching and learning. Sia & Adamu (2021, p. 266) confirmed that "education has changed dramatically with the distinctive rise of online learning, where teachings are done remotely on digital platforms. In Malaysia, implementing the MCO in the middle of March 2020 resulted in HEIs fully switching to online learning with unprecedented challenges." The pandemic irremediably altered a long-lasting attitude about teacher-centred learning practices due to students having to engage with teaching and curriculum delivery predominantly through ICT because of the closure of physical premises. With many HEIs introducing fully online courses and blended learning, educators had to be trained rapidly.

They provided adequate guidance in effectively using online learning tools for online classes to be seamlessly carried out.

## Initiatives to Boost ICT-Intensive Strategies in Education

The pandemic phase highlighted the digital unpreparedness of many HEIs due to their limitations concerning possessing adequate resources and infrastructure for supporting ICT-intensive curriculum delivery strategies, teaching and learning. The *Twelfth Malaysia Plan* (2021, p. 377) acknowledges this issue:

> Digital infrastructure will be provided to schools to support digital teaching and learning. This will include improving internet connectivity, upgrading local area network (LAN) and provisioning 'fit-for-purpose' digital equipment for schools and students. [...]. The closure of HEIs due to the COVID-19 pandemic has shifted learning and teaching activities from face-to-face interactions to online learning. This has necessitated HEIs to change in their learning and teaching delivery to ensure quality education. The HEIs will strengthen remote learning approaches to ensure continuity in learning and teaching. Academic staff and students of HEIs will be equipped with digital skills to further improve learning outcomes. Measures will also be undertaken to improve the Rating for Higher Education Institutions (SETARA) and Malaysian Quality Evaluation System for Private College (MyQUEST), by incorporating technology indicator in the assessment criteria.

ICT factors are henceforth receiving more attention from educational leaders, considering their critical role in implementing ICT-intensive strategies. It is imperative for HEIs to promptly assess and regularly evaluate their level of technological preparedness to pinpoint any deficiencies and subsequently revise their tactics in the implementation of e-learning systems (Al-araibi et al., 2019).

The study by Tan and Muna (2011) on the role of universities in building prosperous knowledge cities in Malaysia reveals that even though there have been tangible achievements in spatial development, such as the transformation of agricultural land towards knowledge-intensive land exploitation and activities in Cyberjaya for example—a town with a science park, IT industry and universities as the core of the Multimedia Super Corridor—there is still a need to call for more concerted and coordinated joint efforts between academia, public and private sectors to further foster the development of a more inclusive 'knowledge economy' and 'knowledge society' for all sections of the population. It should be noted that the implementation of ICT-intensive strategies has not occurred in equal terms across the Malaysian education landscape. Political factors and issues about geographical location and socioeconomic status have contributed to an uneven distribution of resources and the emergence of 'digital divides' across the country. As confirmed in the *Twelfth Malaysia Plan* (2021, p. 387),

> the digital divide among the *rakyat* [people/citizens] has created inequality in economic opportunities and widened the rich-poor gap. Lack of accessibility is among the main factors contributing to the widening of the digital divide. The challenging geographical terrain in rural areas has constrained efforts in ensuring coverage of digital infrastructure and services, resulting in low participation in the digital economy among rural communities.

While the country might boast over 80% Internet penetration, there is still a major discrepancy in infrastructure between East and West Malaysia. "For instance, people living in the capital city (West Malaysia) are enjoying high-speed Internet up to 800 megabytes per second compared with Sabah and Sarawak (East Malaysia) with slower speed, with some areas without access to the Internet" (Sia & Adamu, 2021, p. 266). Such a state-of-affairs negatively impacts students' proper access to online education and academic performance. Jafar et al. (2022, p. 2) argue that because "almost all states in Malaysia, especially Sabah, are still lagging in the availability of educational facilities" and are characterised by poor internet access and limited ownership of electronic devices, a strategy of empowerment that concentrates on vulnerable students should be put in place "to ensure inclusiveness for all individuals in getting educational opportunities, regardless of their geographical location and socioeconomic status." Individuals without adequate access to ICT are marginalised and do not experience the benefits from the progress being made towards achieving a 'knowledge economy' and a 'knowledge society.'

The gap between the 'information rich' and the 'information poor' in Malaysian society will continue to widen into an unbridgeable chasm if no adequate action is taken to confront it effectively. Furthermore, the pandemic has further heightened the urgency to intensify efforts in bridging the digital divide across the nation. As the Twelfth Malaysia Plan (2021, p.396) proposed, "a nationwide provision of digital infrastructure will enhance digital connectivity as well as unlock new economic potential and opportunities. In this regard, efforts will focus on ensuring equitable access and facilitating the adoption of emerging and alternative technologies." Better, reliable and affordable high-speed broadband connectivity is paramount for future-ready sectors to remain competitive and attract significant foreign investment into Malaysia. The National Fiberisation and Connectivity Plan (NFCP) 2019–2023 was launched to improve broadband quality and coverage, reduce broadband prices and provide Internet access across all spectrums of society (Flanders Investment & Trade, 2022).

## Educational Leadership in Post-Pandemic Malaysia

Educational leadership in Malaysia faces the considerable task of re-envisioning curriculum delivery, teaching and learning, which, while excellent for previous generations, might not be meeting the needs and aspirations of Malaysian digital natives who prefer more flexibility in how, when and where they learn in a post-pandemic world that digital ICT is inexorably transforming. Conventional strategies need to be transformed to suit new generations of HEI students (Yadegaridehkordi et al., 2019; Thomas, 2011), and educators and learners need to end up speaking the same language for effective curriculum delivery, teaching and learning to occur.

How are educational leaders to prepare educators and students for a digital future? Educational leaders should first fully acknowledge that access to information and knowledge is no longer confined to what could previously be found only within classroom or school walls. Increased connectivity, superfast wireless technologies, online social networking, cloud computing and artificial intelligence enable students and educators to instantly access large amounts of data from anywhere via smartphones, tablets or portable computers. Educational leaders should recognise that the expertise and practical knowledge in implementing ICT-intensive strategies are within the operational level.

While HEIs are 'information rich,' this information must be organised and managed before it can become knowledge. Knowledge management is paramount regarding the skills required to coordinate and motivate individuals to share their knowledge and experience of effectively implementing ICT-intensive strategies. To attain these goals, educational leaders need to develop suitable organisational structures, such as a hybrid organic and mechanistic framework which facilitates easier coordination, enhances flexibility and accelerates decision-making, ultimately resulting in improved performance. For instance, investing in a peer review approach would be highly productive for educational leaders. The peer review of the implementation of

ICT-intensive strategies would generate valuable feedback about the quality of what is being done in different HEI environments.

Emerging technologies tend to change quite rapidly. The rapid evolution of technology and the Internet has reduced ICT life cycles to an estimated average of twelve months. Ideas, designs, production and development happen at accelerated speeds due to ever-increasing technological convergence and connectivity. This means that when educational leaders formulate and implement strategies to seize the advantages of ICT for effective curriculum delivery, teaching and learning, they need to be equally concerned that something more advanced may supersede what they are adopting within a brief period. To transform decades of set educational practices as well as to convince upper levels of management of the need for change, educational leaders in Malaysian HEIs have to acquire an excellent sense of the full capabilities of emerging ICT, be personally proficient in the use of ICT and be in a position to nurture an educational culture that perceives very positively the implementation of ICT-intensive strategies.

Given the lack of a one-size-fits-all leadership model for higher education, finding the right leadership style to implement ICT-intensive strategies effectively can pose a significant challenge. Educational leaders must emphasise their role as technology-savvy facilitators rather than merely disseminators (Bottery, 2006). This particular approach would indeed fulfil the requirements of what Mercurius (2006) aptly refers to as 'digital-age leadership' whereby the focus is on leaders who "are confident, knowledgeable, systematic and strategic, organised, able to communicate and motivate, able to facilitate and cultivate, attuned to the benefits of globalisation, and infused with technological-savvy" (Litz, 2011, p. 58). For their part, Riggio and Newstead (2023) distil five essential leadership competencies to handle critical changes and events: sensemaking, tactful decision-making, coordinating teamwork, facilitating learning and communicating. Those competencies are particularly needed by educational leaders transforming the educational landscape by implementing ICT-intensive strategies. However, the latter transformational leadership style could be at odds with an enduring instructional face-to-face style, which has been a dominant paradigm in educational leadership in Malaysia for decades. "Malaysian university staff work within powerful academic and managerial hierarchies with role-boundaries that are clear and respected, while at the same time, working relationships tend to be based on collectivism and maintaining social harmony at all costs," according to Harland et al. (2014, p. 39) (Merriam & Mohammed, 2000). A significant challenge for those adopting a transformational leadership style would then be to overcome 'conservative' attitudes shaped by decades of instructional leadership in many HEIs.

"Transformational leaders appear to bring value and motivation to produce excellent workplace relationships, leading to effective work outcomes," and they operate as caretakers to promote and maintain workplace social networks, both lateral and vertical, which will increase task performance and dynamic community participation (Rosnizah et al., 2022, p. 56). A transformational style of leadership attempts to influence the conditions that directly impact the quality of curriculum delivery and teaching instruction to students in the classroom, targets variables in the change process, using such strategies as encouraging continuous learning among staff, sharing learning throughout the organisation, and working with the community towards achieving broader organisational goals (Onorato, 2013). Transformational leadership would be the most productive approach to implementing ICT-intensive strategies—to benefit contemporary learners engaged in the post-pandemic Malaysian higher education system.

## ICT-Intensive Strategies in the Post-Pandemic Phase: Some Issues and Challenges

Considering how they effectively facilitate understanding and retention of complex concepts and improve how students learn, ICT-intensive strategies need careful designing so that student's interest in and knowledge about intended learning outcomes and skills associated with the discipline concerned are well cultivated (Tice et al., 2021). "The success in implementing online learning is dependent on four pillars, which are online academic support, technological support, personal well-being and sense of belongingness," as highlighted by Abdullah et al. (2022, p. 5). For their part, Adams et al. (2020, p. 517) refer to one of the main initiatives in the *Malaysian Education Blueprint 2015–2025* (Higher Education) about the use of blended learning "as a conduit for transforming existing pedagogy. It states that blended learning models will become a staple pedagogical approach in all higher learning institutions. Key initiatives include making online learning an integral component of higher education and lifelong learning, requiring up to 70% of programmes to use blended learning models."

More productive outcomes are expected in HEIs through blended e-learning methods, which combine traditional forms of learning and ICT-intensive strategies. For Adams et al. (2020, p. 516), "the widespread global pandemic has presented challenges that drastically changed the way higher education institutions operate today, necessitating the forced shift to e-learning and blended learning modes as opposed to traditional classes." Inayatullah and Milojević (2014) assert that applying modern technologies creates new learning modes and that new cohorts of students will inevitably develop different expectations and needs. It is, therefore, essential in a post-pandemic world for ICT to be "tightly integrated into the curriculum to support multimedia-based teaching, and on-demand access to learning resources has to be readily available to all learners," as argued by Lai and Hong (2015, p. 726).

Ya (2020, p. 5) comments that the pandemic "has shown us that digitisation and globalisation are very much embedded in our society" and that "traditional rote learning and cramming of knowledge for examinations would not prepare students for work in the future." HEIs have been impelled to re-examine the purpose of higher education beyond extensive examination and to update the Malaysian education system more pointedly in the direction of ICT-intensive strategies of curriculum delivery and teaching and to review learning outcomes so that graduates acquire the kind of skills that will enhance their ability to be globally employable. To add value to the marketability of Malaysian graduates, the government must anticipate the needs of tomorrow's emerging global industries. It has indeed "recognised that the system must keep evolving to stay abreast with the main global trends. For instance, disruptive technologies such as advanced robotics, the Internet-of-Things, and the automation of knowledge work are expected to dramatically reshape the business and social landscape from what it is today" (Rangel et al., 2018, p. 38).

There has been some resistance by many pre-digital generation educators to integrate ICT-intensive strategies within their discipline areas. Thang et al. (2015, p. 360) explain that many educators in Malaysian higher education are afraid of technology and would only use technology without commitment when forced to do so: "Many still hold on to the view that technology is not necessary, and the conventional approach is less complicated and more effective. In line with this, their students taught through the conventional mode would assume that it is the norm and their teachers' instruction is crucial for their success."

Although Malaysia has been among the top five countries regarding the number of Facebook accounts created (Ainin et al., 2015), the formal incorporation of Facebook and other social media applications into teaching and learning practices has been somewhat limited in educational contexts. In their study of the role of social media in collaborative learning to improve the academic performance of students in Malaysian higher education, Al-Rahmi et al. (2015, p. 196) point out that "even though social media has the potential to enhance the learning experience, its use has not made significant inroads into classroom usage." Other studies, such as Roblyer et al. (2010) and Ajjan and Hartshorne (2008), have, for their part, highlighted the reluctance of faculty members to include social media tools in curriculum delivery, teaching and learning. This is concurred by one of the main findings of a 2015 study by Lee et al. (2015) on the use of Facebook at a private university in the Klang Valley: both lecturers and students acknowledged that Facebook should not be included in the formal educational curriculum because it is not designed for education. For their part, Noh et al. (2015) identified how educators found it difficult to set up learning environments with Facebook because, in Malaysia, there are no guidelines for applying Facebook in educational contexts. And, following a 2019-study conducted among undergraduates in three private Malaysian universities, the findings of Moorthy et al. (2019, p.102) indicate that:

> most of the students do not perceive that Facebook is useful for learning and thus they do not have any intention to use Facebook for learning. They believe that Facebook is mainly for communication and maintaining relationships. In fact, they may get distracted from their studies, and Facebook may make it hard for them to focus and use it as a learning tool, thus decreasing their academic performance.

Lim et al. (2014) argued that successfully integrating social media tools, like Facebook or YouTube, in Malaysian HEIs is a complex process because institutions, educators and students each have divergent views and understanding of their educational usefulness.

The implementation of ICT-intensive strategies for curriculum delivery and teaching during the pandemic has been accompanied by significant mental stress among educators in Malaysia. Sia and Adamu (2021) highlight the challenges faced by lecturers who had to swiftly adapt to online learning, familiarise themselves with learning management systems and conduct online classes with limited preparation and training. This is concurred by Abdullah et al. (2022, p. 2), among others, who have similarly highlighted that "students' attitudes and satisfaction towards remote online learning exerted no influence on intention to continue using this method" and that "remote online learning poses diverse challenges to instructors and students especially when implemented under the MCO circumstances which could have put them under tremendous pressure."

The shift from traditional face-to-face classes to e-learning modes and blended learning has become necessary due to the pandemic, creating major challenges for HEIs operating in Malaysia. As some educators have limited ICT training, they struggle to fully conceptualise the benefits of ICT-intensive strategies: "work is required to increase the readiness of academic staff, students, and the infrastructure for a successful transition to online learning" and "staff must cope with increased preparatory work, difficulty gauging students' understanding, and encouraging students' class participation" (Azizan et al., 2022, p. 246). Because educators do not often exchange ideas about problems faced, educational leaders face the complex task of transforming resistive attitudes to ICT to inculcate the pursuit of continuous improvement in teaching practice and nurturing the habit of sharing problems and solutions.

A significant challenge for educational leaders would be adequately supporting educators as they learn, explore, share and experiment with diverse ways of integrating ICT in authentic and meaningful ways in curriculum delivery, teaching and learning (Crawford, 2023). They must provide necessary resources as well as motivate and guide those educators in a post-pandemic world in order for them to become proficient in designing courses that promote online learning while maintaining control of virtual teaching and learning environments. The pandemic created dramatic enough circumstances for educational leaders to urgently convince educators that investing their energy and time in implementing ICT-intensive strategies is valuable.

Within many HEI settings, there is the unrealistic expectation that someone possessing minimal ICT expertise can still successfully make significant financial, pedagogical and developmental decisions. While they may be well-versed in educational programme development and the management of curriculum delivery, teaching and learning, many educational leaders in Malaysia might not always have sufficient ICT expertise to make correct choices and decisions. Educational leaders can often be unprepared in their supplementary role as technology leaders and, as a result, struggle to develop the technological and human resources necessary to implement effectively. The gap in ICT knowledge and lack of leadership preparation about digital literacy for educational environments can cause problems. Educational leaders with limited proficiency in ICT applications might often decide poorly, wasting funds on unnecessary hardware and software or, conversely, not allocating enough funding to purchase the right things.

## Adapting Curriculum Delivery and Teaching to the Post-Pandemic Generation of Learners

It has become primordial for educators in Malaysian HEIs to acquire new knowledge as well as to develop new skills and competencies to handle virtual classrooms, manage ICT effectively and ensure that their students' learning results in the acquisition of appropriate knowledge and skills that will make them employable in a globalised world. Educators are responsible for guiding learners towards a more self-directed style of learning that departs from their preferred learning styles with which they feel more comfortable. As such, students' competence in learning technologies must be considered when designing strategies for learning and facilitating learning.

Lo et al. (2015, p. 844) explain how the findings of their 2015 study of an e-learning system among university students in Malaysia "suggest that when a proper ICT is in place and properly utilised, it could foster and improve teaching and learning and, with that, the instructors or facilitators in the classrooms will have to change their teaching styles and be more technology savvy." According to a study conducted by Al-Rahmi et al. (2018) on the usage of social media in Malaysian higher education, their findings support the notion that it positively impacts collaborative learning and student engagement. The study reveals that students' satisfaction, perceived ease of use and perceived usefulness of social media significantly influence their engagement in collaborative learning activities, consequently leading to improved learning performance. The results highlight the potential benefits of leveraging social media platforms to enhance educational experiences and outcomes.

Although originally created as tools for communicating socially online, Facebook, Twitter and other social media applications have also been utilised in some Malaysian HEIs to facilitate immediateness, sharing information and learner-created content and interaction and engagement outside physical classrooms. Abdullah et al. (2022, p. 5) comment that the "usage of effective collaborative online tools has been found to increase student satisfaction towards online learning as they become more independent and adaptive to the sudden changes" and that "in the long run, social interaction among students in the online environment creates meaningful dialogues and fosters positive relationships."

HEIs are now populated mainly by learners belonging to the 'net generation' who use ICT and social media tools all day. Compared to previous generations of learners, 'net gen' higher education students expect to acquire different knowledge and skills for future life and work after graduation (Yadegaridehkordi et al., 2019). The need to update the teaching strategies to suit newer learners was already recognised before the pandemic. It has become more pertinent in the post-pandemic higher education landscape.

## The Future of Higher Education in Post-Pandemic Malaysia

As online learning continues to develop in the post-pandemic world, according to Abdullah et al. (2022, p. 16):

> necessary adjustments need to be made by HEIs to ensure that courses remain relevant and beneficial for students, and to limit the disruption to the entire education system. With the move of many HEIs in offering online courses, there is an increased responsibility to understand how technology can be harnessed to provide students with the best learning experiences, and to better prepare them for the changing future needs.

There is no doubt about the immense potential of ICT-intensive strategies in Malaysian HEIs to enhance curriculum delivery, teaching and learning outcomes, enabling students to achieve deep understanding. The COVID-19 pandemic has accelerated the adoption of remote, virtual and online teaching methods as a necessary response to ensure continuity of education. As highlighted by Ma et al. (2022), the rapid shift from traditional face-to-face instruction to e-learning has not only served as an emergency measure. However, it has also become a transformative force reshaping the landscape of higher education. "Whether viewed as an emergency pivot or policy expedient, shifting from face-to-face to remote/virtual/distance and/or online teaching […] could become a new (post-pandemic) reality for academics and students alike, changing HE forever" (Ma et al., 2022, p. 842).

Educational leaders in Malaysian HEIs need to recognise the inevitability and urgency of implementing ICT-intensive strategies, immaterial of associated costs and complexities. They must effectively navigate the re-calibration of curriculum delivery, teaching and learning processes. By doing so, they can ensure that students develop the necessary attributes and skills to contribute to an ICT-intensive economy. This proactive approach is essential for fostering a 'knowledge economy' and 'knowledge society' in post-pandemic Malaysia. The objectives will be supported by the promising policies of the latest Twelfth Malaysia Plan 2021–2025 (2021, p. 454) that proposes:

four policy enablers, which encompass developing future talent, accelerating technology adoption and innovation, enhancing connectivity and transport infrastructure, as well as strengthening the public service. As the demand for high-skilled as well as technology and digital savvy workforce increases, the country's education system will be further improved by enhancing digital education.

Even though there have been tangible achievements and good progress so far, it may be argued that the biggest challenge for educational leaders is to permanently alter decades of somewhat 'negative' pre-digital mindsets and attitudes in HEIs towards the implementation of ICT-intensive strategies and ultimately to re-invent Malaysian higher education to suit a post-pandemic world.

## References

Abdullah, S. I. N. W., Arokiyasamy, K., Goh, S. L., Culas, A. J., & Manaf, N. M. A. (2022). University students' satisfaction and future outlook towards forced remote learning during a global pandemic. *Smart Learning Environments, 9*(15), 1–21. https://doi.org/10.1186/s40561-022-00197-8

Adams, D., Hwee, M. J. T., & Sumintono, B. (2020). Students' readiness for blended learning in a leading Malaysian private higher education institution. *Interactive Technology and Smart Education, 17*(2), 117–129.

Ainin, S., Naqshbandi, M. M., Moghavvemi, S., & Jaafar, N. I. (2015). Facebook usage, socialization and academic performance. *Computers & Education, 83*, 64–73.

Ajjan, H., & Hartshorne, R. (2008). Investigating faculty decisions to adopt web 2.0 technologies: Theory and empirical tests. *The Internet and Higher Education, 11*(2), 71–80.

Al-Rahmi, W. M., Alias, N., Othman, M. S., Marin, V., & Tur, G. (2018). A model of factors affecting learning performance through the use of social media in Malaysian higher education. *Computers & Education, 121*, 59–72.

Al-Rahmi, W. M., Othman, M. S., & Yusuf, L. M. (2015). The role of social media for collaborative learning to improve academic performance of students and researchers in Malaysian higher education. *International Review of Research in Open and Distributed Learning, 16*(4), 177–204.

Al-araibi, A. A. M., Mahrin, M. N., Yusoff, R. C. M., & Chuprat, S. B. (2019). A model for technological aspect of e-learning readiness in higher education. *Education and Information Technologies, 24*, 1395–1431.

Azizan, S. N., Lee, A. S. H., Crosling, G., Atherton, G., Arulanandam, B. V., Lee, C. E., & Rahim, R. B. A. (2022). Online learning and COVID-19 in higher education: The value of IT models in assessing students' satisfaction. *ASEAN Journal of Teaching & Learning in Higher Education, 17*(3), 245–278.

Bajunid, I. A. (2011). Leadership in the reform of Malaysian universities: Analysing the strategic role of the Malaysian qualifications agency. *Journal of Higher Education Policy and Management, 33*(3), 253–265.

Bottery, M. (2006). Educational leaders in a globalising world: A new set of priorities? *School Leadership & Management, 26*(1), 5–22.

Crawford, J. (2023). COVID-19 and higher education: A pandemic response model from rapid adaption to consolidation and restoration. *International Education Journal: Comparative Perspectives, 22*(1), 7–29.

Flanders Investment and Trade. (2022). *Coronavirus—The situation in Malaysia.* https://www.flandersinvestmentandtrade.com/export/nieuws/coronavirus-%E2%80%93-situation-malaysia

Harland, T., Hussain, R. M., & Abu Bakar, A. (2014). The scholarship of teaching and learning: Challenges for Malaysian academics. *Teaching in Higher Education, 19*(1), 38–48.

Inayatullah, S., & Milojević, I. (2014). Augmented reality, the murabbi and the democratization of higher education: Alternative futures of higher education in Malaysia. *On the Horizon, 22*(2), 110–126.

Jafar, A., Dollah, R., Dambul, R., Mittal, P., Ahmad, S. A., Sakke, N., Mapa, M. T., Joko, E. P., Eboy, O. V., Jamru, L. R., & Andika, A. W. (2022). Virtual learning during COVID-19: Exploring challenges and identifying highly vulnerable groups based on location. *International Journal of Environmental Research and Public Health, 19*. https://doi.org/10.3390/ijerph191711108

Lai, K. W., & Hong, K. S. (2015). Technology use and learning characteristics of students in higher education: Do generational differences exist? *British Journal of Educational Technology, 46*(4), 725–738.

Lee, C. E. C., Sooria, V., Kutty, S., & Wong, S. P. (2015). Exploring the use of Facebook in the classroom: A Malaysian case study. In *Proceedings of the European conference on e-learning* (pp. 262–260).

Lim, J. S. Y., Agostinho, S., Harper, B., & Chicharo, J. F. (2014). The engagement of social media technologies by undergraduate informatics students for academic purpose in Malaysia. *Journal of Information, Communication and Ethics in Society, 12*(3), 177–194.

Litz, D. (2011). Globalisation and the changing face of educational leadership: Current trends and emerging dilemmas. *International Education Studies, 4*(3), 47–61.

Lo, M. C., Thurasamy, R., & Mohamad, A. A. (2015). Does intention really lead to actual use of technology? A study of an e-learning system among university students in Malaysia. *Croatian Journal of Education, 17*(3), 835–863.

Ma, G., Black, K., Blenkinsopp, J., Charlton, H., Hookham, C., Wei, F. P., Bee, C. S., & Alkarabsheh, O. H. M. (2022). Higher education under threat: China, Malaysia, and the UK respond to the COVID-19 pandemic. *Compare: A Journal of Comparative and International Education, 52*(5), 841–857. https://doi.org/10.1080/03057925.2021.1879479

Mercurius, N. (2006). *Leadership: Become a digital-age thinker*. Tech and Learning. http://www.techlearning.com/story/showArticle.jhtml?articleID=180204173

Merriam, S. B., & Mohammed, M. (2000). How cultural values shape learning in older adulthood: The case of Malaysia. *Adult Education Quarterly, 51*(1), 45–63.

Ministry of Higher Education (MOHE). (2007). *Ministry of national education action plan (2007–2010)*. MOHE.

Ministry of Higher Education (MOHE). (2015). *Malaysia education blueprint 2015–2025 (higher education)*. MOHE.

Moorthy, K., Loh, C. T., Khor, M. W., Tan, P. Z. M., Chai, Y. Y., Lim, K. J. W., & Yue, M. X. (2019). Is Facebook useful for learning? A study in private universities in Malaysia. *Computers & Education, 130*, 94–104.

Multimedia Super Corridor Development Corporation. (2008). *MSC Malaysia national rollout 2020*. http://www.mscmalaysia.my/

National Information Technology Council (NITC). (2019a). *National information technology agenda*. http://www.nitc.org.my/resources/integratedplatform.html

National Information Technology Council (NITC). (2019b). *Strategic trusts agenda*. http://www.nitc.org.com

Noh, N. M., Siraj, S., Jamil, M. R. M., Husin, Z., & Sapar, A. A. (2015). Design of guideline on the learning psychology in the use of Facebook as a medium for teaching and learning in secondary school. *The Turkish Online Journal of Educational Technology, 14*(1), 39–44.

Onorato, M. (2013). Transformational leadership style in the educational sector: An empirical study of corporate managers and educational leaders. *Academy of Educational Leadership Journal, 17*(1), 33–47.

Rangel, E., Sueyoshi, A., & Samsudin, R. S. (2018). Similarities and differences on higher education policy across the Pacific Rim: Japan, Malaysia and Mexico. *Pacific-Asian Education, 30*, 33–46.

Riggio, R. E., & Newstead, T. (2023). Crisis leadership. *Annual Review of Organizational Psychology and Organizational Behavior, 10*, 201–224.

Roblyer, D., McDaniel, M., Webb, M., Herman, J., & Witty, V. (2010). Findings on Facebook in higher education: A Comparison of college faculty and student uses and perceptions of social networking sites. *The Internet and Higher Education, 13*(3), 134–140.

Rosnizah, S., Diyana, K., Soon-Yew, J., & Haziman, Z. (2022). Effects of leadership types on job satisfaction among Malaysian higher education institutions. *Asian Journal of Instruction, 10*(1), 54–70. https://doi.org/10.47215/aji.1020324

Selvaratnam, V. (2016). Malaysia's higher education and quest for developed nation status by 2020. *Southeast Asia Affairs*, 199–222.

Sia, J., & Adamu, A. (2021). Facing the unknown: Pandemic and higher education in Malaysia. *Asian Education and Development Studies, 10*(2), 263–275.

Sofiadin, A. B. M. (2014). Sustainable development, e-learning and web 3.0—A descriptive literature review. *Journal of Information, Communication and Ethics in Society, 12*(3), 157–176.
Tan, Y., & Muna, S. (2011). The role of universities in building prosperous knowledge cities: The Malaysian experience. *Built Environment, 37*(3), 260–280.
Thang, S. M., Nambiar, R., Wong, F. F., Jaafar, N. M., & Amir, Z. (2015). A clamour for more technology in universities: What does an investigation into the ICT use and learning styles of Malaysian 'digital natives' tell us? *Asia-Pacific Education Research, 24*(2), 353–361.
Thomas, P. Y. (2011). Cloud computing: A potential paradigm for practising the scholarship of teaching and learning. *Electronic Library, 29*(2), 214–224.
Tice, D., Baumeister, R., Crawford, J., Allen, K. A., & Percy, A. (2021). Student belongingness in higher education: Lessons for Professors from the COVID-19 pandemic. *Journal of University Teaching & Learning Practice, 18*(4), 2. https://doi.org/10.53761/1.18.4.2
*Twelfth Malaysia Plan 2021–2025*—Prime Minister's Department. (2021). *Twelfth Malaysia plan 2021–2025*. Percetakan Nasional Malaysia Berhad. https://rmke12.epu.gov.my/en
Wan, C. D., Chapman, D., Hutcheson, S., Lee, M., Austin, A., & Ahmad, N. M. Z. (2017). Changing higher education practice in Malaysia: The conundrum of incentives. *Studies in Higher Education, 42*(11), 2134–2152.
Ya, S. W. (2020). *Education during COVID-19*. Institute for Democracy and Economic Affairs. https://www.researchgate.net/publication/340860261_Education_during_COVID-19
Yadegaridehkordi, E., Shuib, L., Nilash, M., & Asadi, S. A. (2019). Decision to adopt online collaborative learning tools in higher education: A case of top Malaysian universities. *Education Information Technology, 24*, 79–102.
Yusuf, S., & Nabeshima, K. (2009). *Tiger economies under threat: A comparative analysis of Malaysia's industrial prospects and policy options*. World Bank.
Zain, N. M., Aspah, V., Mohmud, N. A., Abdullah, N., & Ebrahimi, M. (2017). Challenges and evolution of higher education in Malaysia. *International Journal of Islamic and Civilisational Studies, 4*(1), 78–87.

# Higher Education in Mozambique in the Post-pandemic: Lessons Learned and the Future of Education

Hélio Rogério Martins, José Luis Sousa Manjate, and Iolanda Filipa Rodrigues Cavaleiro Tinga

## Introduction

Mozambique is located in the eastern part of Southern Africa, bordering the Indian Ocean on the east (Government of Mozambique, 2023). Estimates from the National Institute of Statistics (2023) indicate a population of over 32,400,000 inhabitants, with about two-thirds living in rural areas. According to the 2021–2022 Human Development Index, Mozambique ranks 185 out of 191 countries evaluated, thus being considered a country of low human development, with an average life expectancy of around 60 years (The United Nations Development Programme, 2022).

As in most African countries, Mozambique confirmed the first case of COVID-19 several weeks after the outbreak in China and subsequent spread worldwide. More specifically, the first case of COVID-19 in the country was confirmed on March 22, 2020 (Ministry of Health, 2020). Three days later, the government established a technical-scientific commission with the mandate to advise and assist in the response to COVID-19 (Ministry of Health, 2021a). To contain the spread of the disease in the country, on March 30, 2020, a state of emergency was declared for 30 days (Bulletin

H. R. Martins (✉) · I. F. R. C. Tinga
Instituto Superior de Ciências de Saúde, Maputo, Mozambique
e-mail: heliorogerio.martins@gmail.com

J. L. S. Manjate
Ministry of Education and Human Development, Maputo, Mozambique



J. Rudolph et al. (eds.), *The Palgrave Handbook of Crisis Leadership in Higher Education*,
https://doi.org/10.1007/978-3-031-54509-2_21

of the Republic, 2020b). The choice made by the Mozambican Government was guided by the epidemiological situation in the nations hit hardest by the virus, since at the moment of this pronouncement the country had documented eight cases of COVID-19 (National Health Observatory, 2021).

The National Health Observatory (2021) indicates that during the first year of the pandemic in Mozambique (from March 2020 to March 2021), there were two waves, the first between September and November 2020, with an average of 143 cases per day and the second between January and March 2021, with 536 cases on daily average (National Health Observatory, 2021). From the time of the first case notification until April 19, 2023, Mozambique documented 233,334 COVID-19 cases, resulting in 2242 fatalities, indicating a lethality rate of below 1% (World Health Organization [WHO], 2023). Concerning vaccinations, WHO reports that approximately 13 million vaccine doses had been distributed across the country by mid-April 2023. However, the number of individuals covered was not specified (WHO, 2023). Nevertheless, the national vaccination plan outlined to vaccinate about 17 million people, approximately 55% of the country's population, which did not include children under 15 years of age and pregnant women, as at the time, there was a lack of information on the efficacy and safety of vaccines in these groups (MISAU, 2021). Although Mozambique faced a milder epidemic when compared to other countries in the region, the national response plan points out weaknesses in terms of human and financial resources, infrastructure and capacity to manage public health emergencies (Ministry of Health, 2021b).

Regarding the economy, estimates indicate that the gross domestic product grew 3.6% less than it would have grown without COVID-19, and the employment rate was reduced by around 2% (Betho et al., 2021). A survey on the impact of COVID-19 on urban households indicates that two-thirds of respondents stated that they did not have a job in the seven days prior to the survey from July to November 2020, with between 12 and 17% being people who worked before COVID-19 (da Maia et al., 2021).

This chapter was written based on the literature review and official information from the Government of Mozambique on the evolution and impact of COVID-19 in the country and research by various entities in the health and education sectors. We also relied on our experience as university lecturers who had to adapt the teaching and learning process during a health emergency never before experienced in the country vis-a-vis an attempt to adjust our duties to the recommendations issued by the Ministry of Higher Education. To better frame and understand the problem, we described the onset and evolution of higher education in Mozambique. We believe the current status reflects the historical higher education process that began in the colonial era.

The COVID-19 pandemic was a landmark event in all spheres of social life in the country, and in this chapter, we seek to discuss the impact and lessons learned during the pandemic. More than a mere academic exercise or a recording of an unprecedented historical event, this research can contribute to a broad reflection on higher education in Mozambique and its role in society.

## Context

Higher education in Mozambique began in 1962, still in the colonial era, with the establishment of the General and University Studies of Mozambique, which later evolved into the University of Lourenço Marques (1968). After the independence in 1975, the University of Lourenço Marques was renamed Eduardo Mondlane University and remained the only higher education institution until 1985, when the Higher Pedagogical Institute was established (Langa, 2014; Taimo, 2010), today renamed Pedagogical University of Maputo. Until 1990, the socialist system was in force in Mozambique, and, as a result, there were no private educational institutions.

When the country adopted the democratic system in the 1990 constitution, legislative reforms became possible, and private entities could act in education. This is how the first private higher education institutions (HEIs) were established in the country in 1995 (Langa, 2014). From then on, higher education entered an era of rapid expansion, with the establishment of several public and private HEIs, rising the number to 38 in 2010 (Ministry of Education, 2012). Currently, Mozambique has 53 Higher Education Institutions, 31 of which are private and 22 are public (Minister of Science, Technology and Higher Education [MCTES], 2023).

Higher education in Mozambique had a period of rapid expansion in a context where the regulatory institutions were not firmly established (Rosário, 2013). With about sixty years of existence, higher education in Mozambique can be described as a traditional model based on face-to-face classes, where the use of digital resources and distance learning is still limited and with gaps in terms of expansion and regulation (Brito, 2010; Mombassa & Arruda, 2018). Despite this, records of the first experiences with distance learning date back to the 1980s and 90s, when primary school teachers were trained through correspondence and printed material (Neeleman & Nhavoto, 2003). In a more structured format, distance learning entered a new era with the creation of the National Institute of Distance Education (INED) in 2006. INED was created as a coordinating institution to develop policies, regulations, strategies and technological infrastructures to implement a quality distance learning system in Mozambique (Bulletin of the Republic, 2006).

In 2013, the government released the Distance Education Strategy (2014–2018), acknowledging that distance learning was in its early stages during that period. This era was marked by a preference for printed materials over information and communication technologies (ICT). Nevertheless, certain Higher Education Institutions (HEIs) have begun incorporating ICT despite facing challenges from students and educators (Republic of Mozambique, 2013). The strategy also indicates a prevailing shortage of specialised personnel in distance learning and scepticism about this teaching model.

## Teaching and Learning During COVID-19 in Mozambique

### Early Measures to Contain the Spread of COVID-19

Mozambique is part of the last group of countries to notify the first cases of COVID-19 when there was already more evidence about the nature of the disease and preventive measures. There were also experiences from other countries that could serve as examples, with the necessary adaptations to the local context. Therefore, the officials decided not to wait for the uncontrolled spread of the disease and put in place the first measures considered more impactful in preventing the transmission of COVID-19, such as the control of migratory movements and the suspension and or limitation of all events that led to massive gatherings of people.

On March 20, 2020, the Mozambican Government suspended in-person classes for thirty days, effective from March 23 (MCTESTP, 2020). This was one of the initial measures taken to mitigate the spread of COVID-19, just prior to the nation confirming its first case of the illness. More comprehensive measures were introduced through a presidential decree declaring a state of emergency, effective April 1, 2020. Alongside suspending on-site classes ranging from preschool to higher education, the government also imposed restrictions on or suspended activities involving large gatherings, including sports, cultural, religious and commercial events and public transportation norms. Furthermore, certain activities were subjected to stringent protocols to be permitted (Bulletin of the Republic, 2020b).

Initially scheduled to last 30 days, the suspension of face-to-face classes ended up being extended for the rest of the first semester, given the continuous increase in the number of cases and the spread of the epidemic in the country, which led the government to extend the state of emergency for three times (Bulletin of the Republic, 2020a). The United Nations estimates indicate that the suspension of classes covered around 8,530,000 students across the country, of which 101,000 were in preschool education, 6,900,000 in primary education, 1,250,000 in secondary education, 85,000 in technical-professional education and around 200,000 in higher education (The United Nations in Mozambique, 2020).

## Strategies for Continuity with Classes

In order to maintain the progression of classes during the suspension of in-person activities, the Ministry of Science, Technology, and Higher Education issued an official communication instructing higher education institutions to create plans for this period. They were advised to utilise digital tools like email, Google Classroom and WhatsApp to ensure the continuation of instructional activities (MCTESTP, 2020). The government's guidelines for sustaining the teaching and learning process involved the development of plans to recuperate missed classes and engage students in academic pursuits. In contrast, face-to-face classes were put on hold. This implies that the government initially anticipated a brief pause in on-site classes. Consequently, the initial directives were not intended to facilitate continuous adherence to the syllabus for teaching and learning.

The progression of the COVID-19 pandemic, both within the country and globally, indicated that the prompt reinstatement of classes was becoming progressively uncertain. As a result, the academic calendar was poised to be influenced until the eventual return to in-person instruction. Consequently, the implementation of remote teaching and learning was initiated. The effectiveness and timing of these instructional activities were determined by the individual institution's capabilities and organisational readiness, governing how and when remote teaching would proceed.

## Prior Experience with Online Classes

According to Cristóvão and Jr (2021), of the 53 HEIs in the country, only 11 had experience with distance learning when COVID-19 started, eight of which were private and three public; the first to be established in the country.

The rest of HEI experienced the process of online teaching for the first time. An online survey on the teaching and learning process during the pandemic period, carried out in May 2020 and answered by 6224 students of 43 public and private HEIs, showed that about 51% of these used digital platforms for the first time in the teaching and learning process during the epidemic (Martins et al., 2021a). Given that this was the first time where slightly more than half of the students utilised digital tools to engage in classes, approximately 64% displayed limited or moderate confidence in employing these platforms for online sessions. Furthermore, around 87% of students encountered internet-related challenges during the initial months when classes were suspended (Martins et al., 2021a).

Regarding student satisfaction with the remote teaching and learning process, about 80% felt difficulties adapting, and approximately 65% perceived that quality had been reduced (Martins et al., 2021a). The perception of quality problems in remote teaching leads to questioning the competencies that these students acquired during that period. However, this is not a problem exclusive to Mozambique, as similar issues were also evident in other countries, where there was not much sympathy for online classes and assessments, and students felt that their intellectual capacity and abilities were questioned (Dey & Alamman, 2021).

Several factors may have influenced poor satisfaction with online classes. On the one hand, there were hardships related to the quality of the internet and confidence in using digital platforms, as mentioned above. However, on the other hand, this transition was made without preparation, and students received little to almost no assistance with the difficulties they encountered. Coupled with the pandemic's impact on student well-being, encompassing feelings of anxiety, stress and despair were recognised (Bao, 2020; Baticulon et al., 2020; Hasan & Bao, 2020). These may have created an unfavourable environment for an effective learning process.

On the teachers' side, the survey carried out by the National Council for Quality Assessment indicated that in 80% of the 890 courses offered in higher education, 76–100% of teachers were able to switch to online teaching, and in about 16% of courses 51–75% of teachers did not move to online classes (Cristóvão & Jr, 2021). Data from another online survey by 417 teachers about their experience with remote teaching and learning during the pandemic indicates that 71% received instructions from their institutions about continuing online classes. However, only 50% could teach all subjects in this modality. Among those who could not, the obstacles were the internet and the difficulty of adapting and teaching some content in the virtual system (Martins et al., 2021b). Almost 80% felt that the teaching and learning process quality had been affected, with 77% stating that their students' performance was low or reasonable. However, just over half (55%) of teachers assumed that they did not adapt well to migrating to online teaching (Martins et al., 2021b).

During the emergency period, most Higher Education Institutions (HEIs) utilised multiple platforms for teaching. Notably, several studies underline that the prominent platforms for online classes during the Mozambican COVID-19 period encompassed Google Classroom, WhatsApp, email, Zoom, and Skype (Cristóvão & Jr, 2021; Martins et al., 2021b; Zunguze & Tsambe, 2020). Adopting various platforms was expected due to HEIs lacking prior experience with this instructional approach (Cristóvão & Jr, 2021). Nevertheless, the utilisation of these platforms was not notably significant, even when the institution's designated learning platform was available.

The study by Zunguze and Tsambe (2020) at the Pedagogical University of Maputo, the second largest in the country and with experience in distance learning, shows that the institution's specific learning platform falls in third place (after WhatsApp and email). These findings are linked to over half (52%) of educators not being trained to utilise the institution's designated teaching and learning platform. Furthermore, a significant portion of students can solely access the internet through their mobile phones, resulting in limitations when attempting more intricate activities such as engaging with learning platforms.

## Return to Face-to-Face Classes

The resumption of on-site classes in all education subsystems was allowed by decree 21/2020 and occurred in two phases (Bulletin of the Republic, 2020a). Specifically for higher education, the enactment established that, in the first stage, only the last two levels of the courses would return to in-class activities, and the remaining levels would do so later. This measure intended to have a more controlled process that would not pose significant risks in the event of transmission of COVID-19 in the academic community. The Ministry of Science, Technology, and Higher Education established a mechanism to monitor cases of COVID-19 in HEIs, and the most recent data indicate that 752 positive cases were registered from January 31 to February 4, 2022 (this number refers to the university community, not just the students). The situation remained unchanged from May 16 to 20, according to the last update on the Ministry's official website (MCTES, 2022).

Returning to in-site classes was quite heterogeneous in the Mozambican HEIs. Between fears of rapid transmission of COVID-19 in the university space and the need to return to the 'old normality' activities, each institution returned to on-site classes. In the first phase of the recovery, with only the last two levels returning, the university community would not be more than 50%, and all students could attend their classes in rooms where a minimum distance of 1 to 1.5 m between them was possible. However, this is not the reality of most HEIs, as many struggle to provide adequate infrastructure (Langa, 2014; Ministry of Education, 2012).

What happened in some cases, if not many, was the adoption of a kind of hybrid model, where part of the class had face-to-face classes at the institution (with the recommended minimum distance), and the others had lessons from home, using digital platforms. Therefore, the teacher was simultaneously teaching face-to-face and online classes. It is legitimate to assume that students who attended the classes from the university were at some advantage compared to their peers who learned via online classes. The students on-site did not suffer internet instabilities, interferences or distractions in their houses. In addition, teachers tend to pay more attention to those in the classroom, as this was the teaching modality they were used to. They could keep eye contact, read non-verbal language and have more direct interaction with them. Some institutions implemented a method to infuse more dynamism into the process by using a rotation system among class groups. This arrangement ensured that each group experienced in-person and online classes every other week.

Also noteworthy in this process of resuming classes was the recommendation issued by the health entities to instal hand washing and disinfection points in HEIs, apart from the mandatory use of facemasks. Many HEIs did accomplish these guidelines and placed hand washing and disinfection points, especially at the entrances of the institutions. Many HEIs also took action to measure students' temperatures and approach those whose temperature was suggestive of fever. Some HEIs suspended activities to proceed with the disinfection of facilities, especially when positive cases were confirmed in the academic community.

## Higher Education Post-COVID-19

One of the most prominent aspects of the post-pandemic period are the hybrid or virtual events in academic spaces, such as meetings and scientific events. In terms of teaching and learning, there is a tendency towards an almost absolute return to the face-to-face model in most institutions. However, some adopted hybrid teaching to manage the limited number of classrooms they have. During COVID-19, the higher education law (law 27/

2009 of September 29) went to revision due to the need to adjust various matters related to teaching and research, including teaching modalities in the digital era (O País, 2022). Although COVID-19 was not a direct reason for this review, as the debate on digital transformation and the use of ICT in teaching and learning was already underway, it may have acted as a wake-up call for more effective action. Nevertheless, these matters have been part of several higher education policy and management documents in Mozambique before the pandemic, and their implementation has systematically fallen short.

The new higher education law highlights the technological infrastructure as an essential component and a requirement for the opening and functioning of new HEIs, as well as the existence of a qualified teaching staff adjusted to the teaching model that the institution intends to follow, whether face-to-face, hybrid or distance learning (Assembly of the Republic, 2023). This represents strengthening the regulatory mechanisms for higher education, which could favour institutions' compliance with the minimum quality requirements.

We envision a post-COVID-19 period where students and teachers are more familiar with virtual teaching environments and are open to taking advantage of the facilities provided by these tools. Due to various limitations, such as access to stable internet and access to devices at affordable costs, academics and institutions are more reluctant to adopt a hybrid teaching modality. However, due to its interactive advantage and because it enables quick interaction and shortens distances, virtual teaching can now constitute a viable alternative with more supporters but not a total substitute for face-to-face teaching. Moreover, the number of distance courses in HEIs is increasing, possibly because of the demystification of their disadvantages and/or the growth of their credibility derived from their use during the COVID-19 pandemic.

The courses offered in the face-to-face modality need to have their organisation restructured to accommodate the needs and potentialities of hybrid teaching, especially regarding assessments. There is still a great reluctance to assess students virtually because teachers are suspicious of their behaviour or because it is an obstacle for students with inadequate mastery. By experiencing learning in the pandemic context, we believe that the prognosis is favourable to overcome the handicaps that may arise from the academic environment, namely the management of time and space for learning.

In short, despite the gaps and challenges that were noted in the teaching and learning process during the pandemic, from the structural problems of lack of electronic devices and low coverage and stability of the internet to the challenges related to the preparation of teachers and students to use this teaching modality, the experience of HEIs with COVID-19 stresses the importance of HEIs creating or strengthening their capacity to teach using the hybrid model and could dictate a paradigm shift in online teaching.

## Discussion

Looking at teaching and learning after the pandemic, we can say that COVID-19 highlighted the importance of investing in digital resources for teaching activities, as it has uncovered the weaknesses of the infrastructures and digital resources that the institutions had. The first guidelines issued when the government suspended face-to-face classes show that the officials expected that the COVID-19 pandemic would be surpassed quickly. The rationale behind the recommendations was to formulate strategies for compensating for missed classes and engaging students in educational endeavours while schools were inaccessible. These suggestions underscore the conventional framework on which the Mozambican education system relies, centred around in-person instruction. Simultaneously, they acknowledge the absence of suitable circumstances for a seamless shift from traditional face-to-face teaching to remote methods.

This challenge in transitioning and adjusting to remote learning was evident in the prolonged planned activities from the 2020 academic year to 2021. In numerous Higher Education Institutions (HEIs), the academic year, usually from February to November/December, stretches until March or April of 2021. This delay had lasting effects, extending into the initial months of 2023, with certain institutions still finalising tasks related to the second semester of the 2022 academic year.

The difficulties faced during the COVID-19 pandemic can be easily attributed to the country's financial constraints that mainly affect public HEI, which have limited budgets to invest in their infrastructures. However, for a long time, the HEI grew in number, and policies reveal that the primary concern of the government entities was to expand access to higher education to increase the number of skilled labourers and reduce the country's asymmetries. In recent years, it has been possible to pay more attention to quality issues, from infrastructure to the qualification of the teaching staff. Thus, the longstanding lack of investment in technology and infrastructure explains why students and teachers were less confident in using ICT in the teaching and learning process during COVID-19.

Although Mozambique has taken advantage of controlling the pandemic by being one of the last countries to register the first cases of the COVID-19 pandemic, in the field of education, this has not translated into substantial advantages in terms of the strategies taken by government officials for the continuity of the teaching and learning process, as the measures taken have not found a favourable environment and infrastructure for the use of ICT in education. Thus, leadership could have been more assertive in analysing the pre-pandemic reality and indicating the resources and adaptations HEIs should have made for a more effective transition.

In Mozambique, with the measures to contain the COVID-19 pandemic decreasing and with the necessary adjustments on the academic calendar, it was possible to restore normality in the teaching–learning process in most higher education institutions after about two academic years, characterised by the predominant return of face-to-face teaching activities. Containment measures such as using masks and alcohol or proper hand washing were maintained in the institutional spaces to prevent possible cases of COVID-19.

Higher education institutions realise, more than ever, the importance of acquiring and operating functional institutional platforms for current demands and the need to make virtual bibliography available. As for teachers, some institutions are already looking for e-learning qualified professionals or training their current staff to become apt for distance learning, and curricula for face-to-face teaching courses tend to include blended learning methodologies, as it is now a requirement for the accreditation of courses in higher education.

Although the main agenda of public entities is the resumption of economic, social and cultural activities that could not be accomplished while COVID-19 remained a public health emergency, debates on building resilience are common as a way to withstand the impact of adverse events such as what happened with the pandemic, but also the impact of extreme weather events that increasingly affect the country. Hence, the lessons learned from COVID-19 will always be considered in general teaching and higher education decision-making processes.

## References

Assembly of the Republic. (2023). *Law 1/2023: Law establishing the legal framework of the higher education subsystem and repealing law 27/2009 of 29 September* (H. Martins, Trans.). (Original document published 2023).

Bao, W. (2020). COVID-19 and online teaching in higher education: A case study of Peking University. *Human Behavior and Emerging Technologies, 2*(2), 113–115. https://doi.org/10.1002/hbe2.191

Baticulon, R. E., Alberto, N. R. I., Baron, M. B. C., Mabulay, R. E. C., Rizada, L. G. T., Sy, J. J., Tiu, C. J. S., Clarion, C. A., & Reyes, J. C. B. (2020). Barriers to online learning in the time of COVID-19: A national survey of medical students in the Philippines. *Medical Science Educator, 31*, 615–626. https://doi.org/10.1101/2020.07.16.20155747

Betho, R., Chelengo, M., Jones, S., Keller, M., Mussagy, I. H., van Seventer D., & Tarp F. (2021). *The macroeconomic impact of COVID-19 in Mozambique: A social accounting matrix-based approach* (WIDER Working Paper 2021/93). UNU-WIDER.

Brito, C. E. (2010). *Distance education in higher education in Mozambique* (H. Martins, Trans.). 252.

Bulletin of the Republic. (2006). *Decree 49/2006: Creates the national institute for distance education* (H. Martins, Trans.).

Bulletin of the Republic. (2020a). *Presidential decree No. 11/2020: Declares a state of emergency for reasons of public calamity time* (H. Martins, Trans.). Presidency of the Republic.

Bulletin of the Republic. (2020b). *Decree 51/2020 of 1 July: Extends the state of emergency for reasons of public calamity throughout the national territory for the third time* (H. Martins, Trans.). National Press of Mozambique.

Cristóvão, L., & Jr, P. M. (2021). Higher education in Mozambique during Covid-19. *Journal of Progressive Research in Social Sciences, 11*(1) 1–6.

da Maia, C., Myers, C., Negre, M., Tiroso, C., Duce, P., & Dade, A. (2021). *Report of the survey on the impact of Covid-19 on urban households in Mozambique, June-November 2020* (H. Martins, Trans.). National Institute of Statistics & World Bank.

Dey, S., & Alamman, P. (2021). 'Covid batch': A case study on unethical assessment practices in selected higher educational institutions in Assam and West Bengal, India. *Journal of Applied Learning and Teaching, 4*(2), 130–134. https://doi.org/10.37074/jalt.2021.4.2.11

Government of Mozambique. (2023). *Geography of Mozambique/Mozambique/home-portal of the government of Mozambique* (H. Martins, Trans.). https://www.portaldogoverno.gov.mz/por/Mocambique/Geografia-de-Mocambique

Hasan, N., & Bao, Y. (2020). Impact of "e-Learning crack-up" perception on psychological distress among college students during COVID-19 pandemic: A mediating role of "fear of academic year loss." *Children and Youth Services Review, 118*, 105355. https://doi.org/10.1016/j.childyouth.2020.105355

Langa, P. V. (2014). *Some challenges for higher education in Mozambique: From experiential knowledge to the need to produce scientific knowledge* (H. Martins, Trans.). Institute of Social and Economic Studies—Challenges for Mozambique.

Martins, H. R., Manjate, J. L., Tinga, I. C., Matusse, A. P. X., & Sitoe, L. C. A. (2021a). Online learning and COVID-19 outbreak in Mozambique-academics' experience during suspension of face-to-face classes. *Interactive Learning Environments*, 1–10. https://doi.org/10.1080/10494820.2021.1969954

Martins, H. R., Tinga, I. C., Manjate, J. L., Sitoe, L. C., & Matusse, A. P. X. (2021b). Online learning during COVID-19 emergency—A descriptive study of university students experience in Mozambique. *Journal of Applied Learning & Teaching, 4*(1), 29–37. https://doi.org/10.37074/jalt.2021.4.1.16

Minister of Science, Technology and Higher Education. (2022). *Status report on monitoring the effects of COVID-19 on higher education institutions* (H. Martins, Trans.). https://www.mctes.gov.mz/ponto-de-situacao-sobre-a-monitoria-dos-efeitos-da-covid-19-nas-instituicoes-de-ensino-superior-5/

Minister of Science, Technology and Higher Education. (2023). *Higher education institutions* (H. Martins, Trans.). https://www.mctes.gov.mz/instituicoes-de-ensino-superior/

Ministry of Science, Technology, Professional Technical and Higher Education.. (2020). *Measures to prevent the coronavirus pandemic (COVID-19) in Higher Education and Professional Technical Institutions* (169/MCTESTP/GM; Issue 169/MCTESTP/GM, p. 2) (H. Martins, Trans.).

Ministry of Education. (2012). *Higher education strategic plan 2012–2020* (p. 133) (H. Martins, Trans.). Ministry of Education.

Ministry of Health. (2020). *COVID-19 daily surveillance bulletin* (H. Martins, Trans.). https://www.misau.gov.mz/index.php/covid-19-boletins-diarios?start=620

Ministry of Health. (2021a, February 28). *COVID-19 Mozambique monthly bulletin* (H. Martins, Trans.).

Ministry of Health. (2021b). *National response plan for the COVID-19 pandemic* (H. Martins, Trans.). MISAU.

Mombassa, A. Z. B., & Arruda, E. P. (2018). History of distance education in Mozambique: Current perspectives and contributions from Brazil (H. Martins, Trans.). *Praxis Educativa, 13*(3) 643–660. https://doi.org/10.5212/PraxEduc.v.13i3.0001

National Health Observatory. (2021). *COVID-19 in Mozambique: First year report* (H. Martins, Trans.) MISAU.

National Institute of Statistics. (2023). *Demographic and social indicators*. http://www.ine.gov.mz.

Neeleman, W., & Nhavoto, A. (2003). Distance education in Mozambique (H. Martins, Trans.). *Brazilian Journal of Open and Distance Learning*, 1–8. https://doi.org/10.17143/rbaad.v2i0.132

O País. (2022, March 2). *National council for higher education approves revision of higher education law* (H. Martins, Trans.). Jornal o Pais. https://opais.co.mz/cnes-aprova-revisao-da-lei-do-ensino-superior/

Republic of Mozambique. (2013). *Distance education strategy 2014–2018* (H. Martins, Trans.). Conselho de Ministros.

Rosário, L. J. da C. (2013). Higher education in Africa: Mozambican universities and the future of Mozambique (H. Martins, Trans.). *Ensino Superior Unicamp, 10*, 46–55.

Taimo, J. U. (2010). *Higher education in Mozambique: History, policy and management* (H. Martins, Trans.). Ph.D. Thesis in Education, Faculty of Humanities at the Methodist University of Piracicaba, São Paulo. https://www.unimep.br/phpg/bibdig/pdfs/2006/USQUKAQXVOQD.pdf

The United Nations Development Programme. (2022). *Human development report 2021/2022: Uncertain times, unsettled lives. Shaping our future in a transforming world*. The United Nations Development Programme.

The United Nations in Mozambique. (2020). *United Nations multisectoral COVID-19 response plan* (H. Martins, Trans.).

World Health Organization. (2023). *Mozambique: WHO coronavirus disease (COVID-19) dashboard with vaccination data*. https://covid19.who.int

Zunguze, M. C., & Tsambe, M. Z. A. (2020). Perception of teachers in the use of electronic platforms to support face-to-face teaching during the term of the state of emergency due to Covid-19: Case of the pedagogical university of Maputo. *Renote, 18*(2), 2. https://doi.org/10.22456/1679-1916.110195

# Prospecting Educational Leadership in the Wake of COVID-19: An Aotearoa/New Zealand Narrative Study

Martin Andrew and Oonagh McGirr

## Introduction

Our Chapter shares voiced stories of a time of uncertainty and crisis from a small island-nation in the South Pacific, Aotearoa (New Zealand). We recount experiences of national governance and public-sector leadership in the time of Coronavirus (2019 onwards). Motivated by the need to narrate real-time, real-life experiences of peers and colleagues employed in higher education (HE) in our Vocational Education and Training (VET) sector, our interest is twofold. Narratives depict leadership in a time of unknown futures, characterised by an unexpected health emergency and a legislated sector recalibration. They recount the effects and consequences of a national reform from a practitioner perspective, providing hitherto unchartered embodied understandings of a group of tertiary education professionals in Aotearoa.

Since the outbreak of COVID-19, the concept of 'leadership' has been placed in sharp relief, with a universal focus on identity, practice, and behaviours (Fernandez & Shaw, 2020; Riggio & Newstead, 2023). Ongoing commentary debates the merits of anti-hegemonic governance models with

M. Andrew (✉)
College of Work-Based Learning, Otago Polytechnic|Te Kura Matatini ki Otago (Te Pūkenga), Dunedin 9022, New Zealand
e-mail: martin.andrew@op.ac.nz

O. McGirr
University of Leicester Global Study Centre, Leicester, UK
e-mail: oonaghmcgirr@gmail.com





J. Rudolph et al. (eds.), *The Palgrave Handbook of Crisis Leadership in Higher Education*,
https://doi.org/10.1007/978-3-031-54509-2_22

an emphasis on the ethical qualities required to deliver effective stewardship at a time of unprecedented uncertainty (Brown & Treviño, 2006). We note the rise of the ideal visionary leader—the pragmatic decision-maker, informed by kindness, who deploys a communications-led approach.

In 2023, Aotearoa's HE leaders continue to experience the effects of the global pandemic and wrestle with how to lead in this era of continuous change, revision, and recalibration, particularly regarding the national VET reform (Andrew, 2023; Kenny, 2023). In this Chapter, we consider how to meet the omnipresent needs of persistent crisis management. We explore the context of pandemic leadership, uncovering opportunities exemplified by shifts in thinking and ways of working whilst outlining the lessons learned for the future (Rother, 2019). We examine the experiences of educational leaders during the pandemic and reflect on capabilities highlighted as crucial for a *new* leadership approach. Deploying a critical reflective autoethnographic narrative methodology, we cast our learnings through the multiple lenses of local, national, and international HE leaders, drawing on stories and testimonials from a range of sources. A companion piece, eviscerating the university sector at this time (Andrew, 2023), extends the *kōrero* (story), we outline here. The chapter advocates for the adaptation of a leadership model which encompasses *tikanga* (practices), is informed by organisational *whakapapa* (heritage), acknowledges leaders' feedback, and deploys inclusive, consistent communication. Finally, specific and ideal leadership traits required for the enduring pandemic era in Aotearoa's imagined future, and for successful leadership of its tertiary education sector, are presented as a model for practice.

## Context

At the time of writing (2023), in the so-called 'post-pandemic' era, Aotearoa finds itself at an unenviable juncture. The political landscape signals change, schism, and uncertainty as the country embraces pre-election campaigning. The shock resignation of the universally popular and 'inspirational' (Lock & Henley, 2023) Prime Minister (PM), Jacinda Ardern was met with reactions of bewilderment and sadness by the electorate (Reuters, 2023). Chris Hipkins, then Minister of Education, swiftly took up the PM mantle, unopposed.

Hipkins, architect of faltering major reforms of the Health, Environment, and VET sectors, acknowledged in his inaugural speech (2018) the challenging time faced by Aotearoa, citing the dual crises of COVID-19 and economic downturn as major issues for his government to address. Three months from election, polls indicated a decline in popularity, auguring the loss of parliamentary majority held by Labour, and a diminishing possibility of maintaining the current Labour-Green coalition. In parallel, the HE landscape is experiencing a state of general malaise (Stewart, et al., 2022). We discern the convergence of political uncertainty and economic instability. Looming recession and workforce shortages exacerbate pressures on essential services, worn thin by the incremental demands of the pandemic era. The 2019 Reform of Vocational Education (ROVE) represents further disruption. The proclaimed ROVE transformation promised an inclusive, responsive, and harmonised system (Hipkins, 2019) to address the extant skills shortages and raise knowledge and capability in Aotearoa's low-wage, low-productivity economy (New Zealand Ministry of Education, 2019).

## COVID-19

Aotearoa took an early, decisive approach to combat the spread of COVID-19, communicating governmental focus on protecting the nation initially and containing the virus upon its late arrival in the country in March 2021. The precautionary government response was underpinned by four key measures: closure of all land and sea borders, restriction of movement across national territory, imposition of strict isolation for all residents, and establishment of robust quarantine criteria for those (re)entering Aotearoa (Wilson, 2020). A rigorous contact tracing and testing regime was implemented to identify and isolate potential Coronavirus cases (Wiles & Morris, 2020). Deployment of crisis communications through daily televised briefings and weekly updates on evolving guidance provided the public with detailed instructions concerning protocols, policy, and legislative safeguarding measures. Initially, Aotearoa's response was widely praised (Wilson, 2020). The country was able to contain case numbers, which were amongst the lowest in the world. Nevertheless, the government encountered criticism (Vance, 2020) regarding the draconian nature of measures enacted, the lack of timely action responding to the arrival of the virus onshore, the dearth of wide-scale testing, and the delay in delivering a comprehensive vaccine rollout.

## Higher Education: Impact and Evolution

Like many essential services around the world, Aotearoa's HE institutions (HEIs)—eight universities, Te Pūkenga-NZIST's network of 16 former institutes of technology and polytechnics (ITPS), 21 industry training organisations (ITOs), and three *Wānanga* (publicly-owned entities which provide education in a Māori cultural context)—were placed in full lockdown on March 25, 2020. The government assumed full control of the tertiary sector during the pandemic (Ross, 2020a, 2020b). Mandatory indefinite closure of campuses was announced (New Zealand Ministry of Education, 2019) with cessation of on-campus activity. The delivery of face-to-face, in-situ teaching was rendered impossible. Emergency Response Teaching (ERT) was enacted as learners and staff settled into their home 'bubbles', and preparations were made for remote delivery and engagement with a blended online learning methodology (Godber & Atkins, 2021). HEIs reported a swift shift to remote learning and teaching, hosted on virtual learning environment platforms—video conferencing, virtual examination proctoring (Blackboard, Canvas by Instructure, Collaborate, Microsoft Teams, Moodle, Panopto, ProctorU, Schoology, Skype, Socrative, Zoom, etc.) sparking a proliferation of e-learning (Scherman & Snow, 2021; Connor et al., 2021).

*Kaimahi* (staff) and *ākonga* (learners, students) grappled with the dual challenges of social confinement and a burgeoning health crisis. The realisation that ERT bore little resemblance to intentionally created online learning and teaching collateral posed challenges to both instructors and students, being accustomed to physical practical tuition, traditional assessment methods, in-person interactions and blended models of engagement (Scherman & Snow, 2021). As Godber and Atkins report (2021), the restrictive parameters set by the government in its bid to *go hard and... go fast* (Prime Minister's COVID-19 Daily Announcement, March 23, 2020) in the face of a rapidly escalating global pandemic, affected the rhythm, nature and focus of educators and learners across Aotearoa (Wilson, 2020).

## Dual Disruption: Vocational Education Reform

In 2019, the PM introduced what was to become a *dual disruptor* for the post-secondary education community. On February 14th, Jacinda Ardern announced the launch of the ROVE. The proposed transformation, rooted in aspirational purpose for the good of all citizens, intended to provide high-quality education and training to meet the needs of learners, industry, and the wider community (assuming this might not have been the case previously).

This unapologetically ambitious aim would be fulfilled, Ardern said, by offering an array of learning opportunities from foundation to postgraduate level, across a range of subjects and disciplines, enabled by the creation of a more flexible and responsive system. An overarching single entity would be better positioned to furnish the requirements of industry and the changing nature of work. This symbiotic alignment would be realised by working closely with employer stakeholder groups to identify and respond to their needs (Rudolph et al., 2023). Further, it would equip learners with the skills and knowledge for the ever-changing workforce (Maurice-Takerei & Anderson, 2021). Governed by a board of directors, with representation from industry, Māori, and the wider community, it would be supported by a network of regional teams, responsible for the delivery of VET in their respective areas (North, South, East, and West). The formal establishment of this entity, Te Pūkenga-New Zealand Institute of Skills and Technology (NZIST) some 14 months later, exemplified the Minister of Education's desire to change significantly the way in which VET was delivered in Aotearoa, espousing what, with a neoliberal flourish, Hipkins called a focus on collaboration, innovation, and excellence.

In his Letter of Expectations (n.d.), Hipkins outlined his government's aspirations for a hitherto (allegedly) underperforming sector. His vision, predicated on network cohesion, strong delivery, and enhanced capability constituted a blueprint to address the sector's lack of responsiveness, poor financial performance, and failure to meet citizens' needs in their journey of *lifewide* learning. This would be resolved by establishing a single network of service provision for the delivery of innovative tailored, targeted learning to all comers (Hipkins, 2019). At the heart of ROVE was the desire to embed quality, equity, and transparency (see Fig. 1) and a focus on giving full effect to the nation's founding document, *Te Tiriti Te Waitangi* (the Treaty of Waitangi)—foregrounding meaningful partnership as crucial to full participation and co-governance. He acknowledged the creation of a robust and flexible operating model was crucial, indeed fundamental, to long-term success (Hipkins, 2019): "...a cornerstone of the reform...(was)... the design and implementation of NZIST's... operating model to create a sustainable national network of accessible vocational education and training... responsive to the needs of the regions of New Zealand".

**Fig. 1** Summary of core expectations and features of ROVE (McGirr, 2023)

## Contexts of Leadership

Leadership is a "real and a vastly consequential phenomenon" (Hogan & Kaiser, 2005). As McCaffrey contends, those at the helm of our organisations tasked with influencing outcomes and shaping direction, carry considerable responsibility for the well-being of the entity and the people who populate it—employees, clients, and myriad stakeholders (Carruci, 2021; McCaffrey, 2019). In the case of academic institutions, the learners, their families, and all those vested in a successful completion of studies and a meaningful educational experience look to academic leaders for consistent, credible stewardship, whilst governance bodies demand a return on investment amidst ever-growing neoliberal demands of doing "more…with less" (McCaffrey, 2019, p. 1).

The extensive canon of leadership research reveals a steady shift in focus and interest in the subject matter across decades and centuries from the initial scoping of the theory and practice of *good* versus *bad* (transactional) in the latter half of the twentieth century; through the nature of governance, systems of management and organisational frameworks for best practice (transformational), to the relatively recent conceptualisation of ethics, morality, and compassion as core values, deemed integral to success and efficacy in modern times. Many of the more recent works speak of variations on Hogan and Kaiser's (2005) theme of *moral leadership*, values-oriented authentic leadership (Gardner et al., 2011), standards-informed leadership (Brown & Treviño, 2006), stakeholder-focused servant leadership (Liden et al., 2014), and notably, in the Aotearoa-specific context, kindness as leadership (Craig, 2021). This change in emphasis invites us to examine the behaviours as well as the competencies, qualities, and attributes required, whilst pondering the pursuit and attainment of inclusive excellence.

## Crisis Leadership

In the face of disruption, crisis leadership becomes ever more pertinent, as organisations seek to understand the implications of "specific, unexpected and non-routine" event(s) that create "high levels of uncertainty… which threaten the organisation" (Ulmer et al., 2007, p. 7), whilst simultaneously seeking to outperform the irruptions and revert to a type of 'new normal'. Boin et al. (2005) posit such leadership as individual in nature, characterised by a series of critical tasks which permit the organisation to respond to disruption, rationalise it, deal with it, and ultimately resolve it so that complete restoration of service and function of the business is effected. Typically, such crises are defined as organisational transgressions, events, or disruptions which sit outside the control of the entity.

The proliferation of accounts and analyses of COVID-19 crisis leadership charts the impact of the global pandemic on daily life—the disruption to local and regional economies and compromises made to ensure the continuation of frontline essential services. In the case of Aotearoa, academic and media commentators focused on the positively couched and often binary leadership style of Jacinda Ardern—citing a mixture of control (Cheng, 2020) compassion (Craig, 2021), kindness (Wilson, 2020), and performative efficiency (Friedman, 2020) as characteristic of her stewardship.

The simultaneous unravelling of COVID-19 and the Reform of Vocational Education (ROVE) presented concurrent challenges to public leadership in Aotearoa. The twin disruptors of crisis and change; an unprecedented and seemingly unending global pandemic in almost perfect tandem with the upending of the post-secondary VET norms and practices posed countless complexities and demands at a time of unparalleled worldwide uncertainty. This conjunction of crises placed those in public leadership under significant pressure to ensure public safety and deliver a range of emergency health services whilst remodelling an entire sector under extraordinary and anomalous working conditions.

Riggio and Newstead's (2023) synthesis-analysis of crisis leadership invokes the qualities required for success when dealing with the unexpected in circumstances which are abnormal and unstable, behoving leaders to manage the unpredictable through thoughtful response to that which is disruptive, ambiguous, and emotionally charged in nature. Faced with such an infrequent occurrence, leaders must work rapidly to call others to action, focusing on recovery, adjustment, and balance. An important distinction is made regarding the type of crisis faced—either one-off (crisis event) or enduring (crisis-as-process). Crisis leadership is, in either case, subject to intense scrutiny of all actions and (re)actions. It demands a set of core competencies to be deployed with care and consideration: decision-making, sense-making, communication, (team) coordination, and the facilitation of stakeholder learning.

## Change Leadership

The practice and theory of change leadership are well-populated in the canon of literature. Miles (2002) reminds us that all change affects every level of the business entity, irrespective of the nature of business. company-level transformation demands strategic thinking and business modelling; at the operational level, there is the need to consider culture as an overarching tenant of associated layers of the organisation: structure, facilities, resources, services, and products (Lewis, 2016). Disruptive change and aspirational transformation frequently produce changes in reporting lines, departmental mergers, directorate expansion or contraction, and the assimilation of new services, products, technology, and people into the organisation. Biech (2007) reminds us of the inherent complexity of change leadership, noting the collective responsibility borne by all leaders within the hierarchy, and the high-stakes accountability of the top tier of executive leadership. Equally, directors, managers, supervisors, and project leads charged with implementing change processes also carry the impact of institutional disruption, dealing with the myriad reactions of colleagues and coworkers, and the subsequent effects on well-being and staff morale. In this sense, whilst executive leaders take accountability for the strategic planning, vision, and mission setting, it is the front-line worker who is immersed in a churn of operational execution and at risk of becoming trapped in a cycle of lack of progress, poor engagement and an absence of conviction (Carruci, 2021).

Wheatley (1992) and Rousseau (1995) conceive uncertainty as a key feature of organisational change, in terms of behaviours, responses, and outcomes. Transitional change may cause confusion and ambiguity as far as position boundaries and expectations are concerned—and so can affect levels of harmony, productivity, and quality of work–-life balance (Wrzesniewski & Dutton, 2001). Kuhn (1970) proffers three classifications of leadership: transformational, transitional, or developmental. In the transitional domain, adjustments are deemed as incremental or gradual and often linked to policy, protocol, or process modifications, typically implemented at the micro (departmental) level. The transformational domain equates to macro-level whole-of-organisation modifications, with a radical organisational shift in mind—such as a change in function, purpose, and/or direction of the business. The developmental sphere, which has gained much traction in organisational leadership in the past twenty years, speaks to continuous improvement and growth for maintaining primacy within a sector or market.

Andersen (2022) advocates for this type of dynamic and philosophical shift as manageable and most likely to bring successful outcomes, contingent upon the continuous scanning of the environment, consistent communication, and a deep understanding on the part of leadership of the difficulties that change presents. A fundamental aspect of successful developmental leadership is the commitment to transparency, rewarding progress and innovation, and avoidance of one-way, top-down communications (Gilley & Maycunich, 2000). Confronted with such vicissitudes, we do well to remember the oft-repeated quote—"culture eats strategy for breakfast" (Engel, 2018, p. 1). In directing substantial organisational transformation, we encounter the important challenge of modifying, enhancing, or replacing the extant culture of the entity and simultaneously driving the requisite mandated change.

## Method

Our post-qualitative, ethnographic approach of presenting our study can be described as a critically reflective form, best labelled subjective academic narrative (Arnold, 2015). This mode of representation is autoethnographic in that our goal is to contribute to socio-political and cultural understanding of crisis leadership as observed and experienced during a time of major crisis in Aotearoa, with the COVID-19 pandemic as a partial catalyst (Godber & Atkins, 2021). It is 'subjective' in that the authors, as academic leaders within tertiary education during this juncture, convene and curate the multiple real-world materials available to us into a cogent narrative of our own direction. It is 'academic' in that we use a literature review as a method to aggregate understanding and scholarship on key issues in our sector and point to key concerns and gaps, at the same drawing on what we experience and encounter as legitimate data within our understandings and perceptions of 'the academy'. By 'the academy' we refer to HE organisations such as universities/polyversities, polytechnics, and private training establishments. Clandinin and Connelly

(2000, p. 60) claim we meet 'ourselves' in our writings; in academic texts, this is both unavoidable and inevitable (Arnold, 2015).

Sparkes (2000) wrote that autoethnographies "are highly personalised accounts that draw upon the experience of the author/researcher for the purposes of extending sociological understanding" (p. 21). We unashamedly draw upon our understandings, positioned with a socio-political comprehension that these are constructions of our own experiences, perceptions, ideologies, and other factors. Crucially, autoethnography "transcends mere narration of self to engage in cultural analysis and interpretation" (Chang, 2008, p. 43). Following Sparkes (2000; 2004), Wall (2008) believed that autoethnographies begin with a personal story. However, the story we record as leaders/researchers/authors is one of shared experience, with ourselves as decoders, perceivers, understanders, and portrayers of data, both our own and others'. We are curator–narrators, and what we share here comes from being deeply ingrained in narrative enquiry and narrative as enquiry (Polkinghorne, 1995); that is, we both (re)present stories, recognising our implicitness in them, and we reflect critically on them as part of the fabric of our narrative. Our text is a patchwork of embodied memories, our own and others' (Sparkes, 2004).

Our interpretation of events is inseparable from the acts of (re)telling or (re)presenting. As such, we reject the notion that we need findings and discussion, standing with Sparkes (2013) to reject the rise of methodological fundamentalism and a resurgent scientism, to stand for embodied forms of understanding. This approach honours the post-qualitative ethos of working differently with data. Ours is a response to the challenge of eschewing "methodolatry", allowing *thinking-writing* to lead to the "creation of the new" (St. Pierre, 2019, p. 3).

We present our narrative in a form of critically reflective analytic autoethnography (Anderson, 2006; Ellis & Bochner, 2006), with, perhaps, a little less 'auto' because *our* stories are absorbed as experiences, observations, and retellings; and a little more 'ethno', since we speak as members of a community to which we belong and curate voices and narrated experiences of stakeholders within those communities. Thus, we use empirical data "to gain insight into some broader set of social phenomena than those provided by the data themselves" (Anderson, 2006, p. 387). Using reflexivity as a consolidatory strategy, we aim to propagate the voices and viewpoints embedded in our data sources, whilst acknowledging the creative dominance of the researcher/writer (Mauthner & Doucet, 2003).

Our method of *collecting* data comes from the same world. What we share in this enquiry are our collaborative learnings, cast through the multiple lenses of local, national, and international higher educational leaders, drawing on the stories and testimonials from a range of sources. We draw upon a core dataset of reflections and accounts of practice from currently active practitioners in Te Pūkenga-NZIST's network of subsidiaries across the north and south islands of Aotearoa. In the primary method, a cloud-based platform Kobo Toolbox was used to provide a safe and ethical interface between the eight purposively sampled participants and the researcher. The sample population included colleagues and peers who, by dint of their role title, held a leadership position within the VET network in 2020. Criterion sampling was employed to identify colleagues who met the requirements for participation. Post-2021, snowball sampling and opportunistic sampling enabled participants who were recommended or who self-nominated by expressing an interest in participating (as awareness of the project grew) to engage with the project.

This platform enables secure and asynchronous data collection, protection of participants and provides for efficient data collection in limited contexts. We supplement this with a bricolage of discourses: document analysis of public domain editorials, discussion documents, collaborative online forums, stakeholder commentaries, and a wide range of published media both print and audio-visual. This project has been reviewed and approved by the Otago Polytechnic Research Ethics Committee (Ethics Application # 861).

The words of the accounts are supplemented and supported by the lived experiences, perceptions, and beliefs of the two authors, who curate the bricolage into a themed narrative of change leadership, coming to rest on a high-stakes case: the case of change leadership within the emerging and all-encompassing super-Polytechnic, Te Pūkenga. The wicked problems it faced changed by the day. This is the backstory informing the headline 'Te Pūkenga Leadership have failed' (TEU, 2023). Our study addresses the kinds of wicked problems facing HE and VET education today (Ramaley, 2014).

The wicked problems we create this commentary around are:

- What distinctive features mark change leadership in higher education in Aotearoa New Zealand around the time of the COVID-19 pandemic?
- What are the elements of the backstory to the narrative of the failure of leadership in vocational higher education in Aotearoa New Zealand?
- What are the marks of leadership in Higher Education that might assure a positive future for the sector in Aotearoa New Zealand?

In our subjective academic narrative on "imagination, creativity, and commitment to the common good", we stand with Ramaley (2014, p. 8):

> These challenges require us to rethink what it means to be educated in today's world and to explore ways to provide a coherent and meaningful educational experience in the face of the turbulence, uncertainty, and fragmentation that characterize much of higher education today. We have faced times like this before, and our imagination, creativity, and commitment to the common good have helped us through.

## Findings: Asynchronous Voices of Unravelling

The courses of COVID-19 and ROVE unfolded, for a time, in a similar vein. Our colleagues, co-workers, professional-friends, and fellow citizens, shared their concerns, articulated their fears, and embraced the binary disruptions which irrupted into our daily lives with obedience and optimism between 2020 and 2022. Our collated voices, collected between 2020 and 2023, narrate a growing sense of uncertainty, and a loss of confidence in the oft-espoused vision of long-term success for the aspirational new world of VET which chimes with the broadcast and social media critiques. By early 2023, we had observed a lack of conviction in terms of stakeholder perception, tangible outcomes, and public opinion.

The response to the pandemic was underpinned by an initial elimination strategy and lockdown which all but eradicated the first wave of the virus in 2020. By the end of 2021, the nationwide strategy, led by public health experts and disseminated through regular structured press conferences (initially daily) moved to one of mitigation as the Omicron virus swept the country. By 2022, (inter)national media expressed admiration for Ardern's leadership (Friedman, 2020; Lock & Henley, 2023; Mueller et al., 2022) applauding the unexpected economic growth and low unemployment. Media and public expressed appreciation for "leadership that listens to science (with) a focus on equity and partnership with Māori…and…the use of the precautionary principle in the face of uncertainty for…healthcare and public health systems" (Baker & Wilson, 2022).

ROVE, led by Hipkins (who assumed the COVID-19 Response portfolio in 2022) has been less lauded, experiencing an incrementally negative reception. A review of organisational activity between 2019 and 2023 reveals a prevailing focus on mobilising the entity (2019) by setting up a head office (2020 to 2023), refreshing and expanding the ever-changing executive leadership (2021 to 2023) mirrored by an ever-expanding head office team, far exceeding, with a headcount of 200 plus, the anticipated lean central operational hub. Inconsistent stakeholder consultation, the continuous production of organisational frameworks, and constant shifts in staffing at a local level (new hires, retiring or leaving the sector, internal promotions, and secondments) have created a perfect storm of confusion, uncertainty, and fear. A whistleblower attributes this to "poor oversight, decision-making and a lack of transparency" redolent of deficient crisis leadership (Kenny, 2023).

## Discussion

Leadership is an important aspect of management, reified by the deployment of strategy in concrete response to governance demands and directives: "today's university leaders have to respond to external demands with business-like efficiency and accountability, while navigating the maze of diverging cultural norms, narratives and work ethos of academic environments" (Kligyte & Barrie, 2014, p. 161). Assuming that the academic culture of cohesive collegial expertise is differentiated from that of conventional business entities (Knight & Trowler, 2000), we observe that coupled with the disturbance of COVID-19, the ambitions of ROVE were likely compromised at the outset. Given the sheer magnitude of the proposed reform, the consequent pandemic-induced pressure on government resources, and the multiplicity of organisational cultures in existence within the network of entities, the articulated desire to deliver substantial sector and organisational change in a relatively brief period of four years seems logically unattainable in the lived context of Aotearoa.

The response to COVID-19 was one of collective, mono-directional focus, based on a shared perception of the 'team of five million' (Ardern's daily Churchillian petition in early 2020), and a unique multi-stakeholder focus, predicated on all-party agreement which enabled a positive and successful deployment of a well-communicated strategy (Baker & Wilson, 2022). Conversely, the communications emanating from the Te Pūkenga/NZIST spoke of marshalling resources and expertise to effect a radical transformation by, as one colleague commented, "building the plane as we fly it". Faced with detracting headlines and sector stakeholders who report diminished confidence in Te Pūkenga's viability, there are several features of the proposed transformation which merit consideration.

## COVID-19 and Aotearoa Higher Education: Crisis, What Crisis?

Our colleagues and peers report a lack of attention to the unique values of the VET sector entities, a loss of collegiality, and the absence of the erstwhile cohesive institutional and local culture(s). A programme leader shared "I say hello to our (new) leaders, and they look straight past me. Our previous CEO knew us all by name and always stopped to have a chat. Our happy culture has died—and no one cares". Similarly, as the country returned to a semblance of normality after the first lockdown, peers shared stories of increasing unhappiness with ROVE and its impact on professional identity and job satisfaction: "I've worked in this sector for my whole professional life, and I have loved it. But the last two years have been terrible". Several colleagues described the absence of faith in job security: "I do not trust anyone…not even my colleagues…at this point, we are all worried about our jobs…with the recent announcement of redundancies…we have to think about ourselves first. It's my family's livelihood at stake".

The universally admired and oft-cited empathy of Ardern's leadership in the face of COVID-19 is not observed within the Te Pūkenga stakeholder network leadership. As a professorial colleague noted when asked about executive leadership in general, "our CEO tells us they are just helping out; our leadership team sends instructions about what ***not*** to do…and little else…I am not sure they know what to do, to be honest". At macro-level, stakeholders continue to express a lack of conviction, despite reassurances from the executive that they are *doing the right thing* (or words to that effect). A college leader commented:

> I'm waiting for the election (in October 2023), and I will be voting against this government. It's the only way we'll be able to stop the destruction…we went into this with open minds…but as time has passed, we haven't been able to find out what will happen to us or our jobs…they keep telling us we are all in this together. I don't believe that. Most of the ones who believed that have left or now work for the head office (sic).

Peer leaders from subsidiaries in the north and south islands expressed their disappointment at lack of and contradictory communication commenting "we hear nothing…it's worrying" and "I'm not sure what or who to listen to…we receive messages and newsletters less than we did before…no one seems to know what is happening". When describing the opportunities to challenge or question the process of Reform, a colleague noted "we speak in whispers about the changes, we try to work out what is happening…when we ask, we get the same answer....we are all in this together...I am not convinced". One fellow leader summarised declining interest in updates and notifications from local leadership:

> ...our staff newsletter... I used to enjoy reading it. Now it's just a list of announcements of who is leading who, and who sits where in the hierarchy and who is doing wonderful things in the land of make-believe VET...I have set the incoming notifications to divert to the trash folder... as it tells me nothing, frankly speaking', similarly a department head shared 'It's gone eerily quiet. We hear nothing'.

Voices from the chalk face tell us of the harm experienced by the constant exit and replacement of (more experienced) staff across the network (Kenny, 2023). A colleague recounted in late 2022, "...we've lost all of our great staff, especially those who had strong experience. New staff seem to arrive every week... most of them have not worked in our sector and it shows. I say nothing. I keep my head down and hope things will get better. But I doubt it".

These combined narratives speak of well-being diminished by fear—of the future, the present, and of failure (of ROVE). A team leader shared their view in late 2022, "a culture of ...blind optimism prevails. I don't believe anything or anyone", and said, "I wonder about my future and my career. I've been diagnosed with acute depression. I am too scared to tell (anyone) in case I lose my job..." A sense of futility is expressed more frequently as ROVE progresses. A long-serving curriculum leader confided: "we're waiting for the storm to pass. We have no faith in the leadership, even those who jumped ship from our Polytech...it's a farce. We don't believe anything they tell us". A colleague employed in an industry-facing department revealed in early 2023: "we don't have an operating model, and nobody can tell us when we will have one. It's farcical".

When describing the experience of leadership, fellow sector professionals pinpoint a lack of trust in staff: "it's a cancel culture...say nothing...keep your head down...they are monitoring everything, including our emails". They point to uncertainty regarding the appointed leadership cohort's capability when tasked with pathfinding during the prolonged period of ambiguity: "what do I look for in a leader? Erm...exactly the opposite of what we have. They don't tell us much, and when they do, it's contradictory or it's a non-answer. I have zero confidence in this bunch of...mandarins".

Declarations of the Tertiary Education Union (TEU, 2023) on behalf of the membership outlined collective disappointment at the announcement of imminent redundancies in June 2023. The Union leadership highlighted the perceived breach of the documented 'no surprises' approach of the Te Pūkenga Executive—and its continuous miscommunication. The spokesperson emphasised the findings of the institutional pulse-check in March 2023 as revealing sector-wide despondency and limited confidence in the future of the entity. In effect, this capstone commentary lays bare the reach of the change, which touches every employee (Carruci, 2021).

## Discussion: Upon Reflection

Drawing on recent analyses of Aotearoa's leadership of the complex Coronavirus crisis, Wilson (2020) proffers a model of leadership engagement and practice which mirrors the needs (and lacks) identified by our emerging thematic voices.

Strategic or higher-level aspects of successful leadership identified relate to fostering purpose and building trust by the deployment of specific practices across three domains: (i) drawing on evidence-based advice, guidance and expertise, (ii) mobilising the (people) collective through clear communication of direction and ongoing, open feedback, and (iii) building capability and capacity throughout the change process to support meaning-making and creative solutions. Riggio and Newstead (2023) and Wilson (2020) advocate for reciprocal learning and sharing of expertise as crucial in leading through a human-centred crisis. This approach is supported by crisis management models developed internationally during the pandemic (Balasubramanian & Fernandes, 2022).

The concerns raised by VET sector colleagues evoke the importance of leaders needing to "give academics time for growth and reflection" (Kligyte & Barrie, 2014, p. 167). Failure to appreciate extant culture recalls Wilson's (2020) notion of fostering a shared purpose through and by trust. As ROVE approaches the end of its fourth year, the flagship entity of Te Pūkenga is still grappling with the detail of its operating model, the first version of which was communicated for consultation in July 2023. We question, in light of peers' shared commentary, whether there is a common purpose at operational level. We are reminded of Carruci's (2021) posit that when not robustly scoped, prepared, nor communicated, aspiring transformations risk becoming part of the 70% of those which end in failure. Such a sweeping reform, established without a business plan may well exemplify 'scope naiveté' on the part of the ideator (Carrucci, 2021); that is, an absence of full understanding of the enormity of effort and resources required. Such naiveté is reflected here in the accounts of our peers and TEU (2023).

Furthermore, our peer-leaders narrate an incremental effect of concurrent crises that culminates in unhappiness, fear, a decline in well-being, diminishment of *mana* (prestige) and a fear of the future, which, as recounted, appear to have gone unheard by leadership. We see COVID-19 receding as ROVE takes centre-stage. What was communicated as a whole-of-sector-transformation has in fact become a series of incrementally implemented changes, executed with limited consideration for the risk of communication and change fatigue, and inadequate thought for individual entity cultures.

## Conclusion

Contemplating the stories of peers' experiences of leadership at a time of complex and differentiated crises, we invoke the richness of embodied understandings to remind us of the importance of experience as a mediating force. It is important that Aotearoa's public-sector leaders contemplate the impact of their actions in exceptionally challenging circumstances of parallel crises—the crisis event of the disruptive Coronavirus and the emerging and enduring crisis-as-process, ROVE. Loss of the follower-centred kindness approach (Craig, 2021) is at risk. There is a promise of a strong emphasis on *tikanga* (practices), and hopefully also learning from organisational *whakapapa* (heritage) and cultural memory. In addition to the imperative for Māori voices, there is a need to listen to educator voices (Berg & Zoellick, 2019; Carruci, 2021; Maurice-Takerei & Anderson, 2021), likely to accentuate belongingness and trust (Connor et al., 2021; Crawford, 2022; Crawford et al., 2023; Tice et al., 2021) and maintain quality services (Camilleri, 2021; Dagiene et al., 2022).

A further conclusion that can be drawn from the data collected and (re)presented in this bricolage of stories is that national leadership of the health crisis was, in part, deemed as successful by those who shared their experience via a range of media. At this point, there is a dearth of positive commentary regarding the leadership of ROVE. A commentary of absence reminds us of the behaviours and competencies required of the authentic leader. They build trust in a common purpose by harnessing team expertise, leading through shared learning, enabling sense-making through clearly communicated decision-making, and mutual discussion and debate.

To that end, we encourage higher education leaders to pay careful attention to communication as a vehicle for genuine consultation, a key feature of transformational crisis leadership (Ulmer et al., 2022; Dwiedienawati et al., 2021), along with follower-centred compassion (Balasubramanian & Fernandes, 2022). We urge them to place greater emphasis on full stakeholder engagement and authentic feedback. We contend the insights gained from peer interaction are important for understanding made through this storytelling and remind leaders that investment of time and emotion cannot be underestimated in the epoch of intersectional crises, such as the twin disruptions lived in Aotearoa since 2019.

## References

Andersen, E. (2022, April 7). Change is hard. Here's how to make it less painful. *Harvard Business Review.* https://hbr.org/2022/04/change-is-hard-heres-how-to-make-it-less-painful

Anderson, L. (2006). Analytic autoethnography. *Journal of Contemporary Ethnography, 35*, 373–395.

Andrew, M. (2023). Neo-neoliberalist capitalism, intensification by stealth and campus real estate in the modern university in Aotearoa/New Zealand. *Journal of Applied Learning and Teaching, 6*(2), 1–9. https://doi.org/10.37074/jalt.2023.6.2.16

Arnold, J. (2015). Research as stories: An academic subjective analysis. *Advances in Research, 4*(1), 59–66. https://doi.org/10.9734/AIR/2015/13050

Baker, M., & Wilson, N. (2022, April 5). New Zealand's Covid strategy was one of the world's most successful—What can we learn from it? *The Guardian. World Edition.* https://www.theguardian.com/world/commentisfree/2022/apr/05/new-zealands-covid-strategy-was-one-of-the-worlds-most-successful-what-can-it-learn-from-it

Biech, E. (2007). *Thriving through change: A leader's practical guide to change mastery.* ASTD Press.

Boin, A., Hart, P., Stern, E., & Sundelius, B. (2005). *The politics of crisis management: Public leadership under pressure*. Cambridge University Press.

Berg, J. H., & Zoellick, B. (2019). Teacher leadership: Toward a new conceptual framework. *Journal of Professional Capital and Community, 4*(1), 2–13. https://doi.org/10.1108/JPCC-06-2018-0017

Brown, M. E., & Treviño, L. K. (2006). Ethical leadership: A review and future directions. *The Leadership Quarterly, 17*(6), 595–616.

Camilleri, M. A. (2021). Evaluating service quality and performance of higher education institutions: A systematic review and a post-COVID-19 outlook. *International Journal of Quality and Service Sciences, 13*(2), 268–281.

Carruci, R. (2021, April 30). How leaders get in the way of organizational change. *Harvard Business Review*. https://hbr.org/2021/04/how-leaders-get-in-the-way-of-organizational-change

Chang, H. (2008). *Autoethnography as method.* Left Coast Press.

Cheng, D. (2020, May 10). The jagging order from Jacinda Ardern's office—Cynical, arrogant and unnecessary. *NZ Herald*. https://www.nzherald.co.nz/nz/news/article.cfm?c_id=1&objectid=12330745

Clandinin, D., & Connelly, F. M. (2000). *Narrative inquiry: Experience and story in qualitative research.* Jossey-Bass.

Connor, M., Mueller, B., Mann, S., & Andrew, M. (2021). Pivots, pirouettes and practicalities: Actions and reactions of work-integrated learning practitioners. *Journal of University Teaching & Learning Practice, 18*(5), 1–19. https://doi.org/10.53761/1.18.5.2

Craig, G. (2021). Kindness and control: The political leadership of Jacinda Ardern in the Aotearoa New Zealand COVID-19 media conferences. *Journalism and Media, 2*(2), 288–304.

Crawford, J. (2022). *Defining post-pandemic work and organizations: The need for team belongingness and trust*. InTech Open.

Crawford, J., Allen, K.-A., Sanders, T., Baumeister, R., Parker, P. D., Saunders, C., & Tice, D. M. (2023). Sense of belonging in higher education students: An Australian longitudinal study from 2013 to 2019. *Studies in Higher Education*.https://doi.org/10.1080/03075079.2023.2238006

Dagiene, V., Jasute, E., Navickiene, V., Butkiene, R., & Gudoniene, D. (2022). Opportunities, quality factors, and required changes during the pandemic based on higher education leaders' perspective. *Sustainability, 14*, 1933. https://doi.org/10.3390/su14031933

Dwiedienawati, D., Tjahjana, D., Faisal, M., Gandasari, D., & Abdinagoro, S. B. (2021). Determinants of perceived effectiveness in crisis management and company reputation during the COVID-19 pandemic. *Cogent Business & Management, 8*(1). https://doi.org/10.1080/23311975.2021.1912523

Ellis, C., & Bochner, A. (2006). Analyzing analytic autoethnography: An autopsy. *Journal of Contemporary Ethnography, 35*, 429–449. https://doi.org/10.1177/0891241606286979

Engel, J. M. (2018, April 22). Why does culture eat strategy for breakfast? *Forbes.* https://www.forbes.com/sites/forbescoachescouncil/2018/11/20/why-does-culture-eat-strategy-for-breakfast/?sh=bcec8ef1e098

Fernandez, A., & Shaw, G. (2020). Academic leadership in a time of crisis: The coronavirus and COVID-19. *Journal of Leadership Studies, 14*(1), 39–45.

Friedman, U. (2020, April 20). New Zealand's Prime Minister may be the most effective leader on the planet. *The Atlantic*. https://www.theatlantic.com/politics/archive/2020/04/jacinda-ardern-new-zealand-leadership-coronavirus/610237/

Gardner, W. L., Cogliser, C. C., Davis, K. M., & Dickens, M. P. (2011). Authentic leadership: A review of the literature and research agenda. *The Leadership Quarterly, 22*, 1120–1145.

Hipkins, C. (n.d.). *New Zealand institute of skills and technology: Letter of expectations*. https://xn--tepkenga-szb.ac.nz/assets/Publications/NZIST-Letter-of-Expectations.pdf

Gilley, J. W., & Maycunich, A. (2000). *Beyond the learning organization: Creating a culture of continuous growth and development through state-of-the-art human resource practices*. Perseus.

Godber, K. A., & Atkins D. R. (2021). COVID-19 impacts on teaching and learning: A collaborative autoethnography by two higher education lecturers. *Frontiers in Education, 6*. https://www.frontiersin.org/articles/10.3389/feduc.2021.647524/full

Hipkins, C. (2018). *Maiden statements*. https://www.parliament.nz/en/pb/hansard-debates/rhr/document/49HansS_20081216_00001004/hipkins-chris-maiden-statements

Hipkins, C. (2019, 26 August). *Curriculum, progress and achievement: Initial actions*. Cabinet paper released by the Ministry of Education.

Hogan, J., & Kaiser, B. (2005). What we know about leadership. *Review of General Psychology, 9*(2), 169–180.

Kenny, L. (2023, March 15). Former polytech boss launches petition to 'remove Te Pūkenga's board and CEO'. *Stuff*. https://www.stuff.co.nz/national/education/131500072/former-polytech-boss-launches-petition-to-remove-te-pkengas-board-and-ceo

Kligyte, G., & Barrie, S. (2014). Collegiality: Leading us into fantasy—The paradoxical resilience of collegiality in academic leadership. *Higher Education Research & Development, 33*(1), 157–169. https://doi.org/10.1080/07294360.2013.864613

Knight, P., & Trowler, P. (2000). Department level cultures and the improvement of learning and teaching. *Studies in Higher Education, 25*(1), 69–83.

Kuhn, T. (1970). *The structure of scientific revolutions*. University of Chicago Press.

Lewis, S. (2016). *Positive psychology and change: How leadership, collaboration, and appreciative inquiry create transformational results*. Wiley-Blackwell. https://doi.org/10.1002/9781118818480

Liden, R. C., Wayne, S. J., Liao, C., & Meuser, J. D. (2014). Servant leadership and serving culture: Influence on individual and unit performance. *Academy of Management Journal, 57*(5), 1434–1452.

Lock, S., & Henley, J. (2023, January 20). An inspiring leader: World reacts to Jacinda Ardern's resignation as New Zealand PM. *The Guardian*. https://www.theguardian.com/world/2023/jan/19/an-inspiring-leader-world-reacts-to-jacinda-arderns-resignation-as-new-zealand-prime-minister

Maurice-Takerei, L., & Anderson, H. (2021). Vocational education and training reform in Aotearoa New Zealand: The value of educators and education in a new VET environment. *New Zealand Annual Review of Education, 27*, 116–130.

Mauthner, N. S., & Doucet, A. (2003). Reflexive accounts and accounts of reflexivity in qualitative data analysis. *Sociology, 37*, 413–431.

McCaffrey, P. (2019). *The higher education manager's handbook: Effective leadership and management in universities and colleges*. Routledge.

McGirr, O. (2023, April 22). *Aspirations of transformation: A New Zealand leadership case study*. WFCP Leadership Summit, CICAN World Congress – Collective Intelligence, Montreal, Canada. https://conference.collegesinstitutes.ca/

Miles, M. T. (2002). The relative impact of principal instructional and transformational leadership on school culture. *Dissertation Abstracts International, 63*(05)A, AAI3052200.

Mueller, B., Andrew, M. B., & Connor, M. (2022). Building belonging in online WIL environments-lessons (re) learnt in the pandemic age: A collaborative enquiry. *Journal of University Teaching and Learning Practice, 19*(4), 16.

New Zealand Ministry of Education. (2019). *A unified system for all vocational education*. Wellington, New Zealand. https://conversation.education.govt.nz›AoC.

Polkinghorne, D. (1995). Narrative configuration in qualitative analysis. In J. A. Hatch & R. Wisniewski (Eds.), *Life history and narrative* (pp. 5–23). Falmer.

Ramaley, J. A. (2014). The changing role of higher education: Learning to deal with wicked problems. *Journal of Higher Education Outreach and Engagement, 18*(3), 7–21.

Reuters. (2023, January 19). *Reaction to NZ PM Jacinda Ardern's shock resignation announcement*. https://www.reuters.com/world/asia-pacific/reaction-jacinda-arderns-shock-resignation-announcement-2023-01-19/

Riggio, R. E., & Newstead, T. (2023). Crisis leadership. *Annual Review of Organizational Psychology and Organizational Behavior, 1*, 201–224.

Rother, N. (2019). *Hands-on: New suggestions to reform the vocational sector in New Zealand.* New Zealand Initiative. https://www.nzinitiative.org.nz/reports-and-media/reports/hands-on-new-suggestions-to-reform-the-vocational-sector-in-new-zealand/

Ross, J. (2020a, March 27). New Zealand government assumes power over universities. *Times Higher Education.* https://timeshighereducation.com/news/new-zealand-government-assumes-power-over-universities

Ross, J. (2020b, May 14). More student enrolments bankrolled in New Zealand budget. *Times Higher Education.* https://www.timeshighereducation.com/news/more-student-enrolments-bankrolled-new-zealand-budget

Rousseau, D. M. (1995). *Psychological contracts in organizations: Understanding written and unwritten agreements.* Sage.

Rudolph, J., Tan, S., Crawford, J., & Butler-Henderson, K. (2023). Perceived quality of online learning during COVID-19 in higher education in Singapore: Perspectives from students, lecturers, and academic leaders. *Educational Research for Policy and Practice, 22*(1), 171–191.

Sparkes, A. C. (2000). Autoethnography and narratives of self: Reflections on criteria in action. *Sociology of Sport Journal, 17*, 21–43.

Sparkes, A. (2004). From performance to impairment: A patchwork of embodied memories. In J. Evans, B. Davies, & J. Wright (Eds.), *Body knowledge and control: Studies in the sociology of physical education and health* (pp. 157–172). Routledge.

Sparkes, A. C. (2013). Qualitative research in sport, exercise and health in the era of neoliberalism, audit and new public management: Understanding the conditions for the (im)possibilities of a new paradigm dialogue. *Qualitative Research in Sport, 5*(3), 440–459.

Scherman, R. M., & Snow, N. E. (2021). Defending campus culture against the threat of perennial online instruction in a post-COVID-19 world. *Frontiers in Education, 6*. https://www.frontiersin.org/articles/10.3389/feduc.2021.607655/full

Balasubramanian, S., & Fernandes, C. (2022). Confirmation of a crisis leadership model and its effectiveness: Lessons from the COVID-19 pandemic. *Cogent Business & Management, 9*(1). https://doi.org/10.1080/23311975.2021.2022824

Stewart, G. T., Couch, D. B., & Devine, N. (2022). A general malaise: Education in post-Covid times. *NZ Journal of Educational Studies, 57*, 301–304.

St. Pierre, E. A. (2019). Post qualitative inquiry, the refusal of method, and the risk of the new. *Qualitative Inquiry, 27*(1), 1–7. https://doi.org/10.1177/1077800419863

TEU. (2023, March 31). *Te Pūkenga leadership have failed*. https://teu.ac.nz/news/te-p%C5%ABkenga-leadership-have-failed/

Tice, D., Baumeister, R., Crawford, J., Allen, K. A., & Percy, A. (2021). Student belongingness in higher education: Lessons for Professors from the COVID-19 pandemic. *Journal of University Teaching & Learning Practice, 18*(4), 2. https://doi.org/10.53761/1.18.4.2

Ulmer, R. R., Seeger, M. W., & Sellnow, T. L. (2007). Post-crisis communication and renewal: Expanding the parameters of post-crisis discourse. *Public Relations Review, 33*(2), 130–134.

Ulmer, R. R., Sellnow, T. L., & Seeger, M. W. (2022). *Effective crisis communication: Moving from crisis to opportunity*. SAGE Publications.

Vance, A. (2020, April 12). Coronavirus: How Jacinda Ardern is using soft propaganda to beat Covid-19. *Stuff*. https://www.stuff.co.nz/national/politics/opinion/120959519/coronavirus-how-jacinda-ardern-is-using-softpropaganda-to-beat-covid19

Wall, S. (2008). Easier said than done: Writing an autoethnography. *International Journal of Qualitative Methods, 7*(1), 38–53.

Wheatley, M. J. (1992). *Leadership and the new science: Learning about organizations from an orderly universe*. Berrett-Koehler.

Wilson, S. (2020). Pandemic leadership: Lessons from NZ's approach to COVID-19. *Leadership, 16*(3). https://doi.org/10.1177/1742715020929151

Wiles, S., & Morris, T. (2020). The three phases of Covid-19—And how we can make it manageable. *The Spinoff*. https://thespinoff.co.nz/society/09-03-2020/the-three-phases-of-covid-19-and-how-we-can-make-it-manageable/

Wrzesniewski, A., & Dutton, J. E. (2001). Crafting a job: Revisioning employees as active crafters of their work. *Academy of Management Review, 26*(2), 179–201.

# Impacts of the COVID-19 Pandemic on Nigeria's Higher Education System

Olaniyi Felix Sanni and Abike Elizabeth Sanni

## Introduction

Nigeria, a West African country, shares borders with Niger, the Atlantic Ocean, Cameroon, and Benin. Known as the "giant of Africa," it boasts a population of over 200 million, growing annually at around three per cent (Federal Ministry of Health, 2020). Nigeria comprises six zones, 36 states, and a federal capital territory divided into approximately 770 Local Government Areas.

With Africa's highest population and extensive global travel and commercial links, the presence of COVID-19 in Nigeria was inevitable (WHO, 2021). The pandemic disrupted all aspects of Nigerian life, prompting a government-imposed lockdown. This measure affected schools, businesses, and religious institutions and banned gatherings of over 20 individuals, halting physical contact-based economic activities (CDC, 2020). Nigeria has grappled with the virus's overwhelming effects since the first COVID-19 case on 27 February 2020 (Ibrahim et al., 2020).

A study by Human Rights Watch and Justice & Empowerment Initiatives (JEI) revealed that the economic fallout of the pandemic exacerbated the plight of impoverished Nigerian families, leaving many unable to afford food

O. F. Sanni (✉)
Fescosof Data Solutions, Ota, Ogun State, Nigeria
e-mail: feslix@gmail.com

A. E. Sanni
Destiny Assurance School, Ota, Ogun State, Nigeria



J. Rudolph et al. (eds.), *The Palgrave Handbook of Crisis Leadership in Higher Education*,
https://doi.org/10.1007/978-3-031-54509-2_23

and necessities (Human Rights Watch, 2021). During the outbreak, hunger rates surged, particularly in Lagos, Nigeria's most populated city, where rising food prices and a prolonged economic downturn devastated informal workers and low-income urban families (Human Rights Watch, 2021).

COVID-19 also claimed lives in Nigeria, with the Nigeria Centre for Disease Control (NCDC) reporting 3146 deaths since the first case (Olu-Abiodun et al., 2022). Lagos (102,008), the Federal Capital Territory (28,880), and Rivers (17,020) recorded the highest cases among Nigerian states. Despite the urgent need for COVID-19 vaccination, communities show widespread indifference and reluctance (Olu-Abiodun et al., 2022). Consequently, vaccination rates remain low; as of 28 February 2022, over 17 million individuals received the initial vaccine dose, but only 8 million received the second, translating to 8.4% of the population receiving one dose and 3.8% fully vaccinated (NPHCDA, 2022).

## Crisis Leadership and Leadership Evolution in Higher Education Amidst the COVID-19 Pandemic

In our rapidly evolving global landscape, crisis leadership is acknowledged but still largely uncharted within scholarly exploration. Crisis leadership is the art of steering an organisation through unforeseen threats that endanger its operations, reputation, or existence (Firestone, 2020). It encompasses a range of critical attributes, including the ability to make swift and resolute decisions, the capacity to adapt to ever-changing circumstances, the skill of effective communication, and the knack for efficiently organising diverse groups (Deitchman, 2013; Mutch, 2020).

The emergence of the COVID-19 pandemic exerted immense pressure on leaders in higher education, demanding rapid decision-making and a high degree of adaptability (McNamara, 2021). The importance of certain leadership traits, such as adept communication, fostering collaboration, demonstrating empathy, and embracing flexibility, became glaringly evident (Alholiby, 2021; Nugroho et al., 2021). Notably, the pandemic catalysed personal and societal development, amplifying educators' agency and leadership capacities (Hudson et al., 2021).

This crisis also hastened the adoption of decentralised and networked leadership approaches within educational institutions (Harris, 2020). Attributes such as empathy, vulnerability, and agility have become essential to effective leadership (Lawton-Misra & Pretorius, 2021). In response to the unique challenges posed by the pandemic, various leadership models tailored to this context have been proposed (Yokuş, 2022). These models underscore the intricate interplay between entrepreneurial and operational mindsets, demonstrating how they can foster innovation, including the successful transition to remote and blended learning methods.

## Education During the COVID-19 Pandemic (2020 to 2022)

### The Impact of the COVID-19 Pandemic on Education

The advent of the COVID-19 pandemic brought about significant adverse effects on society, particularly within education. The rapid transmission of the virus had a crippling impact on the educational landscape, leading to the closure of numerous educational institutions (Handebo et al., 2021; Rahmon, 2020; UNDP, 2020). On the 19th of March 2020, in response to the escalating threat posed by the disease, the Federal Ministry of Education in Nigeria took the unprecedented step of ordering the immediate closure of all universities, secondary schools, and elementary schools nationwide (*The Guardian*, 2020).

While the primary objective behind these school closures was to contain the virus's spread within the educational environment, shield vulnerable populations from potential exposure, and safeguard public health, the consequences of these closures have been profound, particularly in terms of students' educational progress (Baldwin & Mauro, 2020; Lindzon, 2020). The repercussions of widespread social isolation, coupled with the stringent lockdown measures and protracted school closures, have cast a long shadow over the educational sector, raising concerns about the potential lasting impact on the educational system (Nicola et al., 2020; Yinka & Adebayo, 2020). It is worth noting that the government enforced these measures for both public and private schools.

In light of the detrimental effects of the COVID-19 shutdown on traditional schooling, the importance of e-learning has been underscored as a critical tool for educational continuity and development. However, these closures have starkly exposed the educational disparities within nations like Nigeria, which, despite being among the world's burgeoning economies, still lags in providing equitable educational facilities for its citizens (Dawadi et al., 2020). The pandemic has unveiled a stark contrast in educational resources among Nigerian institutions. While some private schools have leveraged online education to enhance student engagement, especially in urban centres, many public schools find themselves at a disadvantage, struggling to adapt to this new paradigm (Eze, 2021; Mseleku, 2020).

## Shift to e-Learning in Response to the Pandemic

The pandemic revealed the Nigerian education system's overreliance on traditional classrooms, showcasing the limited integration of technology in many institutions. While some university administrations successfully facilitated online learning and assessments during the COVID-19 lockdown, others were ill-prepared for such disruptions (Olatunde et al., 2021).

Private Nigerian institutions swiftly embraced online learning, necessitating digital training for teachers and students. However, this transition presented challenges in maintaining effective communication between educators and learners, especially in a developing nation like Nigeria, where advanced technology remains underutilised (Amorighoye, 2020). Various factors hindered the adoption of virtual education, including insufficient financial support for public institutions, inadequate information communication technology (ICT) infrastructure, a lack of clear ICT policies, high costs, limited ICT awareness among faculty and students, and unreliable power and internet connections (Olatunde et al., 2021).

In 2021, Professor Abubakar Rasheed, the Executive Secretary of Nigeria's National Universities Commission, reported that over 2.1 million students enrolled in Nigerian higher education institutions (Idoko, 2021). The majority of these students, approximately 94%, attended public tertiary institutions, potentially limiting their access to virtual learning due to infrastructure constraints. Statistics for undergraduates in polytechnics and higher education colleges remain unavailable (Agbola, 2019). Nevertheless, research indicates that alternative forms of education gained traction during the pandemic.

A study on digital education in Nigerian universities identified diverse learning approaches during the COVID-19 pandemic (Egielewa et al., 2022). While only 16% of Nigerian universities adopted paid online education platforms, the remaining 70% relied on accessible tools such as Google Classroom, WhatsApp, and Zoom (Egielewa et al., 2022). Adewole-Odeshi (2014) reported that only one in ten online lectures incorporated shared video feeds, and a similar proportion of students did not participate in online lectures (Qutishat et al., 2022). Universities constituted approximately two-thirds of institutions engaged in online activities during the semester, followed by polytechnics and colleges (Egielewa et al., 2022). Notably, most college students

(75%) experienced reduced academic engagement, with professors deviating from the traditional semester-based format (Egielewa et al., 2022).

## Students' Experience and Challenges Amidst COVID-19

Findings indicated that many university students were content with their online educational experiences during the pandemic (Harunasari et al., 2021). On the other hand, some students voiced their displeasure with online education, indicating that they prefer the face-to-face classroom lecture and that they would rather have that than a hybrid model that combines physical and digital components even after the lockdown (Kovacs et al., 2022; Olawade et al., 2021). However, Kituyi and Tusubira (2013) reported how some university students saw a hybrid approach to education as superior, providing room for more study and experimentation. Several studies have explained issues affecting the adoption of virtual learning, with network problems and a lack of consistent power supply as significant obstacles to the successful adoption of online education in Nigeria (Li & Lalani, 2020; Olaitan & James, 2017). Another impediment to virtual learning during the pandemic was internal issues such as a lack of motivation, boredom, and laziness (Khobragade et al., 2021). Most students are motivated by friends, study groups, and physical discussions with teachers. With COVID-19 restricting movement, these students may have lost their academic drive, making it difficult for virtual learning to bring back. Additionally, since the lockdown restricted people to their homes, distractions from family members may have also affected students' concentration. Adetona et al. (2021) reported poor student attention during the online lectures.

Financial problems such as lack of funds, insufficient data, or access to fast and reliable internet were also listed as problems of e-learning (Adeyeye et al., 2014; Olatunde et al., 2021). Since the pandemic affected the economy, many families found it challenging to feed; hence, affording online services like data or other subscriptions for courses online may have been an extra burden. Research shows that while over half of students have some grasp of the material, the majority grasp it at or below the 50% mark (Adetona et al., 2021). This conclusion makes sense, as most students in Nigeria have experience attending lectures in a classroom setting, where they can better focus on the material at hand because of the presence of peers studying the same material. However, a higher level of focus is required for online learning since students are more likely to be side-tracked by their surroundings and other activities. Nevertheless, it may be said that Nigerian higher education institutions' most significant barrier to effective online learning is the lack of adequate infrastructure, followed by students' limitations in motivation, resources, and technology.

## Government Initiatives, Financial Challenges, and Lessons from the COVID-19 Pandemic in Nigerian Higher Education

During the academic closure in Nigeria, several distance learning initiatives were introduced. In March 2020, the Minister for Education directed all academic institutions to commence online teaching during a teleconference with education sector stakeholders (McKibbin & Fernando, 2020). However, few government-owned institutions adopted this directive, while most public schools did not resume classes. Little action was taken to enhance classroom instruction and student learning in these schools (Ladipo & Adebori, 2020).

The regulatory agency acknowledged that many government entities lacked essential ICT infrastructure and resources (Zar et al., 2020). Additionally, some lecturers lacked the technical skills for virtual teaching, and even if students had personal computers and smart devices, they often faced challenges like unreliable power supply and internet connectivity (Igwe, 2022). This digital divide resulted in the marginalisation of students with fewer resources, delaying their academic progress. Consequently, Nigeria's efforts to prepare its youth for future employment suffered further setbacks due to the pandemic.

The COVID-19 lockdown disrupted the academic calendar for higher institutions, preventing many schools from conducting exams (Akuh, 2020; Ebohon et al., 2021). This impacted their finances as they depended heavily on tuition fees, which were no longer being collected. Upon students' return, the payment of tuition and other fees, a primary revenue source for government and private institutions (Saka, 2021), was uncertain. Most tertiary institutions faced severe financial challenges as they needed to cover staff salaries, infrastructure development, research, and other essential activities to maintain educational standards.

In 2020, the Economic Sustainability Committee (ESC), led by Prof. Yemi Osinbajo, predicted that unemployment in Nigeria could reach 33.6% or $51,005.21 (Ogunmade, 2020). This projection could affect students in both private and public institutions, as parental job loss might force some to drop out of school (Saka, 2021). Private colleges and universities, which rely heavily on tuition, were particularly hard hit, resulting in layoffs of educators (Abubakar, 2020). The ESC also estimated monthly losses of over $200 million, further hindering infrastructure development and essential resources for e-learning (Adeoye et al., 2020).

The pandemic's strain on the healthcare sector diverted funds away from education. Nigeria's primary revenue source, crude oil, saw a price drop, exacerbating funding challenges for higher education (Saka, 2021). In the 2020 National Budget, the federal government allocated only $800 million (6.7% of the total budget) to the educational sector, falling far short of UNESCO's 15–20% recommendation for developing nations. Even before COVID-19, Nigeria's education budget was insufficient, resulting in protests from academic unions over outdated equipment, obsolete textbooks, low lecturer salaries, and a brain drain (Kolawole & Sanusi, 2020). Budgetary allocation in the Nigerian educational sector has been decreasing since 2016, with a drop from 7.05% in 2019 to 6.70% in 2020, partially attributed to the economic impact of the pandemic (Suleiman & Ileyemi, 2022).

The COVID-19 pandemic significantly affected Nigeria's higher education system, necessitating swift measures to ensure learning continuity during the lockdown (Ebohon et al., 2021)—many educational institutions, particularly private ones, transitioned from traditional face-to-face teaching to online education. As the lockdown persisted, more schools adopted exclusive online courses, requiring teachers and students to adapt quickly to this new approach. Adjusting to remote education was challenging, especially in a resource-constrained setting like Nigeria, which had not fully embraced advanced technology in higher education (Ebohon et al., 2021).

## Education Transformation in Nigeria's Post-Pandemic Era

Even in this post-pandemic era, most of Nigeria's educational institutions, such as schools, polytechnics, colleges, and universities, rely solely on conventional teaching and learning methods (Nwachukwu et al., 2021). This indicates that they continue to use the traditional classroom lecture format. However, several academic units have begun to embrace technology to improve academic activities and remodel outdated methods. For example, the face of Nigeria's educational sector is gradually changing, as evident by the apparent advancement of the National Open University of Nigeria (NOUN). It is a distance learning institution whose course delivery is digitally fostered through Web-based modules, textual materials, audio and video tapes, and other media (Nwachukwu et al., 2021).

Many schools were permitted to offer distance learning education and use digital learning tools in their semester exams (National Universities Commission, 2022). However, the level of digital learning in Nigeria remains low throughout this post-pandemic period due to the educational sector's unwillingness to shift from traditional pedagogical techniques to more innovative, technology-based teaching and learning processes (Nwachukwu et al., 2021). Digital learning has several hurdles in Nigeria, including weak digital infrastructure, other socio-economic constraints, and a poorly coordinated educational sector (Agbele & Oyelade, 2020). Due to these factors, Nigeria lags significantly behind other emerging countries in supporting digital learning.

In addition, studies have shown that using ICTs in the classroom is necessary because they capture students' attention, stimulate their creativity and perception, deepen their comprehension, and facilitate student–teacher interactions (Ray et al., 2020; Sangrà & González-Sanmamed, 2010). Students gain social skills, initiative, creativity, and responsibility through e-learning (Ghavifekr & Rosdy, 2015; Ghavifekr et al., 2014). Some university-based library schools lack computer and ICT laboratories for practical courses like the library and information science. Others have outdated labs and poorly maintained ICT tools, and some have labs with no technical support (Adetoun Akinde, 2021). As a result, no good electronic or online teaching or learning can occur without a proper computer laboratory and well-trained and prompt technical support personnel. Nigerian universities are still dealing with a great deal of difficulty today. This may be evident in challenges against effective content delivery and course administration, such as overcrowded lecture auditoriums caused by insufficient infrastructure to accommodate knowledge-hungry young brains (Adetoun Akinde, 2021).

The reinvention of teachers' role in education is expected post-COVID in Nigeria due to what the education sector experienced during the pandemic. This means that the old notion of a teacher being seen as an all-powerful knowledge custodian showering wisdom on students will become obsolete and will not exist in the future. Many students may now obtain material online with a few mouse clicks, all thanks to the pandemic experience, which has deprived them of access to the four walls of the classroom for a long time. In light of this, the nation's higher education institutions explicitly recognise lecturers as facilitators and integrators. They lead and stimulate students as they journey through self-discovery and build new concepts and attitudes as facilitators (Abosede et al., 2021). At the same time, as an integrator, they assist students in bridging the gap between academic knowledge and practical life.

Skill-based learning will likewise take precedence over knowledge-based education in the post-COVID era. The pandemic has highlighted the need for pupils and instructors to acquire vital life skills for crisis survival. As a result, these skills will need to be integrated into all levels of schooling. Emotional intelligence, entrepreneurship, informed decision-making, empathy, and teamwork have all been mentioned as skills, including creativity and critical thinking (Abosede et al., 2021).

Furthermore, due to the pandemic, the future of education in the country may see a rise in private school fees, which some parents may be unable to pay because many individuals have lost their income sources. In contrast, others have experienced a significant fall in salaries. This may cause some students to withdraw from their prominent colleges, jeopardising their academic advancement.

Lastly, parental involvement in their children's academic activities will also significantly increase post-COVID-19. This is because many parents who previously did not dedicate enough time to their children's academics are now more aware of their obligations. Consequently, parents and teachers know their mutual commitments and a common goal: to help the students learn and succeed academically. This will serve as the cornerstone for a solid and long-term partnership.

The most challenging task facing tertiary education administrators is to develop financial resources to integrate information technology (IT) into the educational scheme. Due to a lack of funding, school administrators cannot acquire the facilities that will effectively improve the learning environment in Nigeria (Jacob et al., 2021). That is why academic employees, also known as faculty members, are a critical component of higher education institutions that are always on strike (ASUU, ASUP, among others).

A lack of basic IT facilities is also a barrier to the widespread adoption of computer-generated learning environments in Nigerian institutes in the post-COVID-19 age. This is due to the little funding available to university leaders. Post-COVID-19 tertiary schooling in Nigeria should be IT-driven, necessitating universities to acquire the required infrastructure to facilitate virtual learning.

Furthermore, most ICT devices are powered by electricity, and Nigeria has a low rate of power production and frequent power outages. This is a significant setback in the drive to improve higher education. Because of this power outage, tertiary teachers cannot adequately use the minimal information technology resources accessible at various schools. The money spent on private power generation would have gone into higher-productivity projects at the institutions. Also, other problems include poor motivation, overcrowded classrooms, poor staff development programmes, strike actions, and insecurity (Jacob et al., 2021).

A digital learning environment is required to meet the needs of Nigerian society and remain competitive in the post-COVID-19 era. Therefore, a paradigm shift from the traditional learning environment, which is burdened with overcrowded classrooms and insufficient instructional materials, and where lecturers still interact face-to-face with students via the "talk and chalk" method, should be ousted from our educational system. A "digital learning environment" means Integrating IT with educational pedagogy to create a learner-centred space with sufficient teaching materials. Virtual learning encourages collaborative, creative thinking, and activity-based learning (Wordu, 2021).

The move from paper-based to paperless administration is a planned effort. It is a call to action for educators to evaluate how they might make their classrooms more engaging for students and instructors. There should be no obsolete buildings, insufficient classrooms, or inadequately equipped libraries and labs in the educational environment. The post-COVID-19 learning environment should be student-centred and collaborative rather than the old survival of the fittest technique (Wordu, 2021).

## Student Leadership, Sense of Belonging, and Well-Being During and After the COVID-19 Pandemic

Due to the unplanned transition from classroom to virtual learning during the pandemic, numerous undergraduate students in Nigeria had severe academic issues. Students with strong leadership abilities may inspire, encourage, and build confidence in their peers. It is an essential component required for a university to thrive. Aymoldanovna et al. (2015) argue that including students in the governance system of the institution would provide them with opportunities to enhance management and leadership competencies. These are necessary talents for success and survival in the global economy (Acafoundation, 2020). Despite the challenges and uncertainties caused by the COVID-19 pandemic, such as school closures and social distancing rules, Enactus student teams in Nigeria's tertiary institutions served their communities by demonstrating leadership skills and implementing programmes that helped to mitigate the socio-economic impact of the COVID-19 pandemic.

Enactus is a network of student, academic, and business leaders dedicated to utilising the potential of entrepreneurial action to allow growth for themselves and the communities in which they live (Enactus, 2019). The following are some courageous and remarkable acts by Enactus students in their communities in response to the COVID-19 epidemic.

1. The Kaduna Polytechnic Enactus team assisted its community in remaining safe and healthy by ensuring that individuals have easy access to hand sanitisers and water to wash their hands often but also practise hand washing and the usage of hand sanitisers. The group devised an ingenious plan to recycle discarded materials into functional hand-washing basins fitted with flowing water taps. The group also created cheap hand sanitisers that are readily available and may be used by anybody to defend themselves against the coronavirus.
2. The Enactus team from Kaduna State University set out to manufacture hand sanitisers that were effective and inexpensive, with an alcohol level of 80%, to fulfil the requirements set by the World Health Organization. The team manufactured and sold over 6,000 bottles of hand sanitisers at a price significantly lower than the market rates in collaboration with pharmacies, superstores, and hospitals. In another instance of entrepreneurial initiative, the Kaduna Polytechnic Enactus team created and distributed safe, recyclable face masks at a price lower than currently available.
3. Since schools nationwide have ceased physical operations, the University of Port-Harcourt Enactus team offered free online skill-acquisition programmes for students during the lockdown.
4. The Covenant University Enactus team in Ota, Ogun state, went out to police officers on patrol to thank them for enforcing the government's lockdown order, recognising that they were among the most at-risk members of the community. The Covenant University Enactus team also donated face masks to the local police station to prevent them from contracting a virus while performing their duties.
5. Due to the social distancing instructions, the Federal Polytechnic Idah Enactus team offered their assistance in bridging the distance between purchasers and sellers of food goods. To accomplish this goal, the Enactus team established an online marketplace connecting food vendors (who cannot bring their items to the market since it is closed) with food consumers (who need these goods but must stay safe at home). The Enactus group ensured that goods were delivered to the customers as quickly as possible.

Following the government's announcement of a total lockdown during COVID-19 across the country, strict lockdown procedures were implemented, making any form of face-to-face teaching or learning impossible (Dan-Nwafor et al., 2020). As a result, students experienced a loss of community and a profound sense of alienation from their schools. In the wake of the COVID-19 spread, several higher institutions in the country realised they were unprepared for emergencies such as the pandemic. As a result, many students first felt disengaged from their various educational environments. During the pandemic, students were abandoned, separated from the rest of the school, and unable to progress academically. Since the COVID-19 epidemic often necessitates social isolation and distance education, it was even more challenging for higher institutions to give a sense of belonging to their students. The widespread COVID-19 pandemic made it clear that more significant efforts and innovative approaches were required to foster feelings of exclusion among students. Therefore, several universities employed teaching technologies like Blackboard Collaborate, Moodle, Google Meet, Zoom, Microsoft Team, and others to engage students virtually instead of physical classrooms (Ogunsanya, 2021). Higher institutions that use the aforementioned educational technologies could engage their students, giving them a sense of belonging. These teaching tools allowed students to receive a lecture from their teachers and give feedback on the lessons. Students were treated as if they were in the four walls of a classroom as they were given assignments to work on and provide subsequent feedback. Later, schools adopted the hybrid method as the cases of COVID-19 patients decreased, and measures were taken to keep the situation in check. This method allows students to visit their respective higher institutions for practical classes and, at the same time, attend lectures online. With this measure, students in the country could connect more with themselves and their higher institutions on and off campus, giving them a sense of belonging.

Since the first case was reported on the 27th of February 2020, by the Nigeria Centre for Disease Control (NCDC), the Nigerian government, to curtail the situation, implemented lockdowns, including mobility restrictions and the indefinite shutdown of religious centres and schools, to halt the spread of the coronavirus (Iyanuoluwa, 2020). As a result, the public, particularly students in higher institutions, has experienced extensive psychological repercussions affecting their well-being. Students suffered the unexpected transformation from interactive face-to-face learning to an online mode of teaching, which most Nigerian universities never considered due to a lack of preparedness for anything that may block the education system, such as a pandemic shutdown. Students' mental health deteriorated due to the pandemic and lockdown, which was unavoidable given the school's lack of emergency preparedness.

A study carried out among medical students at the University of Ibadan reported that final-year students were more affected by the lockdown than others. The abrupt school closure and suspension of academic activities led to delayed graduation time and future employment prospects. Therefore, 19% experienced mild to moderate depression, 5% severe to extremely severe depression, 10% had mild to moderate anxiety, 7.5% severe to extremely severe anxiety, and approximately 16% had mild to moderate stress (Adewale et al., 2021). Increased anxiety, depression, stress, and post-traumatic stress disorder (PTSD) related symptoms were associated with increased time on social media, movies, and television, sleep duration, and reduced physical activity (Adewale et al., 2021).

Owing to the pandemic, many higher institutions in Nigeria have shown interest in advanced technology to improve the country's education, which will continue to play a significant role in the educational system in Nigeria in the future (Iyanuoluwa, 2020). It is expected that blended learning, in which digital technologies are utilised to complement conventional learning techniques, would gain acceptance post-COVID. Most educational institutions have realised the importance of creating and maintaining online learning systems to ensure institutional resilience and academic continuity during times of crisis. They will probably remain on this path for a long time. While many educational institutions in the country have been indifferent to changing the traditional 150-year-old classroom model, the pandemic has necessitated adopting the trending learning method (Iyanuoluwa, 2020).

## Recommendations for Rebuilding the Quality of Learning and Teaching Cultures in the Post-Pandemic Period

1. To ensure the long-term viability and enhance the quality of services for Nigeria's tertiary institutions, the federal government should direct the appropriate oversight and regulatory agencies (such as the National Universities Commission, the National Board of Technical Education, and the National Commission for Colleges of Education) to convene a summit of relevant stakeholders and discuss the way forward in securing the future of the nation's tertiary institutions for better service delivery (Akintola, 2022).

2. The government should strive to implement the United Nations Educational, Scientific, and Cultural Organization's (UNESCO) funding recommendation of 26% for education in the country rather than allocating a small portion of the annual budget to education.
3. The higher education curriculum should be modified immediately to incorporate security/safety and health education problems, as entrepreneurial education is established as a mandatory course in the system.
4. Higher education teaching and learning activities should include face-to-face interaction and distance learning using ICT devices. Also, they should improve ICT equipment for connecting instructors and students to continue with the curriculum via social media platforms such as Telegram, Edmodo, Mixir, Webinars, and teleconferencing, among others (Akuh, 2020).
5. The government needs to be prepared to provide additional physical infrastructure, including buildings and other facilities, to aid in developing higher education in the country. Also, ICT equipment and facilities of international standards should be improved in Nigeria's tertiary institutions.

## References

Abosede, C., Oresajo, O., & Akintola, O. (2021). COVID-19 and higher education in Nigeria: The present and the future. *Interdisciplinary Journal of Education, 4*(2), 100–113. https://doi.org/10.53449/ije.v4i2.59

Abubakar, I. (2020). *With COVID-19 cases rising, will Nigeria schools fully reopen in 2020?* https://techcabal.com/2020/08/10/with-covid-19-cases-rising-will-nigerian-schools-fully-reopen-in-2020/·

Acafoundation. (2020). *Enactus Nigeria student teams respond to the COVID-19 pandemic—African capital alliance foundation.* https://www.acafoundation.com/enactus-nigeria-student-teams-respond-to-the-covid-19-pandemic/

Adeoye, I., Adanikin, A., & Adanikin, A. (2020). COVID-19 and e-learning: Nigeria tertiary education system experience. *International Journal of Research and Innovation in Applied Science (IJRIAS), V*, 28–31.

Adetona, Z. A., Ogunyemi, J., & Oduntan, O. E. (2021). Investigating e-learning utilisation during COVID-19 pandemic lockdown in Southwestern Nigeria. *International Journal of Scientific & Engineering Research, 12*(5), 893–899.

Adetoun Akinde, T. (2021). Inhibitors to the electronic teaching and learning of library science in the Nigerian universities of the post-COVID-19 pandemic era and the way forward. *American Journal of Information Science and Technology, 5*(2), 30–39. https://doi.org/10.11648/j.ajist.20210502.13

Adewale, B. A., Adeniyi, Y. C., Adeniyi, O. A., Ojediran, B. C., Aremu, P. S., Odeyemi, O. E., Akintayo, A. D., Oluwadamilare, F. A., Offorbuike, C. B., & Owoeye, I. P. (2021). Psychological impact of COVID-19 pandemic on students at the University of Ibadan in Nigeria. *Journal of Education, Society and Behavioural Science, 34*(1), 79–92. https://doi.org/10.9734/jesbs/2021/v34i130295

Adewole-Odeshi, E. (2014). *Attitude of students towards e-learning in south-west Nigerian universities: An application of technology acceptance model*. http://digitalcommons.unl.edu/cgi/viewcontent.cgi?article=2504andcontext=libphilprac

Adeyeye, O. M., Afolabi, I. T., & Ayo, C. K. (2014). Virtual learning in Nigerian universities: A panacea for enhanced academic standards. *International Journal for Cross-Disciplinary Subjects in Education, 2*(2), 40–49.

Agbele, A. T., & Oyelade, E. A. (2020). Impact of COVID-19 on the Nigerian educational system: Strengths and challenges of online/virtual education. *Asian Journal of Education and Social Studies, 13*, 26–35. https://doi.org/10.9734/ajess/2020/v13i130322

Agbola, B. (2019). 94% of Nigerian students are in public tertiary institutions *Premium Times*. https://www.premiumtimesng.com/news/more-news/336120-94-of-nigerian-students-are-in-public-tertiary-institutions-official.html

Akintola, O. (2022). COVID-19 and higher education in Nigeria : The present and the future. February. https://doi.org/10.53449/ije.v4i2.59

Akuh, E. A. (2020). COVID-19 pandemic and management of education system in Nigeria: Impacts of e-learning programme intervention and google classroom. *International Journal of Innovative Education Research, 8*(4), 118–123.

Alholiby, M. S. (2021). Higher education's leadership soft skills reflected in COVID-19 responses. *Journal of Scientific Research in Education, 22*(9), 540–556. https://doi.org/10.21608/jsre.2021.92771.1361

Amorighoye, T. A. (2020, June). COVID-19 has exposed the education divide in Nigeria. This is how we can close it. In *World economic forum* (Vol. 2, pp. 101–114).

Aymoldanovna, A. A., Zhetpisbaeva, B. A., Kozybaevna, K. U., & Kadirovna, S. M. (2015). Leadership development university students in the activities of student government. *Procedia-Social and Behavioral Sciences, 197*, 2131–2136. https://doi.org/10.1016/j.sbspro.2015.07.336

Baldwin, R., & Mauro, B. W. (2020). Economics in the time of COVID-19. *Economics in the Time of COVID-19*, 105–109.

CDC. (2020). *Coronavirus (COVID-19)*. https://www.cdc.gov/coronavirus/2019-ncov/index.html

Dan-Nwafor, C., Ochu, C. L., Elimian, K., Oladejo, J., Ilori, E., Umeokonkwo, C., Steinhardt, L., Igumbor, E., Wagai, J., Okwor, T., Aderinola, O., Mba, N., Hassan, A., Dalhat, M., Jinadu, K., Badaru, S., Arinze, C., Jafiya, A., Disu, Y., ..., & Ihekweazu, C. (2020). Nigeria's public health response to the COVID-19 pandemic: January to May 2020. *Journal of Global Health, 10*(2), 1–9. https://doi.org/10.7189/JOGH.10.020399

Dawadi, S., Giri, R. A., & Simkhada, P. (2020). *Impact of COVID-19 on the education sector in Nepal: Challenges and coping strategies* (pp. 1–16). Sage Submissions.

Deitchman, S. (2013). Enhancing crisis leadership in public health emergencies. *Disaster Medicine and Public Health Preparedness, 7*(5), 534–540. https://doi.org/10.1017/dmp.2013.81

Ebohon, O., Obienu, A. C., Irabor, F., Amadin, F. I., & Omoregie, E. S. (2021). Evaluating the impact of COVID-19 pandemic lockdown on education in Nigeria: Insights from teachers and students on virtual/online learning. *Bulletin of the National Research Centre, 45*(1). https://doi.org/10.1186/s42269-021-00538-6

Egielewa, P., Idogho, P. O., Iyalomhe, F. O., & Cirella, G. T. (2022). COVID-19 and digitised education: Analysis of online learning in Nigerian higher education. *E-Learning and Digital Media, 19*(1), 19–35. https://doi.org/10.1177/20427530211022808

Enactus. (2019). *About.* UF Warrington College of Business. https://warrington.ufl.edu/enactus/about/

Eze, U. N. (2021). Impact of COVID-19 pandemic on education in Nigeria: Implications for policy and practice of e-learning. *Library Philosophy and Practice (E-Journal),* 5651. https://digitalcommons.unl.edu/libphilprac/5651

Federal Ministry of Health. (2020). *Nigeria family planning blueprint 2020–2024.* https://health.gov.ng/doc/Final-2020-Blueprint.pdf

Firestone, S. (2020). What is crisis leadership? *Biblical Principles of Crisis Leadership, 7–21.* https://doi.org/10.1007/978-3-030-44955-1_2

Ghavifekr, S., Razak, A. Z. A., Ghani, M. F. A., Ran, N. Y., Meixi, Y., & Tengyue, Z. (2014). ICT integration in education: Incorporation for teaching & learning improvement. *Malaysian Online Journal of Educational Technology, 2*(2), 24–45.

Ghavifekr, S., & Rosdy, W. A. W. (2015). Teaching and learning with technology: Effectiveness of ICT integration in schools. *International Journal of Research in Education and Science, 1*(2), 175–191. https://doi.org/10.21890/ijres.23596

Handebo, S., Adugna, A., Kassie, A., & Shitu, K. (2021). Determinants of COVID-19-related knowledge and preventive behaviours among students in reopened secondary schools: Cross-sectional study. *British Medical Journal Open, 11*(4), e050189.

Harris, A. (2020). COVID-19—School leadership in crisis? *Journal of Professional Capital and Community, 5*(3–4), 321–326. https://doi.org/10.1108/JPCC-06-2020-0045

Harunasari, S. Y., Dwigustini, R., Halim, N., & Susillawati, S. (2021). University students' acceptance of online learning during the pandemic in Indonesia. *AL-ISHLAH: Journal Pendidikan, 13*(1), 396–406. https://doi.org/10.35445/alishlah.v13i1.491

Hudson, L., Mahendrarajah, S., Walton, M., Pascaris, M. J., Melim, S., & Ruttenberg-Rozen, R. (2021). Leadership in education during COVID-19: Learning and growing through a crisis. *Journal of Digital Life and Learning, 1*(1), 16–33. https://doi.org/10.51357/jdll.v1i1.113

Human Rights Watch. (2021, July 28). *"Between hunger and the virus" The impact of the Covid-19 pandemic on people living in poverty in Lagos, Nigeria.* https://www.hrw.org/report/2021/07/28/between-hunger-and-virus/impact-covid-19-pandemic-people-living-poverty-lagos

Ibrahim, R. L., Ajide, K. B., & Olatunde, J. O. (2020). Easing of lockdown measures in Nigeria: Implications for the healthcare system. *Health Policy and Technology, 9*(4), 399–404. https://doi.org/10.1016/j.hlpt.2020.09.004

Idoko, C. (2021). 2.1 Million students studying in Nigerian Universities—NUC. *Nigerian Tribune.* https://tribuneonlineng.com/2-1-million-students-studying-in-nigerian-universities-nuc/

Igwe, B. M. (2022). COVID-19 pandemic and education in Nigeria. *Journal of Social Sciences, 8*(1), 25–32.

Iyanuoluwa, S. A. (2020). Coronavirus (COVID-19) and Nigerian education system: Impacts, management, responses, and way forward. *Education Journal, 3*(4), 88–102. https://doi.org/10.31058/j.edu.2020.34009

Jacob, O. N., Jegede, D., & Musa, A. (2021). Problems facing academic staff of Nigerian universities and the way forward. *International Journal on Integrated Education, 4*(1), 230–241.

Khobragade, S., Soe, H., Khobragade, Y., & Abas, A. (2021). Virtual learning during the COVID-19 pandemic: What are the barriers and how to overcome them? *Journal of Education and Health Promotion, 10*(1). https://doi.org/10.4103/jehp.jehp_1422_20

Kituyi, G., & Tusubira, I. (2013). A framework for integrating e-learning in higher education institutions in developing countries. *International Journal of Education and Development Using Information and Communication Technology, 9*(2), 19–36.

Kolawole, W. S., & Sanusi, S. L. (2020). *Post Covid-19 crisis: Effects and transformation of tertiary education system in Nigeria. IV*(Ix), 174–178.

Kovacs, C., Jadin, T., & Ortner, C. (2022). Austrian college students' experiences with digital media learning during the first COVID-19 lockdown. *Frontiers in Psychology, 13*(February). https://doi.org/10.3389/fpsyg.2022.734138

Ladipo, Y. D., & Adebori, A. (2020). COVID-19 is exacerbating the problem of educational inequity in Nigeria. *Nairametrics.* https://nairametrics.com/2020/04/18/covid-19-is-exacerbating-the-problem-of-educational-inequity-in-nigeria/

Lawton-Misra, N., & Pretorius, T. (2021). Leading with heart: Academic leadership during the COVID-19 crisis. *South African Journal of Psychology, 51*(2), 205–214. https://doi.org/10.1177/0081246321992979

Li, C., & Lalani, F. (2020). The COVID-19 pandemic has changed education forever. This is how. *World Economic Forum.* https://www.weforum.org/agenda/2020/04/coronavirus-education-global-covid19-online-digital-learning/

Lindzon, J. (2020). School closures are starting, and they'll have far-reaching economic impacts. *Fast Company*.

McKibbin, W., & Fernando, R. (2020). The economic impact of COVID-19. In R. Baldwin & B. Weder Di Mauro (Red.), *Economics in the time of COVID-19* (pp. 45–51). Centre for Economic Policy Research (CEPR).

McNamara, A. (2021). Crisis management in higher education in the time of COVID-19: The case of actor training. *Education Sciences, 11*(3). https://doi.org/10.3390/educsci11030132

Mseleku, Z. (2020). A literature review of e-learning and e-teaching in the era of Covid-19 Pandemic. *International Journal of Innovative Science and Research Technology, 5*(10), 588–597.

Mutch, C. (2020). Crisis leadership: Evaluating our leadership approaches in the time of COVID-19. *NZCER,* 1–24. https://doi.org/10.18296/em.0058

National Universities Commission. (2022). *Guidelines for open and distance learning in Nigerian universities*. https://www.nuc.edu.ng/distance-learning-centers/

Nicola, M., Alsafi, Z., Sohrabi, C., Kerwan, A., Al-Jabir, A., Iosifidis, C., Agha, M., & Agha, R. (2020). The socio-economic implications of the coronavirus pandemic (COVID-19): A review. *International Journal of Surgery, 78*, 185–193. https://doi.org/10.1016/j.ijsu.2020.04.018

NPHCDA. (2022). *NPHCDA—National Primary Health Care Development Agency*, 19. https://nphcda.gov.ng/

Nugroho, I., Paramita, N., Mengistie, B. T., & Krupskyi, O. P. (2021). Higher education leadership and uncertainty during the COVID-19 pandemic. *Journal of Socioeconomics and Development, 4*(1), 1–7. https://doi.org/10.31328/jsed.v4i1.2274

Nwachukwu, S. T., Ugwu, C. M., & Wogu, J. O. (2021). Digital learning in post COVID-19 era: Policy options and prospects for quality education in Nigeria. *Library Philosophy and Practice, 2021*(March 2022), 1–18.

Ogunmade, O. (2020). *Osinbajo committee projects 39.4m job losses by Dec.* https://www.thisdaylive.com/index.php/2020/06/12/osinbajo-committee-projects-39-4m-job-losses-by-dec/

Ogunsanya, K. (2021, January 18). The future of education post-COVID. *The Guardian.* https://guardian.ng/opinion/the-future-of-education-post-covid/

Olaitan, A., & James, U. (2017). E-learning implementation in higher education: Aspects of infrastructure development challenges and students learning approaches. *INSPIRE (International Conference for Process Improvement, Research and Education),* 83–94. https://pure.ulster.ac.uk/en/publications/e-learning-implementation-in-highereducationaspects-of-infrastru-3

Olatunde, A., Ogunode, N. J., & Eyiolorunse, A. (2021). Assessment of virtual learning during Covid-19 lockdown in Nigerian public universities. *Academia Globe: Inderscience Research, 2*(5), 159–175. https://doi.org/10.17605/OSF.IO/S6N2Q

Olawade, D. B., Wada, O. Z., Asaolu, F. T., Odetayo, A., Akeju, O. O., & Olorunsogbon, O. F. (2021). COVID-19 and students' mental well-being: A cross-sectional study across selected Nigerian universities. *Journal of Education, Society and Behavioural Science, 34*, 176–186. https://doi.org/10.9734/jesbs/2021/v34i1130377

Olu-Abiodun, O., Abiodun, O., & Okafor, N. (2022). COVID-19 vaccination in Nigeria: A rapid review of vaccine acceptance rate and the associated factors. *PLoS ONE, 17*(5), 1–10. https://doi.org/10.1371/journal.pone.0267691

Qutishat, D., Obeidallah, R., & Qawasmeh, Y. (2022). An overview of attendance and participation in online class during the COVID pandemic: A case study. *International Journal of Interactive Mobile Technologies, 16*(4), 103–115. https://doi.org/10.3991/ijim.v16i04.27103

Rahmon, R. (2020). *Education in Ado-Odo Ota local government*. Ado-Odo Ota Local Government.

Ray, A., Bala, P. K., & Dasgupta, S. A. (2020). Psychological analytics based technology adoption model for effective educational marketing. *Digital and Social Media Marketing: Emerging Applications and Theoretical Development*, 163–174.

Saka, A. J. (2021). The effect of COVID-19 on Nigeria tertiary institutions: Challenges and prospects. *Arabian Journal of Business and Management Review, 11*, S7.

Sangrà, A., & González-Sanmamed, M. (2010). The role of information and communication technologies in improving teaching and learning processes in primary and secondary schools. *Australasian Journal of Educational Technology, 26*(8), 207–220. https://doi.org/10.14742/ajet.1020

Suleiman, Q., & Ileyemi, M. (2022, January 11). *2021 Review: How insecurity, COVID-19 hampered Nigeria's education sector*. https://www.premiumtimesng.com/news/top-news/505275-2021-review-how-insecurity-covid-19-hampered-nigerias-education-sector.html

*The Guardian*. (2020, March 19). *COVID-19: FG orders closure of unity schools*. https://guardian.ng/news/covid-19-fg-orders-closure-of-unity-schools/

United Nations Development Programme. (2020). The impact of the Covid-19 pandemic in Nigeria. *UNDP Nigeria*, 1–12.

WHO. (2021). *Arsenic*. https://www.who.int/en/news-room/fact-sheets/detail/arsenic

Wordu, J. A. (2021). Redefining tertiary education learning environment for greater productivity in post COVID-19 era in Nigeria. *Multidisciplinary International Journal of Research and Development (MIJRD)*, 53–63.

Yinka, D. L., & Adebayo, A. (2020). *COVID-19 is exacerbating the problem of educational inequity in Nigeria*. Nairametrics.

Yokuş, G. (2022). Developing a guiding model of educational leadership in higher education during the COVID-19 pandemic: A grounded theory study. *Participatory Educational Research, 9*(1), 362–387. https://doi.org/10.17275/per.22.20.9.1

Zar, H. J., Dawa, J., Fischer, G. B., & Castro-Rodriguez, J. A. (2020). Challenges of COVID-19 in children in low- and middle-income countries. *Paediatric Respiratory Reviews, 35*, 70–74. https://doi.org/10.1016/j.prrv.2020.06.016

# The Impact of COVID-19 on Papua New Guinea's Higher Education

Jerome Oko

## Introduction

The COVID-19 pandemic has caused economic, social and political disruption (Rashid & Yadav, 2020; Toquero, 2020). The borders were closed, and governments worldwide have introduced significant financial measures to support their economies (Cahusac de Caux, 2023; Sin et al., 2023; Khanom, 2023). In most countries, many higher education institutions, such as universities, have faced disruption and significant financial impacts (Schwander-Maire et al., 2023; Salimi et al., 2023). For instance, a study by Rashid and Yadav (2020) reveals that countries such as Australia, Canada, England and the US, where universities mainly relied heavily on inbound fee-paying international students, were affected. In the UK, the pandemic has exposed deep-rooted flaws in public universities' funding. Billions of pounds were lost because of the decrease in international student numbers (Ayling & Luetz, 2023; Roy et al., 2023; Zhang et al., 2022).

The pandemic has exposed multiple levels of inequalities in higher education (Jehi et al., 2022; Bozkurt, 2022). These levels of inequalities include the differential treatment of students based on their background, closed access to knowledge and research results (Marinoni et al., 2020), unevenness in global patterns of research collaboration (Mncube et al., 2021) and lack of access to the basic requirements of digitalised higher education such as devices,

J. Oko (✉)
Divine Word University, Konedobu, NCD, Papua New Guinea
e-mail: joko@dwu.ac.pg


J. Rudolph et al. (eds.), *The Palgrave Handbook of Crisis Leadership in Higher Education*, https://doi.org/10.1007/978-3-031-54509-2_24

internet access and electricity (Zhang et al., 2022; Tilak & Kumar, 2022). The urgency of addressing these inequities must be kept at the forefront as higher education institutions begin to think ahead to create a more equitable post-pandemic world (Camilleri & Camilleri, 2022; Naidoo & Cartwright, 2022; Li & Che, 2022). COVID-19 shows good management practices are based on flexibility, strong communication, crisis team creation, digitalisation and remote work. Services were significantly impacted, and virtual delivery depended on infrastructure availability (Crawford & Cifuentes-Faura, 2022; Selvanathan et al., 2023; Azila-Gbettor et al., 2023). Institutional finances were also impacted. The mental health of students and staff became a significant concern (Marinoni et al., 2020; Mncube et al., 2021).

COVID-19 changed the nature of teaching and learning for students and lecturers to an online model (Agasisti & Soncin, 2021; Shahzad et al., 2021). The sudden transition opened great opportunities for innovation in virtual mobility and collaboration. However, it also impacted the quality of instruction because infrastructure and lecturers lacked previous teaching and learning experience in virtual environments (Camilleri, 2021; Jung et al., 2021). The pandemic has affected research, one of the cornerstones of a country's development prospects (El Said, 2021; Abu Talib et al., 2021). For instance, access to knowledge has widened, but resources were mostly geared towards COVID-19, and fieldwork was disrupted. Female academics, early career researchers and PhD students were the most vulnerable regarding job placements and stability.

## Purpose of the Study

This study aims to discuss the challenges faced by higher education institutions in Papua New Guinea (PNG) during the COVID-19 pandemic. The challenges include the differential treatment of students based on their background, closed access to knowledge and research results (Marinoni et al., 2020), unevenness in global patterns of research collaboration (Mncube et al., 2021) and lack of access to the basic requirements of digitalised higher education such as devices and internet access (Zhang et al., 2022; Tilak & Kumar, 2022). Online learning, dropping enrolment numbers, and financial constraints to adapt to online learning to PNG universities facing financial, emotional and virtual learning adaptation challenges. Providing leadership within these challenges was another challenge for university leaders. As a developing country, PNG university leadership groups were unprepared for the consequences of COVID-19 when it started in the country. However, with international collaboration and university support, they provided leadership with online teaching and learning. Even though there were issues associated with online delivery due to university staff being less prepared to use the online platform, this study addresses some of these issues. It discusses the way forward for post-COVID-19 in higher education.

## Methodology

This paper employs content analysis of popular literature to investigate higher education in PNG and the Pacific Islands during the pandemic. To achieve this, updated reviews of current literature were conducted, utilising governmental reports, news media and other non-academic sources, as there is limited research on COVID-19 in this region. The current literature review has some limitations due to the scarcity of resources, resulting in only a few remarks being identified and analysed. However, there is potential for further exploration of relevant information. More extensive studies could consider developing more inclusive criteria and conducting empirical examinations of the evidence in the literature review.

## PNG's Context of Higher Education Before, During and Beyond the Pandemic

Papua New Guinea (PNG) is one of the Pacific Island countries located north of Australia. PNG has more than 800 languages and different cultural and tribal clans. Additionally, eight million people are living under a democratic government system. Due to its historical colonial influence, this region's education and higher education systems have predominantly been adopted from the Australian education system. PNG has eight universities and other higher education institutions. The universities are University of Papua New Guinea (UPNG), University of Technology (UOT), Divine Word University (DWU), University of Goroka (UOG), University of Natural Resources and Environment (UNRE), Pacific Adventist University (PAU), Western Pacific University (WPU) and Institute of Business Studies University (IBSU). Most of these universities have been using traditional teaching methods without technology. However, when the pandemic came, these universities struggled during the period, and the situation was much more worrying in the eight universities where most students and academics had no access to technology to comfortably switch from traditional on-campus learning to a digitally enhanced mode of learning. The universities were forced to cease their academic business for a while due to genuine panic to control the unforeseen dangers.

Most universities in PNG have indicated that they have online repositories for educational materials in place, centres for e-learning and units that support teachers in digitally enhanced teaching and learning and digital skilling (Ssemugenyi et al., 2021; Nuru et al., 2021). While this is a truism, these centres seemed ill-prepared to tackle the crisis, given the exaggerated nature of the situation alongside strict operational budgets. Divine Word University, "known for digital learning", as Jan Czuba (2020) indicated, also struggled at the outset of the pandemic. The good news is that as soon as institutions of higher learning felt the pulse of the disaster, they intermittently closed down while looking for proactive measures to confront the situation (Raphael et al., 2023; Lau & Sutcliffe, 2021).

The COVID-19 pandemic has disrupted learning for 1.5 billion children, representing over 89% of the world's student population, including all 2.41 million students in PNG (Ssemugenyi et al., 2021; Nuru et al., 2021). The gains in expanding access to education and improving the quality of education are severely compromised (Raphael et al., 2023; Lau & Sutcliffe, 2021). Schools' loss of protection and other support, including school-based health and child protection, also impact children's well-being. Vulnerable children, including girls, children with a disability, poor and other marginalised groups, including those living in remote, hard-to-reach areas, are the most affected (Connell, 2022; Pokhrel & Chhetri, 2021). Due to nationwide lockdowns, the government closed educational institutions temporarily to help contain the spread of the COVID-19 pandemic (Zawacki-Richter, 2021; Elumalai et al., 2021). These nationwide closures impacted almost 70% of the country's student population (Jung et al., 2021; Nuru et al., 2021). Tertiary education was severely marked by the ban on in-person university lectures and examinations and the closing of university facilities, including libraries and canteens (Ssemugenyi & Nuru Seje, 2021; Nuru et al., 2021). These conditions significantly affected young adults, including university students, often causing potentially more stressful lifestyles.

As the pandemic unfolds, its long-lasting effects are far from settled. Studies such as Ssemugenyi and Nuru Seje (2021) and Nuru et al. (2021) have highlighted two key elements. First, the rapid return to in-person teaching and learning and the stabilisation of enrolment patterns suggest the transformation in the core understanding of higher education as a face-to-face endeavour. Second, the resumption of academic-related travel also points to the re-emergence of pre-pandemic era trends regarding the internationalisation of higher education. The good news is that these numbers have started to improve, and student mobility patterns have started to return to pre-COVID-19 levels in PNG ( Ssemugenyi & Nuru Seje, 2021; Nuru et al., 2021). For instance, according to the local media report, PNG witnessed the highest enrollment of students in 2021. The numbers increased from 8000 in 2020 to over 13,000 in 2022 (Ssemugenyi & Nuru Seje, 2021). Though the numbers have improved considerably, the higher education sector will still need to think of ways to build on this momentum (Ssemugenyi & Nuru Seje, 2021). While some experts think higher education in PNG will broadly return to pre-pandemic times in a year or two, others predict the mass extinction of in-person universities. Both are extreme ends of the spectrum. However, somewhere in the middle of these extremes lies the sweet spot for higher education to keep internationalism alive.

## Literature Review on COVID-19 Pandemic

Governments issued restrictions on citizens' movement and social meetings globally starting from March 2020 onward to combat the spread of the coronavirus disease (COVID-19) (Agasisti & Soncin, 2021; García-Peñalvo et al., 2021; Roy et al., 2023). In this setting, higher education providers such as universities were forced to quickly rethink their existing operations (Cahusac de Caux, 2023; Salimi et al., 2023). For example, the changes encompassed various aspects such as modifications to lectures, alterations in library services, adjustments to social meeting places, adaptations to laboratory work, changes to learning support groups and modifications to extracurricular activities like campus sports. These adjustments were made in response to the challenges posed by the COVID-19 pandemic in the higher education setting (Dwyer & Minnegal, 2020). Consequently, students and staff started working from home. Higher education institutions turned to technology and the internet to keep operating under the new circumstances (Ayling & Luetz, 2023; Yamada, 2023; Savage, 2023; Wilkinson & Male, 2023). This rapid transition from traditional to online environments created challenges for the technological solutions, infrastructure, students and teaching and supporting staff. Studies reveal that online learning has characteristics that differentiate it from contact teaching (Ayling & Luetz, 2023; Yamada, 2023; Savage, 2023;Guppy et al., 2022). According to Yamada (2023), the transition to work from home inadvertently required teachers to change their teaching practices. Similarly, students faced new challenges, such as maintaining social relationships with their classmates and self-regulating their learning (Tilak & Kumar, 2022; Jehi et al., 2022; Bartolic et al., 2022).

The restrictions on movement and social gatherings meant changes to the organisation of staff meetings, examinations and support services, among others, according to the perspective of higher education institutions management (Bartolic et al., 2022; Alturki & Aldraiweesh, 2022; García-Peñalvo et al., 2021). Evidence from several studies reveals that the pandemic caused students additional cognitive load due to the holistic changes to their lives and the looming pandemic threat and to reduce any additional cognitive strain (Alturki & Aldraiweesh, 2022; García-Peñalvo et al., 2021). The top-down communication of operating the institutions was less clear (Elumalai et al., 2021; Jung et al., 2021; Cranfield et al., 2021). This situation pressured the management of higher education institutions to quickly conceptualise what was going on and communicate decisions to students and the teaching staff (Riggio & Newstead, 2023). The role of learning technologies and education management systems become significant due to all these changes (De Boer, 2021; Eringfeld, 2021; Iqbal et al., 2022; Wilkinson & Male, 2023).

The higher education sector has prepared to transition into online distance learning (Nuru et al., 2021; Kulikowski et al., 2022; Udeogalanya, 2022). Universities constantly seek ways to improve and optimise their teaching practices, both the content and pedagogy (Cahusac de Caux, 2023; Salimi et al., 2023; Wilkinson & Male, 2023). One of the recent trends in higher education has been the development and use of technological tools, sparking research into areas such as computer-assisted collaborative learning such as educational games and asynchronous online learning (Nuru et al., 2021; Kulikowski et al., 2022; Udeogalanya, 2022). Technological advances and the availability of learning tools have increased the popularity of some pedagogical approaches, such as flipped learning or blended learning, but also provided analytical tools for improving existing teaching (Berdida & Grande, 2023; Almaiah et al., 2022). Before the COVID-19 pandemic, some universities already offered full online degrees. Some offered a few online courses, and others still relied entirely on contact teaching (Mitchell et al., 2023; Olson et al., 2023).

Additionally, it is crucial to consider that courses like chemistry, physics and biology may necessitate in-person presence due to laboratory work (Selvanathan et al., 2023; Thompson & Johnson, 2023). This introduces a potential variation in how different university disciplines adapted to the challenges posed by the COVID-19 pandemic.

It is crucial to acknowledge that the technology required for comprehensive online teaching was available; however, its implementation might have been more complex from an organisational standpoint. Furthermore, the shift to distance learning introduces novel factors that impact student learning (Selvanathan et al., 2023; Thompson & Johnson, 2023; Olson et al., 2023). These factors encompass the influence of students' and instructors' home environments, self-regulation capabilities, technical proficiencies and online social self-efficacy.

The COVID-19 pandemic brought about a sudden change in higher education, presenting numerous challenges that were increasingly expected to be addressed and solved by technology (Jehi et al., 2022; Saeed et al., 2023; Roy et al., 2023). Understanding these challenges is crucial for selecting and designing learning technologies that best suit higher education students' and teachers' needs.

## Findings and Discussion

Universities in Papua New Guinea have acknowledged the necessity of embracing and integrating online learning to confront the demands and challenges of innovation in teaching and learning. As a result, this situation has led to the employment of virtual education settings, which support flexible and active education within a constructivist method. Virtual learning is fetching one of the greatest recurrently applied training means in e-learning applications and combination with blended learning in higher education in PNG. It is progressively accomplishing other levels of education due to its flexible adaptability, interactive, multimedia and decentralised learning. The technology is reinforced by Learning Management Systems (LMS), and the "Moodle" system is one of the most used platforms at some universities in PNG. It acts on a set of components and permits modification by adding or deleting items at various stages. In this web platform, tutors and learners have a high level of technological fulfilment and reception, and tutors are inclined to remark that its use improves instructive practice and represents immeasurable benefits. However, other studies have shown that there is great acceptance of the use of the LMS) Platform (Selvanathan et al., 2023; Thompson & Johnson, 2023), but there is no general evidence that the use of a particular platform causes changes in pedagogical where tutors pass on knowledge rather than develop it or create new knowledge.

The higher education sector in PNG has faced challenges during the COVID-19 pandemic. One of many challenges during the pandemic was to develop innovative strategies that limit face-to-face contact and adhere to social-distancing restrictions. In response to the impacts of COVID-19 on higher education in PNG, some university lecturers have adapted to delivering their courses entirely online for the first time, aligning with the universities' existing blended learning programmes. For students residing on campus, classes have resumed in small group sizes. However, students from remote provinces faced disadvantages as they could not travel to universities without undergoing a mandatory two-week quarantine to participate in blended learning.

Furthermore, students outside major towns lacked reliable internet access, and internet prices were comparatively high, posing technological challenges associated with COVID-19. Consequently, the uncertainty among university staff grew concerning the number of prospective students who would be able to engage in blended learning programmes in 2020. It is evident that though there are so many challenges, this study believes that social-distancing restrictions are an essential opportunity to advance technology in higher education in PNG. The challenges identified in PNG universities are likely similar to those in developed countries such as Australia, England and the US. However, several limitations make universities in PNG unique. There is a lack of paid subscriptions to online platforms, and even the bandwidths are limited. This makes it challenging to deliver lectures via video broadcast. For instance, an hour's Zoom meeting can consume a significant portion of a lecturer's daily data limit. However, universities such as Divine Word University lecturers use Moodle, an Online Learning Management System, to share learning resources and facilitate student discussion via e-forums and chat. The shift to blended and online learning is not without consequences for the student experience. Communication between lectures and students through computer and phone affected the relationship and made students feel isolated. For instance, maintaining and engaging students in learning on a computer screen is difficult. Time management is another challenge to balance effectively, as many students also have multiple responsibilities with family and employment.

Online learning has challenged students to engage in active participation rather than passive listening and requires more student-centred teaching methods. This demand has put stress on universities in PNG to effectively provide training for academic staff to learn new technological and teaching strategy skills. Moreover, academic staff that hold a range of responsibilities in the universities was time-consuming to facilitate online activities. These academics feel that learning and adopting the online system was another additional task added to existing duties.

Another challenge university lecturers face in PNG is student feedback with blended and online learning. Many students claim it is more difficult to understand technical and complex concepts such as calculations without face-to-face interactions with lecturers and coursemates. Similarly, the lecturers observed that students lack basic academic skills, such as note-taking and identifying critical components of academic texts. The limited data and bandwidth also further add complications for moving content online. This has hindered students from submitting assessment tasks on time to the lecturers. Despite these challenges, online learning is convenient, and students can efficiently work at their own pace and learning abilities.

## Recommendations

The COVID-19 pandemic has significantly affected the higher education sector in PNG, and the institutions are still recovering from the ordeal. The following are recommendations for university leaders in Papua New Guinea to consider:

1. *Communicate better:* PNG university leaders must provide updates regarding the status of the shutdown process of COVID-19. These communications must also be delivered with a single voice, as conflicting messages create tension and confusion. Because of time demands put on leaders during a crisis, this study recommends creating a crisis communications team that is directed by and answers to the highest academic officer (e.g. university vice-chancellors and presidents). Faculty, staff and students should be encouraged to ask questions, even if it means going outside the "chain of command". Furthermore, institutions should appoint pandemic ombudspersons to confidentially address individual complaints and concerns. University leaders should communicate among themselves and strategise ways to assist teaching and learning with online learning during the post-COVID-19 period.
2. *Clearly define the role of university leaders in crisis response:* University leaders must deeply recognise their responsibility in safeguarding the well-being of their students during the post-COVID-19 period. This sense of responsibility can also be harnessed to support their communities. It is crucial for governments to establish clear guidelines outlining the expectations of university leaders and to provide the necessary support and resources to enable them to fulfil their roles effectively.

3. *Develop programmes to train and connect university leaders:* Providing robust assistance to university leaders as they navigate the current challenges is paramount. Establishing tailored online professional development initiatives holds significant value in supporting these leaders. Engaging with university leaders through online platforms has emerged as a pivotal avenue for education systems during the COVID-19 pandemic, facilitating peer networks where best practices can be swiftly exchanged. University leaders possess an unparalleled understanding of the specific challenges faced by their respective communities. Many of them have demonstrated impressive innovation and resourcefulness in these trying times. Encouraging leaders to share their unique insights and ideas is a potent way to foster collaborative growth and progress.
4. *Embrace virtual learning:* This includes providing students with PowerPoint slides and recording of lectures or conducting live lectures with recording during regular class time. Lectures might also record a podcast-style lecture for students to follow. Pre-recording can be beneficial for households prone to interruptions. Recording lectures is vital to ensure all students can access the learning materials.
5. Additionally, some students must share technological devices with family members and should not be constrained by time limits. University staff also engage in skills-sharing at a more individual level, offering assistance in hosting Zoom meetings and recording PowerPoint presentations. Lecturers at other universities in the PNG network share ideas to learn how they respond to similar circumstances. Lecturers need to understand the mechanism of how best virtual learning works for the effective delivery of lessons, especially on lessons that involve calculations. The universities should strategise effective ways for lecturers and students to appreciate online learning that promotes teaching and learning.
6. *Internet cost.* The idea to reduce internet expenses for students is to partner with internet service providers to support online learning. Internet service providers with a strong presence in PNG, such as Digicel, could provide students with access to digital learning resources freely or at reduced rates.
7. PNG universities follow the Divine Word University to use a Learning Management System (LMS) such as Moodle for easy lesson delivery.

## Conclusion

Amidst the pandemic, universities in PNG swiftly transitioned to online learning, showcasing a critical shift in educational practices. This transition was not just necessary; it embodied a crucial evolution in education. The universities adapted by offering students various avenues for learning, effectively transforming the virtual learning landscape into a space of safety and inclusiveness.

The COVID-19 pandemic also presented a unique opportunity for students to find purpose and leverage virtual classroom discussions to delve deeper into various issues. This process enhanced their problem-solving and communication skills, fostering active participation in crucial decisions shaping the future. This active engagement encourages them to take guided actions that influence upcoming scenarios.

However, it is essential to acknowledge the challenges students face in underprivileged home-learning environments, where access to necessary tools such as gadgets and reliable internet remains a concern due to economic impacts.

The higher education sector is responsible for delivering academic excellence and producing skilled human resources to cater to societal needs. In this context, the pandemic has inadvertently pushed for considering online and blended learning, offering a chance to shift from passive to active learning approaches. It is an opportunity to transform challenges into blessings and reshape the landscape of education for the better.

## References

Abu Talib, M., Bettayeb, A. M., & Omer, R. I. (2021). Analytical study on the impact of technology in higher education during the age of COVID-19: Systematic literature review. *Education and Information Technologies*, 1–28.

Almaiah, M. A., Ayouni, S., Hajjej, F., Lutfi, A., Almomani, O., & Awad, A. B. (2022). Smart mobile learning success model for higher educational institutions in the context of the COVID-19 pandemic. *Electronics, 11*(8), 1278.

Alturki, U., & Aldraiweesh, A. (2022). Students' perceptions of the actual use of mobile learning during COVID-19 pandemic in higher education. *Sustainability, 14*(3), 1125.

Ayling, D., & Luetz, J. M. (2023). Student voices on the COVID-19 crisis: An Australian Christian higher education study. *Christian Higher Education, 22*(1), 46–71.

Agasisti, T., & Soncin, M. (2021). Higher education in troubled times: On the impact of Covid-19 in Italy. *Studies in Higher Education, 46*(1), 86–95.

Azila-Gbettor, E. M., Abiemo, M. K., & Glate, S. N. (2023). University support and online learning engagement during the Covid-19 period: The role of student vitality. *Heliyon,* e12832.

Bozkurt, A. (2022). Resilience, adaptability, and sustainability of higher education: A systematic mapping study on the impact of the coronavirus (COVID-19) pandemic and the transition to the new normal. *Journal of Learning for Development (JL4D), 9*(1), 1–16.

Bartolic, S. K., Boud, D., Agapito, J., Verpoorten, D., Williams, S., Lutze-Mann, L., et al. (2022). A multi-institutional assessment of changes in higher education teaching and learning in the face of COVID-19. *Educational Review, 74*(3), 517-533.

Berdida, D. J. E., & Grande, R. A. N. (2023). Academic stress, COVID-19 anxiety, and quality of life among nursing students: The mediating role of resilience. *International Nursing Review, 70*(1), 34–42.

Camilleri, M. A., & Camilleri, A. C. (2022). The acceptance of learning management systems and video conferencing technologies: Lessons learned from COVID-19. *Technology, Knowledge and Learning, 27*(4), 1311–1333.

Camilleri, M. A. (2021). Evaluating service quality and performance of higher education institutions: A systematic review and a post-COVID-19 outlook. *International Journal of Quality and Service Sciences, 13*(2), 268–281.

Connell, J. (2022). COVID-19 and culture in Papua New Guinea. Failing to meet the challenges of diversity? In *Coronavirus (COVID-19) outbreaks, vaccination, politics and society: The continuing challenge* (pp. 33–44). Springer International Publishing.

Cahusac de Caux, B. (2023). Introduction to the COVID-19 pandemic and its impact on higher education. In *Research and teaching in a pandemic world: The challenges of establishing academic identities during times of crisis* (pp. 15–24). Springer Nature Singapore.

Crawford, J., & Cifuentes-Faura, J. (2022). Sustainability in higher education during the COVID-19 pandemic: A systematic review. *Sustainability, 14*(3), 1879.

Cranfield, D. J., Tick, A., Venter, I. M., Blignaut, R. J., & Renaud, K. (2021). Higher education students' perceptions of online learning during COVID-19—A comparative study. *Education Sciences, 11*(8), 403.

Czuba, J. (2020). Department keen to digitilise education. available online: https://postcourier.com.pg/departmentkeen-to-digitalise-education.

De Boer, H. (2021). COVID-19 in Dutch higher education. *Studies in Higher Education, 46*(1), 96–106.

Dwyer, P. D., & Minnegal, M. (2020). COVID-19 and Facebook in Papua New Guinea: Fly River Forum. *Asia & the Pacific Policy Studies, 7*(3), 233–246.

Elumalai, K. V., Sankar, J. P., Kalaichelvi, R., John, J. A., Menon, N., Alqahtani, M. S. M., & Abumelha, M. A. (2021). Factors affecting the quality of e-learning during the COVID-19 pandemic from the perspective of higher education students. *COVID-19 and Education: Learning and Teaching in a Pandemic-Constrained Environment, 189*.

El Said, G. R. (2021). How did the COVID-19 pandemic affect higher education learning experience? An empirical investigation of learners' academic performance at a university in a developing country. *Advances in Human-Computer Interaction, 2021*, 1–10.

Eringfeld, S. (2021). Higher education and its post-coronial future: Utopian hopes and dystopian fears at Cambridge University during Covid-19. *Studies in Higher Education, 46*(1), 146–157.

Guppy, N., Verpoorten, D., Boud, D., Lin, L., Tai, J., & Bartolic, S. (2022). The post-COVID-19 future of digital learning in higher education: Views from educators, students, and other professionals in six countries. *British Journal of Educational Technology, 53*(6), 1750–1765.

García-Peñalvo, F. J., Corell, A., Rivero-Ortega, R., Rodríguez-Conde, M. J., & Rodríguez-García, N. (2021). Impact of the COVID-19 on higher education: An experience-based approach. In *Information technology trends for a global and interdisciplinary research community* (pp. 1–18). IGI Global.

Iqbal, S. A., Ashiq, M., Rehman, S. U., Rashid, S., & Tayyab, N. (2022). Students' perceptions and experiences of online education in Pakistani Universities and Higher Education Institutes during COVID-19. *Education Sciences, 12*(3), 166.

Jehi, T., Khan, R., Dos Santos, H., & Majzoub, N. (2022). Effect of COVID-19 outbreak on anxiety among students of higher education: A review of literature. *Current Psychology*, 1–15.

Jung, J., Horta, H., & Postiglione, G. A. (2021). Living in uncertainty: The COVID-19 pandemic and higher education in Hong Kong. *Studies in Higher Education, 46*(1), 107–120.

Li, J., & Che, W. (2022). Challenges and coping strategies of online learning for college students in the context of COVID-19: A survey of Chinese universities. *Sustainable Cities and Society, 83*, 103958.

Lau, J., & Sutcliffe, S. (2021). Of isolation and atolls: Coping with Covid-19 in Manus, Papua New Guinea. In *COVID in the Islands: A comparative perspective on the Caribbean and the Pacific* (pp. 385–401). Palgrave Macmillan.

Marinoni, G., Van't Land, H., & Jensen, T. (2020). The impact of Covid-19 on higher education around the world. *IAU Global Survey Report, 23*, 1–17.

Mitchell, R., Bornstein, S., Piamnok, D., Sebby, W., Kingston, C., Tefatu, R., et al. (2023). Multimodal learning for emergency department triage implementation: Experiences from Papua New Guinea during the COVID-19 pandemic. *The Lancet Regional Health–Western Pacific, 33*, 100683.

Mncube, V., Mutongoza, B. H., & Olawale, E. (2021). Managing higher education institutions in the context of COVID-19 stringency: Experiences of stakeholders at a rural South African university. *Perspectives in Education, 39*(1), 390–409.

Naidoo, P., & Cartwright, D. (2022). Where to from here? Contemplating the impact of COVID-19 on South African students and student counseling services in higher education. *Journal of College Student Psychotherapy, 36*(4), 355–369.

Nuru, S. T., Fred, S., Oyekola, P., & Ngene, C. T. (2021). Resourcing as an antecedent of effective online learning adaptation in the face of COVID-19: The case of Papua New Guinea University of Technology (PNGUoT). *Journal of Education, Society and Behavioural Science, 34*(2), 80–89.

Kulikowski, K., Przytuła, S., & Sułkowski, Ł. (2022). E-learning? Never again! On the unintended consequences of COVID-19 forced e-learning on academic teacher motivational job characteristics. *Higher Education Quarterly, 76*(1), 174–189.

Khanom, N. (2023). Leadership in higher education during COVID-19 in Australia: A critical reflection. In *Innovation, leadership and governance in higher education: Perspectives on the Covid-19 recovery strategies* (pp. 297–314). Springer Nature Singapore.

Olson, R., Fryz, R., Essemiah, J., Crawford, M., King, A., & Fateye, B. (2023). Mental health impacts of COVID-19 lockdown on US college students: Results of a photoelicitation project. *Journal of American College Health, 71*(2), 411–442.

Pokhrel, S., & Chhetri, R. (2021). A literature review on impact of COVID-19 pandemic on teaching and learning. *Higher Education for the Future, 8*(1), 133–141.

Rashid, S., & Yadav, S. S. (2020). Impact of Covid-19 pandemic on higher education and research. *Indian Journal of Human Development, 14*(2), 340–343.

Raphael, M., Kelly-Hanku, A., Heslop, D., Hutchinson, D., Kunasekaran, M., Quigley, A., & MacIntyre, R. (2023). Early pandemic use of face masks in Papua New Guinea under a mask mandate. *Western Pacific Surveillance and Response, 14*(1), 1–6.

Riggio, R. E., & Newstead, T. (2023). Crisis leadership. *Annual Review of Organizational Psychology and Organizational Behavior, 10*, 201–224. https://www.annualreviews.org/doi/pdf/10.1146/annurev-orgpsych-120920-044838

Roy, G., Babu, R., Abul Kalam, M., Yasmin, N., Zafar, T., & Nath, S. R. (2023). Response, readiness and challenges of online teaching amid COVID-19 pandemic: The case of higher education in Bangladesh. *Educational and Developmental Psychologist, 40*(1), 40–50.

Salimi, N., Gere, B., Talley, W., & Irioogbe, B. (2023). College students mental health challenges: Concerns and considerations in the COVID-19 pandemic. *Journal of College Student Psychotherapy, 37*(1), 39–51.

Saeed, H. M., Saad Elghareeb, A., El-Hodhod, M. A. A., & Samy, G. (2023). Assessment of COVID-19 preparedness response plan on higher education students' simulation of WHO intra-action review in Egypt. *Scientific Reports, 13*(1), 741.

Ssemugenyi, F., & Nuru Seje, T. (2021). A decade of unprecedented e-learning adoption and adaptation: Covid-19 revolutionises teaching and learning at Papua New Guinea University of Technology (PNGUoT) "Is it a wave of change or a mere change in the wave?" *Cogent Education, 8*(1), 1989997.

Savage, S. (2023). The experience of mothers as university students and pre-service teachers during Covid-19: Recommendations for ongoing support. *Studies in Continuing Education, 45*(1), 71–85.

Schwander-Maire, F., Querido, A., Cara-Nova, T., Dixe, M. A., Aissaoui, D., Charepe, Z., et al. (2023). Psychological responses and strategies towards the COVID-19 pandemic among higher education students in Portugal and Switzerland: A mixed-methods study. *Frontier Mental Health of Higher Education Students, 16648714*, 135.

Sin, C., Tavares, O., & Aguiar, J. (2023). COVID-19: Threat or opportunity for the Portuguese higher education's attractiveness for international students? *Journal of Studies in International Education, 27*(1), 21–38.

Selvanathan, M., Hussin, N. A. M., & Azazi, N. A. N. (2023). Students learning experiences during COVID-19: Work from home period in Malaysian higher learning institutions. *Teaching Public Administration, 41*(1), 13–22.

Shahzad, A., Hassan, R., Aremu, A. Y., Hussain, A., & Lodhi, R. N. (2021). Effects of COVID-19 in e-learning on higher education institution students: The group comparison between male and female. *Quality & Quantity, 55*, 805–826.

Thompson, S. A., & Johnson, M. W. (2023). The Covid-19 dilemma: A roadmap to surmount future challenges in higher education. In *Innovation, leadership and governance in higher education: Perspectives on the Covid-19 recovery strategies* (pp. 25–44). Springer Nature Singapore.

Tilak, J. B., & Kumar, A. G. (2022). Policy changes in global higher education: What lessons do we learn from the COVID-19 pandemic? *Higher Education Policy, 35*(3), 610–628.

Toquero, C. M. (2020). Challenges and opportunities for higher education amid the COVID-19 pandemic: The Philippine context. *Pedagogical Research, 5*(4), 1–5.

Udeogalanya, V. (2022). Aligning digital literacy and student academic success: Lessons learned from COVID-19 pandemic. *International Journal of Higher Education Management, 8*(2), 54–65.

Wilkinson, J., & Male, T. (2023). Perceptions of women senior leaders in the UK Higher Education during the COVID-19 pandemic. *Educational Management Administration & Leadership*, 1–18.

Yamada, A. (2023). Internationalisation of higher education during the COVID-19 pandemic: A case study of the Japanese digital native generation and social media use. In *Globalisation, values education and teaching democracy* (pp. 57–76). Springer International Publishing.

Zawacki-Richter, O. (2021). The current state and impact of Covid-19 on digital higher education in Germany. *Human Behavior and Emerging Technologies, 3*(1), 218–226.

Zhang, L., Carter, R. A., Jr., Qian, X., Yang, S., Rujimora, J., & Wen, S. (2022). Academia's responses to crisis: A bibliometric analysis of literature on online learning in higher education during COVID-19. *British Journal of Educational Technology, 53*(3), 620–646.

# From Crisis to Learning Leadership? Singapore's Unique Journey Through COVID-19 and Beyond

Jürgen Rudolph, Choon-Yin Sam, and Shannon Tan

## Introduction

When the COVID-19 pandemic became recognised as a serious threat in early 2020, Singapore's universities remained open, teaching online or using hybrid methods. By April 2020, schools and higher education institutions (HEIs) were required to conduct lessons entirely online. Progressively, universities went back to providing on-campus learning with safe management measurements in place to allow students to learn from professors in person, collaborate with peers on projects and experience the social life of campus living. With reference to Crawford's (2023) four-stage-model of pandemic response for higher education institutions (rapid adaptation, improvement, consolidation, and restoration), as of mid-2022, the city-state was in the final stage of restoration, with hybrid learning modalities having become the "new normal".

J. Rudolph · S. Tan (✉)
Kaplan Singapore, Singapore, Singapore
e-mail: shannon.tan@kaplan.com

J. Rudolph
e-mail: Jurgen.Rudolph@kaplan.com

C.-Y. Sam
Kaplan Singapore, Singapore, Singapore
e-mail: choonyin.sam@kaplan.com



J. Rudolph et al. (eds.), *The Palgrave Handbook of Crisis Leadership in Higher Education*,
https://doi.org/10.1007/978-3-031-54509-2_25

Despite some minor setbacks, higher education providers in the city-state handled the situation well, though there were some closures of smaller private education institutions (Training Partners Gateway, 2023a). Overall, Singapore's COVID-19-related mortality rates have been very low, thanks to high vaccination rates and a population that followed a variety of phased advisories. Moreover, the success of higher education institutions (HEIs) in their rapid adaptation was aided by Singapore's smart nation status. The city-state's smart nation strategy refers to her application of digital technology and data for innovation to address long-term strategic issues through a whole-of-government approach and in collaboration with diverse stakeholders (Hoe, 2016).

During the pandemic, many countries experienced a progression towards localised education models to support a period of reduced international access to education and travel (Bonk et al., 2020). For institutions relying heavily on international students, especially in the three main HE import countries (the U.S., the UK, and Australia), there have been drastic social and economic challenges (Marshman & Larkins, 2020). The Singapore education sector has not faced the same drastic challenges, with the majority of HE students being domestic and overall demand for higher education exceeding supply, particularly in the government-funded, corporatised and non-profit Autonomous Universities (S. Tan et al., 2022). The focus on domestic consumption of education mitigates the need for government lobbying for border easing, establishing quarantining arrangements for international students, and allowing legislative changes to allow international student visas to be fulfilled without entrance to the country (S. Tan et al., 2022). Nonetheless, students and teachers suffered from several adverse health effects due to inadequate resources, isolation, experiences of loneliness and overwork (Kwan, 2022; Rudolph, Itangata, et al., 2021).

"Singapore's higher education system is one of Asia's success stories", with its quality "the envy of many nations" (De Meyer & Ang, 2022, p. 1). Its perseverance through the pandemic makes for a unique case study within the context of this Handbook. Singapore's educational achievements are grounded in K-12 education. For instance, in the Programme for International Student Assessment (PISA) 2018, an evaluation of reading, mathematics, and science proficiencies among 15-year-old students, Singapore achieved second place in reading, secured the top position in mathematics, and attained a second rank in science (Teng, 2019). In the Trends in International Mathematics and Science Study (TIMSS) 2019, which evaluates mathematics and science skills among fourth and eighth-grade students, Singapore was ranked first worldwide across both grade levels and subjects

(Ng, 2020). Singapore's post-secondary education landscape encompasses a diverse array of institutions and programmes, including polytechnics, technical institutes, autonomous universities, private educational institutions, and international university campuses. The nation is home to two prominent public universities, the National University of Singapore (NUS) and Nanyang Technological University (NTU), both top 10 Asian universities and top 100 global universities, according to the Times Higher Education World University Rankings 2022 (Tushara, 2023). With high-quality education spanning primary to higher levels, Singapore transitioned from a third-world to a first-world economy. Education was critical in transforming an underdeveloped island with limited resources and high unemployment into a globally competitive hub for finance, professional services, trade, transportation, and advanced manufacturing (De Meyer & Ang, 2022).

Our Chapter highlights local HEIs' experiences during the COVID-19 pandemic and how they evolved beyond it, particularly in terms of educational leadership. It delves into the Singaporean government's efforts to rethink higher education, with the aim of keeping universities up-to-date and effective in the years to come. Our Chapter explores how this vision is being put into action, with examples of innovative programmes and initiatives aimed at aiding students to adapt and thrive in a rapidly changing world. In terms of academic literature on Singapore's higher education landscape during the recent pandemic, there are valuable studies with single institutional responses (e.g., Cleland et al., 2020; Compton et al., 2020; Fung & Lam, 2020; Goh & Sanders, 2020; Kwan, 2022; Müller et al., 2021; Rai, 2020; E. Tan et al., 2022). Moreover, there are articles and book chapters that co-present Singapore's HE with other jurisdictions (Bonk et al., 2020; Crawford et al., 2020; Ewing, 2021; Sidhu et al., 2021; Kefalaki et al., 2021; Rudolph, Itangata, et al., 2021). Rudolph, Tan, et al. (2023) article presents the first multi-stakeholder population qualitative research study (of students, academics, and academic leaders) across all three different types of institutions that provide higher education in Singapore (autonomous universities, international branch campuses, and private education institutions). This article complements an earlier study that explored the higher education landscape during the pandemic in Singapore and focused on case studies of educational institutions and their responses during the various phases of the pandemic based on secondary data content analysis (S. Tan et al., 2022).

Comprehensive literature surveys of the academic literature on COVID-19 and higher education published in 2020 showed that the bulk focused on single-institution and single-country studies (Butler-Henderson et al., 2020, 2021). While the numerous institutional case studies all usefully add to our knowledge of the pandemic, the downside of such approaches is their fragmenting focus on specific local contexts, which could easily lead to a myopic perspective that misses the big picture (e.g., Karalis & Raikou, 2020). We have organised this Chapter as follows. The following section discloses our theoretical frameworks and provides a conceptual discussion of relevant models of leadership. In addition, it describes the methodology that combines the thematic analysis of interviews with educational leaders with the evaluation of pertinent academic literature and credible media sources. Next, we provide an overview of Singapore's higher education landscape with special emphasis on the time during the COVID-19 pandemic. Our findings discuss aspects of leadership during and beyond the pandemic. Finally, we synthesise the findings and consider the practical implications and opportunities (including those for future research) in our conclusions.

## Theoretical Framework

In our Chapter, we use four key theoretical frames in this study. We employ a before, during and beyond narrative (Crawford, 2021) and Crawford's (2023) four phases of pandemic response. In terms of leadership theories, Riggio and Newstead's (2023) crisis leadership and Preskill and Brookfield's (2009) learning leadership theories are key.

The academic literature on leadership is massive, necessitating great selectivity in the following paragraphs. For this Chapter, we focus on the concepts of crisis leadership and learning leadership. Riggio and Newstead (2023, p. 201) observe that despite crises such as the COVID-19 pandemic or global warming being exceedingly complex and of global consequence, crisis leadership "is a relatively underdeveloped field". In order to elucidate the tangled field of crisis leadership, they employ seemingly divergent theories such as crisis management theory, cognitive resource theory (CRT), charismatic leadership theory and complexity leadership theory. According to crisis management theory, "leaders must be prepared to respond adaptively to unexpected crises" (Riggio & Newstead, 2023, p. 210). In line with CRT, urgent crises demand that leaders be directive and take quick action (Fiedler & Garcia, 1987). Charismatic leadership theory indicates that a leader's personal attributes, such as composure, reassurance, optimism, and their ability to articulate a vision of a way out of the crisis, are essential in getting their followers' support (Riggio & Newstead, 2023). COVID-19 has been described as a polycrisis (a convergence of multiple intersecting, simultaneously occurring crises): not just a health crisis but also economic, social, political, and educational crises (Rudolph, Tan, et al. 2021; Tooze, 2021). Complexity leadership theory is particularly apt for such polycrises as they require the coordination of many stakeholders and the provision of "adaptive space for stakeholders to generate novel responses collectively" (Riggio & Newstead, 2023, p. 210).

Riggio and Newstead (2023) arrive at five key competencies for crisis leadership: sensemaking, decision-making, communication, coordinating resources and facilitating teamwork, and facilitating learning. In our context, the facilitation of learning is of particular relevance. Both throughout and after a crisis, crisis leaders "should actively search for lessons that will help their organisation recover and improve" (Riggio & Newstead, 2023, p. 217). This can be directly related to what Preskill and Brookfield (2009) have coined learning leadership.

Learning leadership encompasses a prime responsibility to help others learn. This kind of leadership can be exercised from below, behind, and among, as seen in the different leadership tasks that Preskill and Brookfield (2009) have identified. Among these tasks are learning how to question ourselves and others, sustaining hope in the face of struggle, and creating community. By drawing on models of transformational, symbiotic, developmental, servant, and organic leadership that all focus on enabling change, Preskill and Brookfield (2009) understand leadership not as a collection of personal traits held by uniquely charismatic individuals but as a collaboratively exercised process. They view leadership as the process of galvanising collective action that can happen in a myriad of ways, and anybody can exercise that in any place (Brookfield et al., 2024).

Learning leadership is recognised by its focus on two processes of learning. First, learning leaders deliberately promote the learning, growth, and development of those they work with as their top priority. Second, learning leadership focuses on continually learning about the practice of leadership itself. Many teachers are learning leaders. Teaching entails helping participants move forward with their learning. Good teachers want to develop students' self-confidence and see them claim a sense of their own agency. Learning leadership does not require any positional authority in an organisation (Brookfield et al., 2024; Preskill & Brookfield, 2009). This observation puts learning leadership in proximity with the concept of distributed leadership—the idea that "leadership practice takes shape in the interaction of leaders, followers, and their situations" (Spillane, 2005, p. 149).

## Context

### Singapore's Pre-pandemic Higher Education Landscape

With an estimated population of close to six million, Singapore has a highly developed, open, and pro-business economy and one of the world's highest per capita incomes. The city-state boasts a multicultural population (with an ethnic Chinese majority), a garden city environment, and regional hubs for next to everything. The reasons for Singapore's economic success are multi-layered and complex, but it can also be credited to the government's persistent investments in education. Singapore's positioning as a "Boston of the East" and a "Global Schoolhouse" started in 2003 and successfully attracted international branch campuses from world-class universities from the U.S., France, and India (see S. Tan et al., 2022; Waring, 2014; Ye, 2016). Partially as a result of the Global Financial Crisis (2008–2009), there was a backlash against liberal immigration policies, and "the concept of the Global Schoolhouse was quietly dropped" (De Meyer & Ang, 2022, p. 120). However, the objective of enticing international institutions to establish their presence in Singapore was never abandoned but significantly shifted from aiming for quantity to emphasising quality (De Meyer & Ang, 2022).

High participation in tertiary education in Singapore can be attributed to both Confucian values (Marginson, 2010) and the Singapore government's continuing emphasis and support of lifelong learning in the knowledge economy. The cohort participation rate is around 50%, consisting of approximately 40% subsidised university places for fresh school leavers and 10% for working adults (MOE, 2022). The higher education participation rate does not include students studying at international university transnational satellite campuses and private education institutions (PEIs). The latter are non-government-funded education providers that oftentimes offer post-secondary education, leading to the award of certificates and diplomas (Sam, 2017). In Singapore, there are six autonomous universities, eight international branch campuses (IBCs), and 312 PEIs (Training Partners Gateway, 2023b). Out of 312 PEIs, only 120 are permitted to offer external degree programmes through EduTrust certification (Training Partners Gateway, 2023b).

In February 2022, Education Minister Chan Chun Sing (2022, n.p.) said, "No amount of education frontloading can prepare us for life. Only continual learning can help us remain current and relevant for the rest of our lives". Instead of a cohort participation rate, a higher "lifetime participation rate" in training and education is deemed to be more appropriate to describe what Singapore wants to achieve (De Meyer & Ang, 2022).

To ensure that individuals can acquire the necessary skills and knowledge throughout their career, the government calls for a new model of learning that involves rotating between work and education. This contrasts with the frontloading educational model, where education is concentrated at a young age before entering the workforce. In response, universities must be prepared to accommodate multiple entry points throughout an individual's life instead of focusing solely on full-time education. This could involve offering part-time degree programmes for working adults and modular courses that can be accumulated towards a qualification. By adopting this approach, individuals can continue to develop their skills and knowledge as they progress in their careers, leading to better outcomes for individuals and the macroeconomy (De Meyer & Ang, 2022).

## During and Beyond the Pandemic

As of February 2023, Singapore suffered 1722 COVID-19-related deaths. The city-state's case fatality rate of 0.08% is one of the lowest in the world (Johns Hopkins University of Medicine, 2023). The rapid adaptation response in Singapore was influenced by early detection and high sanitisation and social distancing efforts. In the first quarter of 2020, universities remained open, using online or blended learning approaches. The alarmingly increasing rate of new infections, especially among foreign workers staying in dormitories, led to a nationwide lockdown to contain the spread of COVID-19 from 7 April to 1 June (Bonk et al., 2020). Prior to the lockdown, universities began delivering learning activities online and redesigning summative assessments (e.g. invigilated examinations) into online and take-home modalities. After the lockdown ended, activities were planned to be resumed gradually over three subsequent phases: safe reopening, safe transition, and "the new normal". We provide a brief overview of these phases for context.

Phase 1 ('safe reopening': 2–18 June 2020) saw the recommencement of low-risk economic activities. This included higher education institutions returning to campus for practical and laboratory-based sessions during existing teaching periods, with instructional learning remaining online. However, co-curricular activities, enrichment activities, and tuition did not resume (Gov.sg, 2020). In Phase 2 ('safe transition': 19 June–27 December, 2020), some medium-risk economic and social activities resumed (Ministry of Health Singapore, 2020). Phase 3 (the "new normal") started on 28 December 2020, but there was the occasional easing and re-tightening of stop-start curbs around work and social interaction (Cortez et al., 2021; Ho,

2021). A Preparatory Stage of Transition in August and September 2021 eventually led to a Transition Phase (22 November 2021–25 April 2022) that was followed by the COVID-19 Resilient Nation/Acute Phase (26 April 2022–12 February 2023). As of 13 February, Singapore is in the Endemic Phase, with almost all COVID-19 restrictions lifted (Mohan & Lim, 2023; Lim, 2023).

By January 2023, the city-state achieved a high vaccination rate of more than 90 per cent (Ycharts, 2023). Booster vaccinations were actively encouraged, with "vaccine-differentiated safe management rules" also preventing unvaccinated people from, among other things, eating at food courts and entering shopping malls (Lim & Ho, 2021, n.p.). There was an increase in bilateral arrangements for quarantine-free travel. The highly infectious delta variant had made it impossible to continue a zero-COVID-19 policy that initially had been enacted, and that helped avert the huge loss of lives that many countries saw (Ho, 2021). With the pandemic being redesignated as endemic, Singapore has achieved the rare feat of getting through the COVID-19 pandemic without significant loss of life and safely reopening to the rest of the world (Fig. 1).

Timeline of Singapore government coronavirus lockdowns—January 2020—February 2023 (Mohan & Lim, 2023; Rudolph, Itangata, et al. 2021).

## Method

Our study takes a critical leadership lens to examine Singapore's higher education context. It builds on previous research (especially Rudolph, Itangata, et al., 2021; Rudolph, Tan, et al., 2023; S. Tan et al., 2022) in which we used content analyses of the popular literature, autoethnographic approaches and interviews. In previous research, we needed to extensively refer to news media and other non-academic sources (Bonk et al., 2020; Crawford et al., 2020; S. Tan et al., 2022), due to the initial dearth of academic literature. More than three years after the pandemic's start, we can rely more on academic sources.

We purposively sampled and interviewed four students, four academics, and five academic leaders ($n = 13$) from different local HEI types (Rudolph, Tan, et al., 2023). Students, teachers and academic leaders were involved in learning and teaching modules in biology, business and management, chemistry, engineering, forensics, nursing, psychology, and traditional Chinese medicine. This was to ensure maximal variation between responses (Etikan et al., 2016). For this Chapter, we reference semi-structured interviews

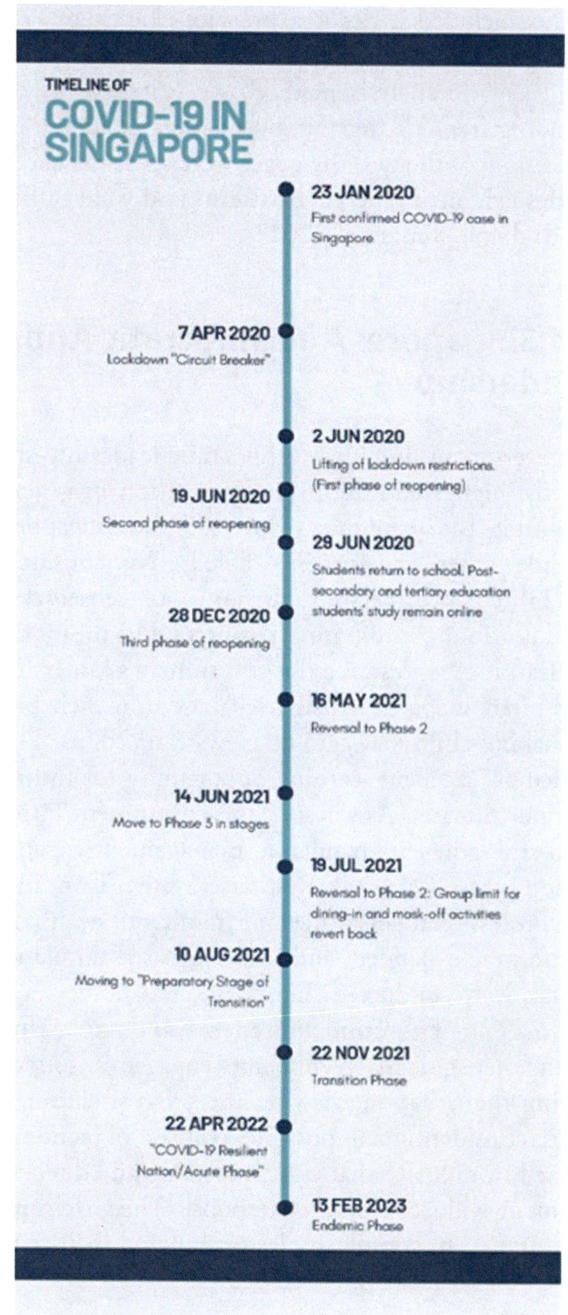


**Fig. 1** Timeline of COVID-19 in Singapore

with leaders, who included a dean, a pro-vice-chancellor, a deputy dean, a vice president, and a transnational education director. Using Braun and Clarke's (2006) thematic analysis method, we searched for themes against a pre-existing coding frame. After the journalling, examination, and careful definition and refining of themes, the codes were sense-checked and reflected upon. These codes exhibited emerging patterns and were gathered to form a mind map (see Rudolph, Tan, et al., 2023).

## The Case of Singapore: A Technocratic Approach to Crisis Leadership

The Singapore government provided technocratic leadership starting in early 2000. Importantly, higher education (and education in general) continued uninterrupted during the pandemic. How did the Singapore government achieve this while other governments failed? We consider Riggio and Newstead's (2023) crisis leadership categories of sensemaking, decision-making, communication, coordinating resources and promoting teamwork, and facilitating learning, to describe the government's leadership.

Crisis leaders often shape the crisis itself based on their previous experience and sensemaking ability (Riggio & Newstead, 2023). The 2003 SARS outbreak provided an excellent learning opportunity for future health crises related to infectious diseases. As a result, the government introduced several key measures to strengthen its pandemic management capabilities. Among other things, the Disease Outbreak Response System Condition framework was established; professional personnel and training of health care workers in outbreak response were expanded; and scenario-based simulation exercises at all public hospitals were conducted (Lin et al., 2020).

The decision-making of government leaders was done carefully, but due to the demanded urgency, quickly. Technocrats engaged in sound reasoning by carefully analysing the situation, viewing the crisis situation from multiple perspectives and considering all possible courses of action. Government leaders had learned from SARS that clear leadership and direction were essential for a government-wide, coordinated response. The government's approach also shows an awareness of complexity leadership and the need to coordinate resources and facilitate teamwork:

> A ministerial committee, first established during the SARS outbreak to provide guidance and decisions on strategies for containment of the outbreak, was convened in the COVID-19 pandemic as a multi-ministry taskforce co-chaired by the Minister for Health and the Minister for National Development… This

> taskforce has the ability to recommend and implement whole-of-government policies to deal with issues related to COVID-19. (Lin et al., 2020, p. 497)

In terms of communication, public engagement and education were crucial via consistent public communication through press releases, media coverage, and an education campaign to educate Singaporeans on the disease and appropriate behaviour to prevent transmission. In June 2020, Prime Minister Lee Hsien Loong (2020, n.p.) spoke about overcoming the "crisis of a generation". He highlighted that despite the complexity of the pandemic (being a public health, economic, social, and political crisis), Singaporeans can be confident due to the country's economic strengths, and the government quickly rolled out successive budgets to protect workers, households and companies. Lee (2020, n.p.) emphasised the need for "unity and resilience of our people". Two years into the crisis, when discussing key takeaways of the crisis, Lee emphasised the need for continuous learning and expressed some humility in not getting everything right:

> We did not get every call right. We have had our share of challenges and setbacks these past two years. But the key is to keep on learning and improving; and as we discover more information, to be prepared to update, revise or even reverse our decisions. (Lee, cited in Channel News Asia, 2022, n.p.).

In communicating clearly and reflecting on the learning lessons from the crisis, the prime minister exemplified honesty, emphasised the need for evidence-based decisions, engendered trust, and instilled confidence. In terms of higher education, the government leadership was instrumental in managing the crisis. Singapore's Education Minister, Chan Chun Sing, has proposed several measures in the 2022 budget to support adult education and help Singaporeans navigate the economic challenges caused by the pandemic. One of the measures includes the SkillsFuture Career Transition Programme, which aims to provide mid-career workers with skills training to help them switch careers. This programme offers modular, industry-oriented training courses lasting three to twelve months, and up to 90% of course fees are subsidised. Another key initiative is the expansion of the SkillsFuture Credit coverage to around 7000 courses, up from the current 300 courses, with a special SkillsFuture Credit of S$500 given to every Singaporean aged 40 to 60. This is to encourage lifelong learning and help individuals stay competitive in the rapidly changing job market. Moreover, the government plans to provide more opportunities for working adults to pursue a degree at any point in their lives to support key growth areas in the economy. Singapore University of Social Sciences is a prime example of this model, which uses a flexible modular curriculum that caters to the unique needs of adult learners. This approach enables learners to choose from a variety of courses based on their interests and career goals, allowing them to upskill or reskill without compromising their work and personal commitments.

Government and university leaders are aware that the future labour market will be characterised by continued disruption driven by the increasing adoption of automation and artificial intelligence. This disruption is expected to affect the white-collar sector and create a need for new skill sets and job roles that incorporate emerging technologies (Rudolph, Tan, Aspland, 2023). The conventional mode of learning, which is linear, disjointed, and compartmentalised, is no longer sufficient to keep pace with the rapid changes required to cultivate a flexible workforce capable of navigating an era of heightened disruption and accelerated change in Singapore. The strategy is not to let external forces disrupt Singapore's plans but rather to take a proactive approach to disrupt herself by adopting innovative thinking. The pandemic is being viewed as an opportunity to re-envision higher education and prepare the economy for the future. There were variations in how institutions implemented the governmental guidelines, but the broad strokes were created by the government (De Meyer & Ang, 2022).

Tan Eng Chye (2021), President of the National University of Singapore (NUS), wrote, "Today, more than ever before, students must be taught to make connections that cut across boundaries, such as those carved out artificially for reasons of administrative efficiency and disciplinary politics—between the arts and the sciences, and between the technical and the human" (n.p.). In December 2020, NUS introduced a new College of Humanities and Sciences, marking a significant departure from the traditional approach to disciplinary learning. The new college is designed to harness the collective expertise of two of the university's faculties—the Faculty of Arts and Social Sciences and the Faculty of Science—and promote interdisciplinary collaboration across a wide range of academic disciplines. The creation of the College of Humanities and Sciences underscores NUS's commitment to fostering a more integrated approach to learning and research. By breaking down traditional silos between disciplines, the college aims to create a more dynamic and collaborative learning environment that better reflects the complex challenges of the modern world.

In 2022, Singapore Management University (SMU) announced the setting up of the College of Integrative Studies to allow students to select an "individualised major", selecting from all modules across six schools—accountancy, business, economics, computing and information systems, law, and social sciences. Students graduate with a bachelor's degree in integrative studies after four years. SMU President Lily Kong said, "The integration of disciplines and domains is how new knowledge is produced. We have set out to develop a new generation of graduates who will be able to combine knowledge domains who can respond to industry disruption in multi-dimensional and non-linear ways" (Teng, 2022, n.p.).

The government has put together a team of "overseas-educated technocrats with strong administrative, professional, academic, technical, and commercial backgrounds" (Tan, 2008, p. 15). The problems posed by the COVID-19 polycrisis were complicated and required specialised knowledge for effective policymaking. Singapore's approach during the pandemic was frequently lauded (Bonk et al., 2020; Kefalaki et al., 2021). The government's technocratic leadership played a key role in this success.

## Discussion: Learning Leadership During Crisis

We complement the concept of crisis leadership with that of learning leadership. The conventional leadership perspective in higher education justifiably focuses on government and university leaders (like education ministers, university presidents and vice-chancellors). In contrast, learning leadership emphasises leaders without positional authority from below, behind, and among.

During the early months and weeks of the pandemic, there was initial resistance to change. Emergency remote teaching (ERT) was a less-than-perfect replacement for face-to-face teaching and learning. It necessitated the rapid deployment of additional EdTech resources, IT support, and professional development needs to enable online teaching. During our interviews, one academic participant praised their EdTech team's responsiveness. Over time, the benefits of online were realised, and online learning became more interactive and improved. The relative success of online—and later hybrid—learning is not attributable to a single entity but the result of distributed learning leadership and a concerted multi-stakeholder effort consisting of government agencies, higher education leaders, teachers, academic support staff and students.

In many countries, online learning exacerbated economic inequalities, as students had no access to suitable digital devices and adequate Internet. While such infrastructural barriers are less of a concern in prosperous Singapore, the government was proactive also in this regard. For instance, the Ministry of Education (MOE) loaned 20,000 devices to low-income facilities and opened school premises for students who needed additional support. Already pre-pandemic, MOE had accelerated the provision of laptops to all students, and it was ensured that all secondary school students would have laptops by 2021 (Hung et al., 2020). Part of Singapore's "smart nation" agenda is to extend broadband access for all households through a stipend (Hung et al., 2020). Significantly, Singapore had a head start in terms of digitalisation, and at the start of the pandemic, the National Institute of Education (n.d.) was quick to come up with an annotated list of suitable educational technology resources. Teachers usually picked up newly required tech skills quickly, with many students being more tech-savvy than them. The pandemic saw the need for more counselling services to help students with anxiety and stress-related mental health issues (Rudolph et al., 2021).

The pandemic has brought rapid changes to the way individuals attain knowledge. In the efforts to prevent disruption of the learning process, some of the leading institutes of higher learning in Singapore, such as NUS or SMU embraced technology well ahead of the curve by integrating online learning in their curriculum (Hutton, 2020). Educational institutes were forced to adapt to full online learning solutions using platforms such as Zoom and Blackboard to facilitate the learning process. Apart from having to adapt to these solutions rapidly, ensuring privacy and security was also a challenge. Early into online learning solutions, there were hacking incidents reported by the Ministry of Education (MOE) where a video-conferencing platform was hijacked by pornographers. While this incident was swiftly resolved, it raised an alert on security and privacy issues (Hutton, 2020). Despite such disruptions during the sudden move from traditional classes to online learning, the pandemic accelerated IT integration in education to eventually become an integral educational component (World Economic Forum, 2020). While COVID created great challenges, it led to long-term opportunities to change higher education. Academic leaders interviewed during our research helped ensure that the pandemic led to accelerated adoption of EdTech and digital pedagogy. For instance, one academic commended the academic support team of her university:

> The Education team… kept emailing me to ask me what kind of support I needed… They did the best they could; they provided us with all the links and accesses and tutorials for Microsoft Teams, Zoom, and Google Classroom… and would say, 'These are things that you can use, see if it works for your class'.

Another important area of learning leadership was the rethinking of assessments and grading. Some academic leaders among our interviewees articulated a temporary simplification of their grading systems to satisfactory/unsatisfactory, in one case only for the first two years of study. Another retained the grading system but excluded subjects completed during 2020 from student Grade Point Average (GPA) computations. Some leaders reported on amendments to assessment designs, including take-home examinations and proctored oral and written online examinations. Others reported pauses in examination delivery. The partial implementation of lockdown browsers and the taking of random pictures every few minutes could not completely address isolated cases of academic offences. One academic leader shared that his University tried:

> to steer unit coordinators away from using exams in some circumstances where we don't think they are appropriate... I think that's been good because it's caused some of our academics in [home campus] to really rethink what they're trying to achieve. How are we trying to test your knowledge? How are we trying to examine the learning objectives? And maybe a single-timed exam is not the best way to do that.

Our research shows that faculty played a key role in learning leadership from below, behind, and among. They were the ones who needed to find out how to deal with sudden and lasting changes and who provided leadership to their students. They needed to question themselves and others, sustain hope while facing a polycrisis, and continue to create community with their students under challenging circumstances. In turn, students were also required to exhibit learning leadership, if only by leading themselves through the new normal of online and hybrid learning.

Although initially event-driven, the move to online delivery provides educators with opportunities to use additional technological tools for innovative educational practices in a post-crisis environment. Despite research evidence to the contrary, online learning has often been stigmatised as being of lower quality as compared with face-to-face learning (Hodges et al., 2020). It is, however, crucial to differentiate well-planned online learning from emergency remote learning in response to a pandemic such as COVID-19. The speed at which the move to online occurred in Singapore and many other countries was astounding and unprecedented. Nevertheless, variations in the designation of "faculty" (from fly-in to land-bound and in-between) may prompt other institutions in other nations to revisit their expectations of the traditional faculty role.

## Conclusion

Singapore has demonstrated strong leadership in coping with the pandemic and its aftermath by implementing various measures in higher education. One example is the implementation of blended learning, which combines online and offline learning to provide students with more flexibility and accessibility while ensuring their safety during the pandemic. Singapore's higher education institutions (HEIs) quickly adapted to the pandemic by transitioning to online learning, allowing students to continue their education remotely. They typically launched a suite of initiatives to support remote learning, including online learning platforms, video-conferencing tools, and online resources.

The COVID-19 pandemic has prompted a rethinking of higher education and has opened up opportunities to explore innovative approaches to teaching and learning. The traditional approach of frontloading education in one's early life is being reviewed. Singapore's Ministry of Education and HEIs have been exploring new approaches to higher education, including modular learning, flexible curricula, and work-integrated learning to encourage individuals to blend learning with work throughout their adult lives. For instance, SMU offers stackable modules that lead to graduate certificates, diplomas, and master's degrees (De Meyer & Ang, 2022).

Another opportunity is the promotion of multidisciplinary studies. The pandemic has highlighted the need for interdisciplinary collaboration to address complex challenges. Universities in Singapore are responding to this need by breaking down disciplinary silos and fostering interdisciplinary research and teaching. Singapore University of Technology and Design (SUTD), despite its focus on technology, requires students to take subjects in humanities and social sciences. NUS, Singapore's oldest university, brought together the Faculty of Arts and Social Sciences and the Faculty of Science to form a College of Humanities and Sciences. NUS president Tan (2020) noted that young adults today need to grapple with "wicked problems", problems that are ill-defined and multi-disciplinary. Overall, Singapore's higher education sector has demonstrated strong leadership during the pandemic by adapting to new challenges and exploring new approaches to education.

The Singapore government is well-known for planning ahead for the long term. Rather than providing a comprehensive overview of the government's public plans for the future (which would go beyond the confines of this Chapter), we offer a few thoughts that we believe are more or less aligned with these plans. Shifting from a teacher-centred to a learner-centred paradigm

(Brookfield et al., 2024), the role of educators is undergoing a transformation, progressing from being a "sage on the stage" to becoming a "guide by the side", adopting the roles of mentors and facilitators. This evolution is significantly influenced by the widespread availability of high-speed Internet and quality open educational resources in Singapore. In addition, given the advancements in generative AI, as highlighted by Tan et al. (2024) and Crawford et al. (2024) in this Handbook, it is of paramount importance that educators must provide insights on distinguishing between "the good, the bad, and the ugly" in terms of content and rethink their assessments.

The importance of online education should be balanced with its limitations, as the pandemic highlighted the unique abilities of human teachers when combined with educational technologies. Teachers offer a superior and personalised learning experience compared to a highly standardised, asynchronous online delivery (Sam, 2022). In addition, efforts to enhance higher education qualifications should continue, acknowledging that student-centricity does not equate to making academic studies overly easy. A conducive learning environment, robust support systems, and a focus on critical thinking and problem-solving are essential for a comprehensive higher education experience (Sam, 2021, 2022). This context also brings forth the opportunity for the continued internationalisation of research—a contribution that our Handbook aspires to make humbly. Further, it is crucial to avoid overly fixating on graduate employability, as exemplified by cases like the prompt engineer with an English major who earns more than USD 300,000 per annum (Bajpal, 2023). This narrative reminds us of the value of the much-poo-pooed humanities, multifaceted pathways and possibilities within the realm of education.

When the whole of Singapore was speedily proceeding to a lockdown, emergency remote teaching was the norm for all but the best-prepared institutions. In the meantime, many potential pedagogical innovations have surfaced, the discussion of which would go well beyond the confines of this article. There are many opportunities for research. Our study is based on qualitative research. More qualitative, quantitative or mixed-methods research is needed to further illuminate the Singapore scenario. This is only the beginning of a new journey. The analysis in this paper identified some institutions having simply digitised their content—taking face-to-face practices and replicating them in an online environment. The next stage will be to incorporate online pedagogical principles to shift from technology being the driver of curriculum design and delivery to technology being the tool of a quality curriculum. This change in practice needs to be driven by whole-of-system policy reform, potentially including a national higher education quality framework, institutional policies for online delivery, digital capability building for academics and students, and reimagining the roles of academics, educational designers and educational technologists in the post-pandemic era.

## References

Bajpai, P. (2023, April 28). How AI helped me land my dream job as an engineer. *Time*. https://time.com/6272103/ai-prompt-engineer-job/

Bonk, R., Kefalaki, M., Rudolph, J., Diamantidaki, F., Rekar Munro, C., Karanicolas, S., Kontoleon, P., & Pogner, K. (2020). Pedagogy in the time of pandemic: From localisation to glocalisation. *Journal of Education, Innovation, and Communication, 2*(SI1), 17–64.

Braun, V., & Clarke, V. (2006). Using thematic analysis in psychology. *Qualitative Research in Psychology, 3*(2), 77–101. https://doi.org/10.1191/1478088706qp063oa

Brookfield, S. D., Rudolph, J., & Tan, S. (2024). *Teaching well*. Routledge.

Butler-Henderson, K., Crawford, J., Rudolph, J., Lalani, K., & Sabu, K. M. (2020). COVID-19 in Higher Education Literature Database (CHELD V1): An open access systematic literature review database with coding rules. *Journal of Applied Learning & Teaching, 3*(2), 11–16. https://doi.org/10.37074/jalt.2020.3.2.11

Butler-Henderson, K., Tan, S., Lalani, K., Mandapam, S., Kemp, T., Rudolph, J., & Crawford, J. (2021). Update of the COVID-19 Higher Education literature database (CHELD v2). *Journal of Applied Learning & Teaching, 4*(1), 134–137. https://doi.org/10.37074/jalt.2021.4.1.22

Chan, C. (2022, February 14). Three Cs for Singapore's Universities to thrive in a post COVID-19 world. *The Straits Times*. https://www.straitstimes.com/opinion/three-cs-for-singapores-universities-to-thrive-in-a-post-covid-19-world

Channel News Asia. (2022, April 12). PM Lee's speech on key takeaways from COVID-19 crisis, Singaporeans' trust in Government. https://www.channelnewsasia.com/singapore/prime-minister-lee-hsien-loong-full-speech-covid-19-public-service-key-takeaways-2621576

Cleland, J., Chee, P., Tham, K., & Low-Beer, N. (2020). How COVID-19 opened up questions of sociomateriality in healthcare education. *Advances in Health Sciences Education, 25*, 479–482. https://doi.org/10.1007/s10459-020-09968-9

Compton, S., Sarraf-Yazdi, S., Rustandy, F., & Krishna, L. (2020). Medical students' preference for returning to the clinical setting during the COVID-19 pandemic. *Medical Education, 54*(10), 943–950. https://doi.org/10.1111/medu.14268

Cortez, M., Moktar, F., & Low, D. (2021, October 15). Singapore confronts the division and fear that come from living with COVID-19. *Bloomberg*. https://www.bloomberg.com/news/articles/2021-10-14/singapore-confronts-division-and-fearbred-by-living-with-COVID-19

Crawford, J. (2021). During and beyond a pandemic: Publishing learning and teaching research through COVID-19. *Journal of University Teaching & Learning Practice, 18*(3), 02.

Crawford, J. (2023). COVID-19 and higher education: A pandemic response model from rapid adaption to consolidation and restoration. *International Education Journal: Comparative Perspectives.* Ahead of Print.

Crawford, J., Butler-Henderson, K., Rudolph, J., Malkawi, B., Glowatz, M., Burton, R., Magni, P., & Lam, S. (2020). COVID-19: 20 countries' higher education intra-period digital pedagogy responses. *Journal of Applied Learning & Teaching, 3*(1), 9–28. https://doi.org/10.37074/jalt.2020.3.1.7

De Meyer, A., & Ang, J. (2022). *Building excellence in higher education.* Routledge.

Etikan, I., Musa, S., & Alkassim, R. (2016). Comparison of convenience sampling and purposive sampling. *American Journal of Theoretical and Applied Statistics, 5*(1), 1–4.

Ewing, L. (2021). Rethinking higher education post COVID-19. In J. Lee & S. H. Han (Eds.), *The future of service post-covid-19 pandemic, volume 1: Rapid adoption of digital service technology* (pp. 37–54). Springer.

Fiedler, F., & Garcia, J. (1987). *New approaches to effective leadership and organisational performance.* Wiley.

Fung, F., & Lam, Y. (2020). How COVID-19 disrupted our "flipped" freshman organic chemistry course: Insights gained from Singapore. *Journal of Chemical Education, 97*(9), 2573–2580. https://doi.org/10.1021/acs.jchemed.0c00590

Goh, P., & Sanders, J. (2020). A vision of the use of technology in medical education after the COVID-19 pandemic. *MedEdPublish, 9*, 1–8. https://doi.org/10.15694/mep.2020.000049.1

Gov.sg. (2020, May 20). *Safe re-opening: How Singapore will resume activities after the circuit breaker.* https://www.gov.sg/article/safe-re-opening-how-singapore-will-resume-activities-after-the-circuit-breaker

Ho, G. (2021, October 9). Zero-COVID-19 strategy no longer feasible due to highly infectious Delta variant: PM Lee. *The Straits Times,* https://www.straitstimes.com/singapore/politics/sporemust-press-on-with-strategy-of-living-with-COVID-19-and-not-be-paralysed-by

Hodges, C., Moore, S., Lockee, B., Trust, T., & Bond, M. (2020). The difference between emergency remote teaching and online learning. *Educause Review.* https://er.educause.edu/articles/2020/3/the-difference-between-emergency-remote-teaching-andonline-learning

Hoe, S. (2016). Defining a smart nation: The case of Singapore. *Journal of Information, Communication & Ethics in Society, 14*(4), 323–333. https://doi.org/10.1108/JICES-02-2016-0005

Hung, D., Huang, D., & Tan, C. (2020). Leadership in times of pandemics: Reflections from Singapore. *International Studies in Educational Administration, 48*(2), 56–63.

Hutton, N. (2020, May 11). Commentary: It is time to rethink how we do online education. *Channel News Asia.* https://www.channelnewsasia.com/news/commentary/onlineeducation-singapore-home-based-learning-school-12707560

Johns Hopkins University of Medicine. (2023, February 23). *COVID-19 mortality analyses.* https://coronavirus.jhu.edu/data/mortality

Karalis, T., & Raikou, N. (2020). Teaching at the times of COVID-19: Inferences and implications for higher education pedagogy. *International Journal of Academic Research in Business and Social Sciences, 10*(5), 479–493.

Kefalaki, M., Rudolph, J., Tan, S., & Diamantidaki, F. (2021). Face masks in education: The cases of Greece and Singapore. *Thesis, 10*(1), 3–42.

Kwan, J. (2022). Academic burnout, resilience level, and campus connectedness among undergraduate students during the Covid-19 pandemic: Evidence from Singapore. *Journal of Applied Learning and Teaching*, *5*(Sp. Iss. 1), 52–63. https://doi.org/10.37074/jalt.2022.5.s1.7

Lee, H. (2020, June 9). Overcoming the crisis of a generation. *Gov.sg.* https://www.gov.sg/article/pm-lee-hsien-loong-overcoming-the-crisis-of-a-generation

Lim, V. (2023, February 9). Singapore to scrap all COVID-19 border measures from Feb 13. *Channel News Asia.* https://www.channelnewsasia.com/singapore/covid-19-border-restrictions-singapore-pre-departure-tests-scrap-3265186

Lim, Y., & Ho, G. (2021, October 10). 10 things you need to know about PM Lee's address and Covid-19 measures. *The Straits Times.* https://www.straitstimes.com/singapore/health/singapores-path-forward-to-a-new-normal-10-takeaways-from-pm-lees-national-address

Lin, R., Lee, T., & Lye, D. (2020). From SARS to COVID-19: The Singapore journey. *The Medical Journal of Australia, 6*. https://www.ncbi.nlm.nih.gov/pmc/articles/PMC7300591/

Marginson, S. (2010). The global knowledge economy and the culture of comparison in higher education. In S. Kaur, M. Sirat, & W. G. Tierney (Eds.), *Addressing critical issues on quality assurance and university rankings in the Asia Pacific* (pp. 23–55).

Marshman, I., & Larkins, F. (2020). *Modelling individual Australian universities resilience in managing overseas student revenue losses from the COVID-19 pandemic.* Centre for the Study of Higher Education. University of Melbourne.

Ministry of Health. (2020). *Roadmap to phase three*. https://www.moh.gov.sg/news-highlights/details/roadmap-to-phase-three

MOE. (2022, March 7). *Expanding pathways & opportunities across a life course: Investing in our learners for life.* https://www.moe.gov.sg/news/press-releases/20220307-expanding-pathways-and-opportunities-across-a-life-course-investing-in-our-learners-for-life

Mohan, M., & Lim, V. (2023, February 9). Mask-wearing no longer mandatory on public transport from Feb 13, as Singapore steps down COVID-19 restrictions. *Channel News Asia.* https://www.channelnewsasia.com/singapore/mask-wearing-feb-13-dorscon-green-mtf-covid-19-3265126

Müller, A., Goh, C., Lim, L., & Gao, X. (2021). Covid-19 emergency elearning and beyond: Experiences and perspectives of university educators. *Education Sciences, 11*(1), 1–15.

National Institute of Education. (n.d.). *eTools@NIE*. https://learn.nie.edu.sg/etools NIE/

Ng, K. (2020, December 8). Singapore students top maths, science rankings for second consecutive edition of international study. *The Straits Times*. https://www.straitstimes.com/singapore/singapore-students-top-maths-science-rankings-for-second-consecutive-edition-of

Preskill, S., & Brookfield, S. (2009). *Learning as a way of leading*. Jossey-Bass.

Rai, B. (2020). A team of instructors' response to remote learning due to COVID-19. A 10.012 Introduction to Biology case study. *Journal of Applied Learning and Teaching, 3*(2), 154–156. https://doi.org/10.37074/jalt.2020.3.2.6

Riggio, R., & Newstead, T. (2023). Crisis leadership. *Annual Review of Organizational Psychology and Organizational Behavior, 10*, 201–224. https://doi.org/10.1146/annurev-orgpsych-120920-044838

Rudolph, J., Itangata, L., Tan, S., Kane, M., Thairo, I., & Tan, T. (2021). Bittersweet' and 'alienating': An extreme comparison of collaborative autoethnographic perspectives from higher education students, non-teaching staff and faculty during the pandemic in the UK and Singapore. *Journal of University Teaching and Learning Practice, 18*(8), 10.

Rudolph, J., Tan, S., & Aspland, T. (2021). Editorial 4(2): Black swan or grey rhino? Reflections on the macro-environment of higher education during the pandemic. *Journal of Applied Learning and Teaching, 4*(2), 6–12. https://doi.org/10.37074/jalt.2021.4.2.1

Rudolph, J., Tan, S., & Aspland, T. (2023). JALT Editorial 6 (1): Fully automated luxury communism or Turing trap? Graduate employability in the generative AI age. *Journal of Applied Learning and Teaching, 6*(1), 7–15. https://doi.org/10.37074/jalt.2023.6.1.35

Rudolph, J., Tan, S., Crawford, J., & Butler-Henderson, K. (2023). Perceived quality of online learning during COVID-19 in higher education in Singapore: Perspectives from students, lecturers, and academic leaders. *Educational Research for Policy and Practice, 22*(1), 171–191.

Sam, C. (2017). *Private education in Singapore: Contemporary issues and challenges*. World Scientific.

Sam, C. (2021). *Teaching higher education to lead: Strategies for the digital age*. Business Expert Press.

Sam, C. (2022). Post-COVID-19 and higher education. *Journal of Applied Learning and Teaching, 5*(1), 156–164. https://doi.org/10.37074/jalt.2022.5.1.21

Sidhu, R., Cheng, Y., Collins, F., Ho, K., & Yeoh, B. (2021). International student mobilities in a contagion: (Im)mobilising higher education? *Geographical Research, 59*(3), 313–323.

Spillane, J. P. (2005, June). Distributed leadership. *The Educational Forum, 69*(2), 143–150. Taylor & Francis Group.

Tan, E. (2020, September 10). Universities need to tear down subject silos. *The Straits Times*. https://www.straitstimes.com/opinion/universities-need-to-tear-down-subject-silos

Tan, E. (2021, January 8). A degree in learning to be human. *The Straits Times*. https://www.nus.edu.sg/newshub/news/2021/2021-01/2021-01-08/HUMAN-st-pA18-8jan.pdf

Tan, K. (2008). Meritocracy and elitism in a global city: Ideological shifts in Singapore. *International Political Science Review, 29*(1), 7–27.

Tan, E., Mwagwabi, F., Lim, T., & Lim, A. (2022). Graduate employability concerns amidst a crisis: Student perspectives from Singapore on COVID-19. *Industry and Higher Education*. https://doi.org/10.1177/09504222221126420

Tan, S., Rudolph, J., Crawford, J., & Butler-Henderson, K. (2022). Emergency remote teaching or andragogical innovation? Higher education in Singapore during the COVID-19 pandemic. *Journal of Applied Learning and Teaching, 5*(Sp. Iss. 1), 64–80. https://doi.org/10.37074/jalt.2022.5.s1.8

Teng, A. (2019, December 3). Pisa 2018: Singapore slips to second place behind China, but still chalks up high scores. *The Straits Times*. https://www.straitstimes.com/singapore/education/pisa-2018-singapore-slips-to-second-place-behind-china-but-still-chalks-up-high

Teng, A. (2022, May 21). New SMU College to let students pick own individualised major. *The Straits Times*. https://www.straitstimes.com/singapore/parenting-education/smu-students-to-get-to-pick-courses-for-their-major-from-2023-under-new-interdisciplinary-college

Tooze, A. (2021). *Shutdown. How Covid shook the world's economy*. Viking.

Training Partners Gateway. (2023a). *Deregistered PEIs*. https://www.tpgateway.gov.sg/resources/information-for-private-education-institutions-(peis)/deregistered-peis

Training Partners Gateway. (2023b). *Permitted courses offered by PEIs*. https://www.tpgateway.gov.sg/resources/information-for-private-education-institutions-(peis)/pei-listing

Tushara, E. (2023, June 23). NUS and NTU among top 5 Asian universities in Times rankings. *The Straits Times*. https://www.straitstimes.com/singapore/nus-and-ntu-among-top-5-asian-universities-in-times-rankings

Waring, P. (2014). Singapore's global schoolhouse strategy: Retreat or recalibration? *Studies in Higher Education, 39*(5), 874–884.

World Economic Forum. (2020*). The COVID-19 pandemic has changed education forever. This is how*. https://www.weforum.org/agenda/2020/04/coronavirus-educationglobal-COVID19-online-digital-learning/

Ycharts. (2023). Singapore coronavirus full vaccination rate. 90.85% for Jan 31, 2023. https://ycharts.com/indicators/singapore_coronavirus_full_vaccination_rate

Ye, R. (2016). Transnational higher education strategies into and out of Singapore: Commodification and consecration. *TRaNS: Trans-Regional and National Studies of Southeast Asia, 4*(1), 85–108.

# Educational Leadership in Times of Crisis: Lessons Learned and the Future of Higher Education in Sri Lanka

Varunadatta Edirisinghe, Sakunthala Yatigammana, Kelum A. A. Gamage, Nanda Gunawardhana, and Leena Seneheweera

## Introduction

The entitlement to education is a basic human right, and education is the key to personal and social growth and development. In this context, educational leadership plays a primary and significant role (Brooks et al., 2021). Higher education (HE) leadership focuses at all times, especially in crises (Weaver et al., 2023), largely on decision-making affecting the pedagogical approaches and the quality of education. These guarantee the personal development and employment success of the current and future students, the community and the country.

The responsibility, therefore, placed on higher educational institutions even under normal circumstances is quite considerable (Broucker et al.,

V. Edirisinghe (✉)
Department of Classical Languages, Faculty of Arts, University of Peradeniya, Peradeniya, Sri Lanka
e-mail: vedirisi@arts.pdn.ac.lk

S. Yatigammana
Department of Education, Faculty of Arts, University of Peradeniya, Peradeniya, Sri Lanka
e-mail: sakuyatigammana@arts.pdn.ac.lk

K. A. A. Gamage
James Watt School of Engineering, University of Glasgow, Glasgow, UK
e-mail: Kelum.Gamage@glasgow.ac.uk





J. Rudolph et al. (eds.), *The Palgrave Handbook of Crisis Leadership in Higher Education*,
https://doi.org/10.1007/978-3-031-54509-2_26

2020), let alone during crises such as the COVID-19 pandemic, the unprecedented global health emergency that first emerged in 2020. In the beginning, and with each intermittent resurgence, the pandemic challenged and moved the boundaries of educational leadership globally in an unprecedented way, highlighting the need for Higher Educational Institutes (HEIs) to assess and reorient leadership attitudes and behaviours in the delivery of quality education (Bergan et al., 2021; Marmolejo & Groccia, 2022; Tilak & Kumar, 2022). In this backdrop, Sri Lanka provides a unique example of a country that has weathered a health crisis since 2020 with a ripple effect in educational, social and economic spheres and endured a state higher education sector that was already beleaguered for decades by pedagogical, administrative, unemployment, militant faction and violence-related crises and challenges.

An examination, therefore, of state higher educational leadership in Sri Lanka in the backdrop of the ongoing three-fold and related crises from 2020 to 2023 is pertinent. It will highlight leadership initiatives (or lack thereof) in facing crises from HEI administrative, academic and student (including students with disabilities) angles in delivering education in tandem with pre-existing "crises". This will enable the country's HE financing, governance and monitoring apparatus and especially the state universities (SUs)—the primary higher education providers of the country—to revisit and reorient their role as higher education leaders in fulfilling their objectives, missions and obligations. The primary objective of this Chapter is to examine educational leadership in selected State and affiliated Universities (SAAUs) in Sri Lanka during the COVID-19 pandemic. It includes the educational, social and economic repercussions in its aftermath through accommodations and adaptations of university administrators, teachers and students using primary and secondary data. Accordingly, the Chapter recommends as viable the crisis leadership framework proposed by Ralph Gigliotti (2017) to surmount current and future crises and challenges while mitigating pre-existing ones. For this purpose, the study refers to past unresolved higher educational crises with a bearing on the present and future. The Chapter contains an account

N. Gunawardhana
Office of International Affairs, SLTC, Padukka, Sri Lanka
e-mail: nandag@sltc.ac.lk

L. Seneheweera
Department of Fine Arts, Faculty of Arts, University of Peradeniya, Peradeniya, Sri Lanka
e-mail: leenas@arts.pdn.ac.lk

of the higher education landscape in Sri Lanka, the research methodology, a review of the literature covering the pandemic and pre-existing crises in SAAUs, and a discussion based on secondary and primary data from the leadership survey. These reiterate the urgency of a viable leadership framework, followed by conclusions and recommendations.

## Context

In Sri Lanka, HE dates back to the education provided by the Buddhist monasteries, followed in modern times by a medical, agriculture and technical college in the mid to late 1800s under British colonial rule. The university education system began with the University College in 1921, renamed the University of Ceylon in 1942 (Ministry of Higher Education, n.d.), and functioned under state patronage. Thereafter, the state was the main provider of HE, and currently, seventeen universities, two campuses, nineteen Institutes and six other government universities and Institutes are under the University Grants Commission (UGC), established in 1978 as per Universities Act No. 16. At national level, administration is hierarchical as UGC plans and coordinates state-funded university education according to national policy, determines funds approved by the Parliament of Sri Lanka, controls expenditure, maintains academic standards and regulates HEIs administration and student admissions (Act, 3-1-5). Under UGC, HEIs enjoy autonomy, which "promotes neither accountability nor performance" (NEC, 2022, p. 122).

State universities (SUs) deliver education free of charge through a competitive district-based selection process at the General Certificate of Education (Advanced Level) Examination. The mismatch between qualified candidates and limited opportunities deprives a large percentage of HE participation, creating a demand for fee-levied private HE (CBSL, 2019; Ministry of Education, 2021). In 2020, 65.98% of Advanced Level candidates were eligible for admission (Department of Examinations, n.d.), whereas the total admission was 22.58% (UGC, 2021). Despite the questionable quality, SUs offer fee-levied distance learning (Dundar et al., 2017; NEC, 2022, p. 194). State sector degree programmes include traditional (with higher enrolments in arts streams [Dundar et al., 2017; UGC, 2021]) and new disciplines catering to the country's economic development. SAAUs also participate in inclusive education with comparatively fewer admissions of students with special needs in a "special category" based on GCE (A/L) performance. The majority in this category belongs to the Humanities and Social Sciences disciplines, while Medicine, Engineering and Management have admitted considerable numbers (INCEDU, 2021). According to Sri Lanka Qualification Framework, study programmes and institutions undergo quality assurance and accreditation procedures regularly (Bandara, 2021). Nevertheless, due to the politicisation of SUs, frequent trade union action by student and staff unions has "strained the internal governance and management of universities" and disrupted SUs frequently (NEC, 2022, p. 204). Trade union action by academics challenging the 2023 tax reforms disrupted teaching and learning in SUs for six weeks (March–April) and the evaluation of the GCE (AL) examination with no solution.

In 2021, the government expenditure on education alone was approximately LKR 154.8 billion. For 2022, it was LKR 200.00 billion (UGC, 2021, p. 120). The share of GDP for education, however, remained low at 2.12% in 2020 (NEC, 2022). Labour force participation with a basic degree or higher from 2017 to 2021 shows a greater percentage (80% and above) for males and females than those with lower educational qualifications (Department of Labor, 2021, p. 33). The Government Budget for 2023 allocated LKR 97 billion for university education, and LKR 15 billion and LKR 392 billion (Ministry of Finance, 2023, n.d.), respectively, for vocational training/skills development and general education, with a greater commitment to the latter. This indicates a reduced focus on overcoming challenges in Technical and Vocational Education Training (NEC, 2022) despite its proven value in labour force participation.

Private Universities and HEIs have been under the Ministry of Education since 2013 (UGC, 2021) and the Company Law of Sri Lanka and have "changed Sri Lanka's educational landscape" since the 1990s (Bandara, 2021; NEC, 2019, p. 92). Nevertheless, they have been unsupervised and "ill-defined" in financial, regulatory and quality assurance aspects (NEC, 2022, p. 203). Nevertheless, a 2018 estimate indicates 65.5% and 66% comparative employability rates for SU and private sector graduates, respectively (UGC, 2018). As an alternative to state/private HE, vocational training institutes (state and private) under the Ministry of Education facilitate human capital for economic development; this, however, despite scarce industry participation (Asian Development Bank, 2016) and access, material and human resources, skills training and quality assurance issues (NEC, 2022).

## Literature Review

Leadership indeed defies definition; over two hundred definitions of the word existed from 1900 to 1990 (Northouse, 2016). From 1900 to 1929, leadership characterised control and centralisation of power. Leadership in the 1930s focused on traits and individual behaviour in directing the group in the 1940s, continuing group focus in the 1950s (and'60s) while adding effectiveness and relationship with shared goals. In the 1970s, it meant organisational behaviour with organisational goals and as a reciprocal process involving leaders and followers. The 1980s used a few definitions: leaders make followers do things, including influence, traits and a transformational process. The twenty-first century conceptualised leadership as a process, the influence of the individual on the group to accomplish goals, and added authentic, spiritual, servant and adaptive leadership perspectives (Northouse, 2016). Leadership literature can be categorised as classical, contemporary, competency and communication (Gigliotti, 2017). The latter is important because of its indispensability to human life and viability in approaching crises (Gigliotti, 2017).

Crises are expected unpredictable occurrences (Coombs, 2015, cited in Gigliotti, 2017, p. 33). Its etymology (Greek κρίσις) denotes a choice, decision, dispute or the event or issue of a thing (Liddell & Scott, 1999) reflecting human deliberation. Crises can affect individual or organisational futures and disrupt the entire organisation (Gigliotti, 2017). The types of crises in HE identified requiring leadership interventions are natural disasters, technical breakdowns and violence (Gigliotti, 2017). Based on particular contexts, however, others, such as management misconduct, confrontation, human breakdowns, organisational misdeeds, challenges and economic and human resources crises, can also generate critical situations (Gigliotti, 2017). Given the disruptive nature of crises, immediate responses are imperative (Gigliotti, 2017). The most useful in this respect is the communicative approach involving internal and external stakeholders and providing a practical guide (Gigliotti, 2017).

HEIs are "value-based organisations" (Gigliotti, 2022, p. 1) that are driven by "moral purposes". The former president of Wellesley College and Duke University observed:

> Colleges and Universities play a crucial part in determining whether humanity will indeed have a future, and what it will be like. Our institutions have significant moral purposes; we are not just collections of loosely affiliated persons, with convergent or conflicting interests, but institutions that make a difference in the world through pursuing our basic goals. (Nannerl Keohane, cited in Gigliotti, 2022, p. 6)

The exact purpose was reiterated in 1852 by Cardinal John Newman when he reinforced the university's primary role of perfecting the intellect, the ideal of education "the clear, calm, accurate vision and comprehension of all things, as far as the finite mind can embrace them" (cited in Gigliotti, 2022, p. 7). Hence, the significance of leadership during crises. In crises, as Riggio and Newstead argue, decision-making through a consultative process is essential: "leaders need to gather relevant information and evidence, seek advice from subject matter experts, and consult with other members of the leadership team and relevant stakeholders" (2022, p. 213). Equally important and more attuned to crisis-ridden HE contexts are the actions of leaders, which, when combined with verbal and non-verbal communication, determine the success or failure of organisations/HEIs. Gigliotti (2020, p. 3), who proposed the framework, noted, "This process is shaped by verbal and nonverbal communication and co-constructed between leaders and followers, and by informal and formal leaders". He reiterated the suitability of its "distributed and communicative process" to address crises in HE because they are "situations that often demand a collective and collaborative response from multiple individuals, units, and organisations" (Gigliotti, 2020, p. 3). The leader frames the situation through communication with the followers: "leadership involves the ability to situate and to make sense of phenomenon in a way that is co-constructed with those individuals whom they lead" (Gigliotti, 2017, p. 134).

The impact of framing crises, Gigliotti noted, is that "it helps to focus attention on a problem of concern and heighten the probability of an expedited response" (2020, p. 12). Viewed this way, crisis leadership is compatible with institutional values because it is "an orientation that positions clarity, consistency, and congruency between the way one leads during the crisis and those core values that are most critical to an institution" (Gigliotti, 2017, p. 140). This is because HE crises "often" challenge "core institutional values" (Gigliotti, 2020, p. 3), and "crises, by their very nature, cause disruption, and they have the potential to threaten the organisation's core mission, purpose, or reason for existence" (Gigliotti, 2022, p. 2). Gigliotti's framework also emphasises the leader who learns by training because "core skills, values, and competencies associated with the practice of crisis leadership in higher education… may be cultivated through formal training and development efforts" (2017, p. iv). The identified skills/competencies include analysis, synthesis, triage, adaptability/flexibility, calmness, care and aftercare, collaboration, confidence and courage, doing right, gathering/dissemination of information, institutional focus, learning, honesty, transparency and trust (2017, pp. 109–125). In delivering its moral mission during crises, HEIs crisis preparedness is crucial, and engagement in flexible, values-based, stakeholder-centred decision-making is compatible with the changed circumstances (Gigliotti, 2020, 2023; Yokus, 2022).

The leadership framework put in place at the University of Johannesburg, South Africa, exemplifies the role of values of social justice, equity, teaching excellence and access in overcoming the COVID-19 pandemic in the backdrop of longstanding equity-based crises (Menon & Motala, 2021). A study of HEI leadership in Indonesia and Ethiopia highlights the significance of leadership through multi-directional communication, empathy, a network of cooperation and a heuristic approach in teaching during the pandemic (Nugroho et al., 2021). Gigliotti reiterates the significance of crisis preparation, perception and core values (principles) in pandemic and post-pandemic scenarios in the hope that crises, known and unknown, will be handled "with care, compassion, clarity, and commitment" (2023, p. 238). Weaver et al. (2023) narrate experiences on U.S. campuses during the pandemic, highlighting the importance of trust, interrelated communication and teamwork while navigating new and pre-existing challenges.

## Methods

This study is based on primary and secondary data on Sri Lanka's HE response to crises with the coronavirus outbreak as a general springboard to examine crisis response. Secondary data cover studies and reports during the pandemic and prior crises and issues in HE. Primary data was collected from questionnaire surveys of administrators ($N$ = 50, 20%), academics ($N$ = 100, 40%) and students ($N$ = 100, 40%) of HEIs under the purview of UGC. The response rate for each category is as follows: academics (online surveys: 14%, paper surveys: 11%), administrators (online surveys: 16%, paper surveys: 10%), undergraduates (online surveys: 24%, paper surveys: none were administered). The questionnaires were modelled on the Multifactor Leadership Questionnaire (MLQ) and consisted of two parts covering the pandemic and post-pandemic scenarios relating to teaching–learning, assessment, leadership roles and education policy, student leadership, well-being and the future of HE with multiple choice and few open-ended questions (Rowold, 2005). The data were analysed using Microsoft Excel. Due to word limit constraints, summaries and percentages of stakeholder responses are tabulated and used, and a major limitation in administering the survey was apparent respondent prejudice against the leadership focus, resulting in poor response rates.

## Discussion

Leadership failures and deficiencies relating to teaching, learning, assessment and wellbeing during the pandemic in Sri Lanka correspond to pre-pandemic times. A brief overview will suffice. Several pandemic and post-pandemic studies of SUs in Sri Lanka highlight the critical role expected of administrative and academic leadership. A decreasing interest in student learning, violence and adverse student politics, declining quality of education and relevance (Udayanga, 2018) require immediate attention. According to Udayanga, HE in Sri Lanka is in crisis, but "the comprehension of that crisis by many stakeholders is not clear and precise" (2018, p. 2). For the first time, Sri Lanka's HEI sector also transitioned to online teaching and learning during the pandemic.

Nevertheless, motivation and attitude change of academics through "strong university administration leadership and incentives will help faculty mindsets" (Hayashi et al., 2020, p. 11), which was also evidenced in primary data (see Table 2). Challenges faced with a World Bank-funded project in one SU have shown the significance of leadership roles, relationships and flexibility for implementation (Munasinghe & Surangi, 2022) and the role of universities in setting up collaborative, cooperative and supportive learning cultures for student-centred curricula is needed (Rasika, 2018). Short-term interventions to ensure the quality of online or blended learning options during crises (Silva & Wickramasinghe, 2022) emphasise the need for university-level leadership. Primary data also complement these findings: with 72%, 88% and 92% of respondents admitting its use throughout the first, second and third waves, respectively, online teaching quickly emerged as the dominant option. More than 60% of instructors preferred the hybrid approach, which combines in-person and online learning. Traditional face-to-face approaches, however, were far less common (36%). A whopping 88% have plans to ensure that teaching and learning continue uninterrupted during future interruptions, with the hybrid model (96%) preferred over only using online techniques (64%). Online testing (68%) is becoming more popular than conventional testing (16%).

Furthermore, they correspond to the suggested crisis leadership framework, emphasising the need for strong academic and institutional leadership (see Tables 1 and 2). Academic and administrative responses on pandemic and post-pandemic leadership equally reveal strengths, weaknesses and hope for the future (see Table 2). Their rating of teaching–learning, assessments, student wellbeing and leadership also reflect indifference as well as genuine commitment and positivity: Students generally described their wellbeing as being only "fair" (60%) or "good" (28%). A "very good" sense of belonging was expressed by about 48% of students, which is highly encouraging. The pandemic's impact on skill development has been inconsistent. COVID-19 has proven crucial in promoting adaptive learning practices even if communication abilities were noticeably hampered. Another 40% of students reported that independent and self-learning had improved, with an improvement in both categories. However, 56% of students rated the impact as "poor" or "satisfactory", suggesting a potential lack of leadership chances in online learning. In contrast, leadership skills showed a decline. In addition, 80% of students expressed anticipation of alterations in student leadership practices, reflecting optimism about the latent transformative potential of this global crisis.

The issues relating to teaching and learning, assessment and wellbeing during the pandemic are similar to pre-pandemic times, emphasising leadership failures and deficiencies. The focus of early HE in English on limited entrants from public schools to create administrators led to a shortage of a skilled labour force for national requirements (Samaranayake, 2016; Tharmaseelan, 2007). The system prevailed despite the subsequent increases in student numbers and study programmes. Changes came at a cost: the access of HE in arts, humanities, social sciences and commerce and management to diverse socio-economic backgrounds created unemployment in the 1960s due to graduates not fitting into the available job market. This resulted in political activism among the affected, and despite policy changes, university curricula, teaching and learning, relevance and quality "remained unchanged" (Samaranayake, 2016, pp. 21–22). Moreover, it was youth unrest in the 1970s–1980s that led to a national policy on education and subsequent "job-oriented" reforms in the HE sector through the establishment of the National Education Commission (NEC) and their proposals in 1997 (Aturupane & Little, 2021; Bandara, 2021).

However, the status quo continues with a mismatch between educational qualifications and labour market needs. According to 2020 estimates, 25% of the total workforce in Sri Lanka was unskilled (Ministry of Education, 2022). In contrast, the graduate unemployment rate in 2019 was 54.8% for Arts (23,040 graduates) and 45.2% for a total of 18,984 "other degree" graduates (Department of Census & Statistics, 2019, p. 25). In comparison, the number of graduates passing out of SUs in 2019 was 18,883, the highest since 2013 being 22,254 in 2015 (Department of Labour, 2020). Unemployment figures reflect failure despite World Bank-funded projects to improve SU undergraduates' soft and entrepreneurial skills (NEC, 2022). The unemployment of arts graduates places the onus of rediscovering the inherent relevance of the arts and humanities disciplines entirely in the hands of the

**Table 1** Teacher leadership and future of HE: student views

| Survey questions | Student responses |
|---|---|
| Most positive influence expected from teachers | • Interest, hard work<br>• Support, patience<br>• Motivation for self-study<br>• Freedom to think/expression<br>• Improvements in practicals<br>• Freedom to question in class<br>• Encouragement during hardships<br>• Technological proficiency<br>• Leadership qualities<br>• Encourage students<br>• Fewer assignments<br>• Good exposure to corporate world, link between examples and theory<br>• Better communication with students<br>• Bring the best in students, teach compassion, organisation, presentation skills<br>• Foster self-esteem to increase motivation, learning<br>• Complete practicals on time |
| Future of higher education in Sri Lanka post-COVID | • Must be in-person<br>• Mental health sensitive, well-rounded education focused on self-development, self-reflection, education should provide assessment of life<br>• In-person university experience for students<br>• Online education good for globalisation<br>• Must be less stressful<br>• More rational, practical<br>• Job oriented education<br>• Improve the hybrid teaching–learning/HEI administration<br>• Self-development, overcoming stressful events<br>• HE more streamlined to prevent unexpected education disruptions<br>• Traditional teaching |

**Table 2** Leadership and future of HE—academic and administrator views

| Survey Questions | Academic responses | Administrator responses |
|---|---|---|
| Teacher leadership | • Students self-learn<br>• Facilitate, inspire<br>• Teacher, guide, advisor, coach, motivator, change agent<br>• Catering to demands of universities<br>• Classroom leadership/beyond<br>• Decision making within regulations, without superior approval<br>• Beyond traditional teacher role<br>• Teaching adjusted to circumstances<br>• Moulding students<br>• Exemplary leading of students | Not applicable |

(continued)

**Table 2** (continued)

| Survey Questions | Academic responses | Administrator responses |
|---|---|---|
| Importance of teacher leadership in education | • Lead, set learning outcomes<br>• Inspire, set achievable goals, assess performance, sensitive to student needs<br>• Process leading to HEI changes to benefit all students<br>• Encourage in class student engagement to follow goals<br>• Guide, Model, groom students to follow targets, role models for the university system<br>• Positively affect students' career<br>• COVID, economic crisis allowed leadership flexibility<br>• Beacon of student success<br>• Teach/prepare for extra curricular activities<br>• Prevents student alienation, provide direction<br>• Mentor, provide learner-centred teaching<br>• Prepares future leaders<br>• Lead students on right path | Not applicable |

| Survey Questions | Academic responses | Administrator responses |
|---|---|---|
| Impact of quality teacher leadership during the pandemic | • Flexibility, adaptability in remote learning<br>• Adapting to crisis to benefit students<br>• No education without it<br>• Promotes learning, shares leadership with parents to direct learning, plans teamwork-based Student Centred Learning, unity among teaching staff, creates desired vision<br>• Sensitive, empathetic towards student needs, encourage students<br>• Closer relations between teachers, students<br>• Empowers student mentality, maintains academic standards | Not applicable |
| Leadership role as a teacher during the pandemic | • Devised outcome based guides for lectures, used activity based assignments on Moodle<br>• Receptive to student needs, motivated them<br>• Worked hard<br>• Realised need for emotional, social support to help students<br>• Empathy<br>• Adapted quickly to remote teaching<br>• Learned online methods, active online<br>• Extra preparation, adjustments<br>• Played coach<br>• Extra vigilant on student vulnerabilities<br>• Creative | Not applicable |

(continued)

**Table 2** (continued)

| Survey Questions | Academic responses | Administrator responses |
|---|---|---|
| Shortcomings in handling of teaching–learning/administration during the pandemic | • Lack of technical knowledge/training in online teaching methods/resources<br>• Teaching without good attitude<br>• Sudden shift to online<br>• Lack of close relationship with new students<br>• Less interactive sessions, feedback/ interaction with students<br>• Loss of individual attention<br>• Inability to stimulate student participation<br>• Planning best online teaching techniques | • Lack of communication/in-person interaction<br>• Delayed decision-making<br>• Semester payment recovery<br>• Difficulties in conducting practicals Internet issues leading to inefficiency |
| Things done well | • Stimulated creativity, motivated students<br>• Kept student interest, interaction, desire to complete<br>• Good attitudes<br>• Finished classes on time<br>• Uninterrupted and consistent teaching,<br>• Quick adaptation to remote teaching<br>• Use of IT<br>• Practical for students' sake<br>• Stimulated online learning<br>• Online tests<br>• understanding student needs<br>• Content delivery<br>• Frequent feedback using online platforms | • Caring for students Quick adoption of online teaching<br>• Video created on practicals<br>• Uninterrupted learning timely communication with students, colleagues |

| Survey Questions | Academic responses | Administrator responses |
| --- | --- | --- |
| What could have been done better | • Use of technology, more practical and activity based learning<br>• Training in online teaching methods<br>• Good attitudes<br>• Networking with students<br>More creative content delivery | • Student welfare workload of administration/non academic staff<br>• Online workshops<br>• Exam management updated information |
| Teacher leadership | • Allow students to adapt, innovate, be creative in learning to achieve goals under any circumstances<br>• Inspires students<br>• Without it students face problems<br>• Balancing everything<br>Quick decisions to ensure uninterrupted learning, quality<br>• Innovative, flexible, practical<br>• Classroom leadership<br>• Leading students to achieve dreams<br>• Critical role of facilitator, advisor of student life | Not applicable |
| Influence of quality teacher leadership | • Not physically evident, impact absolute<br>• Motivates students, role model<br>• Directly affects student grades<br>• Guide student groups/individuals<br>• Influence all aspects of students' lives<br>• Turn students into good products<br>• Creation of emotionally stable high achievers<br>• Takes student achievement to higher levels<br>• | Not applicable |

(continued)

**Table 2** (continued)

| Survey Questions | Academic responses | Administrator responses |
|---|---|---|
| How can educational leaders, restructure quality teaching and learning cultures post-pandemic? | Not applicable | • Culture is returning to old ways<br>• Old method better Interactive sessions Lack of infrastructure alters student mindset in assessments<br>• HEIs should ensure integrity of teaching, learning, assessments |
| Post COVID future of higher education in Sri Lanka | • Opportunities for innovation<br>• Hybrid teaching–learning and administrative environments/in-person evaluation<br>• Need radical change, priority for STEM, more IT facilities, empathy<br>• Online, technical barriers removed<br>• Turn teachers into coaches<br>• Flipped classroom, self-learning<br>• Dynamic, accessible, open for all | • Has and will lag behind region<br>• Dynamic with technical advancement<br>• Online education quick, attitude, socialisation problematic<br>• Limited IT infrastructure affects online teaching-learning, careful planning needed/HEI administrations prepare for future calamities accordingly |

academics, especially in the backdrop of the government initiative in 2023 (Ministry of Education, 2023) to introduce STEAM (Science, Technology, Engineering, Math and the Arts) education in recognition of its potential to enhance higher order thinking skills required at international testing systems (NEC, 2022).

On the other hand, the changing labour market trends present new challenges. Employment statistics for the year 2022, for instance, indicate a private sector preference of only 9% for degree and above qualification or professional/vocational training (Department of Labour, 2022), and the unemployment rate was very low (below 3%) from 2011 to 2020 (except in 2013, 2014 and 2017) among the category with the lowest (Grade 5 and below) education qualifications (Department of Labour, 2020, p. 39). Likewise, in 2022, the highest demand (approximately 50%) was for sewing machine operators, while manufacturing supervisors and labourers took up 20% of the jobs indicating "the changing behavioural pattern of the country's economy" (Department of Labour, 2022, p. 20), and reinforcing the need to assess the merits of public investment and the role of SUs (UGC, 2018, pp. 72–73).

Unemployment also reflects education quality for which SUs have been under the spotlight for decades. Some of the main criticisms revolve around teacher-centred delivery detrimental to adult learning, outdated curricula, assessment methods and knowledge delivery at the expense of application and skills development (NEC, 2022), quality of academic staff (Aturupane, 2018) as evidenced in employer dissatisfaction and reluctance to recruit unemployable graduates, and graduates' own (dis)satisfaction with aspects of teaching and learning leading to employability (UGC, 2018). The UGC tracer study of SU and non-SU graduates from 2014 to 2015 highlights the "not very satisfactory" (UGC, 2018, p. 64) employment rates and notes the challenges caused by the expansion of HE. The study recommended specific knowledge and skills development, industry experience, and needs-based curricular revision, placing the onus of "responsible" decision-making (p. 72) on the SUs. Despite the high literacy rate of 92% in 2022 (World Bank, n.d.), slow development in skills, competitiveness, STEM disciplines and research and innovation in the HE sector remains a challenge to economic growth (CBSL, 2019).

Graduates of SUs also face the hardships of ragging, sexual and gender-based violence that militate against pre- and post-graduation outcomes. A 2008 report on violence on state campuses revealed that given the politicised university setting, widespread student violence and indiscipline are linked with external factors highlighting "deficiencies in the administrative, academic, and managerial aspects of the university system" (Weeramunda, 2008, p. 10). Nevertheless, the status quo continues, as exemplified by recent eruptions, including violent attacks between university student groups (2022–2023), leading to the protracted disruption of all facets of university education. The response of SU authorities in such situations is to close the universities (Bandara, 2021). Moreover, despite legislation passed in the Parliament of Sri Lanka in 1998 due to public agitation—23 years after the first two cases of ragging—and rag prevention mechanisms in SUs, incidents continue unabated.

An undated UGC report on ragging and gender-based violence places greater responsibility on the SUs for enacting legislation activating prevention mechanisms, training, awareness and counselling. It observes that ragging, verbal, psychological and physical harassment on campuses affect students, while gender-based violence affects students and staff. It reports that 21.5% of students do not trust the HEIs rag prevention mechanisms and those against gender-based violence (UGC, n.d.). Among the reasons for the prevalence of ragging were a lack of interest in the academic staff and HEIs, the non-implementation of rules and regulations, and the futility of institutional mechanisms such as disciplinary committees (UGC, n.d.). It also shows that of the students who were ragged once a semester or less, 77.7% sought medical care, 17.4% once a month and 4.8% more than once a month, and similar percentages of students in the "not ragged" category also sought medical attention, of which 5.4% more than once a month (UGC, n.d.), bearing sufficient testimony to the unattended health crises in the SUs. A report on new entrants deprived of education due to ragging also highlights the "passive role" of university administrations (UGC, 2020, p. 11) despite existing legislation and "adverse impacts" on health, academic performance and personality/social development. It defines ragging as the "degenerating disease" (UGC, 2020, p. 28) which continues due to "the longstanding and deep-rooted 'culture of ragging' that has gained political backing" (UGC, 2020, p. 1) and non-implementation of existing preventative mechanisms.

The issue of education policy is also persistent. It centres around the President, NEC, the Ministries of Education and Higher Education, and UGC, and recent student admissions-related decision-making is politically motivated (Alwis, 2021), which in the past has "aggravated the quality issues in the university system" (UGC, 2018, p. 72). Likewise, the 2019–2023 strategic plan to restructure UGC along market trends, resources and environmental considerations with its core values "aimed at creating future knowledge leaders through the state university system" (UGC, n.d., p. iii) is a top-down approach focused on goals and key performer indicators which is likely to garner more resistance than support from the SUs. The centralised funding, salaries and cadre system have already created a lack of motivation in HEI administration and academics to become efficient and cost-effective (UGC, 2018). Moreover, despite deficiencies in implementation, the need for systematic expansion of HE based on "local and international market requirements" (UGC, 2018, p. 71) was a prior recommendation.

Protracted issues and challenges of a critical nature in SU education in Sri Lanka inevitably draw attention to leadership. Despite a scarcity of studies directly focusing on the topic, some have highlighted the need for "visionary leadership, ownership, and a long-term commitment from political authorities and policymakers", albeit in human capital development (Aturupane et al., 2021, p. 131). The pre-pandemic NEC report (2019) summarised the situation succinctly without, however, reference to "crisis" "opportunities for higher education, and where access is available the quality of the education, and student discipline related issues, ragging, violence among students, protests, and clashes with law enforcement which continue to be challenged with no sustainable solutions in sight" (NEC, 2019, p. 4).

Elsewhere in the report, "crisis" occurs eight times, four times about student welfare, once each observing the exclusion of the poor, inadequate access to HE, the mismatch between school, university, employment and lack of professionalism among academics, indicating that not every critical issue is framed as a crisis. Framing was recommended as a remedy because "the ability to take a critical approach to a problem and then choose and implement the right strategy to solve it and patterns of thinking are equally or more important than functional competency" (UGC, 2018, p. 71). Therefore, the need for a viable framework for SUs and education authorities to identify crises and respond accordingly is urgent. Even though Gigliotti's framework discussed above is not a panacea (Gouran, 2020), its focus on framing crises, trainable skills/competencies and value-based communicative approach will certainly provide a new and refreshing alternative to the current status quo in Sri Lanka's SU sector where, as survey responses reveal (see also Tables 1 and 2), there is a general acceptance of the failures, inadequacies and crises, as well as the need for change and remedial action.

## Conclusions and Recommendations

The study focused on crises in the SU system in Sri Lanka, which outweigh its positives. Especially striking is the combination of excessive control and inadequate or absent leadership at national and SU levels manifested in negligible

SU autonomy, inadequate, absent/faulty decision-making, inaction, academic and administrative irresponsibility and failure, lack of professionalism, needs awareness, stakeholder consultation, and importantly, inability to frame (a) particular situation(s) as (a) crisis/crises resulting in their pervasiveness. Inarguably, the current listlessness is detrimental to the future of HE in Sri Lanka. In the backdrop of protracted crises and the absence of remedial initiatives, the takeaways from this study for the future of HE in Sri Lanka are the following: first, the need at all levels for administrative and stakeholder initiative and commitment to identify crises. Second, there is a need for a communication and values-based concrete remedial mechanism to revive the state HE sector in Sri Lanka. The success and sustainability of this sector depend on a system that monitors and acknowledges irregularities and failures and is committed to the training of leadership at various levels to identify and tackle inevitable, critical situations. In a values-based, interrelated, and informed set-up, the trained leader's identification of crises will initiate positive action, superseding the tendency to normalise otherwise critical situations and paving the way for a sustainable state HE sector in Sri Lanka.

The proposed crisis leadership framework recommends the following for education leaders:

1. Identify potential crises through periodic reviews of administrative, academic and student affairs issues and challenges.
2. Adopt an institutional values-based communicative approach to address them.
3. Identify and preserve for future reference appropriate leadership qualities and characteristics appropriate to the time and context.
4. Familiarise with developments in the crisis leadership literature and handling crises in the HE sector elsewhere.
5. Regular training in crisis leadership for all stakeholders to cultivate and develop crisis leadership skills, values and competencies.
6. Adapt to evolving circumstances by revisiting established policies, technologies and learning methods.

## References

Alwis, D. (2021, March). University enrolment to rise by 30% in record intake. *University World News*, 2. https://www.universityworldnews.com/post.php?story=20210318150721888)

Asian Development Bank. (2016). *Innovative strategies in higher education for accelerated human resource development in South Asia: Sri Lanka.*

Aturupane, H. (2018). The evolving landscape of university education in Sri Lanka. *Journal of Economic Research, 5*(2), 3–19.

Aturupane, H., & Little, A. W. (2021). General education in Sri Lanka. In P. M. Sarangapani & R. Pappu (Eds.), *Handbook of education systems in South Asia* (pp. 695–732), Springer. https://doi.org/10.1007/978-981-13-3309-5

Athurupana, A., Higashi, H., Ebenzer, R., Attygalle, R., Dey, S., & Wijesinghe, R. (2021). *Sri Lanka human capital development: Realising the Promise and Potential of Human capital.* World Bank group.

Bandara, D. C. (2021). The Sri Lankan high education journey: From inclusion and improving relevance to acceleration. In P. M. Sarangapani & R. Pappu (Eds.), *Handbook of education systems in South Asia* (pp. 1009–1045). Springer. https://doi.org/10.1007/978-981-13-3309-5

Bergan, S., Munck, R., Gallagher, T., & van't Land, H. (2021). *Higher education's response to the Covid-19 pandemic: Building a more sustainable and democratic future.* Council of Europe.

Brooks, R., Gupta, A., Jayadeva, S., & Abrahams, J. (2021). Students' views about the purpose of higher education. *Higher Education Research and Development, 40*(7), 1375–1388. https://doi.org/10.1080/07294360.2020.1830039

Broucker, B., Borden, V. M. H., & Kallenberg, T. (2020). *Responsibility of higher educationsystems: What? How? Why?* Leiden. https://doi.org/10.1163/978900443 6558

Central Bank of Sri Lanka. (2019). *Annual report 2019. Vol. 1.* Central Bank of Sri Lanka.

Department of Census and Statistics. (2019). *Sri Lanka labour force survey: Annual report 2019.* http://www.statistics.gov.lk/Resource/en/LabourForce/Annual_Rep orts/LFS2019.pdf

Department of Census and Statistics. (2021). *Sri Lanka labour force survey, annual report.* http://www.statistics.gov.lk/Resource/en/LabourForce/Annual_Rep orts/LFS2021.pdf

Department of Examinations. (n.d.). *GCE A/L Examination 2020: New and old syllabi. performance of candidates.* https://www.doenets.lk/images/resources/STAT/POC_AL_final_20050710.10_1620405576468.pdf

Department of Labour. Ministry of Labour. (2020). *Labour statistics Sri Lanka 2020.* https://labourdept.gov.lk/images/PDF_upload/statistics/ls2020.pdf

Department of Labour. Ministry of Labour (2021). *Annual labour statistics report 2021 Sri Lanka.* https://labourdept.gov.lk/images/PDF_upload/statistics/als2021.pdf

Department of Labour, Ministry of Labor. (2022). *Outlook on labor needs of private sector 2022.* https://labourdept.gov.lk/images/PDF_upload/statistics/out look%20on%20requirements%20of%20labour%20demand%202022.pdf

Dundar, H., Millot, B., Riboud, M., Shojo, M., Aturupane, H., Goyal, H., & Raju, D. (2017). *Sri Lanka education sector assessment: Achievements, challenges, and policy.* World Bank Group. https://openknowledge.worldbank.org/entities/publication/c6bf33b7-8fe8-53a0-91bb-d701c45f0758

Gigliotti, R. (2020). Crisis leadership in higher education: Theory and practice. *Rutgers University Press.* https://doi.org/10.1080/19496591.2022.2041428

Gigliotti, R. (2022). Crisis leadership in higher education: Historical overview, organisational considerations, and implications. *The Oxford Encyclopedia of Crisis Analysis.* https://doi.org/10.1093/acref/9780190610623.001.0001,1-17

Gigliotti, R. (2023). Crisis leadership in liberal arts colleges. In I. Jung & K. Mok. (Eds.). *The reinvention of liberal learning around the globe. Crossing cultures: Liberal learning* (pp. 229–239). Springer. https://doi.org/10.1007/978-981-19-8265-1

Gigliotti, R. A. (2017). *The social construction of crises in higher education: Implications for crisis leadership theory and practice* [Doctoral thesis, Rutgers University]. https://rucore.libraries.rutgers.edu/rutgers-lib/53624/PDF/1/play/

Gouran, D. S. (2020). Book review. *International Journal of Communication, 14,* 4548–4551.

Hayashi, R., Garcia, M., Maddawin, A., & Hewagamage, K. P. (2020). *Online learning in Sri Lanka's higher educational institutions during the COVID-19 pandemic.* ADB Briefs. No. 151. https://www.adb.org/sites/default/files/publication/635911/online-learning-sri-lanka-during-covid-19.pdf

INCEDU. (2021). *Developing inclusive education for students with disabilities in Sri Lankan universities.*

Liddell, H. G., & Scott, R. (1999). *An intermediate Greek-English lexicon.* Clarendon Press.

Liyanage, I. M. K. (2014). *Education system of Sri Lanka; strengths and weaknesses.* https://www.ide.go.jp/library/Japanese/Publish/Reports/InterimReport/2013/pdf/C02_ch7.pdf

Marmolejo, F. J., & Groccia, J. E. (2022). Reimagining and redesigning teaching and learning in the post pandemic world. In C. M. Wehlburg (Ed.), *New directions for teaching and learning* (pp. 21–37). John Wiley & Sons.

Menon, K., & Motala, S. (2021). Pandemic leadership in higher education: New horizons, risks and complexities. *Education as Change, 25*(1). http://www.scielo.org.za/scielo.php?script=sci_arttext&pid=S1947-94172021000100008

Ministry of Education (n.d.). *A transformation in Sri Lankan education.* https://moe.gov.lk/wp-content/uploads/2020/06/A-Transformation-in-Sri-Lankan-Education.pdf

Ministry of Education. (2021). *Annual performance report 2021.* https://moe.gov.lk/wp-content/uploads/2022/10/3.-2021-Annual-Report-English.pdf

Ministry of Education. (2022). *Labour market information bulletin 1* (22). https://www.tvec.gov.lk/wp-content/uploads/2023/03/LMI_2022_Jan.pdf

Ministry of Education. (2023, March 30). *STEM education method implemented in 96 countries in the world is included in the education system of this country.* https://moe.gov.lk/stem-education-method-implemented-in-96-countries-in-the-world-is-included-in-the-education-system-of-this-country/

Ministry of Education, Higher Education (n.d.). *Overview.* https://mohe.gov.lk/index.php?option=com_content&view=article&id=66:overview&catid=12&lang=en&Itemid=123

Ministry of Finance. (2021). *Budget brief: Education sector Sri Lanka 2021.* UNICEF. https://www.unicef.org/srilanka/media/2706/file/BUDGET%20BRIEF:%20EDUCATION%20SECTOR%202021.pdf

Ministry of Finance, Economic Stabilization and National Policies. (2023). *Budget highlights 2023.* https://www.treasury.gov.lk/web/budget-highlights-2023/section/budget%20proposal%20-%202023

Ministry of Higher Education (n.d.). *Overview.* https://www.mohe.gov.lk/index.php?option=com_content&view=article&id=66&Itemid=123&lang=en

Ministry of Labour. (2021). *Annual labour statistics report: Sri Lanka 2021.* https://labourdept.gov.lk/images/PDF_upload/statistics/als2021.pdf

Munasinghe, M. A. T. K., & Surangi, H. A. K. N. S. (2022). The World Bank Grants for improving higher education quality in Sri Lanka: AHEAD grant implementation issues and lessons learnt: A case of University of Kelaniya. *Kelaniya Journal of Management, 11*(1), 88–104. https://doi.org/10.4038/kjm.v11i1.7678

National Education Commission. (2019). *National policy proposals on higher education.* http://nec.gov.lk/wp-content/uploads/2020/10/Higher-education-Policy_2019_English.pdf

National Education Commission. (2022). *National education policy framework (2020–2023).* http://nec.gov.lk/wp-content/uploads/2022/10/NATIONAL-EDUCATION-POLICY-FRAMEWORK-2020-2030_Full-Text.pdf

Northouse, P. G. (2016). *Leadership: Theory and practice* (7th ed.). Sage.

Nugroho, I., Paramita, N., Mengistie, B. T., & Krupskyi, O. P. (2021). Higher education leadership and uncertainty during the COVID-19 pandemic. *Journal of Socioeconomics and Development, 4*(1), 1–7.

Rasika, D. G. L. (2018). Student centered curriculum: A higher education case study in Sri Lankan university system. In *Creating a sustainable lens for higher education.*

Riggio, R. E., & Newstead, T. (2022). Crisis leadership. *Annual Review of Organizational Psychology and Organisational Behavior, 10*(1), 201–224.

Rowold, J. (2005). *Multifactor leadership questionnaire.* https://www.mindgarden.com/documents/MLQGermanPsychometric.pdf

Samaranayake, G. (2016). Expansion of university education, graduate unemployment and the knowledge hub in Sri Lanka. *Social Affairs: A Journal for the Social Sciences,* 5–32.

Silva, de T. & https://doi.org/10.1108/IJEM-07-2021-0272

Tharmaseelan, H. (2007). Tertiary education in Sri Lanka: Issues and challenges. *Bulgarian Journal of Science and Education Policy, 1*(1), 173–190. http://bjsep.org/getfile.php?id=42

Tilak, J. B. G., & Kumar A. G. (2022). Policy changes in global higher education: What lessons do we learn from the COVID-19 pandemic? *Higher Education Policy*. Springer. https://doi.org/10.1057/s41307-022-00266-0

The World Bank. (n.d.). *Literacy rate, adult total (% of people ages 15 and above)—Sri Lanka*. https://data.worldbank.org/indicator/SE.ADT.LITR.ZS?locations=LK

Udayanga, S. (2018). Passing the crossroad: An overview on issues and challenges of university education in Sri Lanka. *Global Journal of Human Social Science, 18*(7.1), 1–11.

University Grants Commission. (2018). *Tracer study of graduates: Universities in Sri Lanka*. https://www.ugc.ac.lk/downloads/statistics/webTracer/2018/Tracer%20Study%202018.pdf

University Grants Commission. (2020). *Redressing victims of ragging and providing a regulatory mechanism to prevent ragging related abusive conduct in Sri Lankan state universities and higher educational institutions*. https://www.ugc.ac.lk/downloads/publications/Report%20of%20the%20Rag%20Reliaf%20Committee/Report%20of%20the%20Rag%20Reliaf%20Committee.pdf

University Grants Commission. (2021). *Sri Lanka university statistics* 2021. https://www.ugc.ac.lk/index.php?option=com_content&view=article&id=2404%3As

University Grants Commission. (n.d.). *Prevalence of ragging and sexual and gender-based violence in Sri Lankan state universities*. https://www.unicef.org/srilanka/reports/prevalence-ragging-and-sexual-and-gender-based-violence

University Grants Commission. (n.d.). *Strategic plan 2019–2023*. https://www.ugc.ac.lk/downloads/corporate_plan/University%20Grants%20Commission%20Strategic%20Plan%202019-2023.pdf

Weaver, G. C., Rabbitt, K. M., Summers, S. W., Phillips, R., Hottenstein, K. N., & Cole, J. M. C. (2023). Acute crisis leadership in higher education: Lessons from the pandemic. *Routledge*. https://doi.org/10.4324/9781003239918

Weeramunda, A. J. (2008). *Socio-political impact of student violence and indiscipline in universities and tertiary education institutes*. Research Studies in Tertiary Education Sector. National Education Commission, Sri Lanka.

Yokus, G. (2022). Developing a guiding model of educational leadership in higher education during the COVID-19 pandemic: A grounded theory study. *Participatory Educational Research, 9*(1), 362–387.

# Higher Education and COVID-19: An Adaptive Approach in Thailand

Kaewta Muangasame and Methawee Wongkit

## Introduction

Cases of COVID-19 were first reported in Wuhan, China, in late December 2019. It rapidly spread worldwide and was declared a pandemic by the World Health Organization (WHO) on 11 March 2020 (Marinoni et al., 2020). Thailand was the first country to find a new case of COVID-19 outside of China, with its first confirmed case on 13 January 2020 (Tongkeo, 2020). The COVID-19 outbreak has had a devastating impact on human life. According to statistical records of the WHO (2023), as of 23 March 2023, there have been 761,402,282 confirmed global cases of COVID-19, including 6,887,000 deaths. This pandemic not only affected the health of individuals but also disrupted global economic, social, and education systems, both in developed and developing countries (Rashid & Yadav, 2020). In response to COVID-19, many countries introduced travel restrictions (inward and outward). Several practices suggested by public health

K. Muangasame (✉)
Tourism and Hospitality Management Division, Mahidol University International College, Nakhon Pathom, Thailand
e-mail: kaewta.mua@mahidol.edu

M. Wongkit
Faculty of Commerce and Management, Prince of Songkla University, Trang Campus, Trang, Thailand
e-mail: methawee.w@psu.ac.th


J. Rudolph et al. (eds.), *The Palgrave Handbook of Crisis Leadership in Higher Education*,
https://doi.org/10.1007/978-3-031-54509-2_27

experts and government officials were implemented, such as social distancing, self-isolation or quarantine, and work-at-home policies (Sahu, 2020).

Temporary closures of universities and other academic institutions were implemented by numerous countries worldwide to adhere to social distancing guidelines, aiming to mitigate the spread of the disease and reduce infection rates and fatalities (Toquero, 2020). During the first wave of the pandemic, these closures affected almost 1.38 billion students in 188 countries at all levels of learning—approximately 91.3 per cent of total enrolled students. Many universities either postponed or cancelled all campus events regarding higher education institutions. Concurrently, many shifted their courses and programmes from face-to-face to online delivery mode (Sahu, 2020; Toquero, 2020).

The unprecedented pandemic affected almost 15 million Thai students. When the state emergency was declared on 26 March 2020, and the Thai government announced the first curfew on 3 April 2020, all on-site learning and teaching activities were suspended, and the closure of educational institutions was enforced (Chareonrook, 2023; Susiva, 2021). During that time, the world of online education was abruptly thrust upon the shoulders of educators and learners. While online education has existed for some time (Fuchs, 2021), universities recognised the forthcoming challenge. Pansa, Pojanapunya, and Boonmoh (2022) argued that while all learners were urgently required to adjust themselves from physical classes to online classrooms, the educators also found themselves in a difficult situation that required them to change their teaching plan for the entire semester (Fuchs, 2021). Undoubtedly, the higher education sector in Thailand during the COVID-19 pandemic was confronted with various challenges, such as the lack of intensive practices in some workshop classes, the severing of classmate relationships, difficulties in working or collaborating digitally with peers, inaccessibility of internet, especially for those teachers and learners who lived in remote areas; the inability to meet learning outcomes; and the low level of participation in low-performing students (Chareonrook, 2023; Fuchs, 2021; Pansa et al., 2022; Sansupa et al., 2020; Tongkeo, 2020).

This study aims to shed light on higher education in Thailand during the COVID-19 pandemic and assess the adaptive measures taken within the Thai context. Utilising secondary data and content analysis techniques, this research seeks to identify the strategies employed by Thai educational institutions to deliver education, evaluate their effectiveness in a classroom setting, and explore notable shifts in the country's educational landscape.

## Literature Review

From preschool to senior high school, the Thai government provides education in Thailand through the Ministry of Education. At the same time, universities in Thailand are regulated by the Ministry of Higher Education, Science, Research and Innovation (MHESI). According to the policy and strategy of Thailand's higher education (2020–2027), four platforms have been highlighted for Thailand to become an innovation-driven country: (1) the development of human resources and educational institutions, (2) the improvement of research and innovation to meet society's needs, (3) the enhancement of research and innovation competitiveness and (4) the elevation of research and innovation to reduce inequality (Thailand Science Research & Innovation, 2021). There are 170 public and private higher education institutions in Thailand, which deliver about 4100 curricula ranging from undergraduate and graduate studies to several short training courses (Choompunuch et al., 2021). Public universities remain popular among students and educators among these two categories of institutions. This is partly due to particular challenges private universities face, including concerns about their reputation, high tuition fees, a scarcity of renowned professors with academic credentials, and difficulties in attracting potential academic staff (Kerdbanchan & Jarujittipant, 2019).

Fuchs (2021) asserted that online education has grown continuously since the early 2000s. With the advancement of technology and the creation of educational applications for mobile and tablet devices, some lecturers have begun to employ these technological tools in their classrooms to assist their students in gaining new learning experiences. While technology-enhanced education is not a novel concept, its implementation in many Thai universities has been limited. This limitation is often attributed to various factors, such as students' and instructors' readiness and the budget constraints faced by educational institutions, especially those in remote areas (Pittayapongsakorn, 2020; Sahu, 2020). However, when the World Health Organisation (WHO) declared COVID-19 a Public Health Emergency of International Concern on January 30, 2020, followed by its characterisation as a pandemic on March 11, 2020 (WHO, 2023), the sudden transition to remote learning became an unavoidable reality for Thai educators and students. This rapid shift compelled the entire curriculum to transition from traditional face-to-face instruction to online education (Choompunuch et al., 2021; Fuchs, 2021).

## Higher Education in Thailand During COVID-19

After the announcement of the global pandemic on 11 March 2020 by the WHO, the Thai government passed an emergency decree on 24 March 2020 to slow down the infection and mortality rate. Following the instruction of the Ministry of Health on social distancing, this decree was used to impose travel restrictions (inbound and outbound), suspend business operations and services, encourage home isolation practices, and require the closure of educational institutions at every level (Phuthong, 2021; Sansupa et al., 2020). The overnight shift from on-site classrooms to online lessons significantly impacted Thailand's education system. The response to COVID-19 transformed the teaching delivery methods and learning environments for instructors and learners. The following are significant issues in Thailand's education landscape during the COVID-19 pandemic.

## The First Wave of COVID-19: Shifting from On-site to Online Classes

In remote regions of Thailand, the crucial issue revolved around the affordability and availability of internet access. Since all teaching methods had to switch to online and everybody was asked to stay home, Tongkeo (2020) explained that many Thai households faced challenges supporting high-speed internet for their children. Furthermore, many individuals, especially in rural regions, face challenges in providing their children with high-quality educational devices. This issue arose from parents losing their jobs due to company closures. The lockdown policy and travel restrictions during the beginning of the COVID-19 outbreak caused numerous difficulties for students who relied on part-time jobs in restaurants. Many of them had to stop working owing to the suspension of their workplaces, which led to inadequate income to cover their cost of living (Sumruamrum et al., 2021). Although the universities launched laptop rental programmes for instructors and students, the number of available laptops was limited (Sahu, 2020). Many students lived in an area where they could access the internet, but the problem of internet stability persisted. A study by Siriteerawasu (2021) confirmed that unreliable internet connections were a major obstacle to online learning for Thai students.

During the first wave of the COVID-19 pandemic, some universities had not allocated funds to purchase virtual meeting software licences. Only a few platforms were available and selected by Thai universities to provide online courses during the period, such as Zoom, Google Meet, Microsoft Teams, and WebEx (Susiva, 2021). Although some instructors preferred online platforms provided by their universities, many opted for live broadcasting on social media platforms like Facebook and YouTube. This was because of the large class sizes and the familiarity of both instructors and students with these applications (Chiablaem, 2021).

The ability to transition to online learning during the COVID-19 pandemic posed a significant challenge for numerous students. According to Chareonrook (2023), first-year students encountered more difficulties adjusting to the new learning environment and methods than their more experienced counterparts. This problem also led to social anxiety associated with communicating with strangers they met online. It was not only the students facing this problem in online learning adaptation; many instructors also struggled with teaching on an online platform. Several instructors were concerned that their students would not be able to achieve the intended learning outcomes of their courses due to the social distancing policy. The implementation of this policy forced them to either change their delivery methods or cancel some of the class activities, especially the practical ones (Chareonrook, 2023). Bailey and Lee (2020) also mentioned that language skill classes, such as conversation and listening classes, presented challenges for instructors when transitioning to online teaching, primarily because these subjects necessitated the provision of corrective feedback. Learning adaptability was not the only challenge the students faced. Some teachers had to learn and use various technologies, including social networking sites, to stay in touch with their students and build a network (Pansa et al., 2022; Rashid & Yadav, 2020).

The assessment and evaluation of learners posed another significant challenge. Sahu (2020) asserted that while students were uncertain about the procedure for administering assignments and projects, the instructors had to change almost all assessment types to fit the online mode. Fuchs (2021) discovered that students had doubts concerning the effectiveness of remote teaching, and Thai students, in particular, perceived no benefits when group work had to be done digitally. Furthermore, a study undertaken by Sansupa et al. (2020) uncovered that in courses demanding rigorous practice, like those in the 'Faculty of Education' where students were required to complete practical teaching labs, these assessments brought about a substantial shift in the teaching and learning approach due to students being unable to attend the lab simultaneously. To adhere to social distancing guidelines, the classroom arrangement was redesigned to accommodate only a limited number of students at a time. This modification placed additional demands on instructors, leading to heightened stress levels for students and educators regarding the overall effectiveness of the teaching and learning experience.

## The Transformation of Teaching and Learning: The Hybrid Classroom

Following the initial wave of COVID-19, Thailand's educational landscape entered a new teaching and learning phase. Many Thai scholars often referred to this transition as 'the new normal' by many Thai scholars (Pansa et al., 2022; Phuthong, 2021; Sansupa et al., 2020). Historically, online learning operated through asynchronous communication, where instructors organised lessons on a website, allowing learners to select and engage with these lessons based on their individual scheduling preferences. This method was accommodated by the learning management system (LMS). Nevertheless, the shift to live teaching sessions was swiftly implemented amid the pandemic. Consequently, platforms for synchronous communication, such as Google Meet, Zoom, Microsoft Teams, Slack, and Skype, were adopted for remote teaching and learning (Pansa et al., 2022).

It was recognised that COVID-19 would persist, albeit with a lower severity than the initial wave (Charumilind et al., 2022). Consequently, the MHESI and the Ministry of Public Health of Thailand collaborated around November 2021 to strategically plan the next phase of Thai Higher Education during COVID-19. This plan aimed to facilitate a gradual return to in-person lessons. To facilitate this transition, a prerequisite was that a minimum of 85 per cent of university staff had to be fully vaccinated against COVID-19 with at least two doses. Universities were likewise instructed to supervise environmental health measures in line with the guidelines provided by the Department of Health. These measures encompassed aspects such as indoor ventilation and hazardous waste management.

Additionally, some universities implemented COVID-19 tracking systems to identify potential cases of COVID-19 infection (National News Bureau of Thailand, 2021; Ruangsri et al., 2021). At the onset of hybrid classrooms, many universities initiated class schedules where students from different academic years attended classes on alternate days to reduce overcrowding. They also had to reconfigure and, in some cases, temporarily close specific public spaces that could not be adapted to comply with social distancing guidelines. Stringent cleaning and sanitisation protocols were implemented for all public areas. Additionally, for practical classes, class sizes were significantly reduced. Both students and instructors were required to provide the results of an antigen test kit (ATK) before attending classes or perform self-testing every two weeks (Ruangsri et al., 2021; Yongstar, 2021).

In early 2022, Thai educational institutions received the Covid-free setting guidelines, which covered various aspects, including classroom arrangement, hygiene, and sanitation procedures, guidance on COVID-19 vaccination, recommendations for personal health checks using ATKs before attending classes, protocols for arranging examination spaces, reconfiguring pedestrian flow within buildings and guidelines for isolating students or staff members in case of infection. Following the Thai Stop Covid protocols (Ministry of Public Health of Thailand, 2022), universities were also required to achieve a vaccination compliance rate of over 95 per cent. This mandate led to the implementation of a hybrid classroom approach, necessitating adaptability from both students and instructors in their teaching and learning methods, especially in classroom infections. In instances of infection, the teaching mode automatically shifted from on-site classrooms to online formats for subsequent classes. However, adjustments have since been made, and individuals with mild infections may not necessarily need to undergo home isolation (Ministry of Public Health of Thailand, 2022).

To exemplify the flexible methods, especially in higher education, two universities, namely Mahidol University International College and Prince of Songkla University (PSU), Trang Campus, were chosen in this study because the authors had access to the necessary information.

## Method

We utilised secondary data, including university websites, annual academic reports, and media sources employed by these institutions, to investigate how Thai universities have implemented adaptive approaches across various stakeholder groups and assessed their effectiveness. In this research, we employed purposive sampling, specifically selecting two diverse Thai public universities: Mahidol University International College and PSU, Trang Campus. These universities were chosen based on specific criteria: international and Thai programmes, geographical diversity in urban and rural settings and a renowned focus on medical education with public health policies and plans during the crisis. 56 documents were collected, including Ministry of Higher Education announcements, university policies and plans, and student learning experiences detailing teaching methods and learning outcome adjustments stemming from curriculum revisions. The study summarises the adaptive approach, highlighting the essential changes in response to the evolving circumstances.

Mahidol University International College is part of Mahidol University, established as the University of Medical Science in 1943. Mahidol University established two leading medical schools: the Faculty of Medicine Ramathibodi Hospital and the older school, the Faculty of Medicine Siriraj Hospital. The name of Mahidol University came from Prince Mahidol of Songkla, the medical school's father. Mahidol University International College is the first to offer an international bachelor's degree programme at a public university in Thailand since 1986. Currently, 113 faculties and 273 support staff offer a diverse range of 18 undergraduate majors and 24 minors in the arts, languages, sciences and administration. Mahidol University International College also offers two master's degree programmes for approximately 3200 students.

PSU comprises five campuses situated in southern Thailand: Hat Yai Campus, Pattani Campus, Phuket Campus, Suratthani Campus and Trang Campus. Presently, 35 faculties/colleges confer degrees and provide 326 academic programmes, certifications and graduate studies. Concerning administrative structure, each campus is overseen by a vice president reporting to the university president stationed at the main campus, Hat Yai Campus.

## Results and Discussion

This research aims to analyse the methods utilised by Thai higher education institutions to deliver courses during the COVID-19 pandemic, evaluate how effective these methods were in classroom settings and explore notable changes in the country's educational environment. The study identified an adaptive approach by identifying eight key components derived from the experiences of the two universities. These elements are succinctly presented in the Table 1.

The description of the eight elements in Table 1 makes it evident that an adaptive approach necessitated the participation of the university management team and everyone involved. Recognising the continued presence of COVID-19, albeit with reduced severity compared to the initial wave, this study would like to address three crucial issues that can significantly impact both instructors and learners.

**Table 1** Eight fundamental elements of adaptive responses in higher education during the COVID-19 pandemic

| Fundamental elements | Related persons/groups | Key learning | Adaptive approach responses |
|---|---|---|---|
| 1. Making decisions amidst a crisis | 1. Executive board members or management team of the universities | 1. The COVID-19 crisis necessitated many decisions as numerous pressing matters called for immediate attention. Postponing decisions until solutions or official statements were received from the central campus or local government authorities often resulted in significant delays<br>2. The formation of an interim crisis communication team was vital. This team comprised experts from various domains, including physicians, epidemiologists, psychiatrists and journalists. Their role involved conducting thorough assessments before finalising decisions or presenting their ideas and recommendations to the university's board of directors for decision-making. This approach facilitated decision support and served as a means to enlist expertise from diverse fields to aid in the decision-making process | The management team's choice should take into account the following six factors:<br>1. Awareness of the situation: the management team should clearly understand what is happening and what might affect the choices that need to be made<br>2. Proficiency in communication: during the COVID-19 pandemic, many rumours were wildly spreading. The management team should have the skill and ability to effectively convey important messages to their staff and students clearly, concisely and clearly<br>3. Leadership in collective improvisation refers to the university leaders' ability to effectively guide and coordinate group efforts in uncertain situations where predefined plans may not be applicable. Flexibility, creativity, adaptability and risk management were required to achieve the best possible outcome |

(continued)

**Table 1** (continued)

| Fundamental elements | Related persons/groups | Key learning | Adaptive approach responses |
|---|---|---|---|
| | | 3. COVID-19 has widely proliferated across all regions of Thailand. Therefore, pandemic awareness should not be limited solely to the central campus. Instead, effective crisis communication needs to extend to every campus, and the content should be tailored to align with the comprehension levels of each audience | 4. Making decisive and prompt decisions: in the context of university leadership, the need for decisiveness and speed in decision-making demanded firmness and swiftness in information assessment while ensuring that risk evaluation was an integral part of the decision-making process<br>5. Trying out new solutions through revision meant that the management team had to experiment with and enhance different methods or strategies to handle better or resolve any issues that might arise throughout the semester<br>6. Employing technology for consistent message communication: the management teams should practice using digital tools and platforms to ensure that messages, information, or communications are consistently and reliably delivered to their intended recipients |

| Fundamental elements | Related persons/groups | Key learning | Adaptive approach responses |
|---|---|---|---|
| 2. New practices in curriculum design | 1. Deans and Vice Dean in Academic Affair of each faculty<br>2. All instructors within every academic programme | The curriculum mandated students to pursue overseas study or undertake internships external to the university. Nevertheless, this became problematic during the COVID-19 pandemic, which led to international and domestic travel suspensions | Several methods were redesigned, such as<br>1. Apply online and hybrid classroom management to all courses<br>2. Refund the tuition fees of students required to study abroad and find instructors to teach those students instead<br>3. Find internship placements that allow working online, such as an online marketing team or social media content creator<br>4. Make the evaluation of learning outcomes more flexible based on the situation and student condition<br>5. Project-based learning and consulting projects with students |

(continued)

**Table 1** (continued)

| Fundamental elements | Related persons/groups | Key learning | Adaptive approach responses |
|---|---|---|---|
| 3. Classroom experiences (A shift in learning approaches - transition to online classes) | 1. Deans and Vice Dean in Academic Affair of each faculty<br>2. All instructors within every academic programme | 1. Instructors were introduced to hybrid classrooms, providing flexibility and offering students a diverse learning experience. Furthermore, some instructors received training on video production software to create instructional videos, enabling students to study independently at their convenience. Instructors likewise underwent training in online classroom engagement techniques to facilitate active learning experiences. Dedicated online consultation slots were established for students to meet with instructors for Q&A sessions to enhance interaction<br>2. Numerous instructors with limited online classroom experience resorted to using Facebook or Line applications for live teaching sessions. Consequently, students with unstable internet connections encountered difficulty keeping up with the lessons | The classroom experiences should be aligned with the following specifics:<br>1. The implementation of hybrid classrooms should be accompanied by online training for faculty and students, encompassing setup, readiness, and integrating new teaching styles and methods<br>2. The establishment of financial assistance programmes for university staff and students who urgently require support<br>3. The utilisation of online classrooms or alternative communication platforms, including popular social media channels like Facebook and the Line application for conducting live sessions<br>4. The development of contingency plans to address issues related to unstable internet connectivity and potential distractions in the home environment to ensure that students can maintain their focus during lessons |

| Fundamental elements | Related persons/groups | Key learning | Adaptive approach responses |
|---|---|---|---|
| 4. Student performance evaluation | 1. All instructors within every academic programme | 1. The student evaluation policy was adjusted to offer greater flexibility during the COVID-19 pandemic, encompassing provisions such as a re-exam policy, a no-dismissal policy, and probation, all aimed at facilitating student adaptation. Those students facing financial difficulties sought guidance from advisors and counsellors to assess their circumstances. Additionally, tuition fee deductions were implemented following the submission of student surveys<br>2. The university's management team encouraged instructors to reduce the number of examinations and modify assessment methods to align with course objectives. Nevertheless, some students expressed concerns about an increased workload, as examinations were replaced with reports or assignments | 1. To some extent, the university must consider students' challenges during the crisis. Consequently, the new policy should incorporate flexibility in evaluating student performance, encompassing provisions like a re-exam policy, a no-dismissal policy, and the option to postpone probation<br>2. A financial support policy should be established to assist students during sensitive situations, including tuition fee reductions and the option for tuition fee instalments |

(continued)

**Table 1** (continued)

| Fundamental elements | Related persons/groups | Key learning | Adaptive approach responses |
|---|---|---|---|
| 5. Consultation session | 1. All instructors within every academic programme<br>2. All registration officers<br>3. All students | 1. During COVID-19, the registration officers worked as coordinators among the advisors and advisees. In addition, the university encouraged faculties to have an online advisor day to ensure that students could adapt to the situation. Listening to the conditions and concerns of the students helped with the new policy and plan<br>2. Electronic signatures were deemed unacceptable in the initial phase of the COVID-19 pandemic. Consequently, students who needed their advisors to sign documents had no choice but to send them through postal services. Regrettably, numerous documents did not reach their destinations promptly | Advising sessions significantly shape students' adaptability because they necessitate guidance and consultation. These sessions also offer an excellent opportunity for instructors and students to get acquainted. Especially for students in need of study planning assistance, advisors can offer timely recommendations |

| Fundamental elements | Related persons/groups | Key learning | Adaptive approach responses |
|---|---|---|---|
| 6. Health care benefits for staff and students | 1. All supporting staff who work in the Department of Health Care Services and Property Management | 1. Several strategies were implemented to support students during COVID-19, including offering incentive health care insurance. University Health Insurance allowed access to emergency services at university hospitals<br>2. To ensure safety in hybrid classrooms on campus, air purifiers, alcohol, and cleaning spray were provided in every classroom. Social distancing zones and classroom rearrangements were established to facilitate hybrid learning. Students were also given ATKs every two weeks for health screening before attending class, and designated floors in student dormitories were allocated for self-isolation in case of infections<br>3. Staff members were required to purchase COVID-19 insurance using their personal health budget, which the university annually supports<br>4. A stress management manual designed for the COVID-19 era was introduced and made available online for instructors, staff, and students to access and read | Student health care can be included in the incentive health insurance and connected hospital provision. The pandemic affected all families and communities. Therefore, health care for students, staff, and their families could be considered to provide incentive care and support. Students and their families were affected by COVID-19. The sickness of students and family was set to create a code of conduct: How to deal with COVID-19 in different situations from family, friends, and themselves |

(continued)

**Table 1** (continued)

| Fundamental elements | Related persons/groups | Key learning | Adaptive approach responses |
|---|---|---|---|
| 7. IT support | 1. All supporting staff who work in the IT Department | 1. Many students encountered connectivity issues due to their remote hometowns. The university's management team established several protocols to address this challenge, which included (1) providing funding for internet SIM cards for students, (2) launching a laptop rental programme for students, (3) granting academic staff access to Google Business Suite and Microsoft Education; and (4) partially subsidising an online meeting programme, such as Zoom meeting, for academic staff<br>2. Both universities' learning management system (LMS) has been introduced for several years<br>3. The university introduced a hotline, Line official account, and a downloadable application for receiving emergency information and notifications from the Corporate Communication Division. This allowed all students, faculty, and staff to subscribe to alerts for important announcements and code of conduct updates | The IT support and LMS staff are tasked with maintaining connectivity with all stakeholders, and they utilise a range of tools and services, including:<br>1. Providing financial support as needed<br>2. Offering round-the-clock support through robotic process automation teams<br>3. Facilitating computer rental services and software installations<br>4. Conducting training programmes related to LMS and online classroom techniques<br>5. Implementing an IT system to facilitate urgent communication |

| Fundamental elements | Related persons/groups | Key learning | Adaptive approach responses |
|---|---|---|---|
| 8. Staff support | 1. All support staff, both permanent and casual, at the university | 1. Since the beginning of the pandemic's first year up to the present, all faculty and staff have been permitted to work from home, with the option for flexible work hours on campus<br>2. Health care and mental counselling services were available to students, faculty and staff members who required them<br>3. The pandemic can serve as an opportunity to enhance the skill sets of all university staff and support faculty members in becoming leaders prepared for future pandemics | 1. Support for staff members could focus on health care benefits and family insurance packages. Additionally, addressing mental challenges that may arise during remote work can be made more flexible for everyone. Implementing training programmes like Work–Life Balance, How to Transform Your Home Into An Efficient Workplace, and Time Management can be valuable in assisting staff in managing their work-from-home arrangements effectively<br>2. They are equipping individuals with the ability to adapt and prepare for unpredictable scenarios. These skills should encompass training in embracing the new policy of cultivating a culture of preparedness and encouraging workplace flexibility. The management team should empower faculty members to make decisions that consider their students' distinctive needs. The degree of decision-making authority should be commensurate with the challenges encountered, allowing faculty members to collaborate with their superiors to secure backing for their choices |

## 'Transition to Hybrid Learning' as the Preferred Mode of Course Delivery in the Post-COVID-19 Era

There is clear evidence that the management teams of both universities have been diligently working to establish preparedness and flexible learning environments. These efforts include issuing policies to ensure that each class aligns with course learning objectives, preparing online equipment and broadcasting rooms, making IT staff available for equipment support during teaching, and incorporating a blend of in-class examinations with other suitable assessment methods.

Undoubtedly, hybrid classrooms are significant tools for universities to deal with the COVID-19 crisis (Hasnine et al., 2022). They represent a teaching and learning model that creates interactive learning, crucial in developing analytical thinking skills, communication ability, and teamwork skills. The hybrid classroom model serves a dual purpose: it caters to individual learners with diverse learning styles and supports instructors in enhancing their academic performance. It encourages collaborative learning interactions instead of solely concentrating on transmitting content through traditional teaching strategies. Moreover, hybrid learning aids universities in managing costs by enhancing the efficiency of their investments, particularly at the higher education level. This approach allows instructors and learners to use a comprehensive and effective learning system (Bamrungsetthapong et al., 2020). To some degree, hybrid classrooms in some programmes enable students to engage with local communities for study and practical experience. Through IT support, e-learning and in-person activities, these classrooms foster dynamic learning environments where students are motivated to develop analytical skills, voice their opinions and engage in problem-solving. Hybrid learning also promotes educational equity by allowing students to acquire knowledge and essential skills, enabling them to reach their full potential and ultimately paving the way for their lifelong learning (Bamrungsetthapong et al., 2020). Thus, hybrid learning engages and captivates learners and enhances instructors' teaching abilities and capacity to conduct research, provide academic services, and engage in creative work.

## Students' Educational Behaviour After the COVID-19 Crisis

With the introduction of online learning, many students began attending classes more regularly than in-person classrooms (Hollister et al., 2022). An increased number of students likewise exhibited improved punctuality in attending classes and submitting assignments. Specifically, the students revealed that online teaching was more difficult than face-to-face classes. So, they preferred to attend and prepare themselves before the following classes as they did not want to be left behind in the lessons and assignments. For some students, the online environment did not replicate the experience of sitting in a physical classroom with an instructor. As a result, they found it more comfortable to engage in online activities and felt more confident to answer questions through the chat box feature. These findings align with a study conducted by Hollister et al. (2022), who also noted that many students felt at ease asking and answering questions in online classes.

Although online and hybrid classrooms could benefit instructors and learners in many ways, this study found that some students demonstrated negative behaviours and perceptions. This study discovered that many students who encountered obstacles in internet signal while connecting to the online learning applications would often become frustrated and were more likely to be absent if they could not access their online classes. Taswiyah and Imron (2021) further demonstrated that students exhibited enthusiasm for online learning when accessing a reliable internet connection. Conversely, they encountered challenges and dilemmas when facing poor signal quality. Furthermore, many students hesitated to activate their cameras during class. They cited concerns about their appearance and the potential visibility of their surroundings, including people behind them. This finding is intriguing because it reflects a common perception among students not limited to Thailand.

A study conducted by Castelli and Sarvary (2021) with undergraduates enrolled in the Investigative Biology Laboratory course at Cornell University (Itheca, NY, USA) similarly identified students' concerns about their appearance, the visibility of others, their physical surroundings and unstable internet connections as the primary reasons for choosing to keep their cameras off. The findings of this study were consistent with the research conducted by Azmi et al. (2022), which indicated that some students with poor academic performance frequently experienced a lack of engagement in class and felt left behind without support. Consequently, these students often displayed reduced motivation to participate in-class activities and exhibited signs of stress and anxiety, particularly with examinations.

To promote and nurture positive behaviour in students, it is imperative to establish clear rules and regulations right from the beginning between instructors and students. This fosters professionalism and addresses ethical issues, including teamwork, trust-building, and preventing plagiarism. Creating effective communication channels for monitoring student project and assignment performance is also essential. These measures are vital components of a hybrid classroom setting.

Furthermore, it is essential to consider students' attitudes when designing the curriculum, incorporating elements of professionalism and a code of conduct. The difficulty sustaining students' engagement during the transition to on-campus learning must also be acknowledged. Students often excel in active participation, such as class discussions and project-based activities, rather than passively absorbing lectures. Consequently, any alterations to teaching and learning approaches should aim for a harmonious blend of conventional lectures and interactive methods that stimulate the growth of students' ideas, attitudes, and teamwork abilities within practical contexts.

## Impact of Online Learning on Students' Sense of Belonging to the University Community

Pedler et al. (2022) asserted that a sense of belonging is essential as it incorporates feeling valued, included, and accepted at the university. However, introducing online classrooms during the COVID-19 pandemic has profoundly altered this perspective among students. Engaging in online learning and teaching during the COVID-19 crisis offers significant cost savings by eliminating the need for travel expenses. In this context, students were not restricted to classrooms and study groups within their enrolled courses; instead, they could enrol in courses from various universities based on their interests. Consequently, this study discovered that the traditional sense of belonging to the campus environment may not hold the same significance for our students. Instead, their primary focus lies on aspects like course content, study duration, online sessions, the quality of instructors, and post-graduation career prospects. Recent studies by Morán-Soto et al. (2022) and Tang et al. (2023) also confirmed that the rapid change to an online learning environment threatened the effectiveness of promoting students' sense of belonging. These students missed opportunities to develop meaningful relationships with their peers and professors due to the lack of good communication. To encourage a sense of belonging within the university community, the universities examined in this study have actively encouraged students to engage in extracurricular pursuits, including online workshops, competitions, networking, and seeking guidance from their peers and advisors. Their engagement in both online and offline classes can be documented in their activity records before graduation. Both universities also emphasised the importance of balancing academic pursuits and university involvement, encouraging students to build connections with friends and expand their network. However, according to Tang et al. (2023), preserving a comprehensive sense of connectedness has proven and will continue to prove challenging. This difficulty may arise from the intricacies encountered at various levels of belonging, the severity of the crisis, and each educational institution's specific policies. Hence, it is recommended to implement strategies aimed at fostering a stronger sense of belonging among first-year students. This initiative can significantly contribute to the students feeling valued and embraced by the university community (Tang et al., 2023).

## Conclusion and Recommendations

Coping with a pandemic is not a straightforward task. The emergence of the COVID-19 situation compelled the education sector in Thailand to re-evaluate and adapt its curriculum planning. The adaptive actions of higher education institutions in response to the pandemic are drawn from the experiences of two universities affiliated with medical schools and the Ministry of Public Health. The leadership team plays a pivotal role in guiding and making informed decisions. These decisions should encompass six crucial aspects: situational awareness, effective communication, collaborative improvisation, timely decision-making and action, iterative solution experimentation, and utilisation of technology for consistent messaging. All these aspects are pivotal for steering the university's trajectory. A foundation for adaptability allows all stakeholders to implement and assess their performance. Lessons from this experience may yield positive and negative outcomes, yet leaders should foster a supportive environment and instil a positive outlook to propel organisational success. The management team can adjust curriculum redesign, enhance classroom experiences, and refine the evaluation criteria of student performance accordingly.

Two critical aspects demand the university's vigilant attention within the student community: advising sessions and student health care. Students require heightened support from the university in times of crisis. To address this, the university should devise enhanced support mechanisms, including establishing transparent communication channels, providing accessible advisory services and financial assistance, and demonstrating an understanding of potential mental health challenges stemming from familial circumstances. Maintaining online networking with peers, continued participation in university activities during such situations, and fostering a sense of belonging and engagement in campus life is imperative. Equally vital, the collaborative efforts of faculty and support staff play a pivotal role. By working cohesively, they can offer a holistic support system. IT support, financial assistance, and tailored up-skilling programmes can be recalibrated to empower them to overcome challenges effectively.

In terms of the study limitations, this study is limited in terms of generalising the results from secondary data based on the information from two universities. Future studies should explore this topic in a higher education framework using qualitative and quantitative research approaches. The pandemic changed teaching methods to focus on active learning and adaptation of students and faculties. It is essential to study the insight into changes regarding new policies and plans in higher education after COVID-19.

## References

Azmi, F. M., Khan, H. N., & Azmi, A. M. (2022). The impact of virtual learning on students' educational behavior and pervasiveness of depression among university students due to the COVID-19 pandemic. *Globalisation and Health, 18*, 70. https://doi.org/10.1186/s12992-022-00863-z

Bailey, D. R., & Lee, A. (2020). Learning from experience in the midst of COVID-19: Benefits, challenges, and strategies in online teaching. *Computer-Assisted Language Learning Electronic Journal, 21*(2), 176–196.

Bamrungsetthapong, S., Tharnpanya, P., & Satjaharuthai, K. (2020). Hybrid learning and the quality improvement of Thailand's education. *Narkbhutparitat Journal Nakhon Si Thammarat Rajabhat University, 12*(3), 213–224.

Castelli, F. R., & Sarvary, M. A. (2021). Why students do not turn on their video cameras during online classes and an equitable and inclusive plan to encourage them to do so. *Ecology and Evolution, 11*(8), 3565–3576. https://doi.org/10.1002/ece3.7123

Chareonrook, D. (2023). The adaptability of undergraduate students of Rangsit University during the COVID-19 pandemic. *Journal of Communication Arts Review, 27*(1), 132–140.

Charumilind, S., Craven, S., Lamb, J., Sabow, A., Singhal, S., & Wilson, M. (2022, July 28). *When will the COVID-19 pandemic end?*. McKinsey &

Company. https://www.mckinsey.com/industries/healthcare/our-insights/when-will-the-COVID-19-pandemic-end/

Chiablaem, P. (2021). Enhancing English communication skills of Thai University students through Google Apps for education (GAFE) in a digital era during COVID-19 pandemic. *International Journal of Education, 9*(3), 91–98.

Choompunuch, B., Suksatan, W., Sonsroem, J., Kutawan, S., & In-udom, A. (2021). Stress, adversity quotient, and health behaviors of undergraduate students in a Thai University during COVID-19 outbreak. *Belitung Nursing Journal, 7*(1), 1–7.

Fuchs, K. (2021). Students' perceptions concerning emergency remote teaching during COVID-19: A case study between higher education institutions in Thailand and Finland. *Perspectives on Global Development and Technology, 20*(3), 278–288. https://doi.org/10.1163/15691497-12341595

Hasnine, M. N., Ueda, H., & Ahmed, M. M. H. (2022). Adaptation of AL-TST active learning model in hybrid classroom: Findings from teaching during COVID-19 pandemic in Egypt. *Procedia Computer Science, 207*, 3220–3227.

Hollister, B., Nair, P., Hill-Lindsay, S., & Chukoskie, L. (2022). Engagement in online learning: Student attitudes and behavior during COVID-19. *Frontiers in Education, 7,* 851019. https://doi.org/10.3389/feduc.2022.851019

Kerdbanchan, C., & Jarujittipant, P. (2019). Factors affecting the quality of Thai Private University instructors. *Journal of Social Sciences Srinakharinwirot University, 22*(1), 13–27.

Marinoni, G., Land, H. V., & Jensen, T. (2020). *The impact of COVID-19 on higher education around the world*. International Association of Universities (IAU).

Ministry of Public Health of Thailand. (2022, April 22). *The measures to open classes on-site and live with COVID-19 in educational institutions for the semester 1/2022.* https://apps.hpc.go.th/dl/web/upFile/2022/05-5037-20220510102429/94381362ba15d2bd9a3aa5681e8c590f.pdf (In Thai)

Morán-Soto, G., Marsh, A., Peña, O. I., & G., Sheppard, M., Gómez-Quiñones, J. I., & Benson, L. C. (2022). Effect of the COVID-19 pandemic on the sense of belonging in higher education for STEM students in the United States and Mexico. *Sustainability, 14*, 16627. https://doi.org/10.3390/su142416627

National News Bureau of Thailand. (2021, October 15). *The Ministry of Higher Education, science, research, and innovation is ready for universities across the country to gradually open on-site teaching start from November 1.* https://thainews.prd.go.th/th/news/detail/TCATG211015152110295

Pansa, D., Pojanapunya, P., & Boonmoh, A. (2022). Students' perceptions of classroom learning and emergency online learning during COVID-19 pandemic. *Pasaa Paritat Journal, 37*, 1–23.

Pedler, M. D., Willis, R., & Nieuwoudt, J. E. (2022). A sense of belonging at university: Student retention, motivation and enjoyment. *Journal of Further and Higher Education, 46*(3), 397–408. https://doi.org/10.1080/0309877X.2021.1955844

Phuthong, T. (2021). Antecedents influencing the adoption of collaborative learning social-media platforms among Thai university students during the COVID-19 'new normal' era. *International Journal of Emerging Technologies in Learning, 16*(13), 108–127. https://doi.org/10.3991/ijet.v16i13.18083

Pittayapongsakorn, N. (2020, May 14). *What is new normal of Thai education? When distance learning is not the answer.* Thailand Development Research Institute. https://tdri.or.th/2020/05/desirable-new-normal-for-thailand-education/

Rashid, S., & Yadav, S. S. (2020). Impact of COVID-19 pandemic on higher education and research. *Indian Journal of Human Development, 14*(2), 1–4. https://doi.org/10.1177/0973703020946700

Ruangsri, B., Wisetkan, A., Noonsakun, S., & Rungrangsee, W. (2021). Teaching and learning in the new normal COVID-19 era using the format on-site teaching and learning. *Journal of Human Society, 11*(2), 29–45.

Sahu, P. (2020). Closure of universities due to coronavirus disease 2019 (COVID-19): Impact on education and mental health of students and academic staff. *Cureus, 12*(4), e7541. https://doi.org/10.7759/cureus.7541

Sansupa, K., Kongkranphan, U., Sucaromana, U., & Nantasen, P. (2020). The adjustment of undergraduate student in pandemic COVID-19. *Journal of MCU Humanities Review, 6*(2), 83–97.

Siriteerawasu, W. (2021). Obstacles to online learning for Thai university students in the era of COVID-19 crisis. *Social Sciences and Education Research Review, 8*(2), 107–119. https://doi.org/10.5281/zenodo.5790098

Sumruamrum, N., Muechaiphum, P., Jantapanya, I., & Boonwanna, T. (2021). *Indonesian student in Khon Kaen University: Measures, effects and adaptations during the epidemic of COVID-19.* http://www2.huso.tsu.ac.th/ncom/csd/csdful_pdf/c194.pdf

Susiva, S. (2021). Online learning experience during the COVID-19 pandemic: University students' perspectives. *Journal of Roi Kaensarn Academic, 6*(12), 60–69.

Tang, C., Thyer, L., Bye, R., Kenny, B., Tulliani, N., Peel, N., & Dark, L. (2023). Impact of online learning on sense of belonging among first year clinical health students during COVID-19: Student and academic perspectives. *BMC Medical Education, 23*(1), 100.

Tawiyah, & Imron. A. (2021). *Student behavior towards online learning systems during the COVID-19 pandemic.* https://ssrn.com/abstract=3963078

Thailand Science Research and Innovation. (2021). *Higher education, science, research and innovation policies and strategies (year 2020–2027) and science plan research and innovation (year 2020–2022).* https://backend.tsri.or.th/files/trf/2/docs/Policy_and_Strategy_of_Thailand_HESI_2563-2570_and_Thailand_SRI_Plan_2563-2565.pdf

Tongkeo, T. (2020). New normal based design in education: Impact of COVID-19. *Journal of Teacher Professional Development, 1*(2), 1–10.

Toquero, C. M. (2020). Challenges and opportunities for higher education amid the COVID-19 pandemic: The Philippine context. *Pedagogical Research, 5*(4), 1–5. https://doi.org/10.29333/pr/7947

World Health Organization. (2023, April 5). *WHO coronavirus (COVID-19) dashboard.* https://covid19.who.int/

Yongstar, S. (2021, November 1). COVID-19: First day of school, parents responded the "on-site" study and ready to take risks. *BBC News Thailand.* https://www.bbc.com/thai/international-59115806

# Leaders in Crisis: Philippine Educational Leaders Sustaining Learning in Higher Education Institutions During and Beyond the Pandemic

Cathy Mae Toquero and Ariel Ramos

## Introduction

The COVID-19 pandemic has shed light on various shortcomings and vulnerabilities within educational systems worldwide (Mañero, 2020). According to UNESCO's Global Monitoring Report (2020), a significant number of students, approximately 1,186,127,211 or 67.7% of total enrolled learners, have experienced school closures in 144 countries due to the outbreak of COVID-19. This global crisis has exacerbated existing inequalities (Bešić, 2020; Brown, 2020; Poletti & Raballo, 2020), as many students are unable to access quality education during the period of school closures. Consequently, the lack of face-to-face education and the disproportionate social realities have led to a misalignment of educational values for some students. Governments worldwide are facing intense scrutiny as they grapple with the aftermath of COVID-19 in the education system, seeking effective measures to mitigate its impacts.

Amidst the COVID-19 pandemic, the Philippine Government formed a task force team that sought scientific advice from esteemed institutions, including the University of the Philippines, to guide its pandemic response

C. M. Toquero (✉)
Mindanao State University-General Santos, 9500 General Santos City, Philippines
e-mail: cathymaetoquero@gmail.com

A. Ramos
Cebu Technological University-Argao Campus, 6021 Cebu, Philippines
e-mail: ariel.ramos@ctu.edu.ph



J. Rudolph et al. (eds.), *The Palgrave Handbook of Crisis Leadership in Higher Education*,
https://doi.org/10.1007/978-3-031-54509-2_28

(Vallejo & Ong, 2020). Recognising the importance of education, universities have taken proactive measures to ensure uninterrupted learning. Led by dedicated educational leaders, these institutions have implemented various strategies such as prevention, mitigation, tracking, and testing to navigate the challenges posed by the pandemic. In fact, some universities have even developed their own test kits to contribute to the overall containment efforts (CNN Philippines, 2020).

In response to the challenges posed by the pandemic, educational institutions have embraced alternative approaches to deliver learning opportunities to students. One prominent solution has been the adoption of online learning, allowing students to access education remotely through digital technologies. However, it is important to acknowledge that students from low and middle-income countries face barriers to this form of learning due to limited access to digital devices (Morgan, 2020; Worldbank, 2020). Despite these challenges, educational leaders have worked tirelessly to mitigate the impact on students' learning and support the faculty in adapting to online learning through a blend of traditional and innovative pedagogical approaches (Toquero, 2020).

There is decision-making uncertainty (Ahern & Loh, 2021) as educational leaders are forced to rapidly adapt to confront the universal educational dilemma. Lalani et al. (2021) have pointed out that leadership is a crucial indicator for the success of curriculum transformation, particularly at a time of rapid change. The pandemic challenged leaders to create solutions and address educational gaps. In the Philippines, an early study reported that crisis leaders are 'attending to the person, taking charge and showing the way forward, and sustaining the spirit' (Caringal-Go et al., 2021, p. 630). This means that educational leaders' roles include encouraging spiritual growth, showing transparency and collaboration, steering organisational action, and spearheading solutions during a crisis.

While there is a wealth of studies available on educational leaders in basic education institutions in the country (Chua et al., 2022; Katog, 2022; Malala & Lagos, 2022; San Miguel & Pascual, 2021), the research specifically focusing on academic leaders in higher education is limited. Existing studies in the higher education context primarily revolve around the plans and strategies adopted by colleges and universities during the pandemic, as well as the experiences of students and faculty members (Oducado, 2020; Roncesvalles & Gaerlan, 2021; Torrato et al., 2021). However, in times of crisis, there is a pressing need for sustainable leadership (Crawford, 2023). Therefore, this study aimed to address the following research questions to shed light on the role of academic leaders in higher education during challenging times.

- What are the roles of educational leaders in sustaining higher education during and beyond pandemic?
- What are the initiatives of educational leaders to sustain higher education during and beyond pandemic?

## Context

The pandemic intensified educational gaps, social disparities, digital divides, educational inequalities, and other human divides in the country. In 2020, 'Bayanihan to Recover as One' Act was signed into law as a recovery and response intervention to accelerate socio-economic well-being of Filipinos. Through the COVID-19 tracker, the Department of Health (2022) reported 3,982,965 COVID-19 total cases with 26,003 active cases as of this writing (Fig. 1). The statistics are lower compared to the peak of the pandemic cases in 2020 when intense lockdown and social distancing measures ensued to help curb the novel virus (Ajari et al. 2020).

During the early advancements of the pandemic, the Commission on Higher Education (2020) granted discretionary powers to HEIs to formulate educational responses that could meet the needs of their students. The adoption of Flexible Learning is aligned with the customisation of educational delivery to potentially address the prevailing and unique concerns of the students to access quality education considering economic constraints and technological inaccessibility. Hence, universities implemented asynchronous and synchronous sessions while giving the students flexible assessments and homeschool learning activities which were mostly done through self-learning modules.

Despite the customised curriculum, numerous students experienced difficulties in the deployment of online learning. They experienced unconducive

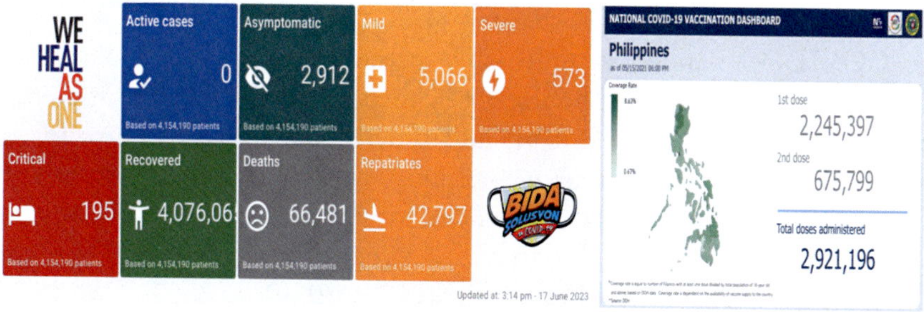


**Fig. 1** COVID-19 Philippines Dashboard as of May 2021

home learning environments (Barrot et al., 2021), poor internet connections, and a lack of technological devices. Other students encountered financial constraints (Acebes et al., 2022) and mental health issues (Toquero & Toquero, 2023) that increased their personal struggles during the pandemic.

Moreover, the grading policies changed in May 2020 as a possible solution to the dilemma of grading students who barely had three months to reach academic deliverables at the tumultuous peak of COVID-19 cases. From 1.0 as the highest mark to 5.0 as the failing mark, instructors gave an alternative rating to students through a binary grading system. For example, in one university, instructors could only give a rating of either 'passed' or 'dropped', with 80% of total attendance as the only criterion, and 'failed' was not part of the binary. Another example is that the highest-ranking university in the Philippines had a grading policy that students should not be given 4.0, 5.0, or INC grades for any courses during the second semester of 2019 to 2020 (between January/February and May/June). The anonymous universities are known for producing passers and topnotchers in state licensure examinations. Other universities throughout the Philippines most likely adopted the modification of the grading system in 2020, following university-wide guidelines.

The leniency in the university grading system impacted the graduating cohorts. Based on observation, some universities achieved an up to 500% increase in Latin honours and awards compared to the previous years. On the other hand, due to the Philippines having one of the longest lockdowns in the world (Cepeda, 2020; de Guzman, 2021; See, 2021), the pandemic graduates had difficulty navigating the employment realm. The pandemic heightened the difficulty of finding employment (Baron, 2023; Cepeda, 2020) due to the lack of proper assessments (de Guzman, 2021) and job readiness skills (de Loyola, 2023; Magsambol, 2023).

## Literature

The COVID-19 pandemic undeniably affected human lives globally and resulted in a new normal. The impact echoed across institutions as government leaders restricted movements and ordered temporary closures for in-person transactions as a mitigating response to minimise the spread of the virus. HEIs crafted contextualised policies for online learning to facilitate the learning activities either synchronously or asynchronously (UNESCO, 2020; Shereen et al., 2020; Shahzad et al., 2021; UN, 2020).

The country had a pandemic response that underwent four stages: rapid adaptation, improvement, consolidation, and restoration (Crawford et al., 2020; Crawford, 2021a, b; Rudolph et al., 2023). Rapid adaptation began as numerous universities adapted the digital platforms for instruction, which was not the case prior to the pandemic. The routine way of performing business has transformed with new modalities. Then came the improvement stage, where most universities applied contextualised teaching and learning to achieve quality education in the home environment. The universities achieved consolidation and restoration that were heavily anchored on the pandemic guidelines and policies of the Philippine Government.

Numerous tertiary institutions have had to adapt and innovate to sustain the learning process amid the crisis (Joaquin et al., 2020; Toquero, 2021), especially the 3.5 million tertiary-level students enrolled in approximately 2,400 HEIs in the Philippines. To sustain learning amid a challenging shift in the academic landscape, educational leaders prioritised the acquisition of learning management systems (LMS) through the re-alignment of budgetary allocation. Universities invested in LMS that provided access to online educational services for teachers, students, and executives (Navarro et al., 2021). The online modality met the immediate demands of the educational sphere in the new normal setting. However, this was only applicable in HEIs with better technological facilities (Bustillo & Aguilos, 2022).

Embarking on a new instructional modality meant difficulties associated with the online curriculum. Some of the challenges in the new normal education include internet connection issues, student engagement (Tarrayo et al., 2021), lack of gadgets, untrained teachers, students' remote location (Toquero, 2023), inadequate LMS, and lack of policies and guidelines for flexible learning (Tuga et al., 2023). A Philippine-wide study (Baticulon et al., 2021) reported that 32% and 22% of the 3670 Filipino students have difficulties adjusting to new learning styles and do not have reliable internet access, respectively. Most students have depression and anxiety due to stress during online classes (Islam et al., 2020). The internet connectivity issue and other problems, such as emotional and psychological aspects revolving around humans, are interconnected and in interplay (Stuart et al., 2020). Academic leaders were ultimately resorting to strategies such as mass promotions, waived requirements, and deferred grades (Yumol, 2020).

Sustaining quality learning became an emergent challenge for educational leaders in the context of planning, implementing, and evaluating teaching and learning. Hénard and Roseveare (2012) argued that achieving quality teaching and learning is a complex endeavour involving multiple dimensions, including the design of curriculum and course content, learning contexts, use of feedback, assessment of learning outcomes, learning environments, and student support services. Educational policies such as the adoption of alternative instructional delivery, re-calibration of faculty with advanced pedagogical competence, and setting a culture of creativity, diversity, and inclusivity for quality educational outcomes are by-products of the pandemic (Ramos & Baldespiñosa, 2021).

## Methods

This research utilised various sources and digital platforms to examine the roles performed by educational leaders during a time of crisis. It also investigated the institutional-wide initiatives or innovations that the educational leaders have carried out to alleviate the educational disparities of emergency remote learning and transition to an inclusive state of teaching and learning. The results came from some of the most recognized educational institutions in the Philippines.

To answer the research questions of this study, a content analysis was performed relative to different sources of information that are accessible online. With the goals of covering many higher education institutions in the Philippines, we find content analysis a suitable analytic method. We include relevant data, particularly on the roles and initiatives of HEIs that were not studied during the pandemic due to the segregated efforts, context-specific actions, and discipline-based interventions of each university. This study would synthesise the prevailing educational innovations of the leaders that were implemented during the pandemic to sustain the delivery of learning despite the complex emergencies in the Philippines.

## Analysis

CHED gave educational leaders the authority to make judgements concerning their institutional endeavours to sustain the learning of their students. The materials used for analysis in the study included various sources, such as peer-reviewed articles by Filipino authors who represent their respective universities. The scientific articles are composed of original research, a literature review, multiple case studies, a policy brief, a monograph, and mixed-method papers. We prioritised looking for published scientific materials that are open access and that are indexed in Scopus and the Web of Science. Due to the limited articles that focused on the educational leaders in the Philippines, we decided to include scientific papers that could supplement inputs from other universities, even though some papers have not been published in Scopus and Web of Science journals. Some secondary data was also collected from nationally recognized online news articles in the Philippines. The researchers also used public information about relevant university-wide initiatives that are available on the websites and Facebook pages of the universities (Table 1).

The researchers initially scanned the scientific literature to determine the scope of existing publications in relation to the current research. Afterwards, the various sources were incorporated into a matrix of secondary sources to list studies about educational leaders in the Philippines. In the matrix, we observed that most studies were about educational leaders affiliated with the

**Table 1** Sources of sample materials used for purposes of data analysis

| Source Type | Number of Articles | Covered Years | Sample University or Affiliations |
|---|---|---|---|
| Research papers | 160 | 2020–2023 | |
| Policy Brief | 1 | 2023 | PNU and 6 TEIs |
| Memoranda | 5 | 2020–2022 | CHED |
| Monograph | 1 | 2021 | UP, La Salle, etc |
| News articles | 8 | 2020 | Rapper |
| University/college Websites | 4 | 2020–2022 | Mindanao State University<br>University of Southern Mindanao<br>Ateneo de Manila University<br>University of the Philippines |
| Government Websites | 2 | 2020–2023 | Philippine Government<br>Commission on Higher Education |
| Social Media | 4 | 2020–2023 | Ateneo de Manila University<br>Philippine Normal University<br>Cebu Technological University<br>Mindanao State University |
| Estimated Total | More or less 30 HEIs | | |

Department of Education (DepEd), the gatekeeper of basic education organisations. We selected articles that deal with educational leaders of universities and the initiatives of HEIs rather than utilise published scientific articles by authors affiliated with basic education institutions. However, similarity exists in the delivery of emergency remote teaching and learning since DepEd and CHED schools generally endorse the same flexible learning curriculum.

## Results

This section presents the professional functions and mitigation efforts of educational leaders to sustain higher education during and beyond the pandemic. The roles of educational leaders during the pandemic are discussed in detail (Table 2). Lastly, the researchers reflected on the initiatives of the educational leaders of HEIs to sustain learning in times of crisis.

**Leaders as gatekeepers.** This role shows that educational leaders value quality outcomes across the mandated areas of instruction, research, and

**Table 2** Concept of roles and specific functions of Philippine Educational Leaders in HEIs

| Concept of Leader Roles | Specific Functions |
|---|---|
| 1. **Gatekeeper**<br>Maintains quality and excellence across mandates through provision and mobilisation of members to provide benefits for the community | ● Executes vision for institutional excellence<br>● Builds pathways for community progress<br>● Spearheads quality of learning and teaching<br>● Assesses situations and makes critical decision for strategic actions |
| 2. **Cultivator**<br>Encourages others to take the creative path by influencing the thinking and practice of academic members | ● Promotes shared goals towards achieving vision<br>● Rewards success and achievement<br>● Empowers professional growth<br>● Shares technological, psychological, and pedagogical support |
| 3. **Incubator**<br>Makes decision through designing, testing, and generating evidence-based insights for optimal utilisation of resources | ● Formulates policies, action plans, and response interventions<br>● Provides opportunities for innovations |
| 4. **Networker**<br>Ensures organisational success through linking resource potentials in the academe | ● Creates international and local linkages for collaborative actions<br>● Shares expert and material resources<br>● Connects in consortia for faculty-student development |

extension regardless of the circumstances. The gatekeeper role revolves around fortifying the academic institutions by meeting the needs of all members and eventually retooling them. The leaders ensure that students received quality education as they re-calibrate the faculty on Outcomes-Based Education (OBE) in a flexible setting, challenging them to contribute to a collective journey, inspiring members to re-think for a collective and effective response, bringing them to a shifted perspective, and linking to quality practice based on existing needs.

Philippine educational leaders strategically meet the needs of the academic community and mobilise its assets, including human, financial, and other resources. Among the tangible supports of educational leaders are the acquisition of high-speed internet connectivity and advanced gadgets to continue instructional delivery, procurement to access electronic databases and libraries for research, and re-alignment of funds to purchase critical materials for extension services that are in line with the context of the pandemic. In addition, intangible support can be seen in the re-calibration of the faculty to help them become adoptive of the situation.

**Leaders as cultivators.** The cultivator role directs the educational leaders to encourage and inspire the academic community to take the creative path of collectively addressing the current context. These leaders influence thinking and practise, and play a critical role as they nurture their members. They challenge and inspire the constituents to create their contribution for the collective success of the institution. The educational leaders support the well-being of their students and promote equity in education. They also inspire the faculty to follow a path of inclusivity and embrace a collective approach to move forward.

**Leaders as incubators.** Their role as an incubator reflects their ability to make decisions through designing, testing, and generating evidence-based insights for optimal utilisation of resources. Educational leaders protect the institution through the formulation and execution of quality policies as a consequence of a thorough process of critical thinking. The leaders choose to address the digital divide, increase access to technology, and provide resources to students in disadvantageous contexts for more inclusive and equitable learning experiences.

**Leaders as networkers**. These educational leaders realised the true meaning of a symbiotic relationship as they shared resources by forging their institutions into acceptable agreements. The synergy drives them to sustain learning despite the tumultuous times of the pandemic. Open communication is significant in building a network of partners. Through this, educational leaders have sought assistance from partner stakeholders and strengthened the linkages among institutions.

Philippine educational leaders applied interventions and innovations to experiment with flexible learning spaces for educational continuity among HEIs. This study takes a microscopic look at different state colleges and universities in the Philippines to explain the pivotal role of educational leaders in their holistic solutions, strategic initiatives, and context-specific actions that have been derived during the pandemic. This study categorised the initiatives of the educational leaders into three main areas (Fig. 2): Flexible Learning Curriculum, New Normal Professional Development, and Contextualised University Support.

Prior to the pandemic, teacher evaluations were done face-to-face, but current adjustments transpire using digital platforms. The students now evaluate the teachers' efficiency through the adaptation of an online platform. The examinations have also been conducted online, resulting in less printing and financial burden for the students during submission as they can submit their work through email or adapted apps of the faculty.

Some universities offer free pedagogical and policy-related courses through their Open University. Faculty with expertise in designing modules and assessment strategies give lectures in webinars to train instructors on dealing with the basic tenets of the Flexible Learning Curriculum. The educational system also made use of low-tech technologies such as radio frequency to enrich the learning needs of those students in far-flung areas. Many hours have been devoted to training the faculty at HEIs through professional certificate courses. Bayanihan spirit emerged as educational leaders spearheaded the initiative for faculty and student training along with safety precautions.

> "Aside from visiting each boarding house in Kabacan, I, together with other volunteers, led the distribution of workbooks to students in far-flung areas during the conduct of online classes," National Outstanding Volunteer and faculty of USM
>
> (Source: Duerme-Mangasar, 2023)
>
> "Truly, we exemplified the Bayanihan spirit by forging unity and cooperation among key stakeholders to vaccinate the members of MMSU family and those from the local communities in a systematic and aggressive manner," MMSU President
>
> (Source: Tapaoan, 2022)

However, the different research studies that we analysed showed that HEIs have neither a clear training framework nor a comprehensive training curriculum. The training of the faculty members is disaggregated, and

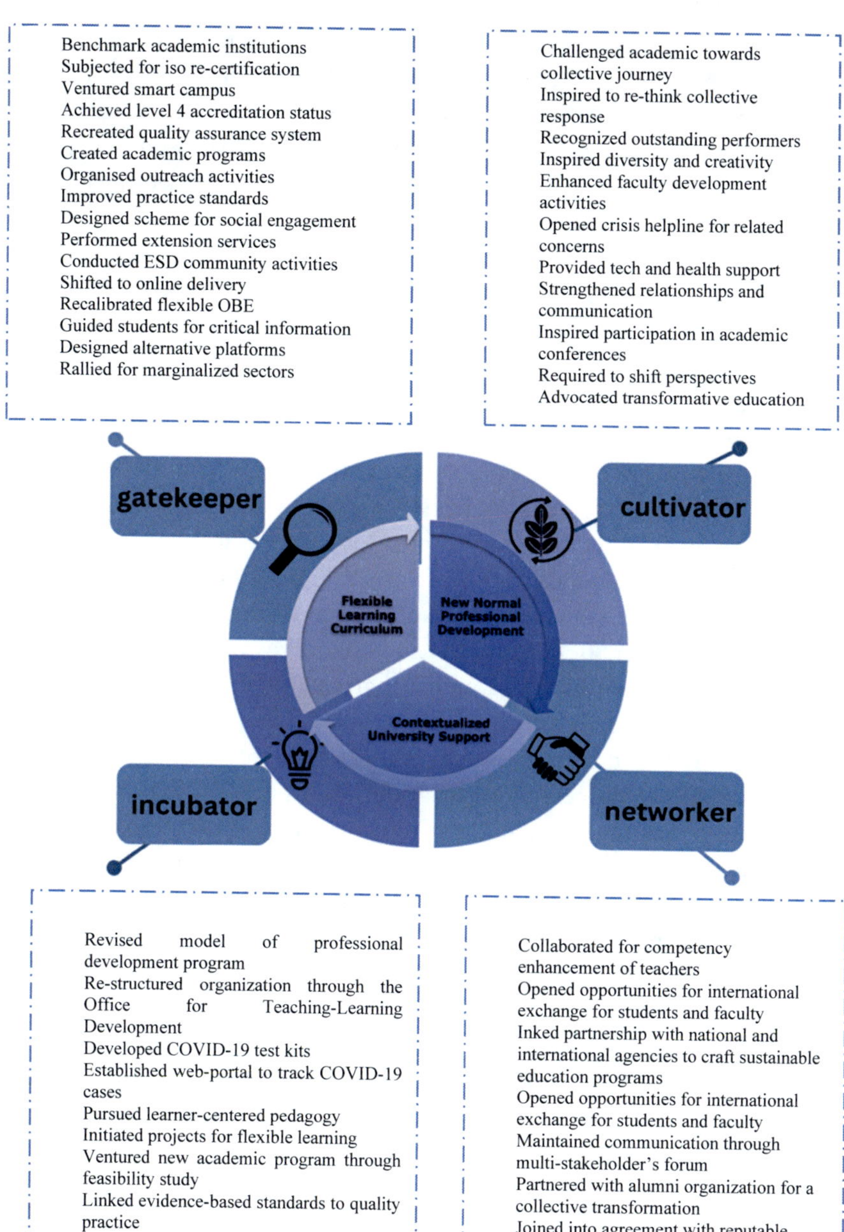

Benchmark academic institutions
Subjected for iso re-certification
Ventured smart campus
Achieved level 4 accreditation status
Recreated quality assurance system
Created academic programs
Organised outreach activities
Improved practice standards
Designed scheme for social engagement
Performed extension services
Conducted ESD community activities
Shifted to online delivery
Recalibrated flexible OBE
Guided students for critical information
Designed alternative platforms
Rallied for marginalized sectors
Challenged academic towards collective journey
Inspired to re-think collective response
Recognized outstanding performers
Inspired diversity and creativity
Enhanced faculty development activities
Opened crisis helpline for related concerns
Provided tech and health support
Strengthened relationships and communication
Inspired participation in academic conferences
Required to shift perspectives
Advocated transformative education
gatekeeper
cultivator
Flexible Learning Curriculum
New Normal Professional Development
Contextualized University Support
incubator
networker
Revised model of professional development program
Re-structured organization through the Office for Teaching-Learning Development
Developed COVID-19 test kits
Established web-portal to track COVID-19 cases
Pursued learner-centered pedagogy
Initiated projects for flexible learning
Ventured new academic program through feasibility study
Linked evidence-based standards to quality practice
Recreated quality assurance system
Collaborated for competency enhancement of teachers
Opened opportunities for international exchange for students and faculty
Inked partnership with national and international agencies to craft sustainable education programs
Opened opportunities for international exchange for students and faculty
Maintained communication through multi-stakeholder's forum
Partnered with alumni organization for a collective transformation
Joined into agreement with reputable international universities


**Fig. 2** Leader roles and outcomes during the pandemic

limited empirical studies were done to determine the efficacy of the courses and training they have undergone through online platforms. Nevertheless, the educational leaders of the top-ranking universities in the Philippines mandated some of their faculty experts to train 26 colleges and universities relative to the principles, assessments, and interventions that were applicable to module-making.

Educational leaders have led innovations in the university's support and services to its constituents. Universities offered psychosocial support to faculty and students through virtual counselling. However, there is a need to strengthen the mental health, sense of belonging, and well-being of the recipients. Educational leaders have applied the mental health break week, which is becoming a practice at a few universities. It is crucial to expand the policies relative to psychosocial support so that students or faculty can realistically gain access to such university services. The implementation of mental health plans, policies, and interventions is a critical component that educational leaders should also prioritise as student support services.

Educational leaders signed memoranda with different organisations to strengthen the universities' research and resource capacities. They also expanded the utilisation of social media, particularly Facebook, to disseminate relevant guidelines and institutional policies. The enrolment procedures in place at many universities combine both face-to-face and online transactions to expedite the process of registration. Incorporating digital platforms has brought about changes and slightly improved some institutional practices. The educational leaders' initiatives supported the strategic implementation of flexible learning curricula (Fig. 3) to sustain learning during the pandemic. Numerous universities in the Philippines demonstrated communal solidarity or 'Bayanihan Spirit', which is a strong hallmark of Filipino resiliency, especially during complex emergencies.

> "Supporting the production of these products is an opportunity for the University to really help the communities in difficult times like this, as we are one with the government and the people in working together to heal as one nation." CLSU President
>
> (Source: Estigoy, 2020)

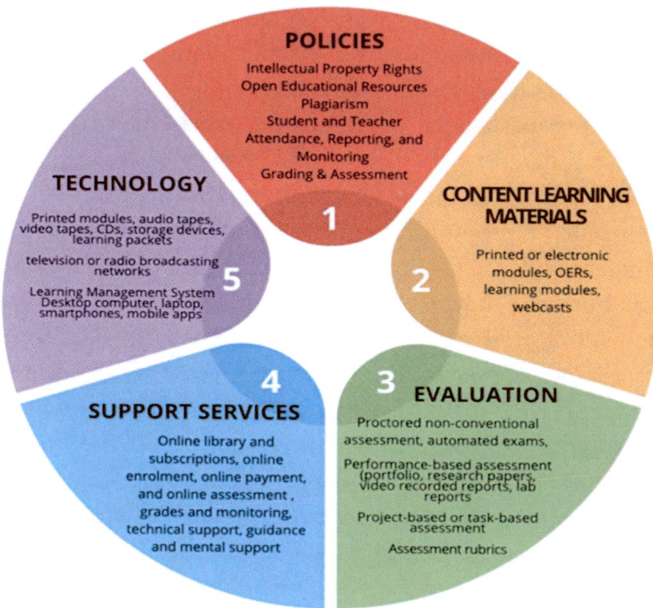


**Fig. 3** Educational leaders' strategic implementation of flexible learning curricula

# Discussion

## Crucial Roles of Academic Leaders

When the pandemic struck the Philippine archipelago, educational leaders' journey during the pandemic tested their competence to overcome the enormous responsibilities in the academe. Findings reveal four types of roles played by leaders of HEIs in the Philippines: gatekeeper, cultivator, incubator, and networker.

The gatekeeper role emphasises how educational leaders maintain quality and excellence across mandates through the provision of resources and mobilisation of members. Their action ensures continuity of quality education because the pandemic spurred educators to deliver instructions from a distance (Alasmari, 2021). Educational leaders also played the role of a cultivator. They fuelled strong transformative advocacies to re-think and re-imagine teaching and learning and shift into a win–win perspective. In the context of supporting well-being, educational leaders possess a holistic perspective on navigating the academic institution by taking actions that involve well-being. This is what Yang et al. (2022) mentioned as the act of supporting inclusive online learning during and beyond the pandemic.

Activities to regulate well-being were established through the utilisation of technology and health support, the establishment of helplines, and the provision of outreach activities for vulnerable groups.

Academic leaders performed as incubators when they recreated quality assurance systems, shared newly discovered knowledge, and committed practices to sustain learning in the academic community. Moreover, their roles reflect the concept of promoting equity in education. The forced shift to online learning provided challenges to administrators and faculty (Rodrigo et al., 2022), but resiliency, knowledge, and competence mitigated these challenges to embrace all students. Lastly, the networker role reflects how educational leaders link potential resources to ensure organisational success. Academic leaders played critical roles in strengthening linkages that resulted in the transformation of teachers (Pinatil & Ramos, 2023). They acknowledge the critical part of collaboration as they connect with potential partners. Their performance demonstrated the critical value of adapting and innovating, as they encouraged faculty to think outside the box and consider different perspectives.

## Strategic Actions to Sustain Learning

CHED has authorised universities to re-think their university trajectories to provide quality instruction to students despite the crisis. Educational leaders ushered in localised academic initiatives and programme policies to address the needs of the local context. They aligned their decision-making based on the pandemic guidelines of CHED and the local mandates to sustain learning.

Flexible learning curricula considered the local context, socio-economic conditions, technological infrastructure, and pedagogical needs of respective universities. The sudden shift to the online learning paradigm prompted educational leaders to redesign delivery, pedagogy, assessment strategies, and feedback mechanisms to accommodate the online learning needs of their students. Pawilen (2021) offered a model that universities can utilise for the effective implementation of flexible learning that considers the types of learners, pace, place, and mode of instruction.

Educational leaders also initiated aligning learning competencies that are essential for students to achieve the programme outcomes of their courses. They required the instructors to contextualise their learning materials and assessment strategies while considering the multiple responsibilities, psychosocial needs, and environmental conditions of the students. They recommended various platforms, such as Zoom, Google Meet, Canvas, LMS,

Facebook, Google Classroom, etc., to accommodate students in class (Acebes et al., 2022; Arciosa, 2022). However, monitoring and evaluation measures of the flexible learning curriculum should prioritise feedback from stakeholders (Arciosa, 2022). A curriculum that meets the context of the learners is crucial for the appropriate evaluation of student learning. Assessing the learning of students is an important element to any educational process (Umar, 2018).

Moreover, Filipino online communities and partnerships are crucial for sustainability during the pandemic since collaboration contributes to social continuity (Joaquin et al., 2020; Maravilla, 2021). Educational leaders demonstrated 'bayanihan' spirit (unity and cooperation) as they synergise with various agencies to achieve desired goals to capacitate the faculty and students for online learning. The 'bayanihan' initiatives reflected their desire to sustain learning and provide educational equity. Crawford and Cifuentes-Faura (2022) argued that the educational landscape should build on the SDGs. At present, there is a disaggregated design of the training curriculum, and some HEIs have no clear design of their framework relative to professional development. It is imperative that educational leaders conceptualise training and anchor such capacity-building activities through research-based results or training needs assessments moving beyond the pandemic.

The leaders renovated the educational system to make it responsive to students' situations and leverage the power of digital platforms to provide services to stakeholders. However, findings indicate a need to strengthen belongingness and improve institutional practices for quality assurance in Philippine universities. Nevertheless, educational leaders demonstrated university-wide initiatives that reflect their situational and crisis leadership. Studies (Caringal-Go et al., 2021; Francisco & Nuqui, 2020) confirm this tendency of leaders in crisis to steer actions and synergise to achieve the desired goals.

## Conclusion

The pandemic has immensely challenged the educational leaders in the country. However, they have led the institutions to maximise their limited resources and envision a way forward beyond the pandemic to improve the academic outcomes of the students. Educational leaders played critical roles in sustaining higher education in the Philippines. They served as gatekeepers to transcend academic continuity while maintaining the standards of quality learning and teaching. As cultivators, they influence the thinking and practices of the academic community to synergise in navigating the treacherous waters of the new normal teaching and learning. The incubator role of educational leaders is a cornerstone for decision-making, policymaking, and designing academic innovations. Lastly, they manifested the networker role through the web of support among universities.

Educational leaders displayed 'bayanihan' (unity and cooperation) spirit as one of the hallmarks of Filipino character. They formulated shared goals of delivering quality outcomes for academic institutions and spearheaded curricular, professional development, and university initiatives to support faculty and student readiness. However, it is an ongoing herculean challenge for educational leaders to formulate a comprehensive re-calibration of the online curriculum, especially since the Philippines is prone to environmental hazards, the HEIs should gear towards a future hyperflex academic transition. Academic leaders should spearhead the formulation of comprehensive faculty development plans and a training curriculum to augment the pedagogical and technological competence of the faculty. Future research should consider conducting a programme evaluation to determine the relevance of the curriculum to respond to the market needs of the current times beyond the pandemic. This study relied on reviews, an empirical study of the good practices and innovations of some universities to sustain student learning is needed. CHED should lead a nationwide study among academic leaders in HEIs for first-account data since most original research on educational leaders is in basic education institutions. Lastly, universities should strengthen their strategies for the belongingness, mental health, and well-being of their students.

## References

Acebes, S. J., Melitante, J., Tuble, N., & Toquero, C. M. D. (2022). Hopes, goals, hindrances, and solutions of students on forced digitalization of course learning amid pandemic. *Journal of Pedagogical Sociology and Psychology, 4*(2), 144–167. https://doi.org/10.33902/JPSP.202218002

Ahern, S., & Loh, E. (2021). Leadership during the COVID-19 pandemic: building and sustaining trust in times of uncertainty. *BMJ Leader, 5*, 266–269. https://bmjleader.bmj.com/content/5/4/266

Ajari, E.E., Kanyike, A.M., Ojilong, D., & Abdulbasit, I.O. (2020), COVID-19 in Uganda: Epidemiology and response. *European Journal of Medical and Educational Technologies, 13*(2). Em2009. https://doi.org/10.30935/ejmets/8269

Alasmari, T. (2021). Learning in the COVID-19 era: Higher education students and Faculty's experience with emergency distance education. *International Journal of Emerging Technologies in Learning (online), 16*(9), 40–62. https://doi.org/10.3991/ijet.v16i09.20711

Arciosa, R. (2022). Effectiveness of flexible learning in teaching college subjects amidst COVID-19 pandemic at CTE, Sultan Kudarat State University, Philippines: Effectiveness of flexible learning. *International Journal of Curriculum and Instruction, 14*(2), 1343–1358. https://ijci.globets.org/index.php/IJCI/article/view/848/489

Baron, G. (2023, April 13). *Study: Pandemic graduates face difficulty finding jobs.* www.ptvnews.ph; PTV news. https://www.ptvnews.ph/study-pandemic-graduates-face-difficulty-finding-jobs/

Barrot, J. S., Llenares, I. I., & del Rosario, L. S. (2021). Students' online learning challenges during the pandemic and how they cope with them: The case of the Philippines. *Education and Information Technologies, 26*, 7321–7338. https://doi.org/10.1007/s10639-021-10589-x

Baticulon, R. E., Sy, J. J., Alberto, N. R. I., Baron, M. B. C., Mabulay, R. E. C., Rizada, L. G. T., Tiu, C. J. S., Clarion, C. A., & Reyes, J. C. B. (2021). Barriers to online learning in the time of COVID-19: A national survey of medical students in the Philippines. *Medical Science Educator, 31*, 615–626. https://doi.org/10.1007/s40670-021-01231-z

Bešić, E. (2020). Intersectionality: A pathway towards inclusive education? *Prospects.* https://doi.org/10.1007/s11125-020-09461-6

Brown, G. (2020). Schooling beyond COVID-19: An Unevenly Distributed Future. *Frontiers in Education, 5*, 82. https://doi.org/10.3389/feduc.2020.00082

Bustillo, E., & Aguilos, M. (2022). The challenges of modular learning in the wake of COVID-19: A digital divide in the Philippine countryside revealed. *Education Sciences, 12*(7), 449. https://doi.org/10.3390/educsci12070449

Caringal-Go, J. F., Teng-Calleja, M., Franco, E. P., Manaois, J. O., & Zantua, R. M. S. (2021). Crisis leadership from the perspective of employees during the COVID-19 pandemic. *Leadership & Organization Development Journal, 42*(4), 630–643. https://doi.org/10.1108/LODJ-07-2020-0284

Cepeda, C. (2020, December 30). *Batch 2020: How Filipino college graduates job-hunted through the pandemic.* INQUIRER.net. https://newsinfo.inquirer.net/1377399/batch-2020-how-filipino-college-graduates-job-hunted-through-the-pandemic

Chua Reyes, V., Hamid, O., & Hardy, I. (2022). When reforms make things worse: School leadership responses to poverty, disasters, and cultures of crises in the Philippine education system. *International Journal of Leadership in Education, 25*(2), 331–344. https://doi.org/10.1080/13603124.2021.2009038

CNN Philippines. (2020, March 10). FDA allows use of coronavirus test kits developed by UP scientists. *CNN*. http://www.cnnphilippines.com/news/2020/3/10/Coronavirus-testing-kit-University-of-the-Philippines-UP-NIS.html

Commission on Higher Education (2020). *COVID-19 Updates*. CHED Advisory: Quezon, Philippines. https://ched.gov.ph/covid-19-advisories/

Crawford, J. (2021a). During and beyond a pandemic: Publishing learning and teaching research through COVID-19. *Journal of University Teaching & Learning Practice, 18*(3), 1–7.

Crawford, J. (2021b). *COVID-19 and higher education: A pandemic response model from rapid adaption to consolidation and restoration.* Unpublished manuscript

Crawford, J. (2023). Introductory chapter: The time for sustainable leadership has arrived. In *Leadership for sustainable and educational advancement—Advancing great leaders and leadership.* IntechOpen. https://www.intechopen.com/chapters/86513

Crawford, J., & Cifuentes-Faura, J. (2022). Sustainability in higher education during the COVID-19 pandemic: A systematic review. *Sustainability, 14*(3), 1879. https://doi.org/10.3390/su14031879

Crawford, J., Butler-Henderson, K., Rudolph, J., Malkawi, B., Glowatz, M., Burton, R., Magni, A. P., & Lam, S. (2020). COVID-19: 20 countries' higher education intra-period digital pedagogy responses. *Journal of Applied Learning & Teaching, 3*(1), 9–27. https://doi.org/10.37074/jalt.2020.3.1.7

de Guzman, C. (2021, December 1). COVID-19 and the Crisis Facing Philippine Schoolchildren. *Time.* https://time.com/6124045/school-closures-covid-education-philippines/

de Loyola, Z. (2023, April 13). Nograles eyes bridging program for "pandemic generation" grads. *Philippine News Agency.* https://www.pna.gov.ph/articles/1199296

Department of Health (2022). *COVID-19 tracker.* Accessed 17 October 2022. https://www.doh.gov.ph/covid19tracker

Duerme-Mangasar S.J. (2023, August). *Reviving Filipino spirit of "Bayanihan" through volunteerism.* Accessed 14 October 2023, https://pia.gov.ph/features/2023/08/14/reviving-filipino-spirit-of-bayanihan-through-volunteerism

Estigoy, M.A. (2020). *CLSU "Bayanihan" spirit shines through amidst Covid-19 crisis: The university gad program grants Php 1.5 M project funds.* Central Luzon State University. Accessed 14 October 2023. https://clsu.edu.ph/news-updates/post.php?slug=clsu-bayanihan-spirit-shines-through-amidst-covid-19-crisis-the-university-gad-program-grants-php-15-m-project-funds

Francisco, C.D.C. & Nuqui, A.V. (2020). Emergence of a situational leadership during COVID- 19 Pandemic called New Normal Leadership. *International Journal of Academic Multidisciplinary Research, 4*(10), 15–19. https://files.eric.ed.gov/fulltext/ED608560.pdf

Hénard, F., & Roseveare, D. (2012). Fostering quality teaching in higher education: Policies and practices. *An IMHE Guide for Higher Education Institutions, 1*(1), 7–11.

Islam, M. A., Barna, S. D., Raihan, H., Khan, M. N. A., & Hossain, M. T. (2020). Depression and anxiety among university students during the COVID-19 pandemic in Bangladesh: A web-based cross-sectional survey. *PLoS ONE, 15*(8), e0238162. https://doi.org/10.1371/journal.pone.0238162

Joaquin, J. J. B., Biana, H. T., & Dacela, M. A. (2020). The Philippine higher education sector in the time of COVID-19. *In Frontiers in Education, 5*, 576371. https://doi.org/10.3389/feduc.2020.576371

Katog, M. S. (2022). Coping with COVID-19: How public secondary school principals adapt to the new normal. *International Journal of Early Childhood*, 1, 2363–2367. https://papers.ssrn.com/sol3/papers.cfm?abstract_id=4104920

Lalani, K., Crawford, J., & Butler-Henderson, K. (2021). Academic leadership during COVID-19 in higher education: Technology adoption and adaptation for online learning during a pandemic. *International Journal of Leadership in Education.* https://doi.org/10.1080/13603124.2021.1988716

Maala, E. B., & Lagos, F. D. (2022). Technological leadership of school heads and teachers' technology integration: Basis for the development of a training program. *International Journal of Multidisciplinary: Applied Business and Education Research, 3*(10), 2074–2089. https://doi.org/10.11594/ijmaber.03.10.19

Magsambol, B. (2023, April 12). *Senators urge "serious effort" in addressing job readiness among students.* RAPPLER. https://www.rappler.com/nation/senators-urge-serious-effort-addressing-job-readiness-students/

Mañero, J. (2020). Post digital brave new world and its educational implications. *Post Digital Science and Education.* https://doi.org/10.1007/s42438-020-00129-0

Maravilla, M. I. (2021). COVID-19 survivors Philippines: Towards the promotion of public health during the COVID-19 pandemic. *Journal of Public Health, 43*(3), e565–e566. https://doi.org/10.1093/pubmed/fdab200

Morgan, H. (2020). Best practices for implementing remote learning during a pandemic, The clearing house. *A Journal of Educational Strategies, Issues and Ideas, 93*(3), 135–141. https://doi.org/10.1080/00098655.2020.1751480

Navarro, M. M., Prasetyo, Y. T., Young, M. N., Nadlifatin, R., Ngurah, A. A., & P. R. (2021). The perceived satisfaction in utilizing learning management system among engineering students during the COVID-19 pandemic: Integrating task technology fit and extended technology acceptance model. *Sustainability, 13*(19), 10669. https://doi.org/10.3390/su131910669

Oducado, R. M. (2020). Faculty perception toward online education in a state college in the Philippines during the coronavirus disease 19 (COVID-19) pandemic. *Universal Journal of Educational Research, 8*(10), 4736–4742. https://doi.org/10.13189/ujer.2020.081044

Pawilen, G. T. (2021). Preparing Philippine higher education institutions for flexible learning during the period of COVID-19 pandemic: Curricular and instructional adjustments, challenges, and issues. *International Journal of Curriculum and Instruction, 13*(3), 2150–2166. http://files.eric.ed.gov/fulltext/EJ1313025.pdf

Pinatil, L., & Ramos, A. (2023). Theory of adaptation of educators teaching technology-based courses. *Recoletos Multidisciplinary Research Journal, 11*(1), 103–118. https://doi.org/10.32871/rmrj2311.01.08

Poletti, M. & Raballo, A. (2020). Letter to the editor: Evidence on school closure and children's social contact: useful for coronavirus disease (COVID-19)? *Euro*

*Surveill, 25*(17), 2000758. https://doi.org/10.2807/1560-7917.ES.2020.25.17.2000758

Ramos, A., & Baldespiñosa, M. (2021). Bridging between beliefs and needs of language teachers in Philippines: Personal qualities, strategies, and framework during COVID-19 pandemic. REILA: *Journal of Research and Innovation in Language, 3*(3), 194–209. https://doi.org/10.31849/reila.v313.7401

Rodrigo, M. M. T., & Estelle Marie, M. L. (2022). Promoting equity and assuring teaching and learning quality: Magisterial lectures in a Philippine university during the COVID-19 pandemic. *Education Sciences, 12*(2), 146. https://doi.org/10.3390/educsci12020146

Roncesvalles, M. C. T., & Gaerlan, A. A. (2021). The role of authentic leadership and teachers' organizational commitment on organizational citizenship behavior in higher education. *International Journal of Educational Leadership and Management, 9*(2), 92–121. https://files.eric.ed.gov/fulltext/EJ1310299.pdf

Rudolph, J., Tan, S., Crawford, J., et al. (2023). Perceived quality of online learning during COVID-19 in higher education in Singapore: Perspectives from students, lecturers, and academic leaders. *Educ Res Policy Prac, 22*, 171–191. https://doi.org/10.1007/s10671-022-09325-0

San Miguel, N. V., & Pascual, E. A. (2021). School leaders' resilience amidst pandemic in the division of Laguna Philippines. *International Journal for Research Publication, 88*(1), 67–88. https://doi.org/10.47119/IJRP1008811120212390

Shahzad, A., Hassan, R., Aremu, A. Y., Hussain, A., & Lodhi, R. N. (2021). Effects of COVID-19 in E-learning on higher education institution students: The group comparison between male and female. *Quality & Quantity, 55*, 805–826.

See, A. B. (2021, March 15). *Inside One of the World's Longest COVID-19 Lockdowns*. Time. https://time.com/5945616/covid-philippines-pandemic-lockdown/

Shereen, M. A., Khan, S., Kazmi, A., Bashir, N., & Siddique, R. (2020). COVID-19 infection: Emergence, transmission, and characteristics of human coronaviruses. *Journal of Advanced Research, 24*, 91–98.

Stuart, K., Faghy, M. A., Bidmead, E., Browning, R., Roberts, C., Grimwood, S., & Winn-Reed, T. (2020). A biopsychosocial framework for recovery from COVID-19. *International Journal of Sociology and Social Policy, 40*(10), 1021–1039. https://doi.org/10.1108/IJSSP-07-2020-0301

Tapaoan, D. (2022, July 19). *MMSU Is region's best HEI for COVID-19 vaccination program*. Accessed 14 October 2023 https://www.mmsu.edu.ph/news/mmsu-is-regions-best-hei-for-covid-19-vaccination-program

Tarrayo, V. N., Paz, R. M. O., & Gepila, E. C., Jr. (2021). The shift to flexible learning amidst the pandemic: The case of English language teachers in a Philippine state university. *Innovation in Language Learning and Teaching, 17*(1), 130–143. https://doi.org/10.1080/17501229.2021.1944163

Torrato, J. B., Aguja, S. E., & Prudente, M. S. (2021). Using web video conferencing to conduct a program as a proposed model toward teacher leadership and academic vitality in the Philippines. *Education Sciences, 11*(11), 658. https://doi.org/10.3390/educsci11110658

Toquero, C. M. D. (2020). Challenges and opportunities for higher education amid the COVID-19 pandemic: The Philippine context. *Pedagogical Research, 5*(4) https://doi.org/10.29333/pr/7947

Toquero, C. M. D. (2021). Academic silver linings in a Philippine State University amid the early stages of pandemic cases. *Journal of Learning for Development, 8*(2), 448–455. https://doi.org/10.56059/jl4d.v8i2.498

Toquero, C. M. D. (2023). Online learning support to reinforce motivation of university students during homeschool exodus. *Mediterranean Journal of Social & Behavioral Research, 7*(2), 85–91. https://doi.org/10.30935/mjosbr/13039

Toquero, C. M. D., & Toquero, J. P. (2023). Pandemic pedagogy conceptualizations of university students during emergency remote education. *Mediterranean Journal of Social & Behavioral Research, 7*(3), 177–182. https://doi.org/10.30935/mjosbr/13403

Tuga, B., Jocson, J., & Mabunga, R. A. (2023). The impact of COVID-19 on a Philippine university: Challenges and responses towards a new normal in education. *AsTEN Journal of Teacher Education.* Special Issue 1, https://po.pnuresearchportal.org/ejournal/index.php/asten/article/view/1777

Umar, A. T., & Majeed, A. (2018). The impact of assessment for learning on students' achievement in English for specific purposes: a case study of pre-medical students at Khartoum university: Sudan. *English Language Teaching, 11*(2), 15–25.

UNESCO. (2020). *Distance learning solutions*. Accessed on 16 June 2023. Available online: https://en.unesco.org/covid19/educationresponse/solutions

United Nations. (2020). *Policy brief: Education during COVID-19 and beyond/ August 2020, United Nations Sustainable Development Group*. Accessed on 16 June 2023. Available online: https://www.un.org/development/desa/dspd/wp-content/uploads/sites/22/2020/08/sg_policy_brief_covid19_and_education_august_2020.pdf

Vallejo, B. M., Jr., & Ong, R. A. C. (2020). Policy responses and government science advice for the COVID 19 pandemic in the Philippines: January to April 2020. *Progress in Disaster Science, 7*, 100115. https://doi.org/10.1016/j.pdisas.2020.100115

Worldbank (2020). *Guidance note on remote learning and COVID-19 (English)*. World Bank Group. http://documents.worldbank.org/curated/en/531681585957264427/Guidance-Note-on-Remote-Learning-and-COVID-19

Yang, D., Tang, Y. M., Hayashi, R., Ra, S., & Lim, C. P. (2022). Supporting inclusive online higher education in developing countries: Lessons learnt from Sri Lanka's university closure. *Education Sciences, 12*(7), 494. https://doi.org/10.3390/educsci12070494

Yumol, D. T. (2020, April 22). All PLM students to get passing mark amid COVID-19 crisis. *CNN Philippines*. Retrieved from https://www.cnn.ph/news/2020/4/22/all-plm-students-get-passing-mark-covid-crisis.html

# Turkish Higher Education in Crisis: An Analysis of Challenges and Future Prospects

Begüm Burak

## Introduction

Turkish higher education system has faced a number of profound crises. Except for the distance education crisis that derived from the sudden change in learning and teaching as a result of COVID-19, the crises have derived from a variety of causes. These causes have been shaped by various factors including political culture, institutions and structural settings. It can be argued that the lacks of academic freedom and meritocracy have played a significant role in the outbreak and maintenance of the crises in Turkish higher education.

Academic freedom is at the very core of the mission of the university. Universities are often centres of political and intellectual dissent, and governments are reluctant to allow institutions the freedom and autonomy that may contribute to instability (Altbach, 2007). One of the important factors which impede academic freedom is the hierarchical structure and power relationships in the university. As a result, the administration can easily intervene in teaching practices of an academic.

Meritocracy is a social system in which individuals are rewarded based on their talent, intelligence and skills (Castilla, 2008). According to the European Research Area and Innovative Committee (2014), recruitment procedures at European universities characterised as open, transparent and

B. Burak (✉)
İstanbul, Turkey
e-mail: begumburak1984@gmail.com



J. Rudolph et al. (eds.), *The Palgrave Handbook of Crisis Leadership in Higher Education*, https://doi.org/10.1007/978-3-031-54509-2_29

merit-based are regarded as a prerequisite for the realisation of the European research area. The effective hiring of the best academics to fill available positions is believed to ensure better academic performances.

This chapter has a two-fold aim: to provide an analysis of crises in the Turkish higher education system with a special reference to meritocracy and academic freedom; and to make an analysis of challenges and future prospects from a crisis leadership perspective. Wooten & James (2008) make a distinction to account for most crises, providing a typology of crises. Their research provides four types of crises: (a) accidents, (b) scandals, which are events or occurrences that compromise the organisation's reputation, (c) product safety and health incidents and (d) employee-centred crises (Wooten & James, 2008). This chapter argues that many of the crises in Turkish higher education can be regarded as "scandals" that compromise the organisation's reputation and a holistic model like complexity leadership can offer remedies. Complexity Leadership Theory (CLT) focuses on emergent processes within complex systems and suggests that leadership needs to operate at all levels in a contextual and interactive fashion (Marion & Uhl-Bien, 2001).

The organisation of the chapter is as follows: Firstly, the historical background section provides information about Türkiye. In this section the impact of COVID-19 is covered while mentioning the pandemic-driven crisis observed in Turkish higher education institutions (HEIs). Secondly, an overview of Turkish higher education system is presented. Thirdly, the theoretical framework section focuses on the relevant literature about crisis and crisis leadership. Finally, a critical examination of the mentioned crises is made. This section also provides discussion about challenges and future prospects from a crisis leadership perspective. The chapter employs a qualitative research methodology using a variety of resources, including dissertations, books, along with non-academic resources such as news articles and reports published by the Turkish government and international organisations.

## Türkiye: Context and History

Türkiye was founded by Atatürk in 1923 on the ashes of the Ottoman Empire. After single-party rule, the country switched to multi-party politics in 1946 and since then there has been democratic politics—at least in procedural terms—despite some interruptions due to military interventions that broke out in 1960, 1971, 1980, 1997 and 2007. The electoral victory of Recep Tayyip Erdoğan's Justice and Development Party (AKP) in 2002 has changed Türkiye's political and economic landscape to an important degree democratising civil-military relations on the one hand, but also undermining certain civil liberties and democratic principles like free speech and media freedom on the other hand.

The failed coup attempt that occurred on July 15, 2016 caused major changes in the country. Two years later, Türkiye adopted the presidential regime. This moved the country away from democracy by replacing its parliamentary system and concentrating all power in the presidency. In the aftermath of the failed coup, the state authorities subsequently detained thousands of judges, teachers, soldiers, civil servants and academics on suspicion of involvement in the coup attempt which Erdoğan said was carried out by "FETO". In addition, several private universities affiliated with Gülenists including the university where the author of this chapter earned her Ph.D. degree from were closed down. (Since 2016, "Fethullahist terrorist organisation-FETO" has been the new label coined by the state authorities to refer to the Fethullah Gülen network.)

For more than two decades AKP has been ruling the country as a single-party government. On May 28, 2023, Erdoğan won presidency in a runoff election with 52.14% of the votes (*The Guardian*, 2023) and became the president again for another period of 5 years. Türkiye has a strategically important geo-political location at the crossroads between Europe and Asia. The country gained official candidacy status for the European Union in 1999. The membership talks were launched in 2005 (Aybet, 2006). However, since 2016, accession negotiations have stalled. The EU has criticised Türkiye for human rights violations (Dam, 2021). Türkiye currently has deteriorating relations with the Western world and this leads it to seek stronger ties with countries like Russia and China (Dalay, 2022). However Türkiye is a key NATO member and holds a significant role in world politics as observed in Sweden's NATO membership.

The population of the country has been 86,750,408 as of March 2023 (Worldometer, 2023). The population is relatively young, with 22.4% aged between 0 and 14 (Turkish Statistical Institute, 2021). After the outbreak of the Syrian civil war in 2011, a huge influx of refugees came. Some cities in the southern region like Kilis have a Syrian population with the ratio of around 38% as of 2022 (Turkish Ministry of Interior Affairs, 2022). With a GDP of roughly $906 billion, as of 2023, Türkiye is the 19th-largest economy in the world (World Bank, 2023). The Koç Group and Sabancı Group are the country's largest companies which also own private universities namely Koç University and Sabancı University. Both of these universities are research-intensive institutions and they are among the top 7 universities in Türkiye (Times Higher Education, 2023).

## Türkiye's COVID-19 Experiment

The outbreak of COVID-19 caused a major impact on Türkiye as it did for almost all the countries across the world. The first case in the country was shared with the public on March 11, 2020 (TRT, 2020). The Government took important steps in the fight against COVID-19. One of them was the establishment of pandemic hospitals. In 2020, a total of 17 hospitals were built (Anadolu Agency, 2021). Despite the success in health sector, Türkiye also saw a serious financial crisis during the second quarter of 2020. To combat this, the government initiated a national solidarity campaign (Sputnik, 2020) creating public bank accounts to collect donations from citizens.

COVID-19 put enormous changes in education and paved the way for the shift to distance education (Tice et al., 2021). During the pandemic, many countries experienced a progression towards localised education models to support a period of reduced international access to education and travel (Bonk et al., 2020). Numerous HEIs over the world employed distance education through digital tools in this period (Crawford, 2023; Crawford et al., 2020). In a similar way, Türkiye suspended face-to-face education for several months. On March 16, HEIs took a three-week-long break which was extended further (Anadolu Agency, 2020). On April 3, lockdown measures were taken for the people under the age of 20 (Turkish Ministry of Interior Affairs, 2020). Despite the start of online programmes through "Digital transformation project at universities" two years before the pandemic (Saraç, 2021) a major setback emerged which can be seen as a "distance education crisis". Pandemic reduced academic integrity and ultimately caused a loss in teaching efficiency.

## Turkish Higher Education System: History and Structure

There was not a strong tradition of higher education in the Ottoman Empire. The first university was founded in 1773 (Şimşek, 1999). The Ottomans lagged 800 years behind Europe, considering the fact that prototypes of modern European higher education were founded in the eleventh century (Gürüz et al., 1994). However it should be noted that during its 600-year existence, the Ottomans made significant advances in science and technology (Aydüz, 2008). The first Ottoman University was founded in 1900. This institution was to be later named as Istanbul University in 1933. Istanbul

University had been the "Darülfunun" (School of Sciences) in Ottoman times (Akyüz, 2001; Timur, 2000; Tural, 2004). As the first university before the Republic was established to create an Ottoman identity, the aim of the education reform in early years of the Republic was to form a national identity (Güçlü 2020).

In 1946, a new law on universities (no. 4936) came into effect. (Erden, 2006) and new universities were established including Istanbul Technical University and Ankara University (Akyüz, 2001). After transition to multi-party politics, increases in the demand for higher education led to the founding of new universities including Aegean University and Middle East Technical University (ODTÜ). These universities have been the first campus universities to be based on the American land-grant model (Akar, 2010). Also, Robert College which had been founded by the American missionary Cyrus Hamlin in 1863 became Boğaziçi University in 1971 (Freely, 2000).

Türkiye witnessed political violence and bloody street clashes in the late 1970s. Tense violence was also evident among university youth and to put an end to this unrest, the military staged a coup in 1980. This coup caused major change in politics, society, economics and higher education. After the 1980 military coup, in a similar fashion to Margaret Thatcher in the U.K. and Ronald Reagan in the U.S. Türkiye under Turgut Özal rule adopted economic and political liberalisation policies. The neo-liberal economic regulations led to privatisation in educational policies (Burak, 2022). Türkiye's first private university Bilkent University was founded in 1985 in Ankara (Erden, 2006). As a major structural development, Law 2547 established the YÖK (The Council of Turkish Higher Education) in 1981 in order to direct the activities of higher education.

The establishment of YÖK paved the way for a major reorganisation of HEIs (YÖK, 2005). YÖK represents the top organisational structure of Turkish higher education. It is responsible for preparing plans for the development, and realisation of educational activities of HEIs. In addition, it evaluates the training of teaching staff to ensure that it is in line with the principles set forth in its law, and supervises the resources allocated to HEIs (YÖK, n.d).

Triggered by the neo-liberal politico-economic measures, the 1990s witnessed the increase in the number of private universities. In these years, Türkiye's EU candidacy process led to important steps for responding to the demands of the Copenhagen Criteria (Sozen & Shaw, 2003). In 2001, HEIs became part of the Bologna Process which aims to strengthen the competitiveness of HEIs and to foster student mobility. YÖK has implemented many reforms for that. Areas of reform include approval of the European credit transfer system (Visakorpi et al., 2008) and accreditation (Akduman et al., 2001). However these changes remained bureaucratic due to the democratic deficit in the implementation.

Access to higher education in Türkiye is determined by centrally administered entrance examinations. Certain areas, including the arts and physical education, accept students based on a talent exam in addition to the examination scores (Wilson et al., 2020). Higher education is almost totally financed by the government (Dündar & Lewis, 1999). Private HEIs charge fees. As of 2023 Türkiye has 208 universities (YÖK, n.d.) and holds the largest higher education student population in the European Higher Education Area with a total of nearly 8 million students (Saraç, 2021). However, due to unplanned opening of some departments, the abundance of graduates leads to an increase in unemployment rate.

## Theoretical Framework: Crisis Leadership and Scandals as Crisis

This chapter focuses on the concepts of crisis leadership and scandals as crisis. A crisis can be more challenging than other organisational events, as it often requires leaders to exercise their skills in not only minimising potential disruptions, but also capitalising on opportunities for positive change while balancing competing demands from stakeholders (Wu et al., 2021). The concept of crisis implies a difficult or dangerous situation. Crises threaten the fundamental operation or viability of an organisation (Hermann, 1963) and have low probability (Weick, 1988) meaning their occurrence is rare, they are also morally and ethically laden (Riggio & Newstad, 2023). The consequences create time pressures, because if not addressed rapidly, the impact can cause the demise of the organisation.

Early crisis research treated crises as discrete events to be prevented in order to protect organisational functioning and reputation (Wooten & James, 2008). Over the years, the ways crises are studied have taken significant turns. Riggio and Newstead (2023, p. 201) note that despite crises such as global warming being highly complex and of global consequence, crisis leadership "is a relatively underdeveloped field".

Preskill and Brookfield (2009) regard leadership not as a collection of personal characteristics held by charismatic individuals but as a collaboratively exercised process. Their work addresses different models of servant, symbiotic, transformational, developmental and organic leadership that all focus on enabling change. Leadership dynamics involve multiple levels and can produce both top-down and bottom-up emergent outcomes at higher and lower levels of analysis (cited in Dihn et al., 2014). In traditional leadership theory, the unit of analysis is oftentimes the leader, the leader and follower, the leader and group and so forth. Today, the field of leadership focuses not only on the leader, but also on "*followers, peers, supervisors, work setting/context, and culture, including a much broader array of individuals representing the entire spectrum of diversity, public, private, and not-for-profit organisations*" (Avolio et al., 2009, p. 422). Such a holistic approach is significant for analysing the role of leadership in the management of crises in higher education.

It can be argued that most of the crises in Turkish higher education can be regarded as scandals. Scandals are defined as not discrete events, most of the time they have obscure origins and damage the reputations of perpetrators and of their organisation—for example, a bribery scandal (Riggio & Newstad, 2023). In a scandal, denying responsibility cannot be credible because complex technological systems do not engender scandals. Rather, they are the results of human and organisational inadequacies. The environment that breeds scandals often is one in which excuses like "everyone is doing it" abound (Marcus & Goodman, 1991). It can be argued that most of the crises in Turkish higher education do not have obscure origins; they derive mainly from institutional and cultural factors and behind them lie corruption and greed.

According to Riggio and Newstead (2023) the key competencies for crisis leadership are communication, decision-making, coordinating resources, sense-making, facilitating teamwork and facilitating learning. In the context of this chapter, decision-making and coordinating resources are of relevance because most of the crises in Turkish higher education are related to both. This chapter argues that Complexity Leadership Theory (CLT) as one of the newly emerging leadership models can help to deal with crises in Turkish higher education. According to CLT, leadership should be seen "*not only as position and authority but also as an emergent, interactive dynamic—a complex interplay from which a collective impetus for action and change emerges when heterogeneous agents interact in networks in ways that produce new patterns of behaviour or new modes of operating*" (cited in Uhl-Bien et al., 2007, p. 299). This model distinguishes leadership from managerial positions and sees leadership as an activity that occurs throughout the organisation.

The fundamental unit of analysis in complexity leadership is referred to as a complex adaptive system, or CAS. This leadership is viewed as an interactive system of dynamic, unpredictable agents that interact with each other in complex feedback networks which can then produce adaptive outcomes such as knowledge dissemination, learning, innovation, and further adaptation to change (Uhl-Bien et al., 2007). CLT has been developed to explain how CAS operates in a bureaucratic organisation, and it identifies three broad types of leadership: adaptive (i.e. bottom-up oriented), enabling and administrative (i.e. top-down oriented). Adaptive leadership emerges within a complex milieu of mechanisms and contexts. CLT exists in complex network contexts and produces (and also is produced by) complex mechanisms. Enabling leadership is useful for the conditions to address creative problem solving, adaptability and learning while administrative leadership refers to the actions of individuals in formal managerial roles (Uhl-Bien et al., 2007). In CLT, these three leadership functions are intertwined in a way that is known as entanglement. Entanglement refers to a dynamic relationship between the formal top-down forces (i.e., bureaucracy) and the informal, adaptive emergent forces (i.e., CAS) of social systems (Kontopoulos, 1993). Despite being a systems theory, the leadership component itself in CLT has an important role: whenever an event occurs and people react and adapt to it, innovation and creativity can happen (Schophuizen et al., 2022).

Today's world is based on knowledge economy and this era wherein HEIs operate is driven by globalisation, technology, deregulation and democratisation. CLT sees leadership as an emergent, interactive dynamic that is productive of adaptive outcomes while providing space for change and innovation (Uhl-Bien & Arena 2017). CLT sees social networks as the driving force behind performance and change which require autonomy and self-responsibility. Now that production of knowledge and innovation is critical to organisational survival in the contemporary world such a leadership model can cope with complex crises faced today including the ones in HEIs.

## An Analysis of Crises in Turkish Higher Education

In Turkish higher education, most of the crises have derived from a variety of causes such as lack of meritocracy. It can be said that the crises most of the time have derived from the flaws of administrative agents (i.e. government or university management). In addition to that, it is not hard to observe that the leadership cadres of Turkish HEIs including rectors, deans, heads of departments and even the YÖK members (The Council of Turkish Higher Education) are far from implementing the principles required by complexity leadership model. University leadership practices in Türkiye have been products of top-down, bureaucratic mentality and they are not well-suited for a knowledge-oriented higher education sector that is evident in today's knowledge era.

## The Distance Education Crisis

After the outbreak of COVID-19, the repeated lockdowns caused the suspension of in-person education. The lockdown measures compelled educators and learners to utilise online tools through a shift to distance education. YÖK made a number of arrangements in order to achieve the new standard in the functioning of HEIs. On 23 March 2020, the digital course contents were published on YÖK courses platform. The digital course materials of 27 undergraduate, 47 associate degrees and 7 undergraduate completion programmes were published (YÖK, 2020). The distance education that has been carried out through digital platforms since the outbreak of the pandemic finished in 2022 fall term.

A second shift to distance education happened in February 2023 after a major earthquake with a magnitude of 7.8 near the Syria border had hit the country causing tens of thousands of casualties. As such natural disasters disrupt academic operations, after the earthquake, Erdoğan announced that all universities would be closed until summer and their residence halls would be used to accommodate the earthquake victims. Subsequently, YÖK (2023) declared that the universities will shift to distance education while stating that if certain conditions are met, the hybrid education option, which also offers face-to-face education will be taken into consideration. This second shift to distance education caused reactions centred on the argument of learning losses that ld should have been bewared. Many protested government's decision of using university residence halls for earthquake victims and they argued that hotels can be used to this aim. The distance education crisis experienced during the pandemic has not been experienced only in Türkiye. Many other countries faced similar challenges as a result of the sudden shift to online teaching. The crisis did not occur as a result of long-lasting problems in higher education like that of meritocracy problem.

## Lack of Meritocracy in Appointments

Meritocracy is a system of management and organisation in which appointments and placements are made based on job-related suitability, knowledge and qualifications rather than unwarranted bases such as wealth, and political power (Sealy, 2010). In meritocratic systems, it is accepted that merit is the most fundamental condition for the appointment of individuals, thus social discrimination is to be eliminated and only the merit of individuals is to be considered (Tannock, 2008). However in the Turkish context, in most cases, the appointment of academics is far from meritocracy (Demirbilek, 2023). Many rector appointments which cause scandalous outcomes not only threaten the fundamental operation of universities but also compromise universities' reputations.

In the period between 1992 and 2016, rectors in Türkiye were appointed in a three-stage system. Firstly, faculty members elected six rector candidates and three of the candidates were selected by YÖK and presented to the president. The president used to appoint one of the candidates. After the failed coup attempt, this system changed and an amendment based on a state of emergency decree revision was made (Gözler, 2019). Rectors have been appointed directly by the president since 2018. With a decree law dated July 2018 YÖK's authority to propose candidates was terminated (Gözler, 2019). In this system, arbitrariness, favouritism and patronage are inevitable and this leads to a decrease in the quality of education. Karadağ who examined the rectors of 197 universities (127 public and 70 private universities) in Türkiye showed the qualitative and quantitative decrease in international rankings of the universities. According to Karadağ (2021) 29% of the rectors had no citations in Scopus, and 36% had no citations in Web of Science. Especially since 2018, some of the rectors have been appointed based on their loyalty to ruling elites rather than their academic qualifications.

## Boğaziçi University Rectorate Crisis

On January 1, 2021, Erdoğan appointed Melih Bulu as the rector of Boğaziçi University. Bulu who had previously applied to be a candidate for AKP was the first rector appointed from outside the university's community. Boğaziçi University had informally held internal elections for rector appointment, but after the failed coup attempt this process changed.

Boğaziçi University has been seen as the best state university by many due to its high-quality education and history stretching back 150 years. Bulu as the first rector appointed from outside university's community was regarded as a "trustee" rector and his appointment sparked months of protests causing hundreds of arrests. 159 people were detained over protests in February 2021 (Reuters, 2021). Due to the pressure created by continuous protests, Bulu was eventually removed from his position in the same way as he was placed there, that is by a presidential decree (Middle East Eye, 2021). Instead of Bulu, Naci İnci was appointed in August 2021 and following that, the acting-deans were replaced by permanent appointees from outside the university, once again in violation of Boğaziçi's long-standing traditions. The lack of merit-based appointments in academia caused crises which have devastating impacts such as the decrease in international rankings of the universities and the weakening of academic freedoms.

## Academic Freedom Besieged by Pressure and Censorship

Academic freedom guarantees the existence and protection of a scientific atmosphere (UNESCO, 1992). An important requirement of academic freedom is that academics should be able to publish freely. Pressure negatively affects the intellectual development of academics. More than half of all academics in Türkiye do not feel free while sharing their opinions and findings in their publications (Taştan et al., 2020). Academic Freedom Index notes that for the period between 2011 and 2021 major declines in academic freedom were evident in Brazil, Türkiye and Thailand (Kinzelbach et al., 2023). Based on this fact, it is not hard to say that academics in Türkiye cannot freely express their thoughts.

Academic freedom and academic autonomy are generally defined as interrelated but they are separate concepts. Academic autonomy is described as "*the independence of institutions of higher education from the State and all other forces of society, to make decisions regarding its internal government, finance, administration, and to establish its policies of education, research, extension work and other related activities*" (cited in Taştan et al., 2020, p. 15). Academic autonomy is recognised as a right and authority of HEIs while academic freedom is accepted as an individual right.

It is known that academic research in Türkiye has been under the shadow of a number of politically controversial topics like the Kurdish question. Academics are either censored or self-censored while publishing about these topics. Furthermore, the existence of an institution called CIMER (Presidential Communication Center) has been one of the main factors for censorship and self-censorship. This institution emerged as an organ targeting the transmission of wishes and complaints to the presidency. Everything taught in class risks being transmitted to this institution. Not surprisingly, this has caused self-censorship among many academics.

To question or oppose the dominant ideology may result in job loss, mobbing or even detentions. Academic activity "*has been penalized, oppressed and finally dismissed at every instance when it is deemed to be contrary to the* de facto *principles determined by political, financial, ideological and cultural norms*" (Taştan et al., 2020, p. 1). The lack of academic freedom is not a new problem. After the first military coup in 1960, several academics were dismissed. Similar purges occurred after 1971 military intervention and 1980 military coup as well. The academics who had been dismissed after 1980 could return to their posts only by a court decision in 1990 (Okçabol, 2007). A massive wave of university purges took place in the aftermath of the failed coup attempt of 2016. The number of academics expelled from universities by statutory decrees after the coup attempt exceeds 20 times the number of academics purged in all coup periods. The number of dismissed academics is more than 5000 (T24, 2017). A total of 4811 academics have been sacked with a string of executive decrees approximately 20 times more than the number of academics who lost their jobs in all the military coups combined (cited in Özkırımlı, 2017). Among these academics, the criminalised academics who signed a petition in 2016 is an important case (The Case of Academics for Peace) to be mentioned.

## The Case of Academics for Peace

The criminalisation of 1128 academics and Ph.D. students started after the petition "We will not be a party to this crime" was made public in January 2016. The petition was penned as a reaction to the government's anti-terror operations in Kurdish-dominated towns from August 2015 to January 2016. In the petition, the academics sought a negotiated solution to the protracted military conflict between the Turkish state and the PKK (Kurdistan Workers' Party). The signatories demanded the Turkish state "*to abandon the deliberate massacre and deportation*" of Kurdish and other peoples in the region (Butler & Ertür, 2017, p. 1). Erdoğan called the petitioners "pseudo-intellectuals, full of darkness" (Agos Daily, 2016). Hundreds of academics have lost their jobs by signing this petition. Some academics were sentenced to prison terms ranging from 15 to 36 months. For example Prof. Füsun Üstel went to prison on May 8, 2019. On July 26, 2019, the General Assembly of the Constitutional Court concluded in the application of "Üstel and others" that the freedom of expression was violated (Human Rights Foundation of Türkiye, 2020).

### Şehir University Closure

Şehir University was founded in 2008 whose founders included Ahmet Davutoğlu, who served as a foreign minister and prime minister but then left AKP and set up his own political party. Şehir University was once a beacon for conservatives before the University got closed down in June 2020 after a midnight decree issued by Erdoğan. The stated justification for the decision was the financial incapacity of the university to continue its activities. State-led bank Halkbank had declared the collateral for the loan worthless based on the administrative stay, and proceeded to freeze the university's accounts. Despite having millions of dollars in income, the university found itself unable to pay the salaries of its professors. The timing of the asset freeze, soon after Davutoğlu withdrew from the AKP led to speculation that the action was politically motivated (Middle East Eye, 2020). According to Hasan Kösebalaban (2020) who previously worked as a professor in Şehir University, the closure of Şehir can be seen as a sort of punishment and it is a blow to academic freedom.

## Conclusion

This chapter has addressed the crises of Turkish higher education from a historical perspective. It can be argued that many of the crises mentioned can be seen as scandals and behind them lie corruption and greed. Several factors including political situation, structural factors and cultural mechanisms have played a role in the outbreak and maintenance of the crises; however lacks of academic freedom and meritocracy have had a huge impact. In countries like Türkiye wherein universities are under government control, and there are many restrictions on academics. The challenge of instituting academic freedom is considerable. In addition to academic freedom, another critical factor that fed the crises is lack of meritocracy. The appointment of rectors by the president alone has most of the time been witnessed in authoritarian regimes, during periods of emergencies such as military coups. In such cases, an obedience-based hierarchical ruling system similar to autocracy exists. The principles of justice, equity and merit are easily disregarded, and the person or institution holding the authority to appoint can appoint and dismiss any person they want. In fact, much of the hiring process in academia is not based on meritocracy and this ultimately creates a crisis characterised by the diminish in academic integrity and quality.

The problems arising from current crises had a dramatic impact on the universities. The increasing patronage relations and nepotism have played a key role in the diminishing of academic freedoms. To combat with the mentioned crises requires not only the transformation of universities but also the transformation of mentality, political structure and existing institutions. Even though the crises have derived from the decisions made by administrative agents the remedies can come into being through a strong and innovative leadership model. Complexity leadership moves beyond the logics of the industrial age to meet the new leadership requirements of the knowledge era. Complexity leadership recognises the dynamic interactions that take place within organisations and puts a focus on complex relationships and network interaction rather than controlling, standardising and autocracy (Uhl-Bien & Marion, 2009). With the help of this model, educational leaders can seek out practices, values and ideas beyond the university's walls. In such a way, the universities can become capable of responding to interconnected political, financial and social challenges.

Whether the inescapable global crisis such as COVID-19 or other crises on a smaller scale all require a leadership model that meets the demands and needs of today's world which can be defined as "knowledge era". This era requires the kind of leaders who can enable learning and innovation in complex environments such as universities. This requires a move from the top-down-oriented managerial structures to the bottom-up and interactive processes. If the leaders can balance top-down coordination (administrative leadership) and bottom-up informal emergence (adaptive leadership) they can enable innovative capacity and manage the crises more efficiently.

## References

Agos Daily. (2016, December 1). Erdoğan targets "Academics for Peace": You are ignorant, June 15, 2023. https://www.agos.com.tr/en/article/13978/erdogan-targets-academics-for-peace-you-are-ignorant

Akar, H. (2010). Globalization and its challenges for developing countries: The case of Turkish higher education. *Asia Pacific Education Review, 11*(3), 447–457. https://doi.org/10.1007/s12564-010-9086-0

Akduman, I., Özkale, L., & Ekinci, E. (2001). Accreditation in Turkish universities. *European Journal of Engineering Education, 26*(3), 231–239. https://doi.org/10.1080/03043790110053374

Akyüz, Y. (2001). *Türk eğitim tarihi* [*Turkish education history*]. Alf.

Altbach, P. (2007). Academic freedom: International realities and challenges. In *Tradition and transition* (pp. 49–66). Brill.

Anadolu Agency. (2020, March 12). İbrahim Kalın 'koronavirüs' toplantısında alınan tedbirleri açıkladı. [İbrahim Kalın announced the measures taken at the 'coronavirus' meeting]. March 20, 2023. https://www.aa.com.tr/tr/koronavirus/ibrahim-kalin-koronavirus-toplantisinda-alinan-tedbirleri-acikladi/1763918

Anadolu Agency. (2021, January 5). Türiye fights COVID-19 with 17 new hospitals. March 20, 2023. https://www.aa.com.tr/en/health/turkey-fights-covid-19-with-17-new-hospitals/2098332

Avolio, B., Walumbwa, F., & Weber, T. (2009). Leadership: Current theories, research, and future directions. *Annual Review of Psychology, 60*, 421–449. https://doi.org/10.1146/annurev.psych.60.110707.163621

Aybet, G. (2006). Türkiye and the EU after the first year of negotiations: Reconciling internal and external policy challenges. *Security Dialogue, 37*(4), 529–549. https://doi.org/10.1177/0967010606072947

Aydüz, S. (2008). Ottoman contributions to science and technology. March 21, 2023. https://muslimheritage.com/ottoman-contributions-to-science-and-technology/

Bonk, R., Kefalaki, M., Rudolph, J., Diamantidaki, F., Munro, C., Karanicolas, S., Kontoleon, P., & Pogner, K. (2020). Pedagogy in the time of pandemic: From localisation to glocalisation. *Journal of Education, Innovation, and Communication, 2*(SI1), 17–64. https://doi.org/10.34097/jeicom_SP_june2020_1

Burak, B. (2022). Teaching nation-building and nationalism: A critical perspective of Turkish academia. *Journal of Applied Learning and Teaching*, *5*(1), 89–98. https://doi.org/10.37074/jalt.2022.5.1.10

Butler, J., & Ertür, B. (2017). Trials begin in Turkey for academics for peace. http://criticallegalthinking.com/2017/12/11/Trials-Begin-Turkey-Academics-Peace/

Castilla, E. (2008). Gender, race, and meritocracy in organisational careers. *American Journal of Sociology, 113*(6), 1479–1526.

Crawford, J. (2023). COVID-19 and higher education: A pandemic response model from rapid adaption to consolidation and restoration. *International Education Journal: Comparative Perspectives, 22*(1), 7–29.

Crawford, J., Butler-Henderson, K., Rudolph, J., Malkawi, B., Glowatz, M., Burton, R. Magni P., & Lam, S. (2020). COVID-19: 20 countries' higher education intra-period digital pedagogy responses. *Journal of Applied Learning & Teaching*, *3*(1), 1–20. https://doi.org/10.1680/geot.2008.T.003

Dalay, G. (2022). Deciphering Turkey's geopolitical balancing and anti-westernism in its relations with Russia. April 20, 2023. https://www.swp-berlin.org/en/publication/deciphering-turkeys-geopolitical-balancing-and-anti-westernism-in-its-relations-with-russia

Dam P. (2021). EU should make human rights core in agenda with Turkey. March 10, 2023. https://www.hrw.org/news/2021/06/22/eu-should-make-human-rights-core-agenda-turkey

Demirbilek, N. (2023). Academics look on the concept of "merit." *Smart Learning Environments, 10*(17), 1–13. https://doi.org/10.1186/s40561-023-00238-w

Dinh, J., Lord, R., Gardner, W., Meuser, J., Liden, R., & Hu, J. (2014). Leadership theory and research in the new millennium: Current theoretical trends and changing perspectives. *The Leadership Quarterly, 25*(1), 36–62. https://doi.org/10.1016/j.leaqua.2013.11.005

Dündar, H., & Lewis, D. (1999). Equity, quality and efficiency effects of reform in Turkish higher education. *Higher Education Policy, 12*(4), 343–366. https://doi.org/10.1016/S0952-8733(99)00016-1

Erden, Z. (2006). *Histories, institutional regimes and educational organisations: The case of Turkish higher education* [Unpublished Ph.D. thesis, Sabancı University].

European Research Area and Innovative Committee. (2014). *Open, merit-based and transparent recruitment*. Final paper for the 2014 ERAC mutual learning workshop on Human Resources and Mobility. April 5, 2023. https://euraxess.ec.europa.eu/sites/default/files/policy_library/report_on_open.pdf

Freely, J. (2000). *A history of Robert college: The American college for girls, and Boğaziçi university* (p. 1). YKY.

Gözler, K. (2019). Türkiye'de 1992'den günümüze rektör atama sistemi [Rector appointment system in Türkiye from 1992 up to today]. April 5, 2023. https://www.anayasa.gen.tr/cbhs-ek-8.pdf

Güçlü, M. (2020). How Turkish universities have evolved through constitutional changes. *Educational Research and Reviews, 15*(3), 86–94. https://doi.org/10.5897/ERR2019.3867

Gürüz, K., Suhubi, E., Surgor, A., Turker, K., & Yurtsever, E. (1994). Higher education, science and technology in Turkey and in the world. *Turkish Industrialist and Businessmen Association (TÜSIAD) Pub*, 6–167.

Hermann, C. F. (1963). Some consequences of crisis which limit the viability of organisations. *Administrative Science Quarterly, 8*(1), 61–82.

Human Rights Foundation of Türkiye. (2020). Academics for peace: report on the current situation. April 8, 2023. https://tihvakademi.org/wp-content/uploads/2020/09/AfP_Current_Situation_August_2020.pdf

Karadağ, E. (2021). Academic (dis) qualifications of Turkish rectors: Their career paths, H-index, and the number of articles and citations. *Higher Education, 81*(2), 301–323. https://doi.org/10.1007/s10734-020-00542-1

Kinzelbach, K., Lindberg, S., Pelke, L., & Spannagel, J. (2023). Academic freedom index–2023 update.

Kontopoulos, K. (1993). *The logics of social structure* (pp. 243–267). Cambridge University Press.

Kösebalaban, H. (2020, July 10). The Turkish government closed a university because it fears free speech. March 5, 2023. https://foreignpolicy.com/2020/07/10/the-turkish-government-closed-a-university-because-it-fears-free-speech/

Marcus, A., & Goodman, R. S. (1991). Victims and shareholders: The dilemmas of presenting corporate policy during a crisis. *Academy of Management Journal, 34*(2), 281–305.

Marion, R., & Uhl-Bien, M. (2001). Leadership in complex organisations. *Leadership Quarterly, 12*, 389–418. https://doi.org/10.1016/S1048-9843(01)00092-3

Middle East Eye. (2020, June 30). Erdogan shuts down Turkish university linked to rival Davutoglu. April 2, 2023. https://www.middleeasteye.net/news/turkey-erdogan-davutoglu-istanbul-sehir-university

Middle East Eye. (2021, July 15). Türkiye: Erdogan rescinds controversial appointment of Bogazici University rector. February 5, 2023. https://www.middleeasteye.net/news/turkey-bogazici-university-erdogan-melih-bulu-rector

Okçabol, R. (2007). *Tarihsel süreçte yükseköğretim, yükseköğretim sistemimiz* [*Higher education in historical process, our higher education system*]. Ütopya.

Özkirimli, U. (2017). How to liquidate a people? Academic freedom in Turkey and beyond. *Globalizations, 14*(6), 851–856. https://doi.org/10.1080/14747731.2017.1325171

Preskill, S., & Brookfield, S. (2009). *Learning as a way of leading*. Jossey-Bass.

Reuters. (2021, February 2). Turkish police detain 159 people at protests over Erdogan-appointed university head. April 6, 2023. https://www.reuters.com/article/us-turkey-security-bogazici-idUSKBN2A13P6

Riggio, R., & Newstead, T. (2023). Crisis leadership. *Annual Review of Organisational Psychology and Organisational Behavior, 10*, 201–224. https://doi.org/10.1146/annurev-orgpsych-120920-044838

Saraç, Y. (2021, March 3). The impact of online education during COVID-19 pandemic in Turkish higher education. April 6, 2023. https://www.aa.com.tr/en/analysis/analysis-the-impact-of-online-education-during-covid-19-pandemic-in-turkish-higher-education/2163525

Schophuizen, M., Kelly, A., Utama, C., Specht, M., & Kalz, M. (2022). Enabling educational innovation through complexity leadership? Perspectives from four Dutch universities. *Tertiary Education and Management, 29*, 471–490. https://doi.org/10.1007/s11233-022-09105-8

Sealy, R. (2010). Changing perceptions of meritocracy in senior women's careers. *Gender in Management: An International Journal, 25*(3), 184–197. https://doi.org/10.1108/17542411011036392

Sputnik. (2020, March 30). Erdoğan milli dayanışma kampanyasını duyurdu [Erdoğan announced national solidarity campaign]. April 10, 2023. https://web.archive.org/web/20200331103822/https:/tr.sputniknews.com/turkiye/202003301041721380-cumhurbaskani-erdogan-aciklama-yapiyor/

Şimşek, H. (1999). 1990'lı yıllarda Türk eğitim sistemi. [Turkish education system in 1990s]. April 6, 2023. https://www.um.edu.mt/library/oar/bitstream/123456789/18873/1/Turkish%20higher%20education%20system%20in%20the%201990s.pdf

Sozen, S., & Shaw, I. (2003). Turkey and the European Union: Modernizing a traditional state? *Social Policy & Administration, 37*(2), 108–120. https://doi.org/10.1111/1467-9515.00328

T24. (2017, February 10). 15 Temmuz KHK'larıyla ihraç edilen akademisyen sayısı tüm darbe dönemlerindeki ihracın 20 katı! [The number of academics dismissed through the July 15 decree laws is 20 times higher than the number of dismissals in all coup periods!]. April 6,

2023. https://t24.com.tr/haber/15-temmuz-khklariyla-ihrac-edilen-akademisyen-sayisi-tum-darbe-donemlerindeki-ihracin-20-kati,388022

Tannock, S. (2008). The problem of education-based discrimination. *British Journal of Sociology of Education, 29*(5), 439–449. https://doi.org/10.1080/01425690802326846

Taştan, İ., Ördek, A., & Öz, F. (2020). *A report on academic freedoms in Turkey in the period of the state of emergency*. Kaged. https://www.ohchr.org/sites/default/files/Documents/Issues/Opinion/Submissions/Academics/INSAN_HAKLARI_OKULU3.pdf

The Guardian. (2023, May 29). Turkey election 2023 live: Erdoğan declared victor in presidential election—As it happened. June 3, 2023. https://www.theguardian.com/world/live/2023/may/28/turkey-election-live-recep-tayyip-erdogan-kemal-kilicdaroglu-turkish-president-runoff

Tice, D., Baumeister, R., Crawford, J., Allen, K. A., & Percy, A. (2021). Student belongingness in higher education: Lessons for Professors from the COVID-19 pandemic. *Journal of University Teaching & Learning Practice, 18*(4), 2. https://doi.org/10.53761/1.18.4.2

Times Higher Education. (2023). Best Universities in Turkey in 2023. June 24, 2023. https://www.timeshighereducation.com/student/best-universities/best-universities-turkey

Timur, T. (2000). *Toplumsal degişme ve üniversiteler* (*Societal change and universities*). Imge.

TRT. (2020, March 11). Türkiye'de ilk koronavirüs vakası tespit edildi. [The first case of coronavirus was detected in Türkiye]. April 6, 2023. https://www.trthaber.com/haber/gundem/turkiyede-ilk-koronavirus-vakasi-tespit-edildi-466216.html

Tural, N. (2004). *Küreselleşme ve üniversiteler* [*Globalization and universities*]. Kök.

Turkish Ministry of Interior Affairs. (2020). Şehir giriş/çıkış tebirleri ve yaş sınırlaması. [City entry/exit regulations and age limitation]. April 10, 2023. https://www.icisleri.gov.tr/sehir-giriscikis-tebirleri-ve-yas-sinirlamasi

Turkish Ministry of Interior Affairs. (2022). Kilis Valiliği'nden Suriyeli sayısı iddialarına cevap [Reply from the Kilis Governorate to the claims of the number of Syrians]. August 16, 2023.

Turkish Statistical Institute. (2021). Population report for 2021. April 6, 2023. https://data.tuik.gov.tr/Bulten/Index?p=The-Results-of-Address-Based-Population-Registration-System-2021-45500

Uhl-Bien, M., Marion, R., & McKelvey, B. (2007). Complexity leadership theory: Shifting leadership from the industrial age to the knowledge era. *The Leadership Quarterly, 18*(4), 298–318. https://doi.org/10.1016/j.leaqua.2007.04.002

Uhl-Bien, M., & Arena, M. (2017). Complexity leadership. *Organisational Dynamics, 46*, 30–58. https://doi.org/10.1016/j.orgdyn.2016.12.001

Uhl-Bien, M., & Marion, R. (2009). Complexity leadership in bureaucratic forms of organizing: A meso model. *The Leadership Quarterly, 20*, 631–650. https://doi.org/10.1016/j.leaqua.2009.04.007

UNESCO. (1992). Academic freedom and university autonomy: Proceedings of the international conference 5–7 May 1992, Sinaia, Romania.

Visakorpi, J., Stankovic F., Pedrosa J., & Rozsnyai C. (2008). *Higher education in Turkey: Trends, challenges, opportunities* (EUA European University Association, TUSIAD, Publication No: T-2008-10/473).

Weick, K. (1988). Enacted sensemaking in crisis situations. *Journal of Management Studies, 25*(4), 305–317.

Wooten, L., & James, E. (2008). Linking crisis management and leadership competencies: The role of human resource development. *Advances in Developing Human Resources, 10*(3), 352–379. https://doi.org/10.1177/1523422308316450

World Bank. (2023). Turkey overview. September 21, 2023. https://www.worldbank.org/en/country/turkey/overview

Worldometer. (2023). Worldometer elaboration of the latest UN data for Turkey's population. April 6, 2023. https://www.worldometers.info/world-population/turkey-population/

Wilson, S., Tan, S., Knox, M., Ong, A., Crawford, J., & Rudolph, J. (2020). Enabling cross-cultural student voice during COVID-19: A collective autoethnography. *Journal of University Teaching & Learning Practice, 17*(5), 3. https://doi.org/10.53761/1.17.5.3

Wu, Y., Shao, B., Newman, A., & Schwarz, G. (2021). Crisis leadership: A review and future research agenda. *The Leadership Quarterly, 32*(6), 101518. https://doi.org/10.1016/j.leaqua.2021.101518

YÖK. (n.d.). History. April 10, 2023. https://www.yok.gov.tr/en/institutional/history

YÖK. (n.d.). Universities in Türkiye. August 18, 2023. https://www.yok.gov.tr/universiteler/universitelerimiz

YÖK. (2005). Türk yüksek ögretiminin bugünkü durumu. [The current status of Turkish higher education]. April 6, 2023. https://www.yok.gov.tr/Documents/Yayinlar/Yayinlarimiz/Turk-yuksekogretiminin-bugunku-durumu-kasim-2005.pdf

YÖK. (2020). YÖK dersleri platformu öğrencilerin erişimine açıldı [YÖK courses platform open to students' access]. April 6, 2023. https://www.yok.gov.tr/HaberBelgeleri/BasinDuyurusu/2020/yok-dersleri-platformu-erisime-acildi.pdf

YÖK. (2023). Statement of Erol Özvar. April 6, 2023. https://www.yok.gov.tr/en/Sayfalar/news/2023/cohe-president-erol-ozvar-s-statement-regarding-spring-term-of-2022-2023-academic-year.aspx

# Management of Higher Education Learning and Teaching Through Crisis: A Benchmark for Improved Future Learning in Uganda

Kizito Omona, Jonathan Kizito Ssuka, Richard Ouma, Kizito Nalela, Jane Florence Amoding, Susan Arayo, and Modest O.'dama Kayi

## Introduction: Crisis Leadership in Higher Education Institutions

Crisis leadership is the ability of employees, managers, or individual stakeholders to deal with an emergency. Such leadership is usually characterised by (a) a threat to the organisation, (b) the element of surprise or emergency, (c) a

K. Omona (✉)
Faculty of Health Sciences, Uganda Martyrs University, Kampala, Uganda
e-mail: komona@umu.ac.ug

J. K. Ssuka
Public Health Department, VODA, Mukono, Uganda

R. Ouma
Department of Programme Accreditation, National Council for Higher Education, Kampala, Uganda

K. Nalela · J. F. Amoding
Faculty of Business Administration and Management, Uganda Martyrs University, Kampala, Uganda

S. Arayo
Department of Governance, Peace and International Studies at School of Arts and Social Sciences, Uganda Martyrs University, Kampala, Uganda

M. O. Kayi
Faculty of Education, Uganda Martyrs University, Kampala, Uganda



J. Rudolph et al. (eds.), *The Palgrave Handbook of Crisis Leadership in Higher Education*, https://doi.org/10.1007/978-3-031-54509-2_30

short decision time, and (d) a need for change. Ngubane (2017) defined crisis leadership as the process by which an organisation deals with a major unpredictable event(s) that threatens to cripple the organisation, its stakeholders, or the public. It applies strategies to help an institution or organisation deal with a sudden and significant adverse event.

In ideal circumstances (Brookfield et al., 2023; Fiedler & Garcia, 1987), effective education leaders should know how to manage change effectively whether teaching in the classroom, leading an education institution, an early learner programming, or even helping to improve large scale education systems in the wake of crisis. They should listen, guide, and motivate others using change to leverage innovative thinking and inspire lasting positive reforms (Brookfield et al., 2023). Impactful leaders work with integrity and are accountable to those they serve. Most importantly, they use their skills to support equity, inclusivity, and fairness to ensure the well-being of all (Bonk et al., 2020; Schechter et al., 2022; Smith & Riley, 2012).

In a study in Singapore, Bonk et al. (2020) asserted that responses to the COVID-19 pandemic required leadership from all to leverage a firm. It needed steady presence, care, and compassion for each other, and prudent decision-making. They found that changes to courses and curricula needed to respond to the emotional needs of the students when transitioning from face-to-face (or hybrid) to online delivery, and administration or leaders must ensure that academic rigour is not sacrificed in the process. Secondly, the mission and value of higher education must indicate that institutions will recommit to faculty support beyond emergency remote teaching. Thirdly, the needs of students and faculty must drive the choices of technology when determining how to transition to online deliveries (Bonk et al., 2020; Rudolph et al., 2022).

In crisis leadership, we strive to keep true to the mission but are flexible in strategies and structures (O'day, 2022; Schechter et al., 2022). For sustained successful crisis leadership, the leader must be adaptable, empathetic, prepared, resilient, transparent, and trustworthy (Gigliotti, 2023). However, it must also be noted that crises can lead to opportunities for innovation and improvement (Crawford et al., 2020; Ngubane, 2017; O'day, 2022). This is coined in the mastery of teaching well, which requires good knowledge of the classroom dynamic. It means the willingness to do anything that helps students learn and delving into investigating the fundamental principle of what teaching effectively entails by exploring the critical dynamics of a learning-centred classroom (Brookfield et al., 2023).

# A Year Without Precedent in Uganda: COVID-19 Experience of Higher Education Institutions

## Background of Ugandan Universities

Uganda has both public and private universities. A public university is a higher education institution established by the Ministry of Education and Sports with approval by Parliament under section 22 and is maintained by public funds (UHEQF, 2016). The reverse is valid for a private university in Uganda. Public universities are situated in the social-public paradigm, which refers to a system or education organisation built on common ideas or standards. In a more expanded form, it implies a philosophy guiding a specific educational institution. The social-public paradigm examines the government's role in providing social services, including education. It is divided into two sub-paradigms: the restrictive and liberal categories. The restrictive category implies that only the government provides university education, whereas the liberal category implies that the government accommodates co-sharing in funding or providing university education (Muwagga, 2006; Nawangwe et al., 2021). Meanwhile, private universities in Uganda have diverse paradigmatic pivots; some are for-profit, whereas others have some social and community dimensions, especially those owned by religious organisations and non-governmental organisations (Muwagga, 2006).

## Higher Education Challenges Prior to Covid-19

Prior to the COVID-19 crisis, Uganda's education system had some significant challenges (Kibalirwandi & Mwesigye, 2021; Omona, 2021) which affected the educational system:

1. Inequalities in access to higher education; Wide gap between the urban and rural population
2. Low funding of research and publication
3. Weak educational philosophy: Many education stakeholders do not explicitly know Uganda's university education philosophy. An education philosophy pivots on a nation's heritage, values, beliefs, people's perceptions and aspirations for their current and future life, and the world outlook.
4. Low morale of employees due to low remuneration or compensation
5. Job insecurity
6. Ineffective promotion in academic ranks
7. Employee mobility high

8. Community Outreach and Engagement during the COVID-19 was difficult
9. Research and innovation were varied; some institutions were high, and others were low.

So, by implication, when the COVID-19 pandemic struck the education system, it lacked the navigation devices for survival. Almost all private and newly created public universities went into disarray during the lockdown.

## Higher Education Experiences of COVID-19

Higher education experiences were classified into three categories: shift in education policy, experiences directly related to COVID-19 challenges and emerging post-COVID-19 realities.

a. **Shift in education policy**: Uganda had one of the most prolonged school closures worldwide as a response measure during the COVID-19 pandemic (two years). More than 73,200 schools and institutions closed, forcing over 15 million learners to stay home (Atwine, 2021). As the government locked down all sectors, including closing all schools at the peak of the coronavirus pandemic in 2020 and 2021, the ministry and NCHE pushed for the countrywide adoption of online and distance learning (ODeL) to facilitate continued learning during the lockdown (Maberi, 2022). The government had to explore various methods to keep children learning via radio, television (TV), and online learning using computers, phones, and the internet.
b. **COVID-19 challenges:** Before COVID-19, e-learning was weak and taken as a leisure activity. Experiences directly related to COVID-19 challenges and e-learning adoption resulted in the following:
    - Confusion and stress for lecturers: The closure was unexpected, and for unknown durations, lecturers were often unsure of their obligations and how to maintain connections with students to support learning. Transitions to distance learning platforms were messy and frustrating, causing lecturers' confusion and stress.
    - Loss of jobs: Many lecturers lost their jobs as universities tried to downsize the number of their employees to survive the COVID-19 period.
    - Challenges in creating, maintaining, and improving distance learning: Demand for distance learning skyrocketed, and remote education

portals were overwhelmed. Learning was moved from classrooms to homes at an accelerated pace.

- High economic costs: Lecturers missed work to take care of their other family responsibilities, resulting in wage loss and negatively impacting productivity. There was a lack of research, including collaborations across institutions, borders, and disciplines (World Bank, 2020).
- Challenges measuring and validating learning; calendar assessments, such as high-stakes examinations, were discontinued. Disruptions to assessments resulted in stress for students and their families and triggered disengagement.

c. **Post-COVID-19 realities**: A study of 109 health professional students at Clarke International University found that 71 (65.1%) adopted e-learning even though there were low odds of adoption of e-learning among participants in the first year (aOR, 0.34: 95%CI, 0.14–0.79), that is 66% less likely, low e-learning expectations (aOR, 0.01: 95%CI, 0.01–0.34) and no confidence in using IT devices (aOR, 0.16: 95%CI, 0.00–0.77), among others (Komuhangi et al., 2022). Many institutions are currently adopting a blended approach to learning (both online and physical) as a modality to survive in the post-Covid era. In some universities, students wedged strikes to abolish online learning (ODeL) from their university educational system.

## Ugandan Perspectives of E-learning in the COVID-19 Era

### What is E-learning?

Arbaugh (2002) and Arbaugh &Duray (2002)defined e-learning as the use of the internet by users to learn specific content. Meanwhile, Selim (2007) defined e-learning as using modern information and communications technology (ICT) and computers to deliver instruction, information, and learning content (Selim, 2007). Stakeholders of e-learning include learners, instructors, administrators, technical staff, and other employers (Fiedler & Garcia, 1987; Ozkan & Koseler, 2009). E-learning in Uganda flourished in the Covid era because there was no other alternative (Biira et al., 2021). Knowing how to lead through a crisis requires leaders to know what crises are, but establishing clear parameters around what constitutes a crisis is an elusive task. Unstable internet connectivity and power supply are among the hindrances to online learning, among other factors such as the cost of internet bundles, ICT gadgets familiarity, and others (Biira et al., 2021).

## What Are the Critical Success Drivers of E-learning in the Post-COVID-19 Era?

The critical success factors are based on three major theories: social cognitive theory, IS success model, and motivation theory. There are seven dimensions for e-learning success (Crawford, 2023; Schrum & Hong, 2002): learners' characteristics, instructors' characteristics, E-learning environment, institution and service quality, infrastructure and system quality, course, and information quality and lastly, motivation. See Fig. 1 for illustration:

1. **Information quality:** This is the quality of course content delivered through the course management system. Course content quality is the student's judgement of the degree to which course content management systems are provided with valuable content concerning the defined needs of the students. Information quality measures include personalisation, completeness, ease of understanding, security, timeliness, availability, relevance, and format of course contents delivered through the e-learning systems. Studies have shown that information quality significantly impacts the perceived usefulness of e-learning systems (Chen, 2010; Cheng, 2012). Thus, the quality of course content may be an essential reason for students to perceive the usefulness of e-learning systems and to have higher levels of satisfaction with using e-learning systems.

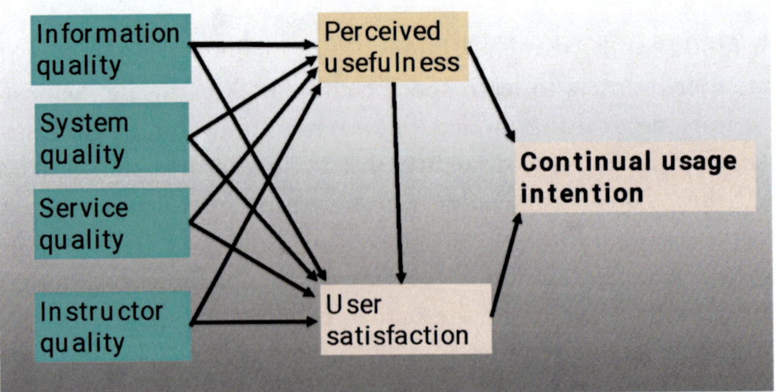


**Fig. 1** Critical success drivers of e-learning in the post-COVID-19 era

2. **System quality:** System quality measures the desired characteristics of the e-learning system. The metrics for system quality include responsiveness, usability, availability, reliability, and adaptability (Delone & Mclean, 2004). Studies showed that system quality is a significant predictor of the perceived usefulness of an e-learning system (Chen, 2010; Cheng, 2012). Consequently, system quality significantly determines user satisfaction with e-learning systems. Thus, the more students believe that web-based learning management systems are reliable, available, and easy to use, the more they will use them.
3. **Service quality:** Service quality refers to the overall support provided by the service provider, such as the ICT department, a specific unit in an organisation, or outsourced services (Delone & Mclean, 2004). Measures for service quality include responsiveness, effectiveness, and availability of technical support personnel. Cheng (2012) found service quality to be a valuable determinant of perceived usefulness in e-learning systems usage. Service quality is linked to previous experiences with information and communication technologies (Shih et al., 2006)
4. **Instructor quality:** Instructors are essential for shaping learners' behaviour in the e-learning course, and thus, their attitude may affect learners' behaviour (Cheng, 2012). Metrics of instructor's quality include instructor's response timeliness, teaching style, and explanation/help towards learners through the e-learning system. Studies found that instructor attitudes towards e-learners had a significant positive relationship with the perceived usefulness of the e-learning system (Cheng, 2012; Lee et al., 2009).
5. **Perceived usefulness:** This represents a perceptual signal of how much a stakeholder perceives that utilising a specific system has improved their job performance or the performance of their group or organisation (Seddon, 1997). In this case, perceived usefulness relates to the degree to which the students believe using the e-learning system will improve their learning performances. Several studies have acknowledged the strength of the perceived usefulness in determining the continual usage intention in technology acceptance (Pušnik et al., 2011; Venkatesh et al., 2003) and e-learning systems studies (Cheng, 2012). Also, prior studies showed that perceived usefulness significantly impacts user satisfaction with e-learning systems (Chen, 2010; Lin & Wang, 2012; Roca et al., 2006). Learners can more readily accept an e-learning system once they believe it will help them achieve their academic goals.
6. **User satisfaction:** This construct is a perception of a user's satisfaction with a system about what the user expected upon first use of the

system (Seddon, 1997). Satisfaction measures include adequacy, effectiveness, relevance, dependability, and usefulness (Urbach & Müller, 2012). Indeed, user satisfaction has a significant positive relationship with the continual usage intention of e-learning systems (Chen, 2010; Cho et al., 2009; Lee, 2010; Lin & Wang, 2012; Roca et al., 2006; Wang & Chiu, 2011).

## Impact of COVID-19 Pandemic on Educational Leadership and Management

Crises are "events perceived by leaders and organisational stakeholders as unexpected, highly salient, and potentially disruptive" (Wu et al., 2021, p. 2). Amidst the COVID-19 lockdown, every university in Uganda faced the task of conducting effective teaching and learning. Private universities encountered even more significant challenges, leading them to revoke employment agreements to prevent potential legal disputes with their staff (Nawangwe et al., 2021). Meanwhile, there is no situation where leadership is more critical than during a crisis, yet crisis leadership is a relatively underdeveloped field (Riggio & Newstead, 2023). So, knowing how to lead through a crisis requires leaders to know what crises are. One needs to consider the different causes and consequences of crises such as COVID-19 to see the complexity of delineating it precisely. Crisis implies difficulty and danger. Hermann (1963) defined crises as threatening an organisation's fundamental operation or viability. Crises are characterised by their low probability, indicating their infrequent nature. As a result, they often arise unexpectedly and with rare occurrences.

Nevertheless, these crises have significant repercussions, severely threatening an organisation's existence or core functioning (Hermann, 1963). The substantial impact of crises' consequences introduces time constraints; failing to address them swiftly affects the institution's survival. This precise scenario unfolded in Uganda, endangering the continued existence of numerous higher educational establishments and their leadership. Zawacki-Richter (2021) asserted that the unexpected COVID-19 pandemic created a setback for Higher Education Instructions and raised the question of whether the current practice of emergency remote teaching in the online term will lead to an acceleration of the digitalisation of teaching and learning and what we can build upon in this development. The discourse surrounding face-to-face teaching was somewhat illusory, as there was minimal evidence of it being under scrutiny. Despite this, not all universities swiftly became exclusively distance learning institutions. Nevertheless, it is crucial to highlight that employing digital media for teaching and learning always has advantages and disadvantages. For specific demographics, the availability of higher education through digital platforms, irrespective of temporal and spatial constraints, is the sole means of access.

In another study, Sá and Serpa (2020) and Rudolph et al. (2022) established that the educational dimension has also been affected by the universities' regular functioning and the impediment of face-to-face classes. It was argued that these challenging conditions could be a pivotal moment of opportunity for reshaping higher education with the implementation, development, and diffusion, among academics and students, of digital technologies. A similar finding (Ahmed, 2020) reached the undeniable conclusion that numerous online opportunities exist, surpassing the justifications concocted for not utilising them. In a study focused on transforming universities into interactive digital platforms, Habib et al. (2021) noted that, despite challenges, there has been a rise in the number of higher education institutions that have enthusiastically adopted ICT-driven educational systems.

## Government Responses to COVID-19 and Their Impact on Higher Education

The impact of COVID-19 extended beyond the global well-being and economies of countries; it also directly influenced academic domains worldwide, including Uganda. Nawangwe et al. (2021) indicated that by the time of the outbreak, almost all universities were ill-prepared for the pandemic, which resulted in multiple effects on higher education institutions countrywide. In response to the COVID-19 pandemic, the Ugandan government, working through the Ministries of Health and Education and Sports, implemented comprehensive national strategies to mitigate the spread of the virus within the population. When COVID-19 emerged in the country, there were a total of 314,548 students enrolled across 49 universities, along with 1543 students in various other tertiary institutions in Uganda (NCHE, 2020). As a result, under the Ministry of Health, the government established standard operating procedures (SOPs) that guided the re-opening of educational institutions after a prolonged closure period. To ensure strict adherence to these SOPs, the Ministry of Education also formulated guidelines distributed to school administrators, facilitating the effective implementation of measures (MoES, 2020).

The guidelines were designed to offer clear direction to all stakeholders within the education sector, ensuring the resumption of academic activities without contributing to the ongoing spread of the disease. These instructions encompassed several vital points, including a gradual approach to re-opening educational institutions. This approach dictated that only students in their final years or candidate classes could return to school (MoES, 2020). Additionally, the ministry encouraged educational institutions to establish accessible hand-washing facilities and emphasised the importance of students bringing their face masks. Furthermore, social distancing measures were strongly recommended as part of the health and hygiene protocols.

It cautioned learning institutions not to allow intruders or strangers into learning institutions to control the spread of the disease through contact. It advised that all visitors to learning institutions should be restricted and be registered for accessible case locations in case of any suspected infection. However, some of these measures had remarkable effects on higher education institutions, especially the private ones whose financial muscle depends on students' tuition and functional fees (Nawangwe et al., 2021; Tweheyo & Mugarura, 2021).

With this, many administrators had no option but to close the universities or downsize the number of staff to contain the financial costs. Both of these measures affected the workers in the said institutions. Furthermore, the reduction in the number of staff forced the institutions to increase the workload per staff, which was not commensurate with the remuneration and this demoralised workers in some institutions.

> "[...] we were forced to reduce the number of staff and instead increase the workload per staff." [an administrator from a private university around Kampala]

The reduced staff size made most casual university workers lose jobs through forced termination of their contracts to remain in the system by the institutions. This also affected those working under probation or whose approvals for the jobs were in the process in many of these institutions. It affected almost all private universities' teaching and non-teaching staff (Nawangwe et al., 2021).

> "[...] With the outbreak of the COVID-19 pandemic, university employees whose employment contracts were not permanent and pensionable were withdrawn [...]." (NCHE, 2021)

Further still, in a bid to ensure continuity of learning, the government advised administrators of higher institutions of learning to adopt the Open Distance and e-Learning (ODeL) model to minimise the risk of over-crowding and contacts with and among students in the typical classroom setting (NCHE, 2020). However, this also had challenges since most institutions had not yet installed robust IT systems, especially the private universities. There is still poor infrastructure to facilitate Internet and e-Learning as it was proposed by the Ministry of Education and Sports (Kaahwa et al., 2022). This coupled with the uneven distribution of electricity and lack of connection access equipment by the majority of students, especially from rural settings, made it harder for e-learning to be effective (Nawangwe et al., 2021; Tweheyo & Mugarura, 2021).

Moreover, a significant challenge arose as many students voiced concerns about the data costs imposed by the government. This situation hindered their ability to access learning materials and participate in lessons through the Open Distance and e-learning model, which had been highlighted as an essential approach. These and other factors collectively contributed to the complexities of implementing e-learning. A student attending a health professionals' college in the vicinity of Kampala was quoted expressing their experience, stating:

> "they used to send us work via the internet but at times, many of us couldn't afford data since we were not working and parents were looking for what to eat with the little they could get" (A student from a health professional college in Kampala)

Nevertheless, these standard operating procedures drastically impacted the running of higher education institutions due to the financial crisis. Many of the students left school for work and never returned. This affected many private higher learning institutions whose income depended on tuition fees. The prolonging of graduations for the finalists due to the pandemic came with much-unexplained pain to many students, with some resorting to other programmes and others dropping education even after the lockdown (Tweheyo & Mugarura, 2021).

Besides the closure of educational institutions, the government restricted the movement of people from one district to another and across borders, making it difficult for international and national students who were doing their research to interact with their supervisors physically. Students were only required to interact with their supervisors via the internet and phone, limited to those in towns and constrained by the economic crisis. In addition to poor internet infrastructure countrywide, only a few students could afford internet charges (Kara, 2021; World Bank, 2020).

Although the government tried to support its citizens with food relief, the educational workforce was left out, especially in private institutions. They tried to lobby the government, tutors, and lecturers in higher learning institutions to help without any positive results (Nawangwe et al., 2021). To uphold the integrity of the education curriculum, the government collaborated with the Ministry of Education and Sports and the National Curriculum Development Centre to create and disseminate learning materials for elementary and lower secondary schools (MoES, 2020). However, these efforts primarily focused on students in primary and lower secondary grades, with limited direct assistance from higher education institutions, particularly those in the private sector. Additionally, the government introduced remote learning initiatives through radio and television broadcasts tailored for learners at primary and secondary levels.

Although the government organised a remote learning programme for elementary and lower secondary levels, it mainly benefited the urban dwellers. This means its impact was limited to elementary levels (Kaahwa et al., 2022; NCHE, 2020; Tweheyo & Mugarura, 2021). Students' capacity to adapt to e-learning was low. Many, if not most, students are not experienced as online learners. While they may be quick to adapt, students face challenges that lead to dissatisfaction with their academic experience. Student feedback can be leveraged to strengthen teaching, but feedback can also risk exposing challenging frustrations (World Bank, 2020). However, while the closure of schools and other gatherings seemed to have a logical solution in enforcing social distancing in communities, it created social vulnerability, especially among disadvantaged students whose educational sustenance depended upon guardians' income (Tweheyo & Mugarura, 2021). This issue was projected to worsen beyond the pandemic, particularly among the most marginalised youth and adults (United Nations, 2020).

## Benchmarking and Quality Assurance for E-learning in Higher Education Institutions (HEIs) in Post-COVID-19 Era

Until March 2020, online learning was uncommon in Uganda's higher education institutions. After implementing lockdown measures in the country to prevent the spread of COVID-19, online learning became the dominant form of teaching and learning in Ugandan higher education institutions (HEIs).

However, the introduction of e-learning led to several problems related to quality assurance. Since the adoption of an increased usage of e-learning by higher education institutions (HEIs), studies have shown that most graduates failed to meet industry expectations due to an explicit mismatch between the industry expectations and HEIs offering (Yeung et al., 2019). Most academic institutions increasingly use learning management systems (Rudolph et al., 2022), also known as e-learning software, Course Management System (CMS), online learning software, or Virtual Learning Environment (VLE). Performance benchmarking and quality assurance are noticeably missing in most institutions of higher learning in Uganda (Masengu et al., 2023). Subsequent research validated that factors contributing to a lower ranking on the list of high-performing African universities might encompass, but are not restricted to, insufficient research funding and publication, reduced employee motivation owing to inadequate remuneration, job instability, ineffective promotion mechanisms within academic hierarchies, and limited employee mobility (Kibalirwandi & Mwesigye, 2021).

Benchmarking is commonly used to enhance quality and has been applied increasingly in various sectors. The concept of benchmarking refers to comparing processes, businesses, and performance metrics with the best practices of others. However, quality is multifaceted. According to Ossiannilsson (2023), "Its definition depends on who defines it, the context in which it is defined, and the maturity of those who define both the concept and its implications". In order to elevate the quality of Higher Education Institutions (HEIs), the guiding principles for e-learning should be organised into four distinct categories: (1) e-learning should be designed for active and effective learning; (2) e-learning should support the needs of learners; (3) the provider of e-learning should develop and maintain the technological and human infrastructure so that learners and learning facilitators are supported in their use of technologies; (4) e-learning programmes should be sustained by administrative and organisational commitment (Crawford, 2023).

In order to affect the four guiding principles stated above, four categories of benchmarks are required:

1. **Course development benchmarks**

   Guidelines for minimum set standards are required for e-learning course development, design, and delivery, whereas learning outcomes determine the technology used to deliver course content. Instructional materials need to be reviewed periodically to ensure they meet programme-set standards. The courses should be designed to require students to engage in analysis, synthesis, and evaluation as part of their course and programme requirements (Omona, 2022).

2. **Teaching/learning process benchmarks**

   Students' interaction with instructors and other students is essential in this benchmark. It is facilitated through various ways, including voice mail, e-mail, or other online tools such as Moodle. Feedback on student assignments and questions is constructive and provided promptly to the learners (Omona, 2022). Students are instructed in the proper methods of practical research, including assessment of validity issues.

3. **Course structure benchmarks**

   In the course structure benchmarks, before starting the online programme, learners are advised to determine (1) if they possess the self-motivation and commitment to learn online and (2) if they have access to the minimal technology required by the course design. Students are also provided with supplemental course information that outlines course objectives, concepts, ideas, and learning outcomes for each course. These are summarised in a clearly stated and straightforward manner. Students should be allowed to have access to sufficient library resources required. Lastly, instructors and learners must agree on the expectations regarding times for assignment completion and the instructor's response.

4. **Benchmarks for quality issues**

   An online course review rubric may be required to benchmark quality (Hong, 2008; Omona, 2022). The rubric may be composed of several elements under several categories of set standards. A review process will be appropriate, and the review is not about individual instructor and faculty evaluation but should focus on course design and improvement. There are eight set standards of best practice, which include: (1) course overview and introduction; (2) learning objectives; (3) assessment and measurement; (4) resources and materials; (5) learner interaction; (6) course technology; (7) learner support; (8) and accessibility (Crawford, 2023; Kibalirwandi & Mwesigye, 2021; Schrum & Hong, 2002). These quality issue benchmarks help to address active learning, personal interactions, timely feedback, and appropriate instructional materials (Kibalirwandi & Mwesigye, 2021). This marks the quality assurance in online education and enhance the critical success factors (Bhuasiri et al., 2012; Lwoga, 2014; Naveed et al., 2020).

## Conclusion

Online and distance learning forced massive adaptations in how information is delivered and how students must learn. Higher education leaders and stakeholders must seek and produce evidence from the learning sciences while embracing technological innovations to ensure this push to change the delivery of teaching to online platforms delivers on the promise of learning and skills development. Such changes must be studied for efficacy and to understand best what works and does not and for whom. To date, most online learning approaches do not have comparable evidence-based foundations. While leading higher education systems into the post-crisis world, policymakers and practitioners alike will need to focus their efforts on the most vulnerable students and ensure that teaching and learning solutions, technological set-up, infrastructure investments, and funding modalities are geared towards keeping these students engaged and connected and support their learning process and outcomes. It is, thus, highly imperative that those in a position to think beyond immediate survival keep an eye on core values in any higher education sector so that when the crisis abates, values remain within the mission of all higher education systems. Strengthening the resilience of education systems enables countries to respond to the immediate challenges of safely re-opening schools and positions them to better cope with future crises.

## Recommendations

The authors recommend the following:

1. The government should support the universities, especially private universities, in installing internet systems to allow the growth of e-learning across all universities, even in the post-COVID-19 era. This can be done by subsidising the installation cost or reducing the tax imposed to attract higher education institutions to connect to the Internet.
2. The government should also consider tax exemption for private universities, especially the private-not-for-profit private universities and other higher institutions of learning whose intention is primarily to promote socio-economic well-being.
3. The government should consider top-up salaries for academics and other staff in private and public universities.

4. Universities should mobilise mobile, readily available, and scalable resources widely on e-learning.
5. Universities should consider curating existing content and gathering feedback on its usefulness as they roll out e-learning in the post-COVID era.
6. Universities should continuously communicate with faculty, students, and other stakeholders to provide comfortable and guiding learning environments.
7. Universities should consider building the academic staff capacity to deliver remote courses. Faculty are often underprepared to deploy content. While some faculty members may be active online, many had not taught in the online mode before this crisis. So, whereas there is much material online, there is little 24/7 technical and pedagogical support available for them. In the medium and short terms, academic staff will need digital skills training.

## References

Ahmed, A. (2020). Synchronising pedagogy and technology in post-COVID scenario. *International Journal of Creative Research Thoughts, 8*(6), 243–246.

Arbaugh, J. B. (2002). Managing the on-line classroom: A study of technological and behavioral characteristics of web-based MBA courses. *Journal of High Technology Management Research, 13*(2), 203–223. https://doi.org/10.1016/S1047-8310(02)00049-4

Arbaugh, J. B., & Duray, R. (2002). Technological and Structural Characteristics, Student Learning and Satisfaction with Web-Based Courses. *Management Learning, 33*(3). https://doi.org/10.1177/1350507602333003

Atwine, B. (2021). *COVID-19 and e-learning in Uganda: How can the education access inequality gap be closed?* https://eprcug.Org/press-releases/covid-19-and-e-learning-in-uganda-how-can-the-education-access-inequality-gap-be-closed/

Bhuasiri, W., Xaymoungkhoun, O., Zo, H., Rho, J. J., & Ciganek, A. P. (2012). Critical success factors for e-learning in developing countries: A comparative analysis between ICT experts and faculty. *Computers & Education, 58*(2), 843–855. https://doi.org/10.1016/j.Compedu.2011.10.010

Biira, S., Gimugunic, L., Ocen, G., Bwire, F., Waako, P., & Wamakote, L. (2021). COVID-19 and students' readiness for online learning in higher education institutions in Uganda: A case study of Busitema university. *Uganda Higher Education Review, 9*(2), 21–33.

Bonk, R. J., Kefalaki, M., Rudolph, J., Diamantidaki, F., Rekar Munro, C., Karanicolas, S., & Kontoleon, P. (2020). Pedagogy in the time of pandemic: From localisation to glocalisation. *Journal of Education, Innovation, and Communication,* (SI), 17–64. https://doi.org/10.34097/jeicom_SP_june2020

Brookfield, S. D., Rudolph, J., & Tan, S. (2023). *Teaching well: understanding key dynamics of learning-centered classrooms* (1st ed.). Routledge. https://doi.org/10.4324/9781003447467

Chen, H. (2010). Linking employees' e-learning system use to their overall job outcomes: An empirical study based on the IS success model. *Computers & Education, 55*(4), 1628–1639. https://doi.org/10.1016/j.compedu.2010.07.005

Cheng, Y. M. (2012). Effects of quality antecedents on e-learning acceptance. *Internet Research, 22*(3), 361-390.

Cho, V., Cheng, T. C. E., & Lai, W. M. J. (2009). The role of perceived user-interface design in continued usage intention of self-paced e-learning tools. *Computers & Education, 53*(2), 216–227. https://doi.org/10.1016/j.compedu.2009.01.014

Crawford, J. (2023). COVID-19 and higher education: A pandemic response model from rapid adaptation to consolidation and restoration. *The International Education Journal: Comparative Perspectives, 22*(1), 7–29.

Crawford, J., Butler-Henderson, K., Rudolph, J., Malkawi, B., Glowatz, M., Burton, R., Magni, P. A., & Lam, S. (2020). COVID-19: 20 countries' higher education intra-period digital pedagogy responses. *Journal of Applied Learning & Teaching, 3*(1), 9–28. https://doi.org/10.37074/jalt.2020.3.1.7

DeLone, W. H., & McLean, E. R. (2004). Measuring e-Commerce success: Applying the DeLone & McLean information systems success model. *International Journal of Electronic Commerce, 9*(1), 31–47. https://doi.org/10.1080/10864415.2004.11044317

Fiedler, F. E., & Garcia, J. E. (1987). *New approaches to effective leadership and organisational performance*. Wiley.

Gigliotti, R. (2023). *6 critical components of effective crisis leadership.* https://icma.org/articles/article/6-critical-components-effective-crisis-leadership

Habib, M. N., Jamal, W., Khalil, U., & Khan, Z. (2021). Transforming universities in interactive digital platform: Case of city university of science and information technology. *Education and Information Technologies, 26*, 517–541.

Hermann, C. F. (1963). Some consequences of crisis which limit the viability of organisations. *Administrative Science Quarterly*, 61–82.

Hong, W. (2008). Benchmarks and quality assurance for online course development in higher education. *US-China Education Review, 5*(3), 31–34. https://files.eric.ed.gov/fulltext/ED503008.pdf

Kaahwa, Y. E., Muwanguzi, S. T., Flavia, N., & Florence, N. (2022). Digital divide related educational inequalities in Uganda: Alternative learning modalities during the COVID-19 learning period. *International Journal of Innovative Research and Knowledge, 7*(11), 55–64. https://www.researchgate.net/publication/366393328

Kara, A. (2021). Covid-19 pandemic and possible trends for the future of higher education: A review. *Journal of Education and Educational Development, 8*(1), 9–26. https://doi.org/10.22555/joeed.v8i1.183

Kibalirwandi, M. M., & Mwesigye, A. R. (2021). Financial strategies and quality assurance implementation in universities under the COVID-19 pandemic. *Journal of the National Council for Higher Education, 9*(2), 1–20. https://unche.or.ug/wp-content/uploads/2021/09/NCHE-Journal-Vol.-9-Issue-2-August-2021-FINAL-COPY-1.pdf

Komuhangi, A., Mpirirwe, H., Lubanga, R., Githinji, F. W., & Nanyonga, R. C. (2022). Predictors for adoption of e-learning among health professional students during the COVID-19 lockdown in a private university in uganda. *BMC Medical Education, 22*, 671. https://doi.org/10.1186/s12909-022-03735-7

Lee, B., Yoon, J,. & Lee, I. (2009). Learners' acceptance of e-learning in South Korea: Theories and results. *Computers & Education, 53*(4), 1320–1329. https://doi.org/10.1016/j.compedu.2009.06.014

Lee, M. C. (2010). Explaining and predicting users' continuance intention toward e-learning: An extension of the expectation-confirmation model. *Computers & Education, 54*(2), 506–516. https://doi.org/10.1016/j.compedu.2009.09.002

Lin, W. S., & Wang, C. H. (2012). Antecedences to continued intentions of adopting e-learning system in blended learning instruction: A contingency framework based on models of information system success and task-technology fit. *Computers & Education, 58*(1), 88–99. https://doi.org/10.1016/j.compedu.2011.07.008

Lwoga, E. T. (2014). Critical success factors for adoption of web-based learning management systems in Tanzania. *International Journal of Education and Development using Information and Communication Technology, 10*(1), 4–21. https://files.eric.ed.gov/fulltext/EJ1071193.pdf

Maberi, N. (2022). *Ugandan schools must continue with e-learning post-covid, govt insists*. https://allafrica.com/stories/202209270241.html

Masengu, R., Muchenje, C., Ruzive, B., & Hadian, A. (2023). E-learning quality assurance is an act of symbolic control in Higher Education Institutions (HEIs). In *SHS web of conferences* (Vol. 156). https://doi.org/10.1051/shsconf/202315606001

Ministry of Education and Sports (MoES). (2020). *Guidelines for re-opening of education institutions and implementation of standard operating procedures for education institutions during COVID-19 period.* https://www.education.go.ug./wp-content/uploads/2020/05/Preparedness-and-Response-Plan-for-COVID19-MAY-2020.pdf

Muwagga, M. A. (2006). *The philosophical implications of the liberalisation of university education in Uganda* (Published PhD Thesis). Makerere University.

Naveed, Q. N., Qureshi, M. R. N., Tairan, N., Mohammad, A., Shaikh, A., Alsayed, A. O., & Alotaibi, F. M. (2020). Evaluating critical success factors in implementing E-learning system using multi-criteria decision-making. *PLoS ONE, 15*(5), e0231465.

Nawangwe, B., Muwagga, A. M., Buyinza, M., & Masagazi, F. M. (2021). Reflections on university education in Uganda and the COVID-19 pandemic shock:

Responses and lessons learned. *Alliance for African Partnership Perspectives, 1*, 17–25. https://Www.Muse.Jhu.Edu/Article/837359.

NCHE. (2020). *Guidance to universities and tertiary institutions in Uganda during the COVID-19 lockdown.* NCHE.

NCHE. (2021). *The Uganda higher education review. NCHE*. https://unche.or.ug/wpcontent/uploads/2021/09/NCHE-Journal-Vol.-9-Issue-2-August-2021-FINAL-COPY-1.pdf

Ngubane, M. (2017). *Crisis leadership: Rising to the challenge.* https://icma.org/sites/default/files/CONF2017-Crisis%20Leadership-Ngubane_Mpilo_0.pdf

O'day, J. (2022). *Educational leadership in crisis: Reflections from a pandemic.* https://files.eric.ed.gov/fulltext/ED622164.pdf

Omona, K. (2021). Effects of school closures in COVID-19 era: Evidence from Uganda Martyrs University. *Journal of Applied Learning & Teaching, 4*(2), 46–53. https://doi.org/10.37074/jalt.2021.4.2.5

Omona, K. (2022). Addressing virtual learning challenges in higher institutions of learning: A systematic review and meta-analysis. *Journal of STEAM Education, 5*(2), 104–116. https://doi.org/10.55290/steam.1076766

Ossiannilsson, E. S. I. (2023). Benchmarking: A method for quality assessment and enhancement in higher education. In M. J. Spector, B. B. Lockee, & M. D. Childress (Eds.), *Learning, design, and technology*. Springer. https://doi.org/10.1007/978-3-319-17727-4_52-3

Ozkan, S., & Koseler, R. (2009). Multi-dimensional students' evaluation of e-learning systems in the higher education context: An empirical investigation. *Computers & Education, 53*(4), 1285–1296. https://doi.org/10.1016/j.compedu.2009.06.011

Riggio, R. E., & Newstead, T. (2023). Crisis leadership. *Annual Review of Organizational Psychology and Organizational Behavior, 10*. https://doi.org/10.1146/annurev-orgpsych-120920-044838

Roca, J. C., Chiu, C., & Martínez, F. J. (2006), Understanding e-learning continuance intention: An extension of the technology acceptance model. *International Journal of Human-Computer Studies, 64*(8), 683–696. https://doi.org/10.1016/j.ijhcs.2006.01.003

Rudolph, J., Tan, S., Crawford, J., & Butler-Henderson, K. (2022). Perceived quality of online learning during COVID-19 in higher education in Singapore: Perspectives from students, lecturers, and academic leaders. *Educational Research for Policy and Practice, 22*, 171–191. https://doi.org/10.1007/s10671-022-09325-0

Sá, M. J., & Serpa, S. (2020). The COVID-19 pandemic as an opportunity to foster the sustainable development of teaching in higher education. *Sustainability, 12*(20), 8525.

Schechter, C., Da'as, R., & Qadach, M. (2022). Crisis leadership: Leading schools in a global pandemic. *Management in Education.* https://doi.org/10.1177/08920206221084050

Schrum, L., & Hong, S. (2002). Dimensions and strategies for online success: Voices from experienced educators. *JALN, 6*(1), 57–67. https://olj.onlinelearningconsortium.org/index.php/olj/article/view/1872/703

Seddon, P. B. (1997). A respecification and extension of the DeLone and McLean model of IS success. *Journal of Information Systems Research, 8*(3), 240–253. https://doi.org/10.1287/isre.8.3.240

Selim, H. M. (2007). Critical success factors for e-learning acceptance: Confirmatory factor models. *Computers & Education, 49*(2), 396–413. https://doi.org/10.1016/j.Compedu.2005.09.004

Shih, P., Muñoz, D., & Sánchez, F. (2006). The effect of previous experience with information and communication technologies on performance in a web-based learning program. *Computers in Human Behavior, 22*(6), 962–970. https://doi.org/10.1016/j.chb.2004.03.016

Smith, L., & Riley, D. (2012). School leadership in times of crisis. *School Leadership and Management, 32*(1), 57–71. https://doi.org/10.1080/13632434.2011.614941

Tweheyo, G., & Mugarura, A. (2021). Strategic responses to crisis: Case study of universities in Uganda during Covid-19. *International Journal of Social Science and Economic Research, 6*(4). https://doi.org/10.46609/IJSSER.2021.v06i04.009

UHEQF. (2016). *The Uganda higher education qualifications framework: A publication of Uganda national council for higher education.* https://iuea.ac.ug/sitepad-data/uploads/2021/03/Uganda-Higher-Education-Qualifications-Framework-2016.pdf

United Nations. (2020). *Policy brief. Education during Covid-19 and beyond.* UN. https://www.un.org/development/desa/dspd/wp-content/uploads/sites/22/2020/08/sg_policy_brief_covid-19_and_education_august_2020.pdf

Urbach, N., & Müller, B. (2012). The updated DeLone and McLean model of information systems success. In: Y. K. Dwivedi, M. Wade, S. Schneberger, (Eds.). Information Systems Theory. *Integrated Series in Information Systems*, (vol. 28). Springer. https://doi.org/10.1007/978-1-4419-6108-2_1

Venkatesh, V., Morris, M. G., Davis, G. B., & Davis, F. D. (2003). User acceptance of information technology: Toward a unified view. *MIS Quarterly, 27*(3), 425–478. https://doi.org/10.2307/30036540

Wang, H. C., & Chiu, Y. F. (2011). Assessing e-learning 2.0 system success. *Computers & Education, 57*(2), 1790–1800. https://doi.org/10.1016/j.compedu.2011.03.009

World Bank. (2020). The COVID-19 crisis response: Supporting tertiary education for continuity, adaptation, and innovation. World Bank. https://documents1.worldbank.org/curated/en/621991586463915490/The-COVID-19-Crisis-Response-Supporting-Tertiary-Education-for-Continuity-Adaptation-and-Innovation.pdf

Wu, Y. L., Shao, B., Newman, A., & Schwarz, G. (2021). Crisis leadership: A review and future research agenda. *Leadership Quarterly, 32*(6), 101518.

Yeung, C. L., Zhou, L., & Armatas, C. (2019). An overview of benchmarks regarding quality assurance for e-learning in higher education. In *2019 IEEE conference on e-learning, e-management & e-services (IC3e)* (pp. 1–6). https://doi.org/10.1109/IC3e47558.2019.8971808

Zawacki-Richter, O. (2021). The current state and impact of Covid-19 on digital higher education in Germany. *Human Behavior and Emerging Technologies, 3*(1), 218–226.

# New Wine in Old Skin: How the Pandemic Changed the U.K. Higher Education Leadership

Lena Itangata and Michelle Kane

## Introduction

The U.K. reported its first two COVID-19 cases on 29 January 2020. As of 1 March 2023, there have been 20,629,892 cases and 186,138 deaths (U.K. Health Security Agency, 2023). 90% of people aged 12 or over have received two vaccines; however, 1 in 13 people in England were infected with the virus in March 2022 (Office for National Statistics, 2020).

### Three years on…

As one walks down a regular U.K. high street, COVID-19 seems like a distant memory, and the use of face masks and social distancing has faded. Nonetheless, the visible scars of boarded-up shop windows and prominent brands visibly missing serve as a reminder of the COVID-19 pandemic. However, the campus's main street is bustling with student activity back to pre-pandemic days as they have opted out of stay-at-home learning.

L. Itangata
School of Accounting, Economics and Finance, University of Portsmouth, Portsmouth, UK
e-mail: lena.itangata@port.ac.uk

M. Kane (✉)
Faculty of Business and Law, University of Portsmouth, Portsmouth, UK
e-mail: michelle.kane@port.ac.uk


J. Rudolph et al. (eds.), *The Palgrave Handbook of Crisis Leadership in Higher Education*, https://doi.org/10.1007/978-3-031-54509-2_31

Additionally, investors and student accommodation providers display confidence in future demand. There were 2,413,155 students in Universities U.K. (UUK) member institutions in 2019–2020 (Castell & Wake, 2022). Despite COVID-19 disrupting the education of millions, student numbers increased by 8% over 2019/2020. This increase was primarily driven by UK-based first degrees, up 8%, and postgraduate taught degrees, up 16% (Van Essen-Fishman, 2022). The remnants of online activities synonymous with the pandemic are staff meetings and personal tutorials.

However, the deeper scars of the pandemic remain, particularly among higher education staff. A unanimous agreement exists among numerous scholars and higher education leaders that the well-being and mental health of the majority of staff were negatively impacted by the pandemic (Kassem, 2022; Rudolph et al., 2021; Watermeyer et al., 2021; Wray & Kinman, 2021). In addition, industrial strife by University College Union (UCU) announcing 19 days of strike action symbolises some remnants of the pressures of the COVID-19 pandemic, particularly concerning overworked staff and pay conditions (Lewis, 2023).

## U.K. Background

### COVID-19

Two years of COVID-19 in the U.K. can be summarised into five phases, based on the three national lockdowns (stay-at-home order), the road map out of lockdown and living with COVID-19 (Sherrington, 2022). The U.K. Prime Minister announced the first national lockdown on 23 March 2020. Government agencies were working frantically behind the scenes to offer support services to the public. Universities and colleges were closed in March 2020 (Hubble et al., 2021). Many students left their accommodations and returned home as institutions began offering online courses. Schools, however, had been closed indefinitely three days earlier on 18 March 2020 (Sample, 2021). A conditional lifting of restrictions was announced in May, and schools reopened on 1 June 2020 (Institute for Government Analysis, 2022).

The second lockdown (phase) was driven by the dominant Alpha strain of the virus that came into force on 5 November 2020 (Sherrington, 2022). During this time, university learning was online. The third national lockdown announced on 6 January 2021 closely followed the second while learning for schools and universities remained online (Rudolph et al., 2021). The fourth phase (or the road map out of lockdown published on 22 February) began on 8 March when schools in England reopened for students (Institute for Government Analysis, 2022), although universities continued with online delivery. By 14 July 2021, the final sector of the economy had opened. However, later in November 2021, the Omicron variant became dominant (U.K. Health Security Agency, 2023), resulting in restrictions such as face masks in public indoor venues and the NHS COVID-pass was introduced in some venues.

## U.K. Higher Education

Before the pandemic, the U.K. had a diverse range of universities, from prestigious research-intensive institutions to others offering a wide range of courses and degrees, contributing to the U.K.'s reputation for high-quality tertiary education. U.K. universities also had a solid international presence and welcomed students from around the world, contributing to cultural diversity and leading to research partnerships and international collaborations. Before the introduction of tuition fees for U.K. and E.U. students, funding came from the government funding councils (Bolton & Hubble, 2021). A report by the Institute for Fiscal Studies (Hubble & Bolton, 2018) believed university funding by students was at its highest level. However, the freeze of tuition fees and higher inflation rates have increased financial pressures for universities and a greater focus on attracting international students.

## Literature: U.K. Higher Education Response to the COVID-19 Pandemic

Effective leadership is paramount in unexpected crises to avoid potential disruptions. It is recommended for leaders to have critical competencies utilised throughout the crisis lifecycle—sensemaking, decision-making, coordinating teamwork, and facilitating learning and communication (Riggio & Newstead, 2023). It is, therefore, essential for organisations and governments to have proactive contingency plans and for leaders to have sufficient experience to deal with the crisis (Fiedler, 1967) and be flexible and adaptable (Yukl & Mahsud, 2010).

Recent research has highlighted how leadership within UK HE responded during and after the global pandemic. Ikpehai (2022) says the pandemic "was one of the most disruptive periods in living memory" (para. 3), and institutions worked to minimise damage to the student learning journey using virtual technology (Abdur Rehman et al., 2021). Previously identified changes within UK HE occurred before the COVID-19 pandemic (Ransom, 2022), such as adapting to new technology and the role of estates. COVID-19 changes, however, demanded faster decisions and timeframes than the sector was previously used to (Saxton, 2021), forcing institutions to become less risk-averse (Robson et al., 2022). Leadership needed to move away from traditional traits, identify the reasons for the problems and respond decisively (Yukl & Mahsud, 2010). Emergency Management Theory (EMT) was one of the tools used by HE policymakers to help tackle the new problems (Soroya et al., 2020), and there were significant opportunities for those institutions that were able to respond quickly (Ransom, 2022).

Despite a notable interest, only limited research has been conducted on crisis management. However, Rolph (2022) brought attention to the stages of crisis management: Reaction, Response, Reflect and Reset/Return. These stages allow the crisis to be managed while building an infrastructure and developing a strategic response. This is similar to Crawford's (2023) four stages of pandemic response: Rapid adaptation, Improvement, Consolidation and Restoration. Crawford's four stages aimed to show how universities and countries progressed from pre-pandemic to the 'new normal' after COVID-19 (Butler-Henderson et al., 2020). Rolph's (2022) crisis management model was based on schools. However, similarities exist between primary, secondary and tertiary education. Once the lockdowns had begun to ease, universities could reflect on their responses and move forward into recovery mode, post-pandemic.

While the theories applied to UK HE leadership, times of crisis can also be used to force people to make previously unfavourable choices, such as working from campus or online (Anderson, 2021). Some saw university leaders as deceitful as they projected the image of a benevolent employer while increasing workloads and, in some cases, making job cuts (Watermeyer et al., 2021). Forecasts were also made regarding the potential loss of home and international tuition fees, causing sector-wide concern, especially for those institutions reliant on international students (Adams, 2020). There was limited, short-term support from the U.K. Government, which came with strings attached. The government would only intervene to keep a university open as a last resort (Foster, 2020). This led to most universities instituting immediate spending constraints to avoid significant short and medium-term financial losses (Hillman, 2022). This change in circumstances, the threat of redundancies, and voluntary severance increased job insecurity and a culture of fear among some academics (Watermeyer et al., 2021).

Transition during the first COVID-19 lockdown was challenging as faculty members needed to become more accustomed to online delivery: up to 70% of academics had yet to teach online beforehand (International Association of Universities, 2020). In addition, they felt they needed to be more mentally prepared. The transition to immediate online teaching revealed that some lecturers were not as technologically confident as their students, necessitating staff upskilling (Isles, 2021; Times Higher Education, 2023). Frequent communication was vital during the lockdown periods. Online communication, though, can be draining and limit the ability to read body language (Saxton, 2021), resulting in miscommunication. In addition, the increased workloads and the prioritising of digital teaching and research affected staff mental health and well-being (Watermeyer et al., 2021).

Increased rates of COVID-19 were experienced in university towns, with students returning to their university accommodation (Hordosy & McLean, 2021), causing stress for the university and local communities. It had been assumed that students would return to their homes to study (Hillman, 2022) during the lockdown periods. However, the majority of full-time undergraduate students remained in their term-time accommodation. Discussions regarding the university's duty of care for the well-being of students became more urgent (Green et al., 2020) as students reported loneliness and isolation. This was especially true for some international students, away from their families and friends.

At the beginning of the subsequent lockdown in November 2020, the Office for National Statistics (2020) reported that three out of every ten students had stayed in their accommodation seven days before completing the survey. More than 50% of students also reported worsening mental health symptoms. There was a reported fall in concentration levels by 39% of surveyed students (Bashir et al., 2021), which may be correlated to the effect of online learning and the restrictions imposed, as well as the associated stress of the pandemic. The heightened engagement of students with digital tools (Times Higher Education, 2023) led to a corresponding rise in digital poverty within certain disadvantaged regions (Isles, 2021). This was due to issues arising from a lack of technology and internet access, which posed challenges for some students.

Moving out of the pandemic has highlighted the need for staff to be flexible and adaptable to change (Saxton, 2021). Institutions are re-evaluating their priorities as pedagogical changes made during lockdowns may signal the beginning of educational reform (Robson et al., 2022). The significance of new initiatives becomes evident with suggestions that five to ten years of learning have been disrupted (Times Higher Education, 2023). Therefore, there is a need for adaptive measures to recover the time that has been lost. To assist with this, the U.K. government is encouraging people of any age to learn new skills via the lifelong loan entitlement (Kernohan, 2023), and 12 new investment zones are being established. These will provide funding for a partnership between local government and universities or research institutes once a location has been identified (H.M. Treasury, 2023).

## Methodology

The chapter employs desk-based research to investigate how UK HE Institutions navigated the COVID-19 pandemic and its aftermath, utilising secondary data from UK HE agencies such as Higher Education Statistics Agency (HESA), Higher Education Policy Institute (HEPI), Higher Education, regulators such as Office for Students (OFS), the U.K. government websites and agencies, reputable news agencies, newspapers and other internet sources. The research methodology was interpretivism, as qualitative information was used within an inductive research type (Saunders et al., 2023). The research design used inductive reasoning, where the data was used to identify themes and patterns.

## U.K. Politics and Higher Education

### A Government in Chaos

During times of crisis, a charismatic leader can emerge and influence attitudes and motivation through verbal and non-verbal behaviours (Weber, 1964). Crisis events of "low probability and high consequence" need to be addressed rapidly and publicly with "immediate corrective action" (James & Wooten, 2010, p. 17). The U.K., however, did not enter into a national lockdown until 23 March 2020, even though the U.K. Scientific Advisory Group for Emergencies (SAGE) advised social distancing and school closures could cut transmission by 50% to 60% in February. The World Health Organisation (WHO) declared COVID-19 a pandemic on 11 March (Sample, 2021).

At the start of the COVID-19 pandemic, the U.K. Prime Minister, elected during the Brexit negotiations, used their charisma to influence attitudes and motivate followers. Cognitive resource theory states that leaders need quick, decisive and directive behaviour with enough experience to deal with the crisis (Fiedler, 1967). The U.K. government seemed hesitant to consider the worst-case scenarios, which resulted in the pandemic causing significant disruptions. In contrast, countries like New Zealand took prompt action to contain the virus, leading to only 3249 deaths by August 2023 (World Health Organisation, 2023).

After the lockdown, U.K. government members, including the Prime Minister, were investigated for breaking lockdown rules (Durrant, 2022; Haddon, 2022). In January 2022, an investigation brought forth the removal of the U.K.'s Prime Minister, leading to a rift between supporters and opponents. Since then, the country has experienced three leaders, one holding the position for 49 days. Furthermore, the education ministry has been wrought with troubles, going through six secretaries in the same period, with five changes occurring in 2022 alone. These events hint at a government and education system grappling to keep themselves steady. In a Guardian article, opposition parties and teaching unions accused the ministers of "presiding over a carousel of education secretaries… in a particularly turbulent time for the education sector, including the unprecedented disruption to schools, nurseries, and higher education because of COVID, and often severe funding and staffing issues" (Walker, 2022, para. 6).

University staff have been striking since February 2018 over pension reforms, pay and working conditions (Lewis, 2023). A total of 36 days of strike action, curtailed due to COVID-19, then resumed in December 2021. Following three days of strikes in November 2022, 19 days of strike action were announced for February and March 2023 (UCU, 2023). The industrial action has not been restricted to university staff. The first quarter of 2023 has seen industrial action from nurses, teachers, lecturers, doctors, postal workers and many more, staging the biggest walkout in three decades on 15 March (*Sky News*, 2023). However, the cost-of-living crisis due to inflation rising continuously from early 2021 (from under 1% to 11.1%) to late 2022 may also have exacerbated workers' strife. The drivers were strong global demand for consumer goods and related supply chain disruption due to COVID-19 and soaring energy prices due to the Russia-Ukraine war that began in February 2022 (Harari et al., 2023).

## Brexit and COVID

Following a majority vote by the U.K. population to leave the European Union (E.U.) in June 2016, the U.K. withdrew from the E.U. on 31 January 2020. The transition ended on 31 December 2020 when the U.K. left the E.U. single market and customs union. As a result, new students arriving from the E.U. to start courses in August 2021 were no longer eligible for

U.K. (home) status, meaning they had to pay international fees and did not qualify for tuition fee loans (Bolton & Lewis, 2022). According to a report by Conlon et al. (2021), it was estimated that U.K. universities would lose £62.5 million per year in tuition fees due to losing more than half of their first-year E.U. students. Between 2017/2018 and 2020/2021, EU-domiciled first-year students numbered about 65,000 and plummeted to 31,400 in 2021/2022 (Kreier, 2023), a 53% drop from 2020/2021 to 2021/2022 (Mantle, 2023).

Around the same time as the E.U. exit, the first two positive cases of COVID-19 in the U.K. were reported. The first national lockdown saw all teaching in HE moved online as universities and colleges were closed (Hubble et al., 2021). In a middle-ground scenario, Drayton and Waltmann (2020) estimated that the COVID-19 crisis would cost the U.K. university sector around £11 billion in the long term, £4.1 billion of which would be losses resulting from fewer student enrolment and £1.5 billion from accommodation and catering. Despite this, the first-year student population for 2020/2021 rose approximately 10% over 2019/2020 (Van Essen-Fishman, 2022). The number of first-year non-EU international students increased from 189,500 in 2017/2018 to more than 350,300 in 2021/2022 (Kreier, 2023), and the total number of international students full-time in 2021/2022 was 636,060. In the same period, the U.K.-domiciled first-year student enrolment decreased by 2%. Overall, non-EU first-year enrolment rose by 32% (Mantle, 2023), primarily driven by students enrolling on postgraduate taught courses.

## University Finances

According to UUK (2022), universities in England supported 815,000 jobs and contributed £95 billion in gross output to the U.K. economy in 2018–2019. In addition, the HE sector grew GDP by £52 billion from 2014–2015 to 2018–2019 (UUK, 2022). The sector's 2018/2019 total income was £40.5 billion; the expenditure was £39.1 billion, with a surplus of £1.4 billion or 3.4% of income. Income from tuition fees and education contracts was 49% of the total. Details varied between institutions; 47 out of 178 providers had a deficit, with 15 at more than 5%, and 64 had a surplus of more than 5% (Bolton & Hubble, 2021). The income in 2019/2020 and 2020/2021 was £36.15 billion and £37.31 billion respectively (OFS, 2022).

U.K. home student fees have been fixed at £9250 per student since 2017 (Waltmann, 2022). This successive freeze in tuition fee cap has reduced the real-term value of teaching resources by 11% between 2017 and 2021, taking the spending per student back to the same real-term level as in 1990

(Drayton et al., 2022). The policy to freeze tuition fees will continue until 2025, with no additional funding to cover the higher-than-expected inflation—the Consumer Price Index (CPI) rose by 10.1% in the 12 months to March 2023 (Gooding, 2023), driving the real value spending further down. This has caused some English universities to rely heavily on international students' fees (Adams, 2022). According to a recent report on the Transparent Approach to Costing (TRAC), teaching non-publicly funded primarily overseas students has resulted in a significant surplus of £2724 million for the academic year 2021–2022, compared to £2299 million for the previous year. However, publicly funded teaching and research have incurred a deficit of £955 million and £4482 million, respectively (OFS, 2023).

In a letter to the Public Accounts Committee (PAC), the Interim Chief Executive highlights the financial pressures on universities, colleges and other higher education providers (Lapworth, 2022). Despite a positive picture across the HE sector, a total income of £37.31 billion recorded in 2020–2021 and a forecast of £45.72 billion for 2024–2025, the OFS has warned of the financial risk inherent in the overreliance on income from overseas students (OFS, 2022). Recent data shows the economic benefit from international students to the U.K. across the 2021/2022 cohort to be £41.9 billion. Additionally, PAC has reported that 80 higher education institutions have experienced annual deficits. 20 institutions faced deficits for three or more years (Adams, 2022).

## Staff and Students

The move to online learning and remote working was sudden for the HE sector (Saxton, 2021). It became clear that new policies and edicts were required to move through this unprecedented time. HE leaders needed to make tough choices in line with government mandates and in short timeframes; they needed to manage the crisis to be robust, astute, adaptive and innovative (Yukl & Mahsud, 2010).

Before the first lockdown, some government debates took place (Soroya et al., 2020), and several universities brought forward the end of the term to provide time for decisions to be made. However, at the beginning of March, most universities planned to stay open and continue face-to-face teaching (Baker, 2020). When the first lockdown was announced, with little warning, staff and students were expected to continue their teaching and learning remotely. The shift to online learning posed challenges for staff and students, especially those without access to suitable equipment and a quiet space in which to study. Suddenly, the 'kitchen table' became the centre of the house, especially where households did not have a spare room for an office (Al-Habaibeh et al., 2021). Where other house members were also working from home, it became difficult to ensure privacy.

Additionally, extra impetus and time were required when staff and students had children requiring home-schooling. Where possible, universities provided resources, such as computers or furniture. However, this did not mitigate other issues, such as a lack of space. As most teaching took place face-to-face before the first lockdown, some modules and courses did not use the virtual learning environment (VLE) for teaching, only as a repository. The short timescale generally requires time to introduce or modify digital technology, but there was no time to prepare for online activities or resource modifications. Because of this, staff experienced many changes to their working conditions during the lockdown, affecting their mental and physical health, including remote working, meaning staff worked longer hours and had to adapt (Watermeyer et al., 2021) their ways of teaching and engaging students online.

The lockdowns also meant communication methods changed. During the lockdowns, HE leaders knew frequent and transparent interchange would be essential (Times Higher Education, 2022); software such as Google Meet and Zoom was rapidly introduced and used with email. However, communication became sporadic when students were not comfortable with blended learning or confident with digital technology. Some students refused to communicate online, not engaging with their studies or participating in classes (Catling et al., 2022). The rise in sedentary behaviour exacerbated the challenge of student engagement, resulting in heightened feelings of anxiety and depression. To support students who may be at risk, universities were recommended to perform routine follow-ups, aligning with the recommendations provided by ONS (2020). Well-being services were accessible to both students and staff. However, the absence of social integration in daily routines and the resulting loneliness and detachment from peers ultimately led to significant mental health concerns.

With the shift to online teaching and learning, online exams were introduced for staff and students. However, students were more accustomed to in-person tests at school and college, and taking exams online caused uncertainty and stress. This also added to staff workloads, as papers and questions had to be transferred to the VLE and sometimes rewritten. Familiar assessments like essays were used instead of exams when possible to make things easier. However, for online exams, some students faced issues with technology, internet access, and the time pressure of a traditional exam. Additionally, setting up online exams increased the workload for staff, who were also responsible for invigilating and monitoring the exams while assisting those with technical or subject difficulties.

The lockdowns had financial implications for individuals as well. While some saved on commuting and office-related expenses, others faced economic challenges due to reduced working hours. Certain furloughed staff members received only the government-mandated minimum pay, while unfortunate others lost their jobs. Nevertheless, more had concerns about job security, pay cuts and hiring freezes, especially when initial forecasts showed the number of students enrolling in the following year would drop, prompting some course reviews. Many students also experienced financial difficulties, especially those who relied on part-time work to help with their cost of living and tuition fees. Students still in term-time accommodation were provided with the basics required, such as food and some toiletries. However, this would not have provided any luxuries or treats.

## Resources

Technology played a big part during the lockdowns, with the move to online learning and teaching. Although virtual learning environments such as Moodle or Blackboard had been available for several years, many staff used them as a material repository rather than as part of blended learning. A survey by the International Association of Universities (2020) showed that up to 70% of academic staff had not taught online before the lockdowns. Likewise, a surge in student engagement with digital tools, as noted by Times Higher Education (2023), underscores the necessity for training specific individuals within institutions. To address digital poverty, certain universities permitted staff and students to bring home computer equipment to which they might not be accustomed, however, some institutions lacked adequate technical personnel to support these new resources. As a result, those staff members who were proficient in using the technology experienced abrupt and heightened workloads as they attempted to teach the new software while interacting online with individuals unfamiliar with video calls.

Changes were also needed during the lockdowns to enable students from different time zones to engage with the staff and their peers. Deadlines for assessments were extended to help with caring responsibilities, internet access and religious observances, and lectures were delivered both asynchronously and synchronously, usually supported by interactive components. Recording of lectures and seminars enabled students to be flexible in their learning times and styles (Robson et al., 2022). Although controversial before the pandemic, lecture capture became important. At the beginning of the lockdowns, Tesar

(2020) said, "we have no longer debated whether online teaching and learning was the future of education. The answer was here" (p. 557).

## Leadership Priorities for the Future

University leaders surveyed in 2021 agree that managing change and complexity is critical for HE leaders (Dunn & Stuart, 2022), with 50% of the respondents feeling that the complexity of issues facing universities was the top challenge. This is a change from pre-pandemic, when continual change and complexity dominated the surveys. In addition, 37% felt there was too much demand on their time, dealing with continual change and uncertainties (34%). Managing external changes was the priority (46%), followed by financial stability (32%) and dealing with internal changes a distant third (10%). The survey showed leaders found staff motivation less of an issue as they were willing to do things differently and adapt. A survey conducted by the UCU of its members (7000 respondents) in higher education found that many felt deeply undervalued by university leaders, and 88% were not optimistic about the sector's future (UCU, 2022). In addition, many respondents highlighted problems with university governance as a critical reason for dissatisfaction. Dunn and Stuart's (2022) report reveals that given the widespread disruption, navigating financial uncertainty and staff well-being topped the priorities for higher education leaders in the next two years. University leaders all agree that the nature of leadership has changed since the pandemic's start.

# Conclusions and Recommendations

The U.K. government is responsible for protecting the country's position as the second most popular destination for higher education globally. Therefore, they should review their migration policy to ensure it is competitive, firm, and friendly. While the government could aim to restrict migration numbers, they should avoid using language that may be perceived as unwelcoming. In addition to following government policies, U.K. universities must focus on maintaining competitive and appealing portfolios to sustain their status as top-tier higher education institutions. Furthermore, they must prioritise innovation in providing higher education to international students.

The government's decision to implement the student graduate route visa as part of its efforts to limit migration via the points-based migration system has been successful. The visa has helped to exceed the target of 600,000 students a decade ahead of schedule (by 2020), significantly since Brexit has reduced the number of E.U. students. Despite the perception of a disorganised government, there appears to be a clear and effective plan in place. However, while a few top research-intensive universities have adequate financial resources, most face deficits. Relying on international student enrolment to fund these deficits is risky, as it heavily depends on government policies that can change quickly and unexpectedly. Additionally, the financial risk to universities will persist if a cap on publicly funded student fees remains.

In today's competitive job market, students expect to receive their money's worth as customers. However, they also face the added challenge of high living expenses, which have worsened due to the COVID-19 pandemic's impact on university life. The need for suitable housing also rises with the number of students. Therefore, it is the responsibility of the U.K. government and universities to ensure that students have access to appropriate accommodations. Students are also tired of experiencing strikes before and after the pandemic. While financial concerns are essential for university leaders, it is equally important to consider staff morale when adopting new operational strategies. The high cost of living adversely affects staff income, resulting in low morale among them.

The COVID-19 pandemic led to a shift to online learning; and the emergence of A.I. platforms like ChatGPT, which have created a constantly evolving environment, leading to exhaustion among staff. The higher education industry requires dedicated staff to maintain the U.K.'s global appeal as a provider of higher education, and this should be taken into consideration as the hard work of staff members helps maintain a university's reputation and rankings. Leaders who make poor decisions should not blame their staff for their lack of success and dare to take responsibility for their mistakes.

COVID-19 is expected to affect institutions and their staff for years, and universities may not see stability for a few years. It can be estimated that the pandemic disrupted five to ten years of student learning, and universities and students must adapt to make up for this potentially lost time (Times Higher Education, 2023). Following the lockdowns and removing social distancing guidelines, institutions have tried to return to 'normal' where possible. Face-to-face teaching has resumed, and students and staff are encouraged to be on campus. Nonetheless, online instruction and learning continue to play a significant role in the updated curriculum, with technologies like video conferencing and lecture recording being widely utilised. However, not all students lean towards exclusively in-person lectures and seminars. A 2022 UUK survey highlighted that 66% of students prefer blended learning. This can profoundly shape the future trajectory for educators and students in the post-pandemic landscape, offering avenues to re-evaluate working methodologies, pivot priorities and nurture heightened flexibility and adaptability within work environments. Moreover, universities must reassess their physical campuses, as traditional buildings might not be as essential if hybrid learning gains prominence (Saxton, 2021).

## References

Abdur, M., Soroya, H. S., Abbas, Z., Mirza, F., & Mahmood, K. (2021). Understanding the challenges of e-learning during the global pandemic emergency: The students' perspective. *Quality Assurance in Education, 29*(2/3), 259–276.

Adams, R. (2022, June 15). English universities over-reliant on overseas students' fees, report warns. *The Guardian*. https://www.theguardian.com/education/2022/jun/15/english-universities-over-reliant-on-overseas-students-fees-report-warns

Adams, R. (2020, April 23). Coronavirus U.K.: Universities face £2.5bn tuition fee loss next year. *The Guardian*. https://www.theguardian.com/education/2020/apr/23/coronavirus-uk-universities-face-25bn-tuition-fee-loss-next-year

Al-Habaibeh, A., Watkins, M., Waried, K., & Javareshk, B. M. (2021). Challenges and opportunities of remotely working from home during Covid-19 pandemic. *Global Transitions, 3*, 99–108. https://doi.org/10.1016/j.glt.2021.11.001

Anderson, W. (2021). The model crisis, or how to have critical promiscuity in the time of Covid-19. *Social Studies of Science, 51*(2), 167–188. https://doi.org/10.1177/0306312721996053

Baker, S. (2020, March 13). Coronavirus: Growing number of U.K. universities move to online teaching. *Times Higher Education*. https://www.timeshighereducation.com/news/coronavirus-growing-number-uk-universities-move-online-teaching

Bashir, A., Bashir, S., Rana, K., Lambert, P., & Vernallis, A. (2021). Post-COVID-19 adaptations: The shifts towards online learning, hybrid course delivery and the implications for Biosciences courses in the higher education setting. *Frontiers in Education, 6*, 1–13. https://doi.org/10.3389/feduc.2021.711619

Bolton, P., & Hubble, S. (2021). *Coronavirus: Financial impact on higher education*. U.K. Parliament: House of Commons Library. https://commonslibrary.parliament.uk/research-briefings/cbp-8954/

Bolton, P., & Lewis, J. (2022). *International students in U.K. higher education: FAQs*. U.K. Parliament: House of Commons Library. https://commonslibrary.parliament.uk/research-briefings/cbp-7976/

Butler-Henderson, K., Crawford, J., Rudolph, J., Lalani, K., & Sabu, K. M. (2020). COVID-19 in higher education literature database (CHELD V1): An open access systematic literature review database with coding rules. *Journal of Applied Learning & Teaching, 3*(2), 11–16. https://doi.org/10.37074/jalt.2020.3.2.11

Castell, E., & Wake, D. (2022, December 20). *Higher education in facts and figures: 2021.* Universities U.K. https://www.universitiesuk.ac.uk/what-we-do/policy-and-research/publications/higher-education-facts-and-figures-2021

Catling, J. C., Bayley, A., Begum, Z., Wardzinski, C., & Wood, A. (2022). Effects of the COVID-19 lockdown on mental health in a U.K. student sample. *BMC Psychology, 10.* https://doi.org/10.1186/s40359-022-00732-9

Conlon, G., Lader, R., Halterbeck, M., & Hedges, S. (2021). *E.U. exit: Estimating the impact on higher education.* U.K. Department for Education.

Crawford, J. (2023). COVID-19 and higher education: A pandemic response model from rapid adaption to consolidation and restoration. *International Education Journal: Comparative Perspectives.* Ahead of Print.

Drayton, E., Farquharson, C., Ogden, K., Sibieta, L., Tahir, I., & Waltmann, B. (2022). *Autumn statement leaves colleges, nurseries and universities out in the cold.* Institute for Fiscal Studies.

Drayton, E., & Waltmann, B. (2020). *Will universities need a bailout to survive the COVID-19 crisis?* The Institute for Fiscal Studies.

Dunn, I., & Stuart, M. (2022). *The 2022 NCEE leadership survey: How the pandemic will shape university leaders and their institutions.* The National Centre for Entrepreneurship in Education (NCEE).

Durrant, T. (2022, March 30). "Partygate" investigations. *Institute for Government.* https://www.instituteforgovernment.org.uk/article/explainer/partygate-investigations

Fiedler, F. E. (1967). *A theory of leadership effectiveness.* McGraw-Hill.

Foster, P. (2020, May 4). Ministers unveil package to shore up U.K. universities' cash flow. *Financial Times.* https://www.ft.com/content/540683b5-ed3d-4d5a-ae41-7d8cc3b4e4c4

Gooding, P. (2023). *Consumer price inflation, U.K.: March 2023.* Office for National Statistics.

Gov.UK Coronavirus. (2022, February). *Guidance COVID-19 response: Living with COVID-19.* https://www.gov.uk/government/publications/covid-19-response-living-with-covid-19/covid-19-response-living-with-covid-19#introduction

Green, W., Anderson, V., Tait, K., & Thi Tran, L. (2020). Precarity, fear and hop: Reflecting and imagining in higher education during a global pandemic. *Higher Education Research & Development, 39*(7), 1309–1312. https://doi.org/10.1080/07294360.2020.1826029

Haddon, C. (2022, January 14). *Sue Gray investigation.* Institute for government. https://www.instituteforgovernment.org.uk/article/explainer/sue-gray-investigation

Harari, D., Bolton, P., Francis-Devine, B., & Keep, M. (2023). *Rising cost of living in the UK.* House of Commons Library.

Hillman, N. (2022, January 18). Five common predictions about COVID and education that now appear to be wrong. *Hepi.* https://www.hepi.ac.uk/2022/01/18/five-predictions-about-covid-and-education-that-tuhubblerned-out-to-be-wrong/

H.M. Treasury. (2023, March 2023). *Spring budget 2023 speech*. Gov.uk. https://www.gov.uk/government/speeches/spring-budget-2023-speech

Hordosy, R., & McLean, M. (2021). The future of the research and teaching nexus in a post-pandemic world. *Educational Review, 74*(3), 378–401. https://doi.org/10.1080/00131911.2021.2014786

Hubble, S., Bolton, P., & Baker, C. (2021). *Coronavirus: Higher and further education back to campus in England in 2020/21?* The House of Commons Library. https://commonslibrary.parliament.uk/research-briefings/cbp-9030/

Hubble, S., & Bolton, P. (2018). *Higher education tuition fees in England*. The House of Commons Library. https://commonslibrary.parliament.uk/research-briefings/cbp-8151/

Ikpehai, F. (2022). *Change management in higher education: Pre, during and post-pandemic*. SUMS Consulting. https://sums.org.uk/change-management-in-higher-education-pre-during-and-post-pandemic/

Institute for Government Analysis. (2022, 9 December). *Timeline of U.K. government coronavirus lockdowns and restrictions*. https://www.instituteforgovernment.org.uk/sites/default/files/2022-12/timeline-coronavirus-lockdown-december-2021.pdf

International Association of Universities. (2020). *Regional/national perspectives on the impact of COVID-19 on higher education* (guide). https://www.iau-aiu.net/IMG/pdf/iau_covid-19_regional_perspectives_on_the_impact_of_covid-19_on_he_july_2020_.pdf

Isles, N. (2021, March 15). Evolve or die—The challenge for HE leadership in the post-pandemic world. *WONKHE*. https://wonkhe.com/blogs/evolve-or-die-the-challenge-for-he-leadership-in-the-post-pandemic-world/

James, E. H., & Wooten, L. P. (2010). *Leading under pressure: From surviving to thriving before, during, and after a crisis*. Routledge.

Kassem, R. (2022, October 4). How did COVID-19 impact staff in U.K. higher education? *Higher Education Policy Institute (HEPI)*. https://www.hepi.ac.uk/2022/10/04/how-did-covid-19-impact-staff-in-uk-higher-education/

Kernohan, D. (2023, March 15). The lifelong loan entitlement could get very expensive for learners. *WONKHE*. https://wonkhe.com/blogs/the-lifelong-loan-entitlement-could-get-very-expensive-for-learners/?utm_medium=email&utm_campaign=Wonkhe%20Mondays%20-%2020%20March&utm_content=Wonkhe%20Mondays%20-%2020%20March+CID_db1d90f1833a0696eb8cbc31303c2696&utm_source=Email%20marketing%20software&utm_term=David%20Kernohan%20built%20a%20model

Kreier, F. (2023, January 26). U.K. universities report sharp post-Brexit drop in E.U. students. *Nature*. https://www.nature.com/articles/d41586-023-00214-x#:~:text=During%20the%20academic%20years%202017,see%20'Brexit%20effect')

Lapworth, S. (2022, July 27). *Letter to the public accounts committee—Financial sustainability of the higher education sector in England*. Office for Students.

https://www.officeforstudents.org.uk/publications/letter-to-the-public-accounts-committee-financial-sustainability-of-the-higher-education-sector-in-england/

Lewis, J. (2023, March 13). *University strike action in the UK.* House of Commons Library. https://commonslibrary.parliament.uk/research-briefings/cbp-9387/

Mantle, R. (2023, January 19). *Higher education student statistics: U.K., 2021/22—Where students come from and go to study.* Higher Education Statistics Agency. https://www.hesa.ac.uk/news/19-01-2023/sb265-higher-education-student-statistics/location

Office For Students. (2023, May 25). *Annual TRAC 2021–22: Sector summary and analysis by TRAC peer group.* Office for Students. https://www.officeforstudents.org.uk/publications/annual-trac-2021-22/

Office For Students. (2022, June 30). *Universities have managed finances well during pandemic but risks remain.* https://www.officeforstudents.org.uk/news-blog-and-events/press-and-media/universities-have-managed-finances-well-during-pandemic-but-risks-remain/

Office for National Statistics (ONS). (2020). *Coronavirus and the impact on students in higher education.* https://www.ons.gov.uk/peoplepopulationandcommunity/educationandchildcare/articles/coronavirusandtheimpactonstudentsinhighereducationinenglandseptembertodecember2020/2020-12-21

Ransom, J. (2022, February 28). How the pandemic will shape university leaders and their institutions. *Hepi.* https://www.hepi.ac.uk/2022/02/28/how-the-pandemic-will-shape-university-leaders-and-their-institutions/

Riggio, R. E., & Newstead, T. (2023). Crisis management. *Annual Review of Organizational Psychology and Organizational Behavior, 10*, 201–224. https://doi.org/10.1146/annurev-orgpsych-120920-044838

Robson, L., Gardner, B., & Dommett, E. J. (2022). The post-pandemic lecture: Views from academic staff across the U.K. *Education Sciences, 12*(2), 123. https://doi.org/10.3390/educsci12020123

Rolph, C. (2022, February 16). Post-pandemic: Return or reset? *BERA.* https://www.bera.ac.uk/blog/post-pandemic-return-or-reset

Rudolph, J., Itangata, L., Tan, S., Kane, M., Thairo, I., & Tan, T. (2021). 'Bittersweet' and 'alienating': An extreme comparison of collaborative autoethnographic perspectives from higher education students, non-teaching staff and faculty during the pandemic in the U.K. and Singapore. *Journal of University Teaching and Learning Practice, 8*(18). https://doi.org/10.53761/1.18.8.10

Sample, I. (2021, October 12). Covid timeline: The weeks leading up to first U.K. lockdown. *The Guardian.* https://www.theguardian.com/world/2021/oct/12/covid-timeline-the-weeks-leading-up-to-first-uk-lockdown

Saunders, M., Lewis, P., & Thornhill, A. (2023). *Research methods for business students* (9th ed.). Pearson.

Saxton, B. (2021). *COVID—A catalyst in HEI leadership?* https://www.saxbam.com/wp-content/uploads/2022/02/Covid-a-catalyst-in-HEI-leadership_Saxton-Bampfylde-2021.pdf

Sherrington, A. (2022, July 25). *2 Years of COVID-19.* GOV.U.K. https://gds.blog.gov.uk/2022/07/25/2-years-of-covid-19-on-gov-uk/

*Sky News.* (2023, March 31). Strikes: Who is taking industrial action in 2023 and when? https://news.sky.com/story/strikes-who-is-taking-industrial-action-in-2023-and-when-12778841

Soroya, H. S., Abdur Rehman, M., Abbas, Z., Mirza, F., & Mahmood, K. (2020). Emergency management in higher education during COVID-19 pandemic: A phenomenology inquiry comparing a developed and developing country. *Library Philosophy and Practice (e-journal),* 4720.

Tesar, M. (2020). Towards a post-covid-19 'new normality?': Physical and social distancing, the move to online and higher education. *Policy Futures in Education, 18*(5), 556–559. https://doi.org/10.1177/1478210320935671

*Times Higher Education.* (2023). How can we adapt university leadership for a post-pandemic future? https://www.timeshighereducation.com/hub/pwc/p/how-can-we-adapt-university-leadership-post-pandemic-future

*Times Higher Education.* (2022). The leadership and management summit. https://www.timeshighereducation.com/hub/leadership-and-management-summit/p/what-does-it-take-be-vice-chancellor-these-days

UCU. (2023, January 23). *University strike dates in February and March confirmed.* https://www.ucu.org.uk/article/12759/University-strike-dates-in-February-and-March-confirmed

UCU. (2022). *U.K. higher education A workforce in crisis.* University and College Union.

U.K. Health Security Agency. (2023, March 9). *Coronavirus (COVID-19) in the U.K.: Cases in England.* https://coronavirus.data.gov.uk/details/cases?areaType=nation&areaName=England

UUK. (2022, December 20). *Huge economic contribution of universities must not be forgotten.* https://www.universitiesuk.ac.uk/what-we-do/creating-voice-our-members/media-releases/huge-economic-contribution-universities

Van Essen-Fishman, L. (2022, January 25). *The impact of the COVID-19 pandemic on 2020/21 Student data.* Higher Education Student Statistics (HESA). https://www.hesa.ac.uk/insight/25-01-2022/impact-covid-19-2021-student-data

Walker, P. (2022, September 7). 'Carousel of education secretaries' as Kit Malthouse becomes fifth in a year. *The Guardian.* https://www.theguardian.com/politics/2022/sep/07/kit-malthouse-becomes-tories-fifth-education-secretary-in-a-year

Waltmann, B. (2022, February 10). *Government uses high inflation as cover for hitting students, graduates and universities.* Institute for Fiscal Studies (IFS). https://ifs.org.uk/articles/government-uses-high-inflation-cover-hitting-students-graduates-and-universities

Watermeyer, R., Shankar, K., Crick, T., Knight, C., McGaughey, F., Hardman, J., Ratnadeep Suri, V., Chung R., & Phelan, D. (2021). 'Pandemia': A reckoning of U.K. universities' corporate response to COVID-19 and its academic fallout. *British Journal of Sociology of Education, 42*(5), 651–666. https://doi.org/10.1080/01425692.2021.1937058

Weber, M., & Parsons, T. (1964). *The theory of social and economic organisation.* Free Press.

World Health Organisation. (2023). *New Zealand: WHO coronavirus disease dashboard.* https://covid19.who.int/region/wpro/country/nz

Wray, S., & Kinman, G. (2021). *Supporting staff well-being in higher education.* Education Support.

Yukl, G., & Mahsud, R. (2010). Why flexible and adaptive leadership is essential. *Consulting Psychology Journal: Practice and Research, 62*(2), 81–93. https://doi.org/10.1037/a0019835

# U.S. Higher Education in Crisis: A Study of Leadership Challenges in a Post-Pandemic World

Michael Anibal Altamirano

## An Unexpected Reality

The COVID-19 pandemic has affected every corner of the world resoundingly. This study focuses on the impact on higher education within the United States and how leadership has met the challenges of the pandemic. The aforementioned pandemic has forced institutions to change their views and practices of what traditional higher education was and currently is (Rapanta et al., 2021). Many institutions are entering a post-pandemic world full of uncertainty that has forced leaders to strategise and change their policies and procedures regarding management, hiring, employee engagement, enrollment, teaching pedagogy, academic offerings, and mental health.

Universally, most academic leaders do not view higher education as a business. Nonetheless, it is (Mekvabidze, 2020). This business of higher education straddles both sides of the non-profit and for-profit sectors. The North American Industry Classification System (NAICS), the U.S. standard system for classifying business entities, recognises higher education as an official industry classified with code 611310. This industry classification represents institutions actively offering educational courses and granting undergraduate and graduate degrees (NAICS, 2023). Unfortunately, the lack of recognition that higher education is a business has historically fostered ineffective leadership and management (Jais et al., 2023). Part of the reason for this perspective

M. A. Altamirano (✉)
School of Business, King Graduate School, Monroe College, Bronx, NY, USA
e-mail: maltamirano@monroecollege.edu





J. Rudolph et al. (eds.), *The Palgrave Handbook of Crisis Leadership in Higher Education*, https://doi.org/10.1007/978-3-031-54509-2_32

is that until 2019, enrollment at most institutions has always been steady. Those promoted to leadership positions have traditionally been academicians with educational credentials but limited business/organisational experience (Jais et al., 2023). Therefore, many educational leaders were organisationally and strategically unprepared for the pandemic's unforeseen and volatile environmental shift.

During the pandemic, institutions needed to close their doors to staff and faculty as they followed the lead of municipalities and many businesses by adhering to national protocols on safety and social distancing (Crawford & Cifuentes-Faura, 2022). The dangers and uncertainty were real, hence many government leaders lacked answers and solutions to their newfound problems. In all fairness, most organisations had no answers, as these were unprecedented events. The world began to operate remotely overnight, and almost everyone involved was ill-prepared for what this meant (Taher et al., 2022). Virtual meetings, telecommuting, and independent work became the standard for conducting business. One distinct advantage most educational institutions in the United States had was learning management systems (LMS). LMS is software that facilitates the delivery of course information and assignments (Camilleri & Camilleri, 2022). While popular in the asynchronous educational community, traditional education delivery has slowly evolved (Taher et al., 2022). This slow reaction resulted in two obstacles. First, the lack of familiarity among a significant population of faculty, staff, and students who were not trained to navigate these systems. Second, the need for urgent training in learning management systems while also incorporating video conferencing tools to create virtual lecture settings. Those outside of education would probably view this as a natural and reactionary paradigm shift, whereas many within education viewed this as impactful and, to a certain extent, distressing (Ndzinisa & Dlamini, 2022).

According to Selase & Enyonam (2023), the COVID-19 pandemic would eventually stifle some businesses that leaned on the adage, "if it is not broken, why fix it?" This prevailing attitude challenged educational institutions to react quickly within an industry environment engulfed in tradition (Voinea & Roijakkers, 2023). The United States education system suffered as a result and continues to struggle in the post-pandemic era (Kose et al., 2022). The pandemic would catalyse more environmental impacts, like remote work and learning. From kindergarten to twelfth grade, all schools were forced to go remote. This challenged all members of the American population to be technologically prepared in a country where not everyone has access to personal computers or WIFI (Oberg et al., 2022). Even having access does not guarantee success because there is still the issue of reliability based on regional infrastructure and what type of technology individuals can afford (Oberg et al., 2022).

Before the COVID-19 pandemic, most high school graduates in the United States. were already academically unprepared to succeed in college (Xu et al., 2023). Since the pandemic, initial surveys suggest this percentage has grown more extensive and disparate based on diverse backgrounds (Brown-McKenzie, 2023). The pandemic created a reality of virtual learning that most students were not accustomed to or prepared. The change required a significant aptitude and the ability to learn independently. Asynchronous learning is not for everyone. There is an idealistic difference between independently choosing to learn asynchronously and having it forced upon an individual. Virtual lectures using video conferencing tools are also challenging. Academic researchers have reported largely disengaged students, and many suggest and believe that some students log on to be marked present and then move away from the screen to do other activities (Sharma et al., 2023). If 94% of students were on their smartphones during class before the pandemic, it is probably now close to 100% (Derounian, 2020). Disengaged students are counterintuitive to the underlying goal of education, but for leaders, it is only one aspect of several emerging issues.

## An Exodus to Greener Pastures

For all industries, a universally common reaction to the pandemic was the transition to telecommuting of many job responsibilities. According to a study done by Apollo Technical, globally, 62% of employees aged 22–65 worked remotely during the pandemic (2022). In the United States, 59% of workers report working remotely at least part of the time (Pew Research Center, 2022). Since the pandemic, leaders of colleges and universities in the United States are now trying to open all doors to their institutions, but also realise the value of having many employees work from home at least two days a week. It helps to keep the total population down and reduces exposure to human contact, the primary spreader of most communicable diseases (Parkhomenko & Delventhal, 2023). Work-related stress and burnout are challenging for organisational leaders, especially in higher education. To challenge leaders further, the winter season of 2022/2023 presented heightened cases of COVID-19 and rising cases of the flu, strep throat, and RSV (respiratory syncytial virus) (Hom, 2023).

Employee stress and burnout have become a prevailing after-effect of the COVID-19 pandemic. Organisational leaders were not primed for this challenge at all (Adanaqué-Bravo et al., 2023). Not to suggest occupational stress and burnout did not exist prior, but most people attributed it to poor working conditions, not a global pandemic. The pandemic symbolised uncharted territory for schools to manage; when stress and burnout became a prevailing issue, most institutions were still trying to survive and manage through the epidemic and were inevitably caught off guard. Here are the issues most commonly reported by employees: fear of exposure, isolation, lack of motivation to work from home, lack of communication with management, and the economy (Gerding et al., 2023).

Prior to the pandemic, the general population of the United States already had high rates of diseases directly linked to mortality, such as heart disease, cancer, diabetes, and obesity, to name a few (Thoma & Declercq, 2022). The additional risk of contracting COVID-19 greatly increased employee mental health and well-being concerns (Collins et al., 2021). Consider also the social debate of whether or not to get a vaccine, which half the population does not trust, because of the contrasting political divide prevalent in the United States. Regardless of what side of the political fence one stands on. There is uncertainty because of the vast unknown (Amlani et al., 2023). Employee populations within higher education are only microcosms of the total population. When many schools required employees to be vaccinated before returning to work, some employees complied, some protested, and others resigned or terminated. Those who complied and returned to work wore personal protective equipment (PPE), mandated or voluntarily. Many staff and faculty were returning to work with the added anxiety of potentially contracting COVID-19 because many employees were (Singh et al., 2022). As institutional leaders struggled to address many of these issues, the reality of managing the unknown mandated leaders to seek aid from newly hired healthcare counsellors to help deal with these growing issues. Clinical social workers have become a new normal for universities as they extend themselves to the rising emotional health needs of their students, staff, and faculty (Salimi et al., 2023).

## Decreased Enrollment Post-Pandemic

The higher education business is in turmoil because of decreased enrollment due to rising tuition costs, anxiety, academic unpreparedness, and even the influence of social media. These factors add to the causes of an industry in the financial crisis (Kose et al., 2022).

The cost of tuition continues to rise steadily, and mounting student debt is becoming a source of controversy, complete with divided social opinions. To further exasperate this issue, the country's economy continues to be in crisis, and even more concerning, enrollment in colleges and universities is down considerably. It would be ill-advised to point to the pandemic as the sole cause for this particular priority issue. Instead, there has been a perfect storm of environmental factors, which share the blame here (Boatman et al., 2022).

The United States economy is currently affected by high inflation, rising interest rates, and tightening monetary spending. Experts project that inflation will continue to be an issue past 2024, and interest rates will not drop for at least the next 1–2 years (Visco & Lecture, 2023). Citizens face critical decisions on how and when they spend their money. The cost of attending a private institution of higher learning is economically prohibitive to the average American family, whose income in 2022 was $78,813 (DOJ, 2023). According to a report by U.S. News & World Report (2023), the average tuition cost for attending college in 2022–2023 is $39,723 a year for private institutions compared to $10,423 for public in-state colleges. These average statistics do not account for the extrinsic costs of attending school, which can make these average numbers rise significantly. As an almost punitive result, the Education Data Initiative reports that 30–40% of all undergraduate students take out loans to attend college. This currently accounts for 1.757 trillion dollars in overall student debt in the United States (2023).

Enrollment in higher education was down significantly between 2019 and 2022. Undergraduate enrollment decreased 8%, equal to 1.2 million students, and graduate enrollment decreased 6%, equal to 1.1 million students (US DOE, 2023a). This is indicative of a higher education industry in turmoil. This decrease in enrollment is attributable to several factors. There is the economic reality that causes students to feel hesitant to take out loans in order to attend college.

Apprehension of attending school and being out in public is genuine. Two years of social isolation has shown a rise in psychological disorders such as depression, anxiety, and genuine fear of being out in public (Flesia et al., 2023). While the pandemic created trauma, students adapted quickly. Ironically, now that the pandemic is over, students are experiencing the trauma of "going back" to normality. Many in the United States label themselves "survivors", illustrating the powerful reality of facing a life-or-death traumatic experience (Jehi et al., 2022). This results in many students not wanting to attend college in person, and many institutions have moved away from the synchronous virtual modality they adopted during the pandemic and are back to in-person lectures. Several studies suggest students prefer asynchronous and virtual lessons to attend in-person classes (Zhang et al., 2023). Interestingly, a recent challenge for institutions is presented through emerging studies suggesting that high school students in the United States have lost two years of social/psychological development because of the pandemic (Manuel Prieto et al., 2023). This loss of social/psychological development is another reason universities and students struggle to succeed.

Two years of halted social/psychological maturity can also be described as arrested emotional development. Regardless of how it is labelled, higher education leaders attribute it as a major cause of poor academic performance and disinterested enrollment (Speakes-Lewis et al., 2022). Signs of arrested emotional development for high school and students just entering college are:

- Lack of focus—students lacking maturity struggle with concentrating on tasks
- An inability to accept criticism—an aspect of social development is the ability to receive and accept criticism and learn from it
- Impulsive behaviour—This is indicative of childlike behaviour. Most people grow out of
- Name-calling and/or bullying—normally, mature people do not engage in this type of behaviour
- Avoidance of responsibility—emotionally immature people tend not to see the future clearly and are not prepared to take necessary action to achieve goals and objectives
- Narcissism—The inability to show concern over others because of energy focused on oneself

This issue presents a distinctive strategic challenge for educational leaders in the United States. The pandemic forced organisational leaders to react without adequate preparedness. Similarly, the post-pandemic environment has presented new issues for leaders to manage as they move forward.

School closures during the pandemic were challenging for all American college students, particularly Black and Hispanic students. These populations were most impacted because of the economy, loss of jobs, caregiver issues, emotional distress, and isolation. For high school and college students, the trauma of living through the pandemic is evidenced by poor academic performance and emotional and behavioural problems (Jones et al., 2022). Studies illustrate that students who suffer from depression are twice as likely to drop out of school (2022). The challenge of managing the heightened emotional needs of students has presented another distinct issue for unprepared leaders.

Sociological research describes high school and college-aged students as the largest population group influenced by social media (Popat & Tarrant,

2023). For many, this probably is not a surprise. However, a growing population of social media influencers are spreading a narrative of making easy money, college degrees are useless, and learning a trade or skill is the way to go (Lajnef, 2023). People between the ages of 13 and 22 are very impressionable and are often influenced by influencers who look like them, talk like them, and cleverly pull on the heartstrings of familiarity. All this challenges the roles of parents, guardians, and school leaders, who more often side with the idea of social advancement through higher education.

## Leadership: Uncertainty, Challenges, and Opportunity

In all industries, successful organisations normally approach business processes using strategic management principles. Strategic management occurs when organisations purposely maximise the use of their resources to achieve organisational goals and objectives (Datta & Kulzewski, 2023). This is accomplished through an internal and external environmental analysis process, identifying issues affecting various company functions. In order to succeed, companies manage strategically to gain a competitive advantage over rivals, achieve goals and objectives, accomplish sustainable and steady growth, maintain a unified organisation with members who buy into the culture, and encourage effective management throughout all aspects of the strategic plan (Nayak et al., 2022).

Leaders in higher education in the United States are now challenged with strategically managing their institutions successfully after the pandemic. As previously illustrated, this does not happen without challenges. The idea of managing strategically is ideological. Those organisations that embrace it tend to outperform those that do not (Jayawarna & Dissanayake, 2019). The decision to manage strategically is only one part of the future challenge. In order to do this successfully, leaders must be acutely aware of environmental factors that can affect even the best-laid plans of organisations. The COVID-19 pandemic caught almost everyone off guard. The United States higher education system was greatly affected and continues to struggle as it recovers from a historic catastrophe. Leaders are now faced with the changing landscape that has radically affected their ability to provide a necessary service for young minds (Devlin & Samarawickrema, 2022).

For higher education institutions to forge forward, they must be intuitively aware of certain environmental factors and prepare sound strategies to address them. As a result, complex and unproven decisions need to be made. For example, college enrollment has been down over the last 10 years. The pandemic did not help. Consequently, because of low enrollment, colleges were forced to raise tuition prices to make up for this financial deficit. This creates a dilemma for potential students. The inherent cost of obtaining a degree is so high considering the success rate of those who start and finish. According to the latest statistics by the Department of Education (U.S.), the graduation rate in the United States for those who complete their education within six years of starting is 62% (US DOE, 2023b). The future state of higher education is uncertain in the United States. The past three years must be considered to move forward over the next five years. Leaders must consider several questions and realities as they plan the present and future. They are:

- Is your institution prepared for another pandemic?
- How do institutions account for less academically prepared incoming students?
- How does your institution address the issues of depression, anxiety, fear, and burnout within your community?
- How to address decreased enrollment?
- Retention: what are the strategies for keeping students in school?
- How open is your institution to adapting new learning modalities?
- How can institutions use social media to reach to current and potential students?

These are not easy challenges for institutional leaders. There must be a legitimate paradigm shift concerning policies and procedures (Kang et al., 2022).

Leadership is the ability to influence and inspire others. Leadership in higher education within the United States is perpetually challenged with creating cultures of acceptance, growth, nurturing, and support. According to NCES (2023) statistics, the United States. has nearly 5916 degree-granting colleges and universities. As of 2022, that is a total population of 17.9 million students (NCES, 2023). While enrollment continues to decrease, this can easily be seen as an opportunity for success. An opportunity in business is when an organisation or industry can take advantage of a situation (Haider & Tehseen, 2022). While the business of higher education is currently facing challenges, it is inconceivable that it will remain in this state indefinitely. This situation presents an opportunity for forward-thinking leaders to prepare their organisations for better times ahead. Leaders must consider internal and external environmental factors and use these factors to identify priority issues, which will eventually be the foundation for sound strategic management planning. The culture cannot be one of business as usual. Instead, college and university cultures must adapt to a new social way of life, which is more complex than in the past.

## Conclusion

The post-pandemic landscape in the United States has taken a toll on all stakeholders involved. Institutional leaders are finding themselves unprepared in an ever-changing environment. They must be mindful of this uncertainty as they strategically plan out the future of their organisations. From an economic standpoint, there is decreased enrollment and a nation reeling from economic challenges. Sociologically, they must help students navigate through issues of isolation, fear, depression, and anxiety. Social media has become prevalent in the decision-making of many students. From a political perspective, student debt has become a hot topic that continues to fester. Technology has become prevalent, with rising numbers of asynchronous and virtual courses being offered. Unfortunately, access to technology is not available or affordable to all students. Leaders of higher education institutions have an opportunity to level the playing field for all students. They must do so with purposeful strategic intent, genuine care for their students, and an understanding that today's student is starkly different from the student of 2019 (pre-pandemic). Optimism exists through opportunity. The late Malcolm X once said, "the future belongs to those who prepare for it today".

## References

Adanaqué-Bravo, I., Escobar-Segovia, K., Gómez-Salgado, J., García-Iglesias, J. J., Fagundo-Rivera, J., & Ruiz-Frutos, C. (2023). Relationship between psychological distress, burnout and work engagement in workers during the COVID-19 pandemic: A systematic review. *International Journal of Public Health, 67*, 1605605.

Amlani, S., Kiesel, S., & Butters, R. (2023). Polarisation in COVID-19 vaccine discussion networks. *American Politics Research, 51*(2), 260–273. 1532673X221148670.

Apollo Technical. (2022). *Statistics on remote workers that will surprise you.* https://www.apollotechnical.com/statistics-on-remote-workers/

Boatman, A., Callender, C., & Evans, B. (2022). Comparing high school students' attitudes towards borrowing for higher education in England and the United States: Who are the most loan averse? *European Journal of Education, 57*(2), 199–217.

Brown-McKenzie, C. (2023). *A role for pre-college programs: Cultural capital and school outcomes for black students seeking higher education* [Doctoral dissertation, Georgetown University].

Camilleri, M. A., & Camilleri, A. C. (2022). The acceptance of learning management systems and video conferencing technologies: Lessons learned from COVID-19. *Technology, Knowledge and Learning, 27*(4), 1311–1333.

Collins, C., Mahuron, K., Bongiovanni, T., Lancaster, E., Sosa, J. A., & Wick, E. (2021). Stress and the surgical resident in the COVID-19 pandemic. *Journal of Surgical Education, 78*(2), 422–430.

Crawford, J., & Cifuentes-Faura, J. (2022). Sustainability in higher education during the COVID-19 pandemic: A systematic review. *Sustainability, 14*(3), 1879.

Datta, S., & Kutzewski, T. (2023). The conventional wisdom in strategy. In *Strategic optionality: Pathways through disruptive uncertainty* (pp. 37–90). Springer International Publishing.

Department of Justice. (2023). *Cases filed between April 1, 2022 and May 14, 2022, inclusive.* https://www.justice.gov/ust/eo/bapcpa/20220401/bci_data/median_income_table.htm

Derounian, J. G. (2020). Mobiles in class? *Active Learning in Higher Education, 21*(2), 142–153.

Devlin, M., & Samarawickrema, G. (2022). A commentary on the criteria of effective teaching in post-COVID higher education. *Higher Education Research & Development, 41*(1), 21–32.

Education Data Initiative. (2023). *Student loan debt statistics*. https://educationdata.org/student-loan-debt-statistics

Flesia, L., Adeeb, M., Waseem, A., Helmy, M., & Monaro, M. (2023). Psychological distress related to the COVID-19 pandemic: The protective role of hope. *European Journal of Investigation in Health, Psychology and Education, 13*(1), 67–80.

Gerding, T., Davis, K. G., & Wang, J. (2023). An investigation into occupational related stress of at-risk workers during COVID-19. *Annals of Work Exposures and Health, 67*(1), 118–128.

Haider, S. A., & Tehseen, S. (2022). Role of decision intelligence in strategic business planning. In *Decision intelligence analytics and the implementation of strategic business management* (pp. 125–133). Springer Innovations in Communication and Computing. https://doi.org/10.1007/978-3-030-82763-2_11

Hom, K. (2023). *Last winter's tripledemic: A multi-factorial syndrome of respiratory illness*. The George Washington University.

Jais, I. R. M., Azman, A. M., Abidin, A. S. Z., & Ghani, E. K. (2023). Leadership competency portfolio for universities: A behavioural event-interview approach. *International Journal of Innovative Research and Scientific Studies, 6*(1), 205–211.

Jayawarna, S., & Dissanayake, R. (2019). Strategic planning and organisation performance: A review on conceptual and practice perspectives. *Archives of Business Research, 7*(6), 155–163.

Jehi, T., Khan, R., Dos Santos, H., & Majzoub, N. (2022). Effect of COVID-19 outbreak on anxiety among students of higher education: A review of literature. *Current Psychology*, 1–15.

Jones, S. E., Ethier, K. A., Hertz, M., DeGue, S., Le, V. D., Thornton, J., Lim, C., Dittus, P. J., & Geda, S. (2022). Mental health, suicidality, and connectedness among high school students during the COVID-19 pandemic—Adolescent behaviors and experiences survey, United States, January–June 2021. *MMWR Supplements, 71*(3), 16–21.

Kang, S. P., Chen, Y., Svihla, V., Gallup, A., Ferris, K., & Datye, A. K. (2022). Guiding change in higher education: An emergent, iterative application of Kotter's change model. *Studies in Higher Education, 47*(2), 270–289.

Kose, H. B., Kalanee, I., & Yildirim, Y. (2022). Recovering higher education during and after the pandemic. In *Handbook of research on future of work and education: Implications for curriculum delivery and work design* (pp. 14–26). IGI Global.

Lajnef, K. (2023). The effect of social media influencers' on teenagers behavior: An empirical study using cognitive map technique. *Current Psychology, 42*(22), 19364–19377.

Manuel Prieto, J., Salas Sánchez, J., Tierno Cordón, J., Álvarez-Kurogi, L., González-García, H., & Castro López, R. (2023). Social anxiety and academic performance during COVID-19 in schoolchildren. *PLoS One, 18*(1), e0280194.

Mekvabidze, R. (2020). From business modeling to business management: An exploratory study of the optimal decision making on the modern university level. *Journal of Logistics, Informatics and Service Science, 7*(1), 67–86.

NAICS. (2023). *NAICS code description.* https://www.naics.com/naics-code-description/?code=611310#:~:text=611310%20%2D%20Colleges%2C%20Universities%2C%20and%20Professional%20Schools&text=This%20industry%20comprises%20establishments%20primarily,at%20baccalaureate%20or%20graduate%20levels

NCES. (2023). *Educational institutions.* National Center for Education Statistics. https://nces.ed.gov/fastfacts/display.asp?id=1122

Nayak, B., Bhattacharyya, S. S., & Krishnamoorthy, B. (2022). Exploring the black box of competitive advantage—An integrated bibliometric and chronological literature review approach. *Journal of Business Research, 139*, 964–982.

Ndzinisa, N., & Dlamini, R. (2022). Responsiveness vs. accessibility: Pandemic-driven shift to remote teaching and online learning. *Higher Education Research & Development, 41*(7), 2262–2277.

Oberg, C., Hodges, H. R., Gander, S., Nathawad, R., & Cutts, D. (2022). The impact of COVID-19 on children's lives in the United States: Amplified inequities and a just path to recovery. *Current Problems in Pediatric and Adolescent Health Care, 52*(7), 101181.

Parkhomenko, A., & Delventhal, M. J. (2023). *Spatial implications of telecommuting in the United States. A research report from the national center for sustainable transportation.* National Center for Sustainable Transportation.

Pew Research Center. (2022). *COVID-19 pandemic continues to reshape work in America*. https://www.pewresearch.org/social-trends/2022/02/16/covid-19-pandemic-continues-to-reshape-work-in-america/

Popat, A., & Tarrant, C. (2023). Exploring adolescents' perspectives on social media and mental health and well-being—A qualitative literature review. *Clinical Child Psychology and Psychiatry, 28*(1), 323–337.

Rapanta, C., Botturi, L., Goodyear, P., Guàrdia, L., & Koole, M. (2021). Balancing technology, pedagogy and the new normal: Post-pandemic challenges for higher education. *Postdigital Science and Education, 3*(3), 715–742.

Salimi, N., Gere, B., Talley, W., & Irioogbe, B. (2023). College students mental health challenges: Concerns and considerations in the COVID-19 pandemic. *Journal of College Student Psychotherapy, 37*(1), 39–51.

Selase, A. E., & Enyonam, E. S. (2023). The impact of COVID-19 paroxysm on businesses and markets: A global mire. *Studies in Social Science & Humanities, 2*(1), 36–42.

Sharma, P., Joshi, S., Gautam, S., Maharjan, S., Khanal, S. R., Reis, M. C., Barroso, J., & de Jesus Filipe, V. M. (2023, January). Student engagement detection using emotion analysis, eye tracking and head movement with machine learning. In *Technology and innovation in learning, teaching and education: Third international conference, TECH-EDU 2022, Lisbon, Portugal, August 31–September 2, 2022, Revised selected papers* (pp. 52–68). Springer Nature Switzerland.

Singh, J., Evans, E., Reed, A., Karch, L., Qualey, K., Singh, L., & Wiersma, H. (2022). Online, hybrid, and face-to-face learning through the eyes of faculty, students, administrators, and instructional designers: Lessons learned and directions for the post-vaccine and post-pandemic/COVID-19 world. *Journal of Educational Technology Systems, 50*(3), 301–326.

Speakes-Lewis, A., Meyers, A., & Sollin, C. (2022). Fostering social-emotional learning (SEL) for classroom management. In *Engaging diverse learners: Enhanced approaches to classroom management* (p. 115). Rowman and Littlefield.

Taher, T. M. J., Saadi, R. B., Oraibi, R. R., Ghazi, H. F., Abdul-Rasool, S., Tuma, F., & Oraib, R. R. (2022). E-learning satisfaction and barriers in unprepared and resource-limited systems during the COVID-19 pandemic. *Cureus, 14*(5), e24969. https://doi.org/10.7759/cureus.24969

Thoma, M. E., & Declercq, E. R. (2022). All-cause maternal mortality in the U.S. before vs during the COVID-19 pandemic. *JAMA Network Open, 5*(6), e2219133.

U.S. Department of Education. (2023a). *Undergraduate graduation rates*. https://nces.ed.gov/fastfacts/display.asp?id=40

U.S. Department of Education. (2023b). *Undergraduate and graduate enrollment*. https://nces.ed.gov/programs/coe/indicator/cha

U.S. News & World Report. (2023). *See the average college tuition in 2022–2023*. https://www.usnews.com/education/best-colleges/paying-for-college/articles/paying-for-college-infographic#:~:text=The%20average%20cost%20of%20tuition,respectively%2C%20U.S.%20News%20data%20shows

Visco, I., & Lecture, B. P. (2023). Monetary policy and the return of inflation. In *The Warwick Economic Summit 2003, Bishnodat Persaud Lecture.*

Voinea, C. L., & Roijakkers, N. (2023). Educating for the future. In *Futurology in education and learning* (pp. 1–4). World Scientific.

Xu, Z., Backes, B., & Goldhaber, D. (2023). The impact of transition intervention in high school on pathways through college. *Community College Review, 51*(2), 216–245. 00915521221145325.

Zhang, R., Bi, N. C., & Mercado, T. (2023). Do zoom meetings really help? A comparative analysis of synchronous and asynchronous online learning during COVID-19 pandemic. *Journal of Computer Assisted Learning, 39*(1), 210–217.

# Caution, Conception, and Repercussion: Re-examining Higher Education Leadership in Perilous Times in Uzbekistan

Teck Choon Teo

## Introduction

Schools in Uzbekistan and many other nations were suspended to prevent the spread of the virus. The first instance of coronavirus transmission in Uzbekistan was recorded on March 15, 2020. Two days later, the Ministry of Public Education (MPE) unveiled a distance learning initiative for the country's 6.1 million pupils under quarantine. Ensuring all students have equal access to education during school closures was challenging due to inadequate funding. Assuming that all students would have equal access to internet-based educational resources and opportunities during the quarantine would be an enormous error. Socially marginalised students, the majority of whom reside in rural areas without access to electronic devices such as cellphones, laptops, computers, tablets, and the Internet, are especially vulnerable in the event of a crisis.

Internet access remains difficult for the Uzbek population. The World Bank (2018) reports that nearly one-third of the world's population lacks Internet access. Due to these factors, the World Bank acknowledges that online education cannot guarantee that all students utilise learning resources equitably. With digital television encompassing the entirety of Uzbekistan, the only feasible way to provide distance education to large populations is through television transmission. Despite lingering challenges, the MPE

T. C. Teo (✉)
New Uzbekistan University, Tashkent, Uzbekistan
e-mail: t.teo@newuu.uz





J. Rudolph et al. (eds.), *The Palgrave Handbook of Crisis Leadership in Higher Education*, https://doi.org/10.1007/978-3-031-54509-2_33

swiftly responded to the situation and established distance learning. As a result, 350 video lectures were produced in a matter of days, and on March 30, they were first aired on multiple state television stations. Uzbek and Russian classes are offered, with ASL (American Sign Language) interpretation available. They are also shared on the Ministry of Education and Science's YouTube and Mover.uz channels and on kundalik.com, a system for overseeing the classroom (Meliboeva et al., 2020).

## Background on Uzbekistan

Central Asian countries are particularly vulnerable because students and young adults account for nearly fifty per cent of the citizenry. The coronavirus (COVID-19) pandemic has protracted deleterious consequences on these sovereign states' schooling, human capital quality, and economic growth. The Special Republican Commission decided on March 16, 2020, one day following the first incidence of coronavirus infection discovered in Uzbekistan, to close all preschools, secondary schools, and universities for three weeks as a precautionary measure. Experts worldwide agree that a swift response is crucial, especially in the virus's earliest transmission stages. Almost 80,000 students from across the country attended Tashkent schools then (Davletov, 2020).

Over 8.4 million pupils, the vast majority of whom (almost 6 million individuals) are learners from mainstream classes, remained at home during the lockdown because schools across the country had been closed. Given these realities, the government's primary educational responsibility was maintaining the teaching curriculum. For this reason, the entire republic participated in various forms of distance education. For instance, the MPE geared all classroom instruction towards broadcasting to meet syllabi requirements. The TV lesson schedule was communicated to all classes, and recordings of these lessons are promptly available on the MPE's official Telegram channel UZEDU and a YouTube channel for video hosting. Additionally, the MPE moved swiftly to establish internet resources on higher learning requirements and to introduce the EDUUZ telegram channel, which provides updates on the most recent educational changes and posts educational materials for self-study.

Uzbekistan's presidential decree proposed two economic and social measures to limit coronavirus spread. Education is linked to a variety of acts. New and temporary employees can take annual leave to care for their preschool or primary school-aged children. Parents (or surrogate parents or legal guardians) of children infected with coronavirus or quarantined by the company cannot be dismissed. Moreover, caregivers of children under 14 receive full average-income temporary disability benefits. The decision also ensures prompt payment to K-12 and higher education workers and state-funded sports and cultural organisations that have temporarily ceased activities. Existing solutions address two significant difficulties associated with school closings. Childcare, preschool, and public school students are critical during a quarantine.

## Literature Review

Many students in Uzbekistan who do not live near a university campus can still get a high-quality university education because of the proliferation of online courses and programmes. In addition, the convenience and adaptability of online education have made it possible for people with heavy jobs and personal commitments to pursue and complete postgraduate degrees. While digitalisation in higher education has been ongoing, recent spikes in activity have led to dramatic changes in surprisingly short periods. According to published findings (Arslan & Ulutaş, 2017; Jensen, 2019), many universities have concluded that technological advancements dramatically alter how they teach and assess students. Under these conditions, most students realise that attending classes on a traditional college campus is not viable. Although teachers use digital technology in their personal lives, Johnson et al. (2016) found significant operational, technological, and learning and teaching barriers when implementing it in the classroom.

The worldwide transmission of the COVID-19 virus spurred many learners and educators to participate in their first virtual classroom online learning and instruction. As a result of the abrupt end of face-to-face education, educators and learners were thrust into unfamiliar territory as they had to swiftly adapt to new e-learning scenarios (Carolan et al., 2020). Public health officials issued regulations prohibiting all public gatherings and advising everyone to limit in-person encounters due to the COVID-19 pandemic, immediately and radically altering an educational ecosystem for learners and instructors. The post-pandemic phase, considered the "new normal" (Telli & Aydn, 2021), is expected to bring about enduring changes and incorporate new activities.

Due to COVID-19, online schooling began immediately. The new paradigm required instructors and students to learn technology and posed other difficulties. University administrators and teachers had to handle many obligations at once, including a large number of students, innovative methods of teaching, and public anxiety (Chauhan et al., 2020). Individual faculty staff's online teaching domain likely affected course performance. For some who have never taught online, the pandemic-required online semester was their first encounter. These faculty members required additional time for virtual delivery curriculum planning and development. Selwyn (2007) notes that teachers generally prepare their delivery differently, so technological uniformity and regularity of use depend only on the teacher, leading to inconsistent, uneven integration. Their ambition to offer online courses has become relevant because they were hired so quickly, and the pandemic is dangerous. These conditions caused an unprecedented event. Due to their instructional methods or techniques, online teaching may worry some faculty members. However, personal factors may prevent some from teaching virtually.

The government ordered a massive online education and training initiative in the aftermath of the outbreak of COVID-19. Teachers' perspectives on online education, including their preferences for the virtual classroom, were analysed. Teachers who had never taught online could now discuss their experiences with their colleagues. These faculty members' experiences and relationships may help colleges enhance virtual teaching and classrooms. These interactions could improve online learning for everyone, especially professors and students with little online expertise. The first semester during COVID-19 was especially difficult for faculty who had never taught online. Their pandemic experiences, behaviours, feelings, and perceptions may help them comprehend online faculty dynamics. Higher education's initial response to the emergency can be described as heroic. The future phases will be more unpredictable (Crawford et al., 1998). Policy and economic conditions will determine much. Instead of reversing trends, underlying problems and injustices will be emphasised. These traits are developing (Hazelkorn, 2021).

Instead of debating the efficacy of online education, researchers should investigate why some faculty members find teaching online more challenging and less appealing. Some professors think online learning does not fit their areas or teaching methods. Online education professional development may need to be adjusted to fit diverse fields and personalities. Faculty who believe their teachings or disciplines are unsuitable for online learning may be denied crucial classroom elements. Adapting these aspects of a traditional classroom setting to online teaching requires an instructor. Higher education institutions should consider the factors that shaped faculty members' professional and personal development when they started online instruction during the pandemic quarantine. Owing to its peculiarity, the sentiments experienced simultaneously by numerous academics were never compared to those formed by the mandated online move into teaching in the pandemic semester. Conversations with co-workers who feel they need more online teaching experience before the following semester can provide valuable insight into designing a virtual learning environment that fits one's teaching style, pedagogical approach, and subject area. Higher education is changing. This progression is not a return to business as usual; instead, it is a shift towards a model of education without classroom walls, a rigid curriculum, a physical location, or other traditional restraints (Harris & Santilli, 2021).

Educational leaders should cultivate culturally sensitive learning environments, work with students to increase their knowledge and enthusiasm for learning, act as facilitators who encourage students to work together for the greater good and lead through collaboration and partnership in web-like, non-hierarchical structures (Amey, 2006). A literature review shows that leadership is a hot topic, with an ever-growing number of studies on leadership in schools and universities. These studies tend to focus on more contemporary forms of leadership, such as transformational management (Harris et al., 2004; Jameel & Ahmad, 2019). This research emphasises the significance of adaptable educational leadership during sudden shifts and elevated risk, such as the COVID-19 pandemic. Since leadership in university education is expected to encompass pedagogical, affective, and social dimensions in formal and informal contexts, this study investigates leadership from transformational and socially responsible vantage points.

Leadership is inherently contextual and situational (Antonakis & Schyns, 2012). So, it is not easy to define leadership in a single, concise way, yet the recent literature on educational leadership provides important ideas (Middlehurst et al., 2009). It is worth noting that leadership is becoming increasingly scrutinised in the context of advanced education. For instance, Juntrasook (2014) identifies four primary categories for leadership in higher learning: (1) leadership as status, (2) leadership as efficiency, (3) leadership as an approach, and (4) leadership as professional examples. More representative democratic leadership models are suggested in the literature for higher learning (Bolden et al., 2009; Dugan & Komives, 2010; Harvey et al., 2003; Middlehurstt et al., 2009), including shared action, inspirational motivation, and socially conscious leadership.

Bolden et al. (2009) claim that distributed leadership, which allows collective response, has rhetorical significance in identification, involvement, and influence, and may reasonably embrace the fundamental power dynamics inside universities and is the most effective leadership paradigm. Transformative leadership is another well-received theory in the literature. It is notable for its focus on leaders' charisma, intellectual stimulation, and consideration (Spendlove, 2007). The social change model (Külekçi, 2015; Yokuş, 2018) is also widely used in leadership development programmes at higher education institutions (Dugan & Komives, 2007; Külekçi, 2015; Yokuş, 2018). In light of the COVID-19 pandemic, higher education institutions must adopt a leadership model emphasising social responsibility by teaching self-awareness, teamwork, shared goals, and adaptability.

This research centres on what university students should expect from their institution's leadership during the COVID-19 outbreak. During the pandemic, education takes on a new form, mostly in informal settings like online or offline gatherings in virtual environments. Consequently, exceptional academic leadership is crucial to improving schools and universities and influences curriculum development. In light of the pandemic, a study of the interactions between educators and their students in institutions of higher learning is urgently required. The term "educational leadership," which has been replacing "school leadership," "school management," and "educational administration" for the past three decades, has grown increasingly common and widespread (Carvalho et al., 2021; Mazurkiewicz, 2021). Various actors in the school administrations, including academics, are all examples of educational leaders in higher education. James et al. (2019) define educational leadership as the legitimate engagement in an academic institution meant to improve involvement with the institutional core task. Sellami et al. (2019) posit that educational leadership is often mistakenly thought to refer only to positions of authority held within schools. However, a broader, more inclusive definition is needed. A key challenge for educational leaders in modern higher education is to examine the institution's fundamental aim strategically while also preparing students for learning in the future, making this a timely and pertinent idea. Thinking of present leadership techniques as a band-aid until regular service is restored is a missed opportunity to lead in a new and, perhaps, more effective way (Harris, 2020). Most of the leadership studies that have been done focus on how the actions of school administrators affect students' attitudes, performance, and general contentment at school (Karadag, 2020).

Developing infrastructure for online learning and assessing its efficacy were higher education plan priorities during the lockdown. Internet webinars, instructional videos, interactive, immersive learning, and resources for teachers, parents, and students have caught students' attention in higher education (Pollock, 2020). Students and teachers will benefit from training classes on this distinctive online learning style. These issues require an intellectual approach to education crisis leadership. Gurr and Drysdale (2020) believe leaders must be daring enough to take strategic risks to steer the organisation on the right path. Roache suggests that expert leadership be needed during COVID-19 to implement successful policies that promote the university's vision and mission and give professional growth and training in the new virtual learning mode (Roache et al., 2020). As the COVID-19 situation unfolds, it becomes clear that empathy, sensitivity, self-awareness, and agility are necessary leadership traits. Faculty, staff, and students experiencing emotional discomfort due to the pandemic need (Lawton-Misra & Pretorius, 2021) to lessen the intensity of their feelings (Roy et al., 2020). Dumulescu and Muţiu (2021) argue that higher education managers must respond swiftly to handle large academic communities, catering to the requirements of students, faculty, and staff, as well as those of the larger community. Their research shows that leaders can learn much about themselves, their followers, and the situation during a pandemic.

Lawton-Misra and Pretorius (2021) state that governance during a pandemic necessitates unlearning and relearning particular behaviours. For instance, higher education leaders need to be able to delegate authority, shift from a command-and-control to a follower-centred leadership style, foster a collaborative culture, and respond effectively to change. The COVID-19 pandemic highlights the importance of parallel and coordinated efforts between leaders and followers. As once held by many, the concept of a leader and a follower must be abandoned (Bolden, 2020; Lawton-Misra & Pretorius, 2021). It is possible to execute a form of dispersed leadership in times of crisis that, while slower than other leadership methods, is more effective because it considers more views when making decisions (Fernandez & Shaw, 2020). Antonopoulou et al. (2021) recommend transformational leadership for university education, especially during a pandemic. In order to effectively handle the varied leadership responsibilities that arise in educational settings, transformational leaders emphasise delegating authority to a group of teachers who bring complementary sets of expertise to the table.

What are institutional leadership behaviours essential in higher education during the COVID-19 pandemic? This is the central research question motivating this study. Given this overarching goal, the following research questions are addressed:

1. How to create a framework for institutional leadership amid the COVID-19 pandemic?
2. What do students want from their higher education institution's administration during the COVID-19 pandemic?

3. Amid the COVID-19 pandemic, what are the defining criteria of institutional leadership in higher education?

## Methodology

This research is based on grounded theory. Grounded theory, a qualitative research approach, is widely used in educational studies, especially interpretive research. Bryant (2017) proposes starting an inductive inquiry without hypotheses, studying a new topic, or refining an old problem. Accordingly, preliminary assumptions can only be formulated once knowledge's saturation point is reached. This viewpoint is supported by Bryman and Bell (2007), who contend that grounded theory relies on coding vis-a-vis constant comparing, filtering, and saturation. The new normal in higher education requires a conceptual framework for institutional leadership. This framework uses information gathered from written materials, individual interviews, and discussion groups.

### Group Discussion

A grounded theory study should involve multiple groups to draw findings and create a theory. All groups are college or university students with various majors. The initial focus group contains 23 people affected by COVID-19. After the COVID-19 pandemic, all selected respondents have returned home to their communities, taking advantage of distant learning possibilities like online classes. They are trying their best with the resources they have to fight the global issue, but they need leadership. Table 1 shows the demographics of the two study groups, showing that a representative, diverse sample was selected for theoretical mapping.

The ages of Group Alpha participants vary from 19 to 22, with male ($n$ = 11) and female ($n$ = 12) participants having one to four years of education in their respective majors. University students from various disciplines, such as business, accounting, political science, education, technology, and tourism, have been included to understand multiple perspectives. In Group Beta, 20 university students aged 19–22, male ($n$ = 10) and female ($n$ = 10), were incorporated in data collecting to capture all conceivable perspectives on educational leadership for the new normal. These participants demonstrate a thorough and descriptive knowledge of leadership in institutions for the

**Table 1** Focus group demographic

| | Number | Age | Sex | Cohort | Majors |
|---|---|---|---|---|---|
| Group Alpha | 23 | 19 ($n$ = 7) 20 ($n$ = 11) 21 ($n$ = 3) 22 ($n$ = 2) | Male ($n$ = 11) Female ($n$ = 12) | Freshmen ($n$ = 7) Sophomore ($n$ = 6) Junior ($n$ = 5) Senior ($n$ = 5) | Business ($n$ = 5) Accounting ($n$ = 3 Political Science ($n$ = 3) Education ($n$ = 5) Technology ($n$ = 5) Tourism ($n$ = 2) |
| Group Beta | 20 | 19 ($n$ = 6) 20 ($n$ = 8) 21 ($n$ = 3) 22 ($n$ = 3) | Male ($n$ = 10) Female ($n$ = 10) | Freshmen ($n$ = 4) Sophomore ($n$ = 4) Junior ($n$ = 5) Senior ($n$ = 7) | Business ($n$ = 4) Accounting ($n$ = 2) Political Science ($n$ = 2) Education ($n$ = 5) Technology ($n$ = 4) Tourism ($n$ = 3) |

new normal, subscribe to school leadership in moments of uncertainty and ambiguity, and offer ideas for efficient and effective management.

## Procedure for Data Collecting

To collect data, the first group of participants completed an open-ended survey. Three leadership experts assessed the items and provided feedback, which adjusted a few questions. The final assessment tool consists of six free-form questions that examine students' perspectives on college administration following the global proliferation of COVID-19. The outcomes of this data collection instrument served as the foundation for the follow-up interview questions. Participants in the second study group were interviewed one-on-one over two weeks, utilising a semi-structured online form with seven alternate backup questions. All interviews lasted about twenty minutes.

The pilot study's findings influenced the creation of the semi-structured questionnaire. In addition, two full-time professors reviewed the layout and contents of this form. Finally, the amended material was used in the second round of focus group testing. During online interviews, I made notes and formed opinions. The second focus group had the most qualified and selected people to understand institutional leadership criteria further. The second group (Group Beta) included those with clear and succinct school leadership recommendations. Two sets of respondents discussed mutually interesting themes until it got repetitive. After nearly seven hours of interviews, the researcher reached category saturation, a vital milestone in grounded theory research. The interviews were accurately transcribed and evaluated. Here are the guiding questions for the two groups.

Group Alpha:

1. Could you describe the changes at your school after the pandemic?
2. What comes to mind when you hear "institutional leadership" before and after the pandemic?
3. Are there any educational leaders that you have approached during the pandemic?

Group Beta:

1. Could you explain the qualities of an effective institutional leader in the new normal?
2. How did institutional leaders improve their leadership skills during the pandemic?
3. Which characteristics of institutional leaders inspired you to pursue your studies?

## Findings

In this research on institutional leadership, most respondents named instructors, counsellors, and deans as their institutions' leading members. Respondents value digitisation in the classroom and wish for close partnerships based on personal links from their institutions' leadership. Eighteen codes have emerged thus far in the open coding process, making up the initial codes cluster. The concepts are elevated to preliminary conceptual categories in the subsequent axial coding phase. Five primary groups emerge when 18 open codes/concepts have been processed through the axial coding stage. Each category has its unique set of codes and concepts, and these categories all interact. For instance, the "patience and empathy" grouping has three codes related to two other groups: networking and transparency. The "new normal" institutional leadership is categorised and coded in Table 2.

The grounded theory research identifies five critical leadership themes for the new normal. First, "networking" is the most repeated category

**Table 2** Institutional leadership for higher education's new normal

| Consolidated categories | Frequency | Codes | Frequency |
|---|---|---|---|
| Strengthening educational processes | 149 | Develop a learning atmosphere that is friendly and inclusive | 50 |
| | | Offer instructional materials | 44 |
| | | Include feedback for enhancement | 28 |
| | | Develop an academic achievement plan | 27 |
| Networking | 154 | Promoting online communities | 57 |
| | | Fostering interpersonal contact | 53 |
| | | Community-focused | 44 |
| Systematic and critical thinking | 128 | Data-driven actions | 41 |
| | | Risk management | 30 |
| | | Develop long-term strategies | 29 |
| | | Harness the community's capacity | 28 |
| Patience and empathy | 148 | Leading amid duress | 42 |
| | | Accentuate optimism | 41 |
| | | Attention to students | 32 |
| | | Motivate student learning | 33 |
| Transparency | 110 | Trust | 40 |
| | | Institutional culture | 40 |
| | | Open conversation | 30 |

regarding institutional leadership for the new normal, with components such as promoting online communities, fostering interpersonal contact, and being community-focused directly tied to institutional leadership for the new normal. The second most significant area is "strengthening educational processes," which includes developing a learning atmosphere that is friendly and inclusive, offering instructional materials, including feedback for enhancement, and developing an academic achievement plan. The third essential category is the "patience and empathy" of institutional leaders, which includes leading amid duress, accentuating optimism, attention to students, and motivating student learning. The fourth category, "systematic and critical thinking," includes data-driven actions, risk management, developing long-term strategies, and harnessing the community's capacity. The fifth component is "transparency," which includes trust, institutional culture, and open conversation.

Inferential analysis of data and analysis of social networks using axial and select coding methods help explain educational leadership. Institutional leadership requires networking, improving academic processes, patience, and empathy. Systematic and critical thinking and transparency follow. Systematic and critical thinking, clarity, and socio-emotional variables are crucial for institutional leadership during pandemics. This grounded theory shows that institutional leadership elements are interrelated rather than hierarchical. Data analysis produced a new normal educational leadership theoretical framework.

## Uzbekistan's HE Crisis Leadership During and After COVID

This grounded theory study explores institutional leadership through Uzbek higher education students' perspectives during the COVID-19 pandemic. It creates an approach to identify the new leadership components for the new normal. The data research coded five institutional leadership elements' linkages with eighteen codes. Institutional leadership for the new normal involves strengthening educational procedures, networking, systematic and critical thinking, patience and empathy, and transparency.

### Strengthening Educational Processes

Educational leadership is crucial throughout COVID-19. This includes developing an engaging virtual classroom, providing sufficient learning materials, promoting constructive criticism, and displaying academic accomplishment. Francisco and Nuqui's (2020) COVID-19 research on "new normal leadership" found that leaders must be able to change while being committed, make sound instructional decisions, and have good preparation, attentiveness, and initiative. Education leadership is goal-oriented and driven to mould classroom outcomes that match a desired vision of student performance, pandemic or not. Before the pandemic, education authorities stressed creative approaches to meet academic year and semester goals.

Education leadership is goal-oriented and driven by a vision of student success in the classroom, pandemic or not. Before the pandemic, education leadership concentrated on innovative approaches to meet semester and year targets. The pandemic procedure involves inclusive learning spaces and feedback. Students, educators, and others sought guidance during COVID-19. Interestingly, Gurr and Drysdale (2020) argue that leaders are tasked with setting boundaries during the pandemic while prioritising strategic risk-taking. Leaders must make sense to choose a path and require an understanding of complex situations (Gurr & Drysdale, 2020). Most students expect educational leaders to give online academic support.

Conversely, networking and improving education are valued by institution leaders. Leaders must also equip students with relevant learning aids. Educational leaders have served as resource providers, programme experts, pedagogical champions, creators of human capital, and academic enablers during the COVID-19 pandemic. These strategic choices will benefit the organisation. Fullan et al. (2020) recommend balancing national objectives, school vision, and online distance learning. They suggest integrating remote and school-based instruction during the COVID-19 pandemic. While focusing on academic objectives and benchmarks, this blended approach uses electronic resources to enrich, accelerate, and connect student learning.

## Networking

New normal institutional leadership requires networking. Socialising, creating online communities, and community-mindedness are all part of networking. Pandemics have altered institutions' core functions, straining education leaders (Harris, 2020). Due to the pandemic, educational leaders must first network online. The study shows that higher education institutions, particularly leaders, must build student connections based on shared interests and stimulate social participation under the new normal. Less than half of the respondents stressed community growth and social engagement as signs of the new normal. During quarantine, leaders should permit remote hub students' interaction who may be unable to meet in person.

Institutional leaders should also develop social networks and have a collaborative working team that provides information on educational goals, teaching content, assessment, and evaluation. A good community fosters communication and learning, according to most students. Based on study findings, institutional leaders should promote social involvement and a network rather than isolation and have a community-wide vision. Therefore, institutional leadership must promote community well-being. School leaders work hard during the pandemic to get people to collaborate (Harris, 2020). Networking is vital to educational leadership in the new normal and school development in general. Crisis-induced educational leadership motives vary by student.

Nonetheless, the finding indicates that leadership of the new norm must encourage the collective good while paying attention to the demands of those with diverse issues. Online communities, community-oriented behaviour, and institutional leaders' contributions excite students. In addition, strong communities may lead to the new normal, especially as universities become virtual communities.

## Systematic and Critical Thinking

New normal educational leadership involves systematic and critical thinking. The investigation found that a competent new normal educational leader uses data, plans risks, sets long-term goals, and uses community capacity. Systematic and critical thinking improve institutional leaders' performance during the pandemic. Gurr and Drysdale (2020) found that leadership in the new normal required foresight and calibrated risk-taking. During pandemics, there must be a compromise between risk-taking and risk aversion. This study demonstrates that institutional leadership for the new normal ought to be able to grasp data and make decisions based on data analysis to enhance schools and academic accomplishment. Pandemic uncertainty necessitates a long-term plan rather than a quick fix. It improves education. Effective educational leaders exploit community strengths. The community's capability determines school growth and leadership. University managers must recognise and promote group strengths to maximise benefit and increase results. Learning communities can foster talent during pandemics. Naturally, pandemic leadership shifts from individuals to networks, enhancing involvement, proficiency, and capability for all (Harris, 2020). Competency-based learning paradigms must be enhanced during COVID-19 using community resources. Pandemics encourage talent development. Critical awareness of this challenge may result in education paradigms that are more talent-focused. Institutional leaders can build meaningful relationships that enhance individual and group development based on the findings of this study. Institutional leaders frequently utilise community ability to promote learning, achieve academic goals, and alleviate stress.

## Patience and Empathy

This study indicated that students prefer calm and empathetic educational leaders amid the COVID-19 pandemic. As the pandemic has created mental distress for many university students, Roy et al. (2020) contend that student-centred colleges and universities should assist student health and well-being. Chinese universities counselled first-year students to break up long periods of solitude (Wang et al., 2020). This study found that students want academic leadership to remain composed during critical circumstances. Institutional leadership's patience comprises leading under pressure, motivating positivity, caring for students, and instructing. According to the findings, leaders in the new normal should reduce emotionally charged reasons during pandemics and set acceptable targets while remaining patient and positive. Leaders must be moderate and patient with colleagues (Harris, 2020).

Institutional leaders must support students in the new norm. Informants say kindness underpins educational leadership. Students need adaptive leadership during the COVID-19 pandemic. Participants assert that caring institutional leaders must care about pupils and motivate their learning. Effective educational leadership will promote compassion to accomplish the purpose and curricular objectives. An institution's leadership that completely ignores empathy will fall short of its original goal. Patience and empathy are associated with improved educational practices and transparent educational leadership. Institution leaders would do well in these uncertain post-pandemic times to focus on adding compassionate practices in learning and teaching to reduce the community's overall stress level. Leadership in the classroom should do more than acknowledge students' stress; they should be receptive to criticism, care about others' preferences and expectations, and seek to build a new norm. To retain empathy for students and staff, institution leaders should practice self-compassion. Leaders must demonstrate genuine and effective empathy for their audience. The pandemic highlighted the need for these attributes in institutional leaders, but they are always needed (Lawton-Misra & Pretorius, 2021).

## Transparency

Correspondingly, the research results indicate that students with COVID-19 seek honesty from school administrators. Transparency is crucial to institutional leadership, with its features of trust, corporate culture, and information sharing. The new normal necessitates institutional leaders to be truthful with their students. Additionally, university students want to trust their academic leaders, but they can only do so if they connect through the virtual community. They also wish institutional leaders to develop corporate culture openly, through statements and announcements, rather than through unauthorised individuals. Most students place a high value on trust and school culture. Institutional leaders must be truthful, optimistic, trustworthy, and in command. However, Marshall et al. (2020) note that the COVID-19 pandemic emphasises the importance of consistent, productive discourse in soothing and reassuring relevant parties during times of uncertainty and anxiety. In turbulent times, communications must be precise and timely. Despite COVID-19's complexity and unpredictability, leaders must communicate effectively. Uzbek university leaders in Tashkent routinely shared with stakeholders during the COVID-19 pandemic. This method builds leaders' credibility and reassures stakeholders that the problem is handled carefully (Marshall et al., 2020). Transparency is clearly expressed, enhancing trust since there is nothing to hide. Openness requires more work from educational leaders. The transparency aspect of leadership emphasises the importance of trusting institutional leaders rather than suppressing information.

Furthermore, Bryman (2007) associates good leadership behaviour with explicit instruction. Giving clear direction is intimately linked to institutional culture and open conversation. Institutional leadership, organisational culture, and student trust were strongly linked by Lesinger et al. (2016). Administration improves school atmosphere and employee confidence. Most influential instructors are corporate culture-minded leaders. Institutional leadership in the new normal requires transparency. Although most universities do not think it will boost performance, it is worth investing in. Education leaders should build trust, keep a transparent culture, and communicate with the local community to improve their position with both groups. Academic leaders worry that the government's ambiguous COVID-19 instructions have caused uncertainty. Universities are being asked for more open conversation and cooperation to confront the coronavirus pandemic.

## Conclusions and Recommendations

This grounded theory study examines higher education's new normal leadership during COVID-19. Educational leadership literature during the pandemic supports networking, improving educational processes, patience and empathy, systematic and critical thinking, and transparency (Chisholm-Burns et al., 2021; Fernandez & Shaw, 2020; Gurr & Drysdale, 2020; Lawton-Misra & Pretorius, 2021; Marshall et al., 2020; Pekkola et al., 2021; Samoilovich, 2020; Talu & Nazarov, 2020). School leadership for the new normal emphasises networking, patience, and empathy. According to the study, university students use internet forums to stay updated. Leaders should freely disclose good and bad news and provide feedback to establish trust and organisational culture. Many students rely on their administration to build mutual respect, provide constructive criticism, present an overview of what it means to thrive in higher education, and devise strategies for achieving that success. Education leadership is linked to achieving institutional goals and supporting academic advancement, which influences the quality of education provided by a specific institution. University students suggest integrating it into institutional management to achieve its curricular and administrative goals. Students need institutional leaders who can remain calm under pressure, accentuate the positive, care for their students, and inspire them to learn during a pandemic.

Some students in higher education also require other aspects of institutional leadership, such as motivation to learn, ongoing discussion, planning for risks, and using the community's strengths to their advantage. The participants also assert that effective educational leadership means understanding other people's points of view instead of sticking to the leader's.

## References


Amey, M. (2006). Leadership in higher education. *Change: The Magazine of Higher Learning*, *38*(6), 55–58.

Antonakis, J., Day, V. D., & Schyns, B. (2012). Leadership and individual differences: At the cusp of a renaissance. *The Leadership Quarterly, 23*(4), 643–650.

Antonopoulou, H., Halkiopoulos, C., Barlou, O., & Beligiannis, G. N. (2021). Transformational leadership and digital skills in higher education institutes: During the COVID-19 pandemic. *Emerging Science Journal, 5*(1), 1–15.

Arslan, H., & Ulutaş, M. (2017). Relationship between informatics leadership, learning organisation. In D. Icbay (Ed.), *University culture in higher education in research on education* (pp. 321–337). E-BWN.

Bolden, R. (2020). *Leadership, complexity and change: Learning from the Covid-19 pandemic*. https://blogs.uwe.ac.uk/leadership-and-change/

Bolden, R., Petrov, G., & Gosling, J. (2009). Distributed leadership in higher education: Rhetoric and reality. *Educational Management Administration & Leadership, 37*(2), 257–277.

Bryant, A. (2017). *Grounded theory and grounded theorising: Pragmatism in research practice*. Oxford University Press.

Bryman, A. (2007). Effective leadership in higher education: A literature review. *Studies in Higher Education, 32*(6), 693–710.

Bryman, A., & Bell, E. (2007). *Business research methods*. Oxford University Press.

Carolan, C., Davies, C. L., Crookes, P., McGhee, S., & Rox-Burgh, M. (2020). COVID 19: Disruptive impacts and transformative opportunities in undergraduate nurse education. *Nurse Education in Practice, 46*, 102807.

Carvalho, M., Cabral, I., Verdasca, J. L., & Alves, J. M. (2021). Strategy and strategic leadership in education: A scoping review. *Frontiers in Education., 6*, 1–10. https://doi.org/10.3389/feduc.2021.706608

Chauhan, S., Gupta, P., Palvia, S., & Jaiswal, M. (2020). Information technology transforming higher education: A meta-analytic review. *Journal of Information Technology Case and Application Research, 23*(1), 3–35. https://doi.org/10.1080/15228053.2020.1846480

Chisholm-Burns, M. A., Berg-Poppe, P., Spivey, C. A., Karges-Brown, J., & Pithan, A. (2021). Systematic review of noncognitive factors influence on health professions students' academic performance. *Advances in Health Sciences Education,* 1–73.

Crawford, K., Gordon, S., Nicholas, J., & Prosser, M. (1998). Qualitatively different experiences of collaborative learning: A phenomenographic study of students' conceptions in a small-group setting. In C. Rust (Ed.), *Improving student learning: Improving students as learners* (pp. 146–158). Oxford Centre for Staff and Learning Development.

Davletov, F. (2020, April 23). *Global impact of COVID-19 on the education system* [Web log post]. Review.uz. https://review.uz/ru/post/globalnoe-vliyanie-covid19-na-sistemu-obrazovaniya

Dugan, J. P., & Komives, S. R. (2007). *Developing leadership capacity in college students: Findings from a national study. A report from the multi-institutional study of leadership.* National Clearinghouse for Leadership Programs.

Dugan, P. J., & Komives, R. S. (2010). Influences on college students' capacities for socially responsible leadership. *Journal of College Student Development, 51*(5), 525–549.

Dumulescu, D., & Muţiu, A. I. (2021). Academic leadership in the time of COVID-19—Experiences and perspectives. *Frontiers in Psychology, 12,* 1272.

Fernandez, A. A., & Shaw, G. P. (2020). Academic leadership in a time of crisis: The coronavirus and COVID-19. *Journal of Leadership Studies, 14*(1), 39–45.

Francisco, C. D., & Nuqui, A. V. (2020). Emergence of a situational leadership during COVID-19 pandemic called new normal leadership. *Online Submission, 4*(10), 15–19.

Fullan, M., Quinn, J., Drummy, M., & Gardner, M. (2020). Education reimagined: The future of learning. *A collaborative position paper between New Pedagogies for Deep Learning and Microsoft Education, 1,* 34.

Gurr, D., & Drysdale, L. (2020). Leadership for challenging times. *International Studies in Educational Administration, 48*(1), 24–30.

Harris, A. (2020). COVID-19—School leadership in crisis? *Journal of Professional Capital and Community, 5*(3/4), 321–326. https://doi.org/10.1108/JPCC-06-2020-0045

Harris, J. T., & Santilli, N. R. (2021). Higher education should embrace this liminal moment because there will be no "new normal". In S. Bergan, T. Gallagher, I. Harkavy, R. Munck, & H. van't Land (Eds.), *Higher education's response to the COVID-19 pandemic: Building a more sustainable and democratic future* (pp. 129–136). Council of Europe Higher Education Series No. 25.

Harris, R. P., Moran, T. R., & Moran, V. S. (2004). *Managing cultural differences: Global leadership strategies for the 21st century*. Elsevier.

Harvey, S., Royal, M., & Stout, D. (2003). Instructor's transformational leadership: University student attitudes and ratings. *Psychological Reports, 92*(2), 395–402.

Hazelkorn, E. (2021). Some challenges facing higher education in Europe in view of the Covid-19 pandemic. In S. Bergan, T. Gallagher, I. Harkavy, R. Munck & H.van't Land (Eds.), *Higher education's response to the COVID-19 pandemic: Building a more sustainable and democratic future* (pp. 53–66). Council of Europe Higher Education Series No. 25.

Jameel, S. A., & Ahmad, A. (2019, April). *Leadership and performance of academic staff in developing countries.* Paper presented at the annual meeting of Proceedings of the 33rd International Business Information Management Association Conference, Granada, 6101–6106.

James, C., Connolly, M., & Hawkins, M. (2019). Reconceptualising and redefining educational leadership practice. *International Journal of Leadership in Education*, 1–18. https://doi.org/10.1080/13603124.2019.1591520

Jensen, T. (2019). *Higher education in the digital era: The current state of transformation around the world*. International Association of Universities (IAU).

Johnson, L., Adams, B. S., Cummins, M., Estrada, V., Freeman, A., & Hall, C. (2016). *NMC horizon report: 2016* (Higher Education Edition). The New Media Consortium.

Juntrasook, A. (2014). You do not have to be the boss to be a leader: Contested meanings of leadership in higher education. *Higher Education Research & Development, 33*(1), 19–31.

Karadag, E. (2020). The effect of educational leadership on students' achievement: A cross-cultural meta-analysis research on studies between 2008 and 2018. *Asia Pacific Education Review, 21*, 49–64. https://doi.org/10.1007/s12564-019-09612-1

Külekçi, E. (2015). *Üniversite öğrencilerinin sosyal sorumluluk temelli liderlik becerilerinin geliştirilmesine yönelik deneysel bir çalışma* [An experimental study about developing undergraduate students' socially responsible leadership skills]. (Doctoral Dissertation). Gaziantep University Educational Sciences Institution.

Lawton-Misra, N., & Pretorius, T. (2021). Leading with heart: Academic leadership during the COVID-19 crisis. *South African Journal of Psychology, 51*(2), 205–214.

Lesinger, Y. F., Dagli, G., Gazi, A. Z., Yusoff, B. S., & Altınay, F. (2016). Investigating the relationship between organisational culture, educational leadership and trust in schools. *International Journal of Educational Sciences, 15*(1–2), 178–185.

Marshall, J., Roache, D., & Moody-Marshall, R. (2020). Crisis leadership: A critical examination of educational leadership in higher education in the midst of the COVID-19 pandemic. *International Studies in Educational Administration, 48*(3), 30–37.

Mazurkiewicz, G. (2021). Educational leadership in times of crisis. *Risks, 9*(5), 90. https://doi.org/10.3390/risks9050090

Meliboeva, N., Patrinos, H. A., & Teixeira, J. (2020, April 27). *Prompt provision of the learning process during the period of school closure for quarantine in*

*Uzbekistan*. Blogs Worldbank. https://blogs.worldbank.org/ru/europeandcentralasia/uzbekistan-timely-response-learning-during-school-closures

Middlehurst, R., Goreham, H., & Woodfield, S. (2009). Why research leadership in higher education? Exploring contributions from the UK's leadership foundation for higher education. *Leadership, 5*(3), 311–329.

Pekkola, E., Siekkinen, T., Kujala, E. N., Kanniainen, J. P., & Laihonen, H. (2021). An assessment of COVID-19's impact on Finnish university leadership. *Knowledge Management Research & Practice, 19*(4), 510–516.

Pollock, K. (2020). School leaders' work during the COVID-19 pandemic: A two-pronged approach. *International Studies in Educational Administration, 48*(3), 38–44.

Roache, D., Rowe-Holder, D., & Muschette, R. (2020). Transitioning to online distance learning in the COVID-19 era: A call for skilled leadership in higher education institutions (HEIs). *Proceedings CCEAM*, 103.

Roy, D., Tripathy, S., Kar, S. K., Sharma, N., Verma, S. K., & Kaushal, V. (2020). Study of knowledge, attitude, anxiety & perceived mental healthcare need in Indian population during COVID-19 pandemic. *Asian Journal of Psychiatry, 51*, 1–8.

Samoilovich, D. (2020). Leadership in the time of COVID-19: Reflections of Latin American higher education leaders. *International Higher Education, 102*, 32–34.

Sellami, A. L., Sawalhi, R., Romanowski, H. M., & Amatullah, T. (2019). Definitions of educational leadership–Arab educators' perspectives. *International Journal of Leadership in Education*, 1–20. https://doi.org/10.1080/13603124.2019.1690701

Selwyn, N. (2007). The use of computer technology in university teaching and learning: To critical perspective. *Journal of Computer Assisted Learning, 23*, 83–94. https://doi.org/10.1111/j.1365-2729.2006.00204.x

Spendlove, M. (2007). Competencies for effective leadership in higher education. *International Journal of Educational Management, 21*(5), 407–417.

Talu, S., & Nazarov, A. D. (2020). Challenges and competencies of leadership in Covid-19 Pandemic. *Proceedings of the Research Technologies of Pandemic Coronavirus Impact (RTCOV 2020), Advances in Social Science, Education and Humanities Research, 486*, 518–524.

Telli, S. G., & Aydın, S. (2021). Covid-19 sonrası dönemde işletme bölümlerinin Dijital Çağ'a yönelik hazır bulunuşluğu: Türkiye örneği. *Yükseköğretim Dergisi, 11*(1), 123–138. https://doi.org/10.2399/yod.20.009000

Wang, C., Cheng, Z., Yue, X., & McAleer, M. (2020). Risk management of COVID-19 by universities in China. *Journal of Risk and Financial Management, 13*(2), 36.

Yokuş, G. (2018). *Analysis of online professional learning networks' effect on pre-service teachers' researcherly dispositions, socially responsible leaderships and social networks based learning: Digital teacher community* [Unpublished Doctoral Dissertation, Mersin University Educational Sciences Institution].

# Correction to: The Palgrave Handbook of Crisis Leadership in Higher Education

Jürgen Rudolph, Joseph Crawford, Choon-Yin Sam, and Shannon Tan

**Correction to:**
**Chapters 8 and 18 in: J. Rudolph et al. (eds.), *The Palgrave Handbook of Crisis Leadership in Higher Education*, https://doi.org/10.1007/978-3-031-54509-2**

The original version of the book was inadvertently published with incorrect affiliations for the first and third authors in Chapter 8 and without the second author name in Chapter 18, which have now been corrected. The book and the chapters have been updated with the changes.

The updated versions of these chapters can be found at
https://doi.org/10.1007/978-3-031-54509-2_8
https://doi.org/10.1007/978-3-031-54509-2_18


J. Rudolph et al. (eds.), *The Palgrave Handbook of Crisis Leadership in Higher Education*, https://doi.org/10.1007/978-3-031-54509-2_34

# Index




J. Rudolph et al. (eds.), *The Palgrave Handbook of Crisis Leadership in Higher Education*, https://doi.org/10.1007/978-3-031-54509-2

D

J

Printed in the United States
by Baker & Taylor Publisher Services